Deviant Designations

Crime, Law and Deviance in Canada

Thomas Fleming
L.A. Visano
Editors

Butterworths
Toronto

Deviant Designations
© 1983—Butterworth & Co. (Canada). Ltd.

Printed and bound in Canada
5 4 3 2 1   3 4 5 6 7 8 9/8

Canadian Cataloguing in Publication Data

Main entry under this title:
Deviant designations

Includes bibliographical references.
ISBN 0-409-82984-6

1. Crime and criminals - Canada. 2. Deviant behavior. 3. Criminal justice, Administration of - Canada. I. Fleming, Thomas. II. Visano, L.A.

HV6807.D48 1983   364'.971   C83-098878-5

The Butterworth Group of Companies

Canada:
Butterworth & Co. (Canada) Ltd., Toronto and Vancouver

United Kingdom:
Butterworth & Co. (Publishers) Ltd., London

Australia:
Butterworths Pty. Ltd., Sidney, Melbourne, Brisbane, Adelaide and Perth

New Zealand:
Butterworths of New Zealand Ltd., Wellington and Auckland

Singapore:
Butterworth & Co. (Asia) Pte. Ltd., Singapore

South Africa:
Butterworth & Co. (South Africa) Ltd., Durban and Pretoria

United States:
Butterworth Legal Publishers, Boston, Seattle and Austin
Mason Publishing Company, St. Paul
D & S Publishers, Clearwater

Contents

Preface

The publication of this reader marks a turning point in the study of crime, law, and deviance in Canada. It represents the collaborative effort of almost two dozen academics from one shore of this country to the other. This in itself is an occasion for some celebration given the relative isolation in which most of us work between annual meetings. This a truly Canadian book, with high-calibre contributions from the fields of sociology, criminology, psychology, anthropology, government research, and from those people involved in the struggle to apply or fight against deviant designations.

We have consciously indicated in our title the desire to present material across three areas which we feel are not only related in the day-to-day activities of society but which also represent interconnected features in any serious consideration of designating, controlling, or responding to deviance and crime. To this end the book is divided into four sections: examination of the reaction of communities to crime; some of the issues involved in creating deviant designations and controlling the careers of those deemed deviant or criminal; the response of formal agents and agencies of social control to the discredited (courts, police, and prisons); and finally, some of the emerging theoretical concerns in the fields represented in this book and the problems inherent in attempting to convey this information in an applied form.

Each section of the book is preceded by a short introduction that draws together some of the basic issues covered in the essays which follow. In keeping with the field of inquiry which has had the strongest impact upon the study of crime, law, and deviance in Canada these introductions are sociological in nature. There is no attempt to provide a summary of each section, we feel this to be presumptuous as the articles quite clearly speak for themselves. The introductions for sections I and IV provide a more general analysis of the issues being examined, while those for sections II and III, in keeping with the content of the articles presented, offer an understanding of some of the theoretical underpinnings of the section as a whole. We would not wish to be accused of perpetrating an injustice upon those who are so concerned with justice.

A majority of these articles were written especially for this reader. Others, although printed elsewhere, are almost impossible for the undergraduate reader to ferret out of the library stacks, particularly in an era when cutbacks are likely to present the eager student with an empty shelf. Lecturers from a variety of disciplines will find this book filled with Canadian data on a variety of subjects that are often difficult to find, particularly in this clear and compelling form. Where Canadian research is scarce or in its infancy in new and promising areas of research we have provided quality material (for example, in the case of media presentations of crime and deviance). Bibliographies and informative notes are provided at the end of each chapter so that instructors who wish to assign essay topics may do so, confident not only that the student can find adequate resource material, but also references that are challenging and *interesting*. We are not of the opinion that the study of crime, law, and deviance must constantly disappoint the casual student; rather we feel that this book will do much to satisfy the curiosity, and *increase* the interest of just such a reader.

Thomas Fleming
L.A. Visano

Acknowledgements

A project of this type requires the cooperation and good will of a small army of individuals. Those who have weathered the many storms associated with bringing this book to press deserve our hearty thanks. We are especially grateful to the many contributors from across Canada who cooperated in the production of this book and in giving it its truly national character.

We owe a great debt to Janet Turner who had as much enthusiasm for this book as we did. Patricia O'Reilly-Fleming and Karen Tilford-Visano assisted us at all stages of the work and made contributions to our egos and mental health far exceeding those which should be required of any two persons. Thanks also go to Shirley Corriveau for her patience and very competent editing.

Val Caskey undertook the Hurculean task of typing the manuscript in a short span of time, and did so without complaint. She made our task immeasurably easier. Trudie Smith-Gadacz and Laura C. Hargrave proofread large portions of the book and finished with smiles still on their faces.

Robert Silverman encouraged me in this endeavour and has been a good friend to me in my first year in the "land of stucco" and on our sojourn to Stanford, (commonly known as "that great place"). Tim Hartnagel and Gwynn Nettler, my other criminological colleagues have been generous in their support of me, and it is with some sadness that this passage is being written on the occasion of Gwynn Nettler's retirement dinner. He is an academic, researcher, teacher, and writer of the highest calibre who shall be sorely missed at this university. My good colleagues in the Department of Sociology have provided support, encouragement, and friendship which made this a good place to work and live. Terence Morris of The London School of Economics has been a good friend and wise advisor since my days in London and I wish to thank him for encouraging individual scholarship.

Thomas Fleming
Edmonton, Alberta
May 1983

In addition to the thanks given by Tom Fleming, on his and my behalf, to those who greatly assisted in the academic and technical preparation of this book, I wish to make some personal acknowledgements. This book reflects a recognition of the many long-overdue intellectual debts that I owe to my "significant others". Throughout the current and completed stages of my career as a doctoral student it has been a privilege to know and study under a talented group of outstanding academics who have generously provided challenging, stimulating, and encouraging knowledge. These include Professor R. Ericson, my thesis supervisor; Professor P.J. Giffen, my graduate programme advisor and convenor of my deviance comprehensive examination; and Professor D. Magill, convenor of my urban sociology comprehensive examination.

It would be impossible to acknowledge the many others to whom I am indebted for their unyielding support, advice, and criticisms. The following however, need to be singled out and a special note of thanks extended: Professor J. Lee, Professor C. Shearing, Professor G. West, and Reverend E. Frerichs.

This book is a celebration of the collaborative efforts of not only the two editors and the contributors but also of all those who have sensitized us to the problematics inherent in the analysis of deviant designations.

Livy Anthony Visano,
University of Toronto,
1983.

Part I

Crime and Communities

Introduction

Crime is a phenomenon that constantly taxes both the resources and citizens of every Canadian community. Crime and our fear of it has measurable effect on the quality of life we may enjoy, in our neighbourhoods and even in the sanctity of our homes. Crime confronts us each day in the media. It is the control of crime that forms the mainstay of many politician's campaigns. The cost of crime and of incarcerating criminals has become one of the major problems of modern Western industrialized democracies. We all have common-sense solutions for the "problem" of crime but few of us have had the opportunity to examine the processes involved in the creation of criminal labels, the role of the state in administering justice or many of the other myriad of interactions that result in an activity being defined as criminal and individuals consequently being condemned as criminals.

This is, of course, a natural state of affairs for students in any discipline to find themselves in at the beginning of the learning process. It is simply because we have received so much information concerning crime over the course of our lives as citizens in any community, and because we may be familiar with some forms of criminal endeavour that we feel confident to make pronouncements about "what should be done". We have some sense, as should all citizens about what is "just" in criminal cases which make news across the country. We feel confident in what the right course of action should have been in the case of mass murderer Clifford Olson. Our feelings may be more mixed when we

1

consider other cases in which innocent men and women have languished in our prison system for many years only to be found innocent of wrongdoing. What would we wish to do about the approximately 250,000 young Canadians who now possess a criminal record for simple possession of marijuana for personal use? What would we do with those who drink and drive considering the slaughter which currently is taking place on the roads of our nation? In undergraduate criminology and deviance courses in which 800 students at the University of Alberta were asked whether they had engaged in drinking and driving, 83 percent indicated a positive response (Fleming 1983).

The answers we give to this type of question may have more importance than we may imagine for the type of society we will eventually inhabit. Is an action noncriminal because large numbers of citizens wish to engage in it? Similarly may we mete out light penalties for those who steal with a pen or computer, often very large sums of money, while imprisoning for long periods of time (often longer than the convicted murderer) those who steal with the gun and usually get little for their efforts?

The articles presented in this first section of the book present compelling analyses of the relation of law, crime and deviance in Canada. The article which opens the book by McMullan and Ratner is a historical piece that examines the interplay between political change and crime evidenced in the state's handling of two strikes in British Columbia.

Fleming provides a look at the Toronto gay steambath raids in 1981. His article illustrates that all the steam being let off may not be in the bathhouses, in dissecting the roles of the police, politics, and media and the gay community in what turned out to be the largest arrest in Toronto's history.

The two articles that follow examine two minority groups who have not only suffered undue discrimination and stereotyping in this country, but who have only recently become the subject of serious academic research destined to shatter many common myths about both Native Canadians and Italo-Canadians. Hylton and Visano, two of the leading analysts in these areas, present challenging papers which will no doubt do much to cause debate and, at the same time, reforge out a vision of justice and reality.

In a paper that is sure to fascinate all budding criminologists, Leyton presents his ideas on the social profiles of sexual mass murderers. His practical and disturbing article will be of assistance not only to those who wish to understand more about the lives of those who perpetrate the most heinous of all crimes but also to those who must find such culprits after the commission of their crimes.

Our final paper is by sociologist Robert Prus whose work on the careers of professional gamblers and prostitutes have made him one of the most widely read researchers in Canada. This paper is central to the argument presented in this book in examining how communities react to various behaviours amongst their members. Prus analyzes how deviant behaviours are identified, and how societal reactions attempt to regulate these behaviours. His article also has important information to convey about the careers of deviant individuals.

References

Fleming, Thomas. 1983. Are you valid or are you void?: Self-reported deviance amongst undergraduate students in Edmonton. Unpublished paper.

Chapter 1

State, Labour, and Justice in British Columbia*

John L. McMullan and R.S. Ratner

INTRODUCTION

Contemporary conflict theorists argue that the issue of social justice must be examined in relation to the wider political economy. Within more boldly Marxist orientations, the state is regarded as the direct or at least refracted political expression of the dominant class's control over the means of production. Criminal law is seen as an instrument of the state and the "ruling" (or dominant) class to maintain and perpetuate the existing economic order. Legislation, in general, is viewed as the political outcome of uneven struggles between antithetical class forces, embodying the interests and aspirations of the dominant group.

In this paper we seek to trace the nature and direction of political change in capitalist society through an analysis of two historically specific industrial disputes in the Canadian province of British Columbia. These are disputes which have been marked by state intervention invoking one or more components of the provincial and/or federal criminal justice system; thus, they evidence the role of the state in fortifying the development of capitalist political economy. The aims of the study are to identify the changing forms of state intervention occuring in these industrial disputes, their specific manifestations within the criminal justice system, and the subsequent effects of these inter-

---

* Edited version of a paper presented at the annual meetings of the Academy for Criminal Justice Sciences, 23 to 27 March 1982, The Galt House, Louisville, Kentucky. J. McMullan and R. Ratner, Department of Sociology and Anthropology, University of British Columbia.

ventions on the growth of the state, the restructuration of capital, and the organization of the labour movement.

The particular industrial conflicts that we have selected for study are the Naniamo Coal Strike (1914-1916), and the Blubber Bay lumberworkers' strike (1937-1938). These strikes are viewed as exemplars of the changing role of the capitalist state in relation to its cardinal functions of accumulation, legitimation, and coercion. The strikes embrace a crucial historical conjuncture in the expansion and development of capitalism in British Columbia which resonate with continental economic and political trends, therefore permitting a focused study of the transformations in one facet of the political infrastructure of capitalist economy.

We begin our analysis by outlining the neo-Marxist theories of the capitalist state, drawing particular attention to the role and operations of law and the criminal justice system indicated by each of these perspectives. This is followed by a schematic profile of the provincial economy and labour force of British Columbia since the turn of the century. We then examine the specific industrial disputes chosen for this analysis, contextualizing them within broader economic trends in order to trace convergences in the interplay of capital/labour conflicts with forms of state intervention that entail use of the criminal justice system. From a further scrutiny of these events, we deduce the structural identity of the capitalist state in terms of its evolving representation of ruling-class interests.

A central concern throughout the analysis is the question of the instrumental or relatively autonomous character of the state. Our findings lead us to adopt a modified instrumentalist view on the position of the state as historically revealed in British Columbia, and it is from this perspective that we locate the meaning of "justice" and understand its manifestations in the political economy of British Columbia during the monopolization of capital.

THE CAPITALIST STATE AND CRIMINAL JUSTICE

The rediscovery of the state as a problem in the political economy of Canada has generated, in the last ten years, an array of insights and hypotheses about the nature and impact of state interventions in capital/labour disputes. The following presents a summary of these recent developments in Marxist thinking on the capitalist state. The survey is brief and schematic and highlights the variants of state, law and criminal justice theory. Our purpose is to distill ideas and advance arguments we judge central in understanding *empirically* the relationships between capital, the criminal justice system and labour in British Columbia.

The first variant is the instrumentalist one. In this conception, the state is regarded as the direct instrument of class rule and the law and criminal justice apparatus as tools of class domination (Quinney 1980). According to this perspective, those who dominate economically, rule politically. A correspondence of class power and state power is secured because of the overt similarities in class background, interests and world view between those who shape and run the economy and the personnel of the state and criminal justice system (Miliband 1969). Thus this research agenda focuses on the sociological character of the capitalist class (Domhoff 1967, 70), the mechanisms which link this dominant class to the state (Olson 1980), and the concrete manifestations of class interests in state laws, policies, and programs. At bottom, common class position, close educational ties, family and personal links, shared ideological perspective and close working relationships between the dominant class and intermediary institutions (research units, universities, political organizations and parties) predispose state criminal justice institutions to favour dominant social and economic interests (Miliband 1969; Clement 1973, 1976). The instrumentalist position is confirmed empirically by studies of the class composition and social background of those who hold high judicial offices (Olsen 1980; Zander 1968; Griffith 1972) and by the differential formulation and application of justice to different social classes. The state and the law are particularly lax and ineffective when pursuing corporate tax fraud and business crime, while those at the bottom who "fiddle" welfare are vigorously pursued and sanctioned (Reasons 1976). Similarly, judicial policy varies considerably as between white collar crimes and crimes of the powerful and the crimes of/against the lower classes (Reasons 1981; Platt 1978). In Miliband's terms an abyss separates the world of the bench, bar, and law from ordinary working people and because the dominant class corners the state judiciary (class background and control) differential policies result which dwarf the exercise of justice in favour of capital and against labour (Miliband 1969).

The instrumentalist perspective alerts us to an important source of judicial bias in that it brings to light the direct exercise of state power by members of the capitalist class through the manipulation of the law and the judiciary or indirectly through interest-group pressure on the state. Explanations however, are almost always framed in terms of individuals or interest groups who staff the state or justice apparatus rather than classes defined by their relationship to the means of production. Thus social causes are reduced to the *intentions* of groups or agents and there is little systematic analysis of how the voluntarism of the powerful is shaped and limited by impersonal, invisible structural relations (Gold, Lo, and Wright 1975). Moreover, this position tends to assume a homogeneity of ruling class interests, with an unproblematic translation of economic power to the instrumentalization of state, law and criminal justice. As Quinney asserts,

> The state is established by those who desire to protect their material basis and who have the power to maintain the state. The law in capitalist society gives political recognition to powerful private interests. Moreover, the legal system is an apparatus created to secure the interests of the dominant class. Contrary to conventional belief, the law is the tool of the ruling class (Quinney 1974, 52).

This is a contentious formulation; for aside from its simplicity and reductionism, it does not ascribe a logic to the state of its own in terms of state/civil society relations or in terms of its own mode of administration. There *are* initiatives taken *by* the state for interests broader than, or different from, capital. Thus there are crucial realms of state related strategies that are not the result of capitalist class manoeuvres or co-optations. Indeed the state itself may be an arena of class struggle and areas such as culture, ideology and law do possess a degree of autonomy outside the sphere of simple manipulation (Williams 1978).

The structuralist variant takes a different tack and argues that the correspondences between state, law and economy are *not* a matter of the direct participation of members of the capitalist class in the state criminal justice apparatus. In this view, the state and law in a capitalist society have an objective relationship to classes and to the productive forces. The functions of the state then are determined by the structures of society which cannot be understood primarily in terms of the class background of incumbents in positions of state power (Poulantzas 1969, 245). For structuralists, the state is not an instrument but a *relation*; that is, the state is not a concrete unified thing (i.e., a specific network of institutions) but it is a functional objective interrelationship among institutions, a reality *invisible* behind state institutions, which organizes the power coordinates of class domination and conflict as a whole. For structuralists, the state is seen in terms of its functional utilities (Offe 1975; O'Connor 1973; Panitch 1978). Poulantzas, for example, argues that the state has two major functions. It is a factor of cohesion operating to counteract (1) the combined threats of working class unity and action, and (2) capitalist class fragmentation and disunity; which in turn are based upon the fundamental economic contradiction between the ever-developing social nature of production and the continuing private appropriation of the surplus product. The state is also the site where legitimacy for particular policies is fashioned: above all, the acquiescence of labour in the aims of capital. Thus, in terms of its impact on labour, the state, in this perspective, atomizes the labouring class and disintegrates its political coherence through the transformation of workers into individualized citizens, while simultaneously presenting itself as the *universal* interest of the entire society. Not only does the state tend to exclude laws and policies which favour the collective interests of labour (which may be formulated in terms such as the national or public interest) it also creates, through the institutions of law, democracy, and justice, a juridical subject, with individual rights (as opposed to classes with legal statuses or trade union rights) that estranges labour from its collective class position. Thus for structuralists, the state and the justice system are relatively autonomous from the direct manipulations of specific capitalist class fractions. Not mere tools, law and criminal justice then are potent structures of representation which mask class relations, displace classes into legal individuals and reconstitute them as citizens with formal political and legal rights (Hall and Scraton 1981). Thus, "the public", "due process", "the rule of law", "equality before the law"; these are the basic concepts of the legal ideology, endowing universality and legitimacy in a most subtle way to asymmetrical relations of class power. Mystification, disorganization, coercion, and disunity results for the dominated classes (Poulantzas 1973).

Accordingly, the state is also the guarantor of the long-term interests of capital as a *whole*. Structuralists, as opposed to instrumentalists, stress the fractionated character of the ruling class and the problematic nature of the capital accumulation process. Poulantzas, for example, argues that diverse class fractions of the capitalist class may become divergent unless they are solidified into a power coalition under the tutelage of a particular hegemonic fraction. Moreover this power bloc is frequently precarious and only partially able to produce the means for long-term capital exploitation of labour. Enter the state! But in a radically different form from the instrumentalist state. For, in the view of structuralists, the state is able to transcend internal disputes, parochial capitalist interests, and contradictions within the power bloc, to afford protection and direction for the capitalist class as a whole. The mediation of the state then is on a relatively autonomous plane and not to be seen as in the hands of one capitalist grouping (Poulantzas 1969).

The structural perspective affords a more complex view of the state, albeit at times highly schematic and abstract. Yet, they reduce law and state to a structural necessity and overdraw the functional relationship of long-term reproduction of capital. Indeed, some forms of economic structuralism derive state activities directly out of the logic of capital accumulation, thus ascribing it very little independence. Advantages won from the state by pressures "from below" (e.g., welfare programs, safety and protection laws in the workplace, etc.) are difficult to explain within this perspective and there is a reluctance to perceive resistance and struggle as leading to results contrary to or subversive of capitalist development. Thus class consciousness and agency is almost entirely removed from their analytic framework.

The third variant derives from the influence of Antonio Gramsci (1971) whose work has been used by structuralists though it differs from them in important respects. Unlike Althusser (1971) and Poulantzas (1973), Gramsci places the idea of agency and struggle at the centre of his conception of the state. The role of the state, in his schema, is not only to regulate the economy, but to cohere a field of struggle in an attempt to organize society, civil, moral, and intellectual life around the structural requirements and tendencies set by the economy. However, the economy is not determinant. Nor can it be conceptualized as separate (i.e., base-superstructure distinction) from particular ideological and political conditions. The functional character of the state then is not reducible from some *general* theory of the state's function and practice (Offe, for example). Rather it may be established only by analyzing specific historical conjunctures and unravelling the controversies, the balances, and alliances of power. Thus, Gramsci differentiated a situation where classes were secure within their own limited class interests and boundaries, in which rule depended on the exercise of force, where law was essentially repressive and negative, and where particular class fractions attempted, through the state, to side their interests across society, molding sections of the dominated classes into a "historical bloc" within civil society and state. Moreover, such a "historical bloc" is able to assert an enlarged social authority, and rule is more by leadership than by domination (1971). Leadership then implies the obtaining of support and legitimacy from the subordinated classes in order to create a unity of economic, political, intellectual, and moral aims, thus creating, "not on a corporate but a 'universal' plane, . . . the hegemony of a fundamental social group over a series of subordinate groups" (1971, 58).

The stress on the notion of hegemony in Gramsci's work is reflected in his understanding of state power. While he recognized the coercive character to class and state rule, he also identified and developed an "ethical and educative" conception of law and justice. The "winning of consent" enlarged the role of the state in reshaping civil society; and law and justice were pivotal as "positive civilizing activities", sanctioning, but more importantly educating, moralizing, and rewarding conduct which bolstered the ethical principles and directions of the total social foundation. Thus the state is allied with civil society in attempting to impose a consensus by largely peaceful means in which the subjected become willing partners in their own subordination. Central to this task is state control and manipulation of media, press, church, and schools. But this *process of hegemony* is countered by contrary, emergent and less structured forms of thought, some "non-organic", others potentially counter-hegemonic (Williams 1978). Moreover, the dominated class has its own agents; its "organic" intellectuals working at its behest; not only to equip labour with a new ideology, but to win over, neutralize, or detach from their former allegiances, particularly the traditional intellectuals, who are not committed to either capital or labour. In this way, according to Gramsci, labour may both construct its own counter-ideology and weaken the defences of capital before the struggle for state control.

The implications of Gramsci's writing are important to work such as ours. He abandons the crude division of ideology into "true" and "false", advances on a historical approach that undercuts a priori arguments, provides a specificity and effectivity to the "superstructure" in ways which undermine reductionist, economistic and abstract explanations, and recognizes the complex interplay between class, law and ideology (Thompson 1975; Hagetal 1975; Hall 1978).

The final perspective, the "capital logic" approach, attempts an integration of the previous three. While supportive of the Gramscian "class theoretic" position, they argue that the economic constraints on state hegemony are too loosely formulated. In their view, politics, ideology, and culture must be seen as more *directly* connected to the process of capital accumulation. Thus the ideological character of law and the state derives from the "logic" of the economic relations of capitalism (Holloway and Picciotto 1978). This variant, leans heavily on Marx's economic categories in *Capital*. The first formulation of the capital-logic perspective concentrated almost exclusively on the monetary and legal apparatuses necessary to facilitate the production and exchange of commodities and the accumulation of capital (Altvater 1973). The capitalist state was thus a political force complementing the economic force of competition between forms of capital. State intervention then occured *against* capital (as well as the working class) when fractions of capital threatened the interests of capital in general. Recent work has introduced a greater degree of historical specificity so as to illustrate the role of class struggle and exploitation in the formation of the capitalist state. In this formulation, the efforts of the state to secure the conditions for capital accumulation are subject to changes in economic structure as well as to the influence of class dynamics and to changes in the balance of political forces.

In either version, three historical "moments" of the capitalist state are distinguished: the establishment of the preconditions for accumulation; the "liberal" moment when the full separation of politics and economics takes place; and the contemporary moment when the socialization of production generates the tendency of the rate of profit to fall (Holloway and Picciotto 1978, 1–31). Correspondingly, the nature and function of law and the state change over these three periods. In the phase of primitive accumulation of capital, the capitalist state adopts a relatively laissez-faire role, only intervening to prevent internecine competition between capital and to guarantee the conditions necessary to assure the maximum scope for capital accumulation. In the period of liberal capitalism there is a change in state forms from absolutism to parliamentary democracy, whereby different fractions of capital create a legal code subjecting themselves to the same *general* rules and enforcement, yet asserting a domination over labour. At the same time, law is not only a bourgeois artifice since it also reflects the influence of sustained class struggles, notably in the extension of the franchise to dominated classes. Criminal justice thus appears as the outcome of class struggles over the framing, application, and enforcement of the legal fetishisms arising out of the attempted legitimation of bourgeois hegemony. In the shift to the third phase of monopoly capitalism, the form of state moves from an emphasis on the rule of law to more powerful state bureaucratic interventions enabling direct relations with individual capitals for the purpose of counteracting the trend toward falling profits during the increased socialization of production. The role of parliament declines as major capitalist interests seek direct access to executive and administrative centres of power, and the state becomes the locale of conflict between competing capitals and organized labour, responding frequently to the political crises of accumulation as well as to the actual needs of capital. In this third stage, the state acquires extraparliamentary powers in order to ensure ongoing capital accumulation. State power nevertheless is contained, to some extent, by the "rule of law" legacy established during the period of liberal expansion. These residual contradictions become part of the changing content of class struggle and "criminal justice" becomes anarchronistic in the authoritarian democracies of late capitalist society (Jessop 1977, 353–373).

Ironically, the major problem with this approach is that for all the effort to avoid economistic reductionism by the references to crises and class struggle, the "needs of capital" remain as the only explanatory principle for state interventions, and law is reduced to an effect of the logical self-realization of capital (Gough 1979). This perspective tends, ultimately, to deny law of any effectivity or specificity of its own, since law is treated as a form with a hidden economic content. Its truth therefore lies elsewhere and law is always merely a form of mystification.

These brief critical reviews of neo-Marxist theories of the state indicate the contrast and disagreements between perspectives. Later in the paper we offer a resolution of some of these difficulties as they apply to our case studies. Before so doing we provide an overview of the basic features of the economy of British Columbia, and summary accounts of the industrial strikes that comprise the descriptive base of our analysis.

ECONOMY AND LABOUR IN BRITISH COLUMBIA

In attempting to disentangle and assess the conflicting interpretations of state criminal justice politics on labour, a number of features about the wider context of economy and labour in B.C. must be noted. To start with, economic growth in this region of Canada has always been uneven and unstable. This is so because the backbone of the economy is located in a few resource-based industries that produce primarily for shifting and uncertain foreign export markets. Thus mining in the earlier decades of this century and lumber and construction industries in the last four decades have been highly vulnerable to seasonal and cyclical fluctuations in output and sales, and therefore in wages and employment (Jamieson 1968). There is also a high degree of *external* ownership of major productive industries. Owners and the managerial technostructure of industry as well as the financial and the manufacturing sectors tend to be based in the metropolitan regions of central Canada and the United States. British Columbia thus has a lopsided class structure. A large proportion of workers are in the volatile primary extractive industries, and in service or social service occupations. As Marchak observes, "Thus in B.C. both the owning/directing class and the managerial/professional class are small. . . . The working class includes the vast majority of the population." (1974, 44–45). Of course, institutional divisions may cut across the class structure. Corporations, the state, labour, petty-commodity producers, religious institutions, and the family, divide and fragment the class system. But in British Columbia the conflict between unions and corporations and between unions and the state is entrenched and manifest at the level of ideology. Thus, unlike other regions of Canada there is a relatively unambiguous translation of class/institution conflict in British Columbia which accounts, in some measure, for the concentrated militancy and radicalism of the labour movement, particularly in mining, fishing and lumbering.

Geography is also an important factor in understanding capital and labour relations in B.C. An extension of the larger Pacific Northwest and mountain regions of the United States, B.C. has a similar pattern of industrial development and conflict. Its special topography, resources, and location has preserved many of the features of a frontier region even up to the present day (Jamieson 1976). The province also concentrates industries that have been found elsewhere to be particularly strike prone (i.e., mining, maritime, and lumber). As a result the labour force is highly transient and socially isolated, living in company controlled towns, or workers' ghettos in cities, where labour is segregated from other occupational groups or classes. There are, thus, limited opportunities for stable working, family, and living relationships. Frustrations and grievances abound and often develop into a homogenous "isolated mass" politics hostile to capital, corporations, and the state, (Kerr and Siegel 1954, 193; Jamieson 1976, 233-234). As Robins observes: "The closed nature of many homogenous, single industry mining and lumbering communities with no middle class to mediate industrial conflict, in which class lines are clearly drawn, has contributed to the development of an intense working class consciousness" (1966, 677).

Geography is further affected by wider dimensions of regionalism. British Columbia is a hinterland region of larger metropoli in Canada and the United States. Although, B.C. has become affluent through the extraction of its resources, it is in fact highly dependent on metropolitan centres elsewhere for much of the processing, refining, and manufacturing of raw materials. Thus, it exercises little control over ownership of resources, command of markets, direction of utilities, and access to finance. Because the surplus product and profits are pumped out of the hinterland to the metropolitan centres, it is in these centres where balanced industrialism occurs, and where corporations, unions, and governments have their head offices. For the hinterland region, a truncated economy, a lack of social and cultural services, and a dwarfed occupational structure exists vis-à-vis the metropolitan cores. The metropolis-satellite structure also reproduces itself *within* the B.C. region. As Marchak (1975, 41) notes, "between the most powerful metropolis and the least powerful hinterland there are many regions which are metropolitan vis-à-vis their own resource regions and hinterlands vis-à-vis larger and more powerful regions". The Vancouver-Victoria axis is a typical example. Jamieson (1976, 236) argues that:

> Metropolitan Vancouver, as one of Canada's major seaports and the terminus for nearly all the Western region's major transportation and communication facilities, exerts a degree of centralized control over British Columbia's economic life. . . . This is most immediately apparent in such fields as credit and finance, wholesale trade and distribution, and special professional or technical services as well as in corporate management and trade unions.

The class structure in the Vancouver-Victoria core is thus unlike that of the primary based hinterland. Workers in the extractive industries of mining and lumbering are concentrated in peripheral regions of the province, while the cities attract the larger proportion of workers in state institutions business, trade, finance, and communications. Within the underdeveloped manufacturing sector, the hinterland workers are involved in primary resource refinement; the city workers in clerical and sales occupations (Shearer 1968, 7). Accordingly, this movement towards centralization encourages industrywide bargaining. As a result local communities and organizations are often eclipsed. There are consequences for industrial conflict. Not only are grievances and spontaneous wildcat strikes frequent and a result of social segregation and isolation, but when disputes arise, the Vancouver headquarters of state, labour, and business are too distant to monitor, direct, or service their administrative subordinates effectively. Disputes easily develop into unauthorized, larger, and more prolonged actions necessitating coercive state intervention (Jamieson 1976, 236–237).

The relations between capital and labour have also been shaped by policy and immigration patterns. First there is the prevailing government policy of making grants of land, minerals, and timber, as well as financial subsidies, available to major business interests. As Jamieson (1968, 106–107) notes,

this was a policy that tended to promote corruption the amassing of large
fortunes and indulgence in conspicuous expenditure by the more fortunate
minority of the *nouveaux riches*.

Second, various provincial and federal governments have been
consistent in passing partisan laws supportive of the interests of
capital, and reluctant in producing or enforcing legislation protective of labour. Thus they have regularly resorted to coercive
police actions against miners, fishermen, railwaymen, and
forestry workers. Such economic and legal favouritism generated
displays of resistance and radical opposition from workers in the
hinterland economy of B.C. (Bercuson 1981).

Labour also includes an important race dimension. By the
turn of the century, oriental immigrants constituted a significant
fraction of B.C.'s total labour force. As male sojourners, the first
Chinese, Japanese, and East Indians, for the most part, took
unskilled jobs in mining, railway construction, agriculture,
domestic service and later semiskilled jobs in fishing, canning, and
forestry (Ward 1980). Because of racial prejudice, franchise
restrictions, settlement policies, and language and race barriers in
the workplace, Asians were vulnerable to exploitation by business
and antagonism from white workers. They were resented
especially as a source of cheap labour and as strike breakers.
Indeed, as in the western United States, mass immigration and
employment of Asians was one of the more important factors in
stimulating labour unions. But there did emerge a segregated and
bounded labour market, which fueled unrest, ethnic conflict,
violence, riot, and property damage as well as discriminatory anti-
Oriental legislation (Phillips 1967; Warol 1980).

Finally, British Columbia during the 1890s and early 1900s
and during the 1930s and 1940s was the recipient of, among other
immigrants, three streams that articulated the most radical labour
ideologies of the periods. One stream comprised immigrant
British workers, particularly in coal mining and the building
trades, who were influenced by socialism and industrial unionism
from England. The second stream comprised numerous immigrants from the United States who went into such fields as
mining, logging, and construction work. Many of these workers
espoused revolutionary syndicalism and socialism and set up
unions in mining, railways, construction trades, and lumbering
that were distinctly radical in comparison to unions elsewhere in
Canada (Bercuson 1981; McCormick 1981). The third grouping
was comprised of trade unionists associated with the workers'
unity league and the C.I.O. They also tended to concentrate in
the main extractive industries of logging and sawmilling, mining,

and fishing. In the case of the I.W.A. in the 1930s many of the leading figures in this B.C. union were from the United States and had come up through the struggles of the Lumber Workers Industrial union there (Bergren 1966, 125). Many of these unionists advocated a socialist option at a time in which business unionizing was entrenched in the B.C. labour movement.

From this profile of the main determinants of the economy of British Columbia in the period under review, we shift, in the next sections of the paper, to the more specific events and outcomes of two major industrial strikes in the province: the Nanimo Coal Strike of 1912–14 on Vancouver Island, and the Blubber Bay Lumberworker's Strike of 1937–38 on Texada Island. The account of these disputes is then followed by our interpretation of their significance both in relation to the more general features of the provincial economy and to the evolution of the state in the transitional phase of early monopoly capitalism.

THE NANAIMO COAL STRIKE 1912-14

The Nanaimo coal strike was the longest and most bitter strike in the history of British Columbia. Its significance is emphasized in the fact that it occurred in the province's major industry between 1870 and 1920, and that it required the militia to end the strike almost two full years after it began. It involved property damage, personal injury, collective violence, arrests and imprisonment.

The capital-labour conflict in British Columbia centred in the coal fields of Vancouver Island around the turn of the century, with coal miners struggling for union recognition. The economy of the mid-Island region was heavily reliant on the coal industry, with much of the population employed either directly by the mining companies or in related service industries (Wargo 1962, 11). The largest mining company was the Canadian Collieries (Dunsmuir) Ltd., owners of the Extension and Cumberland mines. Purchased mainly by British capital, its owners, McKenzie and Mann, were also railway magnates tied to the Canadian establishment of central Canada. The Western Fuel Corporation, the second largest company, owned four mines in and around Nanaimo, and was financed mainly by American capital. Financed from the outside, neither corporation felt responsible to the local community and both were concerned almost exclusively with problems which affected the industry's income. These problems included the geological conditions of the Island coal industry, which were adverse for mining and led to relatively high labour costs of extraction; marketing conditions, which were on the decline as a result of the growing inroads of petroleum into the fuel market; and the collective unrest amongst miners who were demanding better wages and safety provisions in the mines. Such changes would have been costly, so the companies resisted union- ization efforts and allowed working conditions in the mines to deteriorate. In the 28 years prior to 1912, 373 men were killed in the mines as a result of coal gas explosions, the last explosion occurring at Extension as late as 1909 (Kavanagh 1914, 1). Company "fire bosses" simply dismissed workers who complained of hazardous working conditions, despite the provisions of the Coal Mines Regulation Act of 1911 which established a formal mechanism for complaint and inquiry. On 15 June 1912 two miners who were representatives on the miners' "gas committee" found gas in #2 mine at Extension. They forwarded their report to the Inspector of Mines who verified their finding shortly after- wards. For this action, one of the two miners was fired. He sub- sequently obtained work at the Comox colliery of the Cumber- land mines, but was dismissed there as well. The Cumberland and Ladysmith miners had taken steps to have the Coal Mines Regula- tion Act invoked against the Canadian Collieries Company, but the Provincial Department of Mines was reluctant to intervene in the dispute. On 15 September 1912 the members of the United Mine Workers of America employed at the Cumberland opera- tions voted to strike until the dismissed employee was reinstated. The miners declared their cessation of work a "holiday" in order to avoid the illegality of declaring a strike prior to asking for an investigation under the Industrial Disputes Investigation Act. The owners responded by ordering a "lockout" the following day. The Ladysmith miners at the Extension mines called a sympathy strike on 18 September and by October 1912, all miners employed by the Canadian Collieries Ltd. had been locked out. The United Mine Workers of American (UMWA), which had reestablished itself as District 28 (with local unions in most of the mining vicinities) after earlier attempts to succeed the Western Federation of Miners had failed to take hold, supported the strike and provided organizers and strike pay. The long-range objective of the UMWA was to establish competitive equality between the Island mines and those of Washington State and the eastern United States, with respect to wage parity, general working conditions, and broader economic contingencies. The miners knew that their grievances could not be resolved without the help of a strong international that would bring union recognition, so despite earlier unsatisfactory settle- ments under the auspices of the Mine and Mine Labourer's Protective Association (1889) and the international Western

Federation of Miners (1903), they looked to the UMWA for the improvements that they desired. Neither the provincial nor the federal government seemed willing to get involved in an attempt to settle the strike, although the latter could not intervene until either of the two contesting parties requested its offices, as per the requirements of the Industrial Disputes Act (IDA). But neither side requested government arbitration, the miners fearing that arbitration would result in a negative verdict as the strike was technically illegal, and the company believing that they could break the strike and thereby deflate the union movement.

The strike took on a violent aspect when the Canadian Collieries Company reopened its Cumberland operation in October 1912, and its Ladysmith Extension operation in January 1913. Some strikers returned to work and the company imported strikebreakers from Edmonton and eastern British Columbia. Tension escalated between striking and working miners, and the owners, through the agency of local police officials, requested the Attorney General to reinforce the control apparatus with a large contingent of special police. Unemployment was widespread, so, many men applied for this duty, further embittering the striking miners. UMWA officials, spurred by the desperation of the striking miners, decided to halt production of all the Island mines. On 1 May the miners called a general strike, and strike notices were posted in the Nanaimo mines as well. Within a week after the strike had been called, nearly all of the men who were striking but who were not yet in the union had joined. Since the two largest companies had modernized their operations to substitute mechanization for striking workers, and had imported Oriental workers (who were easier to manage with threats of deportation), the miners became more truculent. Special police were driven out of the strike zone, working miners and their families were harassed, and "law and order" broke down. Riots ensued against the importation of special constables in Nanaimo, Ladysmith, South Wellington, and Extension (August 13–15), houses and stores were burned, wrecked, or looted, some violence to persons occurred, and on 15 August 1913 Attorney-General Bowser requested that troops be sent to pacify the strike zone. Although martial law was not imposed, over 1,000 of the militia were called in to quell the riots and restore a semblance of order. The danger of large scale violence was over by the end of August, though a reduced contingent of the troops remained on duty in the strike zone until the outbreak of World War I, when they were finally recalled.

In retrospect, company indifference to miners' grievances forced the workers to resort to strikes and walkouts. Management, fiercely opposed to the organizational goals of left-wing labour leaders, responded in kind with blacklisting, lockouts, importation of strikebreakers, and the employment of Oriental labour. The added appearance of over 1,000 special constables forced the union into a position wherein violence and an expansion of the strike became the only means to achieve their ends.

As a result of the August riots, 213 strikers were arrested. Of these, 200 were committed for preliminary trials, and 166 of these were then committed for trial. In the Nanimo trials, 5 miners were sentenced to two years in prison, and 23 others to one year plus. The sentences imposed on the strikers found guilty after trial by jury at New Westminister were less severe. Public reaction to the severity of the Nanaimo sentences was furious, and as a consequence, none of the imprisoned miners served their full time. The district and local presidents of the UMWA were among the last to be released. They were freed on 25 September 1914 and immediately deported. The strike officially came to an end when the B.C. Federation of Labour threatened a referendum on the possibility of calling a general labour strike in order to force more equitable terms for the miners. This prompted Premier McBride to convince officials of Canadian Collieries Co., the Pacific Coal Co., and the Western Fuel Corporation, to move toward ending the great coal strike, presumably in the best interests of the companies, the strikers, and the province. The formerly "non-interventionist" Premier then served as go-between for the UMWA district representative and the companies. On 19 August 1914 the strikers decided to accept the companies' proposal and the two-year strike was over. What labour gained was the companies' agreement not to discriminate against those who belonged to the UMWA; however, they did not secure union recognition. Even the nondiscrimination clause was circumvented by the companies, as a serious decline in the demand for coal in 1914–1915 enabled them to ignore this provision of the agreement. Thus, the miners who had been on strike were not quickly rehired by the companies. After pouring in $16,000 per week and about $1.5 million in total, the strike was broken and the UMWA failed to gain union recognition for the miners. Wages were not appreciably improved as a result of the strike and company blacklisting continued. By the end of 1915, the international union dissolved District 28, withdrew its support from the local unions, and the UMWA disappeared once more from Vancouver Island. The suppression of the August riots and the subsequent arrest and conviction of many of the strikers broke the back of the strike. After two years of strife and privation, the miners surrendered everything but the hope that they would be rehired.

As an ironic aftermath to the strike, the report of the one-man Royal Commission endorsed the principle of the collective bargaining and recommended amendments to the Industrial Disputes Act which would enable the Minister of Labour to initiate arbitration proceedings. The Report also recommended the prevention of discrimination against the miners for belonging to a union and the institution of a penalty against the employer dismissing men for such cause (Wargo 1962, 145–146). These gains however, were trivial as future strikes demonstrated that arbitration without union recognition invariably worked in favour of capital. After WWI, labour in the mining industry was relatively passive, disorganized, and divided over unionist or political strategy. An effective brand of labour radicalism did not emerge in British Columbia until the 1930s.

THE BLUBBER BAY LUMBERWORKERS' STRIKE 1937-38

Blubber Bay is an isolated single-resource hinterland town, located on the northern end of Texada Island. In 1937–38, the town as well as much of the island was dominated by one source of employment — the sawmill and lime quarry owned by Pacific Lime Company, an affiliate of Kingsley Navigation Company and a subsidiary (97 percent owned) of the New York multinational Niagara Alkali. By the mid-thirties, the paternalism of this company town industry was in marked decline. Poor export markets, price fluctuations, a surplus labour population, new militant unionism (C.I.O.) under communist leadership and the rise to political prominence of the socialist Cooperative Commonwealth Federation (CCF) led to wage cuts, layoffs, deterioration of working conditions, and aggressive labour-capital conflicts over union recognition and rights (Jamieson 1968, Ch.V). Earlier company policies of rotating the labour force from quarry to sawmill, providing extra work through freight handling and general clean-up, and rewarding seniority, had produced a loyal and relatively harmonious labour force. By the mid-thirties 80 percent of 150 employees had been on the payroll for at least five years, 10 percent for over fifteen years, only 6 employees were with the company for less than a year (Burnell 1980, 7). But by 1936–37, a change of management to a "dedicated anti-unionist" group further deteriorated already poor health and safety conditions in the pit, fostered a growing antagonism towards workers and again reduced wages (Bergren 1966, 116). The labour force in Blubber Bay responded by reorganizing itself on an industrial basis, integrating lumbering, longshoring and quarry-working within one umbrella union — the Federation of Woodworkers, later to be called (July 1937) the International Woodworkers of America (I.W.A.). Decidedly militant, this new union affiliated with the C.I.O. and was met with forceful resistance from employers, other labour organizations (i.e., T.L.C. in Canada) and the state. The Blubber Bay strikes of 1937 and 1938 were the first tests of the new union (Jamieson 1968, 264–266).

The first dispute occurred over wage levels, working conditions in the pits, and recognition of the union as the legitimate bargaining agency for the work force (Bergren 1966, 117–120). The company refused to negotiate with the union committee and a strike ensued which lasted for seven weeks. There was no arbitration, but a settlement was arrived at which improved wages and provided guarantees that (1) no *new* employees would be hired before the reinstatement of *all* employees on the 23 July payroll (the first day of the strike), and (2) there would be no discrimination against any employee for union activity. Furthermore, the company agreed to collective bargaining with its labour force through a committee elected by its own employees, but the company did not agree to recognize any union affiliation. Between September 1937 and January 1938 a series of violations of the settlement clauses by the company on rehiring policies fueled a combative climate. By the end of January, the company had decided on a course of action. They attempted to form a company union. This failed and the union applied to the provincial minister of labour for a conciliation commissioner to investigate the company's attempt "to force upon the men a negotiating committee unacceptable to the majority of the employees" (Burnell 1980, 14).

This was the first application for a review under the newly passed Industrial, Conciliation and Arbitration Act. This legislation was an extension of the earlier Industrial Disputes Investigation Act. It conceded labour the right to organize and be protected from employers' intimidation and discrimination. It also added to the conciliation "cooling off period" by adding an extra stage. The new act required a conciliation commission to investigate and seek a solution *in advance* of a conciliation board appointment (ICA Act 1937, 93–94). Yet, it was highly ambiguous on entrenching trade union rights. While it did recognize collective bargaining through a committee of the workers' choice, it did not explicitly compel negotiation with an established trade union (Phillips 1967, 115). This opened the door to an array of competing bargaining agents and the company union.

The conciliator investigating the union's complaint found against the company, had the election of the I.W.A. committee ratified by a new ballot, and requested that the company recognize the union committee as the bona fide representative of the employees. The company did not respond favourably. They refused negotiations with the union, did not reemploy all old employees (they did not reinstate fourteen employees) and hired new workers from Vancouver. Once again, the union applied to the labour minister for a conciliation commissioner claiming that the company was effectively blacklisting its members by refusing to rehire laid-off men.

However, before the conciliator arrived, the company fired a union stalwart and a one-day wildcat protest strike ensued. Upon reaching Blubber Bay, the conciliator persuaded the company to reinstate the fired employee and open negotiations with the union committee. The strikers returned promptly to work. Negotiations commenced but broke down three weeks later when the company attempted to enforce its agreement (rejected by the employees) on individual workers under threat of dismissal. The workers committee applied for a conciliation-board arbitration. Before the board met, the company fired nine Chinese employees and replaced them with twenty new men recruited by the local provincial police constable. This triggered a political crisis and the minister of labour intervened and ordered the men reinstated (Burnell 1980, Ch. 2).

The arbitration board considered thirty-two clauses between 29 April and 28 May. The company accepted the arbitrated decision, but the employees rejected it by a vote of three to one. Two clauses were particularly contentious. First, the decision did not guarantee the reemployment of workers who were on the 23 July payroll. So the issue of discrimination was not resolved. Second, the deliberations did not provide for labour's right to be represented by a committee having majority support (as provided in subsection 5 of the I.C.A. Act). Instead, the commissioners opted for separate negotiation and grievance committees to be composed of management, union, and nonunion members. This placed the union, who represented 80 percent of the employees, at a distinct disadvantage. The union did not accept the award and since it was not binding, they gave strike notice for 2 June. A last minute effort to resolve the dispute failed when the company again refused to reinstate the fourteen laid-off men. After four months and four days of negotiation, conciliation, and conflict, the strike began (Burnell 1980, Ch. 2).

Prior to the strike, state strategies were directed towards

arbitration, negotiation, and conciliation. With the onset of the strike, the labour ministry considered another course of action. While admitting that the company was in violation of subsections 5 and 7 of the I.C.A. Act, they attempted to minimize these incidents as not disruptive of the arbitration process and maximize the wildcat action as the *first* break in conciliation and thus the first violation against the I.C.A. Act. Seemingly unable or unwilling to enforce their own legislation against the company, they announced through the media that the strike was the result of employees' obstinacy and irresponsibility (*Vancouver Province* 8 December 1938, 2–3; *Daily Colonist* 18 September 1938, 2). Moreover, as we shall see, the police and the judiciary were soon playing a partisan role in the dispute.

The conflicts between labour and capital were intense. During both strikes, the Pacific Lime Company hired Chinese labourers as strike-breakers, illegally evicted workers from their bunkhouses, denied free access to employees to the post and telegraph offices located on company property, and attempted to establish a new committee of nonstriking employees. Within two months, over 80 percent of the workers and their families had been evicted, some forcibly and with provincial police assistance. The union responded with blacklists of company products, boycotts, picketing and industrial sabotage (i.e., destruction of finished lumber and water supply line). Physical violence between strike-breakers, company officials, strikers, and police occurred on several occasions. Arrests, prosecutions, hearings, trials, fines, convictions, and prison sentences resulted. Altogether thirty-eight strikers were charged with either obstruction, assault, unlawful assembly, or rioting. (Four were charged with unlawful assembly and rioting; twenty-three strike-breakers — some of these apparently company officials — were charged with unlawful assembly, and one company official and a police constable were charged with assault.) Throughout the strike, charges of illegal police intimidation, disorderly conduct, illegal arrests, and provoking a riot were made. Some twenty affidavits were gathered against police practices, a judicial investigation was considered by the Attorney-General, but was overruled by the Premier. Bias in the administration of justice was also evident. Complaints were voiced that the Department of Labour, the Attorney-General's department, the Courts, and the Premier's Office were committed to manipulating legal proceedings in order to obtain a favourable outcome for the company. Certainly the sentencing outcomes were revealing. No strike-breakers or company officials were convicted of any charges, one police constable received a six-month sentence for grievous bodily assault and twenty-two strikers were convicted with sentences ranging from "20 or 30 Days" to six months' hard labour (Burnell 1980, Ch. 3-4).

After the police interventions and the subsequent court hearings, trials, and results, union morale was low. Donations did not cover costs and the expenses of legal proceedings, transportation, food, and the length of the strike, severely weakened the union's financial position. Indeed, by the end of the eleven-month dispute I.W.A. membership had dropped from around 3,500 (in B.C.) in 1937 to below 300 a year later (Bergren 1966, 125). The strike ended in May 1939 production resumed to full capacity, there was no union recognition, and what happened to striking employees is not known. However, the strikes of 1937-38 did have an impact on the state. Labour organizations pressured both federal and provincial governments to amend their labour codes to prevent companies from interfering with the rights of labour to organize and to force companies to recognize unions. The I.C.A. was amended in 1943 to accommodate these reforms. The forestry magnates reluctantly acceded to labour's demands particularly in the favourable circumstances of the war economy and labour shortages (Jamieson 1968, 266). Labour itself was slow to recover. The strike almost destroyed the I.W.A. organization in British Columbia and set back the militant unionism of the C.I.O. The labour movement formally split. The C.I.O. and its affiliates were expelled. Strikes declined in frequency, size, and time loss (Jamieson 1968, 266-269). In the case of the lumberworkers they altered strategies. The main forces of their activities centred around rebuilding their ranks through policy and programs, not in Blubber Bay but in the Queen Charlotte's and Lake Cowichan regions (Bergren 1966, 128-132). However, the events of Blubber Bay did affect, more generally, the activities and policies of organized labour. They deepened labour's mistrust of the state as an oppressor, made apparent the ineffectiveness of conciliatory company unionism, fostered the promotion of an autonomist labour ideology, encouraged a contempt for the law as an entity designed to protect property rather than the person, and made for difficult bargaining in the years after World War II (Jamieson 1968, Ch. V).

Interpretation — State/Justice/Labour

Let us now examine in more detail the activities of state intervention in the Nanaimo and Blubber Bay strikes.

The initial posture of the provincial government in the

Vancouver Island coal miners' strike was noninterventionist. This was characteristic of the government in previous mine strikes (1871–1903), as little aid was given in the working out of settlements. Ostensibly, the sole concern of the government was to maintain observance of the law (Wargo 1962, 16). Thus, Premier McBride, who was also the Minister of Mines, continuously evaded requests from the miners to intervene in the dispute. The professed neutrality of the premier, however, was incongruent with the fact that he allowed a ludicrously simple procedure for calling out the militia to go unchallenged. Under the federal law applying to this procedure, any three justices of the peace could sign an order for the militia to be activated in connection with any disturbance or anticipated disturbance. Moreover, the premier opposed a resolution put by the two Socialist members of the provincial parliament which called for the appointment of a select committee to inquire into the cause of the company lockout. The resolution was defeated by a vote of 35 to 2. In addition, Premier McBride corresponded with colliery owners and managers, keeping them informed about government discussions of strike activities (Report to W.L. Carelson, General Manager of Canadian Collieries (Dunsmuir) Ltd.: Provincial Archives, GR441). Finally, the premier showed little hesitation in approving the call-out of the militia, and no concern for de-activating them while they held the strikers effectively in check.

The federal government appeared to have a more considered interest in stopping the strike, but under the 1907 IDIA Act, the Minister of Labour did not have the power to initiate conciliation proceedings unless it was requested by either of the parties to the dispute. It is curious, however, that the federal government made no attempt to use its influence to persuade the McKenzie-Mann corporation (Canadian Collieries Ltd.) to settle, though at the time of the strike it had granted the company $17,000,000 for the purpose of constructing the Canadian Northern Railway (Silverman 1956, 181). On the other hand, the federal government may have endorsed the use of the militia precisely because it did not want to see the McKenzie-Mann operations preoccupied with damaging work stoppages (Norris 1980, 64). Despite grounds for partisanship, the report of the one-man Royal Commission appointed by the Minister of Labour handed down recommendations seemingly favourable to the miners' aspirations, and led to amendment to the IDIA Act, one of which gave the Minister of Labour the power to initiate arbitration proceedings.

Although the role of the federal government was somewhat ambiguous with respect to the prolongation and sudden ending of the dispute, it is clear that the provincial government eschewed its responsibilities when the Department of Mines failed to investigate the miners' original complaint. This encouraged the companies to believe that they could break the strike, which, in turn, brought on union violence. In all of this, the provincial government underused its own state apparatus for responding to industrial conflict — until the strike got out of control. When capital was threatened, the state mobilized a massive retaliatory response.

The coercive realm of the state is concentrated in its criminal justice system. It is within this ideological sphere that the partisan nature of the state becomes transparent. The instrumentality of the state was brazenly revealed in the Nanaimo Coal Strike once the provincial government crossed the threshold of intervention.

The actions of the special police was discriminatory throughout. Miners were often assaulted by armed strike-breakers, but the police refused to extend the protection of the law to the striking miners. The ties between the special police and the companies were evident in the officiousness of the police on behalf of the company. They served as employment agents in the recruitment of company strike-breakers, and as bank messengers running deposits between the bank and the company office (Kavanagh 1916, 6, 15). In general their conduct was such as to confirm the miners' opinion that the large number of special police dispatched by the Attorney-General was a declaration of war on the strikers.

The discretionary biases of the Courts were no less flagrant and grating on the miners' sensibilities. One magistrate was replaced when the agent for the Attorney-General decided that the cases of strikers charged in connections with incidents between strikers and strike-breakers were being handled "summarily and unsatisfactorily" by the magistrate (Wargo 1962, 91). In connection with the August riots, none of the 213 arrested strikers were granted bail while the preliminary hearings were in progress. One observer commented that,

> . . . at the preliminary hearing in Nanimo, the visitors to the court house were treated to the edifying spectacle of Magistrate Simpson retiring to the judges room in company with Prosecuting Attorney Shoebotham, any time he happened to be in doubt as to what course to pursue (Kavanagh 1914, 13).

Reflecting on the prosecuting attorney's apparent motivation to break the strike, another miner commented, ". . . it is perfectly clear that there are two brands of justice in this province" (Wejr and Smith 1978, 20). Even a Pinkerton hireling was moved to describe the courtroom machinations as a "grotesque travesty" in one of his daily reports (Reports of Operator #29, 21 and 22 December 1913; Provincial Archives of British Columbia, GR68, Vol. 2). In the Nanaimo trials, Judge Howay sentenced two union leaders to two years in the penitentiary although they had not themselves taken part in any violence.

The use of the militia to suppress the strike also gave basis to suspicions of collusion between the government and the companies. On four of six previous occasions when the militia was called out to aid the civil power, it was employed in strike-breaking. In 1890, when the militia was stationed for five months in Wellington, all expense incurred by the militia, including the room and board, and transportation and pay of the men, was paid by Dunsmuir and Sons (Silverman 1956, 160). In 1900, one of the three justices who signed the requisition for the militia to come into the fishermen's strike at Steveston was himself a cannery owner. It was also the case that ". . . no great number of the labouring class were in the militia, its composition being largely of middle-class persons" (Silverman 1956, 180). Furthermore, it was uncertain why the Royal Northwest Mounted Police were not called upon instead of the militia, though it is probable that the militia were preferred since the federal government would not allow the RNMP to come under the direct control of provincial authorities. In sum, the actions of the state criminal justice system in the confrontative stages of the Island coal strike were anything but reassuring to the miners. At every level, the provincial authorities displayed flagrant partiality towards the owners and mine operators. In retrospect, the inaction of the state in the earlier stages of the dispute gave the appearance of a delaying strategy. When the strike widened and industrial productivity was seriously threatened, collusive alliances between government and capital became conspicuous and the class character of the state was nakedly revealed in the coercive and biased application of the criminal justice system.

By the 1930s a considerable state apparatus had emerged to monitor and regulate industrial conflict. At both federal and provincial levels labour codes had come about, in part, to forestall direct workers' actions and allow capital time to prepare for strikes. Thus labour legislation from the Industrial Disputes Investigation Act of 1907 up to the Industrial Relations and Disputes Investigation Act of 1948 increasingly hedged in the rights of unionization and collective bargaining, while simultaneously attempting to solve capital-labour conflicts by means of an innovative "soft" approach. The state central and subcentral units embedded industrial relations in a massive legal structure designed to

prevent or delay strikes and lockouts by means of an investigation
and conciliation process. As Panitch notes (1977, 19)

> This places such tremendous strategy restriction on labour and gives such a
> large role for the law and the courts to play, that the legitimation aspect of
> labour legislation in Canada's case seems at least balanced if not actually
> overshadowed by the coercive aspect.

Yet, the state sought legitimacy of its policies. It attempted to
carve out an autonomous sphere for itself in the arbitration of
industry and in so doing secured consent from fractions of capital
and sections of the trade union movement. Unlike earlier periods,
by the mid-thirties, the state was not an artifice; it was able to
mount counteroffensives with its own adjudicative machinery,
and it had established a fragile legitimacy to counterbalance its
coercive features.

In understanding state intervention in the Blubber Bay
dispute a number of preliminary points should be noted: (1) The
autonomy of the state, exercised vis-à-vis its arbitrator role, was
highly limited. Even in its moment of conciliation, the state acted
to safeguard capital and circumscribe labour. (2) Labour slowly
diagnosed the situation, insisted upon its rights to unionize,
fought back against the employer, and in the *process* the class
character of the state became transparent. (3) Unable to resolve
the dispute through bureaucratic means, the state resorted to
coercive means; the use of police, courts, and prisons, against labour.
That is, criminal justice was differentially applied in order to
further weaken the labour movement.

How then did law and conciliation protect capital and dis-
favour labour? Aside from granting only partial union recognition
and allowing lengthy "cooling off" periods which permitted
employer preparation and stock-piling, the I.C.A. Act was never
enforced against the employer. Employer violations of subsections
5 and 7 of the Act (right of workers to choose their own committee
of representation and protection against employer intimidation)
while investigated, substantiated, and condemned, were never
prosecuted. The only *threat* of prosecution against the company
was when it fired nine men during the conciliation board proceedings. The Pacific Lime Company only reinstated the workers
under direct orders from the Minister of Labour. The arbitration
decision is also notable for its bias. The board reached a unanimous
decision which was not in accord with the recommendations of its
previous commissioner. In particular the arbitration award did not
endorse the earlier position that the company recognize the union
committee as the legitimate bargaining unit, even though it had

the overwhelming majority representation. Thus, the decision
was an adjudicative contrivance. Not only was it inconsistent, it
was itself a violation of the I.C.A. Act, and evidence of the limits
of state autonomy. The conciliation ruling that a separate grievance committee should be formed and that the negotiating
committee,

> . . . shall consist of two members of the unionized employees, namely, the
> president or secretary and one other, and an elected member of which shall
> not be members of the grievance committee. These together with the
> general manager and plant superintendent of the employees shall form the
> committee. . . .

further delimited and compromised the rights of labour to capital
since now the employer would have its own representation on the
negotiating committee with which it was bargaining. The consti-
tution of the grievance committee similarly circumscribed labour
and favoured capital. Since one union, one nonunion, and one
company representative were to form the grievance committee,
this gave the advantage to the employer. Nonunion members
(about 30 out of a work force of 150) were particularly susceptible
to dismissal. Unprotected, and a weak minority, they were easily
manipulated by the company (as had happened in the attempt to
form a company union). The grievance committee and the
negotiating committee attempted to further contain the actions of
organized labour.

The union fought back. They rejected the award by a three-
to-one vote and protested the decision to the Minister of Labour,
countering that what was at issue was the union's right to exist
without discrimination to its members. State sponsored conciliation and arbitration would not act as guarantor for even the *legal*
rights of labour. Indeed, in attempting to resolve the dispute, it
revealed that its bureaucratic *raison d'être* was to bolster the position
of employers and divide the interests of labour. The union called a
strike, which made transparent the partisan nature of the state.
The Minister of Labour reinterpreted events so as to shape a moral
climate more amenable to coercion. In a nutshell, he exonerated
the violations of the employer and portrayed labour as disruptive,
uncompromising, and irresponsible to the point of disregarding
the law. What then was the role of the state criminal justice during
the dispute?

From the onset, police, courts, and state departments
operated in a visibly instrumental procompany manner. Police
constables enforced illegal eviction notices against Chinese
workers so that the company could accommodate strike-breakers.

They actively supported company blacklisting by directly recruiting a labour force of strike-breakers for the company. One constable recruited twenty new men by threatening to cut them off relief. The police further aided the employer by seldom enforcing public access regulations to telephone and telegraph service that were located on company property. Civil rights were not protected, indeed they were abused by illegal intimidation and arrest, and police violence against strikers. Some three months into the strike, and before the major riot in September, the community, the I.W.A., and an opposition political party were calling for a government investigation into the activities of the police. Some twenty affidavits alleged police wrongdoings. Thus through commission and omission the police protected the property interests of the employer and ensured the maintenance of their operations.

Arrest charges are a further area revealing the instrumentality of the criminal justice system. In a minor fracas (separate from the riot to be discussed later) between police, strikers, company officials and strike-breakers, thirteen charges were laid (by the police) against the pickets, two against picket sympathizers, and none against the strike-breakers. It took the police six days to lay the charges. They were assisted in this by the company time-keeper, who was a party in the dispute, and four charges were against top union officials. Ten of the thirteen pickets were convicted of either obstruction or assault (three were top union officials), the two sympathizers were acquitted, and in the one case where the union charged the manager of the company with assault, he was not tried by a stipendiary magistrate, but by a nonprofessional, and was acquitted on the basis of police and company testimony (Burnell 1980, Ch. 4).

The judiciary itself was manipulated in favour of the company. In the aftermath of the riot in September, twenty-three strikers were arrested and charged, fifteen went to trial, three were acquitted, and twelve were convicted (eight for unlawful assembly and four for unlawful assembly and riot). Twenty-three strike-breakers were also charged; ten had hearings, but none went to trial. All were acquitted. The sole police constable facing legal procedures was, however, prosecuted and convicted. The differential outcomes are a result of direct intervention in the criminal justice process (Burnell 1980, Ch. 4). First, the Attorney-General's office appointed judges and prosecutors in such a manner as to secure convictions against the union. They appointed competent lawyers as prosecutors, and selected the father of the Assistant District Prosecutor as trial judge. In the cases of the strike-breakers, they made sure (by order-in-council) that an "anti-strike" judge handled the hearing, and they appointed an elderly, ineffectual lawyer as the prosecutor. Second, they ordered the trials in a sequence that would maximize convictions of union members while minimizing the likelihood that strike-breakers would have to be tried. By having the strikers tried first, then the police constable, and finally preliminary hearings for strike-breakers, they were able to use police testimony (which was a large part of the prosecution's case) before it became suspect. Moreover, by having the strikers prosecuted first, the defense at the preliminary hearings of strike-breakers could present the strikers' testimony as unreliable (since they were convicted) and justify acquittals of all (Burnell 1980, Ch. 4). Third, the Attorney-General refused the request to try the strikers en masse or individually. Instead they opted for multiple trials by three's or four's which allowed frequent repetition of details of participation and grouping of easy convictions with the more problematic. Finally, the summing up of evidence favoured the police position. In the case of the first and only striker tried alone, the judge omitted recounting evidence of police "showdowns" and bolstered the moral character of the force.

> ... the police, Canada's representatives of law and order, were faced with a serious situation at Blubber Bay.... If we had a venal police a corrupt one, or one so cowardly that it would not be prepared to take its life in its hands, then there would be no rule in Canada.

Moreover the same judge stated that the basic fact was whether the strikers were there at the time of the riot. He charged the jury that they should not be concerned with the context or aftermath.

> It's not important to decide who struck the first blow.... The testimony on ambushes does not belong here. . . ."

In contrast, the hearings of strike-breakers did not find against them because they were on the wharf at the time of the riot. On the contrary, the judge provided the context of self-defence:

> Company men did nothing to start trouble when they arrived. The disturbance was provoked by the strikers, and when it began the employees went to the assistance of the police, as it was their duty to do so.

To conclude, the judiciary reinforced the police and the company. Despite a multitude of charges of police misconduct, no summons were issued against them and attempted judicial enquiries were stymied. As Premier Pattullo put it:

What sort of force would we have if every time they took action they were met by irresponsible affidavits. We are not going to destroy their morale by having a threat held over their heads of a judicial enquiry over everything that may happen.

From the above accounts, we can see that there were remarkable similarities and some important differences between the two strikes. In each strike, union recognition was a major objective, along with the resolution of grievances pertaining to working conditions and pay. In each strike, the importation of radical unionist and political ideology was an important factor in the shaping of events toward the eventual confrontations with the state. In each strike, the union was defeated, leading to its dissolution or explusion, and company production resumed without significant concessions to the strikers. Events in both strikes followed a sequential pattern leading to arbitrary exercises of state power. There is a noticeable contrast, however, in the way events unfolded in the early stages of each strike. In the Nanaimo Strike, the state's initial posture was one of nonintervention. The provincial government chose not to enact provisions of the Coal Mines Regulation Act and undertake an inquiry. The federal government was unable to initiate arbitration under the Industrial Disputes Investigation Act due to a technical block (perhaps not accidental), and they made no concerted effort to overcome this hindrance. The state, therefore, appeared content to do nothing, entering the fracas only when the companies seemed to be losing the upper hand in the dispute. At that point, acting on the alleged need to restore law and order, the state intervened in full force. In Blubber Bay, more regulatory procedures were already in place, allowing an administrative intervention in the first phase of the strike. When that failed, as a result of the companies' defiance of legality, the state peeled off its administrative veneer and showed the strikers its mettle. Each case, though different in the first form of state response, reveals the unmistakable direction of state allegiances. The recourse to coercion supplies some of the meaning residing in the superficially benign reactions which preceded it — a veiled instrumentalism which indirectly safeguarded the objectives of capital. While the bureaucratic apparatus of the state was more developed by the time of the Blubber Bay strike, it capitulated on the issue of enforcement, leading to the same displays of state partisanship that characterized the Nanaimo strike. In both cases, the state keyed its responses to the needs of capital. Its legitimation function was undeveloped and barely exercised in the earlier dispute. By the time of the Blubber Bay strike, the legitimation function had acquired a more tangible structure, but when it was unilaterally undermined by capital, the state compliantly shifted into another arena and utilized the manipulable powers of the criminal justice system. In each instance, therefore, regulations were either markedly biased or unenforced. When labour challenged these lapses in legality, the companies cavalierly mocked the rules. The state supported its benefactors. Ironically, the coercive stance of the state was justified on the grounds of law and order.

Our interpretation of the events involved in these two strikes points to the relevance of the instrumentalist conception of the state. At this particular historical conjuncture, forms of capital were not obstructing accumulation, so the legitimation function of the State was not well articulated. Labour, however, was emerging as a counterideology and required pacification, ideally through the widening of consensus. Some legislation was produced as a means of incorporating the working class. The extent and force of that legislation was contingent not only on the needs of capital, but also on the organization of labour, and prevailing economic conditions. The specific impact of labour tactics on the outcomes of each strike cannot be precluded by any reductionist analysis, since local and international union organizers were often in conflict, though the strategies that were finally adopted had a crucial bearing on the sequence of events. Moreover, although the immediate resolutions of the strikes favoured capital, the shift toward legitimation as a concession to the interests of labour was apparent in the subsequent tightening of industrial legislation. As for the structuralist argument, it seems clear that during this period of the monopolization of capital the state enjoyed little autonomy, and that a structuralist conception of these events would be inappropriate. The instrumentalist theory of the state, qualified by the regard for agency (operative in labour as well as capital) and adumbrating the spread of legitimation, is the one which resonates with these events and discovers the ideological content of "justice" at a particular historical moment in the development of capitalist economy.

References

Althusser, Louis. 1971. Ideology and ideological state apparatuses. *Lenin and philosophy and other essays.* New York: Monthly Review Press.

Altvater, E. 1973. Some problems of state intervention, *Kapitalistate* (no. 1 and 2).

Bercuson, David. 1981. Labour radicalism and the western industrial frontier, 1897-1919. In Peter Ward and R.A.J. McDonald, *British Columbia historical readings.* Vancouver: Douglas and McIntyre.

Bergen, Myrtle. 1966. *Touch timber*. London: Progress Books.

Burnell, Tom. 1980. *Labour unrest and justice: The case of Blubber Bay*. Honours Essay, B.A., Department of History, University of British Columbia, Vancouver, B.C.

Clement, Wallace. 1973. *The Canadian corporate elite*. Toronto: McClelland and Stewart.

———. 1976. *Continental corporate power: Economic links between Canada and the United States*. Toronto: McClelland and Stewart.

Domhoff, William. 1976. *Who rules America?* New Jersey: Prentice-Hall.

———. 1970. *The higher circles*. New York: Vintage.

Gold, David, Lo Clarence and Erik Wright. 1975. Recent developments in Marxist theories of the capitalist state. *Monthly Review*, October–November.

Gough, Ian. 1979. *The political economy of the welfare state*. London: MacMillan.

Gramsci, Antonio. 1971. *Prison notebooks*. London: Lawrence and Wishart.

Griffith, J. 1977. *The politics of the judiciary*. London: Fontana.

Hall, Stuart. 1978. *Policing the crisis*. London: MacMillan.

Hall, Stuart and Phil Scranton. 1981. Law, class, and control. In Mike Fitzgerald, Gregory McLennan, and Jennie Pawson (Eds.), *Crime and society*. London: Routledge and Kegan Paul.

Holloway, John and Sol Picciotto. 1978. *State and capital*. London: Edward Arnold.

Hay, D., et al. 1975. *Albion's fatal tree*. London: Allen Lane.

Jamieson, Stuart. 1968. *Times and trouble: Labour unrest and industrial conflict in Canada, 1900–1966*. Ottawa: Information Canada.

———. 1976. Regional factors in industrial conflict: The case of British Columbia. In J. Friesen and H.K. Ralston (Eds.), *Historical essays on British Columbia*. Toronto: McClelland and Stewart.

Jessop, Bob. 1977. Recent theories of the capitalistic state. *Cambridge Journal of Economics*.

Kavanaugh, J. 1914. *The Vancouver Island strike*. B.C. Miners' Liberation League, Vancouver, B.C.

Kerr, Clark and Abraham Siegel. 1954. The inter-industry propensity to strike: An international comparison. In A. Kornhauser, R. Dubin, and A.M. Ross, *Industrial conflict*. New York: McGraw-Hill. 189–212.

McCormack, A.R. No date. The industrial workers of the world in Western Canada, 1905–1914. In Peter Ward and R.A.J. McDonald, *British Columbia: Historical readings*. Vancouver: Douglas and McIntyre.

Marchak, Patricia. 1975. Class, regional, and institutional sources of social conflict in B.C. *B.C. Studies* 27.

Miliband, Ralph. 1969. *The state in capitalist society*. London: Weindenfeld and Nicholson.

Norris, John. 1980. The Vancouver Island coal miners, 1912–1914: A study of an organizational strike. *B.C. Studies* 45.

Provincial Archives of British Columbia. Record Group GR 441, Box 153, Fiel 5. (Carleton letter).

———. Record Group GR68, Vol. 2, and Record Group GR429, Box 19. (Pinkerton Reports).

Olson, Dennis. 1980. *The state elite*. Toronto: McClelland and Stewart.

O'Connor, James. 1973. *The fiscal crisis of the state*. New York: St. Martin's Press.

Panitch, Leo (Ed.) 1977. *The Canadian state: Political economy and political power.* Toronto: University of Toronto Press.

Platt, Tony. 1978. Street crime: A view from the left. *Crime and Social Justice* 19.

Phillips, Paul. 1967. *No power greater.* Vancouver: Boog Foundation.

Poulantzas, Nicos. 1969. The problem of the capitalist state. *New Left Review* 58.

_____. 1973. *Political power and social class.* London: New Left Books.

Quinney, Richard. 1974. *Critique of the legal order.* New York: Little Brown.

_____. 1980. *Class, state and crime.* New York: Longmans.

Reasons, Charles. 1976. *Corporate crime in Canada.* Toronto: Prentice-Hall.

_____. 1981. *Assault on the worker.* Toronto: Butterworths.

Robin, Martin. 1972. The politics of class conflict. In Martin Robin (Ed.), *Canadian provincial parties.* Toronto: Prentice-Hall.

Shearer, Ronald. 1968. The development of the British Columbia economy: The record over the issues. In Ronald Shearer (Ed.), *Exploiting our economic potential: Public policy and the British Columbia economy.* Toronto: Holt, Rinehart and Winston.

Silverman, Peter Guy. 1956. *A history of the militia and defences of British Columbia, 1871-1914.* M.A. Thesis, Department of History, University of British Columbia, Vancouver, B.C.

Thompson, Edward. 1975. *Whigs and hunters.* London: Allen Lane.

Ward, Peter. 1980. Class and race in the social structure of British Columbia, 1870-1939. *B.C. Studies* 45.

Wargo, Alan John. 1962. *The great coal strike: The Vancouver Island miners' strike, 1912-1914.* B.A. Honours Thesis, Department of History, University of British Columbia, Vancouver, B.C.

Wejr, Patricia and Howie Smith (Eds.). 1978. *Fighting for labour: Four decades of work in British Columbia 1910-1950. Sound Heritage* VII(4). Aural History Program. Victoria, B.C.

Williams, Raymond. 1978. *Marxism and literature.* Oxford: Oxford University Press.

Zander, Michael. 1968. *Lawyers and the public interest.* London: Weidenfeld and Nicholson.

Chapter 2

Criminalizing a Marginal Community: the Bawdy House Raids*

T. Fleming

INTRODUCTION

The policing of deviant groups in society, and the role of the media in providing information concerning various forms of deviant behaviour have been two contemporary foci of sociological thought. Recent police action against gay bathhouses in one Canadian city, Toronto, have lead to much public and private discussion of both gay and police behaviour. The 1981 Toronto steambath raids resulted in the largest arrest quota since the War Measures Act was invoked in 1970, and the largest mass arrest in the city's history.

Although sociological knowledge of baths life and activities has been informed by several descriptive analyses (Bell 1977; Williams 1979), these accounts have educated a very circumscribed audience. The general public has relied upon "secondhand" media accounts which thrive upon the presentation of atypical phenomena. This process has been tentatively explored by research on several diverse groups, namely mods and rockers (Cohen 1972), homosexuals (Pearce 1973), and drugtakers (Young 1971, 1974) and with reference to general notions of the creation of deviance and criminalization processes by a number of sociologists, most notably Wilkins (1974), Quinney (1970), and Rock

---

* Paper presented at The Canadian Sociology and Anthropology annual meetings, Ottawa, June 1982. An earlier version of this paper appeared in the student journal, *Canadian Criminology Forum*.

(1973). Progressively more informed "road maps" of the inter-active network of gay social and sexual behaviour, in its various manifestations, have been developed over the last decade (Hooker 1967; Humphreys 1970, 1972; Plummer 1973; Lee 1978; Jay and Young, 1979).

This article presents an analysis of the group interaction involved in the creation of a "new" category of criminal act. Specifically, it examines the interplay between police raiding processes, media images of deviance, politics, and the development of a collective gay response to criminalization. Following Lemert (1972), one would predict that police-gay interaction would be characterized by confusion, uncertainty, and inconsistency. The resultant sporadic nature of crusading by police, coupled with a selective enforcement of law would create a deviancy amplification spiral characterized by ever greater police and gay responses. Our concern will be with what Hall et al. (1978) have termed the *social* nature of crime.[1]

The discussion will address four substantive areas:

1. An examination of symbolic versus latent function of police raids.
2. A descriptive analysis of baths environments, inform-ation dissemination networks, and location in the inter-stices of the urban landscape.
3. A prehistory of police-gay community relations centring upon political, media, and moral linkages.
4. An investigation into media presentation of gay sexuality and baths life.

CEREMONIAL AND LATENT FUNCTIONS OF RAIDS

It is useful to think of symbolic acts as forms of rhetoric, functioning to organize the perceptions, attitudes, and feelings of the observers . . . They are persuasive devices which alter the observer's view of the objects (Gusfield 1969, 170).

Throughout the history of modern police forces, large-scale arrests have been utilized both as extremely profitable economic endeavours and as morale boosting tools. Traditionally, law enforcement agencies have chosen as mass-arrest candidates, groups whose practices and moral standing in the community rendered them relatively powerless. In general, sporting house, speakeasy, and, more recently, baths employees and clientele, have suffered the legal, and more disabling social ramifications of what Hart (1963) termed legal moralism. All three of the aforementioned quasi-criminal pursuits share several common characteristics: a victimless nature (Schur 1965), privatized territory, tainted moral quality, and, more importantly, high detection potential. Interestingly enough, they also possess a resilient character which has allowed them to reopen and continue functioning despite sporadic police invasions.

The willingness of police to utilize untapped stores of deviance to *manufacture* crime problems has been documented by various sociologists (Becker 1963; Skolnick 1966). In this innovatory role, police invoke a crime wave, or perhaps more appropriately a "deviancy flood", portraying reality in a manner which justifies their control campaign, so producing the "self-fulfilling prophecy". The profitable facets of this creative endeavour are apparent to police departments if no one else. Raids inevitably occur when budgets are being proposed, and less frequently when the police are turning over a city to collect information on a particularly heinous crime.

The impression which enforcement authorities wish to convey to the public is that the "problem" is comparatively worse than ever, while at the same time assuring them that this is *not* indicative of a failure in policing techniques. The *problem*, they claim, is a lack of resources. Any of a number of problems may be selected from the urban warehouse of deviance and instantly criminalized, or alternatively, one of the many offence categories with which the public have a fair measure of acquaintance (prostitution or drug-trafficking for instance), may be illuminated by an enforcement and media spotlight. Faced with a self-produced avalanche of immoral acts and actors, the police create a reservoir of deviants which can be employed in future to produce progressively increasing arrest rates (see Table 2.1). By sensitizing themselves to user patterns (raiding on reduced rate nights), developing a practiced sophistication to streamline raid procedures (raiding on cold nights to cut down on public protest) or simply increasing the number of premises raided, the police instantly unveil a new cache of miscreants.

Espousing a generalized notion of Foucault's (1965) "contagion" paradigm, public and media authorities emphasize that deviance can seep out from its holding places, and so contaminate others. Pursuing this argument to its "logical" conclusion, police emphasize that the problem, thus constituted has virtually no limitations. However, containment, but unfortunately not eradication, will be possible with a renewed and increased effort. In this way pockets of deviance help to turn out the public's pockets.

The raiding operation provides a forum, not only for the

Table 2.1 Stages in the Creation of Deviance and Deviants' Response

Raid Target	Police Manpower	Arrests	Gay Response
THE BARRACKS 9 December 1978	20 Officers	23 found-ins 5 keepers	Report to Police Commission Peaceful march of 400 one week following the raid "Right to Privacy" Campaign
THE HOT TUB CLUB 11 September 1979	50 Officers	40 Bawdy House Offs. 20 charges involving minor drugs, theft	Crowd intervenes during raid
1. THE BARRACKS 2. THE RICHMOND STREET HEALTH EMPORIUM 3. THE CLUB BATHS 4. ROMAN'S HEALTH CLUB AND SAUNA 5. February 1981	300 Officers: in the field and processing	289 found-ins 20 keepers 22 minor "drugs" 2 buggery 2 obstructing police 1 assaulting police	— Intervention during raid — March of 3,000 — 6 February — Rally of 1,500 — 11 February — March of 5,00 — 20 February — Rally for Gay Freedom — 6 March — Presentations to the Police Commission, City Council, and Attorney-General by gay rights and civil liberties groups call for independent inquiry — Two Italians chain themselves to Canadian embassy in Rome — Fast by Gay church leader — Slogans; "Enough is Enough" & "No More Shit" adopted by gays — George Hislop enters provincial election campaign as a gay-rights candidate

SOURCES: *The Body Politic. 50 - 70; The Globe and Mall; The Toronto Star; The Toronto Sun; The White and Sheppard Report.*

police to increase production quotas, but also to evoke a general feeling of community crisis or moral panic (Cohen 1973; Halloran et al. 1970). It is also an occasion upon which certain strictures of role, and prohibitions circumventing police behaviour may be relaxed; and so, aggressive feelings held against particular deviant groups may be acted out, by the use of verbal, and *possibly* physical harassment. For police officers, who exist in a world of relative and real social isolation, this may be an event which encourages a collective solidarity, reaffirmation of the essential "rightness" of their cause, and directly promotes morale.

The tendency of police to engage in violations of moral norms occurs not only in drunken behaviour at police banquets (Skolnick 1966), but in reaffirmation ceremonies within the closed environment of the baths, equally secluded from the gaze of onlookers. The considerable damage to baths premises in the Toronto raids, as well as substantial reports of verbal and "physical" abuse,[2] particularly in a system where only police consider complaints of officers' misbehaviour, lends support to this contention (*The White and Sheppard Report* 1981). Indeed, 1980 was fraught with arguments from a myriad of minority groups to set up an independent citizens' complaint bureau to investigate allegations of police brutality and abuses of power. The symbolic image engendered by police swinging hammers and axes to gain entry to baths roomettes and lockers is reminiscent of television portrayals of the work of federal ageents against bootlegging operations during the American prohibition. It is one of the few occasions upon which police *can*, and can be seen, *actually* "smashing" crime.

A supplementary explanation for raids suggests a political dimension to such actions. Bell (1977) argues that crackdowns usually occur immediately preceding elections. Gays have been chosen as targets because of their reluctance to press charges or make complaints, so risking potential publicity and social ostracism. In this manner, the police have been able to turn on the deviance "tap" at convenient times, without the problem of squeaking pipes.

The police have shown a remarkable propensity for raiding immediately following a successful conviction of persons on charges of keeping a common bawdy house (*The Body Politic*, 64), and preceding trials involving similar charges.[3] It is within the realm of possibility to suggest that raids may also act as a form of political protest by enforcement authorities against what they may construe as overly liberal laws, or dissatisfaction with the failure of the courts to convict in important morality cases, such as The Body Politic trial, or the International Steam Baths case.[4]

Moral crusades may be directed not only at what police consider a naive public, but also at a misguided judiciary.

The discrepancy between the symbolic and latent functions of raids is most apparent when a comparison is made between police justifications for raiding and arrest results. A perusal of newspaper accounts of baths raids in Montreal and Toronto during the period 1978–80 reveals that authorities substantiate large-scale, costly operations by invoking recurring themes: suspicions of prostitution in the baths; the involvement of minors in sexual escapades; and, occasionally, the role of organized crime in baths ownership.

The first of these justifications — the allegation of prostitution — serves to alleviate a number of functional problems associated with raids. First, it transforms the private action of engaging in sexual relations into a criminal one requiring police intervention. The charges of prostitution function as a *moral key* allowing the police entry to the baths. Having gained entry, the police find the key is a skeleton, opening a variety of doors. However, when no prostitutes are discovered, and minors are not in evidence, police may automatically revert to charging a large number of persons with being "found in" a bawdy house, and attendants with "keeping" charges.

No evidence exists to support a theory of baths prostitution or juvenile involvement, if the charges made by officials are used as a basis for analysis. The baths environment is barren ground for the cultivation of prostitution:

> Essentially, the baths are where gay men go for sex. They are not whorehouses, and no money changes hands between customers, and almost anyone can find his heart's desire, if he hangs out long enough (Bell 1977, 280).

The mistaken characterization of baths exchange which focuses on middle-aged lechers preying on minors who trade sexual favours for monetary gain, is reminiscent of the widely held belief in the age of Emperor Justinian, that buggery was the chief source of earthquakes (Vidal 1969).

Allegations of prostitution (usually involving minors) allow the easy typification of participants into the widely understood roles of "corrupter" and "corruptible". Police actions may then be cast as morally laudable, and necessary to save minors from older, "wicked" gays (Young 1971). This simple bifurcation acts as a mechanism of social control, warning male minors, the sexually disenchanted, and baths patrons who were *lucky* enough not to be apprehended, of the possible consequences of *being* or *becoming* deviant.

Finally, despite police contentions concerning the financing and control of baths by organized crime, to date there have been no charges to substantiate this connection. The indication by authorities that certain baths are linked to American operations, is about as important a "discovery" as finding that MacDonalds has franchises throughout America.

THE SPATIAL LOCATION OF SITUATED ACTIVITIES

The physical location of pockets of deviance in the urban environment, and its nature, whether public or private, have been major determinants of the effectiveness of preventative legislation, and attempts to alter the moral order (Duster 1970; Becker and Horowitz 1972).

Gay baths in Toronto, and most major North American urban centres, are found in secluded areas of the gay ghetto (Humphreys 1972; Levine 1979), or peripheral industrial areas. This clustering is characteristic of gay bars, bookstores, services, and the location of gay residences. In practical terms, this allows the cruising male to seek partners in a variety of settings. Such neighbourhoods are marked by a greater tolerance of gays, and provide some degree of protection from harassment. Certainly, the time restraints associated with the cruising of closet gays and bisexuals, make such territoriality a practical necessity. Baths locations are also determined by the type of clientele they wish to attract, and adopting Bell's (1979) analysis as a foundation, one may distinguish three types catering to businessmen, students, and S&M devotees respectively. However, much overlapping occurs not only in the character of baths, but also in their respective clienteles.

The first two types of baths tend to locate in the peripheral boundaries of the downtown core close to the entertainment centres of the city, so allowing patrons to pursue other entertainment interests. S&M baths and bars appear in semi-industrial areas, somewhat far removed from the mainstream of nightlife. The relative positioning of baths reflects not only the nature of sexual types and fantasies, but also an ordering of the gay world which indicates the less acceptable nature of S&M pursuits in the gay, as well as, wider community.

Advertisements for the baths are found in gay newspapers, book shops, sexual guides, and occasionally, in university student newspapers. These public notices do not explicate the sexual nature of baths to the uninformed, but rather typically list the various facilities available — lockers, roomettes, sauna, whirlpools, swimming pool, refreshments, colour television, lounge — as well as the cost of admission, and hours of operation. To a passerby, the baths existence is signified by a small sign displaying the name of the facility, or even simply, a street number alone. As Lee (1978) has indicated, the only behaviour which might alert neighbours to the baths' existence, is the incessant coming and going of patrons throughout the evening.

The explanation for "cloaking" the clubs' activities, and their existence, resides in both owners' and users' desire to avoid societal reactions, and "accidental access", a privatization process which Plummer (1973) has dubbed, "the search for anonymity". The baths provide a private, and *usually* safe, environment for casual sex, far removed from the public washroom, and open locations which promote entrapment arrests by police. The desire to *avoid* public identification and stigmatization leads many to the baths. Considering the extensive literature which details the isolation and restrictions of gay life, it is small wonder that baths are so popular (Hooker 1967; Humphreys 1973; Weinberg and Williams 1979; Levine 1979).

In Toronto, public knowledge concerning the location and needs served by baths can be said to have passed through preraid, and postraid phases. The first Barracks raid (1978) created the first public information about gay baths, other than that which could be obtained through various gay information networks, requiring a knowledge of gay symbols and argot. In this manner, police actions may *promote* the existence of a world where casual sex can be had with "more fun and less guilt" (Lee, 1978), almost instantaneously, anonymously, and without the exchange of fees. In a world of deferred gratifications, the "new" knowledge generated by police raids may have directed at least some of the "ungratified" to the baths.

THE PREHISTORY OF POLICE-GAY COMMUNITY RELATIONS

The gay steambath has existed in various forms for at least eighteen years in Toronto (*The White and Sheppard Report* 1981). During the 1970s, baths were opened that emphasized a pleasant recreational club environment, in sharp contrast to the "locker room" atmosphere characteristic of existing facilities (such as The International Steam Baths). Prior to the 1978 Barracks raid, baths had engaged in a large-scale accommodation with the authorities, a pattern which had, at one time, marked the relationship between law enforcers and racketeers. In essence, this association was marked by concessions by baths operators to morality squad members, to maintain an "open door" inspection policy, preferring inspection to invasion. Until 1978, police arrests had generally been confined to homosexual acts in public places — tearooms, parks, and lovers lanes. Certainly, the financial impetus for operators to conform to the *working* requirements of the law, are very great, in terms of potential profit.

Unfortunately, such arrangements are intrinsically prone to instability, so that police-gay interaction assumes a schizophrenic quality, characterized by cooperation, then rejection, aid, then penalty. Indeed, the police body has several heads, and so *even if* morality has an unwritten agreement with baths operators, intelligence may have different ideas about how the law is to be enforced. By shifting the burden of investigation and enforcement to an "outside" department, police departments *may* pave the way for the resumption of normal accommodations after a raiding episode. However, a cycle of sporadic raids, followed by a resumption of accommodations may have certain cut-off points at which deviant groups reject the existing relationship as unworkable, jettisoning a "wait and see" attitude, and opting for the creation of special adaptations to deal with "overwhelming" police actions.

Hate, Fear and Politics

The 1980 municipal elections in Toronto were a focal point in convincing police officials that the public would condone the 1981 raids, and little, if any opposition to their actions would materialize, outside of the gay community. The spectre of gay power, a linking of politics and sex, haunted the campaign — a by-product of gay arguments for the right to counsel in Toronto's schools, and the public's perception of a "mythical hedonist monolith of lesbians and gays threatening public morality" (Sagarin 1972; Casey 1981, 4). Two prominent antigay organizations, Positive Parents and The League Against Homosexuality, promoted ultraright fundamentalist and neo-fascist views of gays. Toronto homes were inundated with hate literature depicting gays as murderers and rapists:

Your child (may be) kidnapped, tortured, raped repeatedly, and finally murdered by sexually depraved deviates that now prowl our schools (League Against Homosexuals Leaflet, 1980).

The groundlessness of these assertions is easily ascertainable by a quick perusal of existing research, and certainly gay sexuality cannot be *logically* equated with pedophilia, or violent sexual psychopathy. However, scenarios calculated to arouse what may be termed "moral linkages" with past cases, particularly those which arouse public support for police crusades, have a power that appeals to emotion, and logic is temporarily if not permanently, displaced. Moreover, although a correlation between the distribution of hate literature and violent acts towards gays may be difficult to prove, the cumulative effects may be very real indeed.

The public remain relatively naive concerning gay sexuality, and if one accepts Stinchcombe's (1963) assertions concerning the anonymity of city life, respect norms about "deliberately not noticing" the conduct of others. The wider community was not buoyed in its knowledge by a gay community which has failed to develop an effective language to communicate the realities of gay sexuality. The hate literature dealt with negative stereotypes designed to "evoke the real concerns and real fear of people caught in a world of confused identities, disintegrating personal relationships, and disappearing community" (Casey 1981), a theme developed over a decade earlier in the work of Klapp (1969). In the absence of *any* counterattack by the political parties, trade unions, or ethnic organizations, the hate campaign proceeded with little resistance.

John Sewell, the incumbent mayor, who adopted a marginal policy of tolerating gays as yet another minority in a pluralistic society, was defeated in his bid for re-election by law and order candidate, accountant Art Eggleton. After the election, Sewell reflected that the media had made his stand on gay rights into the key election issue (Sewell 1981, 68). Certainly the election generated a great deal of public anxiety, assisted by hate literature which characterized gays as menacing, repulsive, irresponsible, self-centred, and obsessed with sex, a tactic recurrently associated with media presentations on the subject (Pearson 1973; Casey 1981). The central assertion of this material was simply that tolerance towards gays represented yet another step toward the destruction of the family system.

The resultant "stirring up of people" was so effective as to cause the New Democratic Party (a provincial opposition party), to retract their support for amendments to human rights legislation which would prohibit discrimination on the basis of sexual orientation. Immediately following the civic elections it became clear that association with "gays" was not politically expedient, but, rather, demonstrably disastrous.

Linkages in Moral Manoeuvering: Rekindling Moral Indignation

A highly effective means of reinforcing moral crusades involves a strategy of linking present crusades to past campaigns that have enjoyed a great measure of public support. This is a concept which may be termed *moral manoeuvering*. Toronto's most recent, and certainly most effective moral campaign, revolved around the Jacques tragedy.[5] The malefactors in the Jacques case sexually abused, strangled, and later drowned the child. The four accused were involved with quasi-criminal pursuits on the Yonge street "sin strip"; a collection of body rub parlours (housing prostitutes), pornography shops, taverns promoting striptease, and run-down cinemas devoted to sex and violence. Public sentiment created an atmosphere which allowed not only the closing of "massage parlours", but also a high-density policing of facilities and street people on the strip. The Jacques crusade focused public attention on immoral behaviours, and particularly their connection with the strip. The "cleaning up" operations engendered widespread support for the police as protectors of public morality, for a stress on *ends* rather than *means*, and produced a "superboost" for police morale. The involvement of male offenders in the criminal episode, who engaged in homosexual acts with Jacques (whether they were "gay" or not) cemented a relationship between gay sexual behaviour and murderous acts in the public mind, subsequently reinvoked in coverage of the 1981 baths raids.

Primary media accounts of the raids concentrated upon a portrayal of gays as "sick" and/or "criminal", engaged in continually expanding the boundaries of gay perversion of propogandizing and proselytizing the young. The *Toronto Sun*, in a series of reports throughout the coverage of the raids, juxtaposed the case of a minor who had been forcibly confined and indecently assaulted by three men. This provided not only a memory jogger with regard to the Jacques case, but a connection of gay sexuality with criminal actions. The net effect for the reader is to produce an "understanding" of a marginal news event in terms of an existing category, so rendering present behaviour familiar, and allowing the option of "trivialising" it (Berger in Rock 1973, 28). In this way, the reality which is made of gay sexuality and baths life may be inaccurate or misleading, the "sense" which is made of it *senseless*, but triviality has been restored, and life may be resumed.

Douglas (1966) and Pearce (1973) demonstrated that "moral tales" ending in natural justice are invariably linked with reports of homosexual behaviour, and one would expect this to be a significant phenomenon in the reporting of baths raids. Following the precedent set by the English tabloids in covering murder cases on the same page as the proceedings of the Wolfenden Committee, the *Toronto Sun* utilized the case of a metro constable who was tragically killed during a tavern robbery to morally manoeuver against public sympathies towards gays. The implication of relating the two was simply: "Who shall we support, gays who engage in bizarre sexual activities, or the police who die to protect us against unscrupulous criminals?" Pearce (1973) and Jones (1974) have argued that such cross references provoke a strong and significant association, lumping gays, criminals, and murderers in one anomalous heap.

Spiral, Amplification and Feedback

The discussion so far, of the various functions of police raids, the political dimensions of gay-police relations, and baths social life serve to underpin an event analysis of the three major Toronto raids. Raids have assumed a sporadic and selective character, related primarily, as I have argued, to economic and political determinants. A close parallel may be found in enforcement techniques which dominated the policy governing "massage parlours" on the Yonge Strip prior to the Jacques murder and reflected the immensely profitable tourist interest which sexually related endeavours attract in a diverse range of economic spheres. It is also indicative of the difficulty of enforcing law in a crusade style in the absence of strong public support, and the facility with which it can be enforced once support is mustered. This remains true even when the symbolic "cleaning up" actions represent no more than a shift of disreputable pleasures from one highly visible and profitable locale, to several alternative avenues (Toronto Gay Community 1979, 14). The police have been pursuing a policy of containment, rather than elimination, although two facilities — The Hot Tub Club, and The Richmond Street Health Emporium — have been closed as a result of the raids (see Table 2.1).

The baths represent a difficult policing problem attributable to several diverse factors. First, the operation of a baths closely parallels that of any hotel. Aside from an entrance fee, and the exclusively male content of sexual activities, one has a great deal of difficulty distinguishing between them. Secondly, much criticism has been made of the costs of police manpower necessary to carry out extensive raid operations that result in a large number of minor charges. Equally, this is an area of behaviour which is not only victimless, but removed from public view. At least one prominent moral "expert" has strongly criticized police actions in both these areas:

> . . . if limited to a private dimension, this practice is hardly a concern of the police force which has or ought to have many more urgent preoccupations.

Finally, there are several questions which arise with regard to the attempt to enforce a law which prohibits "indecent acts", without offering clear guidelines as to the definition assigned to demarcate such behaviours (*Canadian Criminal Code*, Sec. 179(1)). Indeed, one may ask how the average citizen is to "know" what the law prohibits? There is a great measure of ambiguity inherent in a criminal code which legalizes sex between consenting adult males in private, while at the same time allowing their arrest on the grounds that such behaviour is indecent. We shall discover later on in this article that the introduction of a "third party" — the sexual aid, "toy" or "prop" — creates the indecency quotient. One feels that such an argument is as inane as suggesting that children *really* become devils when they put on Halloween costumes.

The sporadic nature of bathhouse raiding in Toronto has created not only a successive amplification of gay response, as we shall find, but an unexpected feedback from a large cross-section of the Toronto community. Each successive raid involved not only substantial police manpower, but a dramatic rise in arrests, and finally, in the number of premises raided. Gay response, at first tentative, and relatively privatized, assumed a collective nature manifested in numerous political and legal protests. As Young (1974) observed, disturbing a previously untouched pocket of deviant actors may yield the opposite result intended by the "intruders":

> Conflict welds an introspective community into a political faction with a critical ideology (Young 1974, 256).

Simply stated, the implication is that there are areas of life where coercion is not effective, but glaringly counterproductive.

Police actions, as reflected in the following event analysis, have produced a transformation in the nature of gay politics in Toronto from a form advocating avoidance and circumvention, to that of assertion and confrontation, characteristic of groups whose goals are thwarted. An additional factor is that they are denied *meaningful* access to socially approved channels for complaint and conflict resolution (Bloch and Prince, 1967).

The Barracks, and S&M baths was the object of the first raid in the history of Toronto's gay baths (*The Body Politic*, 50). The charge of being "found in" a common bawdy house was brought against twenty-three men, and five were charged with the more serious offence of "keeping". The police utilized twenty officers, and, in a pattern which was to characterize subsequent raiding operations, various tools, including hammers and axes, were reportedly used to gain entrance to rooms and lockers.

The Barracks represented a form of testing ground for police intrusion, and the testing of what constitutes "indecent behaviour" under the law due, no doubt, to the S&M nature of sexual activities pursued by its clientele. Media accounts emphasized a "whips and chains" depiction of sexual encounter, provided various anonymous police accounts of their disgust with the practices indulged in, and expressed puzzlement at the function of various sexual aids. One might easily assume that if the police, who deal with deviants everyday are disgusted and confused, so must we be. However, accounts and guides to S&M and related bondage practices and equipment used by heterosexuals, as well as homosexuals can be found in numerous sex guides which have reached sales in the millions (*The Joy of Sex*, for example) and in women's magazines (see *Cosmopolitan* Jan. 81 edition). Certainly the S&M denotation is more discrediting and more interesting than accounts which could be manufactured from the "raw" material available at "normal" gay baths. The axiom, "sleazy targets make easy targets", characterizes the media accounts which concentrated overwhelmingly on the Barracks (the smallest by far of the four baths), and neglected other premises. Gay response to this incident was limited to a peaceful march of some 400 persons a week following the raid, the presentation of a report to the Public Commission, and the opening of a two-way dialogue on policing the baths (see Table 2.1).

In the summer of 1979, fifty police officers invaded the Hot Tub Club in central Toronto. Over sixty charges were laid, of which forty involved typical bawdy house offences. Gay response was immediate, as men in neighbouring bars and a community centre interrupted the raiding process; ". . . this time, a defiant crowd gathered outside to jeer at the cops and chant their support for the men arrested inside" (*The Body Politic*, 58:8). Police were forced to abandon the use of a paddy wagon when protesters blocked its path, and suspects had to be released on their own recognizance.

On Thursday, 5 February 1981 at 11 p.m., approximately 300 officers were involved in a simultaneous raid on the four major Toronto gay baths (see Table 2.1). On this night, 336 men were arrested, representing the largest arrest in Canada since 465 persons were jailed under the War Measures Act in 1970, and a greater number than arrested for any year period from 1974–1980 for similar offences (see Table 2.1 and 2.2).

Table 2.2   Ontario Bawdy House Arrest 1974–80 (June)

Males			
1974	247	1978	176
1975	295	1979	144
1976	235	1980(81)	44
1977	222		

SOURCE: Statistics Canada

Authorities displayed a greater sophistication about baths life culled from six months of investigative work and raided on a half-price night for room rentals, which attracts a large number of patrons (although according to Lee [1978], Saturday nights may be even more popular). Additionally, the police also chose a cold night, "to cut down on protests" (The *Toronto Star*, 6 February 1981). Finally, in order to multiply the number of arrests, four facilities were raided.

Gay supporters gathered outside the baths during the course of the raids jeering and denouncing the police actions. Newspaper accounts in The *Toronto Star* provided, once again, the scenario of crowbars and hammers, plus new innovations including "vaseline jokes" and various verbal insults. Collective gay response was swift, culminating in some of the largest antipolice rallies and marches in the city's history. Various civil rights and human rights groups supported presentations to all levels of government, which resulted in approval by Toronto City Council of the idea of an independent inquiry into police actions. So far, the city has hired another in a series of "moral experts", Arthur Bruner to investigate and bring about improved gay-police relations. The "moral expert" attempts to provide a breathing space for society to readjust, to "cool things out", by providing the image that something is being done. However, if the police response to moral experts is judged by their response to Cardinal Carter's (1977) report, we should expect the moral campaigners to continue the struggle, necessary or not.

"PRESSING" THE PANIC

> Those who control both the propagation and dissemination of moral ideas
> and the machinery of sanctions — the law and the penal system — are in an
> unusually strong position to project their own ideas as being the *only* ones
> (Terence Morris 1976, 33).

Deviance is a phenomenon which excites much public interest
in the press. Accounts of deviant sexual behaviour and desiderata
provide the general public with an opportunity to live through a
forbidden experience, titillated by all the details and salaciousness,
finally condemning the acts. Experiencing deviance in this secondhand manner, the reader has broken no convoluted rules and is
afforded the additional pleasure of moral indignation (Pearce
1973). Press accounts of deviant sexual activities (such as baths
behaviour), may allow certain tensions to be dealt with and
conventionalized, acting to "stretch" the limits of our morals
(Douglas 1970; Nettler 1974). However, lest the story be *too*
appealing, the moral message is *always* clear; the "bad" end
miserably, even if they enjoy themselves on the way, and the
"normal" who forego gratifications, end well. The underlying
message of consenualese is clear:

> The rational is pleasurable, is the handsomely rewarded, is the freely
> chosen, is the meaningful, is the non-deviant; the irrational is the painful,
> the punished, is the determined, is the meaningless, is the deviant (Young
> 1974, 247).

The media may also play an integral role in the initiating of
drives against "new" kinds of deviance (Hagan 1977), and in
attempts to sustain or "save" a faltering crusade.

Media accounts of the 1981 bath raids again concentrated
upon the activities of the Barracks, emphasizing bondage practices,
and the "filthy" conditions of the premises. This form of selective
reporting represents a strategy of persuasion calculated to offer
atypical items or events, which are then presented in a stereotypical fashion contrasted against a backdrop of normality which is
overtypical (Young 1971). In this manner, as Halloran et al. (1970)
have suggested, crime reporting may treat as highly salient what
is, in fact, a peripheral facet of the behaviour, focusing upon
immediately visible or dominant symbols. Indeed, what is newsworthy often tends to be the bizarre or untoward, the very
unrepresentativeness of the item ensuring that it is reported
(Rock 1973).

Through separate accounts ("the other three were steam-baths but not the Barracks"), the press led one to conclude that the presence of steam somehow alters the nature of activities within (perhaps it fogs them). A similar form of characterization to promote a separation of gay interests was applied to those who protested police actions and organized rallies. These persons were portrayed as a "lunatic fringe" unrepresentative of the gay community. "Good" gays in this schema seek out sexual gratifications in normal baths (or their homes) and, if arrested, keep quiet. "Bad" gays attend S&M baths and, if arrested, protest.[6]

The cumulative effect of press coverage of the raids was to emphasize what I have termed the "knowledge gap" which allows press and police alike to present their views in a manner which emphasizes their familiarity with the "awful truth". The implication is that if the public was cognizant of this knowledge, they would not support gays. This gap is not about to be filled by the police, as the public must not only be saved from deviants and deviant temptations, but from exposure to the "truth". The authorities will deal with the deviants, and so totally fulfill the role of moral crusader, refusing to let the contagion spread, in its fullest form, or in any form other than that which they wish to portray.

Unfortunately, police exist in a world of comparative social isolation, and exhibit an overdependence on the sensationalist press which mirrors and motivates conservative, puritanical, and self-righteous views (Box 1977; Pearce 1973). Uncertain of the tenets of this morailty, the police are confronted with doubts and tensions which lead them to overemphasize the traditional con-servative elements of middle-class values, because these are less likely to be contested. Although police espouse an "insider's" expertise based upon daily contact with criminal and quasi-criminal elements in society, their collective isolation carries with it problems of accessibility with regard to the "subterranean currents of moral movements" (Box 1971; Hall et al. 1978). In a world of ever-changing moral boundaries, the policeman is in a position, which severely limits the development of sensitivities to such shifts. Police conceptions of deviance come to depend heavily upon reductionist interpretations founded on role con-ceptions, prejudice, occupational culture, and the interpersonal dynamics of encounter. Transferring Ogburn's (1965) conception to completely nonmaterial terms, the police may be said to suffer from *moral lag*, trying relatively unsuccessfully, to combat con-temporary morality problems with the perspectives and techniques applicable to an earlier era.

The media extended its distorted picture of gay sexuality by concentrating upon a second predominant theme, "the paraphernalia of perversion"; specifically sexual aids, or toys (in gay argot), and various forms of lubricants. Reports stockpiled these items, leaving readers to imagine just how much perversion they could produce. Items seized during the raids included whips and leather bonds, handcuffs, studded thongs, a 40-inch dildo, an enema kit, cricket bat, slides of male pornography, a "vat of cooking grease" (a tin of Crisco), jars of vaseline, and various brands of commercial lubricant.

Since public knowledge concerning gay sexuality is limited, the simple listing of various aids without connection to people, may be construed as an attempt to contribute to a highly imaginative "titillation-revulsion" attitude experienced by the *unexperienced* reader (Jones 1974). The imagination is afforded a great measure of leeway in deciding how two men employ such devices as a 40-inch dildo, and it is the stuff of which ribald party jokes are made (see Morris 1976). However, all of the aids listed in media accounts are readily available to the general public in several Toronto sex shops and the presentation of lubricants such as vaseline, which are utilized by heterosexuals as well as homosexuals, assume a far less sinister tone when reported in the context of a mother applying the preparation to her baby's bottom.

The final theme dominating media coverage was the attempt to present a "filth and disease" portrait of baths life and facilities. This involved, primarily, a concentration upon the legal requirement for the accused, both found-ins and keepers, to undergo venereal disease testing. The Venereal Diseases Prevention Act, Section Four, empowers a medical health officer to *order* persons to submit to a test, if he believes the person to be infected.

Two medical practitioners in the office of health protested the testing, as being unjustified, and were subsequently dismissed ("Docs object to VD tests for arrested", The *Toronto Sun*, 17 February 1981). The presence of a VD clinician from Toronto's Hassle Free Clinic who tested patrons on site (and who was arrested as a found-in) was additionally interpreted as evidence that baths "are incubators of disease and filth" ("Petrosex, maybe?" The *Toronto Sun*, 11 February 1981). Alternatively, one might easily argue that the presence of a VD clinician is indicative of the care and concern which owners realistically take with regard to good health. Further it can be suggested that *anyone* who enjoys a large number of sexual partners, whether male or female, will have a greater chance of contracting venereal disease.

Pearce (1973, 291) has suggested that papers should at least attempt "to be honest and accurate". It would seem more likely that newspapers will continue to dish up a concoction of violence and sex, distorted and misleading as it is, to satisfy a seemingly insatiable public appetite. The message seems clear; the "facts" are boring, fabrication is fascinating.

CONCLUSION: THE COSTS OF CONTROL

Each gives up something and gets something, and to that degree the arrangement becomes stable, the stability itself something both prize (Becker and Horowitz 1972, 353).

No law should give rise to social or personal damage greater than it was designed to protect (*The Ouimet Report, 1969*).

The pursuit of deviant groups and the selection of previously tolerated behaviours for criminalization carry significant costs for society, the criminalized, and police. The process of abandoning accommodations and subjecting a specific group to a moral obloquy coupled with an enforcement of conventional morality may result in a relative flurry of social conflict (see Table 2.1). Indeed, the status quo may suffer, while the cause of homosexual law reform is correspondingly advanced by drawing moral issues into the open for public debate.

In an eclectic society, invasions and what Mill (1947) termed "gross usurpations" in areas of privatized adult morality are becoming increasingly difficult to tolerate without significant negative consequences for all of us. Police hypersensitization to particular forms of deviant behaviour may serve to distance authorities from already distant minorities, making the regular routine of police functions increasingly more problematic. By moulding socially harmless people into criminals, and condoning the intrusion of ever more law into social life, society makes a bad investment, channeling limited police resources away from those who pose a real threat. A costs-benefits analysis indicates a negative balance on the costs side, not unlike that associated with the pursuit of canabis arrests.[8] Rather than limiting our efforts to "blaming" the police, I suggest we try to evaluate just *what* it is we are trying to do. However, it may equally be an occasion for society to pause and consider the crimes which it collectively perpetuates against gay men, across a wide spectrum of their economic and social life. A recurring axiom reflecting the criminalization of gays, is that they suffer relatively minor legal sanctions, but devastating social and occupational ostracism, ridicule, verbal and physical violence. Additionally, they carry the stigma of a criminal record for the rest of their lives. Some, such as one twenty year old found-in in the 1981 raids, find that the only way to escape this assault on the self is through suicide.

The 1981 Toronto baths raids represented an attempt by police authorities to recoup some of the public support that had been lost during 1980. The brutal Schiffler and Tomlinson murders[9] received a great deal of publicity, and remain unsolved. The controversy surrounding the Albert Johnson case[10] has not yet subsided. The police conducted a *mismanaged* moral campaign against gay baths; anticipating little or no public or political support for gay rights, and a limited gay response. Their response, and that of a wide range of supporers, culminated in the largest antipolice rallies and marches in Toronto's history, and the call for an independent inquiry into police actions. Police morale has not benefited, as public support has been mixed, and tentative at best. All that has been accomplished is to crowd an increasingly over-crowded criminal environment.

The baths may represent a relatively marginal and transitional adaptation by men who wish to engage in gay behaviours in this society. However, the wider issues of human freedom and private morality which recent police actions have raised in Toronto, will be a recurring theme in a society whose moral boundaries remain fluid and elusive. Heeding Durkheim's position (1938, 1957) that moral conflicts engendered by deviance may pave the way to their future acceptance in society, we may surmise that the morality resolute will stick to their moral guns *even* against the power of the state. This is especially true in a society where, like "Rubik's cube", it is difficult to return to any given starting point, moral or otherwise.[11]

Notes

1. The following paper should not be seen as a denunciation of one particular group, or as a supportive argument for another. The issues involved have serious implications for all of us.

2.. The White and Sheppard Report (1981) contains excerpts from seventy-five foundations which relate various forms of verbal abuse, and the infliction of various forms of indignities by arresting officers.

3. *The Body Politic*, a Toronto gay newspaper was charged with printing lewd and obscene material centring upon an article which detailed the life and sexual escapades of a pedophile. The International Steam Baths, a rather seedy and run-down baths was raided due to the "mingles" room, (see Lee 1978) on the

premise it was used for sex between more than two men usually, and within the view of other men. There were no convictions in either case.

4. The Intelligence investigation into the raids commenced in the same week as the municipal election campaign began in Toronto. The raids were carried out on one of the few occasions that Pierre Trudeau, who introduced the 1969 amendments, was in Toronto. It was also the midway point of the provincial election campaign in Ontario, and the vote-fetching appeal of the raids to certain segments of society is self-evident, The police budget requested increases for Intelligence operation to $5 million annually and $2.5 million for morality. The budget for homicide investigations was a relatively small $1 million. Are we to infer, that the pursuit of conventional morality has priority over apprehending the perpetrators of homicide?

5. Jacques, a twelve-year-old boy who made money by shining shoes on Yonge Street was found murdered atop a Yonge street massage parlour in August 1977. He had been strangled and drowned after being forced to commit various indecent acts with four men.

6. The treatment accorded patrons on the night of arrest varied considerably in the four locations, further supporting my contention that S&M activities are not only considered marginal in the gay world, but are held to be more reprehensible by police and public alike. See The White and Sheppard Report (1981).

7. One wonders why lesbians have not been the focus of prohibitive legislation, or sustained police actions. For a further discussion, see Ettore (1980).

8. I am indebted to Robert Solomon for this idea. It also brings into question the suitability of enforcing law that has been constructed to control a problem in the past, in the present social environment. The 1917 amendment to the Criminal Code which introduced the concept of "indecent behaviour" into bawdy-house laws may be one example, the laws governing drug use originally introduced to control the activities of a relatively small number of Chinese in Canada during the 1920s may be another.

9. Barbara Schiffler, a thirty-three year old woman was brutally murdered in the lobby of her Beaches apartment on her way home from graduation ceremonies at her law school in April of 1980. Elizabeth Tomlinson, a six-year-old girl was murdered in most horrendous fashion on 26 May 1980. Subsequently, police engaged in one of the largest public manhunts in Toronto's history. Both cases contained a sexual element, and were accompanied by much publicity, and public outcry for solution.

10. Albert Johnson, a West Indian immigrant was shot by police on 26 August 1979. The two constables indicted for manslaughter in the case claimed that Johnson was trying to attack them with a garden implement, and exhibited the behaviour of a mentally ill person. The avalanche of publicity surrounding the case increased tensions between the police force and the black community, in a manner similar to that induced by "SUS" campaigns against black youth in South London, as reported by Hall et al. (1978). The slogan "Don't Johnson me" has become a slogan for the discrimination blacks feel they have and might suffer at the hands of police.

11. Rubik's cube is a three-dimensional cube problem that requires the solver to restore the scrambled colour pieces of a 3″x3″x3″ cube to their proper position. There are over 419 possible combinations.

References

Becker, H.S. 1963. *Outsiders: Studies in the sociology of deviance.* New York Free Press.

Becker, S. and I. Horowitz. 1972. Deviance and democracy in the city. In R. Winslow (Ed.), *The emergence of deviant minorities — Social problems and social change.* New Jersey: Transaction Books.

Bell, A. 1977. The baths life gets respectability. In D. Sanders (Ed.), *Gay source — A catalog for men.* New York: Berkeley Publishing.

Black, D. 1976. *The behavior of law.* New York: Academic Press.

Bloch, H. and M. Prince. 1967. *Social crisis and deviance—Theoretical foundations.* New York: Random House.

Box, S. 1971. *Deviance, reality and society.* London: Holt, Rinehart and Winston.

Carter, Cardinal G.E. 1977. *Report to the civic authorities of Metropolitan Toronto and to its citizens.* Toronto: City of Toronto.

Casey, L. 1981. Toronto the bad: The gays, the NDP and the civic election. *This Magazine.* February-March, 16:1.

Cohen, S. 1972. *Folk devils and moral panics.* London: MacGibbon and Kee.

Devlin, Sir Patrick. 1959. *The enforcement of morals.* London: Oxford University Press.

Douglas, M. 1966. *Purity and danger.* Harmondsworth, Middlesex: Penguin Books.

Douglas, J. 1970. Deviance and respectability: The social construction of moral meanings. In J. Douglas (Ed.), *Deviance and respectability: The social construction of moral meanings.* New York: Basic Books, 3–31.

Durkheim, E. 1938. *The rules of sociological method.* Chicago: University of Chicago Press.

_____. 1957. *Professional ethics and civil morals.* London: Routledge and Kegan Paul.

Erikson, K.T. 1966. *Wayward puritans — A study in the sociology of deviance.* Englewood Cliffs: Prentice-Hall.

Ettore, E.M. 1980. *Lesbians, women and society.* London: Routledge and Kegan Paul.

Foucault, M. 1965. *Madness and civilization.* London: Tavistock.

Garfinkel, H. 1956. Conditions of successful degradation ceremonies. *The American Journal of Sociology.* March, 61:421-2.

Gusfield, J.R. 1969. *Symbolic crusade-Status politics and the American temperance movement.* Urbana: University of Illinois Press.

Hagan, J. 1977. *The disreputable pleasures.* Toronto: McGraw-Hill, Ryerson.

Hall, S. et al. 1978. *Policing the crisis—Mugging, the state, and law and order.* London: Macmillan.

Halloran, J. et al. 1970. *Demonstrations and communications: A case study.* Harmondsworth, Middlesex: Penguin Books.

Hart, H.L.A. 1963. *Law, liberty and morality.* Stanford: Stanford University Press.

Hoffman, M. 1972. Homosexuals and the law. In J.A. McCaffrey (Ed.), *The homosexual dialectic.* Englewood Cliffs: Prentice-Hall.

Hooker, E. 1967. The homosexual community. In J. Gagnon and W. Simon (Eds.), *Sexual deviance.* New York: Harper and Row, 167–184.

Humphreys, L. 1970. *Tearoom trade: A study of homosexual encounters in public places.* London: Duckworth.

_____. 1972. *Out of closets: The sociology of homosexual liberation.* Englewood Cliffs: Prentice-Hall.

Jay, K. and A. Young. 1979. *The gay report*. New York: Summit Books.
Jones, M. 1974. *Justice and journalism*. London: Barry Rose.
Klapp, O.E. 1969. *The collective search for identity*. New York: Holt, Rinehart and Winston.
Lee, John A. 1978. *Getting sex — A new approach: More fun, less guilt*. Don Mills: Musson Books.
Lemert, E. 1972. *Human deviance, social problems and social control*. Englewood Cliffs: Prentice-Hall.
Levine, M.P. 1979. Gay ghetto. In M.P. Levine (Ed.), *Gay men: The sociology of male homosexuality*. New York: Harper and Row, 182-205.
Lofland, J. 1969. *Deviance and identity*. Englewood Cliffs: Prentice-Hall.
Marlowe, K. 1968. Some comments on being homosexual. In C. McCaghy et al. (Eds.), *In their own behalf — Voices from the margin*. New York: Appleton-Century-Crofts, 164-167.
Mill, J.S. 1947. *On liberty*. New York: Random House.
Mills, C.W. 1963. Mass media and public opinion. In C.W. Mills, *Power, politics and people*. New York: Oxford University Press.
Morris, Terence. 1976. *Deviance and control — The secular heresy*. London: Hutchison.
Nettler, G. 1974. *Explaining crime*. New York: McGraw-Hill, Ryerson.
Ogburn, W.F. 1965. *Culture and social change*. Chicago: University of Chicago Press.
Ouimet, R. 1969. *Report of the Canadian Committee on Corrections — Towards unity: Criminal justice and corrections*. Ottawa: Information Canada.
Pearce, F. 1973. How to be immoral and ill, pathetic and dangerous, all at the same time: Mass media and the homosexual. In S. Cohen and J. Young (Eds.), *The manufacture of news: Deviance, social problems and the mass media*. London: Constable, 284-302.
Pearson, G. 1975. Misfit sociology and the politics of socialization. In I. Taylor, P. Walton and J. Young (Eds.) *Critical criminology*. London: Routledge and Kegan Paul, 147-167.
Plummer, K. 1975. *Sexual stigma: An interactionist account*. London: Routledge and Kegan Paul.
Quinney, R. 1970. *The social reality of crime*. Boston: Little, Brown and Co.
Rechy, J. 1977. *The sexual outlaw: A documentary*. New York: Grove Press.
Rock, Paul. 1973. *Deviant behaviour*. London: Hutchison.
Sagarin, E. 1973. Sex raises its revolutionary head. In R. Denisoff and C. McCaghy (Eds.), *Deviance, conflict and criminality*. Chicago: Rand McNally, 174-191.
Schur, E.M. 1965. *Crimes without victims—Deviant behaviour and public policy*. Englewood Cliffs: Prentice-Hall.
Sewell, J. 1981. Sewell on ice: A private reflection on public life: Issues, images and intrigues. *Toronto Life*. Feb. 40-43, 68.
Skolnick, J. 1966. *Justice without trial: Law enforcement in democratic society*. New York: Wiley and Sons.
Stinchcombe, A. 1963. Institutions of privacy in the determination of police administrative practice. *American Journal of Sociology*. 69(2):150-160.
Toronto Gay Community. 1979. *Our police force too*. A brief presented on behalf of the Toronto Gay Community to the Metropolitan Toronto Board of Commissioners of Police, 5 April 1979.
Vaz, E. 1976. *Aspects of deviance*. Scarborough: Prentice-Hall.
Vidal, G. 1969. *Reflections upon a sinking ship*. Boston: Little, Brown.

Weinberg, M.S. and C.J. Williams. 1979. Gay baths and the social organization of impersonal sex. In M.P. Levin (Ed.), *Gay men: The sociology of male sexuality*. New York: Harper and Row.

White, D. and P. Sheppard. 1981. *Report on police raids on gay steambaths*. Prepared by Aldermen David White and Pat Sheppard.

Wilkins, L. 1964. *Social deviance*. London: Tavistock.

Young, J. 1971. The role of the police as amplifiers of deviancy, negotiators of reality and translators of fantasy. In S. Cohen, (Ed.), *Images of deviance*. Harmondsworth, Middlesex: Penguin Books.

_____. 1974. Mass media, drugs and deviance. In P. Rock and M. McIntosh, (Eds.), *Deviance and social control*. London: Tavistock.

Chapter 3

Locking Up Indians in Saskatchewan: Some Recent Findings

*John H. Hylton**

ABSTRACT/RESUME

This paper discusses the results of several studies conducted by the Prairie Justice Research Consortium at the University of Regina which have examined "Natives and Justice" issues in the province of Saskatchewan. The studies focus on the involvement of the Indian-ancestry population with regard to justice issues. The findings from Saskatchewan are generally consistent with results of studies conducted in other Canadian provinces.

It appears, however, that the involvement of the Indian-ancestry population in the provincial correctional system may be more disproportionate than previously believed and that further deterioration may occur in the absence of new justice policies and programs for the Indian-ancestry population.

INTRODUCTION

Human-service professionals on the prairies and elsewhere in Canada have, for many years, been aware that persons of Indian ancestry (Status Indians, Non-Status Indians and Metis) are over-represented on their caseloads. Unfortunately, statistics about the extent of the overrepresentation and the reasons for its occurrence are seldom collected on a routine basis in most agencies. Many

* Saskatchewan Social Services. Revised version of a paper from *Canadian Ethnic Studies* XIII, 3, 1981.

agencies are concerned about the implications for human rights and civil liberties of collecting information about racial and ethnic background. In some instances, the logistical problems associated with the collection of this information are considerable. These impediments have been particularly evident in the criminal justice field.

Fortunately, in Saskatchewan, the Corrections Branch of the Department of Social Services has collected information about the racial and ethnic origin of clients for many years. Recently, the record keeping was computerized and the Prairie Justice Research Consortium at the University of Regina undertook an analysis of the data (Hylton 1980). The results provide a picture both of the number of persons of Indian ancestry who are incarcerated and the reasons for their incarceration. This paper reviews these results and examines some preliminary data respecting the attitudes towards Indians' involvement in the justice system.

ADMISSIONS TO SASKATCHEWAN PROVINCIAL CORRECTIONAL CENTRES IN 1976-1977

In 1976–77, 4,344 males were admitted to provincial correctional centres in Saskatchewan. Of this number, 2.098 (48.3%) were Treaty Indians, 671 (15.4%) were non-status Indians or Metis and 1,575 (36.3%) were non-Natives. In other words, 63.7% of all male admissions were persons of Indian ancestry.

In 1976–1977, 368 females were admitted to provincial correctional centres in Saskatchewan. Of this number, 257 (69.9%) were Treaty Indians, 56 (15.2%) were non-status Indians or Metis and 55 (14.9%) were non-Natives. In other words, 85.1% of all female admissions were persons of Indian ancestry.

It is important to note that in Saskatchewan, the size of the Native and non-Native populations are not the same. Whereas the non-Native population in Saskatchewan was estimated to 847,000 in 1976, the total Native population in this year was estimated to be 90,000, or about ten percent of the total. When these figures are incorporated into the analysis, it can be shown that, in comparison to male non-Natives, male Treaty Indians were 25 times more likely to be admitted to a provincial correctional centre, while non-status Indians or Metis were 8 times more likely to be admitted to a provincial correctional centre. If only the population over 15 years of age is considered, that is, the population eligible to be admitted to provincial correctional centres in Saskatchewan, then male Treaty Indians were 37 times more likely to be admitted, while male non-status Indians were 12 times more likely to be

Table 3.1 Rates of Admission to Saskatchewan Provincial Correctional Centres in 1976–1977 by Sex and Ethnic Legal Status

		Number of Admissions	Total Population	Population Over 15	Rates of Admission (Total Population)	Rates of Admission (Population Over 15)
Males	Treaty Indians	2,098	22,633	11,268	92.7	186.2
	Metis/ Non-Status Indians	671	22,633	11,268	29.6	59.5
	Non-Natives	1,575	426,334	313,964	3.7	5.0
Females	Treaty Indians	257	22,266	10,885	11.5	23.6
	Metis/ Non-Status Indians	56	22,266	10,885	2.5	5.1
	Non-Natives	55	420,468	313,130	0.13	0.18

SOURCE: *Hylton 1980*

admitted. In comparison to female non-Natives, female Treaty Indians were 88 times more likely to be admitted to a provincial correctional centre, while female non-status Indians and Metis were 19 times more likely to be admitted. If only the population over 15 years of age is considered, then female Treaty Indians were 131 times more likely to be admitted, while female non-status Indians and Metis were 28 times more likely to be admitted.

The *information* we obtained from the *information* system maintained by the Saskatchewan correctional authority could also be used to assess the probability of readmission or recidivism to provincial correctional centres. Persons released from provincial correctional centres between 1 April and 31 December 1976, were followed up to 31 December 1978. In this period of two to two-and-a-half years, 60 percent of the Treaty Indians *had recidivated,* 50 percent of the non-status Indians *had recidivated* and 32 percent of the non-Natives *had recidivated.* Thus, Treaty Indians were nearly twice as likely to be recidivists when compared to non-Natives. Of course, if admissions to other correctional programs had been included, the recidivism rate would have been much higher and many individuals were admitted on more than one occasion in the follow-up period.

· It was also possible to calculate the chance of any individual being admitted over a long period. We were interested in knowing what the chance was of a sixteen-year-old male being admitted to a provincial correctional centre at least once by the age of twenty-five. The age range of sixteen to twenty-five was selected because it is one with a high risk of incarceration. We found that a male Treaty Indian turning sixteen in 1976 had a 70 percent chance of at least one incarceration in a provincial correctional centre by the age of twenty-five. The corresponding figure for a male non-status Indian or Metis was 34 percent, while for a non-Native male, the figure was 8 percent. Thus, the chance of a male Treaty Indian being admitted to a provincial correctional centre at least once between sixteen and twenty-five was nine times that for non-Natives, while for non-status and Metis Indians, it was four times that for non-Natives.

These findings that the overrepresentation of persons of Indian ancestry in Saskatchewan provincial correctional centres is partly due to a greater chance of being admitted to a correctional centre at least once, and partly due to a greater chance of being readmitted. In the case of male Treaty Indians, for example, they were nine times more likely to be admitted at least once, and twice as likely to be readmitted, when compared with male non-Natives. These findings indicate that the overrepresentation of Natives is not simply due to a small number of persons being continually readmitted as is often suggested. The recidivism data also document the ineffectiveness of correctional institutions, especially for persons of Indian ancestry.

What offences result in a person being admitted to a provincial correctional centre in Saskatchewan? Table 3.2, which gives the percentage distribution of offences committed by persons admitted to correctional centres in 1976–1977, clearly shows that a substantial proportion of all those incarcerated had committed minor offences. For example, 60 percent of those admitted had committed offences for which a sentence of ninety days or less was given. Furthermore, offences against the persons represented less than 10 percent of all offences. The vast majority of all offences were not against persons and a substantial number, nearly 50 percent, were related to drinking or driving. The magnitude of alcohol and alcohol-related problems among persons of Indian ancestry has been widely documented (Verdun-Jones and Muirhead 1980; Brody 1971; Canadian Corrections Association 1967; Haga

Table 3.2 Percentage Distribution of Offences Committeed by Persons Admitted to Provincial Correctional Centres in 1976–1977

Type of Offence	Sentence Length		
	90 days or less	More than 90 days	Total
Homicide, Kidnapping, etc.	.03	.04	.07
Sex Offences	.09	.46	.55
Robbery and Extortion	.07	.79	.86
Assault and Related	2.22	2.04	4.26
Offences Against Person	1.22	.85	2.07
Total Against Person	3.63	4.54	8.17
Theft, B & E and Related	5.51	12.00	17.51
Fraud and Related	1.21	2.29	3.50
Weapons	.35	.51	.86
Vehicles and/or Alcohol	15.76	6.39	22.15
Escapes, Breach	5.57	4.85	10.42
Drugs	1.09	1.31	2.40
Other Federal Offences	5.20	3.33	8.53
Total Not Against Person	38.32	35.22	73.54
Liquor Acts	12.21	2.23	14.44
Vehicle Acts	8.35	2.29	10.64
Other Provincial/ Municipal	.90	.42	1.32
Total Provincial/ Municipal	21.46	4.94	26.40
TOTAL	60%	40%.	100%

SOURCE: Hylton 1980

1975). Further research is needed to clarify how the profiles for persons of Indian ancestry and for non-Natives differ.

While overrepresentation of Natives in correctional institu-

FIGURE 3.1.

Age Distribution of the Native and Non-Native Population of Saskatchewan — 1977 (Standardized Scores)

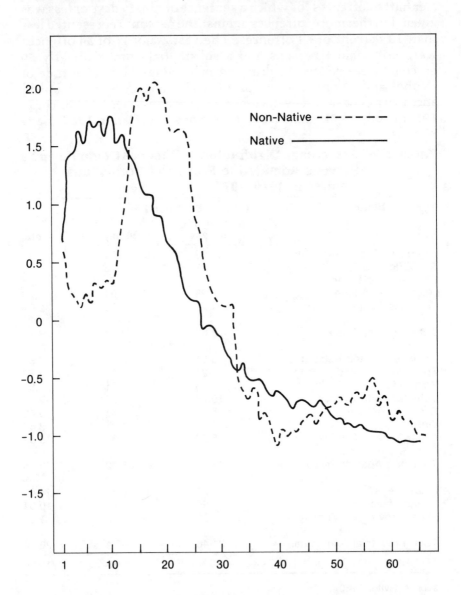

tions during 1976–1977 is cause for concern, there is some evidence that the problems may get worse before they get better. The non-Native population in Saskatchewan, unlike the Native population, has been experiencing a declining birth rate over the last fifteen years. Thus, the proportion of the total population under fifteen years is much greater for the Native as opposed to the non-Native population (see Figure 3.1). In the next fifteen years, however, as the population ages, a large proportion of the Native population will grow into the fifteen- to thirty-year age range — the high risk period in terms of admissions to provincial correctional centres. If the criminal justice system continued functioning in the manner it did in 1976, demographic changes alone would cause Native admissions to rise to about 80 percent of all admissions, while the absolute number of non-Native admissions could actually decline. The opening up of northern Saskatchewan, economic development, and increasing urbanization could cause this figure to rise still higher. On the other hand, the settlement of Indian land claims, the introduction of broad social, economic, educational and other programs, the settlement of jurisdictional disputes between the federal and provincial levels of government, reforms within the criminal justice system, and the greater involvement of the Native peoples themselves in determining their own destiny, could result in some overall improvements.

The situation is so serious in Saskatchewan, that even services provided to meet the broader needs of the Native peoples sometimes end up responding to the immediate needs of those being processed through the criminal justice system. This is well illustrated in a recent evaluation of the Regina Native Counsel project conducted by Havemann (1979). This agency was established to provide legal services to Native organizations in Regina; however, the evaluation indicated that the agency was most involved in providing legal services to persons of Indian ancestry appearing before the courts, who otherwise might not have had any legal representation.

SOME PUBLIC ATTITUDES TOWARDS PERSONS OF INDIAN ANCESTRY IN SASKATCHEWAN

To further illustrate the dimensions of the problem confronting policy makers in Saskatchewan, it will be useful to mention two other studies conducted by the Prairie Justice Research Consortium (Hylton and Matonovich 1979a; 1979b). One study surveyed public attitudes about crime and the police in Regina, while the second surveyed members of the Regina Police Department about their job satisfaction and attitudes towards work. Because issues relating to "Natives and Justice" were identified as a key area of concern in Regina, a number of questions to discern attitudes toward the Native community were included in both survey instruments. Some of the responses to these questions, which are reported in more detail elsewhere (Hylton forthcoming), are set out in Table 3.3.

While a variety of opinions were expressed about persons of Indian ancestry, many respondents clearly held negative stereotypes. Nearly two-thirds of the public and over two-thirds of the police did not agree that most Natives respect the law. Only about one in five citizens and one in seven police officers agreed that Natives are basically hardworking. Nearly half of both the public and police sample agreed that most Natives go out of their way to make the job of the police more difficult. About 40% of the public and 60% of the police believed Natives don't help each other. Over a third of the citizens surveyed believed that the importance of Native culture and history is really exaggerated, while nearly two-thirds of the police agreed with this statement. About 40% of the public and nearly half of the police agreed that, all things considered, the best place for Natives was on reservations.

These findings hardly constitute a definitive attitudinal study. Moreover, it is difficult to assess whether or not attitudes have been changing. While evidence from another Saskatchewan city has revealed similar results (Hylton and Mantonovich 1980), it is not clear how attitudes in Regina would compare with those in Canadian cities outside Saskatchewan.

Yet, the findings do indicate some general trends and they have been endorsed by the Native community as indicating the kinds of attitudes they frequently encounter.

CONCLUSION

The findings presented in this paper are not entirely surprising. The first major survey of the needs of Canada's Native peoples, conducted more than a decade ago (Hawthorne 1966), identified many of the same problems. Since that time, there has been much research undertaken to assess the impact of the criminal justice system on persons of Indian ancestry in Canada. Natives in provincial correctional programs, for example, have been the subject of major inquiries in Ontario (Irvine 1978), Manitoba (McCaskill 1970), Alberta (Kirby 1978), and British

Table 3.3 Some Police and Public Attitudes Towards Natives in Regina

Item		Strongly Agree	Agree	Disagree	Strongly Disagree	Number of Respondents
1. Most Natives respect the law?	Public	1.2%	38.5%	41.6%	18.7%	423
	Police	.4%	30.3%	44.0%	25.3%	277
2. Natives are basically hardworking.	Public	.7%	21.6%	56.1%	21.6%	412
	Police	.4%	12.4%	54.7%	32.5%	274
3. Most Natives go out of their way to make the job of the police more difficult?	Public	11.4%	36.8%	48.7%	3.1%	413
	Police	16.8%	30.3%	51.1%	1.8%	274
4. Natives don't help each other.	Public	6.3%	32.1%	53.9%	7.7%	414
	Police	15.1%	44.1%	37.9%	2.9%	272
5. The importance of Native culture and history is really exaggerated.	Public	12.5%	39.2%	39.5%	8.7%	423
	Police	22.7%	42.2%	31.8%	3.2%	277
6. Natives should not be allowed to drink.	Public	8.2%	20.2%	63.5%	8.0%	425
	Police	16.1%	22.6%	56.6%	4.7%	274
7. All things considered the best place for Natives is on reservations.	Public	14.3%	24.9%	50.4%	10.5%	421
	Police	18.5%	30.0%	50.4%	1.1%	270

SOURCE: Adapted from Hylton and Mantonovich 1979a, 1979b.

Columbia (Hartman et al. 1976). In addition, statistics are now routinely collected at the federal level (Rahim 1977). There have been federal-provincial symposia (Ministry of the Solicitor General 1975) and entire issues of scholarly journals have been devoted to a discussion of the problems. That there are problems is hardly a new finding. Our studies have shown, however, that the magnitude of the problems may be greater than has been realized until now and that conditions may continue to deteriorate if traditional policies and programs continue unaltered.

References

Brody, Hugh. 1971. *Indians on skid row*. Ottawa: Information Canada.
Canadian Corrections Association. 1967. Locking up the Indians: A case for law reform. *Canadian Forum 55*, 16–18.
Hartman, D.M. et al. 1976. *Native Indians in the B.C. correctional system*. Victoria: Ministry of the Attorney-General.
Havemann, Paul. 1979. *Legal services for Native organizations in urban areas: A case study of the Regina Native Counsel Project*. Regina: Prairie Justice Research Consortium.
Hawthorne, H.B. 1966. *A survey of the contemporary Indians of Canada*. Ottawa: Queen's Printer.
Hylton, John H. (forthcoming) Some attitudes towards Natives in a prairie city. *Canadian Journal of Criminology*.
———. 1980. *Admissions to Saskatchewan provincial correctional centers: Projections to 1993*. Regina: Prairie Justice Research Consortium.
Hylton, John H. and Raie Matonovich. 1980. *Public attitudes about crime and the police in Moose Jaw*. Regina: Prairie Justice Research Consortium.
———. 1979a. *Job satisfaction in the Regina police department*. Regina: Regina Police Department.
———. 1979b. *Public attitudes towards crime and the police in Regina*. Regina Police Department.
Irvine, M.J. 1978. *The Native inmate in Ontario: A preliminary survey*. Toronto: Ministry of Correctional Services.
Kirby, Mr. Justice W.J.C. et al. 1978. *Native people in the administration of justice in the provincial courts of Alberta*. Edmonton: Provincial Courts Board of Review.
McCaskill, Don. 1970. *A study of needs and resources related to offenders of Native origin in Manitoba*. Ottawa: Ministry of the Solicitor General.
Ministry of the Solicitor General. 1975. *Native people and justice*. Ottawa: Information Canada.
Rahim, M.A. 1977. *Guide to statistics on Native offenders*. Ottawa: Ministry of the Solicitor General.
Verdun-Jones, Simon and Gregory Muirhead. 1980. Natives in the criminal justice system: An overview. *Crime and Justice 7/8*, 3–21.

Chapter 4

Italo-Canadians and the Mafia: A Case of Misplaced Deviant Designation*

L.A. Visano

INTRODUCTION

Analyses of organized crime have focused on isolated individuals, activities, or social control measures. The results have often been reduced to sensational journalism or an equivalent hysterical response by control agencies. Having limited themselves to secondary data with little or no access to current or direct information, extant approaches tend to offer conflicting interpretations, discrepancies, and confusion.

Organized crime, as a profitable enterprise, must have a mass basis; it must secure not only frightened submission but also the active cooperation of many people in a community. Organized crime may be defined in terms of societal reactions. And yet, despite the many appeals from the Quebec Crime Commissions, Ontario Royal Commissions, Police Commissions, etc., for more information or feedback from the public, very little is known about the way in which the public feels about organized crime. In fact, there is a dearth of studies regarding the opinions and interpretations of the community towards organized crime, its activities and the offenders.

---

* The author gratefully acknowledges the generous assistance and advice provided by both Professor J. Wilkens and Professor R. Harney. Special thanks are also due to Delores Abernathy and Janet Chan for their statistical appreciations of the findings. L.A. Visano is Ph.D. Candidate, Department of Sociology, University of Toronto.

Similarly, popular representations often convey the impression that these activities operate only in a separate world of crime and victimize certain ethnic groups.

Caution must be exercised in approaching the public on questions about organized crime. Because of the complexity of this phenomenon, it must be translated into observable events, to specific forms of behaviour or to matters relative to the norms of the population. Consequently, gambling is analyzed because of the integral role it plays within organized crime and because of the social functions it performs within communities. To determine whether people are concerned about, or apathetic towards, organized crime serves little function. To ask if the public is inclined to participate in certain illicit gaming activities is another matter.

By providing an empirical contribution to the writings on organized crime, this paper represents a response to the plea for more information on public attitudes towards organized crime. The general purposes are

1. to explore the level of knowledge held by the public, especially the Italian community on specific matters of organized crime;
2. to probe public attitudes and opinions concerning organized crime; and
3. to explore the connections or associations of attitudes towards organized crime and exposure to gambling.

In ascertaining the interdependence and interrelationships of variables, indices of acculturations, integration, assimilation, socio-economic background, etc., are employed in order to permit within-group analysis as well as segmental comparisons. For the two dependent variables, attitudes towards organized crime and gambling activities, we are primarily concerned with (1) quantity/frequency of the two related phenomena, (2) reasons/definitions, and (3) associations with other activities and views.

METHODOLOGY

This survey research consists of a number of closely related activities that overlap continuously rather than follow a prescribed sequence. Every new step in the investigation presented new and different problems of some complexity.

Briefly, this study was carried out in several phases. The first phase, from November to March 1973 consisted of (a) deciding the aims of the project, the hypotheses, (b) a review of relevant literature, law, newspaper articles, etc., regarding both organized crime and gambling, (c) contacts with key informants, viz., law enforcement agencies, Italian community organizations, individuals; attendance at the Royal Commission on Violence in the construction industry, gaming establishments, horse races, etc., and (d) devising research instruments, methods and techniques, pretests, revisions to the questionnaire. The second phase took place from April to September 1974; it involved (a) the selection and analysis of the sample, (b) field work, data collection and returns, (c) data processing, coding and preparing cards, (d) statistical analysis, tests for significance, (e) results, testing of hypotheses, and (f) write-up, relating findings to other research studies, interpretations and conclusions.

Pretests of forty-seven individuals had, in fact, become a miniature study. Their responses were analyzed in terms of repeated and consistent themes; the prevailing orientations, interests or attitudes of the respondents were investigated to develop a method for approaching the problem. Categories of questions were revised in an attempt to formulate a workable questionnaire. Pretests had also served to give some feeling for how large a sample was necessary. A sizeable Italian community exists in Metropolitan Toronto. This minority group is highly institutionally self-sufficient (Richmond 1967). The Italian community constitutes more than 10 percent of the city's population. In fact, this represents the largest ethnic group next to the British. Italians are a relatively new immigrant group: i.e., seven out of ten are postwar immigrants (Jansen 1971). In 1981, the Canadian *Census* found 300,000 Italians in Metropolitan Toronto region (*Toronto Star* April 1983). For the purposes of its survey, the *1971 Census* defined "Italians" as persons who were born in Italy or who identify with the ethnic or cultural group to which their ancestor (on the male side) belonged when he came to this continent. The language spoken was also used as a guide to determining the person's ethnic group.

A region was carefully determined and deliberately selected with the aid of *1971, 1966, 1961 Canada, Census* statistics; consultations with key informants, and previous studies on ethnic groups. This area is that section of Metropolitan Toronto bounded on the north by Eglinton Avenue, C.N.R. tracks; on the west by C.N.R. tracks just west of Prospect Cemetery; on the south by C.N.R. tracks just north of Davenport Road; on the east by Oakwood Avenue and Vaughan Road; consisting of nine census tracts completely and two partial tracts. Physical landmarks and permanent features were also used as borders. The area is composed of widespread businesses, factories, old residences, interspersed with new highrise apartments, vibrant shopping and recreation facilities.

Since the population was far too large to approach (approximately 15,000 units), a representative sample was drawn. In order to obtain a random sample it was necessary to have available a complete list of all the population concerned. A list was compiled of all residential units (apartments, houses, flats, etc.) from city directories. A table of random numbers was used to ensure a "random" selection of the sample. A sample of 154 was drawn. The eligible respondent, therefore, was any household member of that randomly selected residential unit over the age of eighteen years.

In light of the nature of the subject matter, attitudes towards organized crime, both "fixed" and "open-ended" questions were employed. Admittedly, "fixed" items offered uniform alternatives, suitable for analytic purposes, while "open-ended" questions were less resistant to simplification and offered maximum freedom to the respondent in regards to a few particular items such as the definitions of organized crime and "mafia".

Two rank orders for agreement employed are Spearman's rank correlation "rs" and Kendall's "tau" statistic.

SOME THEORETICAL PERSPECTIVES

Organized crime operates on a number of convenient beliefs. It has become more evident in the field of criminology that the definitions of crime pose serious problems for both theory and research. Professor Sellin (1938) has tersely declared definition to be "the" issue in criminology. In discussing deviance there are no absolute standard definitions to which we may allude; different societies, agencies or individuals define behaviour differently.

Organized crime is not viewed as a static entity but rather as a continuously shaped and reshaped "category" of dynamic processes of social interaction. Therefore, research attention needs to be shifted from the deviator himself to the definers. Organized crime therefore becomes a constructed social reality where relationships, direct or indirect as well as past, present, and future influence continuing social action. Despite the considerable attention given to the agencies of social control, organized crime research has not clarified the complexities of societal reactions. Moreover, glaring deficiencies exist in the empirical study of organized crime. Historically, organized crime has been studied by law. It is impossible, however, to determine what is regarded as criminal behaviour by merely inspecting its external features of which legality serves as one notable trait. What must also be known are the bases of these social interactions and at what point are the participants in an interactional sequence.

Consequently, in order to define an act as criminal it becomes basic to explore the social dynamics of this behaviour. Secondly, many distinctions of what is legitimate and what is perceived as illegitimate are made culturally (Wilkins 1964). A society in which a large proportion of the population regularly practice a given form of behaviour will tend to permit the behaviour and not define it as "deviant". Since perceptions influence behaviour, the definitions or perceptions of the culture have an influence upon the members of the culture and subcultures. Norms are set for the culture, but different segments of that culture may experience greater or lesser difficulties in maintaining conformity. Almost all forms of organized crime, prostitution, gambling, drugs, etc., are collective acts in which group-derived and group-maintained values are constantly preserved.

More specifically, students of organized crime have in recent years witnessed the birth of distinctly conflicting approaches to the study of organized crime. Each different definition or assumption has shed some light on this complicated term, but it also has added to the already existing confusion. Are these different perspectives reconcilable? By alluding to this background of conflicting theories and approaches, we can profit by understanding the relative contributions of each. This is possible because an analysis of organized crime cannot be reduced to any one method because the subject matter is inherently complex and resistant to simplification. The definition of organized crime also includes the constant interplay of numerous factors or forces such as social mobility, abstract morality, consensual crimes or activities, the Sicilian "mafia", the presence of American syndicates, the spirit of society, unequal distribution of resources, etc.

Essentially, there tend to be two schools of thought that reflect the wide span of current thinking on organized crime. Firstly, the "evolutional-centralization" model assumes that criminal syndicates in Canada represent the evolution of an organization which had its roots in Sicily, where it is called the "Mafia". Once established on the American continent it evolved into a national association with a centralized structure. Alternatively, the "departmental-associational" model views the origins and development of syndicated crime in Canada as one emerging from social conditions and factors within the North American society itself. This latter perspective argues that no uniform development of the syndicates exists. Instead, the structure of the syndicates includes not one national centrally organized syndicate but many organizations which may or may not cooperate with each other (Albini 1971).

The basic assertion about organized crime which is open to debate in criminological circles is whether there is a national, more or less centralized organization, which controls its activities across the U.S.A. and Canada (Mann and Hanley 1968). Law enforcement officials, in particular, paint a compelling portrait of a carefully organized "crime conspiracy" with headquarters in at least two continents. Numerous books and articles by government officials and some social scientists support this view. Donald Cressey (1969), a criminologist who worked with the task force on organized crime remains firmly convinced of the presence of an omnipotent mafia. Popular culture and the public press have also given prominence to this view of a crime conspiracy and to the involvement of Italo-Canadians in organized crime. Alan Phillips (1963) the author of a series of articles on organized crime in *Macleans Magazine* suggests that the Mafia controls all organized crime in Montreal rather than existing side by side with other more or less independent criminal gangs. The implication is that any sort of criminal activity is usually referred to as the "Mafia". This designation no doubt helps to sell magazines but it truly skirts around significant issues. At the Charlottetown convention of the Canadian Association of Chiefs of Police held in August 1973, Maurice St. Pierre, a retired director of the Quebec Provincial Police announced that syndicated crime is under the control "of a clever, vicious group of conspirators" (*Toronto Sun* 1973).

Despite all the evidence cited by the government sources, there are still law enforcement officials and social scientists who do not subscribe to this conspiratorial theme. They, in fact, retort that there is still insufficient evidence to support such a conclusion. Commissioner McClellan of the R.C.M.P. note that "there are competing organizations in Canada, so it cannot be said to be controlled by one particular group, Mafia-like or otherwise" (Report A-9, 1964:49). The former Attorney-General of the U.S. Ramsey Clark (1970, 74) elucidates:

> There is no one massive organization that manages all or even most planned and continuing criminal conduct throughout the country. There are hundreds of small operations that engage in organized criminal activity i.e. car theft rings, groups of burglars, etc. . . . they act sporadically and do not monopolize territories. They are essentially joint ventures in crime. Major organized crime in America is committed by large cohesive groups exhibiting similar patterns of activity in cities separated by hundreds of thousands of miles. They are essentially a loose confederation.

Among the most skeptical critics of the "evolutional-centralization" model are the social scientists. Briefly, Professor Daniel Bell (1962) has commented at length on what he calls the "myth of the Mafia"; Professor Norval Morris of the University of Chicago Law School and his colleague criminologist Gordon Hawkins (1969) readily admit the presence of Italian-Americans in organized crime, but are highly suspicious of the existence of a national criminal cartel. Eric Hobsbaum (1965), the British social historian who studied the Mafia in the south of Italy as a generic form of social banditry sees the belief in an American Mafia as a "myth enshrined in the official and public view".

Considerable research on organized crime has been conducted by social scientists serving as consultants to law enforcement agencies. Unfortunately the files studied are often unavailable to other researchers for analysis because of security reasons. Most of the evidence pointing to a national confederation cannot be put to the test of independent examination since it comes from data disseminated by law enforcement personnel who are themselves party to the controversy (Ianni et al. 1972).

Although the analysis of organized crime is not uniform or precise, a general operational definition for the purpose of this paper may be useful. Sutherland and Cressey (1966, 277) describe organized crime as including groups whose size and structure are determined by the type of activity engaged in; these groups are similar in their acceptance of an underworld code of mutual protection and hatred for the law. By employing such a broad conception, Sutherland and Cressey's description includes many types of organized crime. Likewise, George Vold (1958, 222) calls attention to the utility of a "continuum approach" to organized crime.

In principle, organized crime consists of acts that are designated by those in power to be sufficiently inimical to the general welfare as to warrant official punishment. Generally speaking, organized crime may be defined as any criminal activity involving two or more individuals, specialized or nonspecialized, encompassing some form of social structure, with some form of leadership, utilizing certain modes of operation, in which the ultimate purpose of the organization is found in the enterprise of the particular group (Albini 1971).

The etiology of organized crime is related to the complex influences that have called forth, stimulated, tolerated the very elements we designate as criminal. Professor Peter Chimbos contends that:

> One factor which stands out most clearly is the Canadian private profit economy. In a capitalistic and materialistic society like Canada where the people are motivated by the desire to achieve a standard of luxury, the money motive is an important factor of organized criminal activities (1971, 178).

From the start, America was at one and the same time a frontier community where "everything goes". Crime as a growing business was fed by the revenues from prostitution, liquor and gambling that a "wider urban society encouraged and that middle-class Protestant ethos tried to suppress with a ferocity unmatched by any other civilized country" (Bell 1962). Thus, some of the principal causes of organized crime appear to lie in three constituents of western civilization: first, the repression of emotions; second, the aggregation of power, and; third, popular revolution. Professor Emrich (1966, 1) further postulates this thesis by advancing the argument that our North American continent "has been excessively repressive". In addition, there has been considerable violation of this ideal of intense commitment to the production of goods and services. Its lack of acceptance today is indicated by the general popular tolerance for the violation of the laws controlling gambling, narcotics, sexual behaviour, etc. Organized crime has taken advantage of these attitudes to the point where criminality tolerated in business and politics cannot be distinguished easily from the activities of organized crime. The amount of crime in Canada responds to all these forces. The relationship between the syndicate criminal and the community is total. He or she is the product of the sum of our institutions and the product of selective series of influences within them, as are the best and the worst of the noncriminal population. Tannenbaum (1938, 25) adds that "organized crime" is just as much one aspect of America as is baseball or divorce.

Criminal syndicates have emerged and developed from within the social structure and the history of North American society itself. Syndicated crime has been and continues to be the avenue of upward mobility for those groups and individuals who occupy minority or lower-class status. Organized crime, strangely enough, has a "functional" role in providing a "ladder to social mobility in American life" (Bell 1962). A phenomenon of succession of ethnic involvement exists in that "the Italian's bid for wealth and power came from his infiltration and final takeover of organized crime, taking it from the Irish, the Jew and the Pole" (Reckless 1967). Many ethnic groups lacked the means to make their ambition a reality. Many became engaged in numbers, racketeering, bookmaking, loansharking, narcotics, prostitution, etc. As a minority group loses its minority status, members of the group obviously find more legitimate channels of upward mobility. "An era of Italian crime", according to Ianni (1972), "seems to be passing because of the changing nature of the Italian community which resides in American culture and its inclusion in the society." In Canada, other groups are slowly succeeding the Italo-Canadians. In a newspaper article (*Toronto Sun* April 1973) entitled "Immigrant Racket", the involvement of Toronto's Portuguese and Spanish-speaking community in "a black market in work permits" was described.

Since Italian-Americans emerged as the predominantly "designated" community in syndicated crime in the post-1930 developments, let us now briefly examine this particular group's contribution to organized crime. Every government committee investigating organized crime has singled out some organizational links between Italian-American or Italo-Canadian crime syndicates and the Sicilian Mafia. What then facilitated this Italian-American entry into organized crime? Aside from the characteristics of the receiving society, do the Italian immigrants themselves not also provide some contributing factors that merit serious consideration? Looking at the social history of the Italian-Americans from 1900 to 1930, one finds that some elements of southern Italian culture did have a significant effect on the developments of Italian-American criminal syndicates. Furthermore, social and economic developments in Italy have had an equally important role. For example, after Mussolini's all-out attack on the "Sicilian Mafia", a number of "mafiosi" sought refuge with their countrymen in Canada and the U.S. What then is the "Mafia"?

> The word is employed by Sicilians in two different although related senses, on the one hand, it is used to denote an attitude which until recently has been fairly widespread among certain classes of Sicilians, on the other hand, it signifies a number of small criminal bands (Mosca 1933, 36).

The term "mafia" represents an attitude of protest against, and distrust of the state. It is a belief that injustices can and should be corrected by the person or persons who have received them; recourse to the law is both the sign and the method of the weak (Hobsbawn 1969, 32). In adhering to the code of honour or "omerta", those worthy of the name "mafiosi" are seldom considered as criminals. The "mafia" in Sicily, is as Mussolini's Chief of Police, Cesare Mori (1933) admits, a "particular way of looking at things". Luigi Barzini in *The Italians* sums up this concept:

The lower-case "mafia" is a state of mind, a philosophy of life, a conception of society, a moral code, a particular susceptibility, prevailing among all Sicilians. . . . They are taught in the cradle, or are born already knowing, that they must aid each other, side with their friends and fight common enemies even when the friends are wrong and the enemies right; each must defend his dignity at all costs and never allow the smallest slights and insults to go unavenged; they must keep secrets and always beware of official authority and laws. . . . A Sicilian who does not feel these compulsions should no longer consider himself a Sicilian (1965, 254).

Coinciding with this attitude, there also developed an organization called the Mafia in Sicily. This group is not a tightly knit organization of vicious gangsters "who wantonly kill and destroy but rather a bounded network of members who, following a rigid set of rules" and regulations, brought order and peace to a troubled land (Cronin 1970). This strong-arm organization remained in the preindustrial societies not only as an outcast but also as an unofficial mutual defence and legitimate opposition (Hobsbaum 1969). Most important, the mafia continued to survive in Sicily not because of the strength of a relatively few men, as Edward Allen suggests in the *Merchants of Menace* (1962) but because of the strength of its attraction. Most people of Sicily were not landless peasants. Many had land which the tradition of the mafia guaranteed. For example, Don Carlo Vizzini, a Sicilian "mafioso" was appointed mayor of Villalba in 1943 by the American troops in order not to upset the social system (Lewis 1964). The secret societies of the mafia were institutions of great influence among the people in their respective geographical boundaries.

Originally developing as a "Middleman" to collect taxes for the noblemen, the mafia or the new bourgeoisie soon exploited the peasants. Later however with its monopoly over violence, and with its own recognized organization, the mafia became an important force legitimating an economic order.

Similarities between conditions in the south of Italy and the Italian-Canadian community lead us to speculate on a number of possible relationships. Cultures have often preserved some traditional pattern of response to particular kinds of stress. Does it not seem possible that southern Italian immigrants to North America resurrected the "Mafia" model under stress of poverty and alienation? Generally, the three imperatives which shaped southern Italian culture: the primacy of the family, the juxtaposition of church and state, and the ascendancy of personal honour over the laws of the state, were transported to the new country.

The mafia — the attitudes, the village culture and omerta —

not the organization, immigrated. To be successful this Italian culture soon had to be Americanized. Nevertheless the culture and social organization of existing organized crime groups became the model ideal, i.e. the Irish and Jewish gangsters not the old country oriented mafiosi.

> The acculturation process works in crime as elsewhere and the values which activated and enforced the old Mafia model were, by 1930 no longer prized. But while the organizational form of the Mafia disappeared, it could have left a heritage of kinship which still bands crime families and characterizes the involvement of Italian Americans in organized crime (Ianni et al. 1972, 61).

Another salient feature of syndicated crime appears to be in what is called "consensual" enterprises. That is, "they are consensual crime for the most part, desired by the consuming public."

Serving as intermediaries between the legal and the social normative systems, syndicate criminals manage to erect illegal structures that are "functional" within the overall social system. Moreover, the *raison d'être* of organized crime depends upon the quality of its products and upon the loyalty of its satisfied customers. Hence, a network of relationships characterize this implicit cooperation between the functionaries and their clients.

GAMBLING

More specifically, let us briefly examine one of the most lucrative businesses of organized crime in Canada — gambling. The extremely high profits from gambling are continually invested in other criminal activities. A Canadian writer who had received information from persons involved with organized crime reported that "Canada loses from $100–200 million a year. This money reaches the syndicates directly in Ontario or Quebec and indirectly from Manitoba to other large cities of Western Canada" (Phillips 1963). According to Harold Becker (1970) the estimated annual gross revenues from lotteries, off-track betting, sporting events, etc., in the U.S. ranges from $7–50 billion. And yet, for many Canadians, gambling remains as a form of recreation. In spite of the many legal restraints, gambling is universally indulged in — from the bets on horse races to the twenty-five cent numbers racket.

In this regard the public often feels that its interest is often frustrated by the intervention of law enforcement. Consequently, the police are in direct conflict with many "acceptable" citizens who want to gamble. A conflict between popular morality and law inevitably ensues. The public looks upon gambling simply as "taking a chance"; it fails to be alarmed in pouring millions of dollars to finance other illegal activities. Captain William Duffy, former director of the Chicago Police Department Intelligence Division warns: "our biggest obstacle is the refusal of the public even to accept the fact that organized crime exists here" (Fraenkel 1970). Similarly, Frank Kiernan, a former chief of the Justice Department's Organized Crime Unit in Chicago laments:

> To the people of this city, its like a football game – the Cops versus the Mob. They sit in the grandstand sometimes rooting for one side, sometimes for the other – and they don't realize they are right down in the middle of the action with the players (Fraenkel 1970).

In the area of organized crime, therefore, any attempt to employ the criminal law to regulate private morality encounters many difficulties.

Gambling, etymologically, is derived from Middle English "gamen", to amuse oneself. It involves the taking of a chance on the occurrence of some event with rewards flowing from an accurate estimate, and deficits from an inaccurate one (Geis 1972). In other words, gambling basically consists of risking something one possesses in the hope of obtaining something better. This return may range from a free game at a pinball machine to a substantial amount of money from the purchase of a winning lottery ticket.

Essentially, gambling is a human phenomenon which serves to fulfill certain needs or desires, viz., reactions against boredom, economic motivations, etc. It may function by diminishing social distances and by strengthening group bonds. Values of group morale, social amity and fellowship are symbolically expressed through these rituals. Within a large variety of cultural and social systems gaming practices have become ubiquitous. In many societies control is absent. Currently the state has recognized gambling as a easy method for raising revenue. With programs like Super Loto, Wintario, Lottario, Loto 49, Provincial, etc., the state has become a major competitor in an activity it once strongly denounced. Moreover, the issue of whether the criminal law should include such acts as gambling has come under serious question. The point has often been made that these acts are not necessarily harmful to the individuals involved and typically not harmful to others not engaged. A variation in this general assertion is that if harm is done, it is done to the person so engaged. To consider the gambler a "criminal" serves neither the interests of the individual nor those of the larger community. Gambling, per se, therefore is not prohibited. The prohibitions are confined generally to situations where private individuals are able to exploit and profit from their fellow citizens' urge to gamble. It is for example lawful for people to play games of chance in private provided there is no profit in the form of a "rake-off' or fee for playing. It is also a basic tenet of the *Canadian Criminal Code* that the urges of the citizenry to gamble may reasonably be satisfied within lawful limits.

In our present situation law enforcement agencies have been placed in the unenviable position of attempting to enforce a law which does not appear to be supported by the public. In fact, public attitudes tend to vascillate between approbation to prohibition. It must therefore become abundantly clear that legislation alone cannot be expected to substantially reduce "the profitable and socially harmful" involvement of organized crime in gambling. It may, as the Ontario Task Force on Off-Track Betting (1972) suggests, "be far more important to attempt to build respect for the law by providing it with a greater degree of consistency." Betting on horse races has always been legal when one is physically at the race track, and it would therefore seem to be logically indenfensible to assert that it is wrong to bet on the same game when one is physically distant from the track.

The organized crime problem is not strictly owned by the police but it ought to be an academic concern, a community commitment and a public interest. The main question with which this project attempts to deal is the central issue of public attitudes — attitudes of acceptance and affirmation and how they are, in fact, actualized. In retrospect, theories of organized crime fail to link the phenomenon of organized crime with behaviour which people reward. In other words, business through crime is a pattern of behaviour which the public is unwilling to punish. Instead these behaviours are reinforced. The public perhaps refuses to perceive organized crime as a problem. This refusal to see it as a problem has been translated by the police as a form of moral blindness. To restore the public's vision, surgery is often prescribed in the manner of increased intelligence and increased hegemony over definitions of organized crime activities.

Organized crime activities cannot be effectively controlled by public officials in a democratic society. Admittedly, formal social control may keep criminals in prisons but does it eliminate the counterinstitution of organized crime? Organized crime should not be solely construed as a contest between the police and the criminals. The parameters are far more expansive.

This underworld is the product of many forces — socio-economic conditions, laws, customs, etc., which make its business profitable.

A virtual disregard for the participant exists. Whatever the activity, gambling, prostitution or loansharking, the victim's behaviour and perceptions play a willing but critical role in invoking the act against himself. The "injured" may be responsible for his own victimization. With organized crime activities the victim and the perpetrator are often one and the same; their roles are frequently blurred. How then does the offender or the victim view this activity?

It remains far too shortsighted to simply summon more public awareness. The public must be asked to play an active role in controlling both organized crime and the responses to it. A system of educating both the public and the police; a system of mutual exchange of information and a greater degree of confidence to be shown by formal social control agencies to the general community are all warranted. Organized crime is a social phenomenon; the creation of highly trained "troubleshooters" is but one method of dealing with it and evidently quite ineffective at that.

In any event, it seems clear that a criminological analysis of organized crime is long overdue. No longer should this area be relegated to simply punitive remedies. Instead, theoretical perspectives illustrating the significant role of public attitudes and involvements vis-à-vis organized crime, coupled with empirical explorations, findings and interpretations are essential. Moreover there is a proclivity among many social scientists to view this criminality as an individual matter separate from an acceptable substantial theoretical framework.

FINDINGS

It therefore becomes imperative to study public attitudes in order to fully understand the phenomenon of organized crime. Which activities are stigmatized the most, which the least, and by what elements of the population? What does the public think, if anything, about the strange role gambling plays for organized crime?

Gambling

As a preliminary finding the respondents were asked if they participated in any gaming activity. Gambling carries the approval of the bulk of the respondents. Table 4.1 illustrates that 3 out of 4 respondents participate in some form of gambling.

Table 4.1   Respondents' Gambling Involvement

Category	Per cent	Number
Gamble	76.0%	117
Do Not Gamble	15.6%	24
No Response	8.4%	13
TOTAL	100.0%	154

NOTE: N = 154

It was discovered that people seldom limited themselves to one form of gambling; they indulge in other gaming events as well. Sixty-one percent of the respondents wager at various forms of lotteries. Lotteries are the most frequently cited gambling activity. These lotteries may include numerous variations from foreign raffle tickets like the Irish Hospital Sweepstakes, to the national Olympic Canada Lottery, local fraternal organizations raffle, etc. The current trend today towards more legalization of lotteries accompanies a pervasive public's acceptance. Ticket distributions for many government-sponsored lotteries may be found in many accessible locations.

The question whether and to what extent gambling varies with class affiliation is basic and yet few empirical studies on this matter exist. Are members of the lower social strata the most ardent supporters of gambling? How reluctant are the educated or wealthy classes to engage in this practice? Pay-to-play cards was selected not only because of its high popularity, but also because of the peculiar nature of its illegality. Also, it tends to be highly accessible to all classes. The results are thus approached for the purposes of discovering the extent to which socio-economic class levels are associated with card playing for a fee.

Bernard Blishen's socio-economic index of occupation and education was used in operationalizing the concept "prestige" or "social standing". Essentially, the following hypotheses are dealt with: (1) the higher the socio-economic class level, the less the likelihood to gamble, (2) the lower and less advantaged educational background, the greater the likelihood to gamble.

Correlation analysis may provide further support for these relationships. When occupation levels are correlated with frequency of this specific gaming activity we obtain a *tau* value of −.009 (N = 63) and when frequency of this gambling practice is correlated against education we obtain a *tau* value of +.16 (N = 64). That is, as the occupation category presented in descending levels is correlated with frequency, which is also presented in descending levels, a negative association will be yielded. In other words, the lower the occupation category the higher the rate of gambling. Secondly, as the education levels presented in increasing order are correlated with frequency of gambling, which is presented in decreasing order, a positive association will be yielded. (Both tau values are significant at the 1% level.) These data do not provide very strong support for the notion that social class and involvements in gambling are highly related. Thus, although there is a tendency for labourers and the unemployed to be positively correlated with a high frequency, the degree of association is relatively low. Likewise, although the hypotheses that academic background and frequency of involvement are interdependent, the data slightly support the hypothesis. The less educated and the lower occupation levels of respondents therefore, do not differ significantly from the other groups.

As *acculturation* becomes more intense do we find less frequent participation in betting activities? In order to test this hypothesis it is necessary to perform separate analysis for the Italian and non-Italian groups. Numerous variables of acculturation have been studied in our survey of Italian home dwellers. They include English language facility, listening to the ethnic radio programs, reading ethnic newspapers, length of residency, etc. Language was made the criterion of acculturation; that is, current language facility. This single measure tends to do justice to the diversity of ethnic acculturation. Languages are clearly distinct and readily recognizable. Moreover the acquisition of English in a predominantly Italian geographic area illustrates a deliberate attempt by the individual to make available to him or her a multitude of potential avenues — recreation, employment, etc. Thus, as a single measure of acculturation, language serves the purposes of this study. This indicator has been analyzed in terms of certain dependent variables. Table 4.2 examines language facility and frequency at betting. By so doing individuals within the same groupings of ethnicity are compared within their categories, (Italian nongamblers with Italian gamblers, as well as with other categories like non-Italians). Consequently gaming and ethnic differentiations are pursued.

The hypothesis that gambling increases with acculturation is marginally supportd. A more involved participation with the receiving society by the Italian respondent does not invariably correspond with an increase in one's gambling inclinations. Betting may therefore be construed as universally popular for the "newcomers" and the native Canadians alike. Acculturation is not however highly associated with betting activities. In fact the correlation coefficient is .077, (significant at the 1% level). This means that as acculturation increases (language facility in this particular case), betting involvements also increase. With regard to within-group comparisons, no Italian who spoke only Italian preferred to bet daily. In fact most participants belong to that category of Italians who speak both English and Italian. Moreover, most Italians who spoke no English fell in the nonbettors group. The Italians who identified themselves as Italians but spoke only English also preferred not to bet. There tends to be a correlation between less intense acculturation (inability to speak English) and the frequency of gambling of this sort. To elucidate, a large number of "only speaking" Italian respondents did not bet: 10/17 or 58.8%, whereas "English and Italian speaking" respondents (those who scored higher on an assimilation index) numbered 51.2% admitted betting. Dealing with a small sample these dif-

Table 4.2 Acculturation Process as Defined by Language Facility Assigned by Betting Frequency

Betting Frequency		Speaks Italian	Speaks Italian and English	Speaks English Only	Non-Italian	Total
Daily	N	0	1	0	4	5
	%	0.0	20.0	0.0	80.0	3.2
	%	0.0	2.4	0.0	5.3	
2-3 times/ week	N	3	7	1	5	16
	%	18.8	43.8	6.3	31.3	10.4
	%	17.6	16.2	14.3	6.7	
Weekly	N	1	7	0	14	22
	%	4.5	31.8	0.0	63.6	14.3
	%	5.9	17.1	0.0	18.7	
Once every 2-3 weeks	N	1	4	2	5	12
	%	8.3	33.3	16.7	41.7	7.8
	%	5.9	9.8	28.6	6.7	
Monthly	N	1	2	0	0	7
	%	14.3	28.6	0.0	0.0	4.5
	%	5.9	4.9	0.0	0.0	
Does Not Bet	N	10	22	4	43	79
	%	12.7	27.9	5.1	54.4	51.3
	%	58.8	51.2	57.1	57.3	
TOTAL	N	17	43	7	75	154
	%	11.0	17.9	4.5	48.7	100.0

NOTE: Cell percentages are based on (1) row and (2) column sums. These total percentages are based on total sum N = 154. N.R. category consisted of 12 respondents or 7.8%.

ferences must therefore be more seriously examined and appreciated. In fact, most respondents did not place bets (79/154 or 51.3%) *but* those who did gamble belong to (a) non-Italian respondents, and (b) those Italian respondents who spoke English. Correlational analysis reveals that the further the respondents' birthplace is from Toronto, the more inclined is the respondent to have other involvements with fellow gamblers. The Spearman coefficient value is 0.0880 at the 1% significance level. Table 4.3 clearly indicates that 31 out of 55 card players or 56.3% have had involvements with other players. Relationships continue outside of the gambling process or situation. A considerable difference exists between the patterns of Italian and Canadian responses with those of other "foreign" respondents. It follows that respondents from other foreign countries appear to select the "no" response quite regularly in denying that other involvements exist with their fellow players.

Table 4.3   Other Involvements of Respondents with Fellow Players Assigned by Birthplace

Birthplace		Yes	No	Total
Metro Toronto	N	4	1	5
	%	12.8	4.2	
Other Canadian Country	N	6	3	9
	%	19.4	12.5	
North Italy	N	4	2	6
	%	12.9	8.3	
Central Italy	N	2	1	3
	%	6.5	4.2	
South Italy	N	11	7	18
	%	35.5	29.2	
Other Foreign Country	N	4	10	14
	%	12.9	41.6	
TOTAL	N	31	24	55
	%	100.0	100.0	

NOTE: N = 154 Percentages based on column sums.

ATTITUDES

Having thus presented a few findings on the incidence of gambling, let us now briefly consider some of the attitudes towards gambling. In attempting to determine the general direction of beliefs, we asked "Should organizing a place to play cards (for fee or pay) be illegal?" Interestingly 7.8% of the respondents did not know whether it should be against the law. Most responses, as shown by Table 4.4, indicate an opinion that it should not be unlawful. It seems fairly clear that the perceived seriousness of this crime falls short of a level which would identify it as an overwhelming problem.

Table 4.4. Should Organizing a Place to Play Cards (for a Fee) Be Unlawful?

Response Category	%	N
Yes	29.9	46
No	59.9	83
Don't Know	7.8	12
No Response	8.4	13
TOTAL	100.0	154

NOTE: N = 154

The tendency of the more recent immigrants to fall into the less harsh attitude than either the older immigrants or Canadian-born is no doubt a reflection of the attitudes they maintained in their respective homelands. Immigrants, however, in this regard do not form a homogeneous group. As with the language facility the important questions raised by this inquiry are those which concern differences in the rate of adaptations of immigrants to the new society. The Spearman coefficient for the association between length of residence in Canada and the nature of the penalties assigned is –0.0781 (N = 132) with significance level at 0.187.

Length of residence in Canada is not positively related with the assignment of penalties for gamblers. Newly arrived immigrants (arrived within one year of this survey) supported the "No Penalty" category. The immigrants who had lived in Canada for less than five years, as Table 4.4 demonstrates, were evenly split with regards to "No Penalty" and a "Fine" levy.

Furthermore, responses to the question, "what penalties should be given to the player" reveal that approximately 55% of the sample felt that no penalty was appropriate. Table 4.5 clearly points out that although gambling is sanctioned against; it is not treated harshly nor seriously by the public. The dispositions described in Table 4.5 are drawn up from formal criminal law dispositions usually in the context of the formal criminal justice process as opposed to decriminalizing *diversion processes*.

Table 4.5 The Assignment of Penalties for the Gambler Matched by Length of Stay in Canada of the Respondents

Length of Stay (Years)		No Penalty	Fine	Probation	Fine and Probation	Imprisonment	Don't Know	Total
Up to one Year	N	3	1	1	0	0	0	5
	%	3.5	2.8	16.7	0.0	0.0	0.0	
1–5	N	4	4	1	0	0	0	9
	%	4.7	11.1	16.7	0.0	0.0	0.0	
6–10	N	12	6	0	0	3	0	21
	%	14.1	16.7	0.0	0.0	60.0	0.0	
11–15	N	16	5	0	0	0	0	21
	%	18.8	13.9	0.0	0.0	0.0	0.0	
16–20	N	17	8	0	1	1	1	28
	%	20.0	22.2	0.0	100.0	20.0	25.0	
20+/all their lives	N	33	11	4	0	1	3	52
	%	38.8	30.6	66.7	0.0	20.0	75.0	
TOTAL	N	85	35	6	1	5	4	154
	%	55.2	22.7	3.9	0.6	3.2	2.6	100.0

NOTE: N = 154 N.R. 12 or 7.8%. Cell percentages based on column sums.

A gambler or a player is defined as a person who places a bet on a game of chance with a professional gambler or at a gaming establishment. From the results of Tables 4.4 and 4.5 it is obvious that pervasive discrepancies exist in one's approach to the definition of a gambler; legal concerns are no longer necessarily complemented by societal designations. Societal reactions, furthermore vary with different ethnic groups for instance. A striking majority of respondents feel that these events should not come under the rubric of the criminal law. Correlational analysis testifies to the strong relationship between these sets of associations. In the relationship: respondents' view that organizing a place to play is illegal, the coefficient of association is 0.7556 (N = 110), significant at the .001 level. Secondly, with the variables respondents' belief that paying to play cards should be illegal with the respondents' belief that organizing a place to play cards should be illegal the coefficient of this association (Spearman) is 0.8784 (N = 126), significant at the .001 level. Table 4.6 confirms the impression that most of the respondents felt at home with gambling; they appeared to tolerate some of these illicit services. While it may be dangerous to overgeneralize on the basis of the data, certain immediate conclusions may be drawn: the public regards gambling not as a particularly criminal activity. Its legality may be seriously questioned by the public.

Table 4.6   Respondents' Belief that Paying to Play Cards and Organizing a Place to Play Should Be Illegal

Responses	Pay to Play N	%	Organizing a Place to Play N	%
Yes	43	27.9	46	29.9
No	84	54.5	83	53.9
Don't Know	14	9.1	12	7.8
No Response	13	8.4	13	8.4
TOTAL	154	100.0	154	100.0

ORGANIZED CRIME

Gambling assumes a vital role in the operations of organized crime. How then do the respondents define organized crime's involvement in gambling? How diverse are the meanings given to organized crime? Table 4.7 documents the distribution of the sample's definition of organized crime. From this table it may be observed that the highest percentage of respondents view organized crime as the "Mafia" followed closely by the opinion that organized crime is a loose federation of big business consisting of numerous legitimate and illegitimate enterprises. Ten percent see organized crime being just that, organized crime. Thirteen percent of the respondents recognize the complexity of the term and are unable to define it.

Table 4.7   Meanings of Organized Crime

Definitions	N	%
The Mafia	37	24.0
Big Business: Loose Federations/Enterprises	27	17.5
Don't Know — too Difficult to define	21	13.6
No Response	17	11.0
Organized Crime	16	10.4
Big Business: Tight Organization, Monopolistic	14	9.1
Way of Living	13	8.4
Media: Slogan	5	3.2
Other Meanings	4	2.6
TOTAL	154	100.0

NOTE: N = 154

In response to the separate question asking whether the respondent believes organized crime is the "Mafia", Table 4.8 was drawn wherein birthplace was matched.

Table 4.8 further supports the hypothesis that Italians and other Canadians differ slightly in their definitions of organized crime as the "Mafia".

Table 4.8   "Is Organized Crime the Mafia?" by Birthplace

Birthplace	Yes		No		Don't Know	
	N	%	N	%	N	%
Metro. Toronto	8	9.9	4	11.8	3	21.4
Other Can. Cities	12	14.8	4	11.8	5	35.7
South Italy	25	30.9	8	23.6	2	14.3
North Italy	12	14.8	2	5.9	0	0.0
Central Italy	3	3.7	1	2.9	0	0.0
Other Foreign Country	21	25.9	14	41.2	3	21.4
No Response	0	0.0	1	2.9	1	7.1
TOTAL	81	100.0	34	100.0	14	100.0

NOTE: 1. Cell percentages based on column sum. N = 129
2. Seventy-one percent of all respondents born in Canada and 71% of South Italians equate Mafia with organized crime. Similarly 78% of all Italians and 77% of all other Canadians equate Mafia with organized crime.

Table 4.9 reveals that for both the Italian and Canadian groups, 38.4% felt that organized crime does not exist in Toronto. But the Italian group however comprised the largest category to reply "yes" that organized crime exists in Toronto.

Table 4.9 Perception of Presence of Organized Crime in Different Geographic Areas by Ethnicity

		Toronto				
		Yes	No	Don't Know	No Response	Total
Canadian	N	31	5	4	0	40
	%	27.4	38.4	6.25	0.0	25.9
Italian	N	45	5	6	0	56
	%	39.8	38.4	37.5	0.0	36.3
Other Foreign Country	N	34	3	6	0	43
	%	30.0	23.0	37.5	0.0	27.9
No Response	N	3	0	0	12	15
	%	2.6	0.0	0.0	100.0	9.7
TOTAL	N	113	13	16	12	154
	%	73.4	8.4	10.3	7.8	

NOTE: N = 154 Cell percentages based on column sums.

In Table 4.10 the Italian group is the largest unit to perceive this activity in the U.S.A (37.7% of the total "yes" responses). There is a tendency for all groups to perceive its presence in the U.S.A. Table 4.10 illustrates an increasing tendency of respon-

Table 4.10 Perceptions of the Presence of Organized Crime in Geographic Areas by Ethnicity

		U.S.A.				
		Yes	No	Don't Know	No Response	Total
Canadian	N	38	0	2	0	40
	%	29.2	0.0	18.2	0.0	25.9
Italians	N	49	1	6	0	56
	%	37.7	100.0	54.6	0.0	36.3
Other Foreign Country	N	40	0	3	0	43
	%	30.8	0.0	27.3	0.0	27.9
No Response	N	3	0	0	12	15
	%	2.3	0.0	0.0	100.0	9.7
TOTAL	N	130	1	11	12	154
	%	84.4	0.6	7.1	7.8	100.0

NOTE: Cell percentages based on column sums N = 154

dents to view organized crime in the U.S.A. more so than in Toronto. Table 4.11 compares these perceptions for Italy.

Table 4.11   Perceptions of Organized Crime in Different Areas of Ethnicity

| | | Italy | | Don't | No | |
		Yes	No	Know	Response	Total
Canadian	N	29	1	10	0	40
	%	72.5	2.5	25.0	0.0	25.9
Italian	N	48	2	6	0	56
	%	85.7	3.5	10.8	0.0	36.3
Other	N	35	0	8	0	43
Foreign	%	81.4	0.0	18.6	0.0	27.9
Country						
No	N	2	0	0	13	15
Response	%	13.3	0.0	0.0	86.7	9.7
TOTAL	N	114	3	24	13	154
	%	74.0	1.9	15.6	8.4	100.0

NOTE: N = 154. Cell percentages based on row sums.

Whether organized crime is implicated in all gambling activities is an important consideration not only in the attitudes towards, but also in the incidence of, gambling by the respondents. The beliefs held by our respondents are shown in Table 4.12 Over 50% of these respondents perceive the involvement of organized crime. As noted in Table 4.1, 76% of the respondents admitted involvements in gambling despite the fact that they perceived it as illegal and despite the involvement of organized crime.

Table 4.12   Perceived Involvement of Organized Crime in Gambling

Categories of Responses	N	%
Yes	89	57.8
No	34	22.1
Don't Know	12	7.8
No Response	19	12.3
TOTAL	154	100.0

NOTE: N = 154.

CONCLUSIONS

One important conclusion from examination of such pluralistic value situations and differential degrees of participation is that criminal deviations within ethnic minorities can often be explained in the same way as conformity among members of the dominant group. Subcultural behaviour especially with recent immigrants is often reinforced within the group. Conformity to gambling practices should perhaps frequently be interpreted as a function of accommodative relationships. At this juncture, it is possible to bring several ideas so far developed into a somewhat different and peculiarly novel concept of organized crime. This chiefly refers to situations in which persons who are caught in a network of conflicting values choose not direct criminal alternatives but rather behavioural solutions which carry the *risk of criminalty*, such as operating or participating in a gaming house.

It seems almost basic to insist that many forms of organized crime are collective acts in which both group-derived and private values are maintained. Gambling practices however tend to confirm the contention that pressures to deviate transcend geography, class, age, sex, and ethnicity.

The attitudes towards organized crime in general range from mild acquiescence, humorous tolerance to moderate disapproval.

In our society a large proportion of the population regularly participates in some form of gambling. In fact this is permitted and seldom defined as deviant.

Gambling is not perceived as a "problem behaviour" warranting modification. Organized crime is not viewed as a negative phenomenon. Values and opinions seem to transgress beyond legal boundaries. Instead of allowing law enforcement agencies to nibble away at organized crime by arrests and rearrests, a decriminalizing emphasis is long overdue.

Societal reactions were not studied by merely alluding to attitudes. Participation in various forms of behaviour was also analyzed. The emphasis was on both attitudinal and behavioural differences. The prevailing attitude towards organized crime takes on a variety of expressions.

We began with the question "What is organized crime?" We wanted to explore the nature of several associations. In our findings on gambling we discovered that the man on the street does not generally draw any distinctions between legal or illegal gambling. In fact, many of the respondents simply did not know, if, for example paying to play cards is illegal. The person on whose behalf or for whose benefit the laws are enacted and enforced has little notion of the criminality of gambling. Interesting correlations can be seen to exist between legal attitudes — as construed in laws, and social attitudes. Social attitudes have not followed and are not strongly influenced by legal attitudes. Legislative change and education is therefore crucial in the field of gambling and organized crime.

This study was directed towards providing data to support or refute some of the assumptions introduced in our theoretical discussion. Generally, consensus is missing not only among social scientists in their explorations in this field but also among the respondents whom have been approached. Legal considerations apparently seem irrelevant and overruled by conflicting individual moralities. Law and its accompanying enforcement tends to be ineffective in changing behaviour and attitudes regarding organized crime and gambling. They are ineffective in terms of the primary aim of reducing the likelihood of future criminal behaviour. In ascertaining the strengths of diverse relationships, it was clearly demonstrated by our findings that a relatively homogeneous response emerged for most groups with little or no negative attitudes towards gambling in particular.

Hence, this study has attempted to look at the social attitudes towards a seldom studied area of deviant behaviour — organized crime and gambling. This study may presumably serve to be an introduction to studies on organized crime. It is hoped that this study may further serve as an plea for active empirical research and theoretical analysis into organized crime.

What is of particular relevance to this controversy is the manner in which governments have accelerated legalization of gambling, an endeavour once labelled as "deviant" and operated by organized crime concerns. Questions as to what the limits of the law are rather than limits of behaviour ought to be raised.

As evidenced by our findings, participation in organized crime transgresses ethnic and even socio-economic borders. And yet minority groups are quickly designated perpetrators of these crimes.

References

Albini, Joseph. 1971. *The American mafia*. New York: Meredith Corp.

Allen, Edward 1962. *Merchants of menace*. Springfield, Illinois, Charles C. Thomas Ltd.

Attorney General. *Report of the Attorney General's Committee on Enforcement of the Law Related to Gambling*. 5 July 1961, Ontario.

———. *Report of the Task Force on Off-Track Betting*. June 1972, Toronto, Ontario.

Barzini, Luigi. 1965. *The Italians*, New York: Bantam Books.

Becker, Harold. 1970. *Issues in police administration*. Metuchen, Jew Jersey: Scarecrow Press.

Bell, Daniel. 1962. *The end of ideology*. New York: Free Press.

Canada, Information Canada. 1974. *1971 census of Canada: Population ethnic groups by birthplace*. Ottawa: January.

Chimbos, Peter. 1971. Some aspects of organized crime in Canada: A preliminary review. In *Social deviance in Canada*. W.E. Mann (Ed.), Toronto: Copp Clark.

Clark, Ramsey. 1970. *Crime in America*. New York: Simon and Schuster.

Cressey, Donald. 1969. *Theft of a nation*. New York: Harper and Row.

Emrich, Robert. 1966. The basis of organized crime in Western civilizations. Paper submitted to the President's Commission on Law Enforcement and the Administration of Justice, 14 Oct.

Fraenkel, Jack. 1970. *Crime and criminals: What should we do about them?* Englewood Cliffs, New Jersey: Prentice-Hall Ltd.

Geis, Gilbert. 1972. *Not the law's business*. Washington: U.S. Government Office.

Gronin, Constance. 1970. *The siting of change*. Chicago: University of Chicago Press.

Hobsbaum, Eric. 1969. *Bandits*. London: Ebinizer Baylis & Sons Ltd.

_____. 1965. *Primitive rebels*. New York: Norton Co.

Ianni, Francis et al. 1972. *A family business*. New York: Russell Sage Foundation.

Jansen, Clifford. 1971. Assimilation in theory and practice: A case study of Italians in Toronto. In James E. Gallagher and Ronald Lambert (Eds.), *Social process and institution: The Canadian case*. Toronto: Holt, Rinehart & Winston Ltd.

Lewis, Norman. 1964. *The honoured society*. New York: G.P. Putnam & Sons.

Mann, W.E. and Lloyd G. Hanley. 1968. Mafia in Canada. In W.E. Mann (Ed.), *Deviant behaviour in Canada*. Toronto: Social Sciencies Pub.

Mori, Cesare. 1933. *The last struggle with the mafia*. London: Putnam.

Morris, Norval and Gordon Hawkins. 1969. *The honest politicians guide to crime control*. Chicago: University of Chicago Press.

Mosca, Gaetano. 1933. Mafia. In *Encycopedia of social sciences*. London: Macmillan.

Ontario Police Commission. 1964. *Report to the Attorney General for Ontario on organized crime*. Toronto.

Phillips, Allen, 1963. The mafia in Canada. *Macleans Magazine* 24 August.

Reckless, Walter. 1967. *The crime problem*. New York: Meredith Pub. Co.

Richmond, Anthony. 1967. *Immigrants and ethnic groups in Metropolitan Toronto*. Toronto: Ethnic Research Programme, Institute for Behavioural Research, York University.

Sellin, Thorsten. 1938. *Culture, conflict and crime*. New York: Social Science Research Council.

Sutherland, Edwin and Donald Cressey. 1966. *Principles of criminology*. 7th ed. New York: J.P. Lippincott Co.

Tannenbaum, Frank. 1938. *Crime and the community*. New York: Columbia University Press.

Toronto Sun. 1973. Police know who crime bosses are. 30 August.

Toronto Sun. 1973. 17 April.

Toronto Star 1983. 27 April, A18.

Vold, George. 1958. *Theoretical criminology*. New York: Oxford University Press.

Wilkins, Leslie. 1964. *Social deviance*. London: Tavistock Pub.

Chapter 5

A Social Profile of
Sexual Mass Murderers

*Elliott Leyton**

The ultimate obscenity that human beings perpetrate upon one another is murder. It is therefore hardly surprising that the subject is of such intense interest to members of the public; and the hundreds of books and articles that appear each year on murder constitute a testimony to this concern.

Remarkably, however, the subject has received little attention from the academic community. Moreover, with the exception of a few outstanding studies of isolated phenomena — such as Gaddis and Long (1970), or Reinhardt (1960) on individual murderers, or Wolfgang (1958) on murder in one city — the academic material is overwhelmingly *nonsociological*. Indeed, most of the finest studies of murders have been either journalists, as Klausner's (1981) work on David Berkowitz, or Frank's (1965) study of Albert DeSalvo; or they have been dominated entirely by psychiatric and psycho-analytic perspectives, as in Abrahamsen (1973), Wertham (1949), 1966), Guttmacher (1960) or Lunde (1979). Finally, the subject is muddied by an idiosyncratic and often quite unscientific pseudo-biology (cf. Fox 1971), focusing on such peculiar matters as purported criminal chromosomes or the brain temperature of murderers. Neither is the scholar interested in the subject given much encouragement by the authorities. Police data — statistical

---

* Elliott Leyton is President of the Canadian Sociology and Anthropology Association, Professor of Applied Anthropology at the Memorial University of Newfoundland, actively involved in the construction and operation of Canada's first specialized Bachelor's Degree Program in Police Studies, and the author of a series of books and articles on social problems, including *The Myth of Delinquency* (1979), and "Drunk and Disorderly: Changing Crime in Newfoundland" (1983).

or otherwise — are a researcher's nightmare, being crude, unreliable, and frequently unavailable. Astonishingly, no institution exists anywhere in the western world to collect and analyze social data on homicide; and even the renowned FBI Uniform Crime Reporting unit is understaffed, overworked, insecurely funded, and able to supply only the crudest data. Each researcher is thus forced to develop his or her own sources of information; and knowledge so painfully collected is unlikely to be freely shared.[1]

Additionally, the homicide literature is overwhelmingly American. At one level, this is quite appropriate, since the U.S. is, by a huge margin, the most murderous nation in the western industrial world. Yet this has led to an unfortunate neglect of nation-states such as Great Britain and Switzerland, or cultural areas such as the island Newfoundland, which have developed cultural and social mechanisms for repressing violence.

Perhaps the most outstanding dimension of neglect is the matter of *practical* advice to police. Until recent years, the only serious assistance has come from psychiatry and psychology, which have offered psychological profiles of various types of murderers. These profiles predict, sometimes with remarkable accuracy, the motives, fears, and fantasies of the killers. For example, a psychological profile on the Son of Sam correctly described him as "neurotic, schizophrenic and paranoid," accurately guessed that he "regarded himself as a victim of demonic possession," and concluded that he was "probably shy and odd, a loner inept in establishing personal relationships, especially with women" (In Klausner 1981, 160). Unfortunately, these psychological profiles, however accurate, are rarely of practical value to the police. The diagnosis of "paranoia" will not pick anyone out of a lineup; nor will a suspect under interrogation usually reveal his private fears and fantasies: rather, he will insist that he be seen as what he *seems* to be, a shy and devoted family man, or a dedicated profeminist psychological counsellor. Essentially then, the psychological profiles are of limited value to the police because they are subjective and private. What is required are objective and public sets of criteria.

More recent practical help has come from psycholinguistic threat analysis, which has developed a set of most useful techniques for examining the threat "message for clues as to the origin, background, and psychology of the originator" (Miron and Douglas 1979).

Most successful of all are the excellent "psychological profiles" (which are really *behavioural*, not psychological, profiles) which are being developed at the FBI Academy (cf. Ault and Reese, 1980; Ressler et al. 1980). Here, a wide range of behavioural data is being collected on violent offenders, permitting the extrapolation of the murderer's likely personal characteristics from the murderer's behaviour at the crime scene.

What remains largely undeveloped is a truly sociological profile of different types of murderers. Most murders are relatively easy to solve: the inevitable lovers' triangle, or even the bungled robbery, yield a limited number of suspects possessing an appropriate motive or the property of the victim. Further, the murderer's sense of guilt is usually such that a sharp police officer's "intuition" (which is, after all, a blend of intelligence, sensitivity, and experience) will be alerted during an investigation and lead to the murderer's discovery.

THE SEXUAL MASS MURDERER

Regrettably, none of these simple qualities applies to the sexual mass murderer — a type of deviate which seems to be multiplying at an alarming rate in recent years (and everywhere too, even in Canada where the overall homicide rate has been dropping for years), and whose characteristics make him especially difficult for police to identify.[2] Here, there are no obvious links with the victim, and no obvious motive beyond a deranged (and, during interrogation, undetectable) sexuality. Neither do such investigations yield an obvious list of suspects other than those who have been previously arrested for sexual offences: but sexual mass murderers rarely have such a record, and are more likely to be known as pillars of society than as deviates.

Further, the sexual mass murderer often compartmentalizes his thinking, and is usually only dimly aware that he has transformed his fantasies into reality: thus the explanation by the Boston Strangler regarding his disengagement from one homicidal assault after, "I looked in a mirror in the bedroom and there was me — strangling somebody!" (In Frank 1966, 313). Thus the murderer feels little guilt, and as a result he does not release the subtle guilt-based cues on which intuitive officers depend:

> . . . as far as I was concerned, it wasn't me (who murdered). I can't explain it
> to you any other way. It's just so unreal . . . I was there, it was done, and yet
> if you talked to me an hour later, or half hour later, it didn't mean nothing,
> it just didn't mean nothing. (Albert DeSalvo, the "Boston Strangler",
> quoted in Frank 1966, 308).

Little wonder then that "police will tell you that finding a single killer in the vast swarm of a metropolitan area is often impossible without the intervention of luck" (Klausner 1981, 6–7). With a malfunctioning police intuition protecting the actual killer, he escapes close scrutiny for an extended period, and is free to murder dozens of additional women and men. Fortunately, as I shall try to show, sexual mass murderers do seem to have enough in common to bring themselves to the attention of the police with relative speed.

THE PROGRESS OF INVESTIGATIONS

The activities of many sexual mass murderers remain undiscovered until their gigantic graveyards are discovered. As often, however, two or three victims are found relatively early in the killing "spree"; and when police compare the characteristics of the crimes, they usually realize that they have a mass murderer operating in their area (although even this realization may take much longer if the murderer is operating in that "killing ground" that is the highway, killing in separate police jurisdictions, and leaving several local forces thinking they have isolated and unrelated murders on their hands).[3] Usually, however, using modern police investigative techniques, which include the perusal of prior arrest records, the coordination of informant tips, and the monitoring of automobile movements, the police assemble a list of suspects which can number as many as several thousand.

Most often, the name of the actual killer is in that list of suspects; but, given the limited manpower available to the police, it can take months or years before the killer is discovered. If the killer displays behavioural characteristics that are obviously "crazy" in his day-to-day life — as did, for example, David Berkowitz and Clifford Olson — then they are often caught within a year or less. But most of these sexual mass murderers do *not* behave abnormally. On the contrary:

> The sex murderer differs from other psychiatric killers in his ability to keep his terrible daydreams to himself. He keeps quiet about them: he exhibits no odd behaviour. Thus he is able to move among friends and fellow workers without calling attention to himself. Chances were that he might appear bland, pleasant, gentle, ingratiating — even compassionate. No one would think of him as "crazy" (In Frank 1966, 155–156).

Thus if, as is most commonly the case, the killer appears to be normal, even admirable — after all, Los Angeles' Hillside Strangler was a policeman; Albert DeSalvo was a devoted father and husband; Albert Fish was described by those who met him as "articulate", "genteel", and having a "kind and ingratiating face" (in Angelella 1979); and Ted Bundy was a unversity law student, an active member of the Republican Party, and a respected counsellor at Seattle's Crisis Counselling Centre (Rule 1980) — it can be years before the suspicions of the police are aroused. During those years, dozens die horribly.

THE SOCIAL PROFILE

What would be immensely useful to the police then would be any means for winnowing the killer's name out of the list of suspects. If a man's private fantasies are unknowable, his social characteristics are objective and often public. While engaged in background research for a purely academic series of books on multiple murderers, I have stumbled across such an objective set of social characteristics which distinguishes sexual mass murderers from the majority of the population. They will not be surprising to any social scientist: they have simply not been previously articulated. The Social Profile which emerges from these clustered characteristics can be taught easily to police, and if used systematically, should prove to be an efficient and effective new tool for police science.

The superimposition of the Social Profile over the police suspect list would enable the investigator to reduce the list to a more manageable one-fifth, or less, of its original number: thus an original suspect list of 1,000 would be pared quickly to 200, or fewer, high probability suspects. Such a reduction would enable the police to accelerate the investigative process, cut the killer off in mid-career, and save dozens of lives.

The Social Profile can be used in two phases, or Scans. The *First Scan* concentrates on objective social traits, uses information obtainable from municipal, provincial/state, and national data banks — or, failing that, is easily obtained through interrogation — and reduces the suspect list by some four-fifths. Its information picks out those individuals whose families bear the marks of extreme rupture — marks which show up in public records as one or more of the following: adoption, illegitimacy, institutionalization in childhood or adolescence (reformatory or orphanage), having a father or brother charged with violence, or a mother who had married three or more times. These variables occur in perhaps 20 percent of the population, but in 90 percent of sexual mass murderers for whom reliable social histories are available. Thus in

90 percent of sexual mass-murder cases, so long as the name of the killer has appeared in the suspect list, as it usually has, police should be able to concentrate their enquiries among a vastly reduced pool of suspects.

The *Second Scan* focuses on behavioural and life-style characteristics, and supplements or complements the FBI profiling techniques. The Second Scan concentrates on an extreme presentation of self, *either* as "crazed" (as in Charles Manson), or appearing in a "Mr. Perfect" *ensemble* (as in Albert Fish, Ted Bundy, and Albert DeSalvo). Further variables are an obsession with things, generally to the exclusion of all friendships (the classic "loner" syndrome); or a participation in "power" sports (as in DeSalvo's and Olson's boxing; Kemper's guns; or "Collins" motorcycles).[4]

Table 5.1 International Data Base

	First Scan (Social Characteristics)	Second Scan (Behavioral Traits)
John Bianchi (Hillside Strangler)	ADOPTED	MR PERFECT, POLICEMAN
Cliff Olson (B.C. Murders)	INSTITUTIONALIZED (Juvenile Home)	BOXER
David Berkowtiz (Son of Sam)	ILLEGITIMATE; and ADOPTED	MR CRAZY, SECURITY GUARD
Earle Nelson (Manitoba Murders)	ADOPTED	Insuff. Data
Ted Bundy (Seattle)	ILLEGITIMATE	MR PERFECT
Albert Fish (Prewar children)	INSTITUTIONALIZED (orphanage reared)	MR PERFECT
Albert DeSalvo (Boston Strangler)	INSTITUTIONALIZED (Juvenile home); and VIOLENT KIN (both father & brother charged with assault)	BOXER
Peter Sutcliffe (Yorkshire Ripper)	VIOLENT KIN (brother twice charged with grie- vously wounding police)	MR PERFECT
Dean Corll (Houston Murders)	RUPTURED MATERNAL BOND (mother thrice married)	Insuff. Data
"Norman Collins" (Michigan Murders)	RUPTURED MATERNAL BOND (mother thrice married)	MOTORCYCLES

Table 5.1   International Data Base (Continued)

	First Scan (Social Characteristics)	Second Scan (Behavioral Traits)
William Bonin (Freeway Murders)	INSTITUTIONALIZED (in juvenile home from age of eight)	MR CRAZY
Ian Brady (Moors Murders)	ILLEGITIMATE; and INSTITUTIONALIZED (both foster and juvenile homes)	NAZI BUFF
Richard Speck (Chicago Nurses)	INSTITUTIONALIZED (juvenile home)	Insuff. Data
Robert Irwin	INSTITUTIONALIZED (juvenile home)	Insuff. Data
William Heirens (Chicago Murders)	INSTITUTIONALIZED (juvenile home)	NAZI BUFF, GUN NUT
Edmund Kemper III (Santa Cruz Murders)	INSTITUTIONALIZED (mental hospital from age of 15); and RUPTURED MATERNAL BOND (mother thrice married)	GUN & KNIFE NUT
Fritz Haarmann (Prewar German)	INSTITUTIONALIZED (juvenile home)	Insuff. Data
Robert Carr III	INSTITUTIONALIZED (juvenile home)	Insuff, Data
Antone Costa (Cape Cod Murders)	NOT FIT	NOT FIT
John Christie (London Prostitutes)	NOT FIT	POLICEMAN

ANALYSIS

Why should these variables, especially the primary traits revealed in the First Scan, inexorably lead us to a multiple sex killer? What is there about being adopted, or illegitimate, or reared in an institution, or having a close relative convicted of assault, or a much-married mother, that might propel a man towards a "career" in sexual assault and mass murder? The answer is obvious, and lies in some basic social science.

The simple fact of human social life is that in order for individuals to become "normal", to internalize the values and behaviours of their society, they must grow up feeling that they have some place in the social order — that is, a coherent socially constructed identity. The primary agency charged with inculcating this sense of identity is the family. I have discussed this problem elsewhere in my own recent book, *The Myth of Delinquency*, but Thomas Belmonte (1979, 52–59) puts it more succinctly when he writes that we trace our first "connections to the universe through the intermediary relations of the family", and that the family is therefore "the crucible of every human identity." Sometimes, a family malfunctions: the crucible is overturned, and an incomplete or blemished identity is forged. The First Scan's primary traits are extremely useful indices of this failure to forge a complete identity.

Thus the Boston Strangler, a U.S. Army boxing champion and a devoted father, who strangled thirteen women and raped hundreds more, was seen by others as a "mild-mannered, tearful husband and father living quietly with his wife and two children in a Boston suburb . . . A man treated all but contemptuously by his wife and dismissed as a bore and a braggart by his friends" (Frank 1966, 272). He described himself and his activities in these terms:

> I don't want to be the person who did these things. There's no rhyme or reason to it. I'm not a man who can hurt anyone. I can't do it. I'm very emotional. I break up at the least thing. I can't hurt anyone . . . (In Frank 1966, 317–318).

To a sensitive psychiatrist, the Strangler "had never really integrated these experiences, these murders, into his consciousness." Rather, "he had kept them outside himself, and thus had been able to maintain a kind of mental health — had been able to report them as things done by someone whom he recognized was himself yet not done by himself" (Quoted in Frank 1966, 310).

Similarly, David Berkowitz came to believe that he would never be caught because "The Police couldn't see me. I was an illusion . . . someone other than David Berkowitz" (In Klausner 1981, 130).

> "I am the Son of Sam," says David Berkowitz. Illegitimate, adopted David Berkowitz. Looking backward to the cold winter of 1967–77, he says "It wasn't me. It was Sam that was working through me. I mean, me and the Son of Sam, there's just one body, but we weren't the same people. Sam used me as his tool" (In Klausner 1981, 102).

Berkowitz, the anonymous and friendless virgin-bachelor, "seems never to have felt sure of his identity . . . He was phobic as a child and suffered from overwhelming feelings of rejection. His response, both to rejection and to a shaky sense of self, began with bravado. Then, in 1974, David's pathetic, passive fantasy life evolved into something that was not pathetic. If he could not conquer young women by seducing them, he could conquer them with the act of murder" (Klausner 1981, 2–3).

Fortunately for our purposes, this terrible process wherein a man may be denied an identity[5] is discoverable, not just through the examination of his private thoughts, but buried in his family's birth, marital, and police records. As for the behavioural characteristics contained in the Second Scan: as incomplete as they are,[6] it should be clear that such life-styles are sometimes the attributes of individuals suffering from insecurity and rage, and are further clues to the existence of a malformed identity, to the possibility of harbouring the sadistic fantasies that a man without an identity can put into operation — and do so without guilt.

In conclusion, let me make several points. The first is an ethical one and revolves around the problems of invasion of privacy, and potential damage to innocent people bearing First Scan characteristics; but ultimately this can only be solved by social legislation and judicious police practise. Second, it should be clear that similar social profiles could be developed for a variety of criminals, teasing out high-probability offenders in spheres as diverse as rape, assassination, and diplomatic defection. Finally, police should be clearly aware that while proper training in and use of the Social Profile should enhance and quicken the pace of their work, and thus save many lives, it is not a substitute for good police work: there will never be such a substitute.

Notes

1. I must express my own gratitude here to Special Agents Robert K. Ressler and John E. Douglas of the FBI, to Supt. George Powell of the R.C.M.P., to Sgt. Gerald McQueen of the Manhatten Homicide Task Force, to Dr. Don Loee of the Canadian Police College, and to Chief R.J. Roche of the Royal Newfoundland Constabulary, for their support and encouragement of my own research on multiple murder.

2. I do not deal here with other types of multiple murderers, such as family annihilators, political murders such as the Zebra killings in California, gangland murders, nor delusional killing such as the Santa Cruz murders, for each of these types conform to quite different social profiles.

3. This lack of cooperation and tight coordination between regional forces, especially in the U.S., is a tactical handicap of considerable magnitude.

4. It cannot be emphasized too strongly that the characteristics in both First and Second Scans *do not* automatically cause, suggest, or assign abnormality. Many normal and healthy adults are illegitimate or adopted, just as many are

also fond of guns and boxing. These are merely identifiable forces which, *in extreme cases only*, produce or reflect the stress signs we seek.

5. This process of identity-destruction applies of course to both sexes. The relative absence of female participation in mass murder is a phenomenon as yet unexplained; although recent developments in California homicide cases suggest that females may be becoming more active in this sphere.

7. The Behavioural Science team at the FBI Academy in Quantico, Virginia, naturally have access to a much wider range of data, and immediate access to most murderers, and are able to assemble a much more comprehensive picture of this aspect.

References

Abrahamsen, David. 1973. *The murdering mind.* New York: Harper.

Angelella, Michael. 1979. *Trail of blood.* New York: New American Library.

Ault, Richard L. Jr. and James T. Reese. 1980. A psychological assessment of crime profiling. In *FBI Law Enforcement Bulletin.*

Belmonte, Thomas. 1979. *The broken fountain.* New York: Columbia University Press.

Fox, Richard G. 1971. The XYY offender: a modern myth? In *Journal of Criminal Law, Criminology and Police Science.* 62(1).

Frank, Gerold. 1965. *The Boston strangler.* New York: New American Library.

Gaddis, Thomas E. and James O. Long. 1970. *Killer.* New York: Macmillan.

Guttmacher, Manfred. 1960. *The mind of the murderer.* New York: Farrar, Strauss and Cudahy.

Klausner, Lawrence D. 1981. *Son of Sam.* New York: McGraw-Hill.

Leyton, Elliott. 1979. *The myth of deliquency.* Toronto: McClelland and Stewart.

_____. 1983. Drunk and disorderly. In J. Rex Clark (Ed.), *The new Newfoundland.* St. John's: Breakwater.

Lunde, Donald T. 1979. *Murder and madness.* New York: W.W. Norton.

Miron, Murray S. and John E. Douglas. 1979. Threat analysis. In *FBI Law Enforcement Bulletin.*

Reinhardt, James Melvin. 1960. *The murderous trail of Charles Starkweather.* Springfield: Charles C. Thomas.

Ressler, Robert K., John E. Douglas, A. Nicholas Groth and Ann Wolbert Burgess. 1980. Offender profiles. In *FBI Law Enforcement Bulletin.*

Rule, Ann. 1980. *The stranger beside me.* New York: New American Library.

Wertham, Frederic. 1949. *The show of violence.* New York: Doubleday.

_____. 1966. *Dark legend.* New York: Bantam.

Wolfgang, Marvin E. 1958. *Patterns in criminal homicide.* Montclair: Patterson Smith.

Chapter 6

Deviance as Community Activity: Putting "Labelling Theory" in Perspective

Robert Prus*

Using "labeling theory" as a base, this paper presents a process-oriented statement focusing on the ways in which group life shapes "deviance" with respect to: definitions, identities, regulation, and careers. Examining central aspects of "deviance-related activity", this synthesis is designed to clarify and integrate a body of literature of particular significance for those interested in deviance, crime, law, and social order.

Labeling theory has been a major force shaping explanations of crime and deviance over the past two decades. However, there has been relatively little synthesis of the research and insight this tradition has generated. Thus, for people beginning "the study of criminality and deviance", as well as for those actively working in these areas, the literature on labeling (Labelling) theory can be rather perplexing. In addition to problems arising from some misleading critiques (discussed later), one faces the tasks of (1) sorting out differing perspectives on labeling, and (2) integrating the wide range of issues and research foci which have fallen under its umbrella.

Following a discussion of some of the theoretical underpinnings of labeling theory, the paper focuses on the emergence of deviance definitions, the identification of deviants, the informal and formal attempts to regulate deviance, and the careers of people's involvements in deviance. Examining deviance in process,

---

* Paper presented at Canadian Ethnology Society Meetings. Hamilton, Ontario, 7–10 May 1982. Robert Prus, Department of Sociology, University of Waterloo.

it becomes strikingly apparent that *deviance is a social phenomenon* and is best understood in the context of ongoing community life.

LABELING THEORY: THREE FOUNDATIONS

Although labeling theory has become very prominent in recent analysis of deviance and social control, there is some confusion over "what constitutes labeling theory". For our purposes, "labeling theory" may be defined as "that body of literature focusing on the role that community interaction plays in the emergence, regulation, and perpetuation of deviance". To better sort out "what labeling theory is" (as well as to contextualize much of the criticism directed towards "labeling theory"), three streams of labeling theory are delineated: "societal reactions" (social control), functionalism, and symbolic interactionism. These are most readily identified with the works of Edwin Lemert, Kai Erikson, and Howard S. Becker, respectively. There is some overlap among these approaches, but each is characterized by somewhat different concerns. The social control version emphasizes the role control agencies play in the perpetuation of deviance. The functionalists are most concerned with the interplay of system requirements, demands, and capacities for the tolerance and production of "deviant behaviour". The interactionists are concerned with the ways in which people work out all aspects of their lives, including people's involvements in "deviance" and attempts on the part of agencies and persons (individually and in groups) to regulate activities.

Labeling theory has received most attention from the symbolic interactionists. While not with interactionism, the amount of interchange between labeling theory and interactionism has been so great that the two have become largely synonymous in discussions of deviance. Consequently, since labeling theory has broader terms of reference than interactionism, and since interactionism includes components not presently incorporated in labeling theory, we will examine variations of labeling theory and indicate aspects of interactionism having particular significance for labeling theory.

SOCIAL CONTROL CONCERNS: LEMERT'S SOCIETAL RELATIONS

Although others (most notably Durkheim 1895; and Tannenbaum 1938) had earlier introduced material denoting deviance as

---

p. 109, last complete paragraph — Line 2 should read "interactionists. While not synonymous with interactionism, the amount of"

an outcome of community response, these ideas did not have a major impact on the sociological community until Edwin Lemert (1951, 1967) introduced the concepts of "societal reactions" and "secondary deviation".

In contrast to questions of the type, "What's wrong with the individual and/or the society?", Lemert argues that social control responses ("societal reactions") to deviants are the critical features accounting for intensified involvements in deviance. He contends that systematic involvements in deviance reflect the relative options open to formally identified deviants and their attempts to adjust to these conditions. Although the rigour with which persons are identified as "deviants", may vary extensively, persons so differentiated are apt to find themselves somewhat excluded from conventional groupings. Encountering situations preferentially loaded in favour of deviant options, persons may find it easier to become "seondary deviants" (in the process organizing their lives around deviant activities) than to pursue more conventional life-styles in the face of rejection and disrespectability.

Lemert contrasts secondary deviation with "primary deviation", referring in the latter instance to isolated or occasional involvements in deviant activities. He explicitly disavows interest in primary deviation, arguing that sociologists should be most interested in social control efforts and their implications for the subsequent activities of the deviants.[1]

FUNCTIONALIST CONCERNS: ERIKSON ET AL.

Some functional variations of labeling theory can be seen in the works of Erikson (1962; 1966), Conner (1972), Cohen (1973), and Lauderdale (1976). While the functionalists have not played a major role in the development of labeling theory, these authors derive inspiration from an oft neglected statement by Emile Durkheim. Durkheim (1895) posits that (1) deviance is an inevitable aspect of group life, and (2) definitions of deviance are profoundly social, reflecting community reference points. These scholars consider issues such as the "elasticity", "inevitability", and "functionality" of deviance, as well as the conditions affecting labeling endeavours on a general societal level. Working on a larger and often historical level, they indicate the ways in which community responses to deviance are shaped by the forces affecting the social system at large.

INTERACTIONIST CONCERNS: BECKER AND GOFFMAN

While the interactionists have long been interested in deviance and the "underside of society", a major effect of the development of labeling theory was to accentuate the relevance of interactionism for the study of deviance.

Howard Becker

Assuming an interactionist perspective, Becker contends that like other aspects of group life, "deviance" reflects social definitions and interpretations. He posits that deviance is not a quality of an act, but *a quality conferred on an act*. He sees "activities" and their "evaluations" as two logically distinct entities. Notions of deviance are relative to the audience ascribing meanings to the activities under consideration.[2] Becker does not deny that persons engage in activities, but contends that definitions of deviance are not objective or automatic; they are, in every case, problematic. A property conferred on an act (or actor) by some audience, definitions of deviance are perspectival and reflect "social enterprise" (as involved parties attempt to realize their interests).

Using the term "moral entrepreneurs" to refer to persons and/or groups attempting to shape community morality, Becker further distinguishes between "rule creators" and "rule enforcers". While the two roles can be subsumed by the same actor (and agencies), Becker makes it clear that such need not be the case, and this division of activity may be responsible for much inconsistency between the rules and their enforcement. While these distinctions are now considered very basic, these concepts were highly instrumental in sensitizing us to the perspectival, processual, problematic, and negotiable aspects of both deviance definitions and rule enforcement.

Becker also introduces the concept of "career contingencies" in reference to deviance. Referring to the elements affecting one's movements through sets of activities, this concept adds a valuable dimension to deviance research. One might become a "deviant" in a way similar to that by which one might become a doctor, teacher, or cab driver. Utilizing some of his earlier works, Becker illustrates the relevance of this notion in reference to marijuana use and the activities of jazz musicians. The timeliness of *Outsiders* (1963) relative to the emergence of the drug subculture no doubt added to its popularity, but more importantly, Becker indicates that sociologists assuming a labeling orientation need not be confined to "societal reactions" and "secondary deviation" (Lemert). In "On Becoming a Marijuana User", Becker shows that one can, on a purely sociological basis, account for initial involvements in deviance. His discussion of jazz musicians also illustrates that "deviant insiders" can be highly instrumental in affection the continuity of people in deviant life-styles. Rejection by members of conventional society can contribute to deviant involvements, but acceptance within the "deviant community" is an element not to be overlooked. Thus, Becker argues that evidence is best understood as social enterprise (as opposed to "individual" or "societal" failings); one has to take the "contributions of others" into account in any attempt to explain deviance.

Erving Goffman

In what has become a classic, *The Presentation of Self in Everyday Life* (1959), Goffman not only argues that people can influence how others see (type) them, but provides an extensive, meticulous, and well illustrated statement to that effect. In Goffman's scheme, people are not "robots" acting out psychological programs and conditioning, nor are they "billiard balls" whose movements are predetermined by the forces of age, social class, and the like. Everyday life can be likened to stage acting (a "dramaturgical model"), but actors in everyday life have to work out their own identities and develop scripts in conjunction with their interests and those of their associates as "the drama of everyday life unfolds". People are no longer the mere pawns of psychological or sociological forces, but are conceptualized as imaginative, creative, interpreting and planning beings, capable of taking both self and others into account in developing lines of action. Everyday life is not a static or prearranged program; it is a dynamic process, subject to the resourcefulness of the parties involved. From this perspective, deviants (and others) can play an active (although not necessarily successful) role in shaping their social identities (labels) and their destinies.

In *Asylums* (1961), Goffman depicts the underlife of a mental hospital. He shows how "total institutions" (control agencies) can be understood by examining the day-to-day activities of those whose lives intersect therein. Deviants are no longer so much "grist passing through the mill". Not only are "mills" less well defined and rational than formerly typified, but Goffman makes it apparent that the "deviants" can act upon, and independently of, the "mills".

Although Goffman has de-emphasized deviance in his more recent works, *Stigma* (1963) depicts the problematics and strategies of managing the disrepectability associated with deviance. Essentially an application of the dramaturgical model to the life situations of the disrespectable, this monograph further consolidates the links between interactionism and labeling theory. Goffman's writing represents a noteworthy bridge, with readers becoming exposed to social psychology of relevance to both the "deviants" and the "normals".

DEVIANCE AS SOCIAL ACTIVITY

Assuming an interactionist orientation,[3] and viewing deviance as "social activity", we now focus on (1) the emergence of definitions of activities as deviant; (2) the processess by which persons become known as deviants; (3) the ways in which deviance is handled informally; (4) the responses of control agencies to deviants; and (5) the interrelatedness of social control and involvements in deviance.

DEFINING DEVIANCE

Interactionists see definitions of conduct (rules, norms, deviance, crime, and the like) as problematic, emergent, and negotiable aspects of group life. Envisioning definitions as reflecting social enterprise and collective behaviour (Becker 1963; Blumer 1971), they are interested in definitions neither as a means of promoting stable systems, nor as obstacles in replacing one system with another. Their interests lie in uncovering the processes by which definitions of acceptable and unacceptable conduct come about and their implications for ongoing group life.

For our purposes, the term "deviance" may be defined as "any human quality (thought, word, deed, appearance, or other object) considered offensive, disturbing, threatening, or disrespectable by some audience". Working from this definition, it becomes apparent that "any quality" can be simultaneously considered both "deviant" and "acceptable" (or even highly desirable) when two audiences attach different meanings to the quality. Likewise, a single audience could simultaneously judge an acitivty as both "deviant", and "exciting", "fun", or worthwhile/desirable.[4] Definitions of deviance can also vary with respect to the degree of condemnation associated with a quality, the degree of consensus among and within audiences, and the degree of specificity with which qualities are defined as deviant. Consequently, any and all persons may be seen as (1) definers (interpreters of reality) of deviance and (2) promoters of those definitions to the extent they make their definitions known to others. The extent to which others are exposed to these definitions of deviance is problematic. It is apparent, however, that what Becker (1963) terms "moral entrepreneurs" (people attempting to promote or eliminate particular life-styles) can be found in all "levels" and "areas" of society.

While a number of "natural history" accounts of the emergence of legislation (see Cressey 1932; Sutherland 1950; Gusfield 1955, 1963; Lindesmith 1959; Sinclair 1962; Becker 1963; Chambliss 1964; Platt 1969; and Conner 1972) have made some contributions to the understanding of public acceptance of deviance definitions, the most effective model in this area is the one proposed by Blumer.

In "Social Problems as Collective Behavior", Blumer (1971) delineates five components in the process by which situations become publically treated as "social problems". Although "social problems" include things other than "deviance," the following processes are central: (1) emergence (initial awareness and publicity); (2) legitimation (public and official acknowledgement); (3) attempts to mobilize for action (assess information, suggestions, and probabilities); (4) formation of an official plan; and (5) implementation of the official plan (and the problematics of doing so). At each point, Blumer suggests, the process is negotiable and problematic, with outcomes reflecting a myriad of knowledge, beliefs, resources, and political manoeuverings, as persons and groups endeavour to ascertain and promote their interests relative to the issues at hand (and those seemingly related).

Building most specifically on the works of Cressey (1932), Sutherland (1959), Garafinkel (1956), Klapp (1969) and Blumer (1971), we suggest that parties promoting definitions of deviance are most likely to be successful in having their views (and remedies) accepted when they (are seen to) provide more extensive indications that (1) the activity is morally undesirable; (2) the activity represents an immediate, powerful, and active threat to both the public good and widespread individual well being; (3) the definitions proffered have the support of prominent, respected, and knowledgeable figures (and groups) in the community; (4) any opposition is defined as ill informed, irresponsible, selfserving, or otherwise suspect of motive; and (5) the proposed definitions (and other control efforts) could be implemented with a minimum of disruption (money, inconvenience, suffering) to community members. To the extent they are successful, these interested parties have significance not only for promoting "working definitions of deviance", but also for identifying (deviant) targets, and for generating styles (and agencies) of deviance regulation.

THE NAMING PROCESS: REPUTATIONS IN PROCESS

While both Lemert and Becker acknowledge the impact of labels for one's subsequent careers, neither devotes much attention to the processes by which labels become affixed to targets. People working in the labeling tradition recognize the naming process as problematic, and while one finds some material which focuses on "social identities", "type-casting", "impression management", and the like,[5] limited attention has been given to depictions of the naming process.

Of particular value in this respect is a much neglected article by Harold Garfinkel (1956). Viewing public hearings in which persons' identities are called into question as moral battles, Garfinkel posits that degradation ceremonies are most likely to be successful when (1) the alleged *activity* (a) is considered more unusual; (b) is presumed intended by the perpetrator, and (c) is at variance with fundamental group values; (2) the *denouncer* (a) is perceived to act in the interest of the group, (b) has the authority to speak on behalf of the group, and (c) is himself considered an honourable member of the group; (3) *witnesses* to the activity in question are void of personal interests relative to the target; and (4) the *perpetrator* is considered disrespectable in other ways.

Elaborating on the "naming process", Prus (1975a, b, 1982) delineates four processes operative in the formation of social identities: typing; designating; assessing; and resisting. "Typing" refers to the process by which one person (agent) arrives at a private definition of another (target). Not all typings are made known to the target and/or others, and although agents may occasionally "blurt out" their private typings, they are seen to make decisions as to whether or not to make these typings known to others. "Designating" refers to agents providing indications (verbal and/or behavioural) of a somewhat public nature, suggesting that targets are particular types of people. As others (including the target) learn of these designations, they tend to "assess" these for their appropriateness relative to their knowledge and views of the target. Where target references are seen as inappropriate (too soft, too harsh, inaccurate) interested persons then decide whether to "resist" target designations or to let them go unchallenged.

TYPING

In arriving at private definitions of targets, persons may utilize information they themselves encounter directly as well as that disclosed to them by others. On a first hand basis, they may, utilizing cognitive categories and cultural stereotypes, develop impressions of targets reflecting (1) *appearances* (the settings in which the targets are observed; nonaction personal effects such as dress, grooming, and physique); (2) *activities* in which targets were observed (or assumed) participating; (3) *consequences* (of activities) observed directly or attributed to the target; (4) the level of *responsibility* attributed to targets for appearances, activities, or consequences; and (5) *values* (interests, motives) thought to characterize the targets. Where the agent has prior knowledge of the target, incoming information is subjected to this context. Existing typings may provide powerful interpretative frames, particularly when these typings reflect a more complete sense of knowing targets and/or when incoming information is more ambiguous or incomplete. However, when incoming information is seen more extensive, or more central to the agent's interests, it may form a frame in which earlier information is recast.

DESIGNATING

In making target typings known to others, agents may affect not only the social life of the target, but also that of any others with whom the target has contact (including the agent). Given the potential ramifications of disclosures, agents may be selective in making target references. Typically, as agents define the disclosure of target typings as more significant (more newsworthy to others, situationally more relevant, reflecting their duties, or promoting their interests), they seem more desirious of making their typings known to others. However, persons' actual disclosures are moderated by their perceptions of external accountability. In general, as agents envision themselves as (1) more knowledgeable, (2) more esteemed, (3) more powerful, and (4) more independent, they are more likely to make target disclosures in line with their interests.

Should agents wish to make target disclosures, but experience little designating autonomy, they may (1) disclose their typings more selectively, picking and choosing their audiences; (2) soften disclosures, while maintaining much of the essence of their typings (e.g. referring to the target as a "little slow," rather than "dumb"); and (3) obscure accountability for disclosures by presenting these in the context of double talk, humour, and sarcasm.

Other disclosures may come about (1) inadvertently, (2) in conjunction with moral indignation (wherein the agent, sensing injustice, feels less constrained), or (3) as a consequence of consulting a third party regarding difficulties involving the target. Not all disclosures are truthful, and agents (in an attempt to better their position relative to a target) may misrepresent (miscontextualize, distort, or falsify) information concerning a target.

ASSESSING DESIGNATIONS

Regardless of the authenticity of a disclosure, once a target typing is made known to others, these others (including the target) face the prospects of assimilating this incoming information with their other knowledge of the target. Typically, recipients of information seem most comfortable with material that confirms their present images of the target. When inconsistencies appear, the direction of their resolution seems contingent on: the amount, centrality, and internal consistency of the incoming information; and the credibility of the sources.[6] While more recent information may be seen as more relevant, recipients of information seem to attribute greater credibility to sources they envision to (1) have higher community prestige; (2) assume perspectives more similar to those of the recipient's in reference to the target; (3) provide more "verifiable cues" in making the disclosure; (4) act with greater conviction in their designations; (5) be free of "personal motives"; and (6) possess casts of supporting others (multiple others, particularly those seemingly independent of one another, appear more convincing).

RESISTING DESIGNATIONS

Should proposed labels be judged "inappropriate", "undesired", and such, persons and groups may challenge these.[7] It should not be assumed, however, that all undesired or inaccurate labels are challenged by the targets and/or other interested parties. Designations seem more likely to go uncontested as potential resisters anticipate that (1) designations will be less permanent; (2) designations will be less consequential; (3) the costs or risks of resisting the designations will be more extensive; and (4) their challenges are less likely to be successful.

Should interested parties decide to resist target definitions they may (1) contest the validity of the typing as applied to the target (indicate inconsistencies between the typing and the "target as is", deny and/or provide alternative explanations for the "evidence", or contend that the target should not be held responsible for the "evidence"); (2) challenge the agent (vested interests, incompetence); (3) suggest a compromise typing (whereby the agent retracts some, but not all elements of the earlier designation); or (4) ask the agent to retract the designation (by acknowledging the agent's good will and/or indicating the regret of the target, a "repentent sinner"). Should these options (individually or in any combination) be thought or found insufficient, targets may endeavour to resist undesired labels by (5) seeking out others with whom to associate. This latter option seems more effective when the interactive distance between the two sets of audiences is maximized. Targets may also attempt to resist designations by (6) behavioural alignments, thus providing "living demonstrations" of inconsistencies between suggested typings and their everyday routines. While the prominence of earlier, non-reaffirmed typings are apt to fade with time and across audiences, these nevertheless denote interpretative frames in which any subsequent activities may be conceptualized. As a result, much of the effect of targets changing their behaviour may not only be nullified, but targets become much more vulnerable to designations of a related nature (and consequently more subject to manipulation by other persons). As Simmons (1969) notes, one residual effect of negative labels is to reduce the ability of discredited persons to be competitive on many levels. Not only are these persons more apt to be subject to disproportionate surveillance, but their participation in even "innocent activities" can become readily suspect.

While there is direct relationship between labeling persons as deviants and particular styles of response to those targets, once persons are identified as (or suspected of being) "deviants", concerns with the regulation of deviance become prominent.

HANDLING DEVIANCE INFORMALLY

It is ironic that while most of our deviance is handled informally, most of the literature on responses to deviance has focused on formal control systems, such as the police, courts, and psychiatric facilities. Formal control agencies are important elements in the "law and order" theme, and may be seen as handling a large percentage of the "heavy" cases (some become "heavy" only because of agency involvements; others because of the amount of attention they generate). But, as research on both the referral process (Ennis 1967; Block 1974) and the field responses of police officers (e.g. Black 1970; Black and Reiss 1970) suggests, citizens, through their decisions to report crimes and their expressed preference for legal action as complainants, are critical in understanding the crime phenomenon. Also of interest are the "informal" ways in which much of the deviance encountered by formal control agencies is handled. Proportionately little deviance is referred to "formal control agencies", and even then, the chances that it will be handled informally in those settings are much greater than would seem from examining their control mandates.[8]

While labeling theorists may be criticized for not being more systematic in their analysis of the informal regulation of deviance, this subject has received explicit attention in a recent article by Emerson and Messinger (1977). These authors consider not only the problematics of defining "trouble" or "troublemakers" in everyday contexts, but also examine strategies for informally dealing with disruptive behaviour, and the roles third parties may play in the "micro politics of trouble".

In summarizing central themes in this area,[9] four means of informally responding to deviance can be delineated, along with some of the contingencies affecting their usage. Persons may "do nothing", "alter their own behaviour", "attempt to realign the behaviour of the target" and/or "solicit support from others in dealing with the troublesome situation" (referrals of sorts). These options are not mutually exclusive, and may be deployed on a concurrent or sequential basis. Each instance of trouble, however, is best seen in "career" terms, wherein the agent becomes aware of some "problem", but over time may attach varying interpretations and levels of significance of the phenomenon, possibly in the process responding to the inputs of the target and/or other parties. Instances of "trouble" may, thus, range from very situational and short-lived concerns to long-term persistent courses of difficulty for the involved parties.

"Doing nothing" is one of the most common ways of responding to troublesome behaviour. This response seems more likely when agents (1) consider activities to be more inconsequential; (2) perceive themselves as having more pressing interests and/or obligations; (3) perceive activities as less likely to persist; (4)

anticipate that "doing something" would be personally more costly/risky than doing nothing; (5) are more uncertain about how to appropriately respond to the situation; (6) are more concerned with maintaining congenial relationships with the "trouble-makers"; (7) are personally more sympathetic to the activities under consideration; and (8) anticipate less success remedying the troublesome behaviour.[10] However, insofar as agents may become morally incensed (righteous indignation) over an activity, they believe that overlooking an activity may have more extensive negative consequences, or perceive themselves more accountable for upholding principles or rights that the activity is seen to jeopardize, "doing nothing" becomes an undesirable and possibly frustrating manner of coming to terms with the situation.

Agents "altering their own behaviour" in response to deviant others have three major options. First, they may endeavour to avoid the "troublesome other(s)". Secondly, they may get violent (verbally and physically) with the target, possibly as a function of expressing moral indignation (anger), but possibly also as a means of promoting more acceptable behaviour on the part of the target. Thirdly, and particularly in cases where agents wish to sustain more congenial relationships with targets (or feel especially dependent on their continuing good will), agents may alter their own behaviour to accommodate the targets' activities.

If the undesired behaviour seems likely to continue, attempts to "realizing the target's behaviour" emerge as a more likely option. If the target is perceived as someone to whom the agent should be considerate, attempts may be made to explain and justify alternatives that the target might pursue. Likewise, targets defined as more "reasonable" may be given new chances as alternatives are indicated, possibly with the overriding threat of sanctions. Persons may also endeavour to educate ("rehabilitate") troublesome targets by acting violently (e.g. embarrassing, criticizing, hitting) towards targets as well as imposing other sanctions designed to draw attention to their undesired behaviour.

Another option in responding to deviance is that of seeking assistance from other people. Although this may be a last resort, it is quite apparent that agents may seek assistance from others at any number of points in time. Other people may, thus, be involved from the agent's first suspicion (or may even draw the agent's attention to the "problem"), to throughout the career of the "troublesome situation". Third party consultations may result in agents subsequently "doing nothing", "making personal accom-modations", "attempting to educate the deviants", or playing less instrumental roles in determining the target's fate. In general, people seem more likely to seek assistance from others (both

p. 120, second complete paragraph, line 2 — Substitute "realign" for "realizing" informally and with respect to control agencies) when (1) they perceive *third parties* as (a) more accessible, (b) more ready to believe their accounts, and (c) more likely to act in their interests; (2) they perceive the *troublesome situation* as (a) more identifiable, (b) more persistent, (c) more offensive, (d) more threatening, and (e) more difficult to control; (3) they consider the *revelation of trouble* to be less personally costly (e.g. reputation, friendship);[11] and (4) where they hold the *target* in lower esteem (agents are less concerned about any subsequent costs targets may incur as a result of the disclosures).[12]

AGENCY RESPONSES TO DEVIANCE

While purporting to regulate deviance (and trouble more generally), the day-to-day operations of control agencies may be characterized by five central concerns: agency maintenance, access, classification, restoring justice, and maintaining internal order. It is important to consider the ways in which agents do the activities of which these themes are a reflection; how these concerns are realized in the interchanges between control agents and the other involved parties.

AGENCY MAINTENANCE

If an agency is to regulate deviance on any large scale, a fundamental concern is that of achieving public awareness and support. Not all agencies are dependent on governmental funding, but some degree of community acceptance is essential if the agency is to become influential in its regulatory endeavours. Not only does public acceptance provide legitimation, but it also establishes a basis on which to obtain both the funding and the "cases" necessary to keep the program viable. Promotions ("public relations") work may assume a variety of forms, and has in some cases been so effective as to convince the community that the agency (e.g. police, courts) is an essential element of community life.

As Hawkins and Tiedman (1975) suggest, "controlling deviance is big business." Operations may range from counselling services, social work programs and other community assistance projects, to prisons, mental hospital, and other "total institutions" (Goffman, 1961). In each case, however, and regardless of whether the agency approaches deviance from a legal, medical, psychological, welfare, or religious perspective, agencies seem obligated to make some claims about their viability.

To the outside, the public on which they are dependent for support, the agencies endeavour to appear expert, effective, and trustworthy.[13] If there is sharp competition in dealing with particular types of deviance, agencies may endeavour to indicate that they are not only more knowledgeable and reliable than their competitors, but that their programs are also more economical, humane, or achieve other "secondary concerns" more effectively than do the competitors. Agencies may seek out deviants, but they also recruit support for their programs. An agency's publically expressed philosophy may represent ineffectual indications of actual agency operations, but to the extent that the imagery an agency promotes is perceived as representing desired community objectives, it may serve as a basis for generating both community support and "grist for the mill".

ACCESS

Although some of the deviance control agencies encounter comes about as a result of agency surveillance routines (e.g. police patrol), and the more sensational "witch hunting" activities (e.g. Erikson's [1966] depiction of the Salem witch hunt and Conner's [1972] analysis of the Soviet purge of 1936–1938), most of the deviance coming to the attention of formal control agencies reflects complaints, inquiries, and referrals.

Some citizens may be skeptical of the effectiveness of control agencies (Ennis 1967), but others, perhaps out of a sense of desperation, a desire to "follow procedures", or in attempting to restore order or gain retribution relative to the target, will contact, consult, or inform agencies regarding "troublesome situations". In general, and in spite of other indications, referrals and inquiries constitute the bulk of agency encountered deviance (see Black 1970; Black and Reiss 1970; and Rubinstein 1973), it is also apparent that citizens handle a great deal of the deviance they encounter without recourse of agency intervention. Extensive promotions work detailing legal, medical, or welfare programs do appear to increase the likelihood that a given instance of trouble will be referred to a control agency, but even under optimal conditions, it seems unlikely that agencies will ever handle the bulk of the deviance people encounter.

While promotions work enhances the likelihood of agencies obtaining a more complete knowledge of deviance, a fuller notion of access and one typically assumed by control agencies is that they would like sufficient availability of the "deviants" as to enable appropriate classification and processing of all relevant cases.

CLASSIFICATION

Regardless of routing, most agencies require that those they encounter be sorted into "agency specific" categories (e.g. particular legal or psychiatric categories) before they are processed further. This is not to imply that these categories are objective, or are consistently and accurately applied. Research suggests that agency labels are perspectival, negotiable, and subject to assignment on the basis of little (and sometimes conflicting) evidence.[14] The same processes earlier outlined in the four stage model of naming (Pruss 1975a) are relevant here, as is Garfinkel's (1956) discussion of degradation ceremonies. Formats may vary extensively across agencies and targets may have neither the desire nor the opportunity (or resources) to resist labels being affixed to them.

In general, as control agents (1) hold targets in lower esteem, (2) envision themselves as less accountable to targets, (3) anticipate lower levels of subsequent interaction with targets, and (4) perceive a larger number of cases to be processed, target typifications are more likely to reflect agent perceptions of standardized agency case dispositions and tend to be affixed in the most expedient means available.[15] Where agents sense less accountability to the agency (or others), their typifications are particularly likely to reflect individual agent styles and interests. However, to the extent that targets and/or others interested in the target's future are able to intervene in the definitional process, the resulting typings are more likely to be negotiated, and as such, are less apt to reflect the interests of the agency or the particular styles of the agent than would otherwise be the case.

RESTORING JUSTICE

In providing treatment, punishment, or merely establishing a settlement, agencies are engaged a very basic social function, that of "restoring justice". Styles of "realignment" can vary extensively, as do the philosophies underlying their implementation. While reactions are often linked to the definition of trouble, wherein religious agencies handle "sinners", courts handle "criminals", and the like, it should also be noted that many programs may be applicable to the same instance of "trouble". A "violent offender" may find that he is not only a candidate for court, but that he may also be referred to, or sought out by, control agencies with a religious or psychiatric flavour. However, regardless of the actual agency involved, insofar as it is assumed that the agency is "well intentioned", it is likely to have some value in "neutralizing troublesome occurrences".

As "something is being done", those concerned with troublesome cases can return to life as usual. Justice is restored (for the time being) as a consequence of agency intervention. This restoration of moral order, however precarious, may very well be the main effective function of control agencies; that they serve as "buffers between offenders and victims" (or other concerned parties), thereby neutralizing troublesome situations. This is where "punishment", to the extent it restores "social regulation" (Durkheim 1897) or "distributive justice" (Homans 1958), wherein people are rewarded (or punished) in proportion to their conforming behaviour, serves to quell injured and otherwise indignant parties. Likewise, "requiring that deviants receive remedial treatment", in the process suggesting that they weren't fully responsible for their actions, also serves to validate the existing moral order.

One may argue that control agencies are only partially successful in restoring moral order by settlement, confinement, punishment, and the like. However, once one moves past this "peace keeping" function, and examines other control agency roles (e.g. rehabilitation, deterrence), agency effectiveness becomes even more questionable, and these "objectives" must be viewed within the context of keeping order within the agency.

INTERNAL ORDER

While the problematics of achieving internal order becomes especially evident in instances such as prison riots and "unnatural institutional deaths", it is apparent that the problem of keeping internal order also has major implications for agency maintenance, access to targets, classification schemes, and styles of restoring justice. While space prohibits a more developed statement, it should be noted that concerns with "internal order" are operative on a number of levels ranging from interstaff policies and practices, to staff-target interchanges, to exchanges between targets.

Ideally, one might expect to find integrated systems of control agencies (e.g. criminal justice system, welfare programs), with each component working towards a larger system goal, coordinating their activities with those of the other subsystems in such a way as to best handle the cases they encounter. In actuality, this does not happen. Agencies, even those seemingly highly dependent on one another (e.g. police, courts, prison, parole), generally compete for budgets. Concerned with different subgoals, they also utilize different indicators of "successful activity" and will (sometimes deliberately) "block and stall" other agencies as each attempts to pursue its own goals in the midst of overlapping interests and cases. Also, agents in subsystems tend not to be well informed about the daily operations of related functionaires. Upper-level directors may meet to discuss "system integration and operations", but the "actual people-work" is typically done at a very different level. These conditions are further complicated by a lack of consistency within specific programs. As Freidson (1966) and Stoll (1968) note, models of control employed by agents within the same system may vary considerably from one agent to the next. If agents use different models (entailing diverse explanations) as to "how human behaviour comes about" or "what causes people to act in certain ways", one may expect to encounter different interpretations of activities and different response to these "activities". Persons viewing deviance as "self-willed" or "subject to conditioning", for instance, may be more prone to using punishment as a means of rehabilitation than would agents perceiving behaviour as an "illness", the "fault of society", or a "situational occurrence".

While any of these (or other) models may represent central agency enphases, it seems likely that agencies (and agents within) are likely to vacillate somewhat amongst these positions, in this way providing a somewhat inconsistent image to the persons being processed. One may expect even sharper variations across control agencies, wherein, for example, the police may be operating under generally different perceptions of causality than those of probation agents or prison counsellors.

One consequence of this lack of consistency may be that each of the systems may be rendered relatively ineffective in practice. Rather than being "changed" or "rehabilitated", those being processed may simply become more adept at adapting to a variety of perspectives. It would, in this sense, and with concerns for assessing the general effectiveness of programs, be useful to direct more attention to "what various programs and agencies represent to those being processed therein".

In addition to the problematics of working out a solid, consistent "plan of action", control agencies face the additional task of "working with people". Not only does one lack the sort of "quality control" one achieves in working with aluminum or plastics, for example, but as "minded beings", humans can act back on those attempting to work with them. Thus, in addition to having to contend with legal rights and humane treatment concerns, as well as dealing with diverse and complex "materials", those engaging in people-work also deal with phenomena which can attempt to manipulate them. These manipulations (e.g. deception, ingratiation, threats, disturbances) become even more significant when it is recognized that the "deviants" (1) may not want to change (or be changed); (2) may not trust the agents working with them; (3) may not value the particular orientations promoted by the agent; (4) may consider the agent's views appropriate within the agency, but not relevant in the "outside world"; and (5) may find considerable verbal and behavioural support for their positions among other targets of rehabilitation and others with whom they have contact "on the outside". Where these conditions exist, it seems unlikely that rehabilitation agents will extensively achieve the goal of producing "conventional citizens". A longer and more intensive program is likely to result in targets being more knowledgeable about agency life, and it would seem more effective in restoring the earlier disrupted moral order, but unless these other issues are dealt with, rehabilitation seems unlikely to be effective on a large scale.

Agencies also vary in the extent to which their contact with targets is a fleeting or a more extensive one. Typically, both "voluntary agencies" and those engaged in short-term processing of offenders tend to be less concerned with confinement than are the involuntary and long-term agencies. In any event, as containment concerns become more prominent, other objectives (e.g. rehabilitation, humane treatment) become less significant in the daily routines of staff. It is also apparent, however, that a great deal of research remains in reference to both the operations of control agencies and the role "those being processed" play in the process. We have some highly insightful material on the problematics of agency life and routines,[16] but we need to more fully and specifically examine *the ways in which* agencies (1) seek and achieve community support; (2) access prospective deviants; (3) classify targets; (4) restore moral order following disruptive occurrences; and (5) pursue internal order with its ensuing implications for objectives such as deterrence, rehabilitation, and the like.

DEVIANCE INVOLVEMENTS

To this point, we have focused largely on the identification of deviance and deviants, and responses to deviance. We now turn to a related theme, that of accounting for deviant behaviour from a labeling perspective. Especially prominent, in this respect, are the concepts of "secondary deviation" (Lemert, 1951; 1967; 1973) and "career contingencies" (Becker 1963).

SECONDARY DEVIATION

While not attempting to explain initial involvements in deviance, Lemert suggests that the responses of control agencies to (assumed) deviants in the community serve to (1) draw attention to the targets and differentiate them from others, (2) promote community and self-definitions of targets as "deviants", and (3) restructure the targets' options so as to make deviant behaviour comparatively more appealing than was formerly (or would have otherwise been) the case.

Lemert does not see subsequent involvement in deviance as inevitable, but contends that it is more likely to occur when societal reactions are formal and intense. Not only may targets find regular options limited, but as a result of their disrespectable community images may also have less respect for any available conventional routines (thereby making them more receptive to deviant pursuits). Should these other options become rewarding, they are apt to be pursued more intensively. Should targets more fully organize their lives around these activities, they are apt to find it increasingly difficult to "go straight". Lemert indicates that by excluding persons from acceptable avenues of endeavour, control agencies may effectively promote the very sort of behaviour they sought to eliminate.

Certainly, community responses can alter targets' options, and can make other options appear more appealing by contrast. Further, as people more fully organize their lives around particular (deviant) pursuits, it becomes increasingly difficult to become disengaged from those activities. However, in examining the implications of "societal reactions" three issues require further attention: (1) what constitutes "societal reactions"; (2) how do people become defined as "deviants"; and (3) how instrumental are the resulting identities for systematic deviance on the part of those so identified?

Lemert uses the term "societal reactions" fairly synonymously with "social control efforts", including therein the emergence of legislation and the development and operations of control agencies. Lemert apparently includes "informal responses to deviance" on the part of family, friends, co-workers and the like in the category of "societal reactions", but explicitly emphasizes the role of formal control agencies. He also recognizes "informal responses to deviance on the part of control agencies", but in discussing secondary deviation he focuses chiefly on the implications of exclusionary and official agency responses.

In discussing the imputation of deviance, Lemert's agents seem differentially disposed to identifying targets as "deviants", and the targets seem differentially susceptible to imputations of deviance, but he provides very little elaboration of the "naming process", other than to indicate that formal responses often follow a series of unsuccessful attempts to curb the troublesome behaviour.

Lemert also devotes minimal attention to the effects of societal reactions on targets, as these might be qualified by prior experiences, existing options, contacts, or other resources to which targets might have uneven access. Further, although Lemert indicates that outcomes are always problematic (deviance imputations need not result in "secondary deviation"), his model only acknowledges exclusionary effects.[17] It may be the case that exclusionary reactions are more common and more effective in perpetuating deviance, but we want to sort out the varieties of community responses and their implications.[18]

Lemert is also unclear whether "informal responses" to deviance may be sufficient to generate "secondary deviation", but he does contend that official exclusionary responses strongly promote subsequent deviance. Encounters with the police, the courts, and the like may be among the more dramatic and damning reactions experienced, but Lemert's lack of specificity concerning the nature of "societal reactions" makes it difficult to assess the significance of "formal control agencies" for secondary deviation as opposed to, or in conjunction with, "informal responses to deviance".[19]

The matter of deviance stabilization becomes further complicated by (1) Lemert's failure to consider orientations and activities preceding encounters with control agencies, and (2) his tendency to minimize the role that "deviant" others may play in recruiting or otherwise facilitating targets' involvements in activities. While Lemert suggests that the outcast is likely to be rejecting of his condemners and more receptive to deviant behaviour as a result of exclusion, he provides limited commentary on either the conditions affecting success as a "deviant" (is it easy to be thusly successful?) or the elements promoting reentry into conventional routines. It is exceedingly difficult to obtain a clear understanding of when and to what extent "secondary deviation" occurs, and when and how (if ever) one foregoes this role.

In an attempt to articulate some central aspects of social control efforts, relative to subsequent deviance, it is suggested that further involvement in deviance is more likely when the "discrediting sources" (formal or informal) (1) define targets as (a) more villainous (ill intentioned); (b) persistent, and (c) powerful threats; (2) are more highly esteemed in the community; (3) provide more widespread publicity regarding the targets and their "improprieties"; (4) are more exclusionary in their reactions relative to conventional options; and (5) have greater control over community activities (can more effectively neutralize conventional avenues of target support). We suggest, however, that persons interested in the impact of control efforts on systematic deviance not neglect (6) the target's prior experiences, or (7) the affiliational networks (deviant and conventional) to which the target has access (and the target's receptivity therein). Where persons have more intensively engaged in deviance prior to official processing and/or are better connected with networks of deviants, the effects of agency responses may be very different from those experienced by targets who are largely conventional in orientation and whose contacts with the underlife are exceedingly limited.

CAREER CONTINGENCIES

While acknowleding Lemert's contention that official responses to deviance can effectively promote intensified involvements in deviance, Becker views deviance more fundamentally as "social activity" reflecting interchanges between the targets and those with whom (conventional and deviant) they interact.

Although Becker might have stated his position more fully, he posits (using "career contingencies" as his organizing concept) that deviance be examined in process terms, considering the conditions affecting persons' participation in activities over time. From Becker's work, the following issues emerge as having central significance: (1) how definitions of deviance emerge and are enforced; (2) the ways (as opposed to "why") in which persons become involved in deviant activities and groups; (3) how persons may overcome the disrespectability associated with "deviant activities" (on either a personal level or following the reactions of others); (4) how people may avoid getting drawn more exclusively into conventional routines; (5) the implications of any denunciations (and the elements accentuating/dissipating the impact of denunciations) on the targets' subsequent options; and (6) the implications of group interaction in reference to providing support for continuing deviant activities (rationales, motives, ideologies, identities, opportunities, and techniques).

Becker's statement leaves much unsaid regarding involvements in "deviant" activities, but the concept of "career contingencies" avoids many of the dilemmas characterizing "secondary deviation". It allows us to trace people's activities from A to Z, enabling us to examine these involvements in the context of the actors' preceding experiences and their present situations.

Building on Becker's (1963) work, and drawing upon research on card and dice hustlers (Prus and Sharper 1977), violence (Prus 1978), and the hotel community (Prus and Irini 1980), I would like to briefly outline a statement on the contingencies affecting involvements in deviant activities. Career contingencies, thus, are conceptualized in reference to "initial involvements", "continuities", "disinvolvements", "reinvolvements", and "multiple involvements".

Initial Involvements

In discussing involvements in deviance, three routings (seekership, recruitment, and closure) are particularly noteworthy, as is a qualifier, "drift".

Seekership

Not only are persons apt to find it easier to engage in activities that are orientationally compatible with viewpoints that they have developed (over time, through association with others), but they may also explicitly search out activities they define in line with their interests (i.e. those they consider appealing, fascinating, productive, and the like).[20] Thus, as persons define activities as more effective in realizing personal interests, they are more likely to take steps to become involved in those activities.

Insofar as people actively solicit, or willingly incorporate targets into their routines, they may be said, in varying degrees, to "recruit" these targets.[21] By providing definitions favourable to activities, other people can effectively restructure the targets' orientations towards (deviant) activities. However, to the extent these others also represent lines of access to activities otherwise not available to the targets, or explicitly seek to involve the targets in their activities, their roles are even more significant in accounting for initial involvements. Therefore, as persons encounter others promoting their participation in activities, they are more likely to become involved in those activities.

Closure

To the extent an (deviant) activity is seen to represent a solution to a pressing problem, persons may find themselves engaging in activities they might otherwise have avoided. Considering it essential to fulfill certain obligations, people may become "forced into" deviant activities.[22] Accordingly, as persons experience a greater sense of urgency to achieve specific obligations, they are more apt to engage in activities they consider likely to result in the fulfillment of those obligations.[23]

Drift

While the preceding routes of involvement may occur independently, or in any combination, all are contingent on participants overcoming any reservations associated with activities (e.g. moral, physical, legal concerns). As opportunities for "deviance" may occur in any number of contexts, with different audiences present, the extent to which persons "feel responsible for maintaining usual propriety" can vary considerably from one situation to the next.[24] Hence, as persons feel less (situationally) constrained by accountability to themselves and/or others, they will be more likely to engage in activities that they would otherwise have considered "deviant".

Continuities

As with initial involvements, continuity in a given activity is problematic.[25] While the bases on which individuals become

p. 131, Insert heading "Recruitment" before first complete paragraph

initially involved may differentially affect continuity, participants seem more likely to continue their activities when (1) their previous experiences in particular activities have been more effective in realizing recurrent objectives (e.g. money, entertainment); (2) they believe that particular activities offer more exclusive means of achieving desired ends (or fulfilling obligations); (3) they become more committed to an ideology which normalizes otherwise "deviant" behaviour; (4) they perceive more aspects of their lives to be dependent on their involvements in particular activities; (5) they become better known as particular types of practitioners; (6) they more fully (explicitly and centrally) identify themselves as "participants in those activities"; and (7) they more extensively neglect other options and "outsiders".

Disinvolvement

While the very elements promoting success in new life-styles serve to deter disinvolvement, some other concerns have particular effects on participants' abilities to disentangle themselves from activities. Disinvolvement seems most effective when practitioners (1) redefine their interests and/or envision little hopes of their realization through particular activities, thereby minimizing "seekership"; (2) cease effective contact (by choice, chance, or expulsion) with activity associates, hence curtailing "recruitment"; (3) redefine their obligations and/or perceive viable alternatives, hence reducing "closure"; (4) develop new lines of accountability (e.g. significant others, health concerns), nullifying "drift". Targets processed by control agencies are subject to the same concerns as those becoming "voluntarily" disinvolved, although in contrast to the voluntary condition (in which persons become more "spontaneously disenchanted"), targets of control efforts are more likely to be resistant to definitional changes and may become suspect of all those whose orientations seem different from their own.

Reinvolvement

On encountering difficulties in given situations, persons may consider former as well as new activities. Insofar as people are apt to have become somewhat neutralized to former (deviant) activities and associates, concerns with stigma (and other "usual restraints") are less apt to inhibit subsequent (re)involvement in those activities. On experiencing dissatisfaction with their present circumstances, it may be easier for actors to resume former activities than to embark on new lines of action wherein the contacts are problematic and they may have to overcome other reservations. Reinvolvements seem contingent on success in former activities and some anticipated acceptance on the part of one's former associates. Persons seem more likely to resume former activities on encountering difficulties in their present situations when (1) they define themselves as having been more successful in the former lines of action, and (2) anticipate higher levels of receptivity among activity associates.

Multiple Involvements

To a large extent, deviance definitions are seen as having the effect of a "master status" (Becker, 1963), colouring the targets' other experiences by their application. While deviance definitions can make other target attributions pale in contrast, it should also be noted that both deviance definitions and their effects can be moderated by other target attributes. This seems particularly noticeable in reference to other involvements targets have prior to, or concurrent with, their involvements in deviance. In addition to affecting targets' definitions as "deviants", these other involvements may influence not only the targets' initial involvements and continuities, but also their disinvolvements and reinvolvements in deviance.[26]

LABELING THEORY: CENTRAL CRITICISMS

While the preceding discussion has taken into account a number of criticisms commonly directed towards "labeling theory", there remain some other points deserving our attention. These have, it seems, become stumbling blocks of sorts in conceptualizing and assessing the validity of labeling theory.[27]

A major criticism of labeling theory and one mentioned by both those favourable to it (Schur 1971; Goode 1975; Hawkins and Tiedman 1975; Prus 1975a, b; and Cullen and Cullen 1978), as well as those opposed (Gibbs 1966; Hirschi 1973; and Gove 1975), pertains to (1) its lack of theoretical specificity. While this partially represents the impact of three largely undifferentiated themes (control, functionalism, and interactionism) within "labeling theory", some criticism could have been averted had earlier statements regarding labeling been more fully elaborated. While this vagueness constitutes an important backdrop to much (but not all) of the criticism labeling theory has encountered, one cannot help but think that the recent and rapid proliferation of this theoretical perspective makes it appear less theoretically developed than the (longer-established) "traditional" perspectives on deviance.

Another set of criticisms coming mainly from positivistically oriented sociologists revolves around (2) the "substance" and the "measurement" of deviance. Gibbs (1966), Akers (1968), Hirschi (1973), and Gove (1975) charge that labeling theory fails to provide "objective criteria for defining deviance". These sociologists seem exceedingly uncomfortable with the phenomenological (relativistic) position labeling theory assumes.[28] Although not all of one accord, these critics argue that deviance is best defined as "rule breaking activity" and are generally content to rely on official statistics to determine that "deviance has taken place". They seem unconcerned about the emergence of deviance definitions, the problematics of defining deviants, or the ways in which deviant activities take place. They seem not (choose not?) to recognize the exceedingly basic challenge that labeling theory poses for logical-positivist conceptualizations of social life. Seemingly unencumbered by the relativity of deviance definitions one is apt to encounter in one's daily life, they insist on "objective" definitions of deviance.[29]

While quantitatively oriented sociologists have been differentially bothered by the "deviance is relative to the audience" position characterizing much of labeling theory, those attempting research in this area are apt to have difficulty operationalizing labeling theory. Few statements on labeling theory have been presented in propositional format, and the quantitative researchers have been left largely on their own in developing measures of complex labeling processes. Labeling theorists have also been very critical of positivist methodology and the validity of its assumptions (e.g. that official statistics provide reasonably accurate measures of deviant behaviour, or that questionnaire items and responses have standardized meanings). This phenomenological-positivist schism has long been brewing (see Blumer 1969), but it seems to have become more prominent following Becker's (1963) statement on deviance.

A number of other criticisms have been directed towards (3) the labeling process or some variant thereof. It is frequently charged that (a) labeling theorists ignore involvements in deviance prior to official intervention (Gibbs 1966; Schervish 1972; Hirschi 1973; and Gove 1975). This criticism is most appropriately directed towards a control (Lemert) version of labeling theory. The interactionists are sensitive to the impact of official responses for subsequent deviance, but, as Becker's discussion of marijuana users suggests, are also concerned with initial involvements.

A somewhat related issue is (b) whether a label is a "dependent" or "independent" variable (Gove 1975). Although Lemert seems primarily concerned with the effects of labeling, labeling theorists in general would suggest that labels (i) reflect audience assessments of targets (thus, approximating dependent variables), and (ii) represent features suggesting lines of action for subsequent target-audience interactions (ergo, independent variables as well). However, while viewing labels as perspectival, problematic, and negotiable in their application, labeling theorists would also contend that labels, as with other aspects of culture, are subject to interpretation and exchange in their implications.

Continuing along a similar vein, it has been asked (c) to what extent labels represent "master statuses" (Gove 1975). Although (i) not all deviance imputations are equally damning, and (ii) deviance definitions represent only one of multiple labels that targets may simultaneously possess, labeling theorists have given little consideration to this aspect of social identity. In part, this seems to reflect an interest in exclusionary reactions (especially Lemert), but it is clearly a matter to be taken into account in providing a more complete statement on the contingencies affecting labeling. Other target definitions (and involvements) can have important implications for both the problematics of affixing deviance labels to targets and the implications of those labels for the target's subsequent activities.

It has also been alleged that (d) targets of deviant labels are presented as innocent, helpless, passive recipients (Gibbs 1966; Schervish 1972; Hirschi 1973; and Gove 1975). Although partially accurate, these criticisms would seem most readily applied to early statements on labeling wherein little attention was given to the problematics of affixing names on targets. While targets may be variously innocent, helpless, and passive, statements by Goffman (1959, 1961), Davis (1961), Rogers and Buffalo (1974), Hewitt and Stokes (1975), Leviton (1975), and Prus (1975b) indicate that targets and their supporters may play active (although not always effective) roles in deciding what the eventual "labels" will be. Labeling is, in every instance, problematic, with targets varying extensively in reference to vulnerability and resources with which they might challenge imputations of deviance.

Another criticism sometimes directed towards labeling theory centres around (4) the neglect of "power", "social change", and "macro" analysis (Davis 1975). As noted earlier, in the section on defining deviance, labeling theorists have been sensitive to these concerns, although seemingly not as explicitly or exclusively as some have deemed appropriate. Thus, an examination of Lemert (1951, 1974), Becker (1963), Erikson (1966), Blumer (1971), Conner (1972), and Hawkins and Tiedman (1975) indicates that these scholars are not only attuned to the "politics of deviance", but, as Kotarba (1980) notes, appear highly instrumental in connecting "micro" and "macro" concerns with social order.

Labeling theorists have also received some criticism for assuming (5) "moral positions" in presenting their materials. Interestingly, while some have claimed that labeling theorists are (a) "overly sympathetic to the deviants" being studied (Schervish 1972; Hrischi 1973; Lemert 1974; and Glassner and Corzine 1978), others have chastised labeling theorists for (b) "supporting the status quo" (Liazos 1972; Thio 1978).

In the first instance (a), it might be noted that while individual labeling theorists may assume a variety of political positions, they are much more concerned with how social order comes about than attempting to define the forms it should assume. Some other criticisms may reflect the lack of sympathy labeling theorists have displayed for the "corrections perspective on deviance". Thus, in studying control agency practices, the labeling theorists have made few flattering statements about the desirability or efficiency of control agencies (frequently noting extensive discrepancies between agency claims and practices). The resulting dual tendencies of "demystifying control agencies" and "humanizing deviants" may have resulted in some corrections/rehabilitation oriented audiences defining labeling theorists as "anti-establishmentarian".

The second charge (b), predominantly Neo-Marxist in orientation, contends that labeling theorists rely on official definitions of deviance and therefore ignore the "true deviance in society". These critics allege that labeling theorists promote the "status quo", thus operating as agents of the state. Their main thrust is that labeling theorists do not focus on the "evils of capitalism" and the means of eliminating capitalist society. From a labeling perspective, one examines group processes relative to the exchanges taking place between the parties involved. One considers the participants' perspectives, interests, activities, strategies, and counterstrategies as these come into play. One does not "cheer for the 'red team' or the 'blue team' ", but rather focuses on their activities and exchanges as these are worked out by the parties involved. Labeling theorists are concerned with promoting neither "crime control" nor a "new society"; they are interested in understanding how people work out their activities (including deviance) with others.

IN PERSPECTIVE

Examining "deviance as a community phenomenon", one finds that *"deviance"* (1) *is perspectival;* (2) *entails self-reflectivity;* (3) *is best understood in processual terms; and* (4) *is problematic and negotiable in definition, participation, and regulation.* If one acknowledges that one cannot separate the individual from the society, and vice versa, then it becomes evident that "community responses to deviance" cannot be understood without reference to all those involved in the definition of, participation in, and regulation of "deviance".

Notions of community are exceedingly relevant in reference to *the processes by which* (1) definitions of deviance emerge; (2) people become identified as deviants; (3) people (individually and in groups, formally and informally) endeavour to regulate deviant activities; (4) people become involved in, continue, become dis-involved from, and reinvolved in, "deviant activities"; and (5) people go about "doing deviant activities" and organize their lives around those activities (and the other actors involved therein). Challenging "objective", "individualistic", "static", and "highly deterministic" conceptions of deviance, labeling theory has drawn attention to the significance of processual aspects of community life for the understanding of deviance.

Effectively only beginning to indicate (theoretically and contextually) the extent to which "deviance is a social pheno-menon", labeling theory has deep significance for those interested in the study of crime and deviance. While extensively rooted in interactionist thought, labeling theory not only directs our attention to the interpretation, regulation, and organization of "deviant" activities (and the actors involved therein), but it also provides a frame in which to integrate these profoundly social aspects of group life. We do not need one theory for the "deviants" and another for the "normals", but we do need theory sensitive to the problematic and emergent aspects of the exchanges character-izing daily interaction.

Notes

1. Although a great deal of the attention and criticism Lemert has encoun-tered focuses on the concept, "secondary deviation" he attempts to develop a general theory of social control (see Lemert 1951, 21-98). Lemert is centrally concerned with the emergence and enforcement of community priorities (rules, laws) as these intersect with individual interests, opportunities, and activities; the "what and how of social order in the community".

2. Lemert (1951; 1967; 1972; 1974) is inconsistent on this point. He acknowledges the relativity of deviance definitions, but argues that some activities must be deviant by reference to "objective" or "universal" standards. He does not, however, adequately specify these criteria.

3. Readers are referred to Mead (1934), Blumer (1934), McCall and Simmons (1978) and Charon (1979) for statements on interactionist thought.

4. This position is in basic agreement with Sutherland (1939) who in discussing the theory of "differential association", states that persons may simultaneously hold definitions favourable and unfavourable to criminal activity. The tendency to "average out attitudes" may represent a fundamental error in our attempts to understand human behaviour. Persons may also distinguish between the implementation of activities and their consequences. While an activity may be defined as desirable, for instance, some consequences associated with it may be viewed negatively, and vice versa.

5. The works of Goffman (1959; 1963), Klapp (1962; 1969; 1971), and Lofland (1969) represent especially noteworthy contributions to this literature.

6. Generally speaking, negative target information (possibly as a consequence of its disruptive implications) seems more apt to be believed than incoming positive definitions.

7. For other materials on avoiding undesired imputations, see Sykes and Matza (1957), Goffman (1959, 1963), Davis (1961), Klapp (1962, 1969, 1971), Scott and Lyman (1968), Rogers and Buffalo (1972), Hewitt and Stokes (1975), and Prus (1975b).

8. The works of Bittner (1967), Parnas (1967), Daniels (1970), Rubinstein (1973), and Prus and Stratton (1976) are especially relevant in this context.

9. Persons interested in the informal regulation of deviance will find the following materials particularly relevant: Jackson's (1954) analysis of the family reactions to drinking problems; Lemert's (1962) examination of the social basis of paranoia; Kitsuse's (1962) investigation of responses to homosexuality; Roth's (1962) portrayal of doctor-patient relationships in tuberculosis clinics; Rubington's (1968) depiction of the regulation of drinking activities among bottle gang members; Emerson's (1970) treatment of the problematics of managing intimacy in gynecological examinations; Weinberg's (1970) account of the nudist management of respectability; Ross' (1970) analysis of accident insurance-claims adjustment; Martin's (1975) analysis of teacher-pupil negotiations in the classroom; Prus and Irini's (1980) and Irini and Prus' (1982) discussions of peace-keeping in the hotel community.

10. Readers may note the parallels between persons not responding to "trouble" and targets not resisting undesired labels (wherein the agent represents the troublesome individual from the target's perspective).

11. These disclosures (truthful or otherwise) may in some cases be very productive for the "troubled" individuals, enabling them to restore or achieve esteem by indicating the obstacles they have encountered, their suffering, their relative innocence in the venture, and the like.

12. One might also envision some third party disclosures as having the intended function of injuring a target.

13. Insofar as actual levels of effectiveness are difficult to measure with high degrees of accuracy and validity, agencies better able to "present themselves" (Goffman, 1959) as "effective", or otherwise "essential" tend to fare better. The

widespread tendency to use statistics as "indicators of effectiveness" because readily suspect when one investigates "how rates are obtained" (see, for example, Skolnick, 1966; Rubinstein, 1973; and Prus and Stratton, 1976). Cressey (1959) provides a particularly insightful discussion of the dilemnas of evaluative research and accounting strategies. While Cressey speaks most directly to correctional programs, his statement has much more general relevance. Goffman (1961) presents an illustrative analysis on the attempts of total institutions to "manage impressions", during tours, visits, and the like.

14. Examinations of psychiatric practice by Jewell (1952), Scheff (1964), Stachnik and Ulrich (1965), Daniels (1970), Szasz (1970), and Rosenhan (1973) attest to these points. So does research by Skolnick (1966), Bittner (1967), Black (1970), Black and Reiss (1970), and Rubinstein (1973), on the police. Similar trends are evidenced by court materials gathered by Newman (1956), Reiss (1960), Sudnow (1965), Blumberg (1967), and Wiseman (1970). Materials on probation and parole by Emerson (1969), Arnold (1970), and Prus and Stratton (1976) further indicate the extent to which target definitions are problematic, as does research on emergency wards (Sudnow, 1970; Roth, 1972) and coroner assessments of death (Atkinson, 1971).

15. For more complete statements on the typification tendencies of control agencies, see Scheff (1963; 1964; 1966), Black and Reiss (1970), Daniels (1970), Conner (1972), and Prus and Stratton (1976).

16. For a fuller appreciation of the operations of rehabilitation agencies and the problematics of doing people work, see: Goffman's (1961) analysis of the underlife of total institutions; Roth's (1962) depiction of staff-patient relations in a tuberculosis facility; Emerson's (1969) discussion of juvenile probation work; Scott's (1969) treatment of agencies dealing with blind persons: Irwin's (1970) and Carroll's (1974) analyses of prison life; Wiseman's (1970) depiction of the treatment of skid row alcoholics; McCleary's (1975) and Prus and Stratton's (1976) discussion of parole-revocation decision making; and Hall's (1983) portrayal of front-line institutional workers.

17. Noting that negative labels may also promote conventional behaviour on the part of some targets, Thorsell and Klemke (1972) suggest that (1) societal reactions may have different effects on targets depending on when these occur (e.g., early/late) during their careers; (2) confidential reactions are less likely to promote subsequent involvements in deviance than are those of a more public nature; (3) targets accepting of the agent's perspectives are more likely to respond in conventional ways; (4) easily removed labels are more likely to promote conventional behaviour; and (5) targets receiving greater social support (as opposed to exclusion) from conventional sources, are more likely to conform to conventional standards.

18. It should also be recognized that reactions intended as benign, helpful, and the like, may be interpreted quite differently by targets and may (effectively) have exclusionary results.

19. Research on families (Jackson, 1954; Yarrow et al., 1955), drug usage (Becker, 1963), adolescent male prostitution (Reiss, 1961), and work related theft (Horning, 1970; Prus and Irini, 1980) indicates that deviant behaviour may become highly systematic prior to official consultation or intervention.

20. See Lofland and Stark (1965), Klapp (1969), and Prus and Irini (1980).

21. See Lofland and Stark (1965), Prus (1976), Prus and Sharper (1977), and Prus and Irini (1980) for more contextualized statements on seekership.

22. Lemert (1967, 99–108), Prus (1978), and Prus and Irini (1980) provide more extensive statements on closure.

23. As the "necessity of fulfilling specific obligations becomes more acute", and "as the options for doing so become more limited", then the sense of closure becomes more pronounced.

24. For more detailed material on "drift", see Matza (1964), Prus (1978), and Prus and Irini (1980).

25. For more complete statements on continuity, disinvolvement, and reinvolvement, see Prus and Sharper (1977) and Prus and Irini (1980).

26. Our research (Prus and Sharper, 1977; Prus and Irini, 1980) suggests that not only do disinvolvements (from activity A) and involvements (in activity B) often play more significant roles in both respects than is commonly acknowledged in the literature.

27. For some other attempts on the part of "labeling theorists" to come to terms with criticisms of labeling theory, see: Schur (1971, 1975), Lemert 1972, 1974), Becker (1973), Goode (1975, 1978), Kitsuse (1975), Cullen and Cullen (1978), Glassner and Corzine (1978), Suchar (1978), and Kotarba (1980).

28. In contrast to the interactionists and the functionalists involved in labeling theory, Lemert (1972, 1974) also seems somewhat uncomfortable with phenomenological versions of labeling theory.

29. For an insightful rebuttal to the "positivistic school of labeling theory", most singularly represented in the edited collection by Gove (1975), see Petrunik (1980).

References

Akers, Ronald. 1968. Problems in the sociology of deviance: Social definitions and behaviour. *Social Forces* 46:455–465.

Arnold, William R. 1970. *Juveniles on parole*. New York: Random House.

Atkinson, J. Maxwell. 1971. Societal reactions to suicide: The role of coroner's definitions. In Stanley Cohen (Ed.), *Images of deviance*. Baltimore: Penguin, 165–191.

Becker, Howard S. 1963. *Outsiders: Studies in the sociology of deviance*. New York: Free Press.

_____. Social bases of drug induced experiences. *Journal of Health and Social Behaviour* 8:163–76.

Berger, Peter and Thomas Luckmann. 1966. *The social construction of reality*. New York: Doubleday-Anchor.

Bittner, Egon. 1967. The police on Skid Row. *American Sociological Review* 32:699–715.

Black, Donald J. 1970. Production of crime rates. *American Sociological Review* 35:733–747.

Black, Donald J. and Albert J. Reiss, Jr. 1970. Police control of juveniles. *American Sociological Review* 35:63–77.

p. 140, note 26 — Line 3 should read "B) overlap, but that 'other people' (in activities A and B) often play more significant roles in both respects than is commonly acknowl-"

Block, Richard. 1974. Why notify the police: The victim's decision to notify the police of an assault. *Criminology* 11:555–569.

Blumberg, Abraham. 1967. The practice of law as a confidence game: Organizational cooptation of a profession. *Law and Society Review* 1:15–39.

Blumer, Herbert. 1969. *Symbolic interaction.* Englewood Cliffs, New Jersey: Prentice-Hall.

———. 1971. Social problems as collective behavior. *Social Problems* 1:298–306.

Carroll, Leo. 1974. *Hacks, blacks and cons: Race relations in a maximum security prison.* Lexington, Mass.: Lexington Books.

Chambliss, William J. 1964. *A sociological analysis of the law of vagrancy. Social Problems* 12:67–77.

Cohen, Albert. 1974. The elasticity of evil: Changes in the social definition of deviance. Oxford University Penal Research Unit. Occasional Paper Number Seven. Oxford: Basil Blackwell.

Conner, Walter D. 1972. The manufacture of deviance: The case of the Soviet purge, 1936–1938." *American Sociological Review* 37:403–413.

Cressey, Donald. 1958. The nature and effectiveness of correctional techniques. *Law and Contemporary Problems* 23(3):754–771.

Cressey, Paul. 1932. *The Taxi-Dance Hall.* Chicago: University of Chicago Press.

Cullen, Francis T. and John B. Cullen. 1978. *Towards a paradigm of labeling theory.* Lincoln, Nebraska: University of Nebraska Series (no. 58).

Daniels, Arlene Kaplan. 1970. The social construction of military diagnoses. In H.P. Diretzel (Ed.), *Recent Sociology* 2. New York: Macmillan, 181–208.

Davis, Nannett. 1975. *Social constructions of deviance: Perspectives and issues in the field.* Dubuque, Iowa: Wm. C. Brown.

Durkheim, Emile. 1895. *The rules of the sociological method* (Eighth edition, Trans. S.A., Solvay and E.G. Catlin, 1958) New York: Free Press.

———. 18.7. *Suicide.* (Trans. by J.A. Sapulding and G. Simpson, 1951) New York: Free Press.

Emerson, Robert M. 1969. *Judging delinquents.* Chicago: Aldine.

Emerson, Robert M. and Sheldon L. Messinger. 1977. The micro-politics of trouble. *Social Problems* 25:121–134.

Ennis, Philip H. 1967. Criminal victimization in the United States: A report of a national survey. Field Surveys II, President's Commission on Law Enforcement and Administration of Justice Washington, D.C.: U.S. Government. Printing Office.

Erikson, Kai T. 1962. Notes on the sociology of deviance. *Social Problems* 9:307–314.

———. 1966. *Wayward Puritans.* New York: Wiley.

Freidson, Eliot. 1966. Disability as social deviance. In M.B. Sussman (Ed.), *Sociology and rehabilitation.* New York: American Sociological Association, 71–99.

Garfinkel, Harold. 1956. Conditions of successful degradation ceremonies. *American Journal of Sociology* 61:420–424.

Gibbs, Jack P. 1966. Conceptions of deviant behavior: The old and the new. *Pacific Sociological Review* 9:9–14.

Glassnenr, Barry and Jay Corozine. 1978. Can labeling theory be saved? *Symbolic Interactionism* 1:74–89.

Goffman, Erving. 1959. *Presentation of self in everyday life.* New York: Anchor.

———. 1951. *Asylums.* New York: Anchor.

_____. 1963. *Stigma: Notes on the management of spoiled indentity.* Englewood Cliffs, New Jersey: Prentice-Hall.

_____. 1971. *Relations in public.* New York: Harper.

_____. 1974. *Frame analysis.* New York: Harper.

Goode, Erich. 1975. On behalf of labeling theory. *Social Problems* 22:570–583.

_____. 1978. *Deviant behavior: An interactionist approach.* Englewood Cliffs, New Jersey: Prentice-Hall.

Gove, Walter. 1975. *The labeling of deviance.* New York: Wiley.

Gusfield, Joseph R. 1955. Social structure and moral reform: A study of the Woman's Christian Temperance Union. *American Journal of Sociology* 61:221–232.

_____. 1963. *Symbolic crusade: Status politics and the American Temperance Movement.* Urbana: University of Illinois Press.

Hall, Ian. 1983. *Playing for keeps: The careers of front-line workers for developmentally handicapped persons.* Univesity of Waterloo: M.S. Thesis.

Hawkins, Richard and Gary Tiedman. 1975. *The creation of deviance: Interpersonal and organizational determinants.* Columbus, Ohio: Merrill.

Hewitt, John P. and Randall Stokes. 1975. Disclaimers. *American Sociological Review* 40:1–11.

Hirschi, Travis. 1973. Procedural rules and the study of deviant behaviour. *Social Problems* 21:158–173.

Homans, George C. 1958. Social behavior as exchange. *American Journal of Sociology* 63:597–606.

Horning, Donald. 1970. Blue collar theft: Conceptions of property, attitude towards pilfering, and work group norms in a modern industrial plant." In E.O. Smigel and H.L. Ross (Eds.), *Crimes against bureaucracy.* New York: Van Nostrand, 46–64.

Irini, Styllianoss and Robert Prus. 1982. Doing security work: Keeping order in the hotel setting. *Canadian Journal of Criminology* 24:61–82.

Irwin, John. 1970. *The felon.* Englewood Cliffs: New Jersey: Prentice-Hall.

Jackson, Joan. 1954. The adjustment of the family in the crises of alcoholism. *Quarterly Journal of Studies on Alcohol* 15:564–586.

Jewell, Donald P. 1952. A case of a "psychotic" Navaho Indian mate. *Human Organization* 11:32–36.

Kitsuse, John I. Societal reaction to deviant behavior. *Social Problems,* 1975, 9:247–56.

_____. 1975. The "new conception of deviance" and its critics. In W. Gove (Ed.), *The labeling of deviance.* New York: Wiley, 273–284.

Klapp, Orrin. 1962. *Heroes, villains, and fools.* Englewood Cliffs, New Jersey: Prentice-Hall.

_____. 1969. *Collective search for identity.* New York: Holt, Rinehart and Winston.

_____. 1971. *Social types: Process, structure and ethos.* San Diego, California: Aegis

Kortarba, Joseph. 1980. Labelling theory and everyday deviance. In J.D. Douglas (Ed.), *Introduction to the sociologies of everyday life.* Boston: Allyn and Bacon, 82–112.

Lauderdale, Pat. 1976. Deviance and moral boundaries. *American Sociological Review* 41:660–675.

Lemert, Edwin. 1951. *Social pathology.* New York: McGraw-Hill.

_____. 1953. An isolation and closure theory of naive check forgery. *The Journal of Criminal Law, Criminology and Police Science* 44:296–307.

_____. 1962. Paranoia and the dynamics of exclusion. *Sociometry* 25:2–25.

_____. 1967. *Human deviance, social problems and social control.* Englewood Cliffs, New Jersey: Prentice-Hall (also, 1972).

_____. 1974. Beyond Mead: The societal reaction to deviance. *Social Problems* 21:457–468.

Lesieur, Henry R. 1977. *The chase: The career of the professional gambler.* Garden City, New York: Anchor.

Levitan, Teresa. 1975. Deviants as active participants in the labeling process: The visibily handicapped. *Social Problems* 22:548–557.

Liazos, Alexander. 1972. The poverty of the sociology of deviance: Nuts, sluts, and perverts. *Social Problems* 20:103–120.

Lindesmith, Alfred R. 1959. Federal law and drug addiction. *Social Problems* 7:48–57.

Lofland, John. 1969. *Deviance and identity.* Englewood Cliffs, New Jersey: Prentice-Hall.

Lofland, John and Rodney Stark. 1965. Becoming A world saver: A theory of conversion to a deviant perspective. *American Sociological Review* 30:862–875.

Martin, Wilfred. 1975. Teacher-pupil interactions: A negotiation persepctive. *Canadian Review of Sociology and Anthropology* 12:529–540.

Matza, David. 1964. *Delinquency and drift.* New York: Wiley.

McCall, George J. and J.L. Simmons. 1978. *Identities and interaction: An examination of human association in everyday life.* New York: Free Press.

Mead, George H. 1934. *Mind, self and society.* Chicago: Univesity of Chicago Press.

McCleary, Richard. 1975. How structural variables constrain the parole officer's use of discretionary powers. *Social Problems* 23:209–225.

Newman, Donald J. 1956. Pleading guilty for considerations: A study of bargain justice. *The Journal of Criminal Law, Criminology and Police science* 46:780–790.

Parnas, Raymond. 1967. The police response to domestic disturbances. *Wisconsin Law Review 914–960.*

Petrunik, Michael. 1980. The rise and fall of "Labeling Theory": The construction and destruction of a sociological snowman. *The Canadian Journal of Sociology* (5):213–233.

Platt, Anthony. 1969. *The child savers.* Chicago: University of Chicago Press.

Prus, Robert. 1975a. Labeling theory: A reconceptualization and a propositional statement on typing. *Sociological Focus* 8:79–96.

_____. 1975b. Resisting designations: An extension of attribution theory into a negotiated context. *Sociological Inquiry* 4513–14.

_____. 1976. Religious recruitment and the management of dissonance: A sociological perspective. *Sociological Inquiry* 46:127–134.

_____. 1978. From barrooms to bedrooms: Towards a theory of interpersonal violence. In M.A.B. Gammon (Ed.), *Violence in Canada.* Toronto: Methuen, 51–73.

_____. 1982. Designating discretion and openness: The problematics of truthfulness in everyday life. *Canadian Journal of Sociology and Anthropology* (19):70–91.

Prus, Robert and Styllianoss Irini. 1980. *Hookers, rounders, and desk clerks: The social organization of the hotel community.* Toronto: Gage.

Prus, Robert and C.R.D. Sharper. 1977. *Road hustler: The career contingencies of professional card and dice hustlers.* Lexington, Mass: Lexington Books.

Prus, Robert and John Strattono. 1976. Parole revocation related decisions making: private typings and official designations. *Federal Probation* 40:48–53.

Ray, Marsch B. 1961. Abstinence cycles and heroin addicts. *Social Problems* (9):132–140.

Reiss, Albert J., Jr. 1960. Sex offenses: The marginal status of the adolescent. *Law and contemporary problems* 25(2):309–333.

———. 1961. The social integration of queers and peers. *Social Problems* 9:102–120.

Rogers, J.W. and M.D. Buffalo. 1974. Fighting back: Nine modes of adaptation to a deviant label. *Social Problems* 22:101–118.

Rosenhan, David L. 1973. On being sane in insane places. *Science* 179:250–258.

Ross, H. Laurence. 1970. *Settled out of court.* Chicago: Aldine.

Roth, Julius. 1962. The treatment of tuberculosis as a bargaining process. In A. Rose (Ed.), *Human behavior and social process.* Boston: Houghton-Mifflin, 575–588.

———. 1972. Some contingencies of the moral evaluation and control of clientele: The case of the hospital emergency service. *American Journal of Sociology* 77:839–856.

Rubinstein, Jonathon. 1973. *City police.* New York: Balantine.

Rubington, Earl. 1968a. Variations in bottle-gang controls. In E. Rubington and M. Weinberg (Eds.), *Deviance: The interactionist perspective.* New York: Macmillan, 308–316.

Rubington, Earl and Martin Weinberg. 1968. *Deviance: The interactionist perspective.* New York: Macmillan (also 1973, 1978).

Scheff, Thomas J. 1963. Decisions rules, types of error, and their consequences in medical diagnoses. *Behavioural Science* 8:97–107.

———. 1964. The societal reaction to deviance: Ascriptive elements in the psychiatric screening of mental patients in a mid-western state. *Social Problems* 11:401–13.

———. 1966. Typifications in the diagnostic practice of rehabilitation agencies. In M.B. Sussman (Ed.), *Sociology and rehabilitation.* New York: American Sociological Association, 139–144.

Schervish, Paul G. 1973. The labeling perspective: Its bias and potential in the study of political deviance. *American Sociologist* 8:47–57.

Schur, Edwin M. 1971. *Labeling deviant behavior: Its sociological implications.* New York: Harper and Row.

———. 1975. Comments. In W. Gove (Ed.), *The labeling of deviance.* New York: Wiley, 285–294.

Schutz, Alfred. 1971. *Collected papers I.* Maurice Natanson (Ed.), The Hague: Martinus Nijhoff.

Scott, M.B. and S.M. Lyman. 1968. Accounts. *American Sociological Review* 33:46–62.

Scott, Robert. 1969. *The making of blind men: A study of adult socialization.* New York: Russell Sage.

Simmons, J.L. 1969. *Deviants.* Berkeley, Calif.: Glendessary Press.

Skolnick, Jerome. 1966. *Justice without trial.* New York: Wiley.

Stachnik, Thomas and Roger Ulrich. 1965. Psychiatric diagnoses: Some cracks in the crystal ball. *Psychological Reports* 17:989–990.

Stoll, Clarice S. 1968. Images of man and social control. *Social Forces* 47:119–127.

Suchar, Charles S. 1978. *Social deviance: Perspectives and prospects.* New York: Holt, Rinehart and Winston.

Sudnow, David. 1965. Normal crimes: Sociological features of the penal code in a public defender office. *Social Problems* 12:255–276.

_____. 1970. Dead on Arrival. In A. Strauss (Ed.), *Where medicine fails.* Chicago: Aldine, 111–130.

Sutherland, Edwin. 1939. *Principles of criminology.* (Fourth ed.) Philadelphia: Lippincott.

_____. 1950. The diffusion of sexual psychopath laws. *American Journal of Sociology* 56:142–148.

Sykes, Gresham and David Matza. 1957. Techniques of neutralization: A theory of delinquency. *American Journal of Sociology* 22:664–670.

Szasz, Thomas S. 1970. *The manufacture of madness.* New York: Delta.

Tannenbaum, Frank. 1938. *Crime and the community.* New York: columbia University Press.

Thio, Alex. 1978. *Deviant behaviour.* Boston: Houghton Mifflin.

Thorsell, Bernard and Lloyd Kemke. 1972. The labeling process: Reinforcement or deterrent? *Law and Society Review* 6:393–403.

Weinberg, Martin. 1970. The nudist management of respectability: Strategy for, and the consequences of, the construction of a situated morality. In J.D. Douglas (Ed.), *Deviance and respectability.* New York: Basic Books, 375–403.

Wiseman, Jacqueline. 1970. *Stations of the lost: The treatment of Skid Row alcoholics.* Englewood Cliffs, New Jersey: Prentice-Hall.

Yarrow, M.R., C.G. Schwartz, H.S. Murphy and L.C. Deasy. 1955. The psychological meaning of mental illness in the family. *Journal of Social Issues* 11:12–24.

Part II
Social Control and the Community

Introduction

Any conceptual understanding of deviance must direct us to the phenomenon of power. Unless analyses are ultimately addressed to the relationships of control and power, discussions will continue to falter. Invariably, extant studies provide interesting insights on the social consequences of deviance and the social conditions under which control promotes order.

Careful investigation of "deviance and control", however, yields some interesting implications for our understanding of how various environing influences — political, legal, historical, and ideological contexts — are related to behavioural and organizational variations. The emphasis on deviance and control as mutually exclusive models may serve to obfuscate, and mystify power. Regardless of whether the control is defined as punishment or persuasion, an analytic commitment to power provides promising directions.

The study of power is basic to an understanding of the control process and the attendant "problems of order". From the various extant persectives on order and social control a significant theme emerges linking social order to concentrations of greater proportions of power resources. What then do we mean by power and order? A definition of order within these contexts will undoubtedly demonstrate the underlying transformation of control.

Order is an arrangement of institutions with established

147

structures of action and system of tools that define the nature and quality of opportunities to act.

Norm conformity may be historically traced to the development of the concept of peace. Deviance is an intrusion upon certain orders. Irrespective of whether this order is defined by a community's normative values or by specific interest groups, control is politically oriented.

Admittedly, control involves the management of a wide range of the mechanisms and institutions for the maintenance of a certain peace, however defined. Does not control through the use of coercive sanctions approximate more accurately the nature of social relationships within a "power" perspective (Weber 1969, 157)?

The processes and structures of control have been studied by writers and practitioners from many fields; diverse points of view may be discerned within this inquiry. Sociology is no exception; sociologists have discussed many features of sanctions, utilizing a variety of methodological and theoretical approaches. Although research on sanctions continues to grow, especially of a descriptive or exhortative nature, gaps exist with regard to crucial considerations of how sanctions are sustained and challenged; how theories of sanctions are developed, tested and compared; how new questions are provoked especially in relation to measuring the "costs" of sanctions and "to whom"; how easily sanctions may be transformed into mobilized resources controlling other types of deviance; how sanctions transfer and/or exacerbate existing conflicts; to name only a few. Do sanctions, for example, as socially recognized privileges of force, provide fundamental "links" between the structures of authority and the interactional encounters on a more microlevel of analysis?

Essentially, sanctions perform legitimating services designed ultimately to make order possible in a society in which power and privilege are not equally distributed. Complete with articles of faith, sacred symbols, hardware, rituals; powerful images have thus been evoked and the veritable myth of sanctions developed.

Although no society can hope to survive without sanctions, positive or negative, the attempts to manipulate sanctions have been complex.

Informal controls to suppress or isolate disruptive behaviour or to prescribe behaviour in the interests of the "common good" alone become difficult as the variety of social worlds and the size of groupings that are designated as deviant increase. To maintain a minimum "common moral order" among divergent subcultures (Fischer 1977, 238) additional mechanisms have been introduced. Formal methods may however not be more effective in influencing the behaviour, but they have symbolic significance insofar as they are applied consistently to members of differing primary groups.

Stated differently, the coordination of large scale activities itself tends to be a full-time occupation necessitating enormous resources. The relative decline of informal social controls leads to demands for the imposition of formal and institutional controls.

External controls through a series of formal institutions such as law and the socialization of values become perceived as providing qualities of group conformity over a large number of people.

Generally, the literature on sanctions has been primarily, and too narrowly, concerned with the production of norm conformity. The continued emphasis on deterrence or recidivism precludes any careful attention to the extremely significant and larger roles played by sanctions. It is possible that the relative importance of sanctions is "far more complex than has been assumed." Succinctly stated, almost invariably socio-legal studies have been successful in examining in isolation, only fragmented units of the legal system, vis-à-vis, the deterrent effects of sanctions, the interactional and organizational determinants of decision making, the development of specific statutes, the characteristics of the deviants, etc., while concurrently failing to consider the wider context of which these notable elements presumably constitute integral parts. Indeed, these weaknesses in explaining, specifying and interpreting interests, forces, and participants belies an understanding of the dynamic nature of sanctions. Aside from examining the impact of rules, orders and commands on conduct, it further remains incumbent upon us to interpret the contradictions as well as the conflicts arising out of these incompatibilities.

In analyzing the development of legal authority, control is often depicted as rigidly fixed in character. The readings included in this section argue that interactions are maintained via a complexity of contingencies operating on a number of systems — economic, social, political, etc. Similarly, the relationships between the environment and behaviour cannot be considered as static especially since these relationships change, modify, and develop over time.

These contributions are concerned with the holistic nature of interdependent, stabilizing, and boundary-maintaining mechanisms in relation to the problem of order. These recent revisits yield sensitizing conceptual insights by specifying ways in which open systems engage in complicated processes of interchanges with environing systems. Admitting that an immense amount of elaboration and clarification is needed, they note that the central conception and most important characteristic of control is that they are "open". This flexibility used to describe and analyze social interactions refers both to a complex of interdependences between parts, components, and processes that involve discernible regularities of relationship, especially as known and used by actors. They note that control systems are inherently evolving, engaged in processes of interchange with its environment, as well as consisting of interchanges among its internal units.

To elucidate organizational, the environment is construed to be directly and extremely relevant in particular ways not in determining behaviour nor as a passive setting but rather as interacting actively with the behaving individual in such a way that certain environments are more likely to elicit certain behaviours and inhibit others.

How then does the social organization affect the way people lead their lives, what they do and with whom they do it? The political environment is "permissive", providing opportunities for activities to occur within the framework of the institutional environment.

Lastly, although the determinants of social control are usually construed to be centralized or organizationally oriented and independent of local historical needs, there are many behavioural strategies that fit remarkably well with certain characteristics of the local environment. For instance, team policing, neighbourhood policing, or police-community relations presumably involve a development of an understanding of the urban environment. Consequently, police strategies certainly adapt to characteristics of the neighbourhood.

Organized surveillance of public spaces is typically enacted by control-patrol agents; its effectiveness is often only tempered by the technical ability to observe an entire area at the same time. Natural surveillance, that is, neighbourhood residents' alertness to "offenders" and the use of informal controls over these public spaces are being investigated in these readings.

The readings certainly provide useful empirical knowledge about the processes and structures of specific sanctions. Essentially, they examine the objectives of those sanctions which fall within a "general security" perspective and its emphasis on efficient, smooth circulation and control of movements. They document carefully how social control does not exist in a vacuum but occurs within certain environments which to date have been understated. For example, the historical development of control in all its manifestations is integrally related to the parallel development of the modern state. It should therefore be obvious that addressing the issues of sanctions or changes in sanctions will require much work empirically.

From the foregoing it is apparent that power is considered to be central to social control and order. Much of social theorizing, however, has been suggestive of these relationships and it is to a more definitive application of these assumptions of control we now proceed.

Chapter 7

Mad Dogs, Beasts and Raving Nutters: The Presentation of the Mentally Disordered in the British Press *

Thomas Fleming

INTRODUCTION

> Those who control both the propagation and dissemination of moral ideas and the machinery of sanctions — the law and the penal system — are in an unusually strong position to project their own ideas as being the *only ones*.[1]

> Intermediary communications systems have been established so that the direct contact which was essential in earlier times in not now required. . . . The insane, the criminal, and the deviant can now be isolated so that the normal members of the culture do not gain any experience of the non-normal. . . . Thus, apart from indirect experience derived from newspapers and other mass media, our modern culture has led to the isolation (and alienation) of deviant groups. The nature of information obtained from mass media differs in both quality and type.[2]

The ideological dimension of social control culture and the role of the media as information channels for the diffusion of deviance has been tentatively explored by research on several diverse groups (Fleming 1981). The pivotal role of the media in an ideological sense and its relationship to repressive state apparatus however have remained largely unexplored (Hall et al. 1978; Summer 1981).

---

* Edited version of a paper presented to the annual meeting of the Canadian Sociology and Anthropology Association, 1 June 1983, Vancouver, B.C. Not to be quoted or otherwise reproduced without the written permission of the author.

As a major ideological apparatus in contemporary society, the mass media assumes a crucial mediating role in disseminating the dominant ideology. It may be argued that various forms of media assist in producing a consensual image of society, which has importrant consequences for the maintenance of the hegemony of the ruling class and legitimating coercive social control by actively producing popular images and consent. This process is not conspiratorial in fashion according to the model advanced by Hall et al. (1978) but is effected through the structural relationship between social control agencies and the media. An important dimension to this process is the task of "creating" news which confronts the news reporter, each day, and the selection and presentation of deviance.

Research on the mentally disordered offender has traditionally been focused on several broad areas, specifically the development of individual disorder, treatment methods, dangerousness and its prediction, and the legal processing of the offender-patient. A far less frequent topic but one, as I have argued, of no less importance is the postrelease behaviour of the mentally disordered (Fleming 1982). Despite the important life consequences, and role in the creation of public attitudes and opinions the media must play with regard to the offender-patient and the mentally ill, this process has been virtually ignored by researchers of crime and deviance. In 1961, Nunnally (see Cohen and Young 1973) presented his analysis of "popular conceptions of mental health", an article which has remained the sole effort to understand the presentation of mental disorder in the media. This lack of attention by sociologists, and others who spend a great deal of time researching and writing about the mad (psychiatrists, psychologists, social workers, community workers, halfway-house workers, psychotherapists, lawyers, and the like), is at once perplexing and inexplicable. Scheff (1966, 1975), Szasz (1963, 1965, 1971), and Schur (1971), have provided some material on the stereotyping and labelling of the mentally ill, but their efforts have remained confined to passing commentary in the context of specific arguments regarding the aforementioned process.

This paper explores the relationship between the presentation of the mentally disordered offender in the media and public attitudes toward released offender-patients. It is argued that the media has a profound effect on the public image of mentally disordered offenders, largely negative, which effectively encourages limitations upon the life chances of released offender-patients. Media reports, atypical and highly selective in character, provide an unrealistic picture of the lives and deeds of mentally disordered offenders, a portrayal which heightens the processes of stigma that such individuals are subject to in the daily round of adaptations and adjustments that they must make upon returning to the community.

The analysis proceeds from a consideration of the construction of media accounts of crime and deviance generally, to a more specific discussion of the reporting of news events focusing upon the offender-patient. An examination of the news coverage afforded Rampton (Britain's largest psychiatric prison), its patients, and staff in the wake of "The Secret Hospital" program (ITV 22 May 1979) is undertaken to provide specific comparative data on the Rampton sample in the role of "victims" rather than "offenders". Finally an investigation into the legal and social implications of media representations of madness is offered which explicates the central role of the media as an apparatus of social control.

MAKING NEWS: PROFANE INTERPRETATIONS AND MANIPULATIONS

The analysis of the manner in which the mentally disordered are presented in the press begins of necessity, with an examination of the selection and construction of news. More specifically, the focus will be upon the making of crime news by reporters. By implication, it has been suggested that news does not exist as an identifiable entity, nor is it self-created. The selection of those events, happenings, or actions that will eventually become news is dependent upon a process that is instigated by the so-called crime reporter. Chibnall (1977, 1-20) has written that newspapers (and other media forms) are more than mere "monitors" of the real world:

> ... they construct representations and accounts of reality which are shaped by the constraints imposed upon them; constraints emanating from the conventions, ideologies, and organization of journalism and news bureaucracies.

Chibnall's (1977) work, that of Hall et al. (1978), and the Glasgow University Media Group (1978, 1980) have underscored the essential task for sociologists of deviance to understand the way in which media interpretations are constructed and the influences which effect the process. It is often a difficult task to separate reality from media interpretation, and in the absence of other sources of information, such interpretations may come, for many, to represent reality.

Crime reporting involves a great measure of selection of what will eventually arrive on the front pages of the press to become news. This is a form of selective reporting which emphasizes a strategy of persuasion calculated to offer atypical items or events, which are then presented in a stereotypical fashion contrasted against a backdrop of normality which is overtypical (Young 1971). In this manner, as Halloran et al. (1970) have suggested, crime reporting may treat as highly salient what is, in fact, a peripheral facet of the behaviour, focusing upon immediately visible or dominant symbols. Indeed, what is newsworthy often tends to be the bizarre or untoward, the very unrepresentativeness of the item ensuring that it is reported (Rock 1973).

The cumulative effect of press coverage of crime and various forms of deviance is to emphasize what I have termed the *knowledge gap* (Fleming 1981) which allows press and social control agencies alike to present their views in a manner which emphasizes their familiarity with the "awful truth". In fact, theirs is virtually the only "truth" that can be heard, for the socially and politically powerless, those who exist on the margins of society will not be afforded the opportunity to have their views aired in the press. The type of definition of the situation presented allows problematic events to be embued with a widely understood meaning. This form of news is simply a "loose and imprecise piecing together of explanatory fragments" (Hall et al. 1978, 20) from which result pragmatic constructs situated generally within a specific ideological framework. The result of the real world, yet in many ways constituting for the public their vision of "other" worlds, i.e., the underworld, deviant subcultures, the lives of the "mad".

News is essentially a "social construction of reality" which is governed by a number of factors, predominantly organizational constraints represented by the pressure of meeting deadlines each day, commitment to professional ideology, and the heavy reliance on "accredited sources", which are available (see Molotch and Lester 1974; Tuchman 1978). Hence, although reporters are given a free hand to operate, they can do so only in a very limited sense. The real substantive power to control information and define reality lies in the hands of authoritative spokesmen, who coincidentally happen to be social control agents or agency representatives in most instances. It is, therefore, not surprising that new stories seem to be persistently presented in a familiar and conservative tone. Crime stories are consistently "cooked up" rather like television sitcoms: the oft-repeated plot remains generally consistent, only the principal characters and some of the scenery have been changed. Alternate views and dissent that fall outside of the orbit of official agencies are often treated as "heresies" or "irrelevant eccentricities".[4] Chibnall (1977) has clearly underlined the mixed function of crime and deviance for the reporter which comprise simultaneously, "a challenge to newspapers' liberal and consensual view of society and a source of ideological reinforcement", the significance of which was first observed by Durkheim some four decades earlier. Newspapers not only gear their presentation to the reader level they are attempting to retain and attract, but also take great pains to reflect and manipulate sentiments within the communities they reach by their provision of information, comment, and understandings (Hall et al. 1978).

Newspapers are in the position to provide a central noticeboard for their perception of public morality and sentiment:

> A chance not simply to speak to the community but to speak *for* the community, against all that the criminal outsider represents, to delineate the shape of the threat, to advocate a response, to eulogize on conformity to established norms and values, and to warn of the consequences of deviance (Chibnall 1977).

However, there is a reverse flow to this process, for agents of social control, many of whom exist in a world of comparative social isolation, exhibit an overdepedence on the senationalist press which not only mirrors, but motivates conservative, puritannical, and self-righteous views as a plethora of recent writing has conclusively demonstrated.

MEDIA SOURCES, EVENTS AND LIMITATIONS

In this section an analysis of media presentation of the "lives" and activities of the mentally disordered is undertaken. The empirical data which underlies this discussion (and the one in the next section), was collected during research for my doctoral dissertation. This roughly spanned the period fall, 1975 to fall, 1979. All newspaper articles concerned with the activities of released Special Hospital patients, reviews of committee deliberations on the mentally ill, and accounts linking madness and crime were reviewed from a number of newspaper sources: *The Times, The Guardian, Daily Express, Daily Mirror, Daily Mail, Daily Star, The Sun, The Evening Standard, The Evening News, The News of the World, The Retford Times* and *The South London Press*, were helpful sources of articles.

Additional information was gathered from three magazines,

New Society, Private Eye, and *Time Out*, although each of these sources provided only a minimal amount of data suitable for analysis.

Although the analysis developed in this paper encompasses only "press" accounts of the behaviour of offender-patients, television and radio programs were utilized to supplement my understanding of reporting processes, and the presentation of the "mad" in the media. One television program, "The Secret Hospital" broadcast by Yorkshire Television on 22 May 1979 during the midst of my research was tape-recorded and a transcript produced. This program was the catalyst which resulted in the calling of the Boynton Committee to investigate allegations of staff brutality at Rampton. As a researcher, I was already keenly aware of the impact of media on public perceptions of ex-Rampton patients as a result of my initial interviews (see Fleming 1982). "The Secret Hospital" documentary was to have three profound effects on my research: (1) Rampton was to become a household word virtually overnight; (2) my role as a researcher was made more difficult (Fleming 1982); and (3) the central importance of the media as processors of information to effect opinion, law, and response were unmistakably underscored, and could not be ignored in any fruitful analysis.

Although my knowledge of newspaper accounts concerned with offender-patients has been informed by a variety of sources already outlined, my analysis will reflect only a selection of specific news articles. This is a common practice in the major analyses which have grounded sociological attempts to study the media, and media related phenomenon. In the light of structural constraints which effectively limit the style, content, and presentation of news (Chibnall 1977, IX - XIV) such selectivity does not represent a serious drawback to conveying either content, intent, or meaning.

The analysis is strengthened immeasurably by my direct experience of Rampton patients both in the hospital and upon their return to community life. The discussion benefits not only from discussion with ex-Rampton patients and their perceptions, but from their own observations concerning the indirect effects of the media on public perceptions, before and following the media and public event engendered by "The Secret Hospital" documentary.

MAKING NEWS MAKE MADNESS

In point of news, and amusements and pictures, the public always gets what it wants. This is a pity, but this is so.

Anything that gives power to the masses will please the masses.

There was a period, Fiedler (1978) writes, in which "Bethlem" rivalled the "Monster" show at Smithfield as a prime site for a Sunday outing. Conducted tours, the "one penny show", introduced the curious public to a collection of pauper, and later criminal lunatics, who "existed" in the decaying monolith that Bethlem hospital had become with the passage of time. Naked inmates, chained to cell walls for long periods of time, James Norris, in his iron cage, and as Scull, (1979) has graphically written, ". . . the furious, violent, and frenetic" thrown together with mild and convalescent patients. It was a scene which Hogarth captured with disturbing clarity in the eighth scene of The Rake's Progress which was inspired, and painted in the incurable ward in 1733, and in the description penned by the fleeing criminal Jack Shepherd during a visit to his mother in 1720.

Parry-Jones (1972) has instructed the uninformed in the more profitable aspects of private madhousekeeping, the so-called "trade in lunacy". However, there has been a much more profitable form of contemporary "trade" that has drawn from the deeds and sufferings of the mentally ill: the creation of "news" and the sale of newspapers.

"FACTS"

When you shall these unlucky deeds relate, speak of me *as I am*. Nothing extenuate, nor set down ought in malice (William Shakespeare, *Othello*).

Newspapers have played a crucial role in developing public ideas concerning the character, nature, and possible behaviour of mentally disordered offenders. Accounts of the bizarre or violent crimes of released mental patients form the basis for regular front-page news. Such reports contain a number of factual items including the age, sex, marital status, and past/present criminal and/or psychiatric record. Beyond these basic items, the press engages in the creation of "facts" about the offender-patient, which owe more to fiction than to Freud.

Names and labels have an important function in our society; they convey information about a person, allow an audience or prospective audience to organize meanings, and influence our response to individuals. Doctors, we *expect* to assist in healing our bodies, and the vast majority of society have had direct experience with one of the medical profession. So it is that the *cultural identity* of the doctor is conveyed by our direct and indirect information

channels; i.e., informal interaction, media reports, and via institutional channels, particularly schools.

The mentally disordered offenders perhaps more than any
other deviants in society are individuals with whom the overwhelming majority of the population have had no direct experience. Leslie Wilkins (1964) first pointed out this increasingly
important social development some eighteen years ago:

> The insane, the criminal, and the deviant can now be *isolated* from society so
> that the normal members of the culture do not gain any experience of the
> non-normal.

A further dimension which encourages a lack of general
knowledge concerning offender-patients is outlined by Cohen and
Taylor (1976), namely, the "apparatus of secrecy". Extending their
analysis, it may be argued that such mechanism controls not only
research but also available information. According to Cohen and
Taylor (1976), there are five distinct components which make up
this apparatus: (1) over-centralization, (2) legalization of secrecy,
(3) standardization of research, (4) mystification of decisions, and
(5) appeals to the public interest.

The Special Hospital patient is locked away in the highest
security in a "container for the uncontrollable", geographically
and hence socially isolated from society. This is most strikingly the
case with Rampton whose multilayer escape deterrence system
must rank as one of the most efficient in England, of any Special
Hospital or penal[6] establishment. A central tenet of the analysis
undertaken in this paper is that this isolation is further reinforced
by the state social-control system which permeates control
throughout the social world available to released Rampton
patients. Released Rampton patients, like their counterparts from
the other Special Hospitals tend to inhabit an environment shared
by outcasts and marginal individuals in the community including
chronic alcoholics, petty criminals, and the disenfranchised —
unwanted and largely unnoticed.[7]

Newspapers have undertaken the task of filling in the
knowledge gap which results from our lack of direct contact with this
specific form of deviant. How then do newspapers present, and
construct an image of the mentally disordered? Lifting the veil of
secrecy which has been automatically the creation of Special
Hospitals' policies and the resulting social isolation of ex-patients,
newspapers put names to the mentally disordered; set an impression of their character and qualities in the public mind which
targets into the deepest recesses of fear and prejudice. The following is a representative list drawn from London news articles:

"Monster", "pervert", "murderer", "beasts", "fiends", "devil", "mad", "beserk", "dangerous", "mad dog", "sex maniac", and "deranged".

Such names carry with them *exclusion* and *exploitation*. By defining ex-patients in terms of and highlighting them with names associated with harm and horror, by selectively reporting only the most bizarre and antisocial acts of a small minority of ex-Special Hospital patients, papers do not even attempt to present a balanced picture of the lives of these individuals. Most of us, sociologists and prison researchers included, will not confront an offender-patient in the flesh during our lifetimes. Newspapers have now assumed the role once given over to the "one penny" tour of Bethlem. It is an experience open to distortion, far removed from direct experience. The mentally disordered offender, in the same way as the spectacle of the gallows (Foucault 1978), have become phenomenon that we experience second hand. The unknown and the unpredictable have been supplanted by the predictably bizarre and violent. Like Fiedler's (1978) *Freaks*, the accounts of offender-patients in the press simultaneously tempt us both to avert our eyes and to share. It is an occasion not for introspection on the boundary assumed to separate sanity/ insanity, but for reaffirmation of normality.

Since public knowledge concerning released mentally disordered offenders is effectively limited, the *attribution* of negative, vicious qualities may be easily accomplished. In this manner ex-patients are transformed from isolation to illumination under the media spotlight. Individually supplied definitions become wider group definitions; one acts and all have acted; one ex-patient is dangerous so all are not to be trusted, and so on. The argument here does not rely upon a simple deterministic model, that readers' heads are empty vessels (vestibles) which only require filling. However, it recognizes the abilities of readers to, as Roshier says, differentiate and interpret the information they receive. Where it diverges from the argument advanced by Roshier (1976), is in the evaluation of the relative weight given press accounts of crime and criminals upon public perceptions and opinions. In the case of "ordinary" crimes and criminal acts utilized by Roshier's (1976) analysis, one might reasonably expect audiences to have a fair measure of acquaintance with either the type of person who could be involved in illegal activities, or experience as a victim of specific offenses.

Deviance and criminality are not isolated phenomenon, but are present throughout society, assuming various forms and features. Mentally ill offenders comprise but a small fraction of the prison population in England, Canada, and the United States.

In general, the vast majority of the public receive their *only* information on ex-patients through the press, and to a far lesser degree, through the supplementary media sources provided by television, radio, and surprisingly movies.

"ACTS"

> As the book page yields the inside story of the author's mental aventures, so the press page yields the inside story of the community in action and interaction. It is for this reason that the press seems to be performing its function most when revealing the seamy side (Chibnall 1977, 16)

> For us, in a later age, it is easy to be horrified at the heartlessness and stupidity of our ancestors. We might do better to cast a critical eye around and judge how lingering superstitutions about mental illness still affect public attitudes to, say, discharged mental patients (Roberts 1963, 26).

The reporting of the deeds and lives of ex-social hospital patients in the British press has not been marked either by its portrayal of the social reality of the "mad" and "bad", or the rather unremarkable life that the majority lead. Most released special hospital patients do *not* commit crimes involving either violence or children, two themes which predominate in media representations of the "acts" of these persons. The first point, a question of semantics but none the less important to our exploration, is to ensure that the reader realizes that it is an inherently difficult undertaking to discuss mentally disordered offenders as a group, as this is a group composed of strikingly different *individuals*. The news media engage in reductionist activities in this regard on a daily basis, and it should be borne in mind that the individuality of these persons should direct our discussion.

The general public's beliefs and fears concerning the mentally disordered offender and other criminals in society is largely as Box (1971) has argued, "a melange of facts, fabrications and fantasies, with the last making by far the largest contribution, fed by journalists, television reports, police, and occasionally social scientists" (see Box 1981). This has made a major contribution to developing a collective ignorance concerning the objective nature of crime and criminal actors. How then have the media, particularly the press, attempted to present the misdeeds of the offender-patient?

One central tenet of press coverage is that the involvement of sex and crime is a volatile combination at the newstand. This is nowhere more evidenced than in press coverage of the criminally

insane. The daily tabloid cover presents what may arguably be
the best example of the type of reporting that the "acts" of the mad
receive. All of the constitutent elements of the "successful" crime
reporting story are gathered on one page and inform us not only of
what *has* been done in the present context, but what has been done
in the past. These specific components require some explanation:

1. *The imputation of a subhuman status to the offender-patient.*
   Although it might be expected that this would relieve the
   offender of the brunt of blame in the commission of the
   act, this is not the specific intent of this form of labelling.
   Rather it is to establish that offender-patients are
   essentially beast-like by the use of derogatory names and
   devoid of reason (a return to eighteenth-century ideas
   concerning madness) therefore one must anticipate in
   ordinary interaction they will be not only unpredictable,
   but violent.

2. *An element of sexual perversity.* The "SEX MONSTER"
   conjuring images of Mary Shelley's creation, the monster
   Frankenstein. Her intention in creating the monster was
   not unlike that which can be ascribed to modern journalists, ". . . to (write) a story . . . which would speak to the
   mysterious fears of our nature, and awaken . . . horror —
   one to make the reader dread to look around, to curdle the
   blood and quicken the beatings of the heart". Fascination/
   repulsion, a voyeuristic glimpse into the world of sexual
   depravity, and sadism. The linking of sex and violence is a
   part of the crime-story formula.

3. *The mug shot.* The culprit's picture is a prominent signpost
   of the crime story. It not only attempts to provide the
   reader with some measure of acquaintance with the
   criminal, whether this is so or not, but allows feelings to
   be vented, and characteristics ascribed to the offender.
   Does my neighbour look like that? It implies this is what a
   mentally disordered offender looks like, and is never a
   complimentary photograph. A crook who has achieved
   some popular noteriety, as in the case of Ronnie Biggs,
   may however be shown as a sun-bathing *bon vivant*
   enjoying the spoils of crime. A few mug shots have
   become widely recognized images in the publics' conscience, such as the infamous photo booth "snaps" of
   Graham Young, the sullen face and dyed blonde hair of
   Myra Hindley (the paramour of Ian Brady and one of the
   Moors Murderers), the rather pitiful features of Patrick
   David MacKay, and the pictures of Peter Sutcliffe, the
   so-called "Yorkshire Ripper", David Berkowitz, "The Son

of Sam" and that most infamous of assassions Lee Harvey
Oswald. Photographs operate at what Hall et al., (1978,
184-187) have termed the "second level of significance"
being utilized to convey a highly ideological message.
They are presented as "objective" records, and serve to
effectively heighten public outrage and hostility toward
the target of the accusations.

4. *The compounding of images and acts.* The practice of providing
   linkages between acts and actors, present and past, is a
   frequent element in crime reporting. The intended
   message is clear; this has happened before, it will happen
   once again unless *something is done.* The "tragic errors"
   are multiplying, and all of the images are added up as
   being part of the same phenomenon. It is as if it is all part
   of one, mounting, never-ending crime wave.

5. *Affixing the blame.* The question which the headline
   inevitably begs with the majority of reports of the crimes
   of ex-patients is, "RELEASED TO STRIKE AGAIN, BY
   WHOM?" This adds to public fears. If these men were
   considered "cured" then it follows that psychiatrists have
   no idea what they're doing. How many more supposedly
   cured men are on the streets, ready to attack at any time?

6. *Announcing the acts.* The factual acts of the offender are
   tallied up. How many people were harmed? Were any
   children? Were they sexually abused?

7. *Fabricating Public Opinion and Demanding Action.* This case
   highlights growing public concern over crimes committed
   by patients freed from top-security hospitals. If there had
   been no outcry then hopefully there will be one, an-
   nounces the paper by this form of assertion. More to the
   point, we will "lead" that campaign, and increase readership. There is an underlying theme which demands that
   "something must be done". The Daily Mirror on the same
   date carried a similar account (pp. 5–7) with 3" headlines,
   "TWO BEASTS WHO PREYED ON LITTLE BOYS".
   The accompanying picture was captioned, "Face of a
   Fiend; Liar and Pervert". The journalist responsible for
   the article posed the following question, "Did Broadmoor
   slip up by letting them loose?" The indication is that "top
   security patients" have been released "early" (despite the
   indefinite nature of their sentences) only to "go on the
   rampage once again".

8. *A connective link with criminal places.* Certain key places, well
   known to the general public as supposed dens of crime
   and depravity, are mentioned to provide an easy connec-

tive link for the reader. In this incident it happened to be Playland, an amusement arcade off Piccadilly Square, the subject of a major television documentary "Johnny Go Home", and a well known "hangout" for young male prostitutes as documented in Robin Lloyd's expose, *Playland*. It might just as well be "the back alleys of Soho", the "Chinese district", "the docklands", "the Moors", or any number of widely recognized locations. The connection with suspect locations and hence undesirable elements provides a vehicle for the framing of a threat to the existing social order, a phenomenon which will be addressed late in this paper.

9. *Outlining the punishment.* The message is *always* clear as Young (1974, 247) cogently observed, ". . . the irrational is the painful, is the punished, is the determined, is the meaningful, is the deviant."

The overwhelming effect of the accumulation of news reports on the crimes of released special hospital patients is substantial given the almost virtual lack of information which contradicts popular media images; as Peter Thompson (1974, 10) has written:

> The ordinary person, no matter how sympathetic or "liberal", cannot be expected to visualize the circumstances of a mentally ill offender. The media concentrate, for the most part, on the more horrific cases ("Mad Axeman at Large"), and so on, which attaches all kinds of emotional overtones to the names of the Special Hospitals. . . . Obviously people find it very hard to think of the inmates as *people*, or their disorder as very often caused or at least aggravated, by contemporary public and social attitudes towards the mentally ill.

The strength of media images does permeate the reality making of everyday life, and is effective not only in assisting community members to stigmatize released patients, but in causing the patients themselves to engage in various forms of self-labelling which curtails their interactions with other persons upon release (see Fleming 1982). Mental disorder itself has been demonstrated to evoke powerful feelings of fear amongst the general population without the inclusion of a criminal element (Roberts 1966, 6; Scull 1977). Cecil King (1967) in his study of the British press commented upon the fascination of the media audience for this form of reportage. Sadly, he found his countrymen displayed a "Sabbath appetite . . . for stories of crime, the more brutal and sexual the better." Unfortunately (1967, 14), the survey of newspaper reporting of the deeds of released patients, criminals, and other forms of deviants indicate that this is as popular a daily topic of news as it is a Sunday pastime. For those who might wish to argue that it is not significant "what the papers say," because they are simply scandal sheets rather than even-handed news-papers, I would hasten to point out that fully 80 percent of the newspapers sold in England on a daily basis are of *The Sun* tabloid form (Pearce 1973).

The powerful effects of such accounts have been further emphasized by the work of Morris and Blom-Cooper (1967) on the subject of murder. Their analysis has relevance to the argument advanced here, namely, that since media reports of the crimes of released special hospital patients concentrate on ultraviolent acts with bizarre overtones, the ramifications are significantly magni-fied throughout the whole of society:

> The act of murder . . . profoundly unsettles the delicate equilibrium which social devices have achieved, and arouses in individuals the most deep-seated unconscious fears and anxieties. When a murder is accompanied by great violence or sexual sadism these unconscious feelings may be even more deeply disturbed. . . . Murder produces a profound social shock — heightened in our own society by dissemination of the details through the modern mass media (See Jones 1974).

The Glasgow Media Group (1980, 406–407) have suggested that the partial nature of broadcast journalism, which can also be extended to newspaper reportage, favours the views of one group in society at the expense of another. One must always be sensitive to what kind of understanding is being offered, but this can be a difficult task when no strongly argued, widely distributed alter-nate source is at hand. The agenda setting or selection of what is to be presented effectively limits the "range and density of informa-tion" just so that it can be understood within a narrow consensus. The reiteration of well understood frameworks of understanding, "cues" for perceptions and the rekindling of moral indignation promoted by connective links with past acts and actors, are well established features which characterize contemporary journalistic reports of the "acts" of released special hospital patients, and a variety of criminal and deviant actors.

The overwhelming impression that one is eventually, if not immediately left with from this "clusters of impressions, themes, and quasi-explanations, gathered and fused together", (Hall et al. 1978, 118), is that mentally disordered offenders *are* violent, dangerous *individuals*. A group identity is inferred from individual acts, the world is effectively ordered, and the basis for societal reaction decided.

PRESCRIPTIONS

> I can only accept that Broadmoor, Rampton and Moss Side can do little more for them (or for us) than an ordinary mental hospital can. They can, that is to say, keep them locked up, tide them over their recurring crises until they seem to have stopped, and then return them back into society (*TLS* 8 October 1976).

> All (of the ex-patients) were obviously let out too soon — if they should have been let out at all . . . far greater precautions must be taken to ensure they are cured. (*The Daily Mirror* 26 November 1975, 5).

The final function of the newspaper report of crime is to offer prescriptions for the manner in which the deviant is to be handled in future, having provided definition and shape for the social problem. The preceding analysis of the content of news reporting on this general subject area illustrates a further effect of media reportage, the creation of moral indignation. Cohen (1973, 16) has written about the type of societal reaction the journalist's work may produce:

> . . . even if they are not self-consciously engaged in crusading or muck-raking, their very reporting of certain "facts" can be sufficient to generate concern, anxiety, indignation or panic.

The result may be an occasion for new rule creation, "criminaliza-tion" (see Fleming 1981), for social problem definition. This is particularly the case with the reports which are composed with reference to the behaviour of released hospital patients. The cry, "Something must be done," what I have termed the prescriptive function of crime articles, is the resounding note on which most standard articles end. As Hall et al. (1978) and Chibnall (1977) have both observed, the limited sources available to those constructing the news, means that the majority of stories will be written in strikingly similar language, assuming parallel content, form, and ideas. This is simply because crime news reporting is written with a specific "formula" in mind. What "makes" a good crime story is well known to practitioners of the journalist's art. As one of the reporters who covered the "Son of Sam" case commented on the excessive attention given to the details of the crime in the media, "From Shakespeare through history, its always been the gory stories that have fascinated people most," (*Newsweek*, 22 August 1979). Exploitation of tragedy is not only a front page affair, it involves the lives of several *real* people, but the emotional tone, size of the headline accorded the story, and other factors such as front-page status, number of stories on the incident and so on begin to imply that "no one is safe". The contagion has now touched someone else's life, but it may soon touch the reader's life.

The effect of such coverage is to produce what Cohen (1973) has termed "vague feelings" that something should be done. Young (1973) has clearly demonstrated the role that the media play in engendering "normative concerns" in the public and in producing moral directives which have the result of producing instant mix social problems. The potential value of this form of enterprise to those in society whom Becker (1963) termed "moral entrepreneurs", is to elicit response and hopefully support from the uncommitted for a campaign to either wipe out a specific form of deviance, "save" a group from deviant careers (most commonly adolescents from a life of perversion or crime), or radically change the way in which deviants are handled in society in order to "protect" the people.

The message of piling report on report concerning the violent and the bizarre is to produce a feeling in society that there is a crime wave or *deviancy flood* (Fleming 1981) which is swelling to proportions that will soon be uncontrollable. The clear intention of the articles is to produce what Cohen (1973) has termed "moral panic" in society, the feeling that "things are *already* out of hand". It is at this juncture that the newspaper has prepared the reader for prescriptive counselling. The reader as an individual member of society will have feelings of relative powerlessness in regard to having some effect on the situation. "What is to be done" is not readily apparent, solutions may seem difficult, superficial at best, but the journalist is ready to supply "all the answers".

When a released special hospital patient "goes wrong" the prescriptive advice is doled out in a prescribed formula by newspaper journalists who are exceedingly familiar with the tone such counsel must take, the steps that must be taken, and who the *true* culprits are. The first villain (Klapp 1962) is the hospital, and by reference its consultants who have either "made a mistake", "released too soon", been "made a fool of" by the ex-patient in question, or simply "misdiagnosed". In any event, blame is at least partially affixed to the psychiatrist and by implication, the institution. Although it may be said that media articles sometimes do provide sound prescriptions, for example on the current state of after care, "they (patients) must not just be slung out and promptly forgotten," they are not able, or willing, to deal with the specific viewpoint of the various groups involved, i.e., hospital staff, ex-patients themselves, or their families. Relations of victims are typically presented as emotionally distraught (as no doubt they are in most cases), but one wonders at how almost every victim's relation can "call for a government inquiry", (see for example, "Parents' query on killer" *The Guardian,* 8 June 1979) in strikingly similar language. Is it possible that questions are framed to evoke well-recognized and sought-after responses. "Do you think there should be a government inquiry?" requires only a simple "yes" or "no" answer from a distraught relation. New rules are suggested or demanded, "New curbs urged for ex-patient" *The Daily Mirror* 26 November 1975,5), a range of new "precautions" is outlined "Why was killer set free?". (*The Evening Standard,* 29 May 1979), and blame is affixed to the institution and the psychiatrist for their overly liberal stance (FREED! MOTHER WHO KILLED TWICE *The Daily Mirror* 9 October 1975).

"Talking heads", in other words so-called "experts" in an era when as Terence Morris (1976) has pointed out expertise is cheaply sold, are all solicited for their recommendations. Typically, these individuals are neither informed researchers nor members of patients-rights groups, but "an ex-Broadmoor doctor" (anonymous), police inspectors, and local M.P.'s who are both encouraged and eager to respond to the "crisis" situation providing explanations, conclusions, warnings, and prescriptions about what to do. It does little to buoy public confidence when an "ex-Broadmoor doctor" is reportred as saying" . . . their (patients) apparent response to treatment can be one big sham. And no matter how well a patient has responded *he will revert to former ways."* The newspaper warns (as do many academics!) that psychiatrists are bound on a fruitless search, "seeking cures that do not and cannot exist."

Another feature of prescriptive practice is to claim to represent *the people* and their wishes in a given matter. Take this example; dozens could be given and may be drawn to mind by the reader, "Public confidence in the present system (of dealing with the mentally disordered offender) has been dangerously undermined. The Government *MUST* act quickly to restore that confidence." In this argument, at least, newspapers are self-contradictory. First, they assume that the public "had" confidence at some point in time. When did it end? How do we know that it ended? Now that the "final straw", "breaking point" or what have you has been reached, (and this occurs regularly with each new case), the government must act to reestablish public confidence. The obvious solution to various behavioural problems posed by a small number of released special hospital patients is evidently very clear to those who produce crime reports, and self serving experts, "stop the cult of kindness and the showering of blessings on the violent", (Tribunals twiced freed psychopath who killed. *The Times,* 22 November 1975). In other words, the mentally disordered offender should remain locked up, "for good", but we may ask, "who's" good? Some articles have even suggested that former inmates of the special hospitals are so fond of the institutions that they murder simply to gain readmittance, "(he) killed . . . because he was homesick for Broadmoor." (TRAGIC WISH OF A TRIPLE KILLER (1″ headline). *The Sun*, 5 June 1977).

The family and other relatives of the offending ex-patients are not spared attention in the press. An interesting example is provided by the coverage given to the wife of Peter Cook, also known as "The Cambridge Rapist", and a former inmate of Broadmoor. In an article entitled DEVIL IN DISGUISE, 2″ headline (*The Evening News*, 3 October 1975), his wife Margaret is described as the woman "who had everything". Great play is made of the fact that they had a "caravan home" (a basic trailer), that her husband had made a salary of £27 a week (a somewhat less than average wage at the time), and they had among other possessions "a stereo unit and colour television". With so many trappings of success, how could poor Peter have gone wrong? More importantly the underlying implication is that his wife "knew" more about his activities than is being related in the press. So it is that the spouse, and in some instances other relatives of the offender's family become the victims of negative societal reaction despite their protestations of total ignorance and their innocence in the misdeeds of their relation. Readers are encouraged to ask, "How could she have lived with him and not known?" Some recent examples of the vehement form such reactions can take is provided by both the recent English case of Peter Sutcliffe and the Canadian case of Clifford Olson. Sutcliffe, the "Yorkshire Ripper" terrorized and murdered several women over a stretch of many years before being apprehended on a routine police check of his car. His wife found it necessary to divorce him to escape at least some of the pressures imposed by societal reaction. Clifford Olson, the murderer of thirteen children in British Columbia, Canada, had to be paid by the Royal Canadian Mounted Police to reveal the sites where the bodies had been buried. The "reward" money was paid to his wife who then became the brunt of considerable negative social reaction.

For the purposes of newspaper reporting, patients of any of the four special hospitals are completely interchangeable. Although many of the specific cases related in this section refer to released Broadmoor patients, it should be clearly noted that prescriptive advice (calls for reform and inquiries) inevitably "lump" all top-security hospitals and their charges and former charges into one anomalous heap. Faced with this cumulative buildup of damaging information, the extremely few articles which do talk about the postrelease behaviour in factual terms can have very little effect on public perceptions. Typically, stories taking this form are to be found only in newspapers including *The Times, The Observer,* and *The Guardian.* It has already been established that this general class of newspaper, which attempts to present a more balanced view of news, accounts for only 20 percent of daily sales in England. One has to turn well past the front pages to find this type of article. Banner headlines are utilized to declare that there were only *13 violent acts* for which released Broadmoor patients were convicted during the period 1960 to 1975. In an article entitled "Violence by tenth of ex-Broadmoor patients", the excellent work of Anthony Black was reported (*The Times* 5 April 1977), but well into the back pages of the newspaper. His results confirmed the conclusions reached in the work of this author and others (Fleming 1982; Walker and McCabe 1973) that the majority of offenses for which released Special Hospitals come before the courts are of a minor nature. In his sample, one-third appeared before the bench on a minor charge exemplified by such offences as shoplifting, theft, and drunkeness. Although the journalist rightly concluded that Black's figures "go a long way to allaying public fears that patients are being let out too soon", one must obviously wonder how many persons it actually reached.

A few tragic mistakes (see "The Total Banishment of Bedlam" *The Times,* 3 November 1975) *can* and *do* provide the material out of which the media have shaped the general public's picture of the released offender-patient. The work of Steadman and Cocozza (1974, 1–3) spoke to this key point, and very little has changed in the eight years since it was written:

> . . . both public and professional knowledge of *all* the criminally insane tends to be incorrectly inferred from the atypical, but widely publicized NGRI (not guilty by reason of insanity) cases. The other 96 percent of the people included among the criminally insane are primarily routine cases, involving lower-class individuals that rarely command any press coverage. Thus, the criminally insane have become stereotyped as infamous assassins; fierce stranglers; black rapists; or decrepit child molesters. Such is not the case. Those people called criminally insane are predominantly non-violent individuals, charged with the few sex crimes, who suffer the fate of many other stereotyped groups — that is, they are seriously handicapped in their apprehension, custody treatment, and community reintegration by the ignorance and fear of others.

"THE SECRET HOSPITAL" BUILDING INSTITUTIONAL SCANDAL AND REVEALING PRISON SECRETS

> By not inquiring too deeply into what went on behind asylum walls, by not pressing too hard to find out what superintendents actually did with their patients, and by not being too skeptical of the officially constructed reality, people were (are) rewarded with a comforting reassurance about the essentially benign character of their society and the way it dealt (deals) with its deviants and misfits (Scull 1979, 260).

The repressive apparatus of state control is very rarely the subject of newspaper accounts. It is even rarer for mentally disordered offenders to be portrayed as victims in the press. Yet in the midst of this research ventured a television documentary entitled "The Secret Hospital" which was shown on The Independent Television network taking up four hours of prime time over the two-night period, what was described as ". . . unprecedented peak-time exposure for a documentary." The degree of public interest in the programs can be gauged by the report that the programs, the first of which dealt with Rampton, and the second which dealt with the release of a patient from the Balderton Unit, were watched by the largest audience in British television history.

Since the barrier between the institution and society, particularly a high-security facility of which Rampton is a prime example is strongly maintained, public curiosity could have been expected to be aroused. Further to the analysis already presented, it could also be anticipated that the large readership of the tabloid papers which specialize in the reporting of the crimes of released Special Hospital patients, and concentrate upon the projection of a violent and murderous image for such individuals, would respond with interest and curiosity to this form of documentary. Cohen and Taylor (1976, 81–87) suggest that the approach of hospital administrators is characterized by the suppression of as much information as possible. "Trouble" is effectively managed by reverting to the shield of "no comment" or refusal to discuss "individual" inmates. Here too the concept of the knowledge gap, between what the public has in the way of information about the institution and the way it in fact operates may be compared to a similar gap which exists between public knowledge of mentally disordered offenders and their actual behaviour.

Since, as we have seen, newspapers inevitably criticize special hospitals staff and the institution itself whenever acts of violence are carried out by patients released through their gates, without providing any specific varieties of information on the form treatment takes in the institution, how it is organized to carry out its functions, etc., the public, it may be suggested have built up, through fragments of information, a concept of special hospitals as essentially horror-filled places. This could not be otherwise, for it the hospital is filled with "beasts", "monsters", "perverts", "killers", and other nefarious "creatures", it must of necessity be a truly frightening environment, a garbage "bin" (as mental hospitals are referred to by their inmates), holding *all* of the violent, dangerous, and murdering individuals who have been run by the public like one long computer program of disaster through the medium of the press. The documentary was a chance for the public once again to take a one penny tour, to "meet" through the medium of television some of the "monsters" they had been reading about, if not in the flesh, then at least on film.

BACKGROUND KNOWLEDGE: FILM IMAGES OF MADNESS

This is a medium with which the public can be said to have a great feel of familiarity with in receiving input concerning the "facts" and "acts" of the mentally disordered offender. Fictional accounts of the crimes of insane psychopaths and other mentally ill persons have been a dominant and popular feature of the modern film art. *The Cabinet of Dr. Calgari* an early effort, portrayed the madhousekeeper (an early term for the psychiatrist) gone mad. The 1938 film, *Bedlam* starred Boris Karloff as the medical superintendent of Bethlem Hospital, and is a graphic account (quite true to historical fact) of the abuses meted out to patients of the hospital as their daily lot. At the end of the film, Karloff is judged by a jury composed of the asylum's inmates to be "sane, and so not fit to live among (them)." Hitchcock set the tone of the modern genre in his classic *Psycho*. This is basically the story of a psychopathic young man who murders his mother and keeps her mummified body in a room at the Bates Motel, of which he is the attendant. Visiting guests are ritually murdered, and in particular, the death of Vivien Leigh, stabbed to death in the shower in arguably the most famous of all murder scenes in film history, became a part of popular myth concerning the behaviour to be expected of the mad. Many other examples of the violent activities of psychopaths and other criminally insane persons were produced during the 1950s and 1960s including such notable films as *The Bad Seed*, which detailed the life of an adolescent psychopath (parallelling the Mary Bell case); *The Three Faces of Eve* (a study in multiple personality), and *Whatever Happened to Baby Jane?*, a story of violence and insanity.

It was not until the mid-seventies that films portraying the institution as a weapon of overt and covert social control began to emerge. Sympathetic portrayals of the problems of the mentally ill were handled without a resort to the portrayal of violence and murder in films of the type represented by *I Never Promised You a Rose Garden*. However, it was the film *One Flew Over The Cuckoo's Nest*, which most clearly presented the patient's "side" of the story. McMurphy, the restless psychopath, as portrayed by Jack Nicholson in a role which brought him the academy award as best actor, acts out to secure a transfer from a penal farm to state psychiatric facilities because of his dislike for the work of picking peas. There his outrageous antics, a rebellion against the seemingly senseless rules of the ward, caused ever increasingly harsh corrective measures to be imposed upon him, until ultimately the staff resorted to a lobotomy to curtail his activities.

Throughout the late 1970s and early 1980s it has been the film portrayals of violent mental patients which have sold the most box office seats. There have been an absolute plethora of films which have sold "blood, guts, murder, and madness" to tens of millions of filmgoers throughout the world. In the interest of brevity (and good taste), we shall follow Thoreau's dictate and use but one example to illustrate the point. The film trilogy, *Friday the 13th* (will there be more?) is the story of a young horribly disfigured behemoth of a man who murders his family in a most bizarre fashion, and then is sent for treatment in a state mental institution. Some thirteen years later he escapes to murder, murder, and then murder some more in graphic detail, (and in the latest offering in 3-D). The message which filmgoers receive is the criminally insane are *even more* horrifying and dangerous than they had even imagined.

SETTING THE STAGE: BUILDING PUBLIC INTEREST

The role of the media in spotlighting social problems has been a recognized sociological truism for almost a decade. There is another corollary function which is taken on by the media in this realm, and that is the building of public interest in media events. This process is of considerable import to our analysis of the eventual ramifications and widespread reaction that was produced by the Secret Hospital documentary. Can one program significantly affect public perceptions concerning an institution? The following examination demonstrates that with the aid of an effective media "blitz", that is, the production of a large number of stories within a short period of time (and in a showcase position), a groundwork may be laid for promotion of what has been called a "moral crusade". It is a time for posting on the public notice board that the newspaper provides that "something is wrong" and attention should be paid. As Gusfield (1969, 170) has written, this is an occasion which serves a highly functional and significant purpose:

> It is useful to think of symbolic acts as forms of rhetoric, functioning to organize the perceptions, attitudes, and feelings of the observers. . . . They are persuasive devices which alter in the observer's view . . . (in a front page headline 2″ high "RAMPTON TORTURE").

On Wednesday, 16 May 1979 *The Daily Mail* began the symbolic sequence of announcing a forthcoming scandal, and indicating that it *would* produce a "tidal wave of protest".

> A *MAJOR* scandal about allegations of treatment amounting to torture and systematic brutality by nurses at Rampton Hospital in Nottinghamshire is *about to be sparked off* by a television documentary to be shown next Tuesday (emphasis added).

Similarly, the *Evening News* of the same date carried a parallel story under the banner "Guilty Men of Rampton" on page 6, indicating that the conditions described and *presumably* protrayed in the upcoming documentary would shock the viewing audience, ". . . it all sounds more like Belsen or Dachau than a major British psychiatric hospital." The juxtaposing of widely understood images, which evoke very strong public feelings, is a common tool for exciting interest, and this is the strategy being followed in the preceding report. *The Daily Mail* insisted that the program would "cause a shock wave of protest and disgust." Their express intent of this blitz was to fuel public interest, and hopefully ensure that their prediction of a "shock wave" would be realized in a "shelf fulfilling prophecy."

Public curiosity was also played upon in accounts which emphasized the "secret" nature of Rampton hospital procedures and public ignorance of the institution. The facility was described as:

> . . . isolated in maximum security in the countryside . . . cloaked by the Official Secrets Act. Few people other than its 900 patients and 600 nurses, know what goes on inside it (*The Daily Mail* 16 May 1979).

But this was also an occasion upon which the media was about to make a radical shift in its portrayal of the offender-patient as "victim" rather than in the familiar role of the perpetrator of crime. Suddenly the *Evening News* was able to conveniently shift Rampton patients into a "sick" role from the "criminal" role; "for most their only sin has been to fall victim to mental illness." The *Daily Mail* proved just as willing to produce for the first time during the period 1975 to 1979 a statement underlining the "non dangerous" status of a significant proportion of the Rampton population, facts which had been previously ignored in tabloid accounts:

> About half the inmates of Rampton come into this category (subnormal, no crime). About another quarter have committed only minor crimes — such as stealing and breaking windows. *Only* the remaining quarter could be classed as serious, mentally disturbed criminals.

It may be suggested that the media were able to produce this image of the Rampton patient simply because the individuals were inmates of the institution, still contained away from society, and therefore not a danger. This was consistent with the function of special hospitals as holding places for violent individuals as portrayed by the media. The documentary itself and the articles which followed it were of interest to our analysis because they signalled a revolution in the "making" of madness; for the first time patients' views, accounts, and opinions were being considered as a useful news source.

What specific circumstances contributed to the use of patient's stories concerning the ill-treatment meted out at Rampton? Following Hall (1977) there are strong suggestions that this was one of the few occasions upon which the information provided for news was *not* monopolized by law enforcement agencies, courts, or other state officials. Rather than data which was simply "fed" to the media, the documentary form provided a channel for an alternative message to be conveyed to the public about the institutional handling of the deviants and criminals that society had entrusted to their care. Although Scull (1977) rightly points out that citizens develop and maintain not only a psychological but physical distance from prisons, asylums, and other people-processing institutions, the public still harbours a number of vague notions concerning the functions of a facility like Rampton. If the mentally disordered offender is "sick", then naturally he is being treated. It is the *specific nature* of treatment with which the public have no measure of familiarity. "Something" is done to help patients, otherwise they would not be let out, would they? Contrary to the assertions of the Boynton Committee (1980, 135) who maintain that ". . . an obstructive and suspicious attitude almost invariably results in a bad press", Rampton as a top-security institution had not suffered at the hands of the press by remaining behind the veil of secrecy. Rather, it may be suggested that this strategy had worked to allay the type of institutional calamity which might have arisen at an even earlier stage in Rampton's history. As one patient commented quite pointedly, "You can't change the system of brutality. You *can* cover it up."

The inclusion of a number of ex-staff revelations about the conditions and treatment of patients at Rampton lent validity to the assertions of ex-inmates, who were interviewed in the community about these subjects. Former social workers, nurses, and patients at Rampton, in all the selected interviews from over one hundred carried out by the documentary team, were combined to produce the program. The nursing union and staff of Rampton began their campaign to discredit the allegations and testimony of the ex-patients even before the program had been aired. Mr. Rushworth, the Associate Secretary of the P.O.A. (Prison Officer's Association) commented that the nurses, ". . . as interested parties had not been approached." This was a misleading view of events which transpired in the filming of the documentary. The documentary film crew led by John Willis had approached the hospital authorities on three separate occasions in order to obtain permission to film inside Rampton hospital. This was denied because it "breached security regulations" and would "upset the patients". The P.O.A. through its union representation was a party to denying the crew access on what would prove to be unnecessary grounds. In fact, it was the nurses who had cause to be upset, the institutional barrier had been bridged, an alternative was being "exposed" for the first time, and there was cause for alarm among the ranks of the nursing staff.

Mr. Rushworth also attempted to appeal to the popular image of the mentally disordered offender in the press by suggesting, in a discrediting gesture, that ". . . it should be remembered that Rampton is a hospital for *serious mental cases,* some of whom may have *hallucinations.*" Patients are not persons, they are "mental cases" when they wish to challenge the authority of their "keepers". Passing as an authority on deviants is easily accomplished when a knowledge gap exists between what the institution does and what the public knows about its activities. Rushworth continued, "I have not had any reports of complaints nor of nurses being disciplined for ill-treatment of patients." Earlier we discovered that *178 cases* of alleged brutality had to be investigated by in-house senior nurses, and over a five-year period *not one allegation was substantiated.*

Mr. Rushworth's harangue against the reliability of the patient's accusations continued even after the film had been shown, taking a strikingly similar form to his first response, but now placing more emphasis upon the violent nature of most patients:

> Most of the evidence seems to have come from former patients. It must be remembered that they include violent, dangerous and criminal people. Some are dangerous lunatics and others suffer halluncinations.

The intent of his remarks was clearly to shift public attention away from the images relayed to the public during the course of the documentary, and to the extreme situation under which nurses supposedly work, (*The Guardian* 22 May 1979, 1).*The Evening News* of Wednesday, 23 May 1979 ran a second page article entitled, "There is no torture, says Rampton nurse." Again, the theme of patient violence was emphasized to underscore public understandings and provide rationales:

> Many of the patients we deal with are very violent. They come at you, so what can you do? You have to *restrain* them or else they'll beat you to death.

An attempt was made to assure the public that what they had heard and in some cases (through smuggled photographs of the interior of Rampton) seen, was not really what they had heard and seen after all, "If you look at some of the corridors and wards they might look horrific, but in other places the hospital is quite homey." But the point is that the wards and corridors constitute a major portion of the therapeutic environment (Fleming 1982).

The local MP for the Rampton area joined in casting aspersions on the validity of the allegations made by ex-patients. In *The Evening News* of Wednesday, 23 May 1979, p. 2, under the title "I can't believe claims says MP", he indicated that "The credibility of the witnesses leaves something to be desired." He went on further to emphasize once again the violence and criminal identity so well known to the public:

> Yorkshire television didn't mention the criminal records of the people who appeared, or whether they were on drugs at the time it happened.

As the vast majority of Rampton patients received drugs to control behaviour and ease problems of managing large numbers of patients, it would be a foregone conclusion that they would have been receiving some form of medication throughout their stay in hospital. As to the MPs first point, it is enough to point out that the media has provided a substantial body of data on the residents of special hospitals and criminals, lunatics, and "dangerous" people (Prins 1981). The MP quite succinctly summarized both nursing union and his own view of Rampton patients, by indicating that they were ". . . the dregs of society" which staff have to deal with on a daily basis. A further attempt to discredit was effected by the MP's wonder at why the ex-patients ". . . had never made any real complaint to their MP or police until a television camera came along." It was not until the full disclosure that the documentary provided that it could be realized why patients, while still incarcerated in Rampton would not attempt to initiate complaint procedures. They are denied the use of a telephone, as we have seen in the analysis of contemporary Rampton developed in my research (Fleming 1982). Their mail is subject to censorship by hospital staff. Furthermore, as one patient expressing a complaint against a member or members of staff, with full "grapevine" knowledge of the futility of making allegations within the confines of the hospital, and terror of making a complaint while "outside" still being held and controlled by the nursing staff, and likely to be for many years, it would be difficult to find the courage or resources necessary to pursue this form of action. What credence would be allotted to an allegation made by an overly medicated, "violent", "dreg of society" against the protestations of the all-powerful Rampton branch of the P.O.A.? The Yorkshire Television documentary offered the chance for collective action from outside the walls of the institution, far removed from direct contact with the nurses, some of whom as we shall see, engaged in a collective system of repression and violence against Rampton patients.

"HORROR ON THE WARDS": SYSTEMATIC BRUTALITY AND INSTITUTIONALIZED TERROR

To my mind it is an obscene institution which neither cares for nor treats many of its inmates (Ex-Rampton social worker).

Its a system that's been allowed to go rotten (Ex-Rampton patient).

The *irrational system* as I have termed the collection of rules, regulations, treatment practices and policies which characterize the approach taken to "rehabilitating" patients at Rampton was finally exposed by the screening of the "Secret Hospital" documentary (see Fleming 1982). Drawing its data from interviews with ex-patients, their relatives, and former staff members, the program was able to piece together many, most of the components of the "irrational" sytem for the general public. It documented over 500 allegations of staff brutality, in describing what a-mounted to "traditional and well established ill-treatment practices" (*The Guardian* 22 May 1979).

Staff attacks and ill treatment had become so integral a part of the routine that they had been given specific names by ex-patients, that were reiterated by all those interviewed by Willis and his crew:

1. *The Black Aspirin* — "Ex-patients describe being hit for half an hour, punched in the face and stomach, kicked down corridors and flights of stairs, stripped naked and booted between the legs and stomped on."
2. *Punishment cells* — the segregative side rooms. "Women patients describe being locked in them naked, without even a nightdress and no toilet facilities for days at a time." Also known as the "torture chamber".
3. *The Rampton Humpty* — beating the soles of the patient's bare feet with plimsoles (running shoes).
4. *Throttling Out* — applying a towel around the neck of the patient and tightening it until the individual passes out.
5. *Tickling Combs* — a form of straight jacket employed only at Rampton which the patient is put into naked, and then is forced to remain in, without being taken out for relief of bodily waste.
6. *The Rampton Trifle* — mixing the patient's food and tea altogether in one bowl and forcing the patient to eat it all.

These were not the only practices outlined by those interviewed, others included: pouring water over the head of a patient for "a bit of a laugh", and ". . . patients' testicles being stood upon, pubic hair being pulled out with pliers, a man's penis being laid on a billiard table and whacked with a cue, and an incontinent patient's excreta being mixed with his food and fed to him." In all, there were some 527 complaints against 146 of the approximately 600 nurses at Rampton. In *The Evening News* of 23 May, p. 2 an article entitled "I hope to God they do something now" further underlines the allegations of torture and ill-treatment. Staff were described as "brutes", and a father of one of the patients commented "If the treatment my son got was given to a dumb animal there would be an outburst all over the counry." Sandra, an ex-patient featured in the documentary was quoted in an interview in *The Sun*, Tuesday, 22 May 1979, p. 2, entitled "MY THREE YEAR HELL BY SANDRA" as indicating that the whole process of being a patient in Rampton had, as she put it, "put the frighteners on her."

Public response was immediate as "hundreds of viewers" placed "torture calls" to the television network (*The Evening News* 23 May 1979, p. 1). Police investigations of the charges commenced within a few days from the airing of the show, and the Minister of Health called for the appointment of a committee of inquiry that was to become known as The Boynton Committee. Staff response was strangely missing for a number of weeks until 8 June 1979 when a front page article in the local *Retford Times* proclaimed rather ironically "RAMPTON NURSES HIT BACK AT YTV FILM." In a last ditch attempt to throw discredit on the accusations of the ex-patients' allegations, this letter quoted here in part was sent to the Independent Broadcasting Authority:

> Only one patient gave the reason for his admission to Rampton — this could give the impression that they were *upright citizens whose word is to be trusted* — relevant history may well have thrown doubts on their veracity.

The preceding analysis has provided a detailed examination of the bridging of the gap between institutional realities as portrayed by two distinct groups, patients and staff. The latter group has in the past had the political power, position, and backing of administration to convey their reality as the *only* one, also because of society's lack of interest in the workings of Rampton. The former group had not previously been allowed to present their version of reality; that they did so, and the fact that it has been substantiated by several recent convictions of nurses on charges arising out of the police investigations of staff brutality in the hospital, supports the theoretical framework developed by Chibnall and Hall, et al. which underlines the adaptive abilities of newspapers in building and sustaining reactions to crime. The powerful effect that can be produced by the electronic media in this respect has been recently documented by the work of The Glasgow Group, Fishman, and Fleming, and is supported by the analysis presented here.

On 12 November 1980 The Guardian in a front page article reporting on the just released Boynton Committee findings, quoted Harold Jenkins, then Minister of Health as stating that ". . . the conditions revealed in the report were intolerable." Sir John Boynton concluded that "the regime and treatment were those that had been found in other mental hospitals in the country '25 or 30 years ago'". The Committee did not consider any evidence by current or ex-Rampton patients, and so avoided the unpleasant task of commenting on staff brutality.

CONCLUSIONS

The "irrational" system of Rampton is expected by society to produce rational beings. As this paper has shown, Rampton not only was, and is, incapable of "making people better", but perhaps more importantly, of tending to its own sicknesses. Public concern will be shifted by the media to other crises which must be developed, explored, and exploited in the production of "news". But as a society, we must begin to develop mechanisms to ensure that those whom we send for "treatment" at the very least, do not receive punishment by an insane system, through systems of torture, or neglect of need.

Notes

1. Morris, Terence. *Deviance and control — The secular heresy.* London: Hutchinson, 1976, 37. This is amply evidenced in the discussion which follows with reference to control authority and control staff versions of "reality" as presented in press reports. I should like to thank The Canada Council and the Central Research Fund, University of London for their generous support of my research. Terence Morris supervised the thesis and I am grateful for his constant assistance and support.

2. Wilkins, Leslie. *Social deviance.* London: Tavistock, 1964, 63. The isolation imposed upon mentally disordered offenders permeated their everyday life. See Chapter Six.

3. Offender-patient accounts of institutional processing have not been one of these prime foci.

4. Most significantly alternate political views which contradict prevailing ideology.

5. See Fleming, Ibid., 1981; Young, Ibid., 1971, 1973; Ng, Ibid., 1982, for examples of deviants clashes with the media.

6. This sytem includes a 17' perimeter wall, escape "control" centre, sirens, the use of dogs and roadblocks.

7. See the examination of hostel conditions presented in Chapter Six of T. Fleming, 1982. Ibid.

References

Becker, H.S. 1963. *Outsiders: Studies in the sociology of deviance.* New York: Free Press of Glencoe.
Boynton report. 1980. *Report of the review of Rampton hospital.* HMSO: London.
Box, Steven. 1971. *Deviance, reality and society.* London: Holt, Reinhart and Winston (revised edition 1981).

Chibnall, S. 1977. *Law-and-order news*. London: Tavistock.

Cohen, S. 1973. *Folk devils and moral panics-The creation of the Mods and Rockers*. St. Albans: Paladin.

Cohen, S. and L. Taylor. 1976. *Prison secrets*. London: Pluto Press.

Ferry, J. and D. Inwood. 1982. *The Olson murders*. Langley, B.C.: Cameo Books Ltd.

Fiedler, L. 1978. *Freaks: Myths and images of the secret self*. New York: Simon and Schuster.

Fleming, Thomas. 1981. The bawdy house boys: Some notes on media, sporadic moral crusades, and selective law enforcement. In *Canadian Criminology Forum*, Vol. 3, No. 2, Spring 1981.

————. 1982. *the release of psychopathic, mentally disordered and dangerous offenders from Rampton special hospital: A follow-up study*. London School of Economics: Unpublished Ph.D. dissertation.

Foucault, M. 1978. *Discipline and punish, the birth of the prison*. New York: Pantheon.

Glasgow University Media Group. 1978. *Bad news: Vol. I*. London: RKP.

————. 1980. *More bad news: Vol. 2 of bad news*. London: RKP.

Gusfield, J.R. 1963. *Symbolic crusade: Status politics and the American temperance movement*. Urbana, Ill.: University of Illinois.

Hall, S. et al. 1978. *Policing the crisis — Mugging the state, and law and order*, London: Macmillan.

Halloran, J. et al. 1970. *Demonstrations and communications: A case study*. Harmondsworth, Middlesex: Penguin.

Jones, M. 1974. *Justice and journalism*. London: Barry Rose.

King, C. 1967. *The future of the press*. London: MacGibbon.

Klapp, O. 1962. *Heroes, villians and fools*. New Jersey: Prentice-Hall.

Molotch, H. and M. Lester. 1974. News as purposive behavior: On the strategic use of routine events, accidents and scandals. In *The American Sociological Review* 39:101–112.

Morris, T. 1976. *Deviance and control — The secular heresy*. London: Hutchinson.

Morris, T. and Blom-Cooper. 1963. *A calendar of murder*. London: RKP.

Ng, Y. 1981. *The Jacques case: Morality, ideology and power*. Centre of Criminology, Toronto: M.A. Thesis (Advance copy).

Nunnally, J. 1973. Popular conceptions of mental illness: What the media presents. In S. Cohen and J. Young (Eds.), *The manufacture of news. Deviance, socal problems, and mass media*. London: Constable. 136-146.

Parry-Jones, W. 1972. *The trade of lunacy*. London: Routledge and Kegan Paul.

Pearce, F. 1973. How to be immoral and ill, pathetic and dangerous, all at the same time! Mass media and the homosexual. In S. Cohen and J. Young (Eds.), *The manufacture of news. Deviance, social problems, and the mass media*. London: Constable. 284-302.

Prins, H. 1980. *Offenders, deviants or patients?* London: Tavistock.

Rock, P. 1973. *Deviant behavior*. London: Hutchinson.

Roshier, B. 1973. The selection of crime news by the press. In S. Cohen and J. Young (Eds.), *The manufacture of news. Deviance, social problems, and the mass media*. London: Constable. 28-40.

Scheff, T.S. 1966. *Being mentally ill: A sociological theory*. Chicago: Aldine.

————. 1975. *Labeling madness*. Englewood Cliffs, New Jersey: Prentice-Hall.

Schur, E.M. 1971. *Labeling deviant behavior: Its sociological implications*. New York: Harper and Row.

Scull, A. 1979. *Museums of madness: The Social Organization of insanity in nineteenth-century England.* London: Allen Lane.

Steadman, H.J. and Cocozza, J.J. 1974. *Careers of the criminally insane.* Lexington, Mass.: Lexington Books.

Summer, C. 1981. Race, crime and hegemony: A review essay. In *Contemporary Crises* 5:277-291.

Szasz, T.S. 1965. *Law, liberty, and psychiatry.* New York: MacMillan.

_____. 1965. *Psychiatric justice.* New York: MacMillan.

_____. 1971. *The manufacture of madness.* New York: Harper and Row.

Thompson, P. 1974. *Back and Broadmoor.* London: Mowbrays.

Tockman, G. 1978. *Making news: A study in the construction of reality.* New York: Free Press.

Walker, N. and McCabe, S. 1973. *Crime and insanity in England II: New solutions and new problems.* Edinburgh: University Press.

Wilkins, L. 1964. *Social deviance.* London: Tavistock.

Young, J. 1971. The role of police as amplifiers of deviance, negotiators of reality and translators of fantasy. In Cohen, S. (Ed.), *Images of deviance.* Harmondsworth, Middlesex: Penguin. 27-62.

_____. 1974. Mass media, drugs and deviance. In P. Rock and M. McIntosh (Eds.), *Deviance and social control,* London Tavistock. 229-261.

Chapter 8

Lesbian Feminist Protest: A Case Study

*Sharon D. Stone**

INTRODUCTION[1]

Recently there has been growing interest in the sociological study of lesbians and their communities. In particular, research has tended to focus on the experience of being lesbian, methods of coping in a hostile environment, and studies of lesbian identity. Ponse (1978) examines the formation of a lesbian identity and focuses on the importance of the lesbian community to support identity. Ettore (1980) explores the position of lesbians in society and the development of lesbian consciousness. Brooks (1981) discusses how lesbians cope with the stress that results from being labelled inferior and suggests that "positive group identification" helps to mediate stress. In each of these studies, the lesbian community is of interest only insofar as it supports a lesbian identity. That is, the structure and concerns of the lesbian community are of secondary interest to the focus on lesbian identity.

Existing research tends to study lesbians only in relation to nonlesbians, "by comparison, in reaction to, as secret from" (Krieger 1982). With the focus on lesbian identity, considerations of internal structuring of lesbian communities tend to be glossed over.

In contrast, Grevatt's (1975) research has a different theoretical approach to examining lesbianism; it focuses on the emergence of lesbians as a vocal minority group and their involvement in

---

* Undergraduate student majoring in sociology, University of Toronto.

lesbian protest organizations. Her research included an analysis of lesbian/feminism as it took shape in the United States.

INTRODUCING LESBIANS AGAINST THE RIGHT

Social Climate

There are an estimated 63,000 lesbians in the City of Metropolitan Toronto (Bruner 1981). Lesbians Against the Right (LAR), a group of approximately twenty-five lesbians, is only one of several groups in the city with an exclusively lesbian membership. It is, however, the only lesbian group in the city which was not designed to provide social and/or support services for lesbians.

LAR was formed in 1981, in reaction to the increasingly hostile social climate in relation to lesbians. Particularly during the Toronto municipal elections in 1980, with several candidates sympathetic to the concerns of gay constituents, a hate campaign was mobilized against gay people. The campaign was directed by the New Right, personified by individuals who belonged to groups such as The League Against Homosexuals. Numerous handbills were distributed throughout the city, which specifically identified lesbians as a social menace. Early in 1981, the police orchestrated a massive raid on gay baths, charging hundreds of men with being "found-ins" (Sheppard and White 1981). While the bath raids were not a direct attack on lesbians per se (lesbians did not have baths), a growing number of lesbians began to understand their position.

Groups existed that opposed the harrassment of homosexuals, such as Gays and Lesbians Against the Right Everywhere (GLARE),[2] or The Right To Privacy Committee (RTPC). Without exception, however, these groups were male dominated, and either inadequately addressed the concerns of lesbians, or ignored lesbians completely.

Within the lesbian community, the social situation was deteriorating. The year before LAR's formation, the Lesbian Organization Of Toronto (LOOT) had ceased to exist. For several years, LOOT had been renting a house which had served as a lesbian social centre. With the demise of LOOT, lesbians lost an important social institution. Shortly thereafter, lesbians lost the only women's bar in the city. As a result, lesbians were experiencing "a frightening sense of homelessness" (Steiger and Weir 1981).

The Formation of LAR

In the spring of 1981, GLARE sponsored a series of workshops on fighting the New Right. Out of one of the workshops, which was devoted exclusively to the concerns of lesbians, came plans for a day-long forum to address lesbian concerns in more detail.

The forum attracted approximately one hundred lesbians. In one of the speeches given that day, it was noted:

> ... there is still very little that GLARE has to say about lesbians specifically, how the repression is affecting us. But no one lesbian or two or half a dozen can substitute for the collective discussion within our community. All of us need this discussion in order that our identity as lesbians be presented in the framework of the gay movement, and all other movements. . . . In confronting our invisibility within the gay movement, we need to address the intertwined oppression we face both as women and because of the sexual/emotional choice we have made. Our oppression must be understood within the gay movement not just as a result of our sexual orientation but also as women (Gottlieb 1982, 9).

The consensus of the day was that lesbians needed their own organization, where lesbian concerns would not be secondary.

Thus the groundwork for the formation of LAR was laid. LAR was envisioned as both a social organization and a political organization to counterattacks from the New Right.

From the beginning, LAR called itself a lesbian/feminist organization. Founders were interested in developing a lesbian/feminist analysis of their oppression: a theory which would focus on the unique oppression of lesbians and how to combat that oppression.

At the time of writing, LAR has existed for close to two years. This paper focuses exclusively on LAR's first year of existence. During the first year, LAR was in the process of establishing itself as an action-oriented group. Significant activities included organizing the city's first lesbian march, giving speeches at gay events and women's events, participating in broad-based coalitions to oppose the New Right, organizing workshops on issues of concern to lesbians, and organizing cultural events for lesbians.

Theoretical Model

LAR emerged within the context of a repressive social climate, and in essence, was a political organization. As such, LAR can be examined by focusing on the following questions. What motivated lesbians to form LAR? Did everyone have the same reason for joining LAR? How did ideology manifest itself? What form did LAR take, and how did leadership manifest itself? Through what networks was LAR linked to the outside world? What organizational strains emerged and what were the implications of these strains? Finally, how effective was LAR as a political force fighting against oppression?

These questions can be answered with reference to a general model which seeks to explain the emergence of protest groups and social movements (Clark, Grayson and Grayson 1975, 1–35). The model suggests that when two conditions are present — a perception of institutional deficiency and a means of mobilization — there is a high probability that a protest organization will emerge.

The first condition, perception of institutional deficiency, is indicated by dissatisfaction with and opposition to the existing social structure. The second determinant, a means of mobilization, consists of three preconditions: (1) A unifying ideology identifying what is wrong and providing a remedy. Such an ideology can promote coordinated action and increase commitment, insofar as it proposes to remedy the institutional deficiencies perceived by individuals. (2) Willing and able leadership. Leadership can inspire others to follow direction, to achieve goals, plan strategies, and promote the interests of the group. (3) Channels for communication and networks of cooperative relationships. In isolation, individuals have little chance of effectively changing their situation. With open communication channels, the likelihood of forming a strong organizational base is enhanced.

Data Collection and Sample Selection

Data were collected by participant observation supported with tape-recorded, in-depth interviews.[3] Sixteen of the approximately twenty-five members were interviewed at length. Interviews focused on why they joined LAR, what they thought about LAR's ideology, what they thought about LAR's structure and leadership, and what they thought about LAR's relations with others.

Particularly during the first few months of LAR's existence, there was considerable turnover in membership. Upwards of sixty lesbians attended the first few meetings of LAR, but thereafter, the average attendance at meetings was twenty-five. Lesbians came and went throughout the first year, although not in significant numbers. Especially for the first seven months, membership remained relatively stable. Out of the twenty-five members at the end of the year, only ten had been active members throughout the year. Fifteen left at various times, their numbers being replenished with new members. It was discovered that the ten who had been continuous members were the ones who knew the most about LAR, had thought the most about LAR, and were best able to represent the views of the group as a whole.

All ten active members for the full year were interviewed. The other six interviewees had joined at various times after LAR was founded.

Analysis was carried out by examining recurring and repetitive response patterns in the interviews. The terms "several", "many", and "most" are used in place of specific numbers. "Several" refers to up to five people, or as much as one-fifth of the membership, "many" refers to up to fifteen people. "Most" refers to approximately four-fifths of the membership, or up to twenty people.

PERCEIVED INSTITUTIONAL DEFICIENCY

The Membership and Why They Joined LAR

The membership of LAR ranged in age from twenty to forty years old, with most being close to thirty years old, and all but a few over the age of twenty-five.

In terms of occupations, the majority of LAR's members were secretaries, typesetters, or clerks. There was also a number of academics, with most of them attending graduate school and doing university-level teaching. One member held a management position with a large courier company, another had her own therapeutic massage business, and there were two lawyers. Socioeconomic backgrounds were both middle class and working class. Approximately half of the membership had been to university. In short, the membership was not homogeneous.

When LAR first formed, the membership consisted almost entirely of lesbians who had been active in either the gay or feminist movements (often both) for between five and ten years. In addition, many had contributed to the foundation and/or running of LOOT. Several had attended the first Canada-wide lesbian conference in Ottawa in 1976 and in 1979 had organized a second conference in Toronto. Prior to joining the women's movement, many had been active in left-wing political groups. LAR was formed, therefore, by lesbians who had considerable organizational experience and were well-versed in the politics of protest.

The common demoninator amongst the members was that they had not only decisively identified themselves as lesbians, they had also begun to question the validity of the social structure, and were interested in fighting their oppression. Often they were unable to completely articulate what they thought was wrong or even why they thought there was a problem, but at some level, they all believed that the problem was not with them, it was with society. They all shared a sense of the gross injustices they had to face because they were women and lesbians. They refused to passively accept their perceived oppression and injustices. In other words, rather than accepting the inherent "rightness" of the status quo, they challenged its very foundation. In essence, they strongly perceived that the heterosexual institutional structure was oppressive. The nature of this oppression was evident in the reasons they expressed for joining LAR.

Examining reasons given for joining LAR, three distinct themes emerged: historical necessity; frustration over lack of a political outlet; and personal need. Most respondents mentioned each theme. However, which theme an individual emphasized was related both to how much experience she had had in anti-establishment politics, and to her experience in the lesbian community. Without exception, those who emphasized the first two themes had been present at the formation of LAR or joined very shortly thereafter, while those who emphasized the theme of personal need joined much later. In general, those who empha-sized the third theme had only recently begun to identify as lesbians. The following discussion elaborates upon the themes and the connection to past experience.

Historical Necessity

Generally speaking, those who founded LAR had had the most experience with being active members of groups which identified with "the underdog". Their experience led them to believe that if lesbians united for a common cause, they could be far more effective than if they continued to fight individually. This group expressed the most concern about the visible hatred directed towards lesbians. They perceived that Toronto, in its historical development, lacked an autonomous lesbian movement and no lesbian organizations had emerged that could counteract right-wing attacks. Additionally, they were distressed that the recent closings of lesbian meeting places left lesbians with no place they could call their own. As one said: "There was a sense of loss and a fair amount of fear that there was no unity among lesbians." They wanted an organization which would allow lesbians to join together and present a unified front.

Reflecting such historical considerations, the following reasons for founding LAR were expressed:

> Previous to May 9 there was always a large number of lesbian-feminists around who felt that we were a specific political current, although we hadn't defined ourselves as such. We knew that we had specific politics in relation to feminism and our lesbianism and also the way that related to other kinds of politics which made us a current. Many of us had had discussions with other lesbians active across Canada and the United States and realized that it was really important for this politics to have some expression. So LAR was sort of a long time coming. . . . For a long time a group of us had been looking for a vehicle for our politics. Part of it was that we were tired of the homophobia in the straight women's movement and the left and also the political restrictions that being a political lesbian brought. Lesbians were having difficulty getting any political support for themselves as lesbians. We were allowed to work in other movements for other causes but were expected to stay in the closet. We felt that if we were a political organization we could be a real political force that would be a way of being out politically in other areas.

Another member noted:

> I was disturbed by the collapse of LOOT and the closing of the Fly. Two or three years ago we had lots of dances and cultural events but suddenly we had nothing. It was like we had built something and it had been smashed. So in the May 9 workshop I said, "Look, our movement's being taken out from under us and if we don't want to cooperate we've got to do something."

Another observed:

> We definitely felt the threat of the right-wing. Women were scared. Things were becoming more difficult and the level of paranoia was increasing.

FRUSTRATION OVER LACK OF A POLITICAL OUTLET

Frustration over lack of a political outlet cannot be understood outside of a historical context. It is isolated as a separate theme, however, to underscore the fact that for many, the overriding concern was with finding a lesbian group where they could "express their politics". The following views were expressed:

> I've aways been interested in anti-establishment politics and for a long time I've been political about my lesbianism. So I've been looking for a political lesbian group. I had tried to become involved with other lesbian groups but was dissatisfied with the lack of political focus they had. So I was quite excited about LAR and the prospect of having so many politically experienced lesbians all together.

Echoing this frustration:

> When I first came out I wasn't very familiar with feminist theory or lesbian/feminist theory. One of the first things I did was become active in helping to run LOOT. I joined different committees and got to know lots of people but nothing was very political. My feminist consciousness had been growing ever since I came out and it was particularly high when we had the Conference here in Toronto. Then PLOT [Political Lesbians Of Toronto] formed and I was pretty excited, but that [PLOT's existence] didn't last very long. Since PLOT there's been no outlet, no place to go to talk about politics or do anything. So by the time LAR came along I was anxious to get as involved as possible. From the very first meeting I felt that I had finally found what I was looking for. It was wonderful to see so many lesbians in one room seriously discussing lesbian politics.

A third member explained:

> I've theorized about politics since I was a child but I was never active until 1978 when I got involved with WAVAW [Women Against Violence Against Women]. Then in 1979 I got involved in organizing the Lesbian Conference and since then I've been looking for a place to express my politics.

There had been a need for an organization such as LAR for a number of years. Several, when asked why they thought an organization such as LAR did not become viable sooner, said:

> Lesbians have been developing politically in Toronto through going through political experiences together and separately. A certain maturation has taken place. Women coming to individual decisions and finding that those decisions are the same for other lesbians too.

Another observed:

> After the Conference in 1979 there was a growing energy and it took three years to take off. It takes momentum to get these things going.

Personal Need

More recent members of LAR did not put their reasons for joining in a historical context. Many had only recently begun to claim a lesbian identity and so they did not experience the years of frustration for want of a lesbian group referred to by more politically conscious lesbians. By and large, they joined LAR unfamiliar with the history of lesbian politics and unfamiliar with lesbian/feminist theory. Therefore, their reasons for joining were different.

Emphasizing this theme:

I joined LAR basically because I wanted to learn from LAR. I felt that I couldn't offer LAR much because I didn't have the historical background in politics and I had just come out. I wanted to learn about lesbian/feminism and I knew that LAR was the best place for me to learn because it was with other lesbians. I also wanted to meet lesbians I could talk to about lesbian/feminism.

Another explained:

I had just come out a few months before LAR started and though I knew some lesbian/feminists, I never took more than a passing interest in lesbian politics because I didn't consider it relevant to me. But when I came out I became radical pretty fast and I went to LAR all excited because I wanted to have a better grasp of lesbian politics and meet other political lesbians. Also I think that definitely there is a need for an autonomous lesbian force in politics.

Thirdly, another commented:

I came out last summer and I feel that was incredibily connected to coming out politically. Before that I really had a very liberal view of things. It was sort of like an overnight thing of coming out and gaining political consciousness. So I started reading last summer and was real clear that I wanted to be around more political women, and hearing about LAR, that seemed like a possibility of being around them. Now, I thought, do I want to be around them to make great changes in the world, or . . . I just had this real strong identification with political women. I certainly wanted to meet them socially, but social and political are mixed, and I just wanted to learn more.

LAR as a Social Organization

Most members of LAR emphasized the importance of getting to know other members socially. Both original and newer members expressed much the same opinion about socializing. One commented:

> I sometimes think that lesbian groups are fated to disintegrate because we all have such incredible needs to be with other lesbians and to socialize and be accepted. For those of us who don't like the bar too much then the group has to serve that function and you get so caught up in your own personal needs that in some ways it's a lot easier to be active in another group where you don't go to meet your personal lesbian needs, so you are more willing to "serve the cause" so to speak.

Echoing the sentiment that there is a need for acceptance, another argued:

> There's a really strong fear of being alienated from the only group that will accept one as an out lesbian in politics. The group is almost like a community.

As for the social needs that many had, another noted:

> It's a comfortable way to meet other lesbians. I read an article where a woman said that when political lesbians get lonely they organize a group!

Based on these comments, it would appear that lesbians came to LAR with high expectations. LAR was the only organization of its kind in the city and as such, if one was interested in such an organization, there was no choice but to join LAR. As well, there was no place, outside of mixed gay bars, for lesbians to meet. Therefore, the social aspects of LAR took on added significance. Had there been a vibrant lesbian community, with its own institutions, LAR may not have been expected to remedy so many institutional deficiencies.

Thus, lesbians joined LAR for many different reasons which can be interpreted as reflecting institutional deficiencies. Specifically:

1. An oppressive social structure.
2. No ideology to satisfactorily analyze the oppression of lesbians or propose a satisfactory remedy.
3. No autonomous lesbian movement.
4. No organization allowing lesbians to express their politics.
5. No place for lesbians interested in politics to meet or socialize.
6. No public meeting places for lesbians only.

As noted above, the perception of an oppressive social structure is related to a larger theoretical argument — the institution of compulsory heterosexuality (Rich 1980, 631–60). This is an assumption implicit throughout society that all women are or want to be attached to a male. Since every aspect of the larger society operates on this assumption, lesbians have been rendered invisible. Stressing this argument, Adrienne Rich (1980) has observed:

> The assumption that "most women are innately heterosexual" stands as a theoretical and political stumbling block . . . lesbian existence has been written out of history or catalogued under disease; . . . it has been treated as exceptional rather than intrinsic; . . . to acknowledge that for women heterosexuality may not be a "preference" at all but something that has had to be imposed, managed, organized, propagandized, and maintained by force, is an immense step to take . . .

The institution of heterosexuality suppresses the expression of lesbianism. For example, one LAR member made reference to being expected to "stay in the closet". In that instance, the heterosexual groups she referred to did not seem to mind that she was lesbian, but they were not interested in helping her to be comfortable as a lesbian. The institution of heterosexuality, if it does not assume universal heterosexuality, at least makes it appear as though universal heterosexuality exists. It is this which oppresses lesbians, and which lesbians in LAR wanted to oppose.

The other perceptions can be understood by recognizing that theoretically, the lesbian community is a place to retreat from the larger society. Within the community, however, a number of deficiencies were perceived to exist. They may be summed up by saying that the lesbian community lacked sufficient resources to allow lesbians to counter their oppression. By becoming involved with LAR, lesbians demonstrated not only their opposition to the larger society, but also their dissatisfaction with the limiting conditions of their community.

IDEOLOGY

Ideology can be defined in a number of different ways. A common definition is that it is a systematic and rational system of ideas. With regard to social movements, a slightly different definition has been used: ". . . the value-system and the interpretation of events that is unique to a particular social movement" (Grevatt 1975, 206).

In studying LAR, the latter definition is more workable, as it focuses on values and interpretation, and recognizes ideology as firmly rooted in perceptions of past events.

The only time LAR had a discussion explicitly devoted to ideology was at its very first meeting. At that time, the following "basis of unity" was struck:

> We define ourselves as 1) a lesbian/feminist organization; 2) as activists working on social, political, and cultural events; and 3) as women identified-women who work together to fight the right-wing as lesbians from a lesbian perspective.

The statement was prepared prior to the meeting and presented to those assembled for approval. It met with widespread acceptance, as it proposed to remedy all of the deficiencies which were perceived by those assembled. With the use of such phrases as "lesbian/feminist", "right-wing" and "lesbian perspective", it was clearly an ideological statement. However, since it was designed for widespread approval, as a way to unite lesbians, it was too abstract and generalized to serve as a definitive ideology.

Individual members offered their own comments in an effort to overcome the shortcomings of LAR's "basis of unity". One said:

> From my perspective I saw LAR informing and politicizing the lesbian community on one hand and on the other participating in different things. I think it's extremely important not to lose sight of the general social movement; I don't think the liberation of lesbians will be achieved by lesbians alone. I think it's wrong to think that our liberation will come from only our own activity.

Another said:

> LAR has a very basic ideology which I think is that lesbians are oppressed in our society as lesbians as well as being oppressed as women, that hetero-sexism and homophobia are different from sexism, and because of that there is a need to fight against lesbian oppression autonomously.

These statements add to an understanding of the basis of unity. They do not assume that lesbian/feminism is a readily definable ideology, and they identify problems in concrete terms. Nevertheless, they are only individual conceptions. During LAR's first year of existence, ideology was not addressed by the group. It is suggested, therefore, that while individual members subscribed to certain ideologies, LAR as a whole had no ideology in the sense of an inclusive value system with which events could be interpreted. Rather than explicit, LAR's ideology was emergent.

To garner a sense of the emerging ideology, one may examine the perceptions which were shared by members.

Every member identified herself as a feminist, and thought of LAR as a feminist organization. It could be said, therefore, that

LAR's ideology is implicitly feminist. This definition, however, is problematic, particularly because not everyone in LAR had the same conception of feminism.

Most agreed with the feminist edict that oppression is a basic experience of women. Beyond that, however, there were various philosophies about what constitutes oppression, what to do about that oppression, and the feminist solution. For example, most members were aware of being discriminated against because of their femaleness, were aware of the social roots of discrimination, and wanted to do something to change the situation. They defined themselves, therefore, as feminists, but not all had thought through the implications of their beliefs.

Others approached feminism from a socialist perspective which meant that for them, the ideological point of departure was social class. Their solution was to create a radically changed, class-less society with women's concerns in the forefront. Still others defined themselves as radical feminists which meant that they were interested primarily in having all women unite to fight their oppression and overthrow patriarchy.

The emergent ideology was labelled lesbian/feminism, although no one was able to offer a definitive definition of what a lesbian/feminist was, other than she was a lesbian who subscribed to lesbian/feminism. One member's reason for calling herself a lesbian/feminist, which was typical of the others, was as follows:

> I call myself a lesbian/feminist because I'm a feminist who's also lesbian. I'm a feminist because I believe that men in general want to oppress me simply for being a women. But I'm a lesbian/feminist because I judge feminism according to how relevant it is to me as a lesbian.

Others, although they defined themselves as lesbian/feminists, cautioned that lesbian/feminism was still in the process of being defined, and that aside from a critique of the institution of heterosexuality, lesbian/feminism had little to say that was different from feminism. In fact, many said that their lesbianism and their feminism were inextricably linked. Presumably, it was different because it was about the politics of being lesbian, but as one noted:

> It's very difficult to talk about lesbian politics. People are much clearer about what are the roots, the nature and the extent of women's oppression in this society. There are certain things you can definitely point to. Whereas lesbian oppression is something I think that is still ill-defined. It's something where you don't have a series of demands where you can say, "Okay, this is what lesbians want."

Several members pointed out that the only thing which lesbians have in common is their lesbianism, and that even lesbianism could be experienced in different ways. Most LAR members experienced lesbianism in essentially the same way, which meant that they were aware that society discriminated against them, in part by assuming that all women are in some way attached to a male. By recognizing the institution of hetero-sexuality, therefore, and wanting to attack society on that basis, they all shared the beginnings of a common ideology.

Other ideological assumptions became apparent when members explained what they thought lesbian politics was, and the position of lesbians in society.

One said that lesbianism is the "epitome of women's invisibility". She believed that women were made invisible by the structure of the English language with its use of the word "he" and reference to "mankind" as the totality of humanity. Lesbians, she held, were even more invisible than women. They were not talked about even as male homosexuals were talked about, and in a visual sense, lesbians could not be distinguished from other women. For this member, the ideological starting point was that the existence of lesbians was rarely acknowledged which meant that lesbians, to a great extent, were invisible to society at large.

Another position was expressed as follows:

> There is no lesbian politics because an individual can subscribe to any political theory. But lesbian/feminist politics is an understanding of the real conditions of the world, which arises from the real conditions of the world. It's how to fight what the real world does to me not only as a woman but also as a lesbian. Also where it fits in with various attempts at humanizing the world that are going on.

In other words, her ideological starting point was that as a woman and as a lesbian, she found the conditions of the real world to be dehumanizing.

Others said that lesbian politics had to do with social sanctions against lesbianism, such as not being able to show affection in public. Another said that it had to do with attaching a positive meaning to the word "lesbian". She noted that in the early 1970s, many feminists were accused of being lesbians and in that manner, an attempt was made to stop women from uniting with each other to fight their oppression. Calling a woman a lesbian was a way of calling her womanhood into question and making women afraid to associate with each other. Lesbian politics, therefore, was about teaching lesbians that their lesbianism could be a source of pride and strength:

> I don't think of lesbian politics as negative, I think of it as positive. I like being a lesbian, and I want to emphasize what's good about it.

In general, each member stressed different ideological conceptions. They could agree on no systematic and unified lesbian/feminist theory. As will be argued later, this problem created organizational strains.

Goals and Strategy

LAR members had no problem with identifying what was wrong with society. Even though their collective ideology had not been fully articulated, most shared the same basic assumptions. In particular, they all recognized the institution of compulsory heterosexuality as oppressive.

LAR had no collective goals. Individual members had separately articulated goals, which were visions of how they wanted to reorganize the world. One member said:

> I think LAR's goal is to make a better world for lesbians, whether it's through getting our act together so that we can change the external world or whether it's just that we can make a little bit of it for ourselves better.... One of the problems is that LAR hasn't been able to articulate its ideology yet . . . lesbian/feminism is about as hard to define as you can get.

Others said that their goal was to radically change society. A representative comment was:

> The heterosexist assumptions that exist in society are very, very deep, you can see them everywhere. I don't see that we can change just one part of that. I think we have to change the whole thing, the whole way that this society works.

That everyone subscribed to a different ideological conception created a problem for formulating a clear-cut political strategy. That is, if lesbians considered themselves part of an autonomous lesbian movement, then they did not necessarily see heterosexual women as allies in their struggle to create a world where lesbians could be comfortable. Most LAR members subscribed to this view which meant that they spoke of the heterosexual women's movement as "they"; adversaries not to be trusted.

A minority, however, were adamant that there was no lesbian movement separate from the women's movement, but that there were only lesbian organizations within the women's movement. Those who subscribed to this view believed that all women, regardless of sexual preference, were potential allies in the struggle to end the oppression of women in general. This meant that they were more interested in working within the women's movement on issues of concern to all women, rather than focusing specifically on problems faced by lesbians.

In other words, the difference was that some saw themselves as having experiences that were fundamentally different from those of heterosexual women, while others did not see themselves as fundamentally different.

Shortly after LAR first formed, there was another dispute over strategy. The split was over whether LAR should, from the outset, be an action-oriented group, or whether it should concentrate on trying to formulate a clear conception of lesbian/feminist ideology.

One side of the argument was that because LAR was a new group with members who did not know each other well, it was important for theoretical discussions to take place before LAR participated in collective action. The other side of the argument was that if the group tried to theorize from the outside, disagreements would become apparent and lessen the possibilities of finding common ground. In favour of this latter position, several pointed out that neither analysis nor strategy could be developed in a vacuum. As one said:

> It's only through the concrete, practical application of our ideas that we're going to learn stuff and figure stuff out.

Another pointed out that "you learn by doing" and that talking on an abstract level was meaningless. This member believed that "actions speak louder than words."

LAR chose to be action oriented, hoping that politics would evolve through its actions. Those who strongly disagreed with the strategy left the group. All of those who stayed, however, were generally satisfied with the strategy and agreed that the actions had had the effect of providing common experiences that could be evaluated collectively.

The strategy of outwardly focused action had not been clearly mapped out. Although many were pleased with the direction which LAR took, they nevertheless were disappointed that LAR did not take enough time to consider in detail the pros and cons of participating in particular events, or set aside adequate time to evaluate and learn from actions. Rather, it seemed at times as though LAR was participating in events for the sake of participating in events, with no overall direction. One member, who fervently believed that "you have to do stuff in order to be able to enunciate your politics" said:

> I think it's always time to draw lessons from what you've done. There always has to be a balance between activism and evaluating what you've done. This is what theorizing is. I'm not sure that I think LAR has actually done enough of that.

Almost everyone was able to suggest alternative strategies. Many argued in favour of "building the lesbian/feminist case", or in other words, defining lesbian/feminism in concrete terms. Many were interested in using lesbian/feminism to educate those not familiar with it and to allow LAR to proselytize. In this vein, it was held to be of the utmost importance for LAR to develop an analysis and understanding of lesbian oppression. Others wanted to build a lesbian/feminist analysis of society which could be offered to "progressive" social groups in general, and hopefully integrated into the latter's ideology.

Others asserted that LAR should be writing down and distributing its thoughts on lesbian/feminism and what it had to do with, for example, the New Right. Actually, LAR had made a successful attempt at writing. A collection of speeches made when LAR first formed had been put into a pamphlet describing LAR. Most were extremely pleased with the pamphlet and wanted to see LAR do more of the same.

Miscellaneous strategies that were suggested included building and maintaining a strong lesbian presence in other groups and movements, helping to build a strong and unified lesbian community, sharing information with other lesbians to make them aware of issues and hopefully inspire them to take a stand. As discussed later, some of these strategies were adopted.

It was pointed out by several that the catalyst for the formation of LAR had been increased attacks from the New Right, yet LAR had not focused attention on the New Right. They believed that LAR should map out an ongoing struggle against the New Right. One member made concrete suggestions such as monitoring the New Right or finding ways to make their leaders uncomfortable.

Finally, several pointed out that the most important strategy, developing and unifying ideology, was being ignored. There was a lack of open and honest discussion during meetings. Members would give a personal opinion, or make a suggestion, without explaining the basis of the comment. Many sensed that their own ideological positions may not have been in accordance with the positions of others. Rather than ask for a discussion of ideology, however, risking the possibility of having to hash over and try to resolve potentially divisive disagreements, many found it easier to avoid such a discussion.

As a result, the general level of commitment to LAR suffered. Many remained highly committed to the possibilities of LAR, yet others reconsidered their earlier commitment. As one member pointed out:

> How can you be committed to LAR when you don't know what you're committing yourself to? If you don't know what LAR's going to do?

Many believed that LAR would be in a much stronger position if it would, instead of trying to be everything to everybody, look for the commonalities among individual ideologies and build upon them. Almost every member commented on feeling a sense of aimlessness and confusion and wondered which direction LAR would take. Yet openly addressing the confusion continued to be a tactic which was avoided. As a result, LAR remained without a clearly defined set of goals and lacked a unifying political strategy.

LEADERSHIP

The leadership role cannot be understood unless the structure of LAR is first examined. One of the most striking features of LAR was its lack of formal structure: it was informal and non-hierarchical.

There was never a desire at LAR for elected offices such as President or Chairperson. Members were in agreement that hierarchy is restrictive and inevitably authoritarian. They were pleased that LAR operated as a collective, where everyone's opinion (theoretically) carried equal weight, and decisions were not unilateral. As a collective, no one was allowed more power than anyone else.

LAR's distaste for formality was particularly evident when one examined how membership was determined. There was no official process whereby one joined LAR. Meetings were not closed; they were open to any lesbian who cared to attend. After attending a meeting, one had the right to call herself a member if she were so inclined.

A quasi-membership list existed, which included the names and telephone numbers of lesbians interested in attending meetings or participating in activities. To facilitate intragroup communication, members were provided with a copy of the list.

Ostensibly, the list was implemented merely to facilitate information sharing. In reality, however, it also served to give an idea of the size of LAR. When asked how many belonged to LAR, members frequently referred to the list and how many names were on it.

The essence of LAR's philosophy regarding power and structure achieved expression through the procedure followed for chairing meetings. Members took turns chairing. Rotating chairs were instituted at LAR not only to ensure that power was not always vested in the same person, but also to give every lesbian a chance to assume responsibility and learn how to use the temporary power for the good of the organization. The practice was also based on the assumption that any lesbian could be a "good" chairperson, but that it was a skill that must be learned and practiced. No one was forced to chair a meeting if she did not want to, but all were strongly encouraged to periodically chair meetings. In this manner, responsibility was shared and basic skills were acquired by all who wished to learn.

Meetings were semistructured, in that the agenda was drawn up beforehand by a predetermined chairperson. Standard procedures regarding items on the agenda were also followed. For example, meetings always began with announcements, followed by a reading of the minutes of the last meeting (minutes were not read for approval, but to provide continuity between meetings). The sequence of items for discussion was predetermined by the chairperson, although that sequence was not necessarily rigid.

Discussions were informal. One did not need to seek the chair's permission to speak, as it was expected that no one would interrupt anyone else. That expectation was not always valid, however, and frequently the chair was forced to implement a speaker's list as a means of keeping order and ensuring that everyone had a chance to voice their opinions.

Most members regarded the speaker's list as a necessary evil. On the one hand, it was sometimes the only way to avoid total anarchy, but on the other hand, its existence inhibited free-flowing discussion.

One member commented:

> I'm not an anarchist, at least when it comes to discussions. I believe there has to be some sort of order because otherwise it becomes a game of seeing who can talk the loudest and longest. But I don't like speaker's lists. I don't often speak when there's a speaker's list because sometimes I might want to comment on what someone's saying but by the time I get my chance to speak, a couple of other people have changed the subject and whatever I wanted to say is out of context. I think people in LAR should start taking

responsibility for keeping order themselves. They shouldn't expect the chair to do everything.

When decisions had to be made at LAR, they were not always voted on. There was an implicit assumption during discussions that silence meant agreement, so that if a suggestion was put forth, if no one voiced an objection it was assumed that there was agreement. Other times, decisions were reached on the basis of consensus. Often, when decisions were voted on, the count of "yes" versus "no" responses was not necessarily final. After the vote, if those who were outvoted still wished to argue their case, they were free to do so. No decision was considered final until all were willing to abide by it. In practice, this procedure meant that particularly contentious issues either never reached a final decision, or dissenting members left LAR.

This structure was legitimized by LAR's leadership. As one member noted: "structure comes from leadership." That is, it was her opinion that the structure of any organization is totally dependent upon its leadership, and that in looking at structure, one is in essence looking at leadership.

The issue of leadership was never discussed at LAR. Many members expressed frustration that the issue was ignored or disguised during meetings. They believed that by avoiding discussion, LAR was pretending that it was "one big happy family" when in fact, avoidance of the issue was creating dissention.

No one believed that because LAR had no formal leadership, there were no leaders. All recognized that there were unofficial leaders in LAR. There were, however, different interpretations about the reality of unofficial leadership.

Leadership came primarily from founding members, who, because of their past experience, were able to see issues more clearly than those with less experience. Not all of them consciously set themselves up as leaders, but they were nevertheless listened to with a great deal of respect for the ability to articulate issues clearly and put them in perspective. One "leader" had the following to say about this situation:

> . . . the leadership operates at the level of social influence. I don't think that's necessarily bad or unnatural. I'm fairly traditional and I like it when women who are older than me and know more things give direction, if it's done in a way that leaves things open for those with less experience to say what's on their minds, to make objections, to have input.

Other members concurred with the opinion that the more experienced members had a great deal to offer, and agreed that everyone should have the opportunity to express their opinions.

During the first few months of LAR's existence, it was primarily the "leaders" who contributed to discussions at meetings. There were several reasons for the virtual monopolization. One was that the "leaders", because they were sure of what they wanted and were able to articulate what they wanted, never hesitated to voice their opinions. Meanwhile, less experienced people did not feel confident enough to express an opinion. Another factor, however, and perhaps the more important one, was that the "leaders" had known each other prior to the formation of LAR. Generally speaking, they knew each other's thoughts on various issues and knew where there was agreement or disagreement. Additionally, since "leaders" frequently discussed issues amongst themselves, they sometimes brought "hidden agenda" to LAR meetings. Issues, although presented to the general membership for discussion, had in fact already been debated.

This situation put the "leaders" in a position of considerable power vis-à-vis the general membership. "Leaders" had easy access to each other, whereas the general membership usually did not see each other outside meetings (until they got to know each other well).

Many members expressed feelings of frustration about hidden agenda. Some felt that the "leaders", in spite of their experience, and in spite of the initiative they displayed, had no right to exclude any LAR member from discussions. Since they did, however, it appeared the "leaders" were not really interested in hearing the opinions of others, unless others happened to agree with them.

On the other hand, others felt that while hidden agenda were less than desirable, they were nevertheless inevitable and served an important function, particularly while LAR's existence remained on shaky ground. Without a small group of knowledgeable people to direct LAR in the beginning they argued, LAR could not have survived. Additionally it was not possible in the beginning for the "leaders" to include others in their private discussions, simply because they did not know who was willing and able to contribute. Debating amongst themselves was convenient and efficient. No one was certain of the direction LAR would take, and as the idea to form LAR came from the "leaders", they wanted to ensure that LAR evolved the way they wished.

Hidden agenda continued to appear throughout LAR's first year of existence, although as the months went on, this happened less frequently. This suggests that the leadership gradually became more responsible to the general membership.

Many members were concerned that LAR did not have

enough leaders. Their fear was based on the fact that several had dropped out of LAR over the year, and they were worried about the possibility of all of the "leaders" dropping out.

One "leader" took a philosophical approach to the problem of having less than a handful of people who were willing and able to lead. She believed that the problem was that too many people listened to the "leaders" in LAR but very few really understood why they said what they did. Few took the time to do their own careful thinking and analysis. As a result, new "leaders" were not coming forward within LAR, as she thought they should:

> I don't think people are really developing politically. Wanting to be a leader means you have to be willing to take the time and think and develop yourself. You don't just put yourself someplace and say, "Here, I'm a leader, follow me."

She believed that this was a basic problem at LAR, that people wanted the glory of being a leader, but were not willing to develop themselves. As well, she said that if people took the time, there would not be a leadership problem at LAR.

Another, speaking about leadership in general, concurred with the idea that leadership should evolve from within the group. She also concurred that leadership, ideally, should come from within the group:

> If people take a real interest in the group then they're going to think about the issues. That's part of what leadership is about.

> Unfortunately, I think leadership is seen too much in terms of having ideas and speaking about them. But if they don't also take care of the group and make sure it runs, then they're going to be a leader in the bad sense of the word. They're going to be a theoretician who says what's going to be done.

> Good leaders don't push anybody into anything. They take care of the group. A good leader puts the needs of the group ahead of her own particular views.

> A good chair can provide leadership. She can summarize the discussion that has just gone on and say, "Well, I think from the different views we've heard, then this is the consensus that's emerging." That is *so* valuable.

Generally speaking, members other than the founding members had little to say about the leadership role. Without exception, however, members wanted LAR to have more leaders. There was widespread fear of leadership becoming too centralized:

> I don't want one person doing all the political analysis or organizing.... The moment someone takes over a group I have to wonder about what she's doing because that means you think the only way it can work is with your leadership and direction. I can understand that kind of thing happening in a meeting but I don't think that kind of situation with one person carrying the ball should continue past that meeting.

Several members pointed out the responsibility that went with the leadership role, and suggested that people were wary of responsibility. If leadership were shared, then responsibility would be shared.

A few members were in favour of overt leadership. For them, efficiency was high on their list of priorities. That is, LAR was quite inefficient, and this was seen as a direct consequence of not having one person in charge to handle administration.

For example, without authority vested in one person, even to take care of emergencies, quick decisions could not be made. Time was wasted in drawn-out discussions, decisions were postponed, and when made, not followed up on, and the level of frustration was high. The level of frustration became accentuated when individual members had grievances, as there was no office for them to appeal to for redress. Lack of identifiable leadership also meant that leaders did not have to be accountable to the general membership for their actions.

The minority who emphasized these problems were aware of the pitfalls of overt leadership (such as the power struggles uppermost in the minds of those against it), but argued that it did not necessarily have to be destructive. Time wasting and lack of direction were enough of a problem that they were willing to sacrifice the benefits of collective decision making.

Significantly, every member had something to say about the lack of accountability at LAR, even as most said they would resist identifiable leadership. The rationale was that, ideally, there should be accountability to the group "just on general principles", with everyone taking responsibility for the smooth running of the group. Yet accountability was a major stumbling block, with no one clear about how to make sure that everyone answered to LAR for the way they carried out (or did not carry out) LAR's business.

Frequently, someone who had not been to a meeting for quite a while could come to a meeting, listen to the topic for discussion, and then proceed to swing the discussion to what she wanted to talk about, and in some cases, offer to take on a task. No one saw this as a problem if she then proceeded to attend meetings regularly and carry out her task. More often than not, however, members were irresponsible in that they took on tasks without following through. One member commented:

I think they [irresponsible members] should be confronted. There's two ways to look at it. You could say you're really interested but haven't been able to come, but really want to participate in discussions. . . . Then there's the other side of someone hasn't been around and comes in and starts asking what's going on and cutting us up for what we've done.

In sum, LAR lacked a definitive leadership structure; this situation contributed to fragmentation.

CHANNELS FOR COMMUNICATION AND NETWORK OF COOPERATIVE RELATIONSHIPS

From the beginning, LAR had had strong ties with others. Many members belonged to other organizations and when they came to LAR, brought their ties with them, so that LAR as a whole benefitted from a variety of contacts. As LAR began to establish itself, it began forming links with still other organizations, and participated in coalitions with numerous other groups. LAR became a member of broadly based organizations such as the Gay Community Council (GCC) and Citizen's Independent Review of Police Activities (CIRPA). Membership in the former allowed LAR to have a voice in matters regarding the gay community in general, while being represented on the board of CIRPA allowed LAR to have a voice in attempts to reform the police department and raise public awareness about what they saw as unjustified police brutality.

All hoped that these links would strengthen over time and that even more links would be developed, particularly with "grassroots" organizations. All shared the conviction that it was of crucial importance for LAR to stay in touch with what others were doing. No one believed that LAR could be an effective political voice in isolation.

While all valued the contacts LAR had made during its first year, many expressed the hope that LAR would in future be more selective in deciding which groups to work with. The high level of activity gave LAR a high profile and established its credibility (which for many, was an end in itself), but the cost in terms of time and energy had been high. Members wanted in future to have more time to evaluate activities.

Many said that they would like to continue working with all the other groups, but felt that because LAR was relatively small, it would be of more value to define priorities and not try to do everything at once. During the first year, priorities had not been defined; rather, LAR worked with almost every group that had asked. As one member said: "it should be quality that defines who LAR works with, not quantity."

One of the aims shared by founding members had been to maintain a lesbian/feminist presence in anti-establishment politics. These members had previously been active on their own in promoting lesbian visibility. They joined forces in the hope that together, they would make more of an impact on other organizations. As one explained:

> We wanted one of the important parts of LAR to make people aware of lesbian/feminism and to make a lesbian/feminist intervention into the broader political community. . . . I saw LAR as the kind of organization that would go into other organizations and ask questions. Challenging the progressive community on its positions on women and lesbians.

Despite this desire, which was shared not only by the majority of founding members but by others as well, the actual logistics of an interventionist policy were never clearly mapped out or discussed. LAR initiated very few actions. A cynical comment was that everyone in LAR seemed to be waiting for someone else to start something. Everyone wanted to participate but few were willing to do the organizational work involved in planning actions. The precedent of responding to what was already going on, had been set in the first few weeks of LAR's existence.

LAR and Other Lesbians

Most members agreed that if LAR was a group of, by, and for lesbians, then it should be integrated into the lesbian community. The general feeling was that if LAR could not be part of the community from which it originated, then its efforts were in vain. The issue, however, is extremely problematic, especially since there is no universally accepted definition of the lesbian community.

Every lesbian, when she speaks of "the lesbian community" attaches a personal meaning to the term. The person she is speaking to, however, does not necessarily subscribe to the same meaning. For instance, when LAR members were asked to describe what they thought the lesbian community was, answers were as varied as:

> I think the lesbian community is more of a wish or a hope than an actuality.
> It is possible to constitute a lesbian community. It is not a pregiven entity.

The lesbian community has been built over the last ten or fifteen years and I see it as a process of still being built.

Another explained:

There's the lesbian community and then there's the lesbian community. The lesbian community is an interconnection, web or network very loosely tied, of lesbians and women who are women-identified-women. There are also lesbians who have nothing to do with the community but know about it through the few articles in the paper or this or that. And then there's the lesbian community or communities that's worldwide. There's lesbians living as lesbians and there's lesbians living in a closet in the suburbs.

Another maintained:

I don't think there is a community in the true sense of the word. I think there's a bunch of cliques and some of them happen to be interconnected through friendship.

A fourth member added:

The lesbian community is amorphous. It consists more of festivals and cultural events.

Many noted the fragmentation of the community. There were lesbians who went to bars as their only contact with the community, lesbians who only came in contact with the community at cultural events, lesbians who rarely went to bars or cultural events but socialized only with their own circle of friends, lesbians who were well-informed on community events, lesbians who worked in the women's movement, lesbians who worked only with other lesbians. The only commonality was that all were lesbians.

Given that almost every LAR member identified herself as a well-informed lesbian interested in working specifically with other lesbians, it is evident that LAR could not be considered representative of the lesbian community. Actually, no one in LAR believed it was representative. Many, however, expressed the desire for LAR to be more broadly based within the community.

For example, there were many lesbians active in various movements, such as the antinuclear movement or the women's movement, who never went to LAR meetings and displayed only a passing interest in LAR. One member complained:

There are a lot of experienced lesbian/feminists in this city who don't come to LAR. I'm not saying lesbians have to give up everything and come to LAR meetings, but certainly they could participate in our events or occasionally drift into a meeting. It concerns me.

For many, a more broadly based organization also meant having more of an impact upon the lesbian community. While it was recognized that LAR was well known, at least among lesbians interested in community events, it was also recognized that most non-LAR members had only a vague idea of LAR's goals.

Gaining the support, if not the active participation of more lesbians, was something that LAR implicitly recognized as necessary. As one member said: "We have to develop a constituency in the lesbian community." If LAR considered itself an organization for the benefit of all lesbians, then it had a responsibility to stay in touch with those lesbians who were either unwilling or unable to join LAR themselves:

> While it's true that LAR as an organization of twenty-five women could do political work and not really attempt to bring the lesbian community along, I think we have to be careful about that. If we were to sort of go off on our own, there would be a lot of lesbians left behind.

While LAR did not focus on the lesbian community during its first year, it nevertheless organized a number of events for the exclusive benefit of the lesbian community. For example, there was not, at the time, a way for lesbian groups in general to communicate or keep in touch with each other. LAR sponsored, therefore, a workshop which laid the groundwork for the establishment of the Lesbian Network, designed to facilitate communication and the sharing of information among lesbians. In general, LAR was proud of its attempt to break down the isolation of lesbians and lesbians groups, thereby taking a step towards unifying the community.

LAR also made attempts to bring its politics to the lesbian community. For some, this was a very important aspect of LAR's work:

> One of our major goals is to educate and politicize the lesbian community.

In particular, LAR organized Toronto's first lesbian march. To quote LAR's pamphlet:

> We organized Toronto's first lesbian pride march so that lesbians could openly declare our pride and power, happily and without fear. Political dykes, street dykes, bar dykes, gay women, lesbian mothers, socialist feminists, radical feminists, lesbians separatists, working women . . . were

all there, enjoying the bright sun and blue sky. . . . Of course, not every lesbian in Toronto was able and willing to go on the march. But many hundreds heard about it, and as one woman said at the dance later that evening: "I'm a teacher and couldn't go to the march. But I'm so glad it went well!" After it was over, we all knew that it was indeed possible to express ourselves as powerful, visible lesbians, and we were a little less afraid (Gottlieb 1982, 31).

In addition, LAR held a National Day of Action, inviting all lesbians to join in the cultural events and political discussions.

The success of the events which LAR organized for other lesbians (as measured by the numbers who had attended from a variety of backgrounds), led members to be confident that they were making inroads into gaining the support of a variety of lesbians.

Despite internal organizational strains and leadership fragmentation, LAR was able to utilize its numerous contacts to be an effective organization of mobilization.

LAR IN PERSPECTIVE

Summarizing LAR's first year of existence, a member noted:

I think generally that LAR has been much more successful than I ever imagined, in terms of how we've managed to hang together in spite of rough times, and with a fair amount of integrity.

In assessing LAR's ability to "hang together" in spite of "rough times", this paper addressed a number of questions. What motivated lesbians to form LAR? Did everyone have the same reason for joining LAR? How did ideology manifest itself? What form did LAR take, and how did leadership manifest itself? Through what networks was LAR linked to the outside world? What organizational strains emerged and what were the implications of these strains? Finally, how effective was LAR as a political force fighting against oppression?

Lesbians were feeling vulnerable because of the oppressive conditions of the larger society and the lack of resources in the lesbian community. Although there were variations in the individual motivations for joining, there was one central condition which led to its formation — dissatisfaction with the existing social structure.

The lack of unifying ideology, however, and the failure to address the issue, meant that there were various conceptions of theory, goals and strategy. LAR's "basis of unity", defined at its first meeting, provided a sense of group identity, but did not go far enough in identifying problems and outlining solutions.

Among the members, there were various interpretations of both feminism and lesbian/feminism. There was also a difference of opinion regarding whether LAR should work inside or outside the women's movement. There was no agreement on goals and strategies. Aimlessness and confusion resulted, and many left the organization.

LAR's distaste for formality meant that strong leadership was discouraged. Yet strong, visible leadership was clearly what LAR was in need of. The unofficial leadership which existed could only operate on the basis of informal patterns of social influence. With the use of hidden agenda and the monopolization of discussions, leadership was manipulative.[4] The informality of LAR's structure created a lack of accountability. This, in turn, meant that LAR could not count on the presence of leadership.

On the positive side, a basis of political mobilization was emerging from the assumptions shared by members. That is, the establishment of networks of cooperative relationships, and the maintenance of open communication channels, were implicitly assumed to be important. LAR's strength lay in the ability to gather support from the lesbian community, as well as in its connections with other organizations.

Mobilizing others, however, is only a means to an end. The organization and its objectives remained amorphous. Unless LAR addresses the strains which emerged, its effectiveness as a powerful, political force fighting oppression will continue to be undermined.

Clearly, LAR could benefit from a manifesto, and must make a choice in its focus. That is, LAR cold focus on common ideological assumptions, or it could focus on ideological differences. Should LAR choose the latter, it is likely that many will leave. Either way, LAR would be left with a core of individuals committed to concrete goals.

Additionally, strong, visible leadership is warranted. Authority need not be unilateral, but such leadership could do much to direct LAR towards the achievement of goals, and improve morale.

Notes

1. I am grateful to all of the members of LAR who took the time to share their views with me, to make this study possible. I am also grateful to friends who wish to remain anonymous, for helpful comments and criticisms on previous

drafts of this paper. Finally, I owe special thanks to my supervisor, Professor Dennis Magill, Department of Sociology, University of Toronto, for advising me with respect to organization at all stages of this paper, and for helpful comments and criticisms.

2. Shortly after the formation of LAR, GLARE changed its name to Gay Liberation Against the Right Everywhere to reflect the lack of lesbian members.

3. As a member of LAR, attending all meetings, I did not encounter problems which many researchers face such as difficulty in gaining access to the group or lack of credibility and trust during interviews.

4. In J. Freeman, "The Tyranny of Structurelessness," in *Radical Feminism,* eds., A. Koedt and E. Levine (New York: N.Y. Times Book Co., 1973), it is argued that hidden leadership is more manipulative than formal leadership and that democracy cannot exist without structure (pp. 285-89).

References

Brooks, V. 1981. *Minority stress and lesbian women.* Lexington: Mass.: Lexington.

Bruner, A. 1981. *Out of the closet: Study of relations between the homosexual community and the police.* Report to Major Arthur Eggleton and the Council of The City of Toronto.

Clark, S., J. Grayson, and L. Grayson (Eds.). 1975. *Prophecy and protest: Social movements in twentieth-century Canada.* Toronto: Gage Educational Publishing Limited.

Ettore, E. 1980. *Lesbians, women and society,* London: Routledge and Kegan Paul.

Freeman, J. 1973. The tyranny of structurelessness. In A. Koedt and E. Levine (Eds.), *Radical Feminism.* New York: N.Y. Times Book Co.

Gottlieb, A. 1982. The gay movement. In *Lesbians are Everywhere Fighting the Right,* Pamphlet produced by LAR, 9.

Grevatt, M. 1975. Lesbian/feminism: A response to oppression. Ph.D. Diss., Case Western Reserve University.

Krieger, S. 1982. Lesbian identity and community: Recent social science literature. *Signs: Journal of Women in Culture and Society* 8(1) fall, 91–108, esp. 105.

Lesbians Against the Right. 1982. *Lesbians are everywhere fighting the right.* Pamphlet produced by LAR.

Ponse, B. 1978. *Identities in the lesbian world: The social construction of self.* Westport, Conn.: Greenwood.

Rich, A. 1980. Compulsory heterosexuality and lesbian existence. *Signs: Journal of Women in Cultural and Society* 5(4) Summer.

Sheppard, P. and D. White. 1981. *Report on police raids on gay steambaths.* Submitted in Toronto City Council for its Meetings of 26 February.

Steiger, B. and L. Weir. 1981. Lesbian movement: Coming together in a hot gym. *Broadside* 2(10) August/September.

Chapter 9

Tramps, Tricks and Troubles: Street Transients and Their Controls

L.A. Visano*

STREET COMMUNITIES: NETWORKS OF THE "DISAFFILIATED"

Introduction

Interest in street communities is not new. Their genealogy and persistence over time and place is well documented (Katz 1976; Bruns 1970; Brandon et al. 1980). This literature, however, on street communities is replete with many muddled and sketchy assumptions which must be replaced by empirically based knowledge of the place of these communities in urban society. Pathogenic approaches have long argued for the salvation of this "lost" community which must be refashioned to facilitate control. Ordering the activities on the street has become a constant problem for modern urban communities (Pearson 1979, 156; Cohen 1980).

The theme that persists in the literature stresses the disaffiliated state of the people who literally live off the streets whether it involves the masses sleeping on the sidewalks of Calcutta, the squatters of West Berlin or the young hustlers of New York's Times Square. It is this disaffiliation that has rendered them dangerous. In fact, the nineteenth century did not speak of this miscellaneous lot of vagabonds, paupers, squatters, runaways,

---

* Ph.D. Candidate, Department of Sociology, University of Toronto.

throwaways, petty thieves, prostitutes, as deviant but a "dangerous" (Pearson 1979, 148). Prowling on the confines of a docile,
frightened order (Foucault 1977, 301), these social nomads,
homeless outcasts (Booth 1930, 405), these multiple deprivation
populations "undermined the very fabric of a city" (Cohen 1980).
They were seen as hard-core drop-outs (Lupsha 1969) who had no
place in the class hierarchy (Thomas and Znaniecki 1958, 1920:
136) and threatened the social relations of production in capitalist
societies (Spitzer 1975, 642). As Charles Booth commented:

> Their life is the life of savages, with vicissitudes of extreme hardship and
> occasional excess. They render no useful service, they create no wealth,
> more often they destroy it. They degrade whatever they touch; and as
> individuals are perhaps incapable of improvement (1930, 404).

In light of their elusive sociality, fluidity and absence of territorial
fixing, they were not utilizable (Procacci 1978, 64). They failed to
proletarianize (Pasquino 1978, 42).

Interestingly, neither labour nor capital was interested in
advancing the concerns of these communities (Cohen, P. 1979,
125). For Marxists, these groups are fundamentally reactionary.
In a revolutionary situation they would remain apathetic or
become mercenary in the services of the bourgeoisie (Matza 1975,
200). In elaborating upon the conditions and constitutions of the
lumpenproletariat, Fanon notes that these hordes of starving
men, uprooted from their clan (1968, 129) are unable to find a
market for their labour and turn to stealing, debauchery, etc. This
lumpenproletariat which endangers the security of the town and
is a sign of irrevocable decay consists of "classless idlers, hopeless
dregs of humanity" (Fanon 1968, 130). These pimps, hooligans,
unemployed, petty criminals, Fanon adds, are "like a horde of rats;
you may kick them and throw stones at them, but despite your
efforts they'll go gnawing at the root of the tree" (1968, 130).

Historically, these idle rogues were seen as a threat to the
larger society (Giffen 1970, 244) precisely because they were
"disconnected" from normal social control. Street communities
were seen as having no long-term investment in the local community. Their independence and nomadism challenged the
existing order and had to be pacified (Donzelot 1979, 71–72). They
existed in the crevices or the margins of modern society (Matza
1975, 199). Although they were affected by various urban systems
— market economy, housing, education, welfare, etc., (Siegel
1977, 88) their levels of participation in these systems were
restricted, unstable and minimal.

What emerges from this extensive literature on street populations is the simple, and hence all the more seductive, theme of dangerous disaffiliation. This theme has been advanced in supporting their social disorganization. As we learn from Suttles, this outcast and stigmatized community consisting of new residents, ex-felons, aliens and transients fails not only to participate fully in its own governance, but also retreats out of shame, fear, and absence of faith (1972, 239). Essentially, the implications remain normative in that unlike other income groups, this outcast population has freed itself from prevailing value systems. A related normative dimension is provided in the very definition of homelessness which stresses "the absence or attenuation of affiliative bonds that link settled persons to a network of interconnected social structures" (Caplow et al. 1968b, 494). That is, their homelessness connotes a fundamental detachment from societal values and social bonds. For Merton, vagrants, transients, homeless, etc., respond to the strains generated by the disjuncture between societally prescribed goals and available means for achieving these goals by retreatism (1957, 153). This retreatism is further characterized by a weakening or absence of affiliations. Although freed from conventional controls this population was nonetheless treated as territorially confined.

Limited support, for this notion of a spatially confined defeated community, exists in studies of skid row (Wallace 1968; Whitney 1970, 72). Friendship patterns persist only as long as the bottle is shared (Fischer 1976a, 138). In her seminal study of skid row, Wiseman rejects outright the argument that this community is bound by geography (1979, XVII). Rather, members of this street community enjoy dispersed patterns of settlement and adapt equally well to other settings (Lee 1980, 104). Clearly, extensive informal networks, not necessarily limited to a few neighbourhood areas, exist among transients (Caplow 1940; Christian 1973, 52; Cohen 1980, 83; Cohen and Sokolovsky 1981). Generally, street communities involve extensive, loose, permeable, elaborate connections (Carmichael 1975). These homeless, unemployed and transient urbanites are members of interdependent and interrelated social networks. The persistence of street life, in many cases, is structured by the nature and strength of linkages. The partners to an interaction on the street are usually in the same social world and do expect their paths to cross again. These relationships are not fleeting (Merry 1980, 59). Obviously, some contacts may be fluid and diffuse, while others are tight, intense and frequent. Often, there is a tendency for ties based on one kind of relationship to expand, so that the relationship becomes multistranded (Craven and Wellman 1973, 35ff).

With respect to youths living on the street, there are considerable kinds of territorial movements, both temporary and permanent, over various distances (Marchand 1979, 65). When not required to be at home, youths have a capacity to cover larger territories. In turn, they disperse, form and maintain new ties. It is important to note that distance remains a minor barrier for mobile populations in pursuit of their specialized interests (Lee 1979, 181; Farley and Hansel 1981, 40). Continuous population flows do not necessarily erode the sense of community (Friday and Hage 1976, 354).

The Question of Size

Generally, street communities can be found in every urban centre and in almost every part of the city (Bird 1981, 1; Cuff 1981, 2.) Membership is not restricted to any age (Johnson 1981, 10; Marchand 1979, 97), sex (Maychak 1981, 1), or socio-economic backgrounds (Dean 1981, 10). Although statistics tend to be unreliable on a population that usually escapes official counting, some rough estimates have been provided. Anderson estimated that during the winter months of the 1920s the Chicago homeless-man population attained a magnitude of 75,000 (1923, 3). Kearns (1981, 127) notes that the current size of London's homeless families who are awaiting government assisted units is 200,000. Counts of other homeless populations remain conservative — for New York City, 36,000 (Bird 1981, 1); Washington at 10,000; Baltimore, 9,000; Boston, 8,000 (O'Toole 1981, 16), to name only a few cities.

This situation has undoubtedly been exacerbated by increasing unemployment rates and increased programs of de-institutionalization especially from mental hospitals. Approximately 30 percent of the 14,000 annually discharged from Ontario psychiatric hospitals have no place to go (Maychak 1981, A12; Malarek 1980, 5; Scrivener 1981, D5). The size of Metro Toronto's homeless population, considered to be one of the largest skid-row populations in North America, ranges from 10,000 (Whitney 1970, 66) to 3,000 (Maychak 1981, A12).

Likewise, the size of the transient youth population has been subject to various estimates. Throughout Canada's early colonial history, well over 100,000 homeless children were shipped from England to Canada mostly to work (Spina and Hagerty 1979, 31, 82). In 1932, a Chicago University research team reported for the Children's Bureau that there were probably 200,000 juvenile hobos roaming the American highways and railroads (Minehan

1934). In the early 1970s there were a million runaway children in the U.S.A. with an average age of fourteen (Ward 1978, 55). In fact, in 1973, 150,000 to 200,000 persons under seventeen were arrested as runaways (F.B.I. 1973, 131, 134; Sandhu 1977, 123). Countless others were not formally processed nor even reported to the police. Official estimates of the number of vagrant children from 1975 in London were held to be between 25,000 and 30,000. In their "juveniles sweeps" of London's West End, a dozen a week, usually the least resourceful kids are rounded up and sent home. But another twenty-five arrive in London daily (Ward 1978, 64). In Canada a conservative estimate maintains that 30,000 young people are on the road (*Toronto Star* 14 December 1974, B1). In Metro Toronto, 2,000 runaway children are reported annually to the police. Ninety percent of these youths escape from institutions or group homes declared by authorities to be for "their care and protection" (Marchand 1979, 98). The number of under-age runners, sixteen years and under, keeps pace with the increase in population. It usually represents a little over 0.03 percent of the total population (Carey 1976, F1). One inner city youth agency recently reported counselling 2,264 young males from 5 August 1980 through 31 December 1980 (Stone 1981, T5). Gay hustlers between ages of fifteen and twenty along Yonge Street alone, represent well over two hundred transients (Jackson 1981, 7).

Recruiting Networks: "Getting Connected"

To the outsider, the street community appears to involve an increasing isolation and deviation from societal values. To the "street kid", however, getting connected and staying connected are fundamental processes of "survival". As we learn from their accounts (file S9; file S10), the most basic communal characteristic is invariably expressed in terms of survival activities — "making it on the street scene" (field notes, 24 June 1981).

Clearly, life on the streets is trouble laden. Were it not for the many difficulties on the street, it would not be necessary to immediately seek the aid of others. Young migrants to large urban centres quickly discover what help is available in and out of trouble (Farrell 1974, E1). Given their limited work experience, even in unskilled jobs (Harris 1973, 27), and their limited education, street kids must find quick ways to feed, house, and clothe themselves (Maloney 1979) while at the same time avoiding official detection. They have available to them various indispensable structures (Fischer 1976, 149) for attaching themselves to the street. From the outset, the newcomer is typically supplied with a set of inter-personal linkages usually with similarly circumstanced others who help manage the transition (Bogdan 1976, 204). These networks serve as mediating structures (Smith 1979, 174) in facilitating the "adjustment" to new conditions.

Moreover, few newcomers whether they happen to be run-aways or throwaways make their journeys to urban centres in complete isolation with no place to go. In the absence of kinship attachments, these migrants often come under the auspices of friends or acquaintances from their former towns (Tilly and Brown 1967). Generally, many are apprenticed in or familiar with the activities of street before actually hitting the pavements (Wells 1980; Johnson 1981, 10; Dean 1981, 11; files S9, S10, S11). High school counsellors have reported a widespread knowledge of hustling as a source of money, escape, or both, among teenagers (Gandy and Deisher 1970). Likewise, many street prostitutes for example, report having known someone on a fairly intimate basis who was involved in this occupation before they themselves "turned out" (Bryan 1965, 287; Gray 1973, 410).

Friendship-based, and to some extent acquaintance-based, networks provide many benefits. Considerable information is shared concerning the accessibility of sources of help. Assistance is given regarding accommodation — squatting, shelters, hostels, etc.; food; protection from official agencies; as well as direct support, companionship and sociability (Srivaslava 1963; Liebow 1967; Tannenbaum 1974).

A finely tuned communications network awaits them through which vital information travels among transients on the street, alleys, in pinball arcades, coffeeshops, fast-food restaurants, shopping malls, etc. These networks locate, mobilize and maintain resources which, in turn, structure their routes and pathways (Hooker 1961). Although they lack the cohesiveness and formal-ness of kin-based networks, these contacts are highly adaptable and succeed in reducing the anxieties of newcomers. Even twelve year olds with limited street experience, according to Marchand (1979, 65), quickly realize the importance of these networks.

Less-experienced newcomers come to the attention of many inviting and supporting networks (Prus and Sharper 1977; Maloney 1979). This recruitment, which refers to the attempts of others who facilitate "embeddedness" (Prus and Irini 1980, 259) on the street, occurs in a variety of ways. Usually the more seasoned street hustlers befriend and "take under their wings" (Marchand 1979, 97) these newcomers for a host of different reasons ranging from a genuine concern for their new "sisters and brothers" (personal communication, S9, S10), to establishing credit for later repayment. These "experienced" will orient the neophytes to various techniques (Brown 1965, 159; Harris 1973, 39, 29). As Chin describes, "A lot of street kids when they see someone new on the street will observe for a while. They they'll go over and get to know him" (*Globe and Mail* 22 December 1979, 4).

Newcomers also actively seek out persons "in the life" by hanging around and introducing themselves to quick new contacts (Carey 1976, F1). Alternatively, they may gravitate to a group or a person who "offers a measure of security in an alien city" (Adler 1975, 71). Gay hustlers may find their way to gay territories where they will be shown how to dress, approach cars, and watch out for the police (Lee 1978, 208). They may learn, for example, that patrons of leather bars tend to form more closely knit networks than those of regular gay bars (Lee 1979, 81). Generally, hustlers become connected with the help of "friends of friends" (Prus and Irini 1980, 56).

Thus a certain esprit de corps exists on the street. Many of their social contacts centre around those people living off the streets (Gagnon 1968, 594). As Herman Gossfeld, a twenty-two year old hustler in Winnipeg comments: "A lot of people here are friends . . .They've learned to get along. There's a bond between them no matter about their drug problem, their alcohol problem" (Johnson 1981, 10).

Staying Connected

As with many other adolescent friendship patterns, recruitment to street life occurs from a variety of social categories. Homophily (Cohen 1979/80) remains relatively unimportant as a basis for interaction. Although street networks tend to be differentiated, specialized and segregated (Cohen 1980, 85), there are numerous overlapping activities (James 1977, 191) with considerable cross-cutting links (Ward 1978, 62). One such activity on which the street places a high premium — hustling — involves a "multiplicity of ties" (Frankenberg 1966, 17). Briefly, hustling is a comprehensive term denoting many methods of securing a meagre subsistence (Krisberg 1974, 117) for some; and a measure of financial independence for others (Butts 1947; Finestone 1964, 281; Harris 1973: Maloney 1979: Jackson 1981, 7). These activities may include gambling (Polsky 1969), theft, burglary or robbery. But on the street, hustling refers usually to public order offences, notably sexual procurement — solicitation (Ross 1959; Deisher et al. 1969; Coombs 1974; Maloney 1979; Symanski 1981), the purveying of light drugs (Carmichael 1975), or simply panhandling. According to Carmichael, these informal income opportunities are based on a criminal's

> loosely structured sub rosa network comprised of local and migrant criminals flanked on one side by professionals and more organized criminals, and on the other side by essentially pre-criminal youths who are only minimally involved in crime (1975, 141).

Many of these lightweight street hustlers (Sutter 1970, 80) drift into and identify with illicit activities for the express purpose of acquiring money or favours. They remain fairly marginal not only to conventional life-styles but also to criminal careers (Carmichael 1975, 143). Basic to hustling are the processes of locating targets, promoting investments and developing contacts (Prus and Sharper 1977; Prus and Irini 1980, 10). Although the lifestyle appears individualistic in orientation (Gillespie 1974, 279; Krisberg, 1974, 123), involvements with the support from certain links are crucial. Within this "shadow system of values" (Liebow 1967, 213), ties are essential in "learning the ropes" (Maloney 1979, 95), "taking the edge" (personal communication, S9) and in developing a repertoire of manipulative techniques (Harris 1973; Carmichael 1975, 147).

Many young transients have few assets to exploit. It is not surprising that one of them is catering to the sexual tastes of others (Adler 1975, 71; Ward 1978, 62). In return, they are provided with food (Budgen 1981, 9), a place to sleep, drugs, money (Harris 1973) and even love. As one hustler described

> They'd hustle for anything, maybe just some sniff — like a bottle of glue or nail polish . . . maybe money or drugs. In the winter they'd go with guys just so they'd let them sleep in the cars (Johnson 1981, 10).

The most common forms of street prostitution involve females to males (Laner 1974, 408), and males to males (Maloney 1979, 25). Within these sexual marketplaces (Corzine and Kirby 1979, 574) the granting of sexual access on a relatively indiscriminate basis for repayment (Gagnon 1968, 592–98) is made without obligation or commitment (Hooker 1965, 97). Many of these activities lack a cohesive organization and do not have direct connections with organized crime. Young gay hustlers usually connect with older men, especially those from another community, who do not have time to establish contacts. These hustlers are chosen, among other reasons, for their youthfulness (Harris 1973, 113) and for the fact that they protect the identity of their clients (Ross 1959, 15). Gay hustlers, however, enjoy a low status in the gay community (Ross 1959; Bruner 1980) and are often deprecated even by those who use them (Lee 1978, 203).

Violence, robbery, extortion and blackmail are associated with a few hustlers, known generally as "rough trade" (Ross 1959, 15–16; Humphreys 1979, 98). Those in this trade are defiantly "straight" (Coombs 1974; Lee 978, 209) and deny vehemently any enjoyment of these acts (Reiss 1979; Maloney 1979; Marchand 1979, 100). Instead they may brag about luring a "trick" into some alley or his residence and then turn on him with a couple of buddies lying in wait to help assault him and relieve him of his wallet and watch (Marchand 1979, 100; Reiss 1979).

Interestingly, hustling whether in the form of panhandling, prostitution, or drug dealing provides a source of revenue for a network of persons involved in the hustler's role set (Laner 1974, 417). Successful hustlers frequently share their earnings with those with whom they happen to "hang together". As one sixteen year old, Lee, reported (S9):

> The things I do are trying to help my street friends — other kids I go out at night with. My friends, in my head, are first all the time. I help them — they help me especially when I'm in a jam with the cops. I support about two or three, maybe four.

This "network of friends" (Ginsberg 1967; Humphreys 1979, 109) is involved in exchanging skills and capital. Despite the absence of gangs or structured groups (Harris 1973), drugs, accommodation, clothing, etc., will often be shared.

The accessibility to various contacts carries serious implications of how trouble is defined and regulated. The nature of links influence plans of action (Kahne and Schwartz 1978, 472; Levine et al. 1979, 484) and the sense of control in the transients' environments. Having recourse to a great number of informal personal links enhance these urbanites' access to and control of "street knowledge". This street knowledge involves general information on different activities, expectations, client contacts, coping strategies and manipulations which serve to minimize risks (Prus and Irini 1980, 240; Marchand 1979, 100). Street wisdom (Cressey 1932, 94) eventually becomes refined with the help of the well-seasoned travellers (Carey, 1976, F1). Street-smart kids will show a remarkable capacity not only to survive but also to sustain their morale and sense of adventure, resilience and resourcefulness (Wells 1980, 216).

Successful "self packaging" entails the development of a particular "vocabulary of motives" (Mills 1940, 904), and techniques of neutralization. These manipulations exist to deliver the required impressions — deviance disavowal, scapegoating, active defenses, rationalizations, etc. Many "wise" hustlers are astutely aware of the "outside" social order (Finestone 1964, 297). They become adept in "sizing up" outsiders — clients, police and social workers. In fact many learn to expect inferior services from these outsiders and remain especially hostile to them (Polsky 1969, 63; personal communication S9). The seasoned street kid will exchange experience and information with newcomers to the street for money. Billy, an eighteen year old regular described:

> You're always dealing. I'm not the Salvation Army — I'll help a new kid but he better give me something — his coat, his home address, welfare money, anything. I'll teach him the rip-offs and scams. I'm not going to tell him everything. I'll give him names (file S14).

Many seasoned hustlers manage the hazards of their environment by maximizing the information they have about the people they confront at the same time as they minimize the information they give out about themselves (Merry 1980, 172).

Within the street community, members do not interact with everyone in their networks with the same intensity. There are a number of different and continually intersecting networks. As Van Pouke describes, they may be sentiment, interest, or power networks (1979/80, 184).

Within the sentiment network relationships are based on the ends of social action whether for love, friendship or companionship. Actors will often subdue self-interest motives in these relatively fixed, durable and close-knit links. Those with strong bonds are less likely to view themselves as deviant even though they may be involved in sustained patterns of delinquency. For example, Lee, a street transient, has seen her "buddies" daily for six months (S9). They will share the same evaluations of people that their friends have, regardless of whether they've met them.

Interest networks tend to be more prevalent on the street. They are formed as a means to some specific ends — food, shelter, contacts (Granovetter 1973; Van Pouke 1979/80, 185). Once attained, there's no longer the necessity to prolong the relation on a continued basis. Bonds appear and disappear quickly. But many single-stranded ties, based on links with specific instrumental contents, have a tendency to become multi-stranded (Craven and Wellman, 1973). In essence, different social networks elicit different patterns of response for its members. Likewise, network salience varies with the issues at hand and the activities pursued.

Where diffuse, generalized help is available from those with whom one is familiar, there exists little pressure to look beyond one's informal network (Tannenbaum 1974, 42; Ward 1978, 62). When sufficient support is not imminent from their contacts, there follows a greater probability that transients will fall into the hands of formal agents — notably the police and/or social workers. Almost invariably, they subsequently undergo humiliation, they submit to inquiries regarding their street life-style, and eventually become impugned with low moral character. In spite of the "hand-outs" of social services agencies, they are often objects of distrust and exploitation (Mann 1968, 26). A myriad of organizational factors militate against the acceptance of most agencies by street transients — size, impersonality, rigid criteria, endless circle of referrals, lack of understanding, etc. Even after relinquishing control to many agencies, street kids soon discover that they are often declared ineligible for assistance. Others may be unwilling to accept the assistance on the conditions in which it is offered (Goetschius and Tash 1967).

As will later be elaborated there are sharp contrasts among

1. transients who are generally well-connected on the street including links with outside, formal regulative agencies,
2. transients who are generally well-connected on the street excluding links with outside, formal regulative agencies,
3. transients who are generally poorly connected on the street but are linked with outside, formal regulative agencies, and
4. transients who are generally poorly connected on the street as well as little/no ties with outside, formal regulative agencies.

Admittedly, as Jacobs notes, public peace on the streets is "kept primarily by an intricate, almost unconscious network of voluntary controls — and standards among the people" (1961, 32). The implication of this statement is that the street is a stable settlement defined by an occupation of space and time by people and occupations. It is more of a frontier with a host of disciplining institutions (Harris 1973, 32) and their networks, routinely influencing and encroaching upon these communities.

To one observing trends in sociological research, a puzzling characteristic emerges — the relative dearth of systematic analysis of street communities. Substantive gaps persist regarding the place of street communities in urban society; the nature and effect of their networks (James, 1977, 183); their interrelationships with larger structures in which activities occur and resources are secured; and lastly, the involvements of these communities with outside formal interventive systems. As Wolfgang aptly notes "street sociology is very rare" (Cohen 1980, xiii).

Most fundamentally, social order, in this exploratory paper, is presented in terms of the relation of actors and their communities to the means of social control (formal/informal, supportive/coercive). Thus, the structures of control shape and, in turn, are shaped by the nature and quality of social networks.

NETWORKS OF CONTROL: FROM DISCONNECTING TO REFASHIONING THE DANGEROUS "COMMUNITY"

A History of Containment

The modern city with its complex mosaic of specialized areas can function only if there are orderly rhythmic flows of people and goods (Duncan 1957, 297; Lynch 1968, 200). Streets are the "main public places of a city" as well as its "most vital organs" (Jacobs 1961, 129). Unsurprisingly therefore, "the control of the streets means the control of the city" (Wilcox 1094, 29). Throughout history, mechanisms and institutions have expanded at accelerated rates to regulate "improper behaviour in public places" (Bedarida and Sutcliffe 1980). Techniques used to discipline those "living off the streets" consisted of "enclosures" and "partitions" (Foucault 1977, 141–42). That is, access to the streets was controlled by processes of surveillance which enabled authorities "to know where and how to locate individuals" (143) and, ultimately, to territorialize them.

In early feudal England the regulation of public order was local, communal, and mutual (Lee 1971). There existed associations of free men who pledged to preserve local peace. Local constables ensured that idle and disorderly persons (Simpson 1895, 628–30) within their walled towns (Lee 1971, 26) would be regulated. When a "hue and cry" was raised against someone not belonging — a stranger, felon, vagrant, transient, etc., everyone in the community had to lay aside his work and join in the pursuit (Lee 1971, 34).

The Statute of Winchester, 1285 (Lee 1971, 33) required bailiffs of towns to investigate residents in suburbs in an effort to locate "people against the peace" or vagrants. Householders were made responsible for the deeds of those whom they harboured and were punished for indiscriminate almsgiving. Citizen surveillance and informal social controls were expanded.

To further secure the structural linkages of these local economies, the first vagrancy statute in 1349 made it a crime to give alms to anyone unemployed while being of sound mind and body (Chambliss 1973, 257). According to Chambliss (258) the vagrancy law served to control the supply of cheap labour for the benefit of the propertied classes, especially since the Black Death reduced the availability of cheap labour. Those caught wandering, loitering and idle with "no reckoning on how they lawfully" got by, were dealt with severely and quickly. Punishment ranged from fifteen days imprisonment in 1360 (257–58) to the use of pillory, stocks, mutilation, starvation, whipping, and death by 1535 (260–62).

The Act of 1531 decreed that local officials search out and register any destitute deemed to be impotent and provide them with a document authorizing street begging. By 1536 local parishes were to be responsible for the care of this problem population. The penalties for street begging included beatings, branding, enslavement, and execution for repeated offenders (Piven and Cloward 1972, 15). Simultaneously, by 1547 laws provided for even more severe penalties of branding with a letter V (Vagabond), enslavement for two years (Chambliss 1973, 264) for those loitering, wandering by streets, highways, lurking in any house, or for running away from work. Also, in 1571 this list of offenders was expanded to include rogues, vagabonds, and sturdy beggars (263–64).

Further, the Elizabethan Poor Laws of 1572 spelled out more fully these local responsibilities. By 1597, Parliament encouraged the practice of making relatives responsible for paupers (Piven and Cloward 1972). Relief and punishment, controlled by local communities, were recognized by the Poor Laws of 1597 and 1601. But by 1662, Poor Laws legalized power of churchwardens and overseers to apply to two justices of the peace for a warrant for the removal of transients (Price 1971, XXI). Interestingly, links with the secular (Scull 1977, 18) rather than the ecclesiastical authorities were expanding (Price 1971, XXI). In any event, the able-bodied poor had to be put to some kind of work — either returned to his workplace or confined to a house of correction (Price 1971, XXI; Marcus, 1978, 45).

In the early 1700s vagrant, begging and thieving boys on the streets of London were rounded up and shipped to the American colonies (Hawes 1971). An Act of 1744 provided for the employment of male rogues or vagabonds over twelve years of age in his Majesty's military service (Price 1971, XXI). Not only were they vagrants, but according to Henry Fielding, a London magistrate, "these deserted boys were thieves from necessity, their sisters whores from the same cause" (Ward 1978, 57). In 1723 Parliament permitted parishes to establish work houses and to refuse aid to those who would not clean roads, clear forests, break stone, etc. Their payment would be food and clothing (Piven and Cloward 1972, 25). This net was expanded by the Gilbert's Act 1782, which enabled parishes to find work for able-bodied poor of their neighbourhoods (Marcus 1978, 46). The Kingswood Reformatory was established for the confinement of "hordes of unruly children who infested the streets of the new industrial towns of England" (United Nations 1952, 10). Likewise, the founding of the Hospital of St. Michael in Rome, by Pope Clement XI, was "for the correction and instruction of profligate youth, that they who when idle were injurious, may when taught become useful to the state" (United Nations 1952, 9).

The Poor Law of 1834, an important piece of social legislation, established a new model of administrative machinery — it established nationally centralized decision making on substantive issues of policy, professionalized civil servants (Marcus 1978, 53–54), and declared that no outdoor relief was to be given except in workhouses. The poor were to be cured in these Houses of Industry (Ignatieff 1978, 213). These houses were deliberately designed as places of horror, shame, and stigma (Polanyi 1957, 2), and served to instill a fear in the labouring masses of a fate that awaited them should they relax into beggary, pauperism, or transience (Piven and Cloward 1972, 1–4). According to Bentham, these newly created workhouses were to be run like a business; everyone including the physically handicapped (Marcus 1978, 53) would be made useful. In fact, the burgeoning textile industry solved its labour problems during the latter part of the eighteenth century by using parish children, some only four and five years old, as factory operatives (Piven and Cloward 1972, 27).

What becomes apparent from this brief outline is the changing nature of control in the face of major structural transformations in society (Price 1971, X). After 1700 (Tilly 1974, 38) with increased industrial revolutions in science, technology and agriculture, as well as with increased urbanization, the cities of England experienced burgeoning dense populations, massive dislocations, violent riots and popular discontent (McDowell 1972 5). These social changes were immediately organized into alarmist interpretations of disorder by many philanthropic reformers (Ignatieff 1981, 164; 153–54) who argued for new remedies. Thus with urbanization, there was a concomitant "increase in specialized demands" (Martindale 1958, 13). In urban settings, order maintenance eventually became routinized into specialization of roles for new "staffs of functionaries" (Weber 1947) who were given appropriate skills. For example, in 1829 a single police force for Metropolitan London was established consisting of one thousand well-trained uniform constables under the authority of Parliament (McDowell 1975, 8). The relationship of cities and formal control is complex and interwoven. The same forces which created the modern cities were also molding social control. In fact, modern social control was deeply rooted in urban life (Haworth 1973, 32) and was often a convenient urban response to social problems. From 1815 to 1848 (Ignatieff 1981, 171) the rising rates of vagrancy, pauperism, masterless apprentices, unemployed youths, child prostitutes were dealt with, to a large degree, through series of interconnected formal institutions such as law, police and penitentiaries. Provisions of public order services required tremendous investments and coordination.

More significantly, a new discourse — that of political economy was promoted. As Pasquino notes, this new industrial order needed to "subject, intern and banish everything which opposed its advance along the royal road of accumulation and proletarianization" (1978, 42). From 1750–1850, the insane, vagrants, beggars, criminals were rediscovered and became new scientific objects (Procacci 1978, 56–59). They, too, had to be connected and implicated in this order. Given the economic, ideological and social connections between prison reformers and new industrial employers, it is not surprising that reformers assumed that a prison should be run like a "well-ordered manufactory" (Ignatieff 1978, 215). Not only would a transient be socialized into a disciplined work ethic (Donzelot 1979, 82; Scull 1977, 29) but his labour would be a profit. The new total institutions — workhouses, penitentiaries, night refuges, asylums, and monitorial schools were embedded in the overall industrial order (Ignatieff 1978, 215), as well as being linked to each other (Foucault 1977, 209). They were interrelated in function and design as they "marched to the same disciplinary cadence" (Ignatieff 1978, 215). All expressed common belief in the reformative powers of enforced asceticism, hard work, religious instruction and routine (162). This discipline would fix, arrest or regulate movement; it would clear up confusion and dissipate any contact groupings of individuals wandering about the country (Foucault 1977, 219).

In light of the above connections, the support for these institutions rested on a larger social need than simply crime control. Reformers succeeded in presenting institutions as a response not solely to crime or the wickedness of individuals but to the wider strategy of political, social and legal reform designed to establish order as a new foundation (Ignatieff 1978, 210; 1981, 165). Crime was thus treated as a product of a dangerous class (Silver 1967), a class out of control of the old social institutions and beyond the reach of gentlemen, parsons or even employers (Beattie 1980, 15).

Transients were perceived as detached from the community and thought to be responsible for a large proportion of crimes against property (Beattie 1977, 7). These new total institutions were used to control them. They accounted for over 50 percent of the prison population in the 1840s (Ignatieff 1978). In the past they would have been ignored, returned to their master or whipped (Ignatieff 1978). This new punishment, directed at the mind, replaced public punishments of the body (Foucault 1977, 101). Although by the 1850s, 10 percent of the English population were paupers (Hobsbaum 1968, 70), relatively little was done to raise housing, education or sanitary conditions without attempts to colonize their minds (Ignatieff 1978, 214). Writing in the 1860s, Mayhew (1972, 48) argued for the development of "ragged schools" to train the "thousands of neglected children loitering about the low neighbourhoods of the metropolis, and prowling about the streets, begging and stealing for their daily bread". Like their predecessors in industrial schools, transients would be socialized into "virtuous and industrious habits and become more profitable to the state" (51).

Rescuing the Lost Community

Increased intervention in the activities of street communities accompanied the spread of urbanization in the late nineteenth century. A new urban order was taking shape to deal with the many footloose youngsters and unemployed youth (Cohen P. 1979, 126–27). A new mode of deviancy control was advocated whose very success depended on the notion of a lost Gemeinschaft community (Cohen S. 1979a, 342). The intent was to recapture a sense of community in cities. As Pearson suggests: "the dominant concern of the sociological pastoral has been with reclaiming runaways and drop-outs from the urban industrial machines" (1979, 197). The fact of not belonging to a family, and hence the lack of a sociopolitical guarantor continued to pose problems (Donzelot 1979, 49). The widespread presumption was that, if left to follow their own preferences, transient communities will not act in a way which maximizes the welfare of the city as a whole.

Containment of youths who had rebelled against parental authorities and roamed the city was not effective (Donzelot 1979, 82; Mechanic 1969, 54; Report S.G., 1975, 2). Pleas for more intensive supervision of the streets recurred (Gray 1931; Von Hirsch 1976, 14). Crusaders were arguing for protected liberation of this misguided lot. This supervised freedom consisted of shepherding the youth back to spaces where they could be more closely watched — the schools, families, religion (Rogers 1945; Holmes 1972, 84; Donzelot 1979, 4, 47).

Many new middle class missionaries (Platt 1969, 98) soon became concerned with the plight of these "young toughs", "the vagabond boys of the metropolis" (Spergel 1967, XIV) and with "unsupervised street life" (Rothman 1980, 52). The appeal to saving become the "linchpin of a new mechanism of assistance" (Donzelot 1979, XIII). Child welfare, initiated in large urban centres by correctional impulses of evangelism, liberal reform and organized philanthropy (Hillman 1967, 146), was to be met as a communal responsibility (Armitage 1975, 48). The Y.M.C.A., Salvation Army, Jane Adams' Hull House, Boy Scouts, or the settlement movement (McFarlane et al. 1966, 6; Ward 1978, 60) sought to penetrate street communities. Shaw and his associates, for example, used street workers to establish direct contact with "unreached" boys in Chicago and help them find their way back to acceptable norms of conduct (Spergel 1967, XV). In New York, the newly created Children's Aid Society disapproved of indiscriminate almsgiving and, instead, provided lodging houses with evening classes, beds, and meals for which the youths were obligated to pay (Ward 1978, 60). The Children's Aid Society, established in 1891 in Toronto, sought through the efforts of J. Kelso to arouse everyone's consciousness to the cause of these neglected and deprived children (McFarlane 1966, 6; Spina and Hagerty 1979, 55).

A medical-therapeutic, case-work model influenced by psychiatry (Young 1952, XIV; Armstrong and Wilson 1973a, 67; Scull 1977, 5) was used in dealing with these transients. These "sick" and "trapped" youngsters needed to be saved for their own good (Platt 1969, 172, 177; Armitage 1975, 248; Scull 1977, 5; Pearson 1979, 15). This pathological orientation extended to those youths in danger and to dangerous youths (Donzelot 1979, 99). This treatment model maintained that it was not the youth's fault that he was diseased or morally tainted. He was incapable of moral responsibility and was propelled into disaffiliation through circumstances beyond his control. Once reached, vagrant youths were clinicized and often committed in increasing numbers to institutions of "care" (Armstrong and Wilson 1973a, 67). Many

reformers recommended rehabilitation through vocational guidance (Nascher (1909), sterilization (Binder 1916), the establishment of self-supporting agricultural colonies (Lisle 1914/15;
Nylander 1933), or national youth camps (Minehan 1934), rather
than through existing reform schools or industrial workhouses.
Even if rehabilitation failed, these colonies would at least keep
vice, degeneracy and vagrancy off the streets (Ferguson 1911).

Interestingly, these individual special approaches avoided
fundamental and more complex analyses of the problem (Von
Hirsch 1976, 27). Instead, they identified clients and recycled old
palliatives (Langley 1977, 227). They served to overlook institutional sources (Mills 1943), or organizational features of these
social problems and they inhibited recognition of collective vested
interests of these moral crusaders (Schur 1980, 1).

In regulating the city streets, according to humanitarian and
benevolent social services, progressives were far more attentive to
the "needs" of transient youth rather than to their "rights"
(Rothman 1978, 69; Glasser 1978, 107). The new humanism held
firmly to the concept of *parens patriae* — the state as parent, and to
the desire and efficacy of paternalistic interventions (Gaylin et al.
1978, XII; Boli-Bennett and Meyer 1978, 799). The state assumed
the role of a kind, conscientious and protective parent (Report of
the Solicitor General (S.G.) 1975, 3, 11). Following the logic that
parental responsibility served ostensibly the youths' best interests,
liberal reformers maintained that it was not necessary to extend
to youths those same procedural and substantive safeguards
enjoyed by adults. Basically, youths were considered misguided,
misdirected, innocent (Dickens 1978, 206), intellectually incompetent and incapable of taking care of themselves.

The spread of urbanization has witnessed the development of
large treatment bureaucracies (Report, S.G. 1975). Acting in
locus parentis (Langley 1977, 227-28), they succeeded in paving the
way for greater inventions of state intervention in the lives of
children, child-parent relations, education, health, recreation, etc.
(Platt, 1969; Armitage, 1975; Report, S.G. 1975, 3). For example,
the Children's Protection Act of 1893 which provided for the
establishment of Children's Aid Societies, also included provisions
for taking neglected and delinquent children from negative home
situations and placing them into foster homes, and further
justified community action on behalf of the child (McFarlane 1966,
6; Spina and Hagerty 1979, 55). Other agencies, like the Big
Brother and Big Sister organizations, were also supervising
youths (Spina and Hagerty 1979, 32).

Inseparable from and concurrent with these philanthropic

gestures are the "practical demands of admistering institutional systems in the real world" (Rothman 1980, 5). Obviously, the heightened involvements in rehabilitation do not overshadow the importance attached to social control. K. Scott, the president of the benevolent Ontario Children's Aid Societies, drafted the Juvenile Delinquents Act of 1908 (McFarlane 1966, 8). In its preamble the Act notes that the welfare of the community demanded that youthful offenders "be guarded against association with crime and criminals, and should be subjected to such wise care, treatment and control as will tend to check their evil tendencies and to strengthen their better instincts" (18, 51). And by 1929, sexual immorality or any similar form of vice was added to this Act (19). The provisions of the child welfare acts, Juvenile Delinquents Act or the early provisions of the Criminal Code regarding vagrancy (Snow 1901) were not contradictory. In fact, they were all tied to the single purpose of the state — control (Rothman 1974).

Family courts processed for treatment many street youths for their "misbehavings" (Platt 1969, 137) which included truancy, running away or staying out late. Those who had limited resources such as access to tutors or psychologists (Glasser 978, 115) were obviously sent to detention homes. Irrespective of its strategy, social assistance exacted a heavy toll in civil liberties (Djao 1979, 40), by stigmatizing, by increasing dependence on relief for subsistence, and by extending comprehensive controls. These early exercises which were remarkably similar to many other liberal-welfare measures, were designed to discipline (Piven and Cloward 1972, 30) and control unrest (Cuneo 1980, 132).

Redefining the Community: Creating Connections of Control

From the above historical overview, we can easily discern economic and political ideological forces shaping the various interventive strategies (Chan and Ericson 1981, 8–9) of liberal-welfare states. More recent interventions are reflecting a passionate rediscovery of the concept of "community". Throughout the last few decades, viable alternatives "in" the community were being sought in order to minimize the involvements of traditional processes. Community participation in health, education, politics, media, social action, or land development is encouraged to ensure more meaningful and effective interventions (Aronowitz 1973; Christian 1973; Hylton 1981, 200).

Social control was no exception. The concept of community was, and continues to be, marketed wholesale and retail on the basis of its utility and reduced costs. Despite the evidence documenting the high costs associated with diversion (Chan and Ericson 1981, 45, 66), this poorly operationalized concept of community has attained a heightened significance within the new "chatter" (Foucault 1977, 304). The shifts toward community crime prevention, compensation, restitution, victimization or simply returning the bad and the mad (Scull 1977, 41) to the community once again echo a lingering pastoral nostalgia. This intent to invite, identify and involve the private sector and its initiatives is cogently expressed by Prime Minister Trudeau who adds: "Do not leave it to government to do it for you, but government has a responsibility to help you do it" (Canadian Association for Prevention of Crime 1978, 1).

The greater involvements of family, schools, private security, social welfare, etc., in the routine business of prevention, treatment and socialization would serve as supplements to formal incarceration (Greenberg 1975, 8; Rothman 1980, 9). They would, however, be tied to the discretion of formal and centralized apparatuses in a number of ways, particularly in funding. The state becomes implicated and strives not to divert from, but into, and within the control system (Chan and Ericson 1981, 55). Techniques of coercion and control become blurred with those of persuasion and support throughout complicated networks having invisible boundaries. That is, beyond this rhetoric of community, distinctions become meaningless, since it is extremely difficult to know when controls end and supports begin; whether one is half-way in or half-way out in multipurpose centres (Cohen 1979); whether something is done "to" or "for" someone (Hughes 1971, 305). Essentially, "community incarceration" (Klein 1979, 182) or "community absorption" (L.R.C. Working Paper 1975, 4) disperses control and casts a wider net (Cohen 1979a, 347). Sixty percent of those patients discharged from the mental hospitals have no place to go and have little or no assistance in finding shelter (Malarek 1980, 5). It is no wonder that the readmission rate is 75 percent of all released within three to five years. The numbers of those who get into the system in the first place (Ibid. 356) will increase to include those who otherwise would be ignored. These processes serve to legitimate intervention as well as facilitate greater surveillance and information sharing. Whatever the programs — requiring offenders to do work for social agencies that haven't money to hire extra staff to paint or repair hostels; involving those on bail in supervision projects to shovel snow, cut grass or chaffeur the aged, handicapped, etc.; or even paying juveniles to report any vandalism on school property, to name only a few; the basic premise, as articulated for public consumption, is that the community is therapeutic (Report, S.G., 1975, 21-27; Greenberg 1975; *Globe and Mail* 30 September 1981, 17). Within this normative orientation, it is held that these positive and public contributions will facilitate readjustment to community values (Community in Corrections 1979, 5).

In any discussion of community participation, community diversion or de-institutionalization two features stand out: the curious role assigned to space and the accelerated rate of interconnectedness among control networks. The saving/controlling community continues to define street transients narrowly in terms of a confined territory. The former erects and projects spatial boundaries for the community to be saved. Paradoxically, the community doing the saving rarely defines itself according to this imposed characteristic. Seldom does it recognize the presence, role and strength of networks within street communities as extending beyond a localized environment.

SPACE

Closely akin to the new strategies of intervention is the enhanced role assigned to space. Diversion or community treatment does not necessarily imply despatializing. Given that space is not irrelevant for control purposes nor is control spatially random (Stewart 1977, 32), territorial referents remain increasingly crucial in identifying and locating transients. The street community is treated like a "contained colony" (Schur 1980, 90). The "principle of locality" — the scheme for splitting up the vast overgrown city into parochial units, avoids dangerous collisions between the urban propertied classes and the "unruly" (Silver 1967) and allows for the creation of insular zones for the "unwanted" where they are permitted to cluster (Stol 1980, 3). This geographic segregation is seldom the result of self-regulation (Schur 1980, 92), but rather imposed externally in a number of ways. For example, the location of support institutions (Whitney 1970, 70), hostels, mental health centres as well as the reluctance of mayors to allow group homes in residential areas, physically keeps the street community out of sight and out of the way.

Likewise, gentrification, revitalization, renaissance, or rejuvenation — euphemisms for the movement of upper income status groups into the inner city is forcing transients to move elsewhere. This "induced displacement" (Henig 1980) which is

supported by powerful business interests, tax incentives, politicians, professionals and the general public alike, is aptly expressed by a consultant to a municipal planning board who stated, "We
want to give the city back its main street" (Vyhnak 1980, 5). This
scheme which parallels many urban relocation initiatives is
"largely a real estate operation with welfare payments thrown in"
(Clairmont and Magill 1974, 255).

Millions of dollars are being invested in privatizing space.
Toronto City Council, for example, allocated $5 million to revit-
alize its main streets — especially Yonge Street, by adding trees,
benches, better lighting. Private interests continue to develop, at
unprecedented rates, large office, retail and accommodation
complexes in the inner core. Many of these new complexes have
miles of privately controlled interconnected underground walk-
ways. A new downtown community is being refashioned. To
accommodate this anticipated demand of reclaiming the inner
core, well over 16,000 condominium and apartment units have
been approved for construction within blocks of Yonge Street.
This "preventative medicine" will certainly act as a "sociofugal"
setting — inhibiting contacts with the outcast transients as well as
"sociopetal" — fostering contacts among the "respectable" newcomers.

This influx of new housing starts and increased business
interests in the inner city will succeed in driving out cheaper forms
of accommodation — shelters, rooming houses or group homes, to
other areas of the city. More significantly, these trends towards
reclaiming space and its control, result in street transients and
"their turf" being watched more closely by many more eyes. The
attempt to "privatize public space" (Lofland 1973, 118) has become
an important factor in restructuring and directing social behaviour. The manipulations of spatial arrangements in the interests of greater security, with its real or symbolic barriers, combine
to bring the environment under control of its occupants. Ultimately, these many innovations ranging from crime prevention
through environmental design to urban renewal, demonstrate the
"sanctity of property" and the "distribution of power in society"
(Pahl 1970b, 188) expressed in spatial and physical terms.

Integrally related to any inquiry into regulation of the street
community is an analysis of the disciplining system with which it
routinely interacts. The regulation of street life has continued to
be a central responsibility of the police. This police responsibility
involves much more than strict law enforcement. Clearly, it
entails surveillance, that is, a concern with "everything that
happens" on the street including "unimportant events" (Foucault
1977, 213). This unremitting watch is translated in the develop-

ment of "network of relations" (176–77), and ultimately in the typification of areas where the police expect to receive the most difficulty from dangerous elements (Cicourel 1968, 67). For the police, the inner city street life requires the allocation and distribution of different sets of priorities, more aggessive patrols and subsequently greater expenditures. In terms of a hierarchy of spaces, the streets of the downtown are considered "central most" behaviour settings with places of greater mobility, variety of interactions, numerous services and different "catchment areas". By establishing, marking or occupying spaces, policing becomes synonymous with territory. This control of a patrol "beat" or area by the police requires learning of "incongruity procedures" (Sacks 1972, 284): knowing when to simply disperse street transients or permit them to linger on in exchange for information. There are constant confrontations between the police and "street kids". They function as a result of the latter's vulnerability, visibility, lack of privacy and the former's proactive approaches in public areas. In fact, as Gillis and Hagan (1979, 19) note, the perceived impairment of traditional control may require compensatory, or even overcompensatory exercises of discipline by the police. In many instances, however, the police may practice a policy of tolerance combined with containment as long as they remain "in their place" (Lee 1979, 185). Many attempts to spatially define street communities blatantly ignore the fact that street crime is easily exportable, given the networks of acquaintances that exist throughout the urban environment and efficient public transportation systems.

NETWORKS: THE POLICE

Despite the profusion of detailed studies on police sanctioning behaviours, relatively little is known about the specific interface of policing and its networks with street transients. Moreover, the literature is remarkably deficient in analysis directed at elucidating the relationships between policing and larger political, social and environmental orders. What, then, does the literature reveal in terms of policing and community?

Police forces enjoy an impressive range of working relations with a number of agencies, civic associations and institutions. Networks of interacting, but formally independent agencies (Miller 1980, 480), exist within the regulative system or "the social control subculture" (Lemert 1951). That is, "urban pacification" (Cohen P. 1979, 128) and "urban surveillance" (Foucault

1977, 209) are ongoing accomplishments of powerful organizations interacting in many inescapable ways (Greer 1972, 7, 23; Levine et al. 1979, 483). These connections involving formal and informal interactions are often loose and linked at many levels. These relations are based on the premise that members of this "control network" would be better able to draw on other agencies in the network in order to gain useful contacts, provide cooperative strategies, and exchange information. Many will use their position in the network as a base from which to establish ties and channel resources to other organizations outside the network itself. These intra-agency links serve to bring previously dispersed and autonomous resources together in a coordinated joint enterprise with even more knowledge and points of access. This is further facilitated by sophisticated communications, storage, and retrieval systems.

Interestingly, members of these networks claim to regulate as well as "help" street communities. According to street case workers, the police represent their most closely and frequently called upon contact in the community (Spergel 1967, 204; Farrell 1974; Budgen 1981, 9). But these connections remain disguised in order not to lose their clients. A transient under sixteen years of age is warned that the agency must contact the police within twenty-four hours and urge the child to return home (Carey 1976, F1). According to the interviews conducted with street transients (file S12) and their case workers (files W2, W3), it was widely reported that hostels and shelters for transient youths enjoy loose, informal relationships with the police. The staff at a shelter would assist the police locate "suspects". In return, the police would reciprocate the favour in removing unwanted guests. Incidentally, during the 1930s it was recommended that social service agencies fingerprint clients who were vagrants to assure identification and facilitate information sharing with the F.B.I (Guild 1939).

In North York, uniformed police officers regularly visit the schools at the request of the Board of Education in order to allow students and police to become personally acquainted and to help keep "intruders under control" (*Toronto Star* 28 November 1980, A16). Despite budgetary restraints which prevent the expansion of schools in Calgary, school boards allocate considerable funds towards the salaries of visiting police officers (Ibid.) In 1981, boards of education across Ontario have used the court systems to rid themselves of 500 children who have committed offenses no more serious than truancy (Lavigne 1981, 13; Nightingale 1981, 1, 2).

Links with private corporations have also proliferated. Police often urge proprietors and merchants to close down early and to order kids off the street (Budgen 1981, 10). In his report, Bruner documents the use of hidden surveillance devices by the police in washrooms of apartment complexes, hotels, bars, subway stations (1981, 131–33). During a preliminary interview, a young street transient (S9) indicated that she was apprehended by a plain clothes police officer driving a taxicab!

In accordance with the spirit of "community involvement", a considerable number of actors have become interested in assisting the police regulate street communities. It is important to note that the participation of developers, merchants, security guards, media, schools, social workers, and individual citizens have spread the "net" of control wider (Klein 1979, 184) resulting in the gathering of yet larger numbers of transients.

This is not to suggest that at the level of intra-agency inter-action, ignorance, fear or distrust is absent. Conflict between agencies for more information is however often balanced with the demands of cooperation. Aside from going out and informally linking with community agencies, police forces have also been promoting their own community involvement projects.

Police forces have also been active in advancing "the com-munity argument", but in a manner highly compatible with their organizational interests. The police have moved beyond the "liberal tinkering" (Ericson 1981) of trying to "recapture the world we have lost" (Brown and Howes 1975, 5). The police have been extremely adept in ensuring cooperation and community input, in effect, defining community and setting. Moreover, the police have rendered this debate quite useful — it enabled them not only to redefine community, but to set themselves up as the architects and organizers of this community. Ironically, the police have suc-ceeded in promoting an even tighter system of official control which the very rhetoric of the early diversion schemes was designed to avoid.

The Ontario Solicitor-General's Annual Report (1980, 17) lists "dozens of programs promoted by the police community in Ontario". They include block parents, crime prevention, teacher's guide to citizenship and crime prevention, home security, to name only a few. Moreover, in recent years police forces have establish-ed community relations, race relations, ethnic squad, domestic intervention, team policing, bail and parole, youth bureau, citations to helpful citizens, etc. These practices have certainly served to promote the public image of the police. This elevated role of the police within this current community debate is more accurately described by the Ontario Police Commission (1978, 16):

Police Officers realize that community involvement is the best way to achieve our goals. Many of the citizens of the community are concerned, and want to assist, but they need purpose and direction. To a substantial degree, this guidance must emanate from well-organized and aggressive programs and services provided by the police.

Likewise, the conditions under which the police welcome community involvement is summarized well by the reaction of Metro Toronto's Chief of Police to the newly created gay street patrols: "If they go out there as extra eyes and ears and call us as they spot a street assault or robbery that is fine with me . . . We need all the help we can get" (*Toronto Star* 30 June 1981, A4). Given the professional image of the police force and its emphasis on arrests, many officers approach these innovations with very little enthusiasm (James 1979, 74). It's quite obvious that the increased trend toward community participation is certainly useful to the police in terms of effective investigation. In his manual for policing, Horgan (1979) outlines in great detail how the police could use contacts with employers, hotels, taxicabs, doctors and hospitals, welfare agencies, banks, etc., to obtain considerable information.

Thus, this concept of community is conveniently alluded to by a number of control networks, shared perspectives develop through which deviant behaviours are explained, motives easily imputed (Cohen 1972, 74) and the levels of dangerousness are grouped together. The problem of street communities becomes susceptible to exaggeration (cf. Taylor 1981, 60) and ripe for exploitation by a number of agencies with this normative community orientation. Even though many agencies are connected to street communities, this does not necessarily mean that they are organized in support of the street communities' interests. Caretakers and legal authorities alike are compelled to strike a delicate balance among three interests — the interest in order, in formal rationality, and in organizational maintenance (Balbus 1977, XVIII). In other words, the "community saved" position must be manipulated to serve bureaucratic control, functional convenience and organizational survival (Chan and Ericson 1981, 3). Consequently, many saving networks remain insulated and isolated from the very persons they are trying to serve (Christian 1973, 43). To elaborate, eligibility criteria for welfare often disqualify transients — they may be too young or cannot produce an address (Cumming 1968).

Many of these prolonged and recurrent links form power networks (Van Pouke 1980, 186). That is, organizations as power networks are formally structured (187) to secure dependency relations. Access and distributions of rewards or sanctions are carefully coordinated on a continuous basis to effect intended consequences.

LIBERATING LINKAGES OF CARCERAL COMMUNITIES: NEXUS OF CONTROL

Networks and Informants

Conceptually, what has been detailed so far in this paper is a perspective on social order which depicts street transients and agencies as attending to certain features of their respective networks. Upon closer scrutiny, it is evident that neither street networks nor the constant interventive crusades alone account for the regulation of social order. Essentially, the study of these "loose peer clusterings" (West 1978, 175, 177, 180) and their links with organizational networks of controls with whom they routinely interact, is also warranted. As noted previously, order is conditioned and coloured by a variety of many intersecting links (Van Pouke 1980, 187). These very relevant links form the raw material from which problems are solved. But, given the exigencies imposed on different networks which are embedded in larger structures, these interfaces may exacerbate rather than settle difficulties. That is, urbanites generally face the problem of maintaining interactions with a number of people for different reasons and must frequently coordinate conflicting demands (Van Pouke 1980, 188). Street transients are no exception. Their interactions with the police and social service agencies provoke tension because, among other reasons, the "logic of necessity" (Lee and Visano 1981, 231-33) governing these organizations remains incompatible with the interests of transients. These relations seldom reflect "unilinear reciprocation" (Denzin 1970, 129).

The most significant impingements on the street community come from the police. In fact, the police represent the most visible and accessible figure of formal authority. Besides tapping on their existing intra-agency networks police forces actively seek to establish ties with the general public. Without the cooperation of the people with whom he or she deals, the police officer is ineffectual (Banton 1963, 133). Police absorption, penetration and reintegration (Cohen 1979a, 355-56) into the community serve to humanize the face of police work, provide closer ties with the general public and encourage early reporting and surveillance. Many gaps in intelligence and information gathering exist.

Consequently, the police actively seek links with potential trouble makers — street hustlers. The need for strengthening police ties with the street community is even more critical given the insularity of the police (Kelling and Fogel 1968, 168). Despite the police disdain for these "scum" (Shearing 1981, 86) or "assholes" (Van Maanen 1981, 222, 228), the police view them as very fertile sources of information (Rubenstein 1973, 201). Large urban police forces require the resources that only street people can provide — information. This becomes even more obvious with police forces which have adopted a "legalistic style of policing" (Wilson 1968, 172, 185) and where organizational production norms are high (Skolnick 1967, 108). As "intimate and private connections" (Rubenstein 1973, 216) develop, the flow of information increases as does the knowledge of how to exploit this information. To "drum up their business" (Skolnick 1967, 116) or "create crime" (Ericson 1981), police encourage disclosures. Moreover, police officers, like many hustlers from whom they obtained their information, use it as a commodity exchange within their own network to pay debts or even to encourage preferential treatment from the detective office (Rubenstein 1973, 201).

In reference to public order violations, police officers need information that typically does not arise from citizen complaints (Skolnick 1967, 115). The "carceral network", as Foucault (1977, 300) explains, allows for the "recruitment" of delinquents. Street kids are put to good use if only to keep others under surveillance (Foucault 175, 200; 1980(a):45). This reliance on informants make sexual deviance usable and useful.

Usually, the informant-informed relationship is a matter of conditional exchange in which each party stands to gain something from the other. (Skolnick 1967, 124; Cohen 1980, 174). From the informant, the police receive information that assists them to meet organizational norms. The police are allowed covert access into various street activities and expand existing controls.

For their cooperation, informants are rewarded. The information may be collected as "rent for allowing people to operate without arresting them" (Rubenstein 1973, 207). Under the rubric of "protection" for their informants, the police may act with minimal aggression, reduce charges, fail to act as complainant or even offer money (Skolnick 1967, 115; Black 1978). As one skilled police officer describes in Rubenstein's study: "Prostitutes and faggots are good. If you treat 'em right, they will give you what you want. They don't want to get locked up, and you can trade that off for information" (1973, 207). Similarly, Humphreys details the case of Tim, a fourteen year old who was caught shoplifting. Instead of processing him, the police put him to work for the vice-squad as a decoy (1979, 90–92).

The police enjoy considerable discretion in the handling of street transients. Many officers are aware that the law grants them this latitude in dealing with juveniles (Werthman and Piliavin 1967; Black and Reiss 1970; Lundman et al. 1980) and that the law further discriminates against the homeless and jobless (McBarnet 1979, 39).

The street therefore becomes a marketplace where retail customers (street kids) and institutional investors (police and/or social workers) are routinely involved in exchange transactions. To extend this analogy further, the costs of certain commodities reflect conditions of supply and demand. For example, after the slaying of Jacques, a shoe-shine boy in Toronto's downtown, the demand for information by the police was very high. The price exacted involved a sizeable crackdown on street hustlers in the hope that information surrounding the circumstances of the boy's death would be forthcoming (cf. Maloney 1979, 22; files, S9, S10).

This market economy facilitates deviance and its control. These transactions are contingent upon the exchange or non-exchange of another relation and not restricted to dyads (Cook and Emerson 1978, 725). The structure and content of these interactions are crucial since the broker's capital consists of his knowledge, information and personal network of relations (Boissevain 1974, 158–59). But, members to these transactions cannot bargain in good faith especially since very little equity exists (Cook and Emerson 1978, 723) as one party is coerced to play the role by the threat of legal sanctions. One party maximizes its position by using the authority of the State (Skolnick 1967, 12) and the other party is all too familiar with consequences of non-compliance (Budgen 1981, 9). The consent to interference wherein suspects help police officers with their inquiries (Ericson 1981, 136) results also from the former's ignorance of the law (Saunders 1981).

An imbalance exists within these functional "knowledge relations" (Foucault 1977, 27; 1980a, 251; 1980b, 80) between street communities and the police. The structural arrangements which organized these contexts of encounters are based on power and translated into conflict. That is, the ability to compel compliance (Schur 1980, 34) or the probability that one actor within a social relationship will be in a position to carry out his own will despite resistance (Weber 1946) characterizes this asymmetry. What emerges in the links between hustlers, kids and formal agencies is a form of compulsory arbitration. In social workers transient relationships, these street clients are usually seeking something scarce (money, clothing, shelter) and are forced to accept something of general value that they do not necessarily want. Power, a crucial factor in any exchange network (Cook and Emerson 1978, 721) determines which and whose assessment gains ascendancy (Schur 1980, XI).

Liberating Links and the Law

How then does street network affiliation facilitate or inhibit social control.

The severity of sanctions — the invocation of the criminal justice or child welfare system and the withdrawal of welfare assistance are related to the resources one holds. On the basis of the literature reviewed and the preliminary field observations, it may be hypothesized that a decrease in resources among street networks leads to higher rates of conflict. We would further speculate that the broader the base from which street networks operate, the more able they are to secure continuity of "survival of the street". The probability of successful apprehension and discipline depends not only, as Berry suggests (1975, 350–53), on the size and goals of the networks defining deviance, but also on the nature of the networks to be controlled.

The literature is replete with studies documenting the relationship of sanctions and relational networks. The relational networks explored, however, are often specified in terms of conventional commitments and normative bonds especially with the family, school or employment. This approach tends to imply that with higher degrees of involvements with these ties, the lower the probability of coercive treatment (Bittner 1967; Cicourel 1968; Ferdinand and Luchterhand 1970). With street transients many of these conventional links are extremely weak. Consequently, it does not necessarily follow that street hustlers are treated punitively or uniformly by formal agencies.

Many other significant relational ties exist on the street. Attention has been sparse on these differential involvements and their impacts on control. Presumably sanctions will vary depending on the nature of one's network and on the willingness of street hustlers to negotiate or trade their "street ties" with the police as commodities.

Interestingly, those more fully connected to street networks tend to be treated differently (file S9, S10). Thrasher (1963) discovered that members of powerful street groupings were less likely to be booked and charged by the police than those of less powerful networks. Why then are, as Van Maanen observes, "some juveniles hanging out on the street overlooked by the police" (1971, 230)?

As previously indicated, street communities are composed of seasoned regulars who are well-connected on the street, marginals who are poorly connected and "tourists" or "week-enders" (file S11).

Within the first category there are a number of entrepreneurs who take risks in manipulating resources. They may have strategic access to sources of information, specialized knowledge, material goods. They know how to place people in contact with each other; they have learned how to engineer impressions (Goffman 1959) and negotiate identities. These are highly expert network brokers.

The level of information brokerage is related to the centrality of one's position in the network structure. Information as a resource will vary with levels of commitments and involvements including duration, frequency, intensity, salience of links (Cook and Emerson 1978, 735). Those members of the street community enjoying multiple and extensive network links are presumably better situated to avoid apprehension. And once apprehended, they can expect greater immunity from the police if they wish to "make a deal". Those less connected, in all likelihood, become more susceptible and vulnerable to outside agencies. Although prime targets for policing, their levels of exchange will be minimal (S9, S10, S11), given their position in the street community.

Studies have also demonstrated how the probability of arrest increases with levels of disrespect (Black and Reiss 1970; Sykes and Clark 1975, 590; Lundman et al. 1980). These findings are highly applicable to the street community if respect is operationalized to include indicators of acquiescence or compliance in providing the much sought-out information on street activities to the police. Law therefore varies inversely with the nature of networks. That is, the more marginal one's position and connections within the street community, the less liberated from law and its applications.

One case in point involved a nineteen-year-old seasoned runaway, Pete, (file S4) who enjoyed a number of multiple network contacts including weak ties with formal agencies of the police and social welfare. In his routine interactions with the police he was able to manipulate and negotiate his resources for a better deal. When approached by the police regarding his gay hustling activities, he willingly provided information on a drug network. He agreed to keep his eyes open regarding the gay hustle "scene" even

246 DEVIANT DESIGNATIONS: CRIME, LAW AND DEVIANCE IN CANADA

when not requested and proved indispensable to information gathering. To the inventory of many extra-legal factors affecting disposition, one may also add the varying degree of suspect's network manipulations.

On the basis of these links to the police and the manipulation of resources therein, one is reminded of Dahrendorf's comment: "Without community there is no conflict and without conflict there is no community" (1959, 229). The conflicts that exist between street transients and the police are conditioned by the formers' degree of connectedness within the street community.

CONCLUSION

Summary

The argument made in this paper is that the study of networks is extremely relevant in any analysis of the continued support for and control of street communities. These communities and their links which ensure "survival on the street" are also inextricably connected to impinging networks of control.

This paper makes problematic many normative assumptions that have persisted regarding urbanization and its consequences for social order. In fact, the separation of these concepts may be artificial. Social control is embedded in the very structure of social relations: it shapes and is shaped by the nature and quality of networks which are ultimately connected to a number of master institutions.

From this structural perspective, this paper examines historically the broader economic, political and social interest which influence both "the frames of reference and institutional remedies" (Emerson and Messinger 1977, 131) for identifying and dealing with street communities. The State emerges not as a political broker balancing interests but as a interested party (Davis 1975, 192–93).

The common normative assumption underlying intervention is that order in the city has gone awry, that the street transients are "lost" and in need of salvation. The concept of "community" is thus used effectively as an attractive and seemingly innocuous metaphor legitimating greater intervention. Again, in the name of community concern, a proliferation of interests deal with this "disorganized" lot of transients. This further entails active attempts to spatialize or "colonize" them.

The focus in this paper on the relationship of transients to each other and to regulate agencies was meant to direct attention to larger structures of control which form the contexts for the formation of ties. That is, the "carceral" or "punitive city" (Foucalt 1977, 30, 129) consists of "multiple networks of diverse elements" (307–308). Social order and the power to regulate it are not attributable to transients, police, social workers, community interests, etc., but are the "over-all effect that emerges from all these modalities, the concatenation that rests on each of them" (1980b, 93).

Contributions and Policy Implications

This paper purports to "build" on the growing body of scientific research concered with the urbanization — social order relationship, and to clearly indicate how analysis must now move beyond to consider aspects of social networks. The literature of the last few decades within the social network tradition bears considerable relevance in pointing to new directions of inquiry. More significantly, recent contributions further suggest the need to research "the way in which the peculiar combination of freedom and control works in the city" (Wayne 1974, 92).

To date, there has been little analytic concern with how and where communities being regulated "fit" within the sociology of the city. And even less information exists as regards to the nature of their networks. One such community — homeless and jobless transients — remains almost unstudied. Instead various "sociologies of the interesting" (Hagan 1973, 455) have been pursued. These studies of prostitutes, skid row, drug dealers, juvenile gangs, etc., have consistently treated the overall impinging "activities of others in the larger social field" (Kahne and Schwartz 1978, 462; Cohen, 1979a) in a cursory manner. There exists relatively little regarding the role of informal networks in determining pathways to services, utilization of formal agencies or attitudes to them.

The attempt in this paper is to grasp some of the more general patterns of street networks and their consequences for sanctioning behaviour. This requires that the investigation be taken into where transients are located in the urban context vis-à-vis structures of power. In exploring "networks in action", the level of access to the knowledge of resources available to the street community and its controllers is reviewed.

From a public policy perspective, continual reassessments of delivery systems ought to be encouraged but according to different premises. These innumerable evaluation or effectiveness studies concentrating on cost-benefit, target-populations, case-modules, or program monitoring have been far too limited in their immediate concerns of reducing organizational uncertainty regarding social issues.

Whatever the program — urban renewal, community involvement in corrections, community mental health or legal services, police community relations, etc., public policy initiatives fail to grapple with the "impact" of these innovations. This orientation invites explicit considerations of both networks of actors — developers, planners, ratepayers associations, retail merchants, the state, transients, politicians, etc., and networks of remedies — suitable housing, education, legal resources, leisure facilities, etc.

This discussion of the regulation of street communities carries with it a number of implications for social policy. The literature review, the historical analysis of the structural linkages of control and the discussion of the networks of the controlled and controllers presumably yield some insights into our understanding of the directions pursued in public policy initiatives. On the basis of this evidence examined, one may advance the argument that a more minimalist involvement by the state is in order. That is, rather than do more good, agencies ought to be doing less harm (Cohen 1979a, 1979b). Similarly, public policy guided by the "community as normative" ideology which perpetuates the rhetoric of the "lost" community may need to be seriously reinterpreted in terms of its disciplining functions. This undoubtedly warrants steps towards a "reshaping traditional values" (Morris 1957, 197) and extricating public policies from remedial palliatives.

It certainly is an odd state of affairs where research only concerns specific applications of some policy decisions. How policy is made, what happens to it when it is made and how it is connected to other policy decisions are issues that cannot be easily ignored. Irrespective of the political orientations of these outcomes whether it is to advance or temper control, impact research will clarify the contradictions between "care and control", "law and order", "conscience and convenience", and move beyond their rhetorical distinctions.

References

Adler, F. 1975. *Sisters in crime.* New York: McGraw-Hill.
Anderson, N. 1923. *The hobo: The sociology of the homeless man.* Chicago: University of Chicago.

Armitage, A. 1975. *Social welfare in Canada: Ideals and realities.* Toronto: McClelland & Stewart.

Armstrong, G. and M. Wilson. 1973a. City politics and deviancy amplification. In I. Taylor and L. Taylor (Eds.), *Politics and deviance.* Harmondsworth: Penguin.

Aronowaitz, S. 1973. The dialectics of community control. In S. Halebsky (Ed.), *The sociology of the city.* New York: C. Scribner's Sons.

Balbus, I. 1977. *The dialectics of legal repression.* New Brunswick, N. J.: Transaction Books.

Banton, M. 1963. *Policeman in the communtiy.* London: Tavistock.

Beattie, J. 1980. Administering justice without police: Criminal trial procedures in 18th century England. Paper prepared for Law Enforcement and Society Symposium, Canadian Police College, Ottawa.

Bedarida, F. and A. Sutcliffe. 1980. The street in the structure and life of the city. *Journal of Urban History* 6 (August) 4: 379–396.

Boli-Bennett, J. and J.W. Meyer. 1978. The ideology of childhood and the state: Rules distinguishing children in national institutions 1870–1970. *American Sociological Review* 43 (December): 797–812.

Berry, B. and J. Kasarda. 1977. *Contemporary urban ecology.* New York: Macmillan.

Binder, R.M. 1916. The treatment of beggars and vagabonds in Belgium. *Journal of Criminal Law & Criminology* 6 (March): 835–848.

Bittner, E. 1967. The police on Skid Row: A study of peace keeping. *American Sociological Review* 32 (October): 699–715.

Bird, D. 1981. Help is urged for 36,000 homeless in city streets. *New York Times* (March 8): 1, 44.

Black, D. 1978. The mobilization of law. In P. Manning and J. Van Maanen *Policing: View from the street.* Santa Moncia: Goodyear.

Black, D. and A. Reiss. 1970. Police control of juveniles. *American Sociological Review* 35 (February): 63–77.

Bogdan, R. 1976. Youth clubs in a West African City. In P. Meadows and E. Mizruchi (Eds.), *Urbanism, urbanization, and change.* Reading Mass.: Addison-Wesley.

Boissevain, J. 1974. *Friends of friends.* Oxford: Basil Blackwell.

Brandon, D. et al. 1980. *The survivors: A study of homelss young newcomers to London and the responses made to them.* London: Routledge and Kegal Paul.

Brown, C. 1965. *Manchild in the promised land.* New York: Signet.

Brown, J. and G. Howes. 1975. *The police and the community.* Lexington, Mass.: D.C. Heath.

Bruns, R. 1980. *Knights of the road: A hobo history.* New York: Methuen.

Budgen, M. 1981. Street smart. *Today* (April 4): 8.

Butts, W. 1947. Bay prostitutes of the metropolis. *Journal of Clinical Psychopathology* 8 (April) 4: 673–681.

Caplow, T. 1940. Transiency as a cultural pattern. *American Sociological Review* 5 (October): 731–739.

Caplow, T. et al. 1968. Homelessness. In D. Shils (Ed.), *International encyclopedia of the social sciences.* 6, New York: Macmillan.

Carey, A. 1976. The children who run away from home. *Toronto Star* (October 23) F1.

Carmichael, B. 1975. Youth crime in urban communities — A descriptive analysis of street hustlers and their crimes. *Crime and Delinquency* 21(2): 139–148.

Chambliss, W. 1973. A sociological analysis of the law of vagrancy. In R.S. Denisoff and C.W. McCaghy (Eds.), *Deviance, conflict and criminality.* Chicago: Rand McNally.

Chan, J. and R. Ericson. 1981. Decarceration and the economy of penal reform. Toronto: Centre of Criminology, University of Toronto.

Christian, T. 1973. The organized neighbourhood, crime prevention and the criminal justice system. Unpublished doctoral dissertation, Michigan State University.

Cicourel, A. 1968. *The social organization of juvenile justice.* New York: J. Wiley.

Clairmont, D. and D. Magill. 1971. Nova Scotia blacks: Marginal people in a depressed region. In J. Galagher and R. Lambert (Eds.), *Social process and institution: The Canadian case.* Toronto: Holt, Rinehart & Winston.

Clairmont, D. and D. Magill. 1974. *Africville.* Toronto: McClelland & Stewart.

Cohen, B. 1980. *Deviant street networks.* Lexington, Mass.: Lexington Books.

Cohen, C. and J. Sokolovsky. 1981. A re-assessment of the sociability of long-term Skid Row residents: A social network approach. *Social Networks* 3: 93-105.

Cohen, J. 1979/1980. Socio-economic status and high school friendship choice: Elmtown's youth revisited. *Social Networks* 2: 65-74.

Cohen, P. 1979. Policing the working-class city. In R. Fine et al. (Eds.), *Capitalism and the rule of law: From deviancy theory to Marxism.* London: Hutchinson.

Cohen, S. 1979a. The punitive city: Notes on the dispersal of social control. *Contemporary Crises* 3: 339-363.

_____. 1979b. Community control — a new utopia. *New Society* 15 (March).

Cook, K. and R.M. Emerson. 1978. Power, equity and commitment in exchange networks. *American Sociological Review* 43 (October): 721-739.

Coombs, N. 1974. Male prostitution: A psychosocial view of behaviour. *American Journal of Orthopsychiatry* 44(5): 782-789.

Corzine, J. and R. Kirby. 1979. Cruising the truckers: Sexual encounters in a highway rest area. In D. Kelly (Ed.), *Deviant behaviour.* New York: St. Martins.

Craven, P. and B. Wellman. 1973. The network city. Research Paper #59. Toronto: Centre for Urban and Community Studies, University of Toronto.

Cumming, E. 1968. *Systems of social regulation.* New York: Atherton.

Cuneo, J. 1980. State, class and reserve labour: the case of the 1941 Canadian Unemployment Insurance Act. In J.P. Grayson (Ed.), *Class, state, ideology and change.* Toronto: Holt, Rinehart & Winston.

Dahrendorf, R. 1959. *Class and class conflict in industrial society.* Stanford: Stanford University Press.

Davis, N. 1975. *Sociological construction of deviance.* Dubuque: W.C. Brown.

Dean, L. 1981. Throwaway Kids. *Today* (November 7): 10-11.

Deisher, R. et al. 1969. The young male prostitute. *Pediatrics* 43: 936-41.

Denzin, N. 1970. Rules of conduct and the study of deviant behaviour: some notes on the social relationship. In J. Douglas (Ed.), *Deviance and respectability.* New York: Basic.

Dickens, B. 1978. Legal represssion and due process in delinquency proceedings. *Revue De Droit* 9: 201-232.

Djao, A.W. 1979. Social welfare in Canada: Ideology and reality. *Social Praxis* 6(2): 35-53.

Donzelot, J. 1979. *The policing of families.* New York: Pantheon.

Emerson, R. and S. Messinger. 1977. The micro-politics of trouble. *Social Problems* 25 (December) 2.

Ericson, R. 1981. *Making crime.* Toronto: Butterworths.

Fanon, F. 1968. *The wretched of the earth.* New York: Grove Press.

Farrell, A. 1974. Homeless youth must find way to self support. *Toronto Star:* 2 April, E1.

F.B.I. 1973. Uniform Crime *Reports* for U.S. U.S. Government Printing Office: Washington D.C.

Ferdinand, T. and E. Luchterhand. 1970. Inner city youth, the police, the juvenile court and justice. *Social Problems* 17: 511–527.

Ferguson, R. 1911. *The vagrant: What to do with him.* London: J. Nisbet.

Finestone, H. 1964. Cats, kicks and color. In H. Becker (Ed.), *The other side.* New York: Free Press.

Fischer, C. 1976a. *The urban experience.* New York: Harcourt, Brace Jovanovich.

Foucault, M. 1977. *Discipline and punish.* New York: Pantheon.

———. *1980a. Power knowledge: Selected interviews and other writings 1972–1977.* (Ed.) C. Gordon. New York: Pantheon.

———. *1980b. The history of sexuality.* I, New York: Vintage.

Frankenberg, R. 1966. *Communities in Britain.* Baltimore: Penguin.

Friday, P. and J. Hage. 1976. Youth crime in post-industrial societies: an integrated perspective. *Criminology* 14 (November) 3.

Gagnon, J. 1968. Prostitution. In D. Shils (Ed.), *International encyclopedia of social sciences.* 12: 592–598. New York: Macmillan.

Gandy, P. and R. Deisher. 1970. Young male prostitutes — The physician's role in social rehabilitation. *Journal of American Medical Association* 212 (June) 10: 1661–66.

Gaylin, W. et al. 1978. *Doing good: The limits of benevolence.* New York: Pantheon.

Giffen, P.J. 1970. The revolving door. In W.E. Mann (Ed.), *The underside of Toronto.* Toronto: McClelland & Stewart.

Gillespie, C. 1974. The open road for boys: Meet Glenn Young, master shuffle-board hustler. In C. Bryant (Ed.), *Deviant behaviour.* Chicago: Rand McNally.

Gillis, A.R. and J. Hagan. 1979. Density, delinquency and design: Formal and informal control and the built environment. Research Paper #109. Toronto: Centre for Urban and Community Studies. University of Toronto.

Ginsberg, K. 1967. The meat rack: A study of male homosexual prostitute. *American Journal of Psychotherapy* 21(2).

Glasser, I. 1978. Prisoners of benevolence: Power versus liberty in the welfare state. In W. Gaylin et al. *Doing good: The limits of benevolence.* New York: Pantheon.

Globe and Mail. 1979 (December 22) 4.

———. 1981. (September 30) 17.

Goetschius, G. and M.J. Tash. 1967. *Working with unattached youth.* London: Routledge and Kegan Paul.

Goffman, E. 1959. *The presentation of self in everyday life.* Garden City, New York: Doubleday.

Granovetter, M. 1973. The strength of weak ties. *American Journal of Sociology* 78 (May) 6: 1360–79.

Gray, D. 1973. Turning out: A study of teenage prostitution. *Urban Life and Culture* 1(4).

Gray, F. 1931. *The tramp: His meaning and being*. London: J. Dent & Sons.

Greenberg, D. 1975. Problems in community corrections. *Issues in Criminology* 10 (Spring) 1.

Guild, J.P. 1939. Transient in a new disguise. *Social Forces* 17 (March) 366–72.

Hagan, J. 1973. Labelling and deviance: A case study in the sociology of the interesting. *Social Problems* 20 (Spring) 4.

Harris, M. 1973. *The daily boys*. London: Croom Helm Ltd.

Hawes, J. 1971. *Children in urban society: Juvenile delinquency in nineteenth century America*. New York: Oxford University Press.

Haworth, L. 1973. *The good city*. Bloomington: Indiana University Press.

Henig, J. 1980. Gentrification and displacement within cities: A comparative analysis. *Social Science Quarterly* 61 (December) 3/4.

Hillman, A. 1967. Urbanization and the organization of welfare activities in the metropolitan community in Chicago. In E. Burgess and D. Bogue (Eds.), *Urban Sociology*. Chicago: University of Chicago.

Holmes, K.A. 1972. Reflections by gaslight: Prostitution in another age. *Issues in Criminology* 7 (Winter) 1.

Hooker, E. 1961. The homosexual community. *Proceedings* of the XIV International Congress of Applied Psychology: 40–59.

_____. 1965. Male homosexuals and their "worlds". In J. Marmor (Ed.), *Sexual Inverson*. New York: Basic.

Horgan, J. 1979. *Criminal investigation*. New York: McGraw-Hill.

Humphreys, L. 1979. *Tearoom trade*. New York: Aldine.

Hylton, J. 1981. Community corrections and social control: the case of Saskatchewan, Canada. *Contemporary Crises* 5: 193–215.

Ignatieff, M. 1978. *A just measure of pain*. New York: Pantheon.

_____. 1971. State, civil society, and total institutions: A critique of recent social histories of punishment. In M. Tonry and N. Morris (Eds.), *Crime and justice*. Chicago: University of Chicago Press, 1981.

Jackson, E. 1981. Street kids: Nobody's priority. *The Body Politic* (December) 7.

Jacobs, J. 1961. *The death and life of great American cities*. New York: Vintage.

James, D. 1979. Police-black relations: The professional solution. In S. Holdaway (Ed.), *The British police*. London: Edward Arnold.

James, J. 1977. Ethnography and social problems. In R.S. Weppner (Ed.), *Street ethnography*. Beverly Hills: Sage.

Johnson, B. 1981. The kids on Main Street. *Globe and Mail* 28 November, 10.

Kahne, B. 1969. Norms and the manipulation of relationships in a work context. In J.C. Mitchell (Ed.), *Social networks in urban situations*. Manchester: Manchester University Press.

Katz, J. 1976. *Gay american history*. New York: Avon.

Kelling, G. and D. Fogel. 1978. Police patrol — Some future directions. In A. Cohn (Ed.), *Future of policing*. Beverly Hills: Sage.

Klein, M. 1979. Deinstitutionalization and diversion of juvenile offenders: A litany of impediments. In N. Morris and M. Tonry (Eds.), *Crime and justice*. Chicago: University of Chicago.

Krisberg, B. 1974. Gang youth and hustling: The psychology of survival. *Issues in Criminology* 9 (Spring) 1: 115–32.

Laner, M. 1974. Prostitution as an illegal vocation: A sociological overview. In C. Bryant (Ed.), *Deviant behavior*. Chicago: Rand McNally.

Langley, M. 1977. A critical theory of juvenile justice. *Crime and/et Justice* 4 (Febuary) 4.

Lavigne, Y. 1981a. C.A.S. sends youth on own for 6 days to see if he likes it. *Globe and Mail* 5 June.

_____. 1981b. Thousands of children needlessly taken from parents. *Globe and Mail* (23 November) 13.

Law Reform Commission. 1975. Diversion. Working *Paper #7*. Ottawa: Information Canada.

Lee, B. 1980. The disappearance of Skid Row: Some ecological evidence. *Urban Affairs* 16 (September), 1.

Lee, J.A. 1978. *Getting sex*. Don Mills: General Publishers.

_____. 1979. The social organization of sexual risk. *Alternative Lifestyles* 2 (February) 1: 69–100.

Lee, J.A. and L.A. Visano. 1981. Official deviance in the legal system. In H.L. Ross (Ed.), *Law and deviance*. Beverly Hills: Sage.

Lee, M. 1971. *A history of police in England*. Montclair, N.J.: Patterson-Smith.

Lemert, E. 1951. *Social pathology*. New York: McGraw-Hill.

Levine, S. et al. 1979. Emergent themes and priorities. In W. Michelson et al. (Eds.), *The Child in the city: Changes and challenges*. Toronto: University of Toronto Press.

Liebow, E. 1967. *Tally's corner*. Boston: Little, Brown.

Lisle, J. 1914/1915. Vagrancy law: Its faults and their remedy. *Journal of Criminal Law and Criminology* 5: 498–513.

Lofland, L. 1973. *A world of strangers*. New York: Basic Books.

Lundman, R. et al. 1970. Police control of juveniles. In R. Lundman (Ed.), *Police behaviour*. New York: Oxford.

Lupsha, P. 1969. On theories of urban Violence. *Urban Affairs Quartery* 4: 273–96.

Lynch, K. 1968. The city as environment. In D. Flanagan (Ed.), *The cities*. New York: Scientific American & Alfred Knopf.

McDowell, C. 1975. Police in the community. Cincinnatti: W.H. Anderson.

McFarlene, G. et al. 1966. *The development of probation services in Ontario*. Department of Attorney-General, Ontario: Queen's Printer.

Malarek, V. 1980a. Ontario dumps mentaly ill into streets, union charges. *Globe and Mail* (30 September), 5.

Maloney, P. 1979. Street hustling: Growing up gay. Unpublished paper in partial fulfillment of LLB programme, University of Toronto.

Mann, W.E. 1968. The social system of a slum: The lower ward, Toronto. In W. Mann (Ed.), *Deviant behaviour in Canada*. Toronto: Social Science Publications.

Marcus, S. 1978. Their brother's keeper: An episode from English history. In W. Gaylin et al. *Doing good: The limits of benevolence*. New York: Pantheon.

Marchand, P. 1979. Street kids. *Chatelaine* 52 (April) 4: 64–65, 96–98, 105–6, 108.

Matza, D. 1975. The disreputable poor. In F.J. Davis and R. Stivers (Eds.), *The collective definition of deviance*. New York: Free Press.

Maychak, M. Homeless in Metro. *Toronto Star (9 December)* 1.

Mayhew, H. 1972. London labor and the London poor. In S. Sylvester (Ed.), *The heritage of modern criminology*. Cambridge, Mass.: Schenkman.

Mechanic, D. 1969. *Mental health and social policy*. Englewood Cliffs, N.J.: Prentice-Hall.

Merry, S. 1980. Manipulating anonymity: Streetwalker's strategies for safety in the city. *Ethos* 45(III/IV).

Merton, R. 1957. *Social theory and social structure.* Glencoe: Free Press.

Mills, C.W. 1940. Situated actions and vocabulary of motives. *American Sociological Review* (December): 904–913.

Minehan, T. 1934. *Boy and girl tramps of America.* New York: Ferrar & Rinehart.

Morris, T. 1958. *The criminal area.* London: Routledge and Kegan Paul.

Nascher, I. 1909. *The wretches of Propertyville: A sociological study of the Bowery.* Chicago: J.J. Lanzit.

Nightingale, S. 1981. Judges still sending truants to maximum-security centres. *Globe and Mail* (23 May): 1, 2.

Nylander, T. 1933. Wandering youth. *Sociology and Social Research* 17 (July–August): 560–568.

Ontario Police Commission. 1978. *A review of regionalized policing in Ontario.* Toronto: Ministry of the Solicitor-General.

Ontario, Solicitor General Annual *Report.* 1980. Toronto: Queen's Park.

O'Toole, L. 1981. The tattered fabric of the city's homeless. *Macleans* (9 February) p. 16–18.

Pahl, R.E. 1970b. *Patterns of urban life.* London: Longmans.

Pasquino, P. 1978. Theatrum politicum: The genealogy of capital — Police and the state of prosperity. *Ideology and Consciousness* 4 (Autumn): 41–54.

Pearson, G. 1979. *The deviant imagination.* London: Macmillan.

Piven, F. and R. Cloward. 1972. *Regulating the poor.* New York: Vantage.

Platt, A.M. 1969. *The child savers.* Chicago: University of Chicago.

Polany, K. 1957. *The great transformation.* Boston: Beacon Press.

Polsky, N. 1969. *Hustlers, beats and others.* Garden City, N.J.: Anchor.

Price, F. 1971. *The Wigginton's constable book 1691–1836.* London: Phillimore.

Prus, R. and S. Irini. 1980. *Hookers, rounders and desk clerks: The social organization of the hotel community.* Toronto: Gage.

Prus, R. and C.R. Sharper. 1977. *Road hustler.* Lexington, Mass.: D.C. Heath.

Reiss, A.J. 1979. The social integration of queers and peers. In D. Kelly (Ed.), *Deviant behaviour.* New York: St. Martins.

Report of Solicitor General's Committee on the Proposals for New Legislation to Replace the Juvenile Delinquents Act. 1975. Young persons in conflict with the law. Ottawa: Solicitor General.

Ribton-Turner C. 1972. *A history of vagrants & vagrancy and beggars & begging.* Montclair, New Jersey: Patterson Smith.

Rogers, K.H. 1945. *Street gangs in Toronto: a study of the forgotten boy.* Toronto: Ryerson.

Ross, H.L. 1959. The "hustler" in Chicago. *Journal of Student Research* 1 (September) 1: 13–19.

Rothman, D. 1978. The state as parent: Social policy in the progressive era. In W. Gaylin et al. *Doing good: the limits of benevolence.* New York: Pantheon.

———. *Conscience and convenience.* Boston: Little, Brown & Co.

Rubenstein, J. 1973. *City police.* New York: Farrar, Straus & Giroux.

Sacks, H. 1972. Notes on police assessment of moral character. In D. Sudnow (Ed.), *Studies in social interaction.* New York: Free Press.

Sandhu, H.S. 1977. *Juvenile delinquency: Causes, control and prevention.* New York: McGraw-Hill.

Saunders, J. 1981. Ignorance of the law among teenagers: Is it a barrier to the exertion of their rights as citizens. *Adolescence* 16 (Fall) 63.

Schur, E. 1980. *The politics of deviance: Stigma contests and the issue of power.* Englewoods Cliffs, N.J.: Prentice-Hall.

Scrivener, L. 1981. Ex-patients face housing hell. *Toronto Star.* (August 24): D5.

Scull, A. 1977. *Decarceration.* Englewood Cliffs, N.J.: Prentice-Hall.

Shearing, C.D. 1981. Subterranean processes in the maintenance of order. *Canadian Review of Sociology and Anthropology* 18(3): 283-298.

Siegal, H. 1977. Gettin' it together: Some theoretical considerations of Urban ethnography among underclass peoples. In R.S. Weppner (Ed.), *Street ethnography.* Beverly Hills: Sage.

Silver, A. 1967. The demand for order in civil society: A review of some themes in the history of urban crime, police and riot. In D. Bordua (Ed.), *The police.* New York: J. Wiley & Sons.

Simpson, H.B. 1895. The office of constable. *The English Historical Review* 10 (October) XL: 625-641.

Skolnick, J. 1967. *Justice without trial.* New York: J. Wiley & Sons.

Smith, M.P. 1979. *The city and social theory.* New York: St. Martin's Press.

Spergel, I. 1967. *Street gang work.* Garden City, N.Y.: Doubleday.

Spina, A. and L. Hagarty 1979. Children, families and community services. In W. Michelson et al. (Eds.), *The child in the city: Changes and challenges.* Toronto: University of Toronto Press.

Spitzer, S. 1975. Toward a Marxian theory of deviance. *Social Problems* 22 (June): 638-651.

Srivastava, S. 1963. *Juvenile vagrancy: A socio-ecological study of juvenile vagrants in the cities of Kanpur and Lucknow.* London: Area Publ. House.

Stewart, M. (Ed.) 1977. *The city: Problems of planning.* Harmondsworth: Penguin.

Stol, M. 1980. The underside. *The Seed* (December) 3:3.

Stone, L. 1981. Services help teens through the long, hot summer. *Globe and Mail* (25 June): T5.

Sutter, A. 1970. Worlds of drug use on the street scene. In J. McGrath and F. Scarpitti (Eds.), *Youth and drugs.* Glenview, Illinois: Scott, Foresman.

Suttles, G. 1968. *The social order of the slum.* Chicago: University of Chicago Press.

Sykes, R. and J. Clark. 1975. A theory of deference exchange in police-civilian encounters. *American Journal of Sociology* 81(3): 584-600.

Symanski, R. 1981. *The immoral landscape: Female prostitution in Western societies.* Toronto: Butterworths.

Tannenbaum, D. 1974. People With problems: Seeking help in an urban community. Research Paper #64. Toronto: Centre for Urban & Community Studies. University of Toronto.

Taylor, I. 1981. Crime waves in post-war Britain. *Contemporary Crises* 5 (January) 1: 43-62.

Thomas, W. and F. Znaniecki (1920). 1958. *The Polish peasant in Europe and America.* Bostono: R.C. Badger.

Tilly, C. and C.H. Brown. 1967. On uprooting, kinship and the auspices of migration. *International Journal of Comparative Sociology* 8 (September): 139-164.

Toronto Star 1974. 14 December, B1.

———. 1980. 28 November, A16.

———. 1981. 30 June, A4.

United Nations. 1952. *Comparative survey on juvenile delinquency, part I North America.* Division of Social Welfare, Department of Social Affairs, U.N. N.Y.: Columbia University Press.

Van Maanen. 1981. The informant game. *Urban Life* 9 (January) 4: 469–494.

Van Pouke, W. 1980. Network constraints on social action: Preliminaries for a network theory. *Social Networks,* 2:181–190.

Vyhnak, C. 1980. Yonge Street's tacky corridor gets a facelift. *Toronto Star* (9 August): B5.

Wallace, S. 1968. The road to Skid Row. *Social Problems* 16 (Summer) 1: 96–102.

Ward, C. 1978. *The child in the city.* London: Architectural Press.

Weber, M. 1946. Class, status and party. In H. Gerth and C.W. Mills (Ed.), *From Max Weber: Essays in sociology.* New York: Oxford University Press.

———. 1947 *The theory of social and economic organization.* New York: Oxford University Press.

Weitz, D. 1976. We still lock up children. *Toronto Life* (May) 56–61.

Wells, K. 1980. I came for the experience. *New Society* #917 (12 June).

West, W.G. 1978. The short term careers of serious thieves. *Canadian Journal of Criminology* 20(2): 169–190.

Whitney, K. 1970. Skid Row. In W.E. Mann (Ed.), *The underside of Toronto.* Toronto: McClelland & Stewart.

Wilson, J.Q. 1968. *Varieties of police behavior.* Cambridge, Mass.: Harvard University Press.

Wiseman, J. 1979. *Stations of the lost.* Chicago: University of Chicago Press.

Young, P.V. 1952. *Social treatment in probation and delinquency.* New York: McGraw-Hill.

Chapter 10

Serious Theft as an Occupation

*W. Gordon West**

For a number of decades, at least since Sutherland's and Cromwell's *Professional Thief*, sociologists have been analyzing various crimes in terms of the concept occupation. Property criminals have been the favoured although not exclusive topic. Such analyses have separated "real" criminals from amateurs or those of us who occasionally falter, and emphasized the normalcy of criminals in contrast to more psychological accounts. With only a few recent exceptions (e.g., Klein 1974), serious evaluation of the utility of such taken-for-granted conceptualization has been absent; in addition, application of such a concept to crime has not produced a reciprocal pay-off, whereby the unique features of the substantive topic are drawn upon for new conceptual clarification.

Theft and thieves have traditionally been regarded as prototypical forms of deviance, crime, and criminals.[1] Given the theoretical centrality of the nature of social order, property crime presents a challenge to the material basis of such order which is understandably of sociological interest. In addition, property crime is of great practical concern, since it composes about three-quarters of the specified criminal code violations (see Statistics Canada 1969; Bell-Rowbotham and Boydell 1972, 110). Since thieves and thieving have been the most established topics in applications of the occupation concept, problems analyzing this substantive area imply problems regarding other topics.

In considering the utility of conceiving of serious theft as an occupation, this paper uses data from participant observation research to challenge more traditional "professional" depictions, and suggests some modifications in the sociology of work. Such

---

* Ontario Institute for Studies in Education.

257

serious thieves do organize their activities occupationally, as the
professional thief literature suggests. Compared with amateurs,
their substantive activities, methods of acquisition, and organization of distribution indicate their occupational perspective, but
they lack the traditional qualities descriptive of professions and
professional thieves. In addition, because of the lack of formal
organization to their activities, its occupational nature has some
peculiarities, and force an extension of the conceptualization of
occupations.

THE TRADITION

Conceiving of serious theft in occupational terms has distinguished it from petty crime. Amateur theft has been extensively documented recently in self-report surveys (e.g., Byles 1969;
Vaz 1965), and a few other studies (e.g., Cameron 1964; Myerhoff
and Myerhoff 1964). Self-report measurements may be better
indicators than official statistics (e.g., Chimbos 1973) of the
frequency of crime in the general population (see Box, 1971), but
neither they nor the official statistics tell much of thieves or theft
themselves. Both types of research are methodologically flawed in
tending to rely on unsubstantiated verbal reports. A recent work
on *The Hidden Economy* (Henry 1978) affirms how widespread such
pilfering is, but underlines it relatively minor nature by advocating
diversion of such offenders from the official justice system.
Although almost all respondents indicate having committed some
property crimes at some time, most such behaviour has warranted
relatively little social concern. To this point, there are few sophisticated sociological analyses of such apparently random and
relatively isolated acts.

Some minor thefts, however, have been assimilated into a
proposed wider pattern of behaviour inclusive of other types of
deviance. "Irrational" thefts, thefts without a reasonable expectation of monetary gain, thefts committed primarily to incite a
reaction, thefts committed to hurt the former owner or to destroy
property — all these would constitute evidence that theft is not
pursued occupationally. Such characteristics would suggest other
explanations of theft such as mental illness or kleptomania (e.g.,
Eysenck 1964), thrill seeking (e.g., Cohen 1955), assertion of self-
hood (e.g., Matza 1964), or perverse values (e.g., Cloward and
Ohlin 1960). These alternative explanations *may* be satisfactory
explanations of certain kinds of theft, but they seem inadequate
for understanding the serious theft of most practical concern. In

examining serious thieves, criminologists have borrowed from the sociology of work. Symbolic interactionists (e.g., Hughes 1971, 286, 294) have conceived of occupations as clusters of task or work activities which link individuals to the larger society by providing them with a regular income of disposable resources in return for providing a service in economic production or distribution.

A number of characteristics are taken as indicative that an activity is pursued as an occupation. Occupations tend to be efficiently and rationally organized; goals are sought on the basis of an "objective" assessment of pros and cons. Practitioners develop a sensitive appreciation of potential opportunities for business. Risks peculiar to the occupation are collectively minimized; in an illegal job, practitioners disguise the crime and themselves as perpetrators. Routines are developed. In a distributing or marketing job such as theft, customers who are trustworthy, pay well, and handle quantities of goods are cultivated. Since an occupation is a person's main economic role in gaining resources, it must provide him with sufficient income to maintain his life style. Holders of the occupation look upon it as their "job" and share a culture which explains their activities to themselves and others.

This occupational analysis of serious thieves has resulted in a focus on professional thieves. Case studies (e.g., Sutherland and Conwell 1937; King and Chambliss 1972; Miller and Helwig 1972; Pollock 1973; Jackson 1969) and intensive interviews of prison-identified professionals (e.g., Denys 1969; Irwin 1970; Letkemann 1973; Waller 1974; Cressey 1953; Shover 1973; Lemert 1967a, 1967b, 1967c) have produced excellent analyses of the phenomenal worlds of such men. Unfortunately, such research has provided little information as to its generalizability, and relies on interview data with few observations offered as confirming evidence.

Even the most recent summaries still retain Sutherland's and Conwell's definition of the serious thief as a professional:

> The professional thief is one who steals professionally. This means, first, that he makes a regular business of stealing. . . .. Second, every act is carefully planned. . . . Third, the professional thief has techniques, skills, and methods which are different from those of other professional criminals. . . . The thief depends on his approach, front, wits, and in many instances his talking ability. . . . Fourth, the professional thief is generally migratory and may work in all the cities of the United States (Sutherland and Conwell 1973, 4).
> The essential character of the profession of theft are technical skills, status, consensus, differential association, and organization . . . the characteristics of any other permanent group. Certain elements run through these

characteristics which differentiate the professional thieves sharply from other groups (Sutherland and Conwell 1937, 197).

The professional thief makes crime his way of life, identifies himself with the world of crime, and is able to steal for long periods without incarceration (Inciardi 1975, 6). Inciardi identifies professional crime as referring to one type of career crime:

> Career crime can be defined as offence behaviour that is pursued in an occupational context for the purpose of obtaining a steady flow of income. The development of the criminal career begins with initiation and socialization into the world of crime, followed by a maturation process involving the acquisition of the skills, knowledge, and associations appropriate for maintaining the desired occupation (Inciardi 1975, 2).
>
> Professional crime refers to nonviolent forms of criminal occupation pursued with a high degree of skill to maximize financial gain and minimize the possibility of apprehension. The more typical forms of professional crime include pickpocketing, shoplifting, safe and house burglary, forgery and counterfeiting, extortion, sneak-thieving, and confidence swindling (Inciardi 1975, 2).

He then goes on to describe the recruitment and training, professionalization, business opportunities and earnings, fixing cases, and status as much the same as in Sutherland's account. He does admit that codes of ethics have weakened and that professional crime has declined since the 1940s (1975, 76, 132–33). Clinard and Quinney (1973) give a similar account in considering professional criminals as the polar example in their typology.

It is curious, however, that most of the above studies on professional thieves suggest at some point that they are a dying breed and that less skilled practitioners have come to dominate theft. Yet almost nowhere in the literature are accounts on these upstarts available, nor is the implication drawn that the professional conceptualization may be of very limited utility. Rather than assuming or denying such analyses on faith, it would seem advisable to recast research efforts by attempting a basic appreciative description of the life-patterns of serious thieves (Matza 1969). Only then can one assess the validity of conceiving of such criminals as professionals.

METHODOLOGY

In carrying out this research, I used participant observation methods (e.g., McCall and Simmons 1969; Schatzman and Strauss 1972; Becker 1970). Since there is no defined population of serious thieves, random sampling was not feasible. I initially gained access to 200–300 lower and working class delinquent Toronto boys through camp counselling, boys' club work and detached youth work between 1963 and 1969. In 1971, formal research began and I "mapped" this population and gained multiple entry to six main groupings in one area of town. Trading on personal relationships, I adopted the classic participant observer role of casually associating with two of the most delinquent of these groupings, participating in political, family, "work", and leisure time activities (e.g., pool, dances, drinking, etc.), initially emphasizing observation. Living in the neighbourhood over 12 months (in 1969 and 1972), my contacts expanded. Data were collected by observation on 143 days within the 13 months of intensive research, and on 40 additional days during the following year which was devoted mainly to analysis and writing. In addition, some 4 months after beginning the research, I began formal structured in-depth interviews with forty serious thieves, two nonthieving peers, two professional thieves and four "fences". Almost all of these were interviewed at least twice during sessions of from 90 to 120 minutes. Notes were generally recorded immediately after leaving the field; overall, some 750 pages of single-spaced typed notes were accumulated.

Generally, a process of analytic induction (Robinson 1951; Turner 1953) was used to develop "grounded theory" (Glaser and Strauss 1967). On initial entry to the field, I had only a general topic of delinquency and adolescent peer groups in mind. After doing a few initial interviews, it became evident that many of the youths to whom I had access were heavily involved in theft to make a living, and I focussed on this, using studies of occupations (e.g., Hughes 1971) as well as deviance to guide the research questions. After each interview or field observation, I elaborated the evolving analysis, and checked that the new data corroborated it; negating evidence was incorporated in revised hypotheses. By rechecking old notes, and seeking negative cases, the sampling design was elaborated. Reliability was established by retesting hypotheses, and cross-checking interview, observational and documentary data. In learning to live in the neighbourhood and participate in the everyday lives of thieves, I tested my understanding in a pragmatic sense countless times. Seven informants read reports and drafts, suggested modifications and offered new information; one became a veritable "Doc" (cf. Whyte 1955) upon his enrolling in sociology courses on returning to school at an "open-door" college. This method does not provide clearly defensible statements regarding the probability of such a social type as "serious thief" in various populations, but does allow theoretical and empirical analysis of the type (see Zeldich 1969; Sieber 1973).

Focussing on actors labelled as thieves rather than acts labelled as theft (Lemert 1967d), and using a "sensitizing concept" approach (Blumer 1969), I have operationally defined "serious thieves" as those persons having all the following characteristics: (a) being recognized and labelled by themselves as thieves; (b) being recognized and labelled by their peers as thieves; (c) having been officially convicted by courts or labelled by police as thieves; and, (d) having gained at least $500 in profit from theft within a two-year period or less, making at least $100 or at least one third of their total income from theft during any single month in which they were actively thieving (1971–72 figures). These criteria distinguish the subjects from petty or amateur thieves.

This definition gave me thieves who appeared adequately to represent the major characteristics of those figuring most prominently in the official court records, the thieves who occupy public concern. Of these forty studied intensively, all were working class, and from a densely populated Toronto neighbour-hood of high unemployment with many female-headed house-holds. Almost all were Anglo-Saxon or French-Canadian. Their mean schooling was 8.4 grades, most had committed petty theft as juveniles, and eight had been incarcerated as juveniles. The thieves who had left school and spent an average of 40-45 percent of their time unemployed by the time of the interviews, and 91 percent of them were unemployed at least 20 percent of this time. The jobs they obtained were low-paying (averaging $65-70/ week in 1971) and low status menial ones, such as printers' helpers, delivery-boys, etc. They had difficulty maintaining employment, averaging 7.5 months per first job, and 3.9 jobs in the average time of three years between school-leaving and inter-viewing. In sum, they all had economic problems. All thieves studied were male, and averaged 18.8 years at the time of the interviews, ranging from 15 to 23 years. These characteristics of the sample closely approximate those of official thieves as indi-cated in police and court data.

Since self-report studies (e.g., Box 1971) indicate few behavioural differences regarding acts of theft between social strata, the above factors may best be seen as more relevant to the elaboration (by youths and officials) of nondistinguishing petty acts of theft into the status of "serious thief" than simply as causes of "theft".

THE OCCUPATIONAL PERSPECTIVE

My initial concern is to describe the theft activities carried out regularly by the population of serious thieves studies, noting how their characteristics are indicative of an occupation. The thieves studied practised six specialties; I will describe three of these in some detail to indicate the range of behaviour, and highlight similarities and differences regarding other accounts. The interested reader can refer elsewhere (West 1974) for similar detail on houseburglary, vehicle theft, and fraud.[2]

Specialization

Shoplifting (12 practitioners) consists of legitimately entering a commercial goods outlet and stealing goods by removing them without payment (cf. Cameron 1964). It is often done surreptitiously by hiding the items sought in clothing, shopping bags, etc., leaving the proprietor in a state of double ignorance: neither the offender nor the offence is known (at least until inventory). An alternative method is known as "snatch-and-grab", whereby the "boost" is executed by simply running from the store after the item is procured. Clothing and electrical appliances are favoured items. Obviously, many "scores" have to "pulled" since each item is of no great value. Partners are often used to "keep six" (watch) in shoplifting.

This afternoon went with E. on a shoplifting expedition . . . he'd just gotten up at 1:00 when I phoned. . . . He decided on his own to actually boost something he wanted. . . . We walked into X, him about 30 seconds before me, and I looked at items around counters where I could casually observe him. Two clerks approached him to offer help, but he said he could pick out his own size, if it was okay, so they dropped off. Then he picked out the pair of pants he wanted; also a second pair which fit his waist but were too long (I could just make out at the time that it was two pair). He went into the change room and came out with the desired pair down his pants and the other over his arm. The manager approached and I got nervous. He stuck on E. and asked if he wanted the pants. E. said "NO, they're too long. . . ." Then the manager decided to really sell him a pair. . . . E. fended off any attempts at measurement by giving the manager his measurements (since if he taped his waist, he almost certainly would discover the clothes). He took another perfect fitting pair from the manager into the booth, tried them on, then emerged and complained about the price. They had a short talk on price, and E. agreed to look elsewhere, and then return if he couldn't find anything cheaper. Then he left the store. He used to take radios, etc., and tools, but they are very hard to get out in summertime. He mostly hits clothing stores but has stopped going there for money over the last few months. "It's summer and hard to wear big clothes." (He'd put a light wind-shell on today although it was 90, in order to hid the bulge). On normal expeditions though, he would have hit five or six places and taken the tags off and put the clothes into bags. "They can't get us then, they can't prove

where you got the goods. You leave the store after one item in each place"
(Observation 20 July 1972).

Commercial burglary (22 practitioners) is carried out
surreptitiously by breaking-and-entering a store, warehouse, or
factory and stealing expensive items or cash, often from coin-
operated vending machines. Times are selected when proprietors
are absent, usually at night. Entry and "casing" skills become more
important as most establishments make formal attempts to
prevent burglary. As with houses, windows are broken and doors
forced or locks picked; not infrequently, inside employees "set up"
the job for an "end" (or "cut") by failing to lock up property, etc.
Higher gains at $100–300 per thief per "score" reward the more
extended effort. Some thieves specialize further by "hitting" only
certain types of stores or sites, e.g., copper pipe is stolen from
buildings being demolished. Partners assist each other.

Commercial b and e's, sure. I couldn't say how many. Did some before the 3
year stretch, and a few after. We'd be going out night after night, until we
figured we had enough bread. I suppose 100 or 200 of them. Making
anywhere from nothing to 8000 a job. The average would be 300–500 I
suppose, divided 2 or 3 ways. We'd hit any place we thought had money.
Variety stores, restaurants . . . grocery stores, department stores even, a
few times after closing. We walked in there to the warehouse after it closed,
when the store was still open. Went through the tunnel and up over a gate
they had. Security guards tripping around — click, click — just an insane
caper really. Hiding behind counter, then sneaking out to grab coats and
stuff. I was just scared shitless. Then we put them in boxes and just walked
out through the doors in the main store. Oh, man, thinking back, we were
just nuts at times. But we got a few thousand dollars worth of coats
between the three of us. It was good money then. We always had money to
spend, huh, honey? We'd do it at night, when it's dark, get into the place
through windows. Avoid places with alarms and stuff. Places with back
alleys were good. Take a crowbar, maybe a screwdriver. We generally
avoided tips on places, and never went high. All over downtown was our
place. We hit C time after time, right around the corner here. Mistakes?
You could keep going back too much. Or come in on the same score for
another load of goods. That's what we did to get nabbed for the 8000 job.
We were taking out our fourth load of stuff. So the guy happened by and
asked "what you doing here?" I went "Alee!" threw the shit up in the air, he
surprised me so, and ran, saying "Uh, I just wanted a pack of cigarettes!"
And goddamn if there wasn't one car going by with a cop in it! I ran out the
back and was almost away, but he followed me in the snow, and I got
trapped by the subway tracks. I almost jumped, but it was 40 feet or more.
And he pulled a gun and said "Don't jump!" I saw it and said, "Eeee, okay, I
won't" (Group Interview 17 July 1972).

"Clouting" (5 practitioners) consists of stealing goods in transit. Delivery vans are followed, then unloaded while drivers are absent or distracted; warehouses are entered and goods loaded onto legitimate-looking carriers. If well done, with a good "front" (performance in disguise), the victim is unaware of his loss as well as the identity of the criminal. As with commercial burglary, "inside" information helps, as otherwise the packages stolen are of unknown value. Partners are common.

> Did a lot of clouting — especially that year after the three year stint in jail. K. had got very bold at it; we operated around downtown mostly, all those Jewish clothing stores. Occasionally around the post office too. You just have guys keep six down the alley with a parked truck, or car. Your car is around the corner waiting — taxis are too risky. Then you smash the no-draught with a hammer or knock off the locks with crowbars, grab what you want and split. We never stole whole trucks — that's hi-jacking and you get big time for that. For clouting at the loading docks, you just drive up and load stuff onto your car if you think of a place you can get away with it. Or hop inside the warehouse. Best if there are a lot of guys running around, you just fit in as another face among forty guys. If anybody questions you, you just make like you know what you're about — ask him questions. . . . Clouting is really safe. Once only did we have trouble. You see, if you take a factory or warehouse, they usually don't even know you took stuff. Not until they take inventory a year later. If you hit trucks, of course, its different cause the guy knows when he comes back or at the least by night when he tallies up. . . . We'd make maybe a hundred a hit on the average (Group interview 17 July 1972).

None of the forty thieves interviewed practised all six specialties in the sense of making $500 or more per specialty. Yet all were recognized by practitioners of other specialties as thieves, and every specialty was practised by persons who worked in additional specialties as well. Many of the attributes and required skills (most of which are not unique to thieves) are common across specialties. Strength and fighting abilities, speed and agility, sharp eyes and quick wits, and the ability to deceive are commonly valued. Simple entry skills are common to commercial and residential burglars, clouters, and car thieves. General mechanical and automotive skills are useful. This encourages versatility and interchangeability.

There is a tendency to concentrate efforts in one specialty. Interestingly, however, the more successful thieves (those who claimed over $10,000 profit) were more likely to have practiced a number of specialties than the less successful ones. This suggests that no one specialty is sufficiently lucrative to produce success; versatility is required.

Corroborating this versatility, but surprising in terms of other studies (Sutherland and Conwell 1937; King 1972), there is no obvious, commonly shared estimation of the status of most of the types per se.

Appropriation: Interaction with Victims

In seeking a rationally calculated profit, the thieves studied developed definitional skills which indicate their occupational orientation.

Thieves are skilled at perceiving "set-ups"; goods and money are most easily stolen when the owner's control is "weakest".

> We drove up Yonge, chit-chatting about movies and girls. They pointed out some stores that were easy to hit. "That one only has girls in it." Then the talk switched to my car; they could get me bucket seats cheap. We passed a liquor store with open shelves — they plan to return. . . . Back down through Rosedale to look at big houses. (They might have been casing them too?) (Group observation 16 November 1971).

> We went driving over to downtown and cased around the back alleys. . . . It's noticeable that a thief would spend a fair amount of time casing joints if he wanted to do it well. Hours of checking how a particular car lot works. Or what the hours of a shop were, or how often the cops patrolled. Probably half his time could be spent casing places and getting information on them. Also very noticeable that a thief is *continually* assessing places. . . . The kids also have mentioned over and over again that each place is different, each really has its particular thing. And I see how that really is true (Observation 12 June 1972).

Another skill is the ability to accurately calculate the likely results of illegal acts. They carefully estimated the losses against the possible gains to be made.

> Cars? No, I try to stay away from them. . . . Too much risk and too little gain. You gonna get caught pulling stupid little things like that. We tried a few b and e's in houses around here. But nobody around here has any money and nobody has any goods worth anything. (Interview 6 June 1972).

The thief attempts to transform a social situation which has defined property relations into a job-site for work. In doing so, he *ipso facto* seeks to impose another set of property relations, but eschews the force used in violent crimes (e.g., robbery). Since other actors in the situation, especially victims, have a stake in maintaining the previously existing set of relations, and have the ability and legal sanction to invoke force in enforcing *their* definitions (by either using force themselves or by calling their agents, the police), the thief finds it impossible to gain public consensual acceptance of his definitions and actions. He is forced to resort to other means for maintaining control over his work situation (cf. Conwell and Sutherland 1937, 4), such as disguising (a) the criminal act and (b) his status as a criminal. Burglars and car thieves avoid confronting victims; in return for more victims, shoplifters, clouters, and fraud artists develop "fronts".

> I walk into a place and you got to look in all the mirrors. If somebody can see you, you can see them. Once this lady was watching me, and I just looked at her, and talked to her you know, asked her how much this was and how much that. Meanwhile behind my back, I picked up a drill, and put it up my back, buttoned up my coat in front, then said I didn't have enough money, waited until she turned around so nobody would see my back, and then walked out with the drill up my coat. It's really easy sometimes (Group interview 17 September 1971).

They all attempt to minimize the time when they appear as thieves.

The thief develops a number of routine moves should he be discovered in the act; his victim is usually comparatively disadvantaged by the extraordinary character of the interaction.

> Once J. and me opened a car-door with a couple necking in the back. We pretended we were drunk. Grabbed the new car and left (Interview 15 December 1971).

"Mistakes" are claimed, or the situation is abandoned. Bold counterchallenges "up the ante".

> If I got hassled, I'd act as if *they* were at fault. Once I kicked up so much shit in a bank, I had everybody looking and I thought they'd nab me for disturbing the peace. I yelled about how difficult they were to deal with, how I'd change my account and get the damn cheque cashed elsewhere, and stomped out . . . (Interview 21 January 1972).

Confusion may be created.

> We'd go down to the Market. We'd ask how much meat was, and when the lady turned, we'd grab a 20 and con her in. One time we got a place we could slip bills through a wall, and got some. And C. went on the floor with his cash and a guy saw him, and so he just threw the box of money at him and we ran. Money all over the place (Interview 4 November 1971).

Most victims back off at the threat of violence.

> You pick a store with little people in it. I punched a guy out once when he caught me. Other times I just ran and got away. Or jumped fences and moved off (Interview 25 November 1971).

Sometimes running is most effective; if caught, a "sob story" is resorted to.

Distribution: Interaction with Customers

All thieves illegally take possession of other people's money or goods, but only those who consider their theft occupationally are left with a problem of disposing of the goods. Although their methods, job sites, and hours of operation vary, serious thieves are left with the common problem of disposing of these stolen goods and converting them as quickly as possible into money or material that is personally desired.

> After a while, other than cigarettes or the copper, I just took cash since it's much easier to get rid of, to carry and harder to trace. You got to have a immediate buyer if you take goods — otherwise you get caught with them sometimes. I'd not even touch stereos and stuff as you can't always get rid of them (Interview 6 June 1972).

In stealing goods, the thief exploits others' trust of him; in disposing of these goods, being assured that he can trust others becomes a major problem for him; good customers, in contrast to victims, hold a definition of the situation in common with the thief.

There are three main types of customers to whom these thieves sell directly. Some are "legitimate" merchants, perhaps pawnbrokers or keepers of secondhand stores. Such merchants usually deal in only a few lines of goods, and hence, only handle some of the goods obtained by a jack-of-all-trades thief, so he usually needs other connections as well. In addition, the problem of trust is aggravated, as the merchant is more likely to "fink out" under police pressure to identify or entrap the thief while saving his own skin. In addition, they offer only 10-20 percent of the retail value of the goods.

Much more trustworthy are personally known consumers who will use the goods themselves. The thief must know many local people who are potential buyers; geographical stability is thus an asset. No single consumer buys much, but they do pay about 33 to 50 percent of the retail value.

Hence, the best type of customer is the "fence" or receiver of stolen goods (see Messinger 1966; Klockers 1974; Leonard 1974; Hall 1952), who usually maintains some plausible legitimate "front", such as a variety store. Being dependent on ten to thirty thieves for supply, the fence is relatively trustworthy; having three to ten bulk buyers as well as a few hundred consumers means he can dispose of most goods. They usually pay 20 to 30 percent of the retail value. The preference of thieves for the most trustworthy and profitable fences and consumers as customers further indicates the occupational nature of their activities.

The serious thieves studied made enough money to support themselves. Operating expenses (e.g., operating a car) are shaved as much as possible, regular customers are cultivated who can quickly receive hot goods, and bargains are sought in a fast changing market. The thieves studied gained an average income of about $50 per week in some two to twenty-five hours of work/week, approximately what their peers earned in thirty-five hour legitimate jobs available to such uneducated working class youngsters (1971 figures). Their collective gains amounted to an estimated quarter million dollars of profit (a figure which is 10 to 50 percent of the retail loss), and they averaged about $7,000 over their individual careers. The biggest single score was $3,500, but the usual amount varied from nothing to $300 to $400.

As a job, theft has many intrinsic attractions. It is exciting and challenging work, often requiring full use of one's physical and mental capacities. The hours required are small (compared with other jobs); most thieves seem to work from two to twenty-five hours a week. A person can set his own hours. There is a constant variety in the working-setting and tasks. A youth can be his own boss; he is self-employed. He uses his own initiative. His colleagues are usually congenial and often old friends. No formal education is required and admission is not barred by low social class or restrictive unionism.

IMPLICATIONS

As the above quotations suggest, the evidence in my field-notes is overwhelmingly in support of the hypothesis that serious thieves operate according to an occupational perspective. It is nonetheless relatively clear that the serious thieves studied do not readily fit Sutherland's characterization of professional thieves.

Whereas Sutherland claimed that few professionals came from slum or working class backgrounds, all the thieves studied did. Although this occurred primarily because of my sampling procedure, these cases nonetheless suggest that different cate-gorization might be appropriate. My contention is that serious theft of the types described is indeed more attractive to working class youngsters than middle class ones, who may perpetrate more sophisticated thefts (e.g., cheque forgery) and comparatively escape detection. This would explain the apparent paradox that although self-reported *acts* of theft are relatively evenly dis-tributed throughout the various strata of society (see Box 1971; Byles 1969), occupancy of the *status* of thief remains a working class phenomenon.

The predominance of urban adolescent males as serious thieves reflects traditional male role demands of earning a living in combination with serious employment problems and a lack of conventional bonds (see West 1978; Miller 1967). Access to serious theft activities is provided through the adolescent peer group in a relatively stable geographically bounded community (see West 1978). Sutherland's professionals, on the other hand, were older, not recruited through such adolescent groups, and geographically mobile.

Most crucially, it is clear that the skill levels of the serious thieves studied are much lower than that of professionals. As a result, they get much less money per "score", must commit many more deviant acts, and almost inevitably get arrested within a couple of years. As they are not able to "lay a patch" ("fix" cases), multiple convictions threaten long-term incarcerations, and a career crises develops. As described elsewhere (West 1978), this crisis often coincides with the acquisition of conventional bonds (especially a wife and legitimate job opportunities) and the status of serious thief is abandoned. Lack of a firmly committed self-identity assists in this process.

Only a few serious thieves have access to professional thieves and even fewer are able to become more sophisticated criminals, as indicated by my extreme difficulty in contacting professionals directly through my subjects.

A — The difference between the two: well, the guys over there at the poolhall they really make a business out of it. They're organized and they have connections and money to back them up. And they get into some really heavy shit. And they have the angles like I said (Interview 13 June 1972).

E — You talk about guys hitting only their own neighbourhood or city, that's amateur stuff. A lot of what you say is amateur, really, Gordie. . . . Well, it *is* a profession. It's a skilled guy who can pull off the best jobs. . . . You say here they make 50–75 a week. That's peanuts. No pro would settle for that. Boosters make 600–1000 a week. They got to figure in overhead, and the danger of getting pinched. You want to risk doing 18 months for 50 bucks? That's nuts. You couldn't interest me in a job under 10 grand. You need to case the place, maybe pay a few guys. Say each one on salary gets 1500 each. There's nothing left unless its a good sized job. . . .

Me — How many guys are pros like you're describing?

E — Not even 5% of the thieves in and out of jail, that the cops know of. Maybe 20 or 30 in the city. Then they'll work with some 1000 or so semi-professionals. Like I used to be when pulling jobs while I was in my twenties. Guys'll move from town to town, connecting in on jobs. Some of those will be partial amateurs, we'll cut in on jobs sometimes to test them out or while training them. Then there's 50,000 amateurs in Toronto. It's hard to put figures on it, but something like that (Interview 17 June 1973).

The serious thieves studied are basically representative of the majority of those thieves who are of most concern to society. Serious thieves may then be further defined and distinguished from professional thieves: (a) they do not have as highly developed skills, such as safe-cracking, confidence racketeering, pick-pocketing, or counterfeiting; (b) serious thieves are non-migratory; (c) serious thieves can rarely "patch" ("fix") cases that come to the attention of the police; and (d) as a result, serious thieves spend two-thirds to three-quarters of their time locked up (compared with one-quarter to one-third of professionals' time) if they continue thieving for more than a couple of years; (e) serious thieves make much less money, talking of "scores" of hundreds of dollars rather than thousands. Nonetheless, their activities are clearly occupational.

Table 10.1 Evidence for the Occupational Perspective Among Serious Thieves[3]

	Social Status Serious Thief	Other
Occupational Perspective	302	4
Other Perspective	11[4]	24

There would thus appear to be a continuum of thieves. At the most populated but least serious end are amateurs. Almost all juveniles commit some property offences, and may best be thought of as "troublemakers", "excitement seekers", and "status-rebels", best described by Matza (1964) and Werthman (1969) (but see also Cohen 1955; West 1975). At the other, least populated, but most serious end are the professionals; most accounts of such professionals suggest their numbers are declining, and that they might live on more in sociological accounts than in real life, where big criminal money has switched to corporate and organized crime (e.g., Klein 1974; Inciardi 1975, 82, 132–33). These polar types, however, do not encompass the most numerous, serious thieves of public concern.

Occupying a mid-point between amateurs and professionals, serious thieves remain almost ignored in the literature. The least professional subjects in a few studies resemble mine (e.g., Helwig and Miller 1972; Letkemann 1973; Lemert 1967c; Shover 1973). Miller (1967) and Short and Strodtbeck (1965) provide some good observational data, without considering thieves in terms of a status. Perhaps the closest accounts are those few of "hustlers" (e.g., Inciardi 1975, 32ff; Irwin 1970; Irwin 1975), but these tend to emphasize much more integration with other crimes (e.g., re sex, robbery, and drugs) than my subjects display. Clinard's and Quinney's (1972) analytic category of "conventional criminal" is appropriate, but their descriptive references are mainly to studies on juvenile delinquents and gangs. Schwendinger (1963) details similar left markets, but also focusses on delinquency.

Accepting the occupational nature of serious theft also forces some modification of conceptualization in the sociology of work to include short-term occupations in general. The short-term nature of such jobs entails a high turnover of occupants, and makes recruitment a continuous recurring problem. High skill development is impossible during the short incumbency, and so training must precede entry to the occuption if proficiency is required. Occupants tend to "expend" themselves quickly. The turnover of incumbents leaves "rough edges", a certain lack of integration between different positions, and institutional instability. Without a clear career pattern, personal commitment is weak, and self-identification focusses either on one's profession or nonwork roles rather than on the organization.

Many social service jobs (e.g., youth work, international-aid-program jobs), many working class jobs (e.g., "hopping" newspapers, labouring jobs), some other illegal jobs (e.g., prostitution), athletic occupations (e.g., football), and some mobile upper class jobs (e.g., consultants, administrative "trouble-shooters"), all seem to have some of these common characteristics. Such short-term jobs seem to be increasing in the economy. They serve to provide bridges between well-institutionalized career lines, and allow for a certain flexibility in the "free-enterprise" expansion and contraction of certain areas of work.

In some ways, serious theft is an extreme example of such short-term occupations. Its illegal nature precludes formal recognition of occupancy of the status; even in a court of law, one is convicted of an act rather than a status. Maintenance of "fronts" encourages a self-functional distancing. The uncertainty of the term of occupancy further reduces commitment.

Although serious theft is a short-term and age-specific occupation, it reveals that a job need not be long-term to attract incumbents and realize an occupational form. Nor is it necessary for an organization to have long-term positions-incumbents for it to persist (Simmel 1898). Despite the high turnover, the institution carries on.

Notes

1. In Canadian law, a thief is one who is convicted of taking another's property without his permission.

(1) Everyone commits theft who fradulently and without colour of right takes or fradulently and without colour of right converts to his use or to the use of any other person, anything whether animate or inanimate, with intent,
  (a) to deprive, temporarily or absolutely, the owner of it or a person who has special property or interest in it, of the thing, or of his property or interest in it,
  (b) to pledge it or deposit it as security,
  (c) to part with it under condition with respect to its return that the person who parts with it may be unable to perform, or
  (d) to deal with it in such manner that it cannot be restored in the condition in which it was at the time it was taken or converted.
(2) A person commits theft when, with intent to steal anything, he moves it or causes it to move or to be moved, or begins to cause it to become moveable.
(3) A taking or conversion of anything may be fradulent notwithstanding that it is effected without secrecy or attempt at concealment.
(4) For the purposes of this Act, the question whether anything that is converted is taken for the purpose of conversion, or whether it is, at the time it is converted, in the lawful possession of the person who converts it is not material (Martin et al. 1972, Section 283).

2. Houseburglary (twelve practitioners) consists of breaking-and-entering a home and stealing goods or money. Times are selected when the owner is absent or asleep. Entry skills are crucial, as the burglar does not gain access legitimately. Among the thieves studied, however, such skills are only crudely developed, and usually consist of breaking windows or forcing doors or locks. A few thieves develop enough skill to pick locks, or cultivate contacts who obtain master keys for them. Many of the thieves studied concentrated on local dwellings as these were most familiar. Expensive electrical goods, clothing, and money are the usual items stolen. Partners are often used to "keep six" and maintain morale.

Vehicle theft (nine practitioners) consists of stealing expensive bicycles or cars, which (other than houses) are usually the most valuable single items possessed by individuals. High skills (such as "hot-wiring") are unnecessary, since many downtown lots require car owners to leave their keys in the cars in order to repark them bumper-to-bumper. The thieves merely drive cars off the lots without paying, or wait until after closing hours, when the attendants must place the keys back into the car for their owners. The cars are then "stripped down" for parts or searched for goods; no thieves I knew sold the cars whole, and Toronto police statistics indicate about 95 percent of other vehicles are recovered (Statistics Canada 1969, 85–205). As with shoplifting, a number of cars must be stolen to make a profit comparable to burglary, as each car only averages about $10–20 profit. Car theft is often practiced alone.

Fraud and forgery (six practitioners) are the least practised specialties among these thieves. Basically, schemes are elaborated whereby someone else's signature or worthless paper is exchanged for money or goods. Bogus cheques, stolen identification and credit cards, "scams" on returning merchandise, etc., are endlessly elaborated. Operations are usually carried on during regular business hours. Only six of the thieves interviewed practise this solitary specialty, as it seems to require middle class skills and appearances which few can emulate (cf. Lemert 1967c; Denys 1969; Cressey 1953; Jackson 1969).

3. This table has been constructed by counting items of information found in the field notes relevant to the hypotheses. It thus provides a quasi-statistical indication of the weight of data supporting the hypotheses as stated. See Becker et al. (1961) for further examples and elaboration.

4. These 11 negative cases generally consist of incidents when serious thieves reverted to "theft-as-a-lark".

References

Becker, H.S. et al. 1961. *Boys in white.* Chicago: University of Chicago Press.

———. 1970. *Sociological work.* Chicago: Aldine.

Bell-Rowbotham, B. and C.L. Boydell. 1972. Crime in Canada: A distributional analysis. In C.L. Boydell et al., *Deviance and societal reaction in Canada.* Toronto: Holt, Rinehart and Winston.

Blumer, H. 1969. The methodological position of symbolic interactionism. In his *Symbolic interactionism.* Toronto: Prentice-Hall.

Box, S. 1971. *Deviance, reality and society.* Toronto: Holt, Rinehart and Winston.

Byles, J. 1969. *Alienation, deviance, and social control.* Toronto: Interim Research Project on Unreached Youth.

Cameron, M.O. 1964. *The booster and the snitch.* Toronto: Collier-Macmillan.

Chimbos, P.D. 1973. A study of break-and-enter offences in Northern City, Ontario. *Canadian Journal of Criminology and Corrections* XV, 3 (July): 316–25.

Clinard, M.B. and R. Quinney. 1973. *Criminal behaviour systems.* Toronto: Holt, Rinehart and Winston.

Cloward, R. and L. Ohlin. 1960. *Delinquency and opportunity.* Toronto: Collier-Macmillan.

Cohen, A.K. 1955. *Delinquent boys: The culture of the gang.* Toronto: Collier-Macmillan.

Cressey, D.R. 1953. *Other people's money.* Toronto: Collier-Macmillan.

Denys, R.G. 1969. Lady paperhangers. *Canadian Journal of Corrections and Criminology* XI, 165–192.

Eysenck, H.K. 1964. *Crime and personality.* London: Routledge and Kegan Paul.

Glaser, B. and A. Strauss. 1967. *The discovery of grounded theory.* Chicago: Aldine.

Hall, J. 1952. *Theft, law & society.* Chicago: Bobbs-Merrill.

Henry, S. 1978. *The hidden economy.* London: Martin Robertson.

Hughes, E.C. 1971. *The sociological eye.* Chicago: Aldine.

Inciardi, J. 1975. *Careers in crime.* Chicago: Rand McNally.

Irwin, J. 1970. *The felon.* Toronto: Prentice-Hall.

_____. 1975. Symposium on modern hustling. *Urban Life,* 4(2):197.

Jackson, B. 1969. *A thief's primer.* Toronto: Collier-Macmillan.

King, H. and W. Chambliss. 1972. *Box man: A professional thief's journey.* Toronto: Harper (Fitzhenry and Whiteside).

Klein, J.F. 1974. Professional theft: The utility of a concept. *Canadian Journal of Criminology and Corrections. XVI(2):133*–44.

Klockars, 1974. *The professional fence.* Toronto: Collier-Macmillan.

Lemert, E. 1967a. The behavior of the systematic check forger. In his *Human deviance, social problems, and social control.* Toronto: Prentice-Hall.

_____. 1967b. Role enactment, self, and identity in the systematic check forger. *Ibid.*

_____. 1967c. An isolation and closure theory of naive check forgery. *Ibid.*

_____. 1967d. The concept of secondary deviation. *Ibid.*

Leonard, H.B. 1974. The fence: Alive and well. *Criminology made in Canada* 11(1): 13–28.

Letkemann, P. 1973. *Crime as work.* Toronto: Prentice-Hall.

Martin, J.C. et al. 1972. *Martin's annual criminal code.* Agincourt, Ont.: Canada Law Book Ltd.

Matza, D. 1964. *Delinquency and drift.* New York: Wiley.

Matza, D. 1969. *Becoming deviant.* Toronto: Prentice-Hall.

McCall, G. and J. Simmons. 1969. *Issues in participant observation.* Don Mills, Ont.: Addison-Wesley.

Messinger, S. 1966. Some reflections on "professional crime" in West City. Mimeo.

Miller, B. and D. Helwig. 1972. *A book about Billie.* (retitled *Inside and outside*) Ottawa: Oberon.

Miller, W.B. 1967. Theft behavior in city gangs. In M. Klein and B. Myerhoff (Eds.), *Juvenile gangs in context.* Toronto: Prentice-Hall.

Myerhoff, H.L. and B. Myerhoff. 1964. Field observations of middle-class gangs. *Social Forces* 42 (March):328–36.

Polock, D. 1973. *Call me a good thief.* Montreal: Transformation Information Centre.

Robinson, W.S. 1951. The logical structure of analytic introduction. *American Sociological Review* XVI, 6 (December).

Schatzman, L. and A. Strauss. 1973. *Field research.* Toronto: Prentice-Hall.

Schwendinger, H. 1963. *An instrumental theory of delinquency.* Unpublished Ph.D. Dissertation, U.C.L.A.

Short, J. and F. Strodbeck. 1965. *Group process and gang delinquency.* Chicago: University of Chicago Press.

Shover, N. 1973. The social organization of burglary. *Social Problems.* XX(4): 499–514.

Sieber, S. 1973. The integration of fieldwork and survey methods. *American Journal of Sociology* LXXXIX (May).

Simmel, G. 1898. The persistence of social groups. *American Journal of Sociology* 3 (July).

Statistics Canada. 1969. *Census* No. 93–609. Ottawa: Information Canada.

Sutherland, E. and C. Conwell. 1937. *The professional thief.* Chicago: University of Chicago Press.

Turner, R. 1953. The quest for universals in sociological research. *American Sociological Review* XVIII.

Vaz, E. 1965. Middle-class adolescents: Self-reported delinquency and youth culture activities. *Canadian Review of Sociology and Anthropology* 11(1) (February).

Waller, I. 1974. *Men released from prison.* Toronto: University of Toronto Press.

Werthman, C. 1969. Delinquency and moral character. In D. Cressey and D. Ward (Eds.), *Crime, delinquency and social problems.* Evanston: Harper and Row.

West, W.G. 1974. *Serious thieves: Working-class adolescent males in a short-term deviant occupation.* Unpublished Ph.D. Dissertation, Northwestern University.

_____. 1975. Adolescent perspectives: On being a greaser, freak or straight. Paper presented to Annual Meetings of Canadian Sociology and Anthropology Association.

_____. 1978. The short-term careers of serious thieves. *Canadian Journal of Criminology* 20(2), April.

Whyte, W.F. 1955. *Streetcorner society.* Chicago: University of Chicago Press.

Zelditch, M. 1969. Some methodological problems of field studies. In G. McCall and J. Simmons (Eds.), *Issues in participant observation.* Don Mills, Ont.: Addison-Wesley.

Chapter 11

Target Hardening Burglary Prevention and the Problem of Displacement Phenomena

John Lowman*

One of the strategies emerging out of the crime prevention through environmental design literature (Jacobs 1961; Jeffery 1971; Newman 1972) aims at taking the opportunity out of crime by "hardening" targets and increasing the risk of would-be offenders. A number of concerns have been registered about such strategies ranging from criticisms of their philosophical and political implications (particularly the tendency towards developing a fortress mentality) to uncertainty about their actual crime prevention effectiveness. While these two issues are ultimately related, my purpose in this paper is to investigate the latter by examining the effects of a burglary prevention program — "Neighbourhood Watch", introduced to British Columbia in 1976. At the heart of the uncertainty is not so much whether certain crime prevention programs do help to reduce crime opportunities, but that if they do, is this effect achieved simply at the expense of the displacement of crime to other times, locales or types? (Reppetto 1976; Maynew et al. 1976; Winchester 1978; Davidson 1981) The appropriateness of target hardening crime prevention strategies is based on the assumption that certain types of crime are so opportunistic in their commission that the reduction of opportunities will reduce crime much more than it displaces it. This argument is particularly applied to residential burglary, especially because the great majority of known offenders are juveniles (e.g., Reppetto 1976; Hakim and Pengert 1981). In the

* Department of Criminology, Simon Fraser University, British Columbia.

literature, burglary, especially that committed by juveniles, appears as the "opportunistic crime" par excellence, the exemplar of situationally induced, or victim precipatated crime.

While the possibility of displacement of crime in response to target hardening has been raised, the discussion remains at a speculative level and, despite the uncertainty about the effectiveness of such programs, millions of dollars have been devoted to their implementation in North America (Krajick 1979). Although the programs appear to be effective in the homes adopting them, program assessments (in the rare cases where any kind of assessment has been made at all) have not dealt with the possibility of crime displacement. Consequently the uncertainty about the effects of the programs continues. Should an assessment of burglary prevention programs demonstrate the occurrence of displacement phenomena? And especially if this appears to reflect adaptive behaviour of juvenile offenders, then residential burglary may not be opportunistic in the sense that much of the literature conveys. In focusing on the criminal event and the apparently highly opportunistic nature of burglaries (in the study are many breaking and enterings which do not actually involve any "breaking" — entrance is made through an unlocked or open door) the intentionality of the burglar may be, to some extent, misconceived.

These remarks are not meant to suggest that a certain group of individuals will commit crime, any crime, no matter what attempts are made to restrict crime opportunities. Nor are they meant to suggest that crime opportunities can not be restricted. But if significant displacement effects so occur, this finding would seem to suggest the need to reconsider certain aspects of the opportunistic nature of burglary and the intentions of the burglar.

The analysis reported here is restricted to what Mayhew et al. refer to as "specific displacement" — displacement of activity *within* a particular crime category — as opposed to "general displacement" to different types of crime (1976, 5). In Reppetto's terms (1976) the scope of the analysis is restricted to "target" and "place to place" displacements of residential burglary with no attempt to identify any form of "typological" displacement (i.e. general displacement).

Evidence will be offered to suggest that Neighbourhood Watch (and its subcomponent "Operation Identification") prevention programs are in the study areas to prevent burglary, but that this effect appears to be short-lived, and at the expense of the displacement of burglaries to homes not adopting the

p. 278, last paragraph, line 3 — For "prevention programs are in the study areas to prevent burglary" read "prevention programs in the study areas do prevent burglary"

program or neighbouring areas where the program is not implemented.

Because of the type of data available it must be recognized that the evidence for these effects is variable and in no sense conclusive. It is, however, both highly suggestive and cumulative.

"NEIGHBOURHOOD WATCH" IN BRITISH COLUMBIA

In 1976 the first Neighbourhood Watch burglary prevention program to be implemented in the Canadian Province of British Columbia was introduced on an experimental basis in Burnaby, the urban municipality immediately east of the City of Vancouver.

Following the initiative of the Burnaby R.C.M.P. detachment in liaison with the British Columbia Police Commission most of the other provincial police forces, at the behest of the Police Commission, soon followed suit (Robinson 1977). The Vancouver City Police Department was one of the first to do so following the success reported by the personnel responsible for the pilot project in Burnaby. Because of this success, the Burnaby project was extended to cover the remainder of the municipality. The analysis concentrates on the Burnaby and Vancouver programs, although the emphasis on each is not quite the same.

Because of differences in the way the Vancouver and Burnaby Police record and collate reports of burglary, only the Vancouver statistics can be aggregated at a small spatial scale — into area units equivalent to two city blocks. But unfortunately, the Vancouver City Police Department has kept very few records of the Neighbourhood Watch implementation plan. In contrast, the Burnaby R.C.M.P. Police Department had fairly detailed records of the implementation plan, but no facility to spatially aggregate burglary data at any scale smaller than patrol areas. It has thus not been possible in either jurisdiction to examine the effect of the progressive stages of the implementation of Neighbourhood Watch or local burglary patterns in a number of different neighbourhoods. It has, however, been possible in one.

Although the Vancouver program appears to have been implemented in a rather hapharzard fashion, what records are available were collected by one of the police officers responsible for the first phase of the program in Vancouver's "West End", a residential area in which apartment buildings predominate (both low-rise and high-rise and compartmentalized houses) adjacent to the central business district. Because of a program funding problem, its implementation in this area was completed some six months before being extended to surrounding locales. The analysis of Neighbourhood Watch in Vancouver thus concentrates on this small project area in an attempt to assess the impact of the program on local burglary patterns.

Given the information available, the Burnaby program will be used to identify the purpose of Neighbourhood Watch, and the rationale for its implementation in British Columbia in the first place. To the extent that both Burnaby and Vancouver programs were coordinated by the B.C. Police Commission the rationale underlying the Burnaby program can be generalized to describe the Vancouver project. Some of the findings of the Burnaby Police' assessment of their general program will also be discussed in order to assess its crime prevention effectiveness, indications of target displacement, and to act as a backdrop for the analysis of the effectiveness of the Vancouver West End project.

Unfortunately the police assessment of the test project in Burnaby does not address the problem of displacement — rather the study focuses exclusively on the deterrent effect of the program as compared to a "control" area of the same size and roughly similar characteristics in terms of its residential composition. The areas are not contiguous with the result that it is almost impossible to discern geographic displacement effects that might be associated with the experimental program in Burnaby.

"NEIGHBOURHOOD WATCH": THE RATIONALE

"Neighbourhood Watch" (with its subcomponent "Operation Identification") is a "target hardening" strategy aimed at both reducing the opportunity for burglary and increasing the risk to the would-be breaking and entering offender (the terms "burglary" and "breaking and entering" are used interchangeably here). According to the booklet describing Neighbourhood Watch to the public, the program consists of three elements.

1. Neighbourhood Watch — a program of co-operation among families in your area to make your entire neighbourhood more secure.

2. Property Identification — a method of safeguarding your valuable property with non-removable identification (Operation Identification)

3. Home security — a program to protect your home and family through upgrading of the home itself, and tips on personal security within the home (British Columbia Police Commission, 1)

The program aims at developing a "co-operative community effort" between the police and members of the public to reduce crime "at the grass roots" level. As well as "target hardening" strategies, the program is based on the idea that the police cannot reduce crime without the active involvement of the public; to this end the booklet stresses the concept of community cooperation.

> Neighbourhood Watch is a program of mutual assistance among neighbours. . . . Get to know your neighbours. Introduce them to the concept of Neighbourhood Watch. Get involved. A neighbourhood where people are alert to the potential of crime and willing to look out for one another's interests is a neighbourhood where crimes are least likely to occur. . . . Good neighbours working together through Neighbourhood Watch can prevent crimes in their area the most effective way — before it starts (British Columbia Police Commission, 1).

The philosophy of the program clearly derives from the approach first articulated by Jane Jacobs (1961).

In terms of target hardening, "Operation Identification" aims at discouraging the burglar before he/she enters a home. The information booklet describes three basic steps in the target hardening process:

1. Electric engraving pencils are available at your local police agency free of charge. Borrow one of these engravers for a day or two and simply engrave your social insurance number on all items of value in or about your home. These markings cannot be removed, and if the item is stolen it can easily be traced. But, what is more important, burglars hesitate to steal easily traceable goods, and proper identification may well discourage the theft before it takes place.[1]

2. Highly visible tamper-proof decals are also available through your local police. Applied to your valuable items, these decals will further discourage theft by warning burglars that the item has been properly identified and will be easily traced if stolen. It will also alert police that the item has been engraved.

3. Larger decals for use on windows or exterior doors of your home are also available from your local police. They serve to discourage break-ins by warning would-be burglars that the contents of your home have been properly identified and will be easily traced if stolen (British Columbia Police Commission, 2).

The purpose of this target hardening is to upgrade a residence to a point of "minimum security" that would discourage most burglars from breaking in. The information booklet notes that "it is impractical and virtually impossible to make your home completely burglar-proof" but that most burglaries are relatively unsophisticated "crimes of opportunity". The point of minimum security is that where destructive force must be applied to gain access to a residence. On the strength of the apparent effectiveness of several highly localized experimental programs the information booklet suggests that "Neighbourhood Watch ... will, with your cooperation, drastically reduce the incidence of burglary in your area."

Should this information booklet be correct about the opportunistic nature of burglary (it points out that most burglars are under seventeen years of age despite the fact that the only illustrations of burglars are caricatures of adult masked "professionals") then not only should Neighbourhood Watch take the opportunity out of the crime and reduce the number of burglaries, but it should also be unlikely to result in any form of displacement. While the experience of these small-scale intensive programs suggests that they reduce burglary drastically, the displacement effects associated with them have scarcely been researched,[2] particularly when the programs are extended to cover entire municipalities such as Burnaby and Vancouver.

THE BURNABY EXPERIENCE: EVIDENCE FOR THE DETERRENT EFFECT OF SMALL SCALE PROGRAMS

Towards the end of 1975 the Burnaby R.C.M.P. studied the effectiveness of a number of crime prevention programs to see which might be usefully implemented in their jurisdiction. The choice of Neighbourhood Watch was based on the success of similar strategies, particularly the ones in Monterey, California, and Revelstoke, Ontario. In Monterey, 5,500 homes were labelled and approximately the same number left untouched. In the twelve years since the implementation of the program, 2,500 break-ins occurred in the unprotected homes while there were only 29 burglaries at protected residences (*Time Magazine* 26 January 1976). The astonishingly disproportionate magnitude of these figures suggests that a displacement effect may be associated with the program, but without information pertaining to the burglary rates prior to its implementation this must be a highly speculative observation.

The Revelstoke program was conducted on a much smaller scale than its Monterey equivalent. The Ottawa police marked all valuables in the 135 homes in Revelstoke and placed large signs at the entrances to the community indicating that the area was protected by "Operation Identification". Homes were marked with stickers to indicate their participation and extensive news media coverage was given. While the police expected the program to decrease burglaries by 25 percent, not one of the homes participating in the program was burgled in its first eighteen months of operating (Burnaby R.C.M.P., 2).

By virtue of these findings, and other reports of the success of similar programs, the R.C.M.P. decided to implement a pilot project in Burnaby in order to ascertain its effectiveness in a different municipal setting. Following the general failure of other programs which had relied on literature mailed to residents requesting their participation, Neighbourhood Watch was chosen because it involved a direct contact between police or volunteer workers with every household in the pilot project area, and subsequently with as many households in the remainder of the municipality that could be physically contacted (an attempt was subsequently made to contact them all). The police believed that such an approach could effectively overcome the main problem of their less intensive "Stop Thief" program that preceded Neighbourhood Watch — what they perceived as public apathy. To encourage public involvement it appeared to the project organizers that in the implementation of any program the police must display positive crime prevention activity and must initiate public response. To this end Operation Identification appeared to be the solution on three grounds:

a) The program is police-oriented and can be easily controlled.
b) Marking is permanent — apathy cannot erase it.
c) The program can be easily evaluated (Burnaby R.C.M.P., 3).

Unfortunately, the problem of displacement was never considered in the evaluation of the pilot project and, as it turns out, an evaluation in these terms is anything but easy. Indeed, rather than using the pilot project to test the effectiveness of the program, plans were made *before* the pilot project began to extend the program to the remainder of the residences in Burnaby. Had the pilot project proved unsuccessful the police could have presumably aborted the program elsewhere. As it turned out the pilot project appeared to provide dramatic results in terms of its deterrent capacity. The test area was located in a "high-crime" area and contained approximately 800 residences. Between 7 and 31 January 1976, 95 percent of the homes in the area were visited by 47 teams made up of representatives of the R.C.M.P. (both auxillary and regular members) and members of the local Rotary Club. The Burnaby police evaluation of the test area operation over a three month period claimed a 79 percent reduction in break-ins (Burnaby R.C.M.P., 8).

Almost immediately after the completion of Operation Identification in the test area the program was extended to the rest of Burnaby. For organizational purposes the municipality was divided into three "areas", and each of these subdivided into "districts" of approximately 200 homes. The districts were further subdivided into "units" of about 10 homes, with a community volunteer responsible for the implementation of the program in each unit. Three thousand volunteers attended training sessions held at Simon Fraser University run by the Operation Identification staff. Volunteers worked their immediate neighbourhoods only, and loaned an engraver to each household, supplied the resident with a copy of an Operation Identification booklet and small decals to apply to marked property. The large house decals were handed out after the volunteer had checked that household valuables had been engraved (Burnaby R.C.M.P., 10-12).

By early September 1976 some 30,000 of the estimated 48,500 residences in Burnaby had been completed. Most of those residences not completed were low-rise and high-rise apartment units which characteristically have lower breaking and entering rates than single family or two family dwellings.

EFFECTS OF THE GENERAL MUNICIPAL PROGRAMS

During the 1970s in the United States hundreds of millions of dollars were spent on crime prevention programs like Neighbourhood Watch and Operation Identification. The initial elation over their apparent success has given way to a widespread skepticism:

> ... the fact is that most security surveys and target hardening programs, are so undermanned or disorganized that they make hardly any impact. The L.E.A.A. survey of 206 such programs found that in only one of five such programs did police contact more than 10 percent of the households in their jurisdictions (Krajick 1979, 10).

> A large part of the problem is that police agencies around the country have adopted a standard battery of crime prevention programs half-heartedly, or as part of a general public relations and public education effort whose results will never be reflected in any crime statistics (Krajick 1979, 7).

This wholesale indictment of crime prevention programs suggests that when poorly implemented they have very little effect. But evidence presented below shows that the Burnaby and

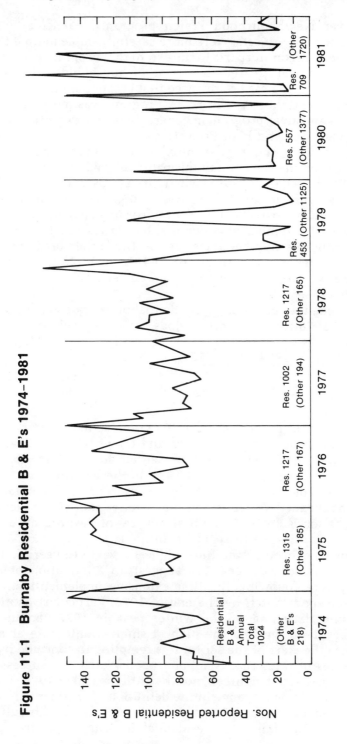

Figure 11.1 Burnaby Residential B & E's 1974–1981

p. 286, third complete paragraph — Delete the fourth sentence and replace it with "In 1977, the first full year of the program in operation, the rates were the lowest in the five-year period apart from the first six-month segment."

Vancouver Neighbourhood Watch programs, particularly the small-scale pilot projects, were more carefully implemented than their American counterparts to the extent that program personnel contacted a much greater proportion of households. The argument will nevertheless be advanced that because of differences in their implementation, the Burnaby program was more effective than the Vancouver program in general (with the exception of the Vancouver West End Pilot Project).

Figure 11.1 shows the number of reported residential burglaries for the Burnaby municipality as a whole. Neighbourhood Watch began in 1976 when there was a total of 1,217 burglaries, while in 1977 there were 1,002. In 1978 the overall number returns to 1,217. In 1979 a recording change appears to take place; the number of residential burglaries falls to 453, but, significantly, the number registered in the "other breaking and entering" category rises from 165 in 1978 to 1,125 to 1979 and their relative proportion of the total number remains equivalent through 1981.[3]

The changes of reported residential burglary rates between 1974 and 1978 for six month periods are shown below:

	1974	1975	1976	1977	1978
Jan.–June	430	573	633	518	567
July–Dec.	588	782	692	486	650

The first six-month period in 1974 represents the first use of the current crime recording system and shows the lowest rate of any of the time segments represented here.[4] The highest segment rate is the latter part of 1975. In the latter part of 1976, the first six-month period of the widespread implementation of Neighbourhood Watch in Burnaby, we see the second highest rate in the series. In 1977, the first full year of the program apart from the first six-month segment. In the latter part of 1978 the rate climbs again to be the third highest level in the series. The trend of this series appears to suggest an attenuation of the burglary rate following the first extensive implementation of Neighbourhood Watch by the end of 1976. Particularly noticeable is the flattening of the winter peak in 1977–78. But in November 1978 we find the highest single-month rate at any time since the start of the series. It is tempting to conclude from the changes in rates that Neighbourhood Watch was successful for a period of about eighteen months until the end of 1978. Then what appears to be a change in the definition of "residential" and "other" breaking and enterings makes interpretation difficult.

Figure 11.2 illustrates residential burglary rates in Van-

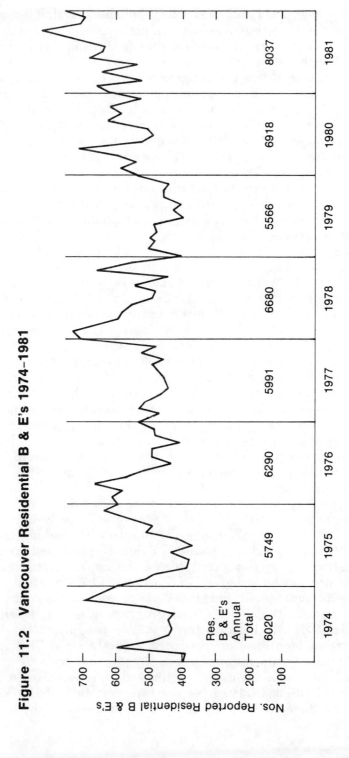

Figure 11.2 Vancouver Residential B & E's 1974–1981

p. 288, last paragraph — Lines 12-14 should read "rates. Because victimization surveys suggest that only a fraction of the actual number of burglaries are reported to the police — the number is usually estimated at between one-third and ⅓DA one-half (Skogan 1976) — the interpretation of the Van-"

288

couver between 1974 and 1981. Neighbourhood Watch began in Vancouver in 1976, but was not comprehensively implemented in the way that it was in Burnaby during this same year. Some areas in Vancouver were not canvassed until 1977 or even later. (In both municipalities the programs have been available on a continuing basis — if a citizen approaches the police department engraving pens are made available. But the implementation of the program was most effective and extensive when citizen groups, and sometimes police officers, actively canvassed an area as was generally the case in Burnaby.)

The Vancouver burglary time-series data are very difficult to interpret with regard to the impact of Neighbourhood Watch. To begin with, every year witnessing a *drop* in the burglary rate (1975, 1977, 1979) is followed by one with an increase in the rate — and vice versa — with the exception of 1981. Neighbourhood Watch began in 1976, and active canvassing continued through 1977 and 1978. There is a reduction in the overall burglary rate in 1977, but in 1978 the rate rises to be the highest in the first five-year period for which data are available. As in Burnaby the drop in 1977 is produced by the "flattening" of the winter season rate "peak". But this rate reduction occurs before the completion of a widespread implementation of Neighbourhood Watch in Vancouver. By the end of 1976 the program in Burnaby was two-thirds complete. While it is impossible to gauge the exact figure in Vancouver, it was nothing like this extensive (the implementation of the program in the test area of Vancouver's West End did not occur until the summer of 1977). From the trend of the Vancouver statistics, no clear pattern emerges as to the deterrent effectiveness of the program — the rate did go down in 1977 slightly, but then it was lower still in both 1975 and 1979.

Two complications should be born in mind when attempting to interpret the meaning of these time-series data. The first concerns the potential effect that a program like Neighbourhood Watch has on the *reporting* of burglary as opposed to its actual effect on burglar behaviour. Evidence presented from a victimization survey conducted during the implementation of a burglary prevention program in Portland, Oregon, suggested that the percentage of burglaries reported to the police increased during the period the program was implemented (Schneider 1976). In Ditton's terms (1979), the implementation of Operation Identification produced a "fantasy-rise" in crime rates. Because victimization surveys suggest that only a fraction of the actual number is usually estimated at between one-third and one-half (Skogan 1976) — the interpretation of the Vancouver and Burnaby burglary time-series profiles is complicated

p. 289, third complete paragraph — Lines 2-3 should read "of the percentage of households adopting the program, the more households adopting the program, the less the possibility of geographic or target displacement occurring. A"

by the possibility that increased reporting rates hide actual reductions in the amount of burglary. We shall return to this problem in the discussion of area displacement effects presented below.

The second complication arises from differences in the Vancouver and Burnaby programs. In general terms the Burnaby program appears to have been better organized than the one in Vancouver. An evaluation of the effectiveness of the first year of the program in Burnaby was conducted by the local police whereas very little in the way of evaluation of their own program was conducted by the Vancouver police. Two pieces of evidence are available which reflect the differing degrees of success of the two programs. The first is in terms of their impact in increasing risk to offenders. An examination of changes in clearance rates tends to demonstrate the different effectiveness of the two municipal programs:

Table 11.1 Percentage of Burglaries Cleared in Vancouver and Burnaby Police Jurisdictions

	Vancouver % cleared*	Burnaby % cleared*
1974	12.9	18.5
1975	11.5	11.2
1976	12.8	16.8
1977	13.3	35.9
1978	11.1	36.8
1979	11.81	36.6
1980	10.5	21.3
1981	8.7	17.0

* Reports unfounded or cleared by charge.

In Burnaby following the introduction of Neighbourhood Watch in 1976, clearance rates approximately doubled for a three-year period and then dropped again in 1980 and 1981 to the level obtaining before the introduction of the program. In Vancouver no particularly significant difference in clearance rates appears to have occured. The differences may reflect the varying success of the two programs.

A second indication of their varying success would be in terms of the percentage of households adopting the program, the less the possibility of geographic or target displacement occuring. A victimization survey conducted by Simon Fraser University's Criminology Research Centre in 1979 included a question on the respondent household's participation in Neighbourhood Watch. Estimates based on the survey sample suggest that 43.2% of the total number of households in Vancouver participated in Neighbourhood Watch, 63.3% in Burnaby. If the Burnaby program is more effective than its Vancouver counterpart by virtue of greater participation then the Burnaby program is more likely to be successful in preventing burglary. This greater degree of success may be apparent in the burglary rates for Burnaby which appear to show a reduction in 1977 and 1978 following the introduction of Neighbourhood Watch. Whatever success the Vancouver program had may be lost in fluctuations in the rate which occur for entirely different reasons, particularly if the smaller percentage of households adopting the program in Vancouver created the greater likelihood of target or geographic displacement. In either case, the displacement of burglary to unprotected homes will obscure the deterrent effect of the program in homes protected by it. For the moment, it is sufficient to note that the potential effect of displacement combined with reporting changes brought about by the program make it very difficult to assess the deterrent effectiveness of Neighbourhood Watch from the municipality level data. It is nevertheless tempting to conclude from the Burnaby data that the program had some deterrent effects and the evidence for the deterrent capacity of a small-scale program, such as the one in Monterey, appears to be unequivocal. What of the evidence for displacement? We begin with evidence for target displacement in Burnaby and then proceed to the problem of geographic displacement as the result of the West End pilot project in Vancouver.

EVIDENCE FOR DISPLACEMENT

Burnaby and the Evidence for Target Displacement

The Burnaby R.C.M.P.'s evaluation of the first year of the Burnaby-wide program (July 1976 — June 1977) includes a detailed description of the numbers of break-ins to residences protected by Operation Identification as compared to the number in unprotected residences. Unfortunately in only 59 percent of the cases through this one year period could it be ascertained from the original crime report form whether a residence was protected by Operation Identification or not. Of the 665 break-ins for which information could be ascertained, 329 occurred in protected residences and 336 in unprotected residences (Burnaby R.C.M.P. 1978, Appendix 1). For the month of June 1977 a survey of the residential burglary crime reports which did not include information about Operation Identification was conducted by visiting the victimized household to check for stickers. The survey showed that 67 percent of these residences were not protected by the program. While it is impossible to attain an exact figure for the number of residences protected by the program in Burnaby, we do know that 30,000 of the 48,500 residential units were contacted by program staff by September 1976 (Burnaby R.C.M.P. 1978). Most of the residences not contacted were apartment buildings which typically experience a lower burglary rate than single and two family homes (apartments are more difficult to burglarize). If the figure for the "unknown" reports for June is indicative of the proportion for the rest of the twelve-month period, a further 313 break-ins occurred in unmarked residences. The cumulative totals would then read 483 break-ins to Operation Identification protected residences, as compared to 649 to unprotected residences.

It should be reiterated, these figures are based on a generalization of the June 1977 ratio of marked to unmarked properties which were not recorded as such on the crime reports — there is no way of knowing whether such a generalization is reliable. Nor is there anyway of establishing the ratio of residential burglaries in apartment building units as compared to single- and two-family dwelling units. The very fact that not much of an attempt was made to implement Operation Identification in apartment buildings is an indication of their comparatively lower break-in rate in general, and confirmation that opportunity does have something to do with the burglar's target selection.

In addition to the aforementioned problems, it is impossible to tell how many of the 30,000 residential units contacted by the Operation Identification personnel actually responded by adopting the program, although the program evaluation report conveys the impression that a large majority did. If this is the case, and if we assume a 70 percent adoption rate, by September of 1976 the *greater* proportion of single- and two-family dwellings in Burnaby had adopted the program in 1978 — by this time there were still households in Burnaby which had not adopted the program. (The victimization survey data reported above suggest that 3 percent of the *total* households in Burnaby had adopted the program in 1978 — by this time there were still households in Burnaby never contacted by program personnel. The Simon Fraser Criminology Research Centre Victimization Survey showed that in 1979, 76 percent of single-family houses had adopted the program, but only 44 percent of the apartments.) If all of these assumptions are correct one is left with the conclusion that while a greater proportion of single- and two-family dwellings had adopted the program,

p. 291, last paragraph — Lines 8-10 should read "had adopted the program. (The victimization survey data reported above suggest that 63 percent"

by far the greatest number of break-ins occurred in those units which had *not* adopted the program. Had the rate of burglary for protected residences been equivalent to the rate for unprotected residences, there would have been 1,052 break-ins to protected residences, and 1,701 burglaries in Burnaby as a whole between June 1976 and July 1977. This latter figure is significantly higher than the burglary rate in Burnaby for any twelve-month period for which data are available. Had the rate in unprotected residences been the same as the rate in the protected residences, there would have been 781 burglaries in Burnaby, a rate lower than at any time between 1974 and 1978. There were in fact 1,122 burglaries reported in Burnaby between July 1976 and June 1977. These hypothetical figures, together with the different rates of victimization of unprotected and protected residences, suggest that Operation Identification does prevent burglaries, but at the expense of a greater victimization of unprotected residences — a target displacement occurs.

From the geographic point of view, what this means is that target displacement of the sort described here may occur instead of or together with geographic displacement (depending upon the percentage of residential units which adopt the program in the first place, and the geographic extent of the program's coverage). *The geographic displacement might thus be between neighbourhoods or within them.*

From the evidence presented to this point, a plausible argument can be made suggesting that target displacement was associated with the Burnaby program once it had been fully implemented. While the pilot project was claimed as being highly successful in reducing crime no means of assessing its effect in displacing burglary to other areas was included. This effect would presumably be most intensive in the vicinity immediately adjacent to the test area, but in lieu of more detailed statistics this hypothesis simply cannot be tested. But the statistics for such a test are available in Vancouver.

The West End Program in Vancouver: Evidence for Area Displacement

Neighbourhood Watch was introduced to Vancouver's West End residential district late in 1976. The program was first advertised in a series of neighbourhood meetings at local community centres and at gatherings of the West End Ratepayers Association in January, February and March 1977. Two police

constables responsible for implementing the program also contacted apartment owners and other local groups in the hope that
they would cooperate. From May to August 1977, six students
were hired to help introduce the program on a door-to-door basis.
Canvassing began in the English Bay area of the West End, and by
the end of the summer the team hoped to complete the area
between Denman, Burrard, Davie and the English Bay shoreline
(see Figure 11.3). By September 1st, 1976, 80 percent of the households in the area had been contacted.

In September the program suffered a temporary setback
when funding for it was suspended by city council. The door-to-
door campaign was discontinued, and residents who wanted to
enter the program had to do so of their own initiative by borrow-
ing marking pens from the local library.

The interruption of funds in this way has created a fortunate
circumstance for examining the spatial impact of Neighbourhood
Watch in Vancouver to the extent that an area where Operation
Identification was systematically implemented by a system of door
to door canvassing is juxtaposed to an area where the program
worked on a purely voluntary basis; as noted earlier a survey of
similar programs in the United States suggests that many more
households adopt such programs if police or their representatives
directly contact householders (Krajick 1979, 13).

In order to assess the impact of Operation Identification we
must ascertain the deterrent effect of the Neighbourhood Watch
program in the test area. As noted above, small-scale intensive
programs have been shown to be successful elsewhere as was the
case with the Monterey program (*Time Magazine* 26 January 1976)
and the results claimed for the first three months of the Burnaby
pilot project indicate a 79 percent reduction in burglary. Also the
available evidence from Burnaby suggests that Operation Identification protected homes are not burglarized at the same rate as
unprotected homes. Although I have not been able to conduct
interviews with burglary offenders, Michael Robinson (1978)
interviewed convicted burglars in Vancouver and Richmond
(another municipality in the greater Vancouver area). Four of the
eight offenders he talked to indicated that they avoided premises
protected by Operation Identification. While it is difficult from the
overall burglary rate in Vancouver to establish the deterrent
effectiveness of the general program, the method of its implementation in the test area is one which elsewhere has had a
considerable measure of success in recruiting residents, and thus
in its general potential for deterring would-be burglars. With
these considerations in mind it seems reasonable to argue that
what appears to be target displacement as a result of the general

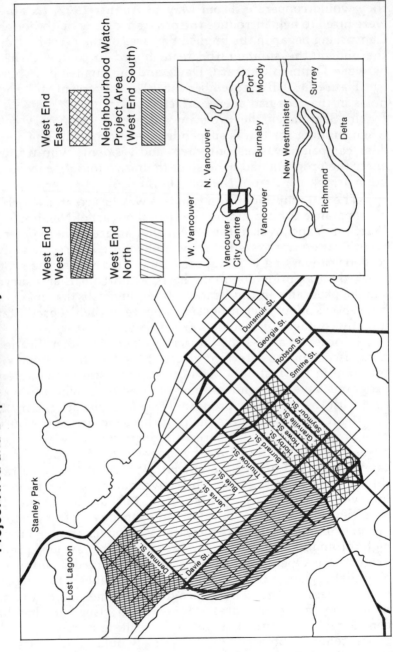

Figure 11.3   Vancouver West End Neighbourhood Watch Project Area and Displacement Study Areas

Burnaby program may translate into an area displacement in the case of geographically restricted pilot projects.

The Neighbourhood Watch Pilot Project Area is shown in Figure 11.3. In searching for displacement effects, burglary rates in three areas adjacent to the project area were examined (West End West, West End North, and West End East). While the Vancouver Police statistics enable the reconstruction of burglary rates for small areas such as these, the records contain no information about which victims were protected by Neighbourhood Watch. Unfortunately, therefore, no assessment of target displacement within the project area can be made. The analysis proceeds on the assumption that while target displacement could occur in the test area (not all the residences contacted would have adopted Operation Identification), it would in this case be more likely to occur geographically — a search for unprotected targets would make some burglars concentrate on unprotected areas, especially in the West End of Vancouver where the project area is located *within* a distinct neighbourhood.

The burglary rates for the four areas depicted in Figure 11.3 are shown in Table 11.2. In the project area the average number of burglaries per month during the twenty-four month period prior to the implementation of Neighbourhood Watch (January 1975 to December 1976) was 10.6. During the first twelve months of Neighbourhood Watch (1977) the monthly average declined by some 20% to 8.0. This rate reduction may be indicative of a deterrent effect of the program, especially if reporting rates increase as a result of its implementation. The rate during the first six months of 1977 was particularly low, however, (just over two burglaries

Table 11.2   Burglary Rates in the West End of Vancouver

					West End North								
	J	**F**	**M**	**A**	**M**	**J**	**J**	**A**	**S**	**O**	**N**	**D**	**Total/ Monthly Average**
1975	22	16	21	12	25	20	23	18	15	15	25	32	242 $x=20$
1976	38	25	27	37	20	28	28	29	39	16	21	15	323 $x=27$
1977	12	15	20	13	22	32	32	29	38	43	38	39	333 $x=27.75$
1978	51	35	36	33	36	27	42	34	40	38	43	24	436 $x=36.3$
1979	36	32	24	23	26	34	25	24	19	20	29	23	315 $x=26.25$
1980	1	32	34	30	29	28	31	40	28	32	25	29	

West End South
(Project Area)

	J	F	M	A	M	J	J	A	S	O	N	D	Total/ Monthly Average
1975	16	7	9	5	7	4	14	11	4	9	12	12	109 $x=9$
1976	21	8	11	11	7	27	25	7	7	10	4	7	145 $x=12$
1977	4	8	4	1	1	8	10	10	11	8	18	14	97 $x=8$
1978	16	11	14	19	13	6	20	16	17	34	12	10	189 $x=15.75$
1979	19	15	8	6	15	7	13	7	9	20	11	22	144 $x=12$
1980	2	15	15	19	22	9	31	12	19	14	14	16	

West End West

	J	F	M	A	M	J	J	A	S	O	N	D	Total/ Monthly Average
1975	1	3	1	0	5	3	3	2	0	0	4	0	22 $x=1.08$
1976	0	0	0	1	1	1	2	3	3	3	0	0	14 $x=1.1$
1977	0	1	1	1	2	2	0	3	2	0	1	1	14 $x=1.1$
1978	1	0	1	4	5	0	1	1	0	3	1	0	17 $x=1.4$
1979	1	0	3	2	11	1	1	1	0	0	1	0	11 $x=0.9$

West End East

	J	F	M	A	M	J	J	A	S	O	N	D	Total/ Monthly Average
1975	0	3	7	6	7	3	8	6	10	6	8	15	79 $x=6.6$
1976	20	13	12	7	8	7	7	7	13	2	2	4	102 $x=8.5$
1977	4	5	7	4	7	9	8	13	10	7	8	7	89 $x=7.4$
1978	22	18	20	19	16	9	6	16	26	14	10	6	182 $x=15$
1979	10	10	3	4	6	10	4	3	3	7	7	6	73 $x=6$

per month) while the rate from July through December was much
higher. Again increased reporting may be responsible for part of
the change.

In 1978, the rate increases to 15.75 burglaries per month, a rate much higher than the preprogram level. But by this time the distinction between levels of adoption of Operation Identification in the project area and surrounding areas would have been significantly reduced — it is noteworthy that the rate in the surrounding areas also increased to a point where it was higher than levels in 1975 and 1976. Once again, this increase may reflect changes in burglary reporting, but such an explanation would not seem to explain the magnitude of rate increases. From her assessment of Operation Identification in Portland, Schneider notes that each increase in reporting (as measured by a victimization survey) was accompanied by an increase in the rate of official burglary (1976, 138). But the increase in reporting which she attributes to the introduction to Operation Identification, if it can be extrapolated to the Vancouver situation, would not be sufficient to explain the rate changes occurring in the West End — Shneider shows a 20% difference in reporting rates while the rate in the project area in 1978 is double the rate it was in 1976, the year immediately prior to the introduction of the program. But in the residential area Schneider studied, only 17% of the households had adopted Operation Identification — in the West End project area the rate of adoption was much higher. The Simon Fraser University Criminology Research Centre Victimization Study estimates that 43.2% of households in Vancouver adopted the program — in the project area the percentage is likely to be higher because of the systematic method of team canvassing used. In the West End there were three follow-up visits if the first one was made when no one was at home. For most of the project area, every residence was visited (the 20% not visited were in a small block area in the south east corner of the project area — the number of burglaries in such a small area is so low that a meaningful analysis of displacement in this area could not be made). There was, then, likely to be a much higher rate of adoption of the program in the West End test area than elsewhere in Vancouver, some of which was not canvassed systematically or not canvassed at all. The rate increase in the project area in the later part of 1977 and the general increase in the West End in 1978 (as more homes in West End North adopted the program), may be at least partly attributable to reporting changes, especially in light of Schneider's evidence that it is adopters of Operation Identification who are responsible for increased reporting (1976); adopters of the program reported 80% of burglaries, nonadopters 65%.[5]

Alternatively, the rates may have changed for entirely different reasons. If burglary rates were increasing in the West End, the introduction of Operation Identification could simply

p. 297, first paragraph, line 29 — Insert "four" after "small" slow the rate of increase. In this case the program would have a deterrent effect, but one hidden by the simple comparison of different rates at different times. From the available data this possibility is difficult to account for. The point is that the deterrent effect on the program cannot simply be measured by comparing rates during the program with rates before the introduction of the program — random fluctuations and seasonal variations make the process of extrapolation difficult. The overall rate in the project area is nevertheless lower in 1977 than in the preceding two year period or thereafter. This is not, however, the case in West End North. A comparison of the rates in the two areas tends to confirm the conclusion that Operation Identification reduced burglaries in the project area, but only at the expense of an increase in West End North (Table 11.2 and Figure 11.4).

In attempting to identify displacement effects I have focused on rate changes in the three areas immediately adjacent to the English Bay Project Area (see Figure 11.2). A short description of each of these areas is warranted.

The area to the northwest of English Bay is largely comprised of high-rise apartments. It has characteristically had a very low burglary rate averaging approximately 1.5 break-ins per month (Table 11.2). It is physically separated from the main part of the Neighbourhood Watch project area except at the south end of Denman Street. During 1977 the burglary rate remained the same as the year before. It seems reasonable to conclude that no displacement of burglary into this area occurred.

The area to the east of the project neighbourhood consists of a mixture of low-rise apartments, duplexes and single-family dwellings, but for the most part is a commercial area. Many of the residential burglaries occurring in this area may be from the rooms of the numerous hotels but, unfortunately no statistics are available to show exactly how many of the burglaries in this area are of this type. For the two years prior to 1977 the monthly average was 7.6 while in 1977 it was 7.4. In 1978 it rose to 15.0, but by this time the area could have been expected to contain more adopters of Neighbourhood Watch. This abrupt increase occurs at the same time as the sharp increase in rates in the program area. In terms of displacement one might not expect to see much of an effect in this area for two reasons: (1) the area as defined only borders the program neighbourhood for a distance of four blocks and two of these were not canvassed by the program personnel; and (2) where the two areas do border each other, they are separated by the North End of the Burrard Street bridge, and this forms a natural boundary to the West End area. Not only is this a physical boundary, but may also form a boundary to social group-

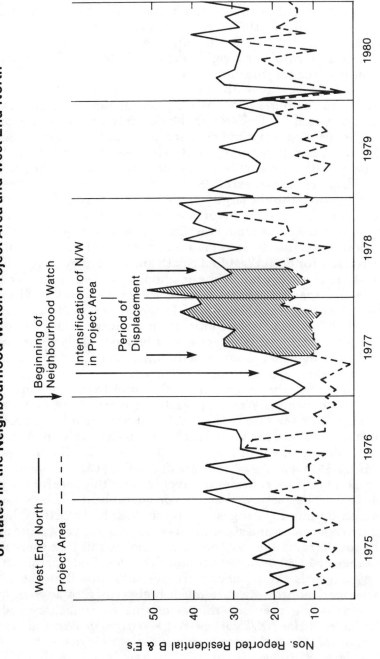

Figure 11.4 Residential Breaking and Entering in Vancouver's West End: A comparison of Rates in the Neighbourhood Watch Project Area and West End North

activity spaces — the schools in the West End area lie in to the north of the project area, and since most burglars are juveniles (over 80 percent of the known burglary offenders in Vancouver between 1978 and 1981 were juveniles), their already developed activity spaces may determine the direction of any displacement of targets as a result of Neighbourhood Watch (in this respect see Brantingham and Brantingham 1981).

This leaves us with the area immediately adjacent to the project to the north. For the purposes of this analysis data have been collected for the area six blocks to the north of the project neighbourhood — a number of studies of burglars have suggested that most burglaries occur relatively close to the offenders home, usually within one mile of it (for a review, see Phillips 1980; Davidson 1981; Herbert 1982). The area described as West End North should thus be large enough for any area displacement to be recognizable. West End North is separated from the project area by Davie Street, the main West End thoroughfare providing access to both areas. Davie Street is a commercial strip, and a focal point of activity for both West End North and the project area. The two areas are thus very much one neighbourhood with a similar mix of high-rise apartments and houses; the two schools servicing the project area are both north of Davie Street. If Neighbourhood Watch did indeed displace burglary, then it is to the area north of Davie Street that the effect would be most likely to be noticed. While the evidence is not exactly unequivocal, a displacement of burglary does appear to have occurred.

In the twenty-four month period prior to the implementation of Neighbourhood Watch in West End North the rate was 23.5. During 1977 the rate rose to 27.5. But one must be careful here, the monthly rate for West End North in the twelve months prior to the development of the program in West End South was 27.0. During 1976 and 1977 the rate did not appear to change much. Not, that is, if we consider the average monthly rate for the whole of 1977. The picture changes considerably if we examine the month-by-month changes by rates in West End North as the team of two policemen and six students gradually canvassed the area to the south from May 1977 onwards. Prior to this time there was an average of 15.5 burglaries per month in West End North. But from May onwards the number increases substantially to 36.5 burglaries per month — a rate much higher than in any six month period in the previous thirty months for which records are available. *As the Neighbourhood Watch program in West End South was implemented through the summer months, residential burglaries appear to have been displaced northwards.* In 1978, when Neighbourhood Watch canvassing was extended into West End North, the burglary rate

may be inflated by reporting changes, especially if most of the increase in reporting is attributable to adopters of the program as Schneider suggests. A victimization survey would be needed to test this hypothesis. But whatever the case, the highest rates in West End North for the six-year period shown in Figure 11.4 occur in the six-month period immediately following the implementation of the test program in the project area.

As well as this evidence for geographical displacement of burglary offences, other evidence suggests that a different form of displacement occurred within the project area. The police officers responsible for the program noted that after the intensive summer campaign a change had occurred. While the number of homes protected by Neighbourhood Watch had been broken into, no marked items had been taken — instead the burglars removed cash and jewelry (West End Courier 15 September 1977). Unfortunately, it has not been possible to gain access to the original crime reports where this information is recorded and so it is not possible to establish the period during which this type of displacement would have remained in effect.

IMPLICATIONS OF THE ANALYSIS

Neighbourhood Watch and Operation Identification do seem to be effective in reducing burglary, particularly when implemented intensively in small areas. Where the plan is implemented at a wider scale, evidence from the Burnaby R.C.M.P. (1978) and the Schneider study (1970) suggest that Operation Identification reduces the rate of burglary for those adopting the program, but evidence in Burnaby suggests that the preventative effect is minimized by target displacement. In the case of a smaller-scale program, target displacement appears to assume a geographic dimension as some burglars concentrate on unprotected areas as a way of concentrating on unprotected homes. Other burglars simply adopt their behaviour by refraining from taking marked items, others are not deterred at all. Whatever preventative effect the program has for those who adopt it is probably short-lived. In Vancouver the program did not seem to affect the clearance rate for residential burglaries, while in Burnaby the effect appears to have been temporary. In keeping with this finding the Burnaby program seemed to have a more noticeable impact in reducing the overall residential burglary rate, despite the evidence for target displacement, than did the program in Vancouver. Because the Burnaby program was adopted in a greater percentage of house-

p. 301, last paragraph, line 12 — Substitute "adapt" for "adopt"

holds than was the case in Vancouver, and because the munici-
pality-wide program in Burnaby was completed in an eight-month
period, its effect in suppressing burglary would be more noticeable
than in Vancouver where it took two years to implement the
program (Vancouver is a much bigger municipality in terms of
both area and population). The declining success of the Burnaby
program and the apparent lack of success of the Vancouver
program as evidenced by changes (or lack of change) in clearance
rates through the Neighbourhood Watch implementation period
may partly reflect problems with the identity number system used
to mark property (see footnote 1). This problem would not,
however, alter the offender's initial perception of the risk created
by Operation Identification.

The evidence for both target and geographic displacement
suggests that the opportunistic nature of burglary may be a little
different from the way it is often conceptualized. The suggestion
that burglary is a highly "opportunistic offence" portrays the
residential burglar, particularly the juvenile, as taking advantage
of opportunities that are happened upon "in the spur of the
moment" (Halcim and Renegert 1981, 12). The usual speculation
has been that if police prevention practices do displace burglary, it
will be the activity of the older burglar that is displaced. This view
may misconceive the nature of juvenile burglary. Unfortunately
in the present analysis it has not been possible to distinguish
between "professional" and juvenile burglary, but given the very
high proportion of juveniles among the known burglars in the
study areas (80 percent) it seems reasonable to conclude that
juvenile burglars do adapt to the problems presented to them by
Operation Identification, that is when it presents any problems
to them at all. Of course the high percentage of juveniles among
known burglars may simply represent their greater apprehension
rate, but, given the average "take" from burglaries (a little over
$200 — hardly the work of professionals) I suspect not. What this
suggests is that although target hardening will influence the
targets chosen, the nature of opportunity is relative. To remove
certain opportunities may only change the way opportunities
are perceived by those wishing to exploit them — opportunity may
be all important in the choice of target, but much less so in the
decision that there is going to be a target in the first place. To infer
the intentions of burglars from the apparently opportunistic
nature of the crime may be to miss the point that juvenile burglary
is a matter of "style", a behaviour which reflects more than just
the opportunistic material acquisition of goods. The potential of
target hardening for displacing burglary could thus be greater
than has generally been thought.

Target displacement appears to be the most likely form of specific displacement, but in the case of small-scale intensively implemented programs, target displacement may assume a recognizable area form. Added to this is the possibility that typological displacement also occurs, a possibility which I have not been able to address. Such an investigation, like the problem of the instrumental meaning of the burglary to the burglar, may only be possible by moving beyond the confines of a phenomenal level of analysis. In this sense the analysis presented here is most certainly incomplete. And even in the case of analysis of specific displacement, a phenomenal level of analysis must ultimately be supplemented by other methodologies and perspectives since area displacement, target displacement, and typological displacement may appear in combination — important in their aggregate effect, but so small individually that they are difficult to recognize and distinguish from the fluctuations that characterize burglary time series data.

Notes

1. The Department of Manpower and Immigration, however, is not allowed to supply names and addresses of social insurance number holders to the police. As a result the use of the numbers does not necessarily allow the police to trace the owners of all stolen goods even when they are engraved!

2. Some research has, however, been conducted on displacement in other contexts. For reviews see Gabor 1979, and Lowman 1983.

3. Whether this is a reporting change is, of course, an empirical question still to be resolved at the time of writing.

4. Because of a change in recording practice the first records (particularly of the first month) may not be reliable. Some of the reports for early 1974 may have been filed for December 1973.

5. Both these reporting rates are higher than those found in other victimization surveys (see generally Skogan 1976). The finding does raise the possibility that reporting rates vary geographically.

References

Brantingham, Patricia L. and P.J. Brantingham. 1981b. Notes on the geometry of crime. *Environmental Criminology*. Beverley Hills: Sage Publications, 27–54.

British Columbia Police Commission. 1976. *Neighbourhood Watch: A home security program*. Published by the B.C. Police Commission and Solicitor General of Canada.

Burnaby R.C.M.P. 1978. *Report on Neighbourhood Watch*. Burnaby R.C.M.P.

Davidson, R.N. 1981. *Crime and environment*. London: Croom Helm.

Ditton, J. 1979. *Controlology: Beyond the new criminology.* London: MacMillan.

Gabor, T. 1978. Crime displacement: The literature and strategies for its investigation. *Crime and Justice* 6(2):100–07.

Hakim, S. and G.F. Rengert. 1981. *Crime spillover.* Beverley Hills and London: Sage Publications.

Herbert, D. 1982. *The geography of urban crime.* London: Longmans.

Jacobs, J. 1961. *The death and life of great American cities.* New York: Random House.

Jeffery, C.R. 1971. *Crime prevention through environmental design.* Beverley Hills: Sage Publications.

Krajick, K. 1979. Preventing crime. *Police Magazine* November.

Lowman, J. *Geography, crime and social control.* Ph.D. Dissertation, Department of Geography, University of British Columbia.

Mayhew, P., R.V.G. Clarke, A. Sturman and J.M. Hough. 1976. *Crime as opportunity.* Home Office Research Study No. 34. London: H.M.S.O.

Newman, O. 1972. *Defensible space.* New York: MacMillan.

Phillips, P.D. 1980. Characteristics and typology of the journey to crime. In D.E. Georges-Abeyie and K.D. Harries (Eds.), *Crime: A spatial perspective.* New York: Columbia University Press.

Reppetto, T.A. 1976. Crime prevention and the displacement phenomenon. *Crime and Delinquency* 22:166–177.

Robinson, M.P. 1977. Reintroducing community responsibility: An issue-oriented evaluation of problems facing crime prevention units in British Columbia. Prepared for the B.C. Police Commission. Unpublished.

Robinson, M.P. 1978. An analysis of two team approaches for dealing with the urban burglar. Report prepared for the B.C. Police Commission.

Schneider, Anne L. 1976. Victimization surveys and criminal justice system evaluation. In W.G. Skogan (Ed.), *Sample surveys of the victims of crime.* Cambridge, Mass.: Ballinger Publishing Co.

Skogan, W.G. 1976. *Sample surveys of the victims of crime.* Cambridge, Mass.: Ballinger Publishing Co.

Winchester, S.W.C. 1978. Two suggestions for developing the geographic study of crime. *Area* Vol. 10, 1978.

Chapter 12

The Crime Displacement Hypothesis: An Empirical Examination

*Thomas Gabor**

Until recently, evaluations of crime prevention programs have shared the underlying assumption that the scope of criminal behaviour is restricted to the terms set by the evaluative study. Such assessments have generally focused only on the form of violation the program was designed to prevent, with little consideration given to the possibility of a concomitant change in the frequency with which other offenses are committed in the area studied. Also, the urban areas under study have been treated as if self-contained, as if offenders are not able to cross the boundaries of the targeted areas for the duration of the study.

The alteration of criminal activity as a consequence of preventive efforts is referred to as crime displacement. An ostensibly effective prevention program may actually lead to changes in criminal behaviour so that offenders can circumvent the preventive measures instituted. Offenders may relocate the site of their activities; they may select different targets within the original site; they may alter the tactics used or the time of their violations; or they may even engage in different forms of criminality (Reppetto 1976, 166–77).

The crime displacement hypothesis is consistent with a hydraulic model of criminal behaviour, whereby the offender is viewed as responding compulsively to adverse biological, psychological, economic, and/or social conditions. The manifestations of this response can be deflected but not eliminated by *ad*

* Department of Criminology, University of Ottawa. This article is a revised edition of a paper from *Crime and Delinquency,* July 1981.

hoc measures. (Vold 1979, 9–10). It is interesting to note that displacement is also explicable under a rationalistic, utility maximization framework, as the offender can be seen to be responding to objective changes in the system of costs and benefits (Palmer 1977, 4–21).

A third possible explanation for displacement, in this case more appropriately termed spurious displacement, may be derived from the criminal justice system's resistance to reductions in crime rates resulting from successful prevention programs. As some persons and groups have a vested interest in stabilizing crime rate, discretionary powers may be used to counteract reductions in certain offenses by more stringent enforcement of others (Schur 1973, 131). In fact, dramatic reductions in certain offenses may result in appeals for criminalization of behaviours not formerly sanctioned (Erikson 1976). This type of stabilization yields what has been referred to as a statutory displacement effect (Planning and Management Corp. 1974).

The concern here is the genuine alternation of offenders' behaviour, rather than the effects of adjustment mechanisms operating in criminal justice systems. A previous review of the literature revealed that displacement has been a neglected aspect of evaluative research; the few studies of displacement that do exist are flawed by numerous methodological problems (Gabor 1978, 100–107). Nevertheless, it should be noted that all five forms of displacement have been observed. By shedding light on the extent of offenders' mobility and flexibility (in committing a variety of offenses and employing different *modus operandi*), displacement studies can aid in effort to assess the usefulness of focused, localized prevention programs.

Peter Lejins has identified three types of prevention programs. The first, punitive prevention, involves the deterrence of potential offenders through the threat of punishment and prevention through incapacitation. The second type, corrective prevention, is the elimination of criminogenic psychosocial conditions. Finally, a third type of preventive activity, mechanical prevention, aims to reduce criminal opportunity through "target hardening" and increased surveillance levels in the community (Lejins 1967, 1–21).

THE STUDY

Selected for the displacement study was the property-marking theft prevention called Operation Identification (0–I). Program participants engrave an identification number on movable property (usually household property, although commercial establishments occasionally are involved), and decals are placed on the front and rear doors of the participant's residence (or place of business) as a warning to prospective intruders. Proponents of O–I claim that its objective, burglary prevention, can be attained because of burglars' reluctance to handle material that is readily identifiable. Possession of marked property (Heller et al. 1975) increases the likelihood of a burglar's apprehension and conviction and makes the disposal or conversion of such property more difficult.

The program is both punitive, in its threat of apprehension and conviction, and also a form of mechanical prevention, in its reduction of criminal opportunity. Since it can be hypothesized that displacement effects are more likely to occur as a result of punitive or mechanical, as opposed to corrective, measures, the O–I program was particularly appropriate for the present study. Evaluations of O–I programs show contradictory findings, although many of these studies lack any type of controls (Heller et al. 1975). Clearly, program effectiveness, in its conventional sense, is a precondition for displacement.

The objective of the study was to determine whether displacement occurred as a consequence of an O–I program implemented in Nepean, a township located south of Ottawa, Ontario. The program began in March 1975 and was monitored through 31 August 1976. One of the nine police patrol zones in Nepean was selected as the site for the study. A police patrol zone was selected rather than a political jurisdiction or census tract because this permitted an assessment of police behaviour in the area during the monitoring period. Changes in enforcement activities could produce a confounding influence on the crime rate, possibly obscuring or exacerbating the effects of O–I. Furthermore, natural geographic boundaries virtually separated this zone from the rest of the township. Thus, it could be assumed more safely than in other areas that program effects would be contained within the zone and the influences of adjacent communities would be minimized.

The extent of program membership in the zone studied also favoured its selection. By the end of the study, 171 of 1,093 (15.6 percent) occupied dwellings were enrolled, while only 1 of the 625 operating businesses in the area was protected by the program. These conditions were conducive to the examination of at least two forms of displacement: first, the possible displacement of burglaries from the dwellings of participants to those of nonparticipants (here referred to as spatial displacement) following the implementation of O–I; and second, target displacement, or the possibility that, because of the relatively high enrollment of households in the program, residences in general would become less desirable as burglary targets, whereas businesses, which did not participate, would become more attractive.

A third form of displacement studied was tactical displacement, or the change among offenders in their *modus operandi* in response to the O-I program. Since marking property does not directly prevent its theft, the tactics discussed here do not refer to the methods used by the offender to secure the property but to the means used in circumventing the preventive measure — which, in this case, involved avoiding marked merchandise. Displacement could be indicated by the increased theft of unmarked items.

The two other forms of displacement identified in the literature were not studied. Temporal displacement was not applicable since the coverage offered by O-I is continuous. Nor was the possibility of displacement from burglary to other offenses studied, because data on numerous types of offenses, specific to the zone studied, were unavailable.

The data used in this study comprised all cases of breaking, entering, and theft in the designated zone reported to the Nepean Police Department from 1970 through 1976. Rates of breaking and entering were computed in terms of occupied units and were adjusted for season and random effects, where applicable (Netter and Wasserman 1966). Each apartment, private house, and commercial establishment was considered as one unit. Premises, rather than population, were used as the base for computing the burglary rates because of the frequent observation that offenses tend to cluster in areas according to the availability of criminal opportunity resented by dwellings and businesses, rather than according to area population size (Engstad 1975, 193–211).

Various procedures have been employed in past studies to probe for displacement. A critical review of these methods has been undertaken elsewhere by the author (Gabor 1978, 100–107). In this study, the possibility of spatial and target displacement was examined through time series analysis, a procedure that enabled assessment of the immediacy, duration, and possible changing character of program effects. Quarterly observations of burglaries were made for all residences and businesses from March 1973, two years before the inception of O-I, through August 1976, eighteen months after implementation. In studying spatial displacement, an attempt was made to ascertain whether residential program participants were becoming significantly less vulnerable to burglary than they had been before O-I and whether unprotected dwellings were becoming significantly more vulnerable as a result of the program. In probing for target displacement, burglary among all residences was compared with burglary among all businesses. If the former exhibited a significant reduction in burglary with the onset of the program and the latter an increase, displacement could be posited. In the study of tactical displacement, items taken during burglaries were examined before and after the program was initiated. In this case, observations were annual rather than quarterly because of the small number of residential burglaries for which items taken were known. This situation precluded the use of inferential statistical techniques.

In probing for spatial and target displacements, two forms of analysis were used to ascertain the effects of 0–I. First, the pre- and postprogram changes in overall burglary rates were examined through Burr's formula for the comparison of trend slopes (Burr 1970). Then, to guage more precisely the dynamics of the suggested displacements, the observed and expected burglary rates were compared at quarterly intervals during the period after the program was begun. The expected rates with which the actual rates were compared were calculated through bivariate, linear regression analysis (Netter and Wasserman 1966).

For the study of spatial displacement, residences were divided into two cohorts: participants and nonparticipants. Membership was determined by a dwelling's status at the final point of observation in the study (August 1976). All residences were monitored for victimizations over the three and one-half years of observation, and the two cohorts were compared. This *ex post facto* method of selecting units and retracing groups' activities over time is referred to as retrospective cohort analysis (MacMahon and Pugh 1970). Changes in burglary rates among the two cohorts, following the onset of 0–I, could be evidence of displacement if participants' rates decreased and nonparticipants' rates increased (taking into consideration the general trend in burglary rates).

The first procedure undertaken in investigating dwelling-to-dwelling displacement was ascertaining 0–I's effects on residences in general. Disregarding the phenomenon of displacement, an effective program would reduce the overall burglary rate for residences. Displacement would be most apparent with a stabilization of this overall rate. However, this was not a prerequisite for a finding of program effectiveness or displacement, because other factors operating independently of the program could have accounted for a change or stabilization in overall burglary rates. The purpose of the trend analyses was to gauge such contemporaneous effects.

After the overall effects of 0–I on residences were determined, dwellings that remained unprotected by the program were compared with protected premises through a difference-of-means

(t) test. Unprotected dwellings, at each point of observation, were those that remained nonparticipant cohort members over the course of the program as well as participant cohort members over the course of the program as well as participant cohort members not yet participating at a given point of observation. Since apparent differences might be due to prior differences in general vulnerability rather than to 0-I, the two cohorts were observed for differences in victimization before the program.

The cohorts were also examined individually for clues as to program efficacy and displacement. Examination of the participant cohort to judge the effects of differing points of entrance into the program extended to (1) the victimization of all units before the onset of the program; (2) burglaries among units that had not yet joined 0-I at the point of observation; and (3) burglaries among this latter group after joining 0-I. Comparisons of (1) with (2) and of (2) with (3) were seen as a way of demonstrating program effects. The results of such comparisons of different cohorts, because of the possible nonequivalence could be reflected in a disproportionate enrollment in the program of the more prudent members of the community.

Finally, the nonparticipant cohort was examined both before and after 0-I's onset. It would be expected that as the number of program participants increased, the more likely it would be that members of the nonparticipant group would become targets of burglary. Members of this cohort would be expected to experience an accelerating increase in burglary as a result of the program.

Target displacement, the suggested shifting of offenders' activity from residences to businesses because of nonparticipation in 0-I among commercial establishments, was studied in a similar fashion. First, changes in the overall community burglary rate (residences and businesses) that were attributable to 0-I were examined. Residences and businesses were then observed separately for 0-I's effects. Theoretically, if displacement did occur, one would expect a stabilization of the overall rate, with a decrease in the residential rate and a concomitant increase in the commercial rate.

Tactical displacement as a result of the program, meaning a change in items taken during burglaries from those marked to those unmarked, could conceivably occur in two ways. First, a burglar, having entered a home and having realized that numerous articles are protected, might select unmarked property. Second, if the offender were aware of such a program, he might shift his attention to other articles in planning the burglary; hence, the program might alter his specific objectives (Heller et al. 1975). Since tactical displacement could occur regardless of the victimized unit's participation in the program, all residential burglaries from 1970 through 1976 were examined for merchandise taken.

RESULTS

Because of the low number of burglaries committed in the area examined, there is a possibility of distortion by "random" events. Consequently, these findings may be regarded with skepticism by those operating from a purely statistical perspective. From a substantive standpoint, however, knowledge of criminal activity in a community of this type, as well as crime-reporting and recording mechanisms in such an environment, may offset such concerns. Demographically stable residential communities such as this are characterized by stable police patrol operations, as well as low turnover in police departments. Both tend to minimize changes in bookkeeping practices. Demographic stability also minimizes numerous potentially confounding influences on crime rates.

The selection of a police patrol zone for analysis permitted the monitoring of police activity in the area, limiting the confounding influences of variability in crime detection and reporting. Also, it will be recalled, the choice of the particular patrol zone studied was made on the basis of its geographic isolation from adjacent zones, minimizing external influences. Finally, well-integrated communities with good relations between police and residents, with large transient populations, and where opinions of police effectiveness are low (Radzinowicz and King 1979, 51–52). Official crime figures in the former type of community more closely depict actual crime rates than do those in the latter type. In Nepean, citizens reported the most trivial offenses imaginable. This lends credence to the comprehensiveness of crime reports in such communities.

Spatial Displacement

In the first part of the study, the burglary rate for all residences was observed. Table 12.1 indicates that, before the intervention period, the seasonally adjusted rates for total residences fluctuated between 1.68 and 4.03 burglaries per 1,000 occupied dwellings per three-month period studied. Following the onset of the program, the rates ranged from 3.73 to 6.54 per 1,000 dwellings. Although burglary rates continued to climb after 0–I's onset, the rate of increase of burglaries declined from an 11.6% quarterly

Table 12.1   Breaking and Entering Offenses for Total Residences and The Participant and Nonparticipant Cohorts (March 1973–August 1976)

Time Period[a]	Total Residences				Eventual Participants			Eventual Nonparticipants		
	B&E's[b]	Total Units	Rate[c]	S.A.R.[d]	B&E's	Total Units	Rate	B&E's	Total Units	Rate
Preprogram										
1	1	889	1.12	1.68	0	131	0	1	758	1.32
2	2	906	2.21	2.31	0	134	0	2	772	2.59
3	3	922	3.25	2.67	0	136	0	3	786	3.82
4	4	961	4.16	3.27	0	142	0	4	819	4.88
5	1	978	1.02	3.97	0	145	0	1	833	1.20
6	7	990	7.07	4.03	1	148	6.76	6	842	7.12
7	4	1,000	4.00	3.99	0	150	0	4	850	4.71
8	4	1,027	3.89	3.34	1	155	6.45	3	872	3.44
Program Commences										
9	1	1,040	.96	3.73	0	151	0	1	882	1.13
10	2	1,049	1.91	5.20	0	147	0	2	889	2.25
11	13	1,058	12.29	5.76	3	129	23.26	10	896	11.16
12	8	1,078	7.42	6.54	1	44	22.73	7	911	7.68
13	2	1,087	1.84	6.48	0	21	0	2	917	2.18
14	8	1,093	7.32	5.37	0	0	0	8	922	8.68

a Three-month intervals starting with March 1973.
b Breaking and entering offenses.
c Rates per 1,000 occupied units.
d Seasonally adjusted rates.

growth to 8.8%. This did not constitute a statistically significant decrease in the trend as a whole (t = .2662; p .05; 10 df). Also, at none of the six observation points in the postprogram period was there a statistically significant departure in the burglary rate from that projected on the basis of the preprogram trend. Therefore, a noticeable, although nonsignificant, decrease in the growth of residential burglary rates accompanied the program.

A comparison of program participants and nonparticipants (the latter group including eventual participants, before participation) reveals distinct differences in the victimization of the two groups (Table 12.2). Although no participant households were burglarized, during the eighteen-month period after the program began, thirty-four burglaries occurred among nonparticipants, providing a mean of 5.79 incidents for 1,000 nonparticipant dwellings for each three-month period. This constituted a significant difference (t = 2.82; p .05; 10 df).

Table 12.2 Breaking and Entering Offenses for Program Participants and Nonparticipants

Time Period[a]	Actual Participants			Actual Non-Participants			
	B&E's[b]	Total Units	Rate[c]	B&E's	Total Units	Rate	S.A.R.[d]
9	0	7	0	1	1033	.97	3.78
10	0	13	0	2	1036	1.93	5.43
11	0	33	0	13	1025	12.68	6.14
12	0	123	0	8	955	8.38	7.12
13	0	149	0	2	938	2.13	7.35
14	0	171	0	8	922	8.68	6.37

a Three-month intervals starting with March 1975.
b Breaking and entering offenses
c Rates per 1,000 occupied units.
d Seasonally adjusted rates.

This apparent indication of program effectiveness and displacement can be attributed, at least in part, to initial differences in vulnerability between the participant and nonparticipant cohorts. As Table 12.1 shows, the participant cohort members had a mean victimization rate of only 1.65 burglaries per 1,000 dwellings before the program, whereas nonparticipant cohort members averaged 3.64 burglaries for the eight points of observation. This difference was found to be significant at the 0.1 level (t = 1.52; 14 df).

The nonequivalence of the two cohorts from the outset made it preferable to gauge program effects through the observation of only one cohort. First, the entire participant cohort was compared before the program's onset with the members of the participant cohort who did not immediately join 0-I (see Table 12.1). Assuming the two groups are fundamentally equivalent, as members of the same cohort, differences could be attributed to the program. The group of dwellings that did not participate immediately would be expected to show a higher burglary rate because they would become more desirable targets as progressively more dwellings entered the program. Indeed, the cohort had a mean burglary rate of 1.65 per 1,000 dwellings before the program; during the program, those cohort members not yet participating had a mean rate of 7.67 incidents. Admittedly, the numbers here are small, precluding inferential analysis and definitive statements on the trend. However, the changes were in the direction predicted.

With respect to this same cohort, program effects were monitored through a comparison of those dwellings yet to join 0-I with those already participating. Consistent with the displacement hypothesis, the former group was victimized at a higher rate (7.67 incidents per 1,000 dwellings) than the latter (no victimizations). Again, although the small figures preclude tests of significance, the differences were in the expected direction.

Finally, the effect of the program on the nonparticipant cohort was examined by comparing the victimizations experienced by the group before and following 0-I's onset. Before the program, the mean burglary rate for this group was 3.64 incidents per 1,000 dwellings; after onset, this increased to a rate of 5.51 incidents. Most suggestive of displacement was the fact that the quarterly growth of burglary rates more than doubled after the program was under way. It will be recalled that residences in general and the participant cohort in particular experienced a reduction in this growth rate and an absolute reduction in incidents, respectively.

Target Displacement

In the overall burglary rates for the region (residences and businesses), the figures fluctuated between 4.79 and 7.29 incidents per 1,000 premises before the program (Table 12.3). After 0-I's onset, the rates varied from 7.04 to 9.94 burglaries per 1,000. The average quarterly rate of increase rose to 6.4% from 6.1% after onset; however, this did not constitute a significant difference (t = .7532; p .05; 10 df). Indeed, at none of the six points of

The Crime Displacement Hypothesis: An Empirical Examination **315**

Table 12.3 Breaking and Entering Offenses for Total Premises, Residences, and Businesses (March 1973–August 1976)

Time Period[a]	Total Premises				Residences				Businesses			
	B&E's[b]	Units	Rate[c]	S.A.R.[d]	B&E's	Total Units	Rate	S.A.R.	B&E's	Units	Rate	S.A.R.
Preprogram												
1	11	1,304	8.44	4.79	1	889	1.12	1.68	10	415	24.10	11.48
2	4	1,331	3.01	5.80	2	906	2.21	2.31	2	425	4.71	13.26
3	7	1,355	5.16	5.73	3	922	3.25	2.67	4	433	9.24	12.21
4	12	1,417	8.46	5.67	4	961	4.16	3.27	8	456	17.54	10.72
5	6	1,449	4.14	6.42	1	978	1.02	3.97	5	471	10.62	11.53
6	10	1,472	6.80	6.85	7	990	7.07	4.03	3	482	6.22	12.62
7	11	1,491	7.38	7.29	4	1,000	4.00	3.99	7	491	14.26	13.86
8	15	1,545	9.72	7.10	4	1,027	3.89	3.34	11	518	21.24	14.53
Program Commences												
9	10	1,576	6.35	7.04	1	1,040	.96	3.73	9	536	16.79	13.55
10	5	1,597	3.13	8.09	2	1,049	1.91	5.20	3	548	5.47	13.61
11	17	1,618	10.51	8.47	13	1,058	12.29	5.76	4	560	7.14	13.48
12	25	1,668	15.01	9.33	8	1,078	7.42	6.54	17	590	28.81	14.32
13	7	1,698	4.12	9.94	2	1,087	1.84	6.48	5	611	8.18	16.04
14	21	1,718	12.22	9.49	8	1,093	7.32	5.37	13	625	20.80	16.59

a Three-month intervals starting with March 1973.
b Breaking and entering offenses.
c Rates per 1,000 occupied units.
d Seasonally adjusted rates.

observation following the program's onset was there a significant departure from the projected rates.

As mentioned above, the quarterly growth rate of burglary among residences in general showed a nonsignificant decline (11.6 to 8.8%) in conjunction with the program's operation. With respect to businesses (Table 12.3), the preprogram rates ranged from 10.72 to 14.53 burglaries per 1,000 premises. Once the program was underway, these rates varied between 13.48 and 16.59 incidents. This incease in the quarterly growth of burglary rates from 3.9% to 4.2% was not significant (t = .9323; p .05; 10 df). Here again, there was an absence of significant deviations from projected rates at any of the six observation points.

Although the changes in the rates for residences and businesses were not significant, the fact that they occurred in the expected direction is noteworthy. The rate of growth of residential burglaries declined and that of businesses increased. Since the 0-I program involved residential participants only (with the exception of one business), these findings can be interpreted in at least three ways.

First, crime may have been displaced from residential to nonresidential premises. An explanation of displacement is insufficient, however, for there were increases in the growth rate of total burglaries (residential plus commercial). A factor in addition to displacement must have produced the rise in the growth rate of commercial burglaries. This may be attributed to a sudden spurt of nonresidential victimizations which coincided with, but was independent of, the introduction of the program. This sudden attractiveness of certain targets to the offender population is referred to as a multiplier effect. (Chaiken et al. 1974). Such an effect may occur without the impetus of specific prevention programs.

Second, a multiplier effect may itself have been responsible for the increased growth rate of burglaries for both businesses and total premises. The decline of the residential burglary growth rate may be attributed to the primary preventive effects of the program (e.g., increased community cohesiveness), to direct deterrent effects, or to both of these.

Finally, the possibility of improved relations between the police and the community brought about by the program may have increased the reporting rate of residential victims. This may have masked a decline in the growth of actual burglary rates that was greater than was apparent from the official data. In that case, the overall burglary rate may have been stabilized, despite the program, and a genuine displacement effect may have occurred.

Tactical Displacement

The items taken in the residential burglaries were examined for the period from 1970 through 1976. It will be recalled that, in this study, the hypothesized tactical displacement referred to a change in objects taken by burglars from markable (property habitually marked in the program) to nonmarkable items.

In 1970, 37.5% of residential burglaries involved the theft of markable merchandise (Table 12.4). In the following year, markable items were taken in 55.6% of the cases. In 1972, no markable items were taken; however, only four burglaries were reported in that year. The years 1973 and 1974 were fairly constant, with 57.1% and 56.3% of burglaries, respectively, involving markable items. In 1975, the year in which the program was initiated, an increase of 61.9% occurred, indicating that the program was not demonstrating tactical displacement effects in its initial nine months of operation. However, in 1976, a 50% decline occurred in the proportion of cases in which markable items were taken. Conversely, cases before 1975 involving the theft of nonmarkable items fluctuated between 14.3% and 100%. During 1975, the first year of the program's operation, the theft of nonmarkable items reached its second lowest point (19%). However, as cases involving the theft of markable items declined in the second year

Table 12.4 Type of Items Taken During Residential Breaking and Entering Offenses (1970-76)

Year	Total B&E's[a]	Markable Items[b]	% of Total	Non-markable Items[c]	% of Total	No Items Taken/ Items Unknown	% of Total
1970	8	3	37.5	5	62.5	0	0
1971	9	5	55.6	3	33.3	1	11.1
1972	4	0	0	4	100.0	0	0
1973	7	4	57.1	1	14.3	2	28.6
1974	16	9	56.3	4	25.0	3	18.7
1975	21	13	61.9	4	19.0	4	19.0
1976	23	7	30.4	13	56.6	3	13.0

a Breaking and entering offenses.
b Cases in which markable items were taken.
c Cases in which nonmarkable items were taken.

NOTE: If both markable and nonmarkable items were taken in a burglary the case was registered under the "markable" column, since it was the number of burglaries involving markable items that was of interest.

of the program (1976), those involving nonmarkable items increased to 56.6%. These changes in the patterns of burglary can be attributed to several factors.

Because there was only one measurement for 1976, random effects cannot be dismissed as explanatory factors. Some external event(s) occurring during 1976 may have been responsible for the abrupt change in the nature of items taken.

Regression effects, or the tendency of extreme figures observed at one point to return toward the mean in subsequent observations (Campbell and Stanley 1963), may provide an alternative or supplementary explanation. Table 12.4 shows that the proportion of markable items taken was not at its lowest point in 1976. In 1972, no cases involved such items (although, as mentioned above, the sample was extremely small), and in 1970, only 7.1% more cases involved markable items. The percentage of burglaries involving markable items tended to increase through 1975, and the 1976 period could be considered to be a normal fluctuation in the direction of the mean. Similarly, even if one discounts 1972 because of the low number of burglaries in that year it can be observed that cases in 1976 involving nonmarkable items did not constitute an all-time high; in 1970, 62.5% of cases involved such theft. Consequently, the sudden increase in 1976 could be attributed to a movement toward the mean after several low years.

Another possible explanation is that a multiplier effect may have been a factor in burglaries during 1975, the first year of the program. In response to the growing membership of the 0–I program, burglars may have specifically sought markable merchandise, knowing that the items would be marked in the near future. At the same time, they may have temporarily avoided nonmarkable items. This could account for an increase in cases involving markable items and the decrease in theft of nonmarkable items in the initial year of the program. It could also account for the sudden change in the following year as burglars' demand for markable items may have been satiated and their interest in nonmarkable goods renewed. However, the increase in cases involving markable items from 1974 to 1975 was only 5.6%, and the decrease in nonmarkable items taken was only 6%, so this explanation is not strong.

Finally, a displacement effect can be postulated, since the change from 1975 to 1976 occurred in the expected direction. The failure of the program to demonstrate effects in the first nine months of the program can be attributed to the scarcity of 0–I participants for that period.

CONCLUSIONS

Notwithstanding the problems of interpretation discussed above, the findings of all three components of the study indicate that displacement is a plausible reaction to prevention programs and should be a part of evaluative studies. The analysis of displacement promises to illuminate offender behaviour patterns and motivation and, consequently, the modes of intervention most appropriate in counteracting antisocial behavior.

References

Burr, Irving W. 1970 *Applied statistical methods.* New York: Academic Press.

Campbell, Donald T. and Julian C. Stanley. 1963. *Experimental and quasi-experimental designs for research.* Chicago: Rand McNally.

Chaiken, Jan M. et al. 1974. *The impact of police activity on crime: Robberies on the New York City subway system.* New York: New York City Rand Institute.

Engstad, Peter A. 1975. Environmental opportunities and the ecology of crime. In Robert A. Silverman and James J. Teevan, Jr., (Eds.),*Crime in Canadian Society.* Toronto, Canada: Butterworths.

Erikson, Kai T. 1966. *Wayward puritans.* New York: John Wiley.

Gabor, Thomas. 1978 Crime displacement: The literature and strategies for its investigation. *Crime and/et Justice* 6 (2).

Heller N.B. et al. 1975. *Phase 1 — Evaluation of Operation Identification.* St. Louis, Mo.: Institute for Public Program Analysis.

Lejins, Peter 1967. The field of prevention. In William E. Amos and Charles F. Wellford (Eds.), *Deliquency Prevention: Theory and Practice.* Englewood Cliffs, N.J.: Prentice-Hall.

MacMahon, Brian and Thomas F. Pugh. 1970. *Epidemiology: principles and methods.* Boston: Little, Brown and Company.

Neter, John A. and William Wasserman. 1966. *Fundamental statistics for business and economics.* Boston: Allyn and Bacon.

Palmer, Jan. 1977. Economic analyses of the deterrent effect of punishment: A review. *Journal of Research in Crime and Delinquency.* January.

Planning and Management Corp. *Planning and Management Consulting Corporation, crime incidence and displacement model.* 1974. Santa Barbara, Calif.:

Radzinowicz, Leon and Joan King. 1979. *The growth of crime: The international experience.* London, England: Cox and Wyman.

Reppetto, Thomas A. 1976. Crime prevention and the displacement phenomenon. *Crime & Delinquency. April.*

Schur, Edwin M. 1973. *Radical nonintervention: Rethinking the delinquency problem.* Englewood Cliffs, N.J.: Prentice-Hall.

Vold, George B. 1979. *Theoretical criminology* 2d ed. New York: Oxford University Press.

Chapter 13

Africville: Community Transformation, and the Emergence of a Deviance Service Centre*

*Donald H. Clairmont and
Dennis William Wilcox-Magill*

INTRODUCTION

Following the War of 1812, approximately two thousand refugee blacks arrived in Nova Scotia; the majority of whom were previous residents of Maryland and Virgina. They settled within a short distance of Halifax, principally at Preston and Hammonds Plains.

In the 1840s a small number of these refugee blacks moved from Preston and Hammonds Plains in order to escape the economic hardships associated with living on small lots of rocky soil and scrubby forest. They moved to an isolated area in the north end of the Halifax peninsula; the community they founded became known as Africville. The first Africville residents lived a rural life style. In later years, however, the community social structure was transformed; part of this transformation was the emergence of a deviance service centre.

Today Africville is part of the pages of history. From 1964 to

* Reprinted by permission of the authors. Originally published in Donald H. Clairmont and Dennis William Magill, 1974. *Africville: The Life and Death of a Canadian Black Community*. Toronto: McClelland and Stewart. Most of the footnotes for this chapter appear in the original publication, pp. 71–72, and p. 134.

1969 the community was relocated following an urban renewal program of planned social change.[1]

RURAL LIFE STYLE

An important factor in Africville's history was that it was isolated from Halifax proper. Africville was set apart from the rest of the city, situated on Bedford Basin and flanked by the railway. Although almost since its first settlement Africville has been linked to Halifax proper by a railway and an unpaved road, it was traditionally more a rural community than an urban neighbourhood.

Africville used to be separated from the rest of the city by bush and rock; one elderly relocate recalled that, prior to the First World War, "all the rest around [Africville] there was a lot of bush, nothing but bush." Long-time residents mentioned the many farm animals (chickens, horses, goats) in Africville around the turn of the century, and a local observer, referring to the same period, has written that the community boasted some of the largest piggeries in the Halifax area. Africville residents never had rich enough soil or sufficient land to engage in substantial farming, but relative isolation and the general ecology of the community did allow them to maintain a meaningful rural image until the First World War. Noncommercial fishing was another traditional activity that contributed to Africville's bucolic character. One Africville relocatee referred to the fishing as follows:

> The fishing! It really hurts to go down to the grocery store and pay really high prices for fish. That really makes me sick. We used to catch almost every kind of fish there is in the Atlantic, right here in Bedford Basin — haddock, cod, mackerel, perch, eels, clams. The only kind of fish we didn't get was smelts.

As the city of Halifax grew in population and in industry, Africville became cluttered with railway tracks and industry and city service depots such as the city dump. By the decade preceding relocation, Africville's rural image had little meaning. City ordinances and the encroachment of industry and government had led to the disappearance of farm animals, and pollution of Bedford Basin had virtually eliminated fishing. Yet, even as late as the early 1960s the editor of a Halifax newspaper felt able to refer to Africville as the "last rural remnant in Halifax peninsula", and several Africville residents could welcome the relocation because, as one relocatee put it, "I'm a city woman." By this time, however,

Africville's ruralness was largely a matter of being located "off the beaten path" and lacking standard city services. This sprawling community of approximately thirteen acres, with its dwellings, sheds, and outdoor privies haphazardly positioned and built, possessed few urban facilities. Residents had to do without paved roads (or even dust deterrent), convenient public transportation, sewerage, water, or garbage collection. The neglect of Africville by city officials was such that, according to one elderly relocatee, "For many years, Africville people were led to believe they were in the County — outside the City limits. It was only when the younger generation came along that we found we were within the City."

Both the sense of historical continuity possessed by Africville residents and the rural characterization of the community by outsiders (and by some residents as well) were congruent with community structure. The population of Africville was always small. In 1851, there were fifty-four blacks living in the area; in 1964, at the time of relocation, the population was approximately four hundred. Much of Africville's population growth took place during the last thirty to forty years of its existence. The majority of this small population were bound together through numerous kinship ties. Approximately 75 percent of the relocated population were associated, either by blood or marriage, with at least one of the five principal families in Africville, families that could trace their Africville ancestry back one hundred years. It is not surprising, under these circumstances, that the social structure of Africville can be characterized as "fluid" — in the sense that kinship and family systems were adaptable and there was a certain interchangeability of personnel. It was common for an older couple to "take in" a grandchild or nephew, and there were numerous instances of adoption, fosterage, and step- and half-kin relationships. The use of intimate kinnship terms, such as "ma", "pa", and "aunt", to refer to more distant relatives, and even to nonrelatives, was common. This structural fluidity and intimacy was compounded, in the several decades preceding the relocation, by an increasing degree of cohabitation and the presence of illegitimate offspring, and was accentuated by the widespread use of nicknames. Haligonians who knew Africville well could often identify its residents by nicknames only; even some of the indigeneous leaders were hard-pressed to identify the proper names of some Africville residents. To the outside (especially to many white Haligonians, welfare workers, city officials, and relocation caretakers) the Africville population appeared to be "jumbled".

An important component of Africville's social structure was the church, and the roles and organizations that it engendered.

The church was as old as the community itself and embodied much of Africville's sense of historical continuity. The Seaview African United Baptist Church contained within itself the principal formal organizations in the community. Through religious services, youth and auxiliary organizations, and a missionary society, it provided residents with a collective identity and fostered sentiments of solidarity. As one Africville resident put it:

> Sunrise Service on Easter morning . . . that was a great thing. You get upon on Easter morning at five o'clock and go to church there. You hear some of the loveliest things you ever wanted to hear, the spirituals; most of the people from Preston, Hammonds Plains, and right in the city here, you hear them say, "If you want to get the spirit, you go to Africville for Sunrise Service on Easter morning, and when you come away from there, you are either lifted up or you're dead!" To tell the truth, when they tore that church down, I cried.

Through the church, Africville residents were linked by traditions to other black communities in Halifax County and to white congregations in the city. Pastors and lay preachers were exchanged, and visiting and other social gatherings were frequent.

Since Africville was not large or wealthy enough to support a resident pastor, leadership and management of the church was left to church members themselves. Involvement in church affairs provided one with status in the community, and the church elders — the deacons, trustees, and leading "sisters" — constituted, as it were, the official representatives. They received communiqués from city officials, petitioned for needed services on behalf of Africville residents, and acted as the vehicle through which philanthropic and other voluntary organizations entered the community.

Africville possessed, in addition to the church, other institutions and roles characteristic of small rural communities. It had a school, a post office, a neighbourhood store, midwives, and political party agents. As early as 1860, Africville residents had petitioned the provincial government for financial aid to support a qualified teacher. Older respondents reported that, prior to 1883, a community resident had taught Africville children in the old Africville church. In 1883, a school was established under the jurisdiction of the city government. This school continued to function until 1953, when it was closed by the city and the children were transferred to larger, racially integrated schools elsewhere in Halifax. Over the years most of the schoolteachers were blacks who resided elsewhere in Halifax.

Since 1936, Africville had its own sub-post office; the two

postmistresses (one served from 3 October 1936 to 31 March 1944; the other, from 1944 to 31 October 1967) were Africville residents. The small neighbourhood stores were a feature of this relatively isolated community since at least early in this century. These stores were owned and operated by community residents who derived from them a modest supplement to family income. At the time of relocation in 1964, two very small stores were operating in Africville. Several Africville women, a few of whom were licensed, carried out the duties of midwife and general "therapist" in the community. These women enjoyed considerable status and were usually proud of their record and their special remedies and techniques. As Africville became less remote from the rest of the city in the decades preceding relocation, and as city health services expanded and local expectations rose, such traditional roles diminished in importance. Like other small communities in Nova Scotia, Africville had its political party agents. They were residents who had established ties with the provincial political parties and who were especially active at election time. Both male and female residents acted as political captains who were responsible for "getting out the vote".

That Africville was a black community is important in explaining how part of a city could develop with the particular characteristics that Africville had and in understanding the changes in social structure that took place during the last thirty to forty years of its existence. Although Africville was always physically part of Halifax, socially it was just an appendage. In this respect it was similar to most of the other black settlements in Nova Scotian towns and cities, and as we have indicated elsewhere, this general pattern reflects the underlying racism that has characterized Nova Scotian society since the abolition of slavery in the nineteenth century. In consequence of the separatist expectations among both blacks and non-blacks and the neglect that accompanied racism, Africville was obliged to develop structures parallel to those found elsewhere in the city. Africville was, traditionally, not merely a rural community, but a segregated black settlement. There was a parallel between governmental policy towards Africville, reinforced by everyday expectations, and its relative geographical isolation.

COMMUNITY TRANSFORMATION

Especially during the last thirty to forty years of its existence, Africville underwent profound changes. From what was described in 1895 as "a community of intelligent young people, much is expected of them," it increasingly became identified as "a national blot on the city of Halifax." Sociologists characterizing communities and forms of social life have often used the term "gemeinschaft", to denote a system of social relationships that can be described as communal, familistic, informal, primary, isolated, and sacred. Gemeinschaft can be applied to the traditional Africville social structure that we have described, but in the several decades preceding relocation, the social structure began to assume a different character. New forms of social differentiation emerged, a mobile heterogeneous population was grafted on to the indigenous group, the encompassing character of the kinship system was attenuated, and there was a significant decline in the leadership role of the church "elders", and in the status of the church as a focal point for community solidarity. There appear to have been three important causes of this transformation; namely, the poverty of Africville, the racism of Nova Scotian society, and the economic and population growth of Halifax.

In discussing the plight of the poor in American society, one sociologist has observed that "they learn that in their communities they can expect only poor and inferior services and protection from such institutions as the police, the courts, the schools, the sanitation department, the landlords, and the merchants."[1] Africville residents were always poor. The historical pattern was that the males worked as labourers on the docks or in small industries and businesses near Africville, and the females worked in low-paid service jobs as domestics in homes or in nearby institutions. Africville residents had been petitioning the city for services available to other residents of Halifax since the middle of the nineteenth century, but successes were few. Although many community delegations met with city officials about water and sewerage, Africville was never linked to the city mains. Residents had to do with makeshift wells that ran dry in the summer months and were a constant threat to health. In addition fire was particularly serious hazard in Africville because of its isolation, the poor housing, and absence of water facilities.

Lack of facilities and of standard public services extended beyond matters of water, sewerage, and fire protection. For instance, Africville lacked recreational facilities although the Halifax Recreation and Playgrounds Commission did provide facilities to other areas of the city. Discrimination by neglect grew increasingly serious as in and around Africville was gradually utilized by government and industry. An editorial in the local newspaper noted that Africville residents "can but contrast public tennis courts in Halifax South, and swimming pools in Halifax

Centre with the complete lack of facilities for recreation and play in their own section of the city." Inadequate police protection was also a matter of long-term complaint of Africville residents. In discussing welfare and other services, most of the inhabitants indicated that their claims were neglected. Local officials and middle-class professionals reiterated their conviction that, at least in the years immediately preceding relocation, a number of Africville people who should have received welfare assistance were not given it. An outside expert in social welfare summed up the situation in asserting that "the delivery system of social service was obviously punitive."

Being poor means not only less likelihood of obtaining necessary facilities and services; it also involves the strong likelihood of receiving negative consideration. For Africville, it meant that the city was less then rigorous in enforcing housing standards and, by declining to issue building permits, in encouraging the orderly residential development of the area. The ultimate negative consideration in Africville's case occurred during the 1950s when the city moved its open dump from within walking distance of Africville to the very doorstep of the community. This action was a "finishing touch" that established Africville clearly as "the slum by the dump". Africville became known as a place to visit if one were interested in observing slum conditions. A prominent city official noted that, when she was a teen-ager:

> A sort of high-school prank was to drive out to Africville on the weekends and turn out your lights and sit on the main road for a few minutes and turn them on and watch the rats run.

Africville residents were oppressed by poverty and neglect, but their plight was not unnoticed. The minutes of the Halifax City Council show that, since the turn of the century, Council repeatedly received petitions and considered taking action about conditions in Africville. In 1945, for example, the Halifax Civic Planning Commission reported that "the residents [of Africville] must, as soon as reasonably possible, be provided with decent minimum standard housing elsewhere." In this and other instances, the matter was shelved and nothing was done. One local black leader complained that Africville people were "objects of pity, not justice." The Chief Justice of the Supreme Court of Nova Scotia was reported in 1966 as describing Africville as a social problem "created by whites because time after time, year after year, municipal councils had ignored the problem." A City official, familiar with the Africville situation since 1945, observed:

I believe that given a little incentive the people of Africville would have had lovely homes and would have made a real effort to come up to a level but, being neglected, forgotten, no sewerage, no water, they did become, they did taken on, the attitude of not caring: "What's the use, the City will do nothing!" I think the people of Africville could have risen very highly.

In accounting for the fact that little was done about the acknowledged plight of Africville, most of its residents and many other concerned Haligonians emphasized that racism, as well as poverty, was responsible. One prominent white businessman described the relationship between Africville and city officials as follows:

I think perhaps the first thing, [Africville] wasn't regarded as part of the city of Halifax . . . and [the City] didn't regard, I suppose, the people as people, certainly not as citizens; and apathy, prejudice, fear, discrimination [existed].

An Africville woman put the matter more explicitly:

The City didn't do anything to improve Africville. All the City did was to try and get it, and they did, in the end. They just did it, too, because we were coloured. If they had been white people down there, the City would have been in there assisting them to build new homes, putting in water and sewers and building the place up . . . There were places around Halifax worse than Africville was, and the City didn't do to them what they did to Africville.

Such judgements are consistent with the general pattern of race relations that has existed in Nova Scotia for the past one hundred and fifty years. Blacks were not, in general, so much subject to direct economic exploitation as to a definition of the situation wherein they were regarded as marginals and outsiders and their deprivation was seen as the ordinary, although perhaps unfortunate, state of affairs.

Generally associated with poverty and racism is a certain "functional autonomy", which, in Africville, meant that the inhabitants had certain "freedoms" unavailable elsewhere in the city. Building codes could be ignored. People could loiter and make excessive noise. A "deviance service centre" could be established in this off-the-beaten-path and poorly policed area. In the thirty to forty years before relocation, Africville became increasingly identified as a place to go for bootleg booze and fun. One social scientist observed, in 1948:

Africville has also been the setting for some low level associations; due to its proximity to Halifax they are probably quite frequent. But as one man expressed it, "Whenever whites want to go on a bat they come to Afric-ville."[2]

Important social structural changes developed in Africville as a consequence of the poverty and racism that its residents experienced. During the several decades preceding relocation, residents became apathetic, lost confidence in the capacity of indigenous leaders to effect desirable change, and lost hope in the viability of the community itself. Pursuit of redress through standard and legitimate avenues had yielded little fruit, and militant collective action by Africville residents would have been hampered by the prevailing political consciousness. The church elders were unable to translate their ties with city officials and outside voluntary groups into substantial gains for the community, and their status in the community declined. Concomitant with this trend was the diminishing role of the church as a focal point of community consciousness and as a generator of solidarity sentiments. By the time that relocation became imminent, the church was a divisive as well as an integrative presence in Africville.

During the last thirty to forty years of its existence, Africville lost much of its close-knit and gemeinschaft quality. A mobile, heterogeneous population of blacks and whites began drifting into Africville, primarily because of the housing shortage elsewhere in Halifax and the exploitative freedom possible in Africville because city policy and practice towards the community had led to a decline in morale. A Halifax alderman, who had grown up near Africville and knew many Africville residents, described the situation as follows:

> As a boy, I knew Africville as a very nice community. It was in the days of the old railway station in the North End, and all the homes in Africville were well-kept, whitewashed or painted white; they had gardens, flowers. From the end of the War on, there seemed to be a general deterioration of the whole area ... the class that got in there sort of ruined the area ... they weren't people who had steady incomes and they couldn't rent in the city of Halifax.

The immigration of this new population complicated and "loosened" Africville's social structure. Africville became socially differentiated in a manner characteristic of slums elsewhere in North America, accomodating temporary and permanent dwellers as well as opportunists. For the most part, the new migrants were not absorbed into the community through kinship ties or church affiliation; rather, new roles and patterns of interaction were grafted on to the crumbling traditional social structure.

DEVIANCE SERVICE CENTRE

Minority group members, if oppressed and discriminated against, often find a mode of adjusting to their situation by performing less desirable and sometimes illegal services for the majority group. Moreover, under these conditions, the minority group members often acquire a certain functional autonomy; that is, not sharing fairly in society's wealth, they are allowed a range of behaviour in their neighbourhoods by the authorities that would not be countenanced elsewhere. Such indulgence by the authorities reflects not liberality but rather the view that the minority people are "different" and a reluctance to expand sufficient resources to control the undersirable behaviour in these areas. This model applies aptly to Africville and to the reaction of Halifax authorities.

It appears that even prior to the First World War it was known in Halifax that Africville, being some distance from the rest of the city and from public surveillance, was a place to go for bootleg booze and conviviality. "One very elderly relocate with kegs of rum and the works. The sailors used to come in and buy from him. After a while he drunk himself to death. Put himself on the bum, you know."

The proximity of Africville to the dockyards and general port activity meant that a pattern was soon established whereby Africville became a deviance centre. Such a development was congruent with the fact that many of the blacks were employed in the service sector, carting away excrement and cleaning the homes of other Haligonians.

It is not known exactly how extensive and how accepted by Africville residents such activity was prior to the First World War. The War greatly stimulated this line of service, causing many Africville residents to write Halifax City Council in 1919 advising it that the community's well-being and reputation was being destroyed and requesting police surveillance. The Africville petitioners were told that "the City Department has no spare men to send such a distance." It was recommended that "the residents of the Africville district form their own police department and anyone they appoint to act as a policeman, the Mayor would swear in as a Special Constable . . . In the event of any serious trouble being reported the Chief is always in a position to send a squad to this district."

The petition, and the response of city authorities to it, may well be taken as signalling the end of that phase of Africville's history in which much was expected of community residents and it was still possible to realize Africville's potential as a good residential district. Residents themselves detected a qualitative change, a new emerging equilibrium, in the community. Their reference to "strangers in our midst" foreshadowed the trend of opportunists and "down-and-outers" who moved into Africville in later years. The response of city authorities illustrates well the kind of negative freedom that they granted the residents; nothing positive was done for the community by City Council, which was always busy figuring out what to do with the land on which Africville residents were located.

As the years went by after the First World War, Africville's reputation as a deviance service centre continued to grow. The predictions of the petitioners of 1919 were borne out as the bootlegging and conviviality gave way to a definition of Africville as a raucous, hazardous place. The process was, however, gradual and incremental; in the wake of the First World War and its aftermath, a new temporary equilibrium was reached inside the community and the rest of Halifax, an equilibrium characterized by a higher visibility of Africville's peculiar service role. This new phase was described by a former Africville resident who migrated from the community prior to the relocation:

> There were more white people than there were coloured in the community. This is a fact. They came and stayed to eat and sleep. And they had their drinks. Some who came down were very prominent people . . . And they had their drinks. Nobody was ever robbed there or anything until . . . them came down there. Look, these well-to-do people came down to Africville . . . they had their drinks, gave us a quarter . . . a quarter was a lot of money in those days, you know . . . and moved on. And when they got drunk and tired and fell down on the road and went to sleep, they would be carried into somebody's house and looked after.

As economic conditions worsened and the city continued to neglect Africville, this deviant aspect became less tolerable. One black outsider observed that "just before relocation the younger ones [in the Africville community] would rob a man when he drank. But a few years back, Africville used to be a wonderful place to go on a drunk. You could flop your head anywhere." Another black non-Africville Haligonian, in referring to these later developments, noted that "the people of all sorts used to go to Africville. It had a kind of attraction because it was kind of weird; no law enforcement. One went out there at one's own risk. It really was the other side of the tracks."

Most Africville residents who complained of these changes identified the turning point from "acceptable" deviance service centre to potentially dangerous place as being around the Second

World War, when Africville received a complement of migrants displaced from the mid-city area. White authorities with some intimate contact with Africville occasionally reiterated this observation concerning a drastic decline in Africville life style and also occasionally linked this development with in-migrants during and after the Second World War. One alderman noted that "the class that settled [in Africville] after the War sort of ruined the area."

There is no doubt that the community changed during its last several decades, but it is too simplistic to explain this development in terms of the relatively small number of later in-migrants. It would be more realistic to see these people as opportunists who, having virtually nowhere else to go, gravitated towards a rapidly deteriorating Africville because of its possibilities for cheap housing, relative freedom and autonomy, and because of contacts established previously with its residents. Most of the outsiders who eventually settled in Africville had, for several years previously, been coming to Africville to drink and to party. Obviously this reinforced the drift of Africville towards a more blatant and hazardous deviance service centre.

The pervasiveness of the simplistic model of change proffered by respectable Africville residents and some white authorities is understandable. Participant models usually are more preservative than explanatory. Respectable Africville residents did not wish to be painted with the same brush as those residents who participated most in "unacceptable behaviours" and, consequently, placed the responsibility for such behaviour primarily on "outsiders". City authorities could find comfort perhaps in a model that interpreted "Africville's problem" in terms of the personality of some of its residents rather than in the historical unfolding of the consequences of city policies, racism, and socio-economic depression. The facts point, however, to the 1919 petitioners' correctness of vision. The relatively small number of in-migrants in the early 1940s neither introduced the deviance service centre nor did they constitute its sole Africville membership.

With the aftermath of the Second World War, a final pre-relocation equilibrium phase was reached within the community and between it and the broader society. Africville became regarded by outsiders as harbouring a risky deviance service centre and being a model of social disorganization. Blacks elsewhere in Halifax advised their children not to go near the community; middle-class whites advised their friends that Africville was an interesting but dangerous place to visit. Inside the community, according to outsiders and some Africville residents, there was a decline in morale; as one Halifax City Council alderman noted:

The character of the area had gone down and the character of some of the people who lived there had changed too. Instead of being a good type of citizen as they were prior to the thirties, they seemed to deteriorate to an extent that they just didn't care; certain activities went on there that didn't lend anything to the area.

Yet it would be unwarranted to see the state of affairs in Africville as socially disorganized and to exaggerate the deviance that occurred. The official crime rate over the past forty years was not particularly high, and only a handful of Africville males were sentenced to terms in prison. The Director of Health Services in Halifax reported that, while venereal disease was not uncommon in Africville in the post-Second World War period, usually the same few people were the only residents involved. Moreover, outsiders continued, at little risk, to visit Africville for booze and conviviality right up to the time of relocation. One frequent black visitor observed: "Everybody had a good time. More bootleggers than you could shake a stick at. Girls available for a good time." A white visitor reported that he and his colleagues at the dockyard always went to the community on payday for "drinking and carousing" and that "it was rough, but if you weren't looking for trouble, it wasn't bad." Other black and white outsiders frequenting the community underlined this observation, indicating that the risks were no greater than one would expect from drinking and carousing anywhere.

Africville residents themselves indicated that they experienced little sense of danger while living in the community. Even those heavily involved in these activities reported that few acts of violence occurred. Africville remained a small community where most residents were related by kinship ties. Adjustment in the community to this higher level of deviance took the form of segmentation of groups and activities. The community did lose its cultural and structural simplicity and homogeneity, but adjustments were made, and Africville was not an unpredictable social jungle.

Notes

1. Rainwater, Lee. "Poverty and Deprivation in the Crisis of the American City." 1966. Occasional paper No. 9, mimeographed. St. Louis, Missouri: Washington University.

2. Brookbank, C.R. "Afro-Canadian Communities in Halifax County, Nova Scotia." 1949. M.A. Thesis, University of Toronto, p. 76.

Part III

Responding to Discredit

Introduction

Social order therefore does not exist independent of social life but unfolds or emerges out of complex interactive processes in which it is embedded.

Analysis of deviant designations may presumably be made conceptually more comprehensive by focussing on the nature of controls constructed by actors in meaningful interaction, the multiple involvements with larger relational communities and, lastly, the relationships with disciplining/sanctioning agencies. The self concept, relational controls and formal controls become inextricably linked. This, therefore, warrants an examination of both the impinging controls of outside structures and the emerging (responding) controls of the community. How do communities make decisions affecting the ordinary rounds of activities? How is the social organization of response affected by pressures inherent in this life-style? Response therefore, includes the necessary and ongoing accomplishments that develop in effective interaction in order to better cope with various problems of adjustments and commitment. That is, in fragmented and differentiated social worlds, actors come into contact and attend to the responses of others. How is response as a purposive and continuous activity, socially organized?

In discovering the nature of their social realities, we will examine how these actors in their mundane and routine forms of interaction create opportunities, regulate difficulties and manage their problems. This leads us to determine the extent to which they acknowledge to themselves and to others symbolic expressions of collectivity. Essentially, this entails an investigation of how they adapt, respond, and make use of their affiliations. In terms of its nature and roles, how does the subculture or community function to secure the flow of resources, information about activity, appropriate self-packaging neutralizations, manipulations and coping strategies; sociability, support, companionship, etc.?

This section examines how communities claim and affirm themselves in light of deviant designations. The manner in which communities respond to the legitimacy of labels is fundamental to an analysis of social control and change. Traditionally these responses have been studied in terms of accommodations and negotiations. From the readings it becomes apparent that a valuable commodity like self-identity is not a negotiable item especially from the perspective of those in subordinate positions. A recognition of their realities is sought. The mechanism used to secure this immediate end is protest or challenge.

Another more expansive interpretation considers deviance generally as an expression of challenges to authority. That is, *all crimes are politically significant acts* in the symbolic or real struggle for power. Regardless of the competing definitions of the foundations or accountability of state — populist, pluralist or elitist — the state must ultimately be perceived within its role as definer. Accordingly, the state is an interested party and loses its neutrality. The legal system is designed to maintain the existing distributions of powerful resources. One such resource is the certification of offenders. Political consciousness on the part of offending members is not a necessary condition of the politicization of deviant protests.

By definition, deviance may also reflect the ineffectiveness of the persuasive and coercive resources of the authority structure in controlling "disorderly" elements. Caution must be exercised in noting that not all protests constitute a challenge to existing social relationships. For example, the label may be conveniently flexible resulting in exaggerated or even understated implications for those in authority. Simply stated, "challengeable" order becomes a pivotal concern in any discussion of protest. Consequently, these mechanisms — whether expressed within the "order-maintenance" idiom of conflict theory, or within the Parsonsian model of "social equilibrium" — do not remain neutral. Whether our concerns are with the "offender" or the "offenders", actors represent meaningful identities denoting their status or their "fit" in the social order.

Traditionally, studies of protests have been discredited

because of rhetoric, sloganeering and failure to consider non-coercive aspects of power. The last few decades, however, have witnessed the growth of the conflict perspective which has provided both substantive breakthroughs in power analyses, and the methodological generation of new data bases. The term has come to denote a wide variety of activities and imputations. Clearly, deviance is the subject of complex interpretations connoting contests of, or more appropriately, challenges to interests and power.

Essentially, fundamental differences in interests and influence, characterize social order. That is, a certain order will obviously satisfy some interest groups and offend others. Whether we accept the notions that normative standards are assented to by the Durkheimian "collectivity" or the Marxian ruling class, social order tends to exact civil disobedience.

In brief, the responses are studied in terms of how they shape and are shaped by the nature and quality of social control. Relatively little attention has been directed to these larger contexts in which response occurs. Little effort has been made in examining how formal social controls stimulate the development of informal controls and how subcultural and community accomplishments affect relations with the outside.

Chapter 14

Native Juveniles in Court: Some Preliminary Observations *

Carol Pitcher LaPrairie

INTRODUCTION

A pressing concern among academics, Native people and agents of the criminal justice system has been, and continues to be, the issue of disparity in the treatment of Native people in the criminal justice system.

The reason for concern is not so much about what the figures tell us, as about what disparity means. The first and most obvious meaning is one which obscures more than it enlightens and is one of overrepresentation. If we know that many more Native people than their population would suggest, are arrested, charged, sentenced to incarceration, and serve longer prison sentences (indeed, the evidence suggests that this is so) does this necessarily imply disparity in the treatment according Native and non-Natives?

What might be the reasons for overrepresentation? The first and most obvious response might be termed extralegal. This argument holds that the explanation must be found in offenders' behaviour, specifically that Native people are disproportionate in their criminal behaviour and/or commit the serious types of crimes that courts deal with most harshly.

A second position focuses on the criminal justice system and how its personnel and agents act with intentional or unintentional

* Dr. Alex Himelfarb contributed to the introduction for this paper. Carol Pitcher LaPrairie, Research Division, The Solicitor General's Office, Ottawa.

338 DEVIANT DESIGNATIONS: CRIME, LAW AND DEVIANCE IN CANADA

discrimination. The behaviour of these agents, the argument goes, makes it more likely that Native people will be designated as deviant, indeed criminal, and will receive the harshest sanctions.

Finally, disparity may focus on fundamental structural differences, i.e., the social segmentation among groups in a way that encompasses both the above two meanings, as the criminal justice system is seen as reflective rather than independent of these cleavages. In its extreme position, the criminal justice system is seen as supportive of inequalities through the reproduction of social order. In this latter view, neither the Natives nor the agents of the criminal justice system are perceived as villians. All are constrained by the same social structure, the same laws of inequality.

Each of the positions outlined asks different empirical questions and suggests different directions for policy. The extra-legal position would recommend action directed toward offenders — ranging from education and resocialization to job training and various programs to enhance the social position of Native people. Its research questions would in turn be directed toward the differences in criminal behaviour among groups rather than toward the criminal justice system response.

The second position, i.e., that which concentrates on the response of the criminal justice system through its agents and roles, would advocate policies directed towards criminal justice agents and agencies, for example, the implementation of a Native courtworkers program, legal protection for Native people, Native representation in the criminal justice system, and the sensitization and training of criminal justice personnel on Native cultural differences.

The final position goes beyond the Native offenders and the criminal justice system and demands a theory of society which focuses on social inequality. The policy concerns which emanate from this position are always long term and are directed toward autonomy and distributive justice. This paper is an empirical exploration of a single court in which Native- and non-Native-offender court interactions are examined. This is not to say that the paper is nonideological or uncommitted. The very choice of the term "disparity", the very focus, suggests a commitment to what often has been termed a conflict perspective of society.

The data presented in this paper is the result of a preliminary study of juvenile court in a northern community. Although limited by sample size, the findings are presented here as a way of identifying issues that may require further exploration.

NATIVE PEOPLE IN CANADIAN SOCIETY: THEORETICAL EXPLANATIONS

A number of theories compete to explain the condition of Native people in Canadian society. Hawthorne, Belshaw and Jamison (1960) identify the culturalist model as creating social disorder and dysfunction for Native people as a result of the clash between the Native subculture and the value system of the dominant culture. For those who support this perspective, the overrepresentation of Native people in the criminal justice system is viewed as evidence of the culture clash.

The culturalist model falls within the rubric of what Reasons (1977, 2) identifies as the order/assimilationist premise, which he describes as follows:

> The order/assimilationist perspective minimizes the significance of power and coercion in everyday life between subordinate and superordinate groups, emphasizing the social psychology of individual and group adaptation to dominant groups values and practices. Society is viewed as made up of competing individuals who carry out their competition within the context of neutral social institutions. Thus, everyone is equal and has equal opportunity.

The structuralist model on the other hand, identifies structural factors as the source of contemporary Native social conditions. Muirhead et al. (1976) describe this in the following way:

> These (structural) explanations assert that a dependency relationship between any unskilled minority group and an industrialized economic social order is the basis for these conflicts. Poverty breeds social and economic dependence, and this dependence perpetuates a cycle of poverty. The normal routes of social mobility are effectively limited for members of unskilled, impoverished and dependent groups. This structure *produces* the "culture" of poverty which is then perceived as the source of the Native population's problems by those advocating the cultural explanation.

As Muirhead (1981, 7) notes, the overrepresentation of Native people in the criminal justice system "should be seen as a reflection of the social conditions applying to *all* social actors defined by these conditions." Moreover, evidence from research provides support for the notion that social structural factors are important determinants of involvement with the criminal justice system (Muirhead 1981, 8; Watkins 1977; Frideres 1974; Hagan 1974).

The structural approach to Native conditions in Canadian society is grounded in the conflict/pluralist explanation of social relations. Both Reasons (1955) and Verdun-Jones and Muirhead (1980) address the overinvolvement of Native people in the criminal justice system from a conflict perspective. These authors suggest that native people form a dominant underclass in Canadian society because of the structure of power relations which has resulted from colonization.

Frideres (1974) in justifying the colonial framework to explain Indian-white relations points to the relevant factors in the colonization process — the taking over a geographical area by a dominant group upon the Native population as well as external political control, economic dependence, and substandard social servicing; and finally, the institutionalization of racism and the establishment of a colour line.

A colonial-structural model explains (a) the emergence of the Indian reserve system and the continued underdevelopment of reserves; and (b) resulting from underdevelopment, the creation of a social structure which produces a "culture" of poverty for Native people.

The social position of Native people as a "marginal underclass" would suggest that they have a higher potential for conflict with the criminal justice system (Muirhead 1981, 8) than do these groups with higher social status and thus more power and authority. The fact that the majority of Native people exist in Canada as members of an underclass suggests that their disproportionate involvement with the criminal justice system is a direct reflection of that status. The lack of awareness of the structural disabilities of Native people coming into contact with the criminal justice system suggests that social inequality is maintained and perpetuated.

NATIVE PEOPLE AND THE CRIMINAL JUSTICE SYSTEM

. . . in the nature of things indigenous persons in modern advanced industrial society will progressively lose out in the political and legal arena. This would seem to become more certain as acculturation continues with industrial development and indigenous minorities increasingly, perhaps inevitably, lose their indigenous lifestyle, their special needs and, in part their rationale for special treatment (Keon-Cohen, 1982, 204).

The effect of this "loss" is most visible in the relationship of many Native people in Canada with the criminal justice system.

This would appear particularly true for those Native people who live in dominantly non-Native communities where traditional ways are assumed to have disappeared and with this, "the rationale and need, for special justice mechanisms" (Keon-Cohen, 1982, 254). Because Native people in these communities have not acquired the prevailing standards of living that one might expect to accompany physical assimilation, they are subject to a system of justice that will judge their ability to be accountable and responsible on the basis of their social structure.

The suggestion of a relationship between the conditions in which Native people in Canada live and their overrepresentation in the criminal justice system is a compelling one. It has now become conventional wisdom that Native people are over-represented at every stage of criminal justice processing — arrests, convictions, carceral sentences. Moreover, the deplorable social and economic conditions of Native people in Canadian society are well documented (Stanbury 1979; DINA 1980; Hylton 1981). The overrepresentation of Native people in the justice system should then be addressed in terms of the effects of structural disadvantages on criminal justice processing. If, for example, as Platt (1969) suggests, the juvenile justice system incorporates the values of the middle class, it may be assumed that it is likely to be more biased toward youth who do not fall within these norms. It may further be hypothesized that while the majority of youths who appear in juvenile court hearings are of low socio-economic status, the ones who most severely suffer the effects of discrimination because of lack of structural supports are Native juveniles.

This same argument may be applied in the various steps of criminal justice processing that affect Native adults — arresting practices, sentencing procedures and parole granting, all of which take into account the social and economic realities of the individuals involved. Even while controlling for seriousness of offence, the public visibility of Native people when drinking for example, may as Harding (1981) suggests, make them more vulnerable to police scrutiny and arrest and account for their vast number of arrests for public drunkeness. The destitution of Native women (Ontario Native Womens' Association 1982) often forces them to try to survive on the streets, where they are highly visible to police (Harding 1982).

The structural differences between the Native and non-Native inmates in the federal penitentiaries has been documented (Planning Branch, Treasury Board Secretariat 1975). Less of the Native population (36.4 percent); only 11.5 percent of the Native inmates as compared to 25.8 percent of the non-Native inmates had received an education above the ninth grade level and 30.5 percent of the Native population compared to 18.9 percent of the non-Native inmate population had either no education or education to the first to sixth level. Native inmates were also younger than non-Native and more likely to be single.

The same report claims that the loss of remission is significantly higher among Native inmates who are young on admission, single or unemployed. Similarly, a failure to earn "Earned Remission" is associated with the same factors.

The Solicitor General's study on conditional release (1981, 117–118) which states that Native offenders have a lower full-parole release rate and higher revocation rate than the population as a whole suggests that while this may not be an indicator of racism in corrections, it may, in many cases, reflect a lack of release plans considered appropriate by releasing authorities. As such, plans are based upon factors which relate to employment, living arrangements, social support systems, etc. Any group which is disadvantaged in these areas, will be disadvantaged in obtaining parole. Moreover, even if granted, Native releases may, again, because of a lack of structural supports, be more vulnerable to having parole revoked.

While the bulk of the research findings which exist to date address the demographic characteristics of Native adults in contact with the criminal justice system, this study demonstrates that the same characteristics apply to Native juveniles appearing in court. What is important in terms of the sentencing of Native juveniles is the significance of social factors in presentence reports and the recommendations of probation officers (see Banton 1976; Emerson 1969; Perry 1958). Again, as a result of the disadvantaged social and economic position of Native juveniles, one must question the appropriateness of applying the same standards to groups with very different structural characteristics, even if the end sentencing result appears to be one of legal equality.

FINDINGS

The research data for this paper were part of a larger study conducted in a northern hinterland community over an eighteen-month period in 1979/80. During that time a number of methodologies were employed to study Native juvenile delinquent offence and offender characteristics. As there is a dearth of research in the area of juvenile delinquency among Native people, this preliminary research sought to document patterns which might exist to differentiate Native and non-Native offenders as well as to document the response of the criminal justice system.

The component of the research that relied on official file material, i.e., court registry, probation and diversion files laid the groundwork for the juvenile court study by identifying key social structural characteristics of Native and non-Native delinquents as well as offences and dispositional data relating to both groups. The findings in the major study were that cases of Native juveniles were vastly overrepresented in the juvenile justice system, that Native juveniles became involved with the system at an earlier age, and that the group was severely disadvantaged in comparison to their non-Native delinquent counterparts in terms of structural supports.

The findings of the juvenile court observation study are presented here as a way of documenting the structural disparities which exist between Native and non-Native juveniles in one court jurisdiction. Not only is the fact of overrepresentation of Native juveniles borne out in this sample, but the apparent inability of the criminal justice system to address the structural disparities between the two groups at the disposition stage is suggested as well.

The overrepresentation of Native juveniles in the criminal justice system was noted in the preliminary delinquency report where probation and court registry data sets were examined (LaPrairie and Griffiths 1982). In the court observation data similar findings occurred. Nearly 39 percent of the total sample was Native although the actual Native population of the community is approximately 10 percent; while 83.1 percent of the sample was male, nearly twice as many Native females as non-Native females appeared in court.

Although the cases of the two groups of juveniles did not differ in their offence histories, i.e., over one-half of the cases of both groups had a prior offence record (including formal and informal contacts with the criminal justice system) some differences were found in the types of prior offences which had been committed. Although the cells are small and no firm conclusions can be drawn there are suggestions from the data that shoplifting involving cases of Native juveniles were more frequent than those for non-Native, while motor vehicle offences were more common in cases of the latter — probably a function of differential access to cars.

In examining present offences, similar patterns emerge. Native juveniles seem to be more involved in minor theft and liquor-related offences but overall there are few differences in types of offences between the two groups (Table 14.1).

Table 14.1   Types of Offences by Juveniles, Native and Non-Native

		Minor Theft	Major Property	Status	MVA	Wilful Damage	Other	Total
Native	No	10	10	5	3	4	0	32
	%	31.3	31.31	15.6	9.4	12.5	0	
Non-	No	7	22	4	8	6	3	50
Native	%	14	44	8	16	12	—	
Total		17	32	9	11	11	3	82

The previous discussion has focused on the characteristics and patterns of offences for eighty-three juveniles who appeared in court over a six-month period in one northern jurisdiction. Although the sample is very limited in number, nonetheless, the findings do suggest that Native juveniles, particularly females, are overrepresented but that no major differences exist in the types of offences committed. The following discussion suggests, however, that there may be major differences between the two groups when examining sociostructural characteristics. These differences do not appear to be reflected in dispositions as no differences in sentences were found.

EMPLOYMENT/SCHOOLING

In examining the school-employment status of all of the juveniles who appeared before the court in this sample, it appears that the Natives are less often students and less frequently employed than are their non-Native counterparts (Table 14.2).

Table 14.2   Occupation of Juveniles by Ethnicity

		Student	Unemployed	Employed	Total
Native	No	11	19	2	32
	%	34.4	59.4	6.3	
Non-	No	28	13	10	51
Native	%	54.9	25.5	19.6	
Total		39	32	12	83

More than twice as many of the Native juveniles were unemployed than the non-Native juveniles and fewer were students. Although they are not characterized by the probation officers as having worse school histories or more behavioural and

academic problems while in school (as both groups are characterized generally as having poor histories and related school problems)
it appears that Native juveniles tend to fall out of the school
system at a disproportionate rate in comparison to the non-Native
juveniles. This is not a result of working as the table demonstrates
the general lack of employment for the Native juveniles.

LIVING ARRANGEMENTS

In examining the living arrangements for the groups two
facts are apparent — fewer Native juveniles are living with both
parents than are the non-Native juveniles and more Native
juveniles are with their mothers only or with one parent and a
step-parent (Table 14.3). Significant levels are achieved when
categories are collapsed (Table 14.4).

Table 14.3 Living Arrangements of Juveniles by Ethnicity

		Both Parents	Mother Only	Father Only	Parent & Step-Parent	Other	Total
Native	No	12	6	1	3	7	29
	%	41.4	20.6	3.4	10.3	23.1	
Non-Native	No	33	2	2	0	9	46
	%	71.7	4.3	4.3	0.0	19.0	
Total		45	8	3	3	16	75

Table 14.4 Living Arrangements of Juveniles by Ethnicity

		Both Parents	Other	Total
Native	No	12	17	29
	%	41.4	58.6	
Non-Native	No	33	13	46
	%	71.7	28.3	
Total		45	30	75

X 6.83 df 1 p. 01

FAMILY LIFE

During the course of the report that is provided by the probation officer (written or verbal but most often verbal) one of the
three critical social factors (i.e., school, employment, and family)

that is taken into account is the assessment of the juvenile's family life. From the following table it appears that the family life of Native juveniles is more often characterized as "bad" then is characterized for the non-Native group (Table 14.5).

Table 14.5 Family Situation of Juvenile by Ethnicity

		Very Bad	Bad	Fair	Good	Total
Native	No	12	5	9	2	28
	%	42.9	17.9	32.1	7.1	
Non-Native	No	10	0	17	16	43
	%	23.3	0.0	39.5	37.2	
Total		22	5	26	18	71

Again, when identifying the type of family problems to the court, probation officers described Native families as having particular problems more often than non-Native families (Table 14.6).

Table 14.6 Family Problems of Juvenile by Ethnicity

		None	Alcohol	Unempl.	Unable to Handle Juv.	Physical/ Mental	Other	Total
Native	No	2	5	3	6	7	6	29
	%	6.9	17.2	10.3	20.7	24.1	20.6	
Non-Native	No	23	2	1	11	8	6	41
	%	45.1	3.9	2.0	21.6	15.7	11.8	
Total		25	7	4	17	15	12	70

Although the problems encountered by Native families are diverse, what is perhaps most interesting about the findings is that so few of these families are seen as having *no* major problems (6.9%) as compared to a much larger percentage (45.1%) of the non-Native families. As assessments of the families are made as a result of interviews with juveniles and the parents (often in conjunction with interviews involving school counsellors and/or teachers, employers) it is expected that the same criteria are used by the probation officers in making the assessments.

The preliminary study of Native delinquency in the same jurisdiction found similar differences in the Native and non-Native cases. An analysis of the data indicated that in cases involving Native juveniles, education achievement was significantly lower than cases involving non-Native juveniles. Over one-half of the Native cases in the probation order data had not progressed past Grade seven, as compared to only one-fourth of the non-Native cases. While 16.8 percent of the non-Native cases in the probation order sample showed completion of Grade eleven or graduation from Grade twelve, only 8 percent of the Native cases reached this senior secondary level (LaPrairie and Griffiths 1982).

The above data demonstrates that major sociostructural disparities exist between the cases of Native and non-Native juveniles in this particular sample when measured by family, living arrangements, employment and school related variables. From the available information it appears that in one jurisdiction, there are differences in the structural support systems cases of Native and non-Native juveniles. In what ways are these differences reflected at the sentencing stage in the court observation study?

At the conclusion of the social history presentations the probation officer may recommend to the court what he/she feels is an appropriate disposition. Normally the recommendations are directed to dispositions so the probation officer will recommend those dispositions and related conditions that reflect his/her assessment concerns. He/she usually suggests probation or containment without specifying a particular period of time.

In examining the recommendations that are given to the court it appears that few distinctions are made by the probation officer between the two groups (Table 14.7).

Table 14.7 Probation Recommendation for Juveniles by Ethnicity

		Terminate	Prob.	Cond.	Susp.	Incar.	Total
Native	No	11	17	1	2	0	31
	%	35.5	54.8	3.2	6.5	0.0	
Non-	No	17	24	2	0	1	44
Native	%	34.7	49.0	4.1	0.0	2.0	
Total		28	41	3	2	1	75

Judges followed the recommendations made by the probation officers in full in 92.1% of the cases and in part in another 6.6% of the cases. This suggests that the above recommendations were carried out at the sentencing stage. There are no differences between the two groups with regard to dispositions given or to conditions such as hours of community service work.

The research reported here is clearly limited as a result of scope and design and thus any conclusions about the findings must necessarily be qualified. Nonetheless, this preliminary study suggests some future research directions and allows for a very general discussion of possible implications of the research findings.

CONCLUSIONS

The social, economic, and political disparities which exist between Native and non-Native people in Canada are most apparent when examining the overrepresentation of Native people in the criminal justice system. While some claim that the social situation for Native offenders is no different from that of similarly placed non-Natives, the reality is that the *majority* of Native people live in these conditions and therefore, poverty overrepresentation is reflected in criminal justice overrepresentation. So long as these conditions exist for Native people we can expect them to maintain a high level of contact with the justice system.

According to the rules of the criminal justice system we can select out no particular villians. What is clear from these and other findings which relate to the overrepresentation and processing of Native people in the criminal justice system is that rules uphold a certain kind of justice. Perhaps the strict adherence to these rules, however, produces a certain kind of injustice as well.

It must be kept in mind that the findings of this research pertain to only one community and that further research is necessary. Below standard-of-living conditions for Native people in Canada, however, have been documented elsewhere (Indian Affairs and Northern Development 1980; Stanbury 1975), so the findings in this research which relate to sociostructural characteristics of Native juvenile are probably representative of similar groups in comparable communities. Given that many Native juveniles reside in communities which share similar characteristics with the one under study, a strong argument is made for focusing further research attention to these areas. It is also important to direct research to both larger urban and more isolated rural areas.

While references are made to the particular situation of juveniles in the presentence reports to the courts, in this small data set we were not able to show that the structural disparities between the groups had an impact at the disposition stage. This should be further tested with a larger data set, since the rehabilitative intent of the court suggests that the structural disparities ought to have an effect on the dispositions.

The findings also suggest some possible policy implications, particularly in light of the proposed Young Offenders Legislation. As an adherence to due process is characteristic of the new legislation, one would hope that the effect of having counsel would result in the presentation of the best possible case for the client and that the emphasis and scope for presentence reports would yield better information to the courts. There are a number of assumptions, however, which underlie these changes. It is assumed that all areas will have access to legal counsel (even though vast disparities exist in the locales in which Native people reside) and that individual counsel will share a common understanding of the particular social and cultural conditions in which Native people live. Furthermore, by presenting better information to the courts through more comprehensive presentence reports it is assumed that judges will be able to make different dispositions than they are able to under the present legislation.

A number of other issues which underlie the new legislation should be addressed. The youth court will have the power to release a young person into the care of a responsible adult when it appears that the adult can exercise control and guarantee the young persons subsequent attendance in court. Will Native parents be perceived as "responsible" by courts and judges by the same standards as non-Native parents or will the legislation ensure a more flexible and culturally based set of guidelines? What will be the implications of the fact that Native juveniles are less likely to be living with their parents? Will judges be made aware of the extended family concept or will Native juveniles be penalized for living in nonparental surroundings?

The principle of personal responsibility is strongly embedded in the Act. Is a common understanding of responsibility implied and does this notion assume a shared value system around measures such as time, demeanour, attitude, and parental concern? Perhaps the major issue that these questions pose is whether or not the Young Offenders Legislation can be operationally sensitive to the "special needs" of particular groups of juveniles.

References

Banton, W.H. 1976. Discretionary decision making in juvenile justice. *Crime and Delinquency* October.

Emerson, Robert M. 1969. *Judging delinquents: Context and process in juvenile court.* Chicago: Aldine.

Frideres, J.S. 1974. *Canadian Indians contemporary conflicts.* Toronto: Prentice Hall.

Hagan, J. 1974. Criminal justice and Native people: A study of incarceration in a Canadian province. *Canadian Review of Sociology and Anthropology*. Special Issue (August):220–236.

Hawthorn, E.B., C.S. Belshaw, and S.M. Jamieson. 1960. *The Indian of British Columbia: A study of contemporary social adjustment.* Toronto: University of Toronto Press and the University of British Columbia.

Hawthorn, E.B. (Ed.). 1966. *A survey of the contemporary Indians of Canada.* 1, Indian Affairs Branch Ottawa.

Indian Affairs and Northern Development. 1980. *Indian conditions: A survey.* Ottawa.

Keon-Cohen, Bryan A. 1982. Native justice in Australia, Canada and the U.S.A.: A comparative analysis. *Native people and justice in Canada.* Special Issue Part II National Legal Aid Research Centre, University of Ottawa: Ottawa, April.

LaPrairie, C.P. and C.T. Griffiths. 1982. *Native Indian juvenile delinquency in a Northwestern Canadian community.* Ministry of the Attorney General, Province of B.C. and Simon Fraser University (unpublished).

Merton, R.K. 1968. *Social theory and social structure.* New York: Free Press.

Muirhead, G.K. 1981. *An analysis of Native over-representation in correctional institutions in B.C.* Ministry of the Attorney General, Corrections Branch, Victoria.

Muirhead, G.K. et al. 1976. *Native Indians in the B.C. correctional system.* Ministry of the Attorney General, Corrections Branch, Victoria.

Perry, Robert L. 1978. An empirical study of juvenile court behaviour in arriving at dispositions. Ann Arbor: University Microfilms International (Dissertation).

Planning Branch. 1975. *The Native inmate within the federal penitentiary system.* Treasury Board Secretariat, January.

Platt, Anthony. 1960. *The child savers: The invention of delinquency.* Chicago: University of Chicago Press.

Reasons, C.E. 1975. Native offenders and correctional policy. *Crime and/et Justice.* 4, 255–267.

Report of the Working Group. 1981. *Solicitor General's study of conditional release.* Ottawa: Solicitor General Canada, March.

Watkins, M. 1977. *Dene Nation — The colony within.* Toronto: University of Toronto Press.

Verdun-Jones, S.N. and G.K. Muirhead. 1980. Natives in the criminal justice system — An overview. *Crime and Justice.* 7/8 (1):3–21 Ottawa: University of Ottawa.

Chapter 15

Speak No Evil, Hear No Evil?: Juveniles and the Language of the Law

Trudie Smith-Gadacz[*]

INTRODUCTION

Lorne V. Stewart (1978,158) writes that "Canada's juvenile courts are essentially criminal courts *calibrated* to the age of its clients and carrying with them the ingredients of a 'fair' hearing through recognized and practiced procedures of due process, but, at the same time bearing the burden and disadvantages attached to criminal court type procedure." In preserving the due process procedure legal language has become the dominant mode of communication in this setting. While such discourse can be argued by its defenders to be more precise than "ordinary" language, skeptical individuals argue that the use of legal language can lead to nothing but disaster (Mellinkoff 1963,295; Matza 1964, 133; Smith-Gadacz 1982) in terms of effectively communicating to the accused the ideas and meanings inherent in legal proceedings. Two key questions arise. First, "Is legal language in fact understood by the accused juvenile or is it for the most part incomprehensible to him/her?" Second, "What do probation officers, lawyers and judges think juveniles understand or should understand about legal language?"

This paper[1] addresses the second question. The findings obtained from focused interviews (Merton, Fiske and Kendall 1956) conducted with probation officers,[2] defense counsel,[3] and judges[4] of the Winnipeg juvenile court[5] (Province of Manitoba,

---

[*] Ph.D. Candidate, Department of Sociology, University of Alberta.

Canada) are presented. The discussion is placed in the context of the juvenile justice system as it functions presently with special attention to the changes currently underway in this court.

THE JUVENILE'S ABILITY TO UNDERSTAND

The governing legislation, the Juvenile Delinquents Act (JDA), suggests that the proceedings of the juvenile court can be informal, as long as there is due regard for procedural fairness and the elements of due process. This position coupled with the implicit and explicit assumptions of Section 38 of the Juvenile Delinquents Act has afforded the court the opportunity to function informally at times. One effect of this has been that there has been the potential for a simple language to be used in legal proceedings. Specifically "Probation docket"[6] courts in Winnipeg allowed for the juvenile to *participate* in the legal process. Juveniles were often afforded the opportunity to speak to the judge and explain their circumstances and concerns in a direct manner. The chance to participate in the courtroom hearing meant that a juvenile had a greater chance to discover the meaning of legal language as it had been used in that particular setting. The move towards a more "legalistic"[7] model of court functioning has changed this situation completely. Under the new system, the juvenile is swept into a milieu characterized by legal vocabulary which for the most part is probably completely foreign to him/her. The presence of lawyers, prosecutors and judges has resulted in an increased use of legal vocabulary. The juvenile who appears before the court tends to become what Erving Goffman has called "a non-person" (Bankowski and Mungham 1976, 88).

The move towards a more legalistic model within the juvenile court raises some critical concerns. One author captured this sentiment quite well when he stated, "The future is clear: law and due process are here to stay in the juvenile court; prosecution and defense counsel have become permanent members of the court's cast of characters; rehabilitation efforts will be pursued within a legal context" (Rubin 1976, 137). Under the Young Offenders Act (YOA), to be proclaimed in the fall of 1983, juveniles are to be held more responsible for their actions and the "protection of society" is to be a key consideration in all dispositions. The key question to be raised is, "Will the proposed legislation take into consideration the juvenile's ability to understand the language and the procedure of the court?" The proposal does state that juveniles should be given an opportunity to participate as fully as possible in the proceedings against them. This attempt to change the role of the juvenile from a silent observer to an "active" participant presupposes that the juvenile has the ability to understand not only the *procedure* of the court but also the *language* of the court.

KEY ACTORS' VIEWS OF JUVENILES' UNDERSTANDING

The literature states that the accused's (in this case the juvenile's) ability to understand legal language is a problem (Ericson and Baranek 1982; Atkinson and Drew 1979; Hackler 1978; Matza 1964). The primary issue is whether or not the individuals (judges, lawyers and probation officers) who ultimately shape the juvenile justice system believe that legal language in fact affects a juvenile's understanding of the courtroom process. When these courtroom participants were interviewed about this issue the general sentiment was that "yes, legal language does affect the juvenile's understanding of the courtroom hearing." Fifty percent of the judges responded positively. Both probation officers and defense counsel agreed with this assessment. As one lawyer succinctly put it, "I just really believe that they [juveniles] are at sea the whole time." This view would suggest that some effort on the part of key legal actors would, or at least should be made to explain certain legal terms and phrases if contact were made with a juvenile. This study assumes that there is contact between the juvenile and legal actors. The key questions which arises is "Whose role is it to explain legal terms and phrases as well as court process to the juvenile?"

ROLES AND FUNCTIONS OF EACH KEY ACTOR GROUP

The probation service functions to provide support and assistance to juveniles who have become involved with the law. The duties and functions within the service range from administrative duties to intake work and later supervision of juveniles placed on probation. To elaborate, of the fifteen probation officers interviewed, seven stated that they had administrative duties, one had to develop new programs, eight do intake, three do later supervision, two are duty probation officers, one does community investigation, one does nonjudicials and two do interagency work. As these figures indicate many probation officers have dual or multifunctions within the system. In accomplishing these tasks most probation officers (86.7 percent) feel that they are helpful to juveniles in dealing with court process. The two major ways in which they perceive themselves as being helpful are in providing the juvenile with an *explanation* of the process and procedures and fulfilling a supportive role.

The role and function of defense counsel in juvenile court is an area which is somewhat more controversial and divided than the role of probation officers. There is widespread disagreement within the legal profession itself about the role of counsel in the juvenile court (Bala and Clarke 1981, 207).

Interviews conducted with fifteen Winnipeg defense counsel produced a number of different responses to the question of role. Lawyers predominantly saw their role as being "adversarial" (73.7 percent). Somewhat synonymous with this was the response "child's advocate" (53.3 percent). In terms of function, three main answers outlined by Bala and Clarke (1981, 2007) found support in this study. First, lawyers felt that they should "ensure that both the parent and the juvenile understand what happened in court" (46.7 percent). Second, "ensure that all relevant facts and law are brought to the judge's attention" (40 percent) and finally "ensure that the child's views are expressed to the court" (46.7 percent). All lawyers interviewed (100 percent) felt that they were helpful to the juvenile. They believe they are able to help them deal with the process, speak for them in court and in general provide support. What is important to note is that defense counsel, unlike probation officers, mention the processing of the charge and protecting client's interests ahead of any translator type of role.

The judge occupies a position different from either defense counsel or a probation officer. His/her contact with juveniles is limited to *within* the courtroom. In his/her profession, a provincial court judge hears matters under the Juvenile Delinquents Act, the Family Maintenance Act and the Child Welfare Act. Only the senior judge performs administrative duties. Some of the judges (50 percent) do related committee work. For the most part however the role and function of the judge is determined by the profession itself.

Given the various roles and functions of the three key actor groups it is important to assess the type and context of the transactions between these persons and juveniles. To accomplish this it is helpful to look at the various phases of the court process.

PRE-FIRST COURT HEARINGS

Initial Contact

The probation service comes into contact with juveniles in eight potential ways. These include: (a) when they get a referral (a charge had been laid by the police and the matter is to be handled judicially), (b) at the time of arrest (meet the juvenile once he has been detained at the Manitoba Youth Centre),[8] (c) when the judge requests a pre-disposition report, (d) a reconsideration is laid, (e) the juvenile and parent call the probation service seeking information about court process and procedure, (f) at the time of the first court appearance, (g) after first court appearance, or alternatively (h) after a plea has been entered by the juvenile to the charge before the court.

The variation in initial contact pattern can be attributed to a number of factors. The most important reason is that the timing of their initial contact is determined by the structure of the juvenile justice system itself. Prior to the October 1981 change in the Winnipeg juvenile court the probation service met each individual that was to appear in the court *prior* to their first court hearing. The rationale was that if a juvenile had not appeared before a judge, had not entered a plea, or was not currently on probation, the service should not be involved at all. Without a finding of delinquency the juvenile is still considered to be innocent. Given that the juvenile might never be found delinquent no inquiry should be made concerning issues such as background, prior record and particularly nothing concerning the nature of the pending charge. Thus the reason for the different points of initial contact.

Defense counsel, unlike probation services, have a clear mandate for being involved with the juvenile from the moment that s/he is drawn into the legal system. It is not surprising that the greatest amount of initial contact occurs when the juvenile is held in detention (75 percent) or when the juvenile and/or parent call the lawyer themselves requesting that s/he become involved in the case (75 percent). A lawyer can also become involved when the legal aid certificate is awarded to them (46.7 percent), after first court (33.3 percent), at the time of first court (13.3 percent), through referrals from the Children's Aid Society (6.7 percent) or after meeting kids at group homes (6.7 percent).

Once contact has been made between the juvenile and

probation officer and/or the juvenile and defense counsel, a first meeting is likely to occur. The first meeting of juvenile and probation officer and/or juvenile and defense counsel is devoted to many topics. The majority of probation officers (86.7 percent) say that the one topic discussed more frequently than any other is court procedure, that is, what is most likely to occur inside the courtroom. Other topics include, nature of the charge (66.7 percent), prior record (60 percent), potential dispositions (60 percent), background information (46.7 percent), a juvenile's right to legal counsel (40 percent), pleas (26.7 percent) and finally, the juvenile's version of what happened (13.3 percent).

A lawyer-client interview seems to focus on rather different issues. The most common matter discussed is background information (75 percent). Other issues raised during this encounter include, how the case is likely to proceed (66.7 percent), prior record (60 percent), information for bail (60 percent), potential dispositions (60 percent), the juvenile's version of the story (13.3 percent), detention (13.3 percent), pleas (13.3 percent), the lawyer's approach in court (6.7 percent), court dates (6.7 percent), and finally, what the juvenile would be facing if s/he were before the adult court (6.7 percent). Clearly there are differences between a probation-juvenile and defense counsel-juvenile interview. Two main themes seem to dominate probation-juvenile interviews. One is "implications of the charge" and related to that "explanation of the procedure". They discuss what is likely to occur inside the courtroom which involves explaining to the juvenile who will be in the courtroom, what the various actors are likely to say and what will be the outcome — an adjournment, a disposition and so on. The second theme "implications of the charge" is revealed by the emphasis on topics such as "nature of the charge", "prior record", and "potential dispositions". If a juvenile's charge is serious in nature then the disposition may be severe. Likewise if the juvenile has a prior record this will influence the outcome. What dispositions a juvenile receives has implications for the juvenile's future. If s/he is fined then the juvenile is left with a formal record. In summary probation-juvenile interviews seem to be concerned with the juvenile's understanding of the court procedure and what effect court will have on the juvenile. Implicit in understanding court procedure is an understanding of legal language. This emphasis arguably reflects probation's supportive role to the juvenile as s/he goes through the process.

A lawyer-client interview seems to emphasize the "strategy" of the case more than anything else. The main topics of discussion: background of the juvenile, how the case is likely to proceed, prior record, information for bail and potential dispositions all relate to this theme. If the juvenile has a good family, no prior record, and has a place to go to if released this will affect the approach the lawyer will take in court. S/he may argue that the juvenile should be released. Likewise at the time of disposition defense might argue in favour of leniency based on this informa- tion. The lawyer points these things out to the juvenile who will then have some grasp of "how the case is likely to proceed". This overwhelming emphasis on strategy is a product of the "adver- sarial" or "child advocate" role lawyers perceive themselves as playing in the juvenile court.

The issue of court procedure, or how the case is likely to proceed seem to be a major concern raised between juvenile and probation officer and juvenile and defense counsel. The question of "Are juveniles normally interested in the proceedings of the court?" revealed an interesting response. Both defense counsel and probation officers responded that juveniles were interested in the proceedings of the court. In each of the two groups, 46.7 percent thought this was the case. Probation officers felt that the main reason that juveniles were interested was "fear of the unknown." Court represents a new and unusual experience for them. Defense lawyers suggest that the key reason for a juvenile's interest is his/her desire to know what is going on. Corroborating the position of probation, counsel maintain that a lack of interest stems from an overwhelming concern with disposition. Lawyers and probation officers said they would provide an explanation if the juvenile was interested. A point which could be made here is

Table 15.1 Describe Procedure Probation Officers

Would you please describe what you would normally tell a juvenile about court procedure?

Describe procedure*	Frequency
Proceedings are confidential	12
Judge is likely to read the charge	8
May have to enter pleas	8
The role of key actors	8
Physical surroundings of courtroom	6
Courtroom actors	6
Role of probation officer	5
Judge may ask you questions	4
Expected behaviour of juvenile	3
Everything is ultimately the judge's decision	2
May have to speak to judge	2
If you deny/admit a certain process follows	2

* Multiple responses permitted
Number of interviewees = 15

that perhaps the concern of these two actor groups with explaining court procedure is client-initiated as opposed to actor-initiated. So it is that if a probation officer or a defense counsel believe that a juvenile is not interested at all in the proceedings of the court then it may be that these actors will be less likely to explain this to juveniles. This has significant implications for any assessment of what a juvenile does not understand. Whatever their motivation, probation officers explained twelve different aspects of procedure, while defense counsel tended to describe only ten elements (See Tables 15.1 and 15.2).

Table 15.2   Describe Procedure Defense Counsel

Would you please describe what you would normally tell a juvenile about court procedure?

Describe procedure*	Frequency
Role of Crown prosecutor	11
Role of judge	10
Role of probation officer	6
What each key actor will likely say	5
Meaning and order of different court hearings	3
Answer to charge	3
Adjournments	3
Potential dispositions	3
Parent must be present at court	2
May have to enter pleas	2

* Multiple responses permitted
Number of interviewees = 15

FIRST COURT HEARING

On the day of the juvenile's first court hearing s/he will appear in front of the judge accompanied by either a probation officer, a lawyer or both. Probation officers maintain that they will generally always appear at the first hearing. They do not attend for two reasons. First, there is a duty probation officer system[9] and secondly the matter has not yet been referred to the probation district office. One point well worth noting here is that some probation officers (20 percent) suggest that their presence is *less* important once defence counsel is involved in the proceedings.

Lawyers also stated that they would generally appear on the day of a juvenile's first court hearing unless one of the following factors were involved: the attorney had never met the juvenile before (6.7 percent), there was a conflict of appointments (33.3 percent), the juvenile was not in custody on these charges (6.7 percent), the juvenile hadn't contacted the lawyer yet (13.3

percent), or there was going to be an adjournment (20 percent). Although each of these five responses was put forth as a reason for not attending the first appearance court with the juvenile, one can see that the number of persons who give any one of these reasons is very small. The only major reason would appear to be a conflict of appointments.

Once inside the courtroom the juvenile is confronted with the charge which has been laid against him/her. Most probation officers (60 percent) felt that juveniles knew what they were charged with before they went to court for the first time. Lawyers (53.3 percent) shared this view. According to these two groups a juvenile's main source of information concerning the charge was the police. Defense counsel said that an equally large number learned what they were charged with from the notice and summons which they received. Probation did not express a similar view.

Before arraigning a juvenile most judges (66.7 percent) interviewed stated that they would directly ask the juvenile if s/he knew why they were there. One of the judges said that s/he would be inclined to do this but in a less direct manner. In this regard, all of the judges in the sample said that they were likely to advise the juvenile of his/her right to counsel if s/he did not have a lawyer or indicated to the court that s/he had not yet spoken to one. Two judges said that they would always do this while the remainder stated that they would sometimes do this. These statements were consistent with my observations of each judge in the courtroom.[10]

The reading of the information to the juvenile can either be verbatim or a paraphrased version. Only one judge stated that s/he would always utilize a verbatim version. Only one judge stated that s/he would always paraphrase the information. Three of the other judges (50 percent) said that they might do this sometimes. In conjunction with this, most judges (66.7 percent) interviewed indicated that they would *not* explain the elements of an information and complaint to a juvenile and yet they (83.3 percent) also felt that most juveniles don't understand what they are charged with when the information is read to them. Further, both defense counsel and probation officers stated that juveniles do not understand the charge at the moment the judge reads the information to them.

Although there seems to be some discrepancy in the views expressed by the judges in regard to the preceding issue these same individuals (83.3 percent) state that they will generally ask the juvenile whether or not s/he understands the charge. The judges said that they would not do this if the juvenile had legal counsel or s/he responded immediately to the charge which had been read.

Once the information has been read the judge will ask the juvenile whether s/he is guilty or not guilty (33.3 percent), whether s/he admits or denies (33.3 percent), did s/he do it or not do it (16.6 percent) or whether the charge is true or false (16.6 percent). If a lawyer is involved in the case and tells the judge that they (juvenile and the lawyer) are entering a plea then of course the judge will not ask for a plea from the juvenile. One sees that in general judges do not ask juveniles how they plead to the charge(s) but rather ask them some version of this question. This is particularly important since both probation officers (46.7 percent) and defense counsel (53.3 percent) maintain that juveniles do not understand what is being asked for if a judge asks them "How do you plead?" They do, according to the key actor groups, understand if the judge asks, "Are you guilty or not guilty?", Did you do it or not?", "Is it true or false?"

An important question raised with each group of actors was "Do you think that it is the judge's role and responsibility to explain the charge, what it means to make a plea, the difference between guilty and not guilty, for example, to the juvenile?" Judges themselves felt that indeed this was their role in part but that defense counsel should assume part of the responsibility if they are involved in the case. They did not mention that probation should assume any of this responsibility. Defense counsel themselves expressed a mixed viewpoint regarding this question. One lawyer felt this should be the judge's role completely. The majority (86.7 percent) saw it as part of the judge's role. This is an interesting position to take since the court time allotted for each case makes the judge the *least* free to explain these things to the juvenile. Likewise, these interviews revealed that juveniles are not likely to ask the judge for clarification concerning any issue. Judges said 0–20 percent of all juveniles who appeared before them would ask any questions when given the opportunity.

Probation service (66.7 percent), on the other hand, felt that indeed this was part of the judge's role and responsibility. They see themselves, defense counsel and the prosecutor as being important in this regard. This position is significantly different from that taken by defense counsel and judges who would give the responsibility of explaining the charge, what it means to make a plea, the difference between guilty and not guilty only to themselves. This attitude demonstrates "how specialized vocabularies can be a way of perpetuating group or professional power" (Probert 1972, 84). Lawyers and judges may feel that they should do all of the explaining in order to preserve and protect their interests in the juvenile court. To have probation officers share in the explaining of these things may create the potential for probation to eventually fulfill this role completely. Probation officers on the other hand, seem to want to maximize the numbers of sources that the juvenile has to have these things explained to him/her. The underlying sentiment seems to be a desire on the part of probation to increase the juvenile's understanding. This could be facilitated by maximizing the juvenile's sources of information.

Although it would seem that other key actors would hold the judge ultimately responsible for whether or not the highly technical vocabulary of the information and plea is explained and understood by the juvenile it would be misleading to leave the discussion of the internal workings of the court at that. As pointed out earlier, legal language is viewed by defense counsel as being necessary for the effective functioning of the juvenile court. An important consideration then is whether or not lawyers who are active in the juvenile court systems *explain* the legal vocabulary they use in the courtroom to their child clients? Most probation officers (40 percent) told me that it had not been their experience that lawyers *appeared* to explain. The other probation officers said that they were unable to reply to this question. Judges had an equally difficult time answering this question. Only two judges (33.3 percent) interviewed said that it had been their experience that lawyers active in the juvenile court system did explain the legal vocabulary they use in court to their child clients. One said that "no" this was not the case. The majority (50 percent) didn't really know. This indecision can be attributed to the position that the judge occupies in the court structure. S/he is unable to observe directly the activities of different lawyers. Seven of the defense lawyers interviewed said that it was their practice to explain the legal vocabulary which they use in court to juveniles while the majority (53.3 percent) said they did not do this. All three groups did agree that it was important for lawyers to explain to juveniles the legal vocabulary used in court.

At the end of the court hearing most judges (83 percent) said that they would never do this. The reasons for not explaining varied. Two (33.3 percent) stated that this was the role of counsel, others maintained that a few kids know the system so well there was no need to explain while some said that this was not a trial or disposition. Almost all of the judges (66.7 percent) said that they do ask juveniles whether or not they understand what has occurred in court that day. The explanation provided is predominantly at the initiation of the judge (83.3 percent).

Judges indicated that one of the main reasons for not explaining to the juvenile what had occurred in court that day was that this was the role of defense counsel. In an independent question I asked judges directly whether or not they would explain if the juvenile had legal counsel. Three (50 percent) of the judges said that they would only explain sometimes if counsel were involved. Two reasons were given for this action. First, these judges wanted the juvenile to understand the disposition completely if one was given. Secondly, they felt that it might get the message across to the juvenile more clearly and consequently the juvenile might take it more seriously.

Given that part of the role of a probation officer is explanatory I questioned judges about whether or not they would explain to the juvenile what had occurred in court if the juvenile's probation officer was present. All responded that indeed they would. First, they felt that it was not the probation officer's role to have to explain court. Second, they shouldn't rely on them to explain legal matters. Third, it was part of the judge's role. Fourth, probation officers have a different perspective and finally, when a disposition was given they should not be explaining that to a juvenile. One point that might be raised here is that although it is questionable whether probation could not or should not be explaining what has happened in court perhaps what judges and lawyers may not realize is that the explanation isn't as complicated as they think it is.

AFTER COURT

The period which follows court can conceivably be viewed as an opportunity for lawyer-client, probation officer-client to spend a few moments discussing what has just occurred in court. It can best be likened to a "debriefing" session. However, certain structural factors often prevent this from happening. A probation officer or a defense lawyer may have cases which come up in court one after another. This makes it impossible for the actor to leave the court to discuss the juvenile's case with him/her.

An explanation of what has occurred is not necessarily given to each and every juvenile processed through the court on any particular day. Probation officers (93.3 percent) and defense lawyers (93.3 percent) said that they would provide an explanation which was always at their initiation. Both lawyers and probation officers informed me that less than 50 percent of all juveniles they deal with would ever ask questions about court once the initial explanation had been provided.

One very revealing aspect of the probation and defense counsel interviews was their respective responses to the question of whether or not they would explain if the other was present. Probation officers (66.7 percent) stated that yes they would explain even if the juvenile had legal counsel. The main reasons given were: the lawyer doesn't always explain adequately (33.3 percent), they provide different information to the juvenile (20 percent), the explanation that counsel provides is too complex (13.3 percent) and finally, they want to make sure that the juvenile understands (6.7 percent). All lawyers interviewed said they would provide an explanation of what had happened in court even if the probation officer was present. Reasons given: probation officers explain from a different perspective (33.3 percent), it's the role of defense counsel (13.3 percent), "I want to scare the kid into believing that this is for real" (6.7 percent), or the juvenile and probation officer have a hostile relationship (6.7 percent). In some instances, a juvenile will very often get the benefit of two accounts. Other juveniles however may end up with no explanation. The fact that probation officers and defense counsel explain to the juvenile in spite of one another's presence indicated some uncertainty as to role and function if not a degree of role conflict or at least role tension. Perhaps this uncertainty has grown out of the changes which have occurred in the Winnipeg juvenile court.

COURT FOLLOW-UP

Given that very few matters are disposed of in the first appearance court the issue of follow-up becomes an important one. I asked both probation officers and defense counsel whether or not they ever followed up a court hearing by writing a letter to the juvenile and/or his/her parent/guardian explaining what took place in court. Some lawyers (33.3 percent) said that they would always do this while the remainder (66.7 percent) said they would only do this sometimes. Only one probation officer (6.7 percent) stated that s/he would always write a letter while eight (53.3 percent) others do this sometimes. For lawyers the most common reason for forwarding a letter was either to remind the juvenile of the next court date or explain the nature of the disposition given. Probation officers shared defense counsel's position in saying that a letter was particularly important when a period of probation was given as a disposition. They feel that the conditions of the probation order need to be thoroughly explained to the juvenile.

If a hearing is adjourned to another court all lawyers said that they would be in touch with a juvenile either by telephone (100 percent), letter (66.7 percent) or personal meeting (46.7 percent).

Probation officers (86.7 percent) were likely to have telephone contact with the juvenile.

IS LEGAL LANGUAGE NECESSARY?

The question of whether or not legal language is necessary for the functioning of the Winnipeg juvenile court is a most critical question in assessing key actors views about what juveniles should understand about legal language. The inquiry produced a variety of responses. Probation officers as a group seemed to feel that legal language was not necessary. They maintain that the court can not only function as effectively with less legal vocabulary but that if less were employed the courtroom experience might be more meaningful for the juvenile. It might have greater impact on him/her.

Not surprisingly, defense lawyers favour the use of legal language arguing that legal language not only serves a very specific purpose but that it also facilitates the process. Judges, for the same reasons advanced by defense counsel, seem to see the need for legal language in juvenile court.

The issue of whether or not the legal language is necessary was most clearly revealed by the question "What in your mind are the most important legal terms or legal phrases that a juvenile has to understand in coming to court?" Whatever their view as to the necessity of legal language within the juvenile court, each actor group isolated legal terms and phrases which they felt were important for the child appearing before the juvenile court to understand. A point to be noted is that each interviewee was provided with a list of legal terms and phrases[11] which had been prepared in advance of the interview. Although the compendium of terms was intended to be as extensive as possible other terms were raised which did not appear on the original list. Most of the responses were promoted. (See Table 15.3, 15.4, and 15.5).

An examination of the tables reveals that probation officers isolated different legal terms and phrases than defense counsel and judges. Probation officers mentioned things like adjourn *sine die*,[12] the charge, the plea, pretrial, and transfer whereas both judges and defense counsel emphasized disposition as being most important. Probation's position seems to reflect their emphasis on the court process and the implications that getting involved has for the juvenile. For example, a juvenile has to understand the charge and what it means to give a plea before s/he goes to court. Likewise if the juvenile's case proceeds to pretrial or transfer then the juvenile's position will change — his/her legal status will be altered. Finally, to have a charge adjourned *sine die*[13] means that the juvenile has received a break. Probation probably view this as important because if the juvenile does not understand that s/he has received a break then this can have serious implications for reinvolvement. To elaborate, when I asked why they selected

Table 15.3   Most Important Legal Terms or Phrases Probation Officers

What in your mind are the most important legal terms or legal phrases which a juvenile has to understand?

Name of Term/Phrase*	Frequency
Adjourn *sine die*	13
Not guilty/Guilty	10
Information and complaint	9
Pretrial court	9
Transfer application	9
Contrary to Section ____ of Criminal Code of Canada	8
Fine	8
Restitution	8
Plea	8
Waive reading of charge	8
Condition discharge	8
Stay of proceedings	8
Committal	8
Probation	8
To be seized of a case	8
Trial	8
Get particulars	8
Allegations	7
Bail application	7
Right to legal counsel	7
Suspend final disposition	7
Withdraw charges	7
Indicated plea	7
Remand	7
Pre-disposition report	6
Not delinquent/Delinquent	6
Reconsideration	6
Period of progress	6
Disposition court	6
Cross-examination	6
To take an oath	6
Ascertain jurisdiction	5
Subpoena	5
Witness	5
Keep the peace and be of good behaviour	5
Finding of delinquency	5

* Multiple responses permitted
Number of interviewees = 15

Table 15.4 Most Important Legal Terms or Legal Phrases Defense Counsel

What in your mind are the most important legal terms or legal phrases which a juvenile has to understand?

Name of Term/Phrase*	Frequency
Delinquent/Not delinquent* Guilty/Not guilty	8
Disposition in general	8
Plea	6
Adjourn *sine die*	6
Transfer application	5
Pre-disposition report	5
Particulars	5
Release	5
Forensic	4
Probation	4
Committal	4
Words in an information	4
Remand/Adjourn	4
Voir dire	4
Placement	4
Restitution	4
Stay of proceedings	4
Release	3
Progress report	2
Trial	2
Plea bargaining	2
Leave application	2
Finding of delinquency	2
Reconsideration	1
Pretrial	1
Party to an offence	1
Curfew	1
Legal vs. moral guilt	1
Failure to appear	1
Children's Aid	1
Juvenile record	1

* Multiple responses permitted
Number of interviewees = 15

these terms as important most (80%) probation offices said they were important because "they affect the juvenile". Some (26.7%) said they were "the basics of the system" and the remainder (26.7%) said they were "used frequently". One point to be made here is that probation officers view many legal terms as being important. For every term or phrase at least 33.3% of all probation officers interviewed saw it as being important. They do not just isolate the disposition terms. This is significant because it suggests that although this group feel that legal terms and phrases should not be used in juvenile court they believe that if they are used then

Table 15.5   Most Important Legal Terms or Legal Phrases
Judges

What in your mind are the most important legal terms or legal phrases which a juvenile has to understand?

Name of Term/Phrase*	Frequency
Disposition	2
Charge	1
Entering a plea	1
Guilty/Not guilty	1
Curfew	1
Know why they are there?	1
Have you seen a lawyer?	1
Record	1
Particulars	1
Stay of proceedings	1
None	1

* Multiple responses permitted
Number of interviewees = 6

juveniles should understand them. They are concerned with the juvenile's comprehension.

Both judges and defense counsel mention disposition as the most important legal terms which a juvenile has to understand. I would argue that this ties in directly with their respective roles. Defense counsel in this study see themselves as "adversarial" or "child's advocate" which accounts for the importance they attach to disposition. Disposition is what the lawyer ultimately works toward. Thus when a disposition is given they want the juvenile to understand and appreciate what it actually means to receive it. Likewise judges act as decision makers who order dispositions in each and every case. Arguably, judges, like defense counsel, view disposition as important for the juvenile to understand because if s/he does not then they may not realize that they have been given a break on a particular charge. Juveniles must also understand the seriousness of the disposition and what implications it has for their future. Clearly this interpretation of the positions of defense counsel and judges was borne out by the answer to the question "Why are these particular terms so important?" Defense counsel said that these were the "basics of the system" (73.3 percent) and that "these terms affect the juvenile" (60 percent). Two defense counsel (13.3 percent) state that these terms were important because they "personified the power of the state" — a point implicit in my observation that lawyers want juveniles to understand and appreciate what a given disposition means. Judges shared the sentiments of defense counsel. The majority (66.7

percent) stated that "these terms affect them" was the most important reason for their selection.

One interesting finding which is well worth noting is that one judge stated that there were no legal terms or legal phrases which a juvenile has to understand. This individual said that it was not the juvenile's responsibility to understand but rather for counsel to take care of this.

CHANGING LEGAL LANGUAGE

Each of the three key actor groups interviewed in this study shared the view that legal language does affect the juvenile's understanding of the courtroom hearing. Acknowledging the impact that the use of this language has on the juvenile who appears before the court, three related questions become important. First, "Do key legal actors feel that the courtroom experience would have greater impact if less legal vocabulary were used?" Second, "Do they feel that simplifying legal language would make the courtroom experience more meaningful for the juvenile?" Third, "If legal language were simplified would the courtroom experience have more of a teaching function?"

Almost all (93.3 percent) of the probation officers interviewed maintain that the courtroom experience would have greater impact if less legal vocabulary was used. This position ties in well with the earlier comments made by this group about the undesirability of having legal language used in the juvenile court. For the probation officer, juvenile court should be more of an "informal court" with greater emphasis placed on "the best interest of the child". Implicit in their conception of an informal court is the use of language which the juvenile can understand. To ensure that the juvenile understands would be to act in the "best interest of the child".

Defense counsel were divided on this issue. The majority (53.3 percent) felt that court would have greater impact if less legal vocabulary were used; however, they place their greatest emphasis on due process which can be accomplished with legal language *and* without the juvenile's comprehension. One point which should be made is that fourteen (93.3 percent) of the lawyers interviewed also told me that it was their position that a lawyer's responsibility was discharged only if s/he had protected the juvenile's rights *and* the juvenile had *understood* what had happened in court, but at the same time they admitted not always explaining.

Only half of the judges (50 percent) in this study said that the impact of court would be greater if less legal vocabulary were used, while three other judges felt that "very little legal vocabulary was being used now so impact could probably not be increased." This view is not surprising given the conflicting position judges express when describing their feelings about the functioning of the juvenile court. Their view of court requires competent case processing by legal actors. From this perspective legal language is an asset.

The second question posed, "Would simplifying legal language make the courtroom experience more meaningful for the juvenile?" gained a variety of responses. Probation officers (93.3 percent) felt that definitely meaningfulness would increase if language were simplified. The majority of attornies (60 percent) shared this optimism. Judges (33.3 percent) were less convinced.

In conjunction with the question of meaningfulness I asked interviewees "If legal language were simplified would the courtroom experience have more of a teaching function?" Not surprisingly, probation officers (86.7 percent) said that it would. I suggest that this very positive response can be linked to their "treatment" approach to dealing with juveniles. Judges (66.7 percent) and lawyers (46.7 percent) responded affirmatively to this question as well.

The simplification of legal language would seem to produce a number of positive results. The critical issue is the feasibility of simplifying legal language into plain and simple English. The criteria used in the assessment of its feasibility are equally important.

Seven (46.7 percent) of the probation officers interviewed thought that simplifying legal language was a feasible proposition. Their reasons included: anything is possible, the court is for the people, all legal words can be replaced with simpler more easily understood words and the most experienced counsel active in the juvenile court always use simple English. The reasons for why such a plan was not seen to be feasible were: some legal terms are essential to the functioning of the court, there is a tradition involved and finally, it would be too time consuming to change everything into Plain English. It is interesting to note that the reasons for why it is not feasible support fully that body of literature which argues against the reform of legal English (Danet 1980, 541; cf. Mellinkoff 1963, 290; Aiken 1960).

Somewhat surprising was the response of juvenile court lawyers to the question of feasibility. Most (80 percent) lawyers felt that such a change *was* feasible. Their reasons are of particular interest. They suggested, first of all, that many lawyers active in the juvenile justice system already do this. My courtroom observations do not corroborate this. Second, they feel that there are plain words for complex legal terms. Third, juvenile court can be informal which implies that a simpler language might be used just as effectively as legalese. Fourth, legal language is really only for the convenience of the judiciary, the prosecution and defense. Finally, they thought that if other areas of law (contract, insurance, etc.) are doing this effectively then there is no reason why criminal law cannot do the same.

The fourth reason given above lies in complete contradiction to much of the literature regarding lawyers views about changing legal language. Specifically, Danet notes in her article, "Language in the Legal Process" that many lawyers would argue adamently that "to change the language of the law is to make it less precise because lawyers and judges know what the words mean; these words have stood the test of time. To change the language is to create new legal issue, to sacrifice the comforts or precedent" (Danet 1980, 541; cf. Mellinkoff 1963, 290). Likewise the work of Zenon Bankowski and Geoff Mungham, "A Power Elite: The Legal Profession in Process" (1976) presents an opposing view.

Judges were divided on the issue of feasibility. Only two (33.3 percent) felt that it was feasible and they provided two reasons. First they believe that "there isn't that much being used now so any changes wouldn't be major ones." Second "other areas of law (contract, insurance, etc.) are already engaged in this process." The judges (33.3 percent) who were opposed said that it was not feasible because "it detracts from the essence of the process — the language as prescribed by the Criminal Code itself", "we are dealing with very specific issues", "we are dealing with the language of the criminal law which is very straight forward" and "one can't substitute simple words for some of the legal ones." The position reflected in these responses falls in line with that taken by supporters for the continued use of legal language (Danet 1980, 541).

The final question raised in the discussion of language change was "What changes would you (each key actor group) propose to simplify legal language?" The answers appear in Tables 15.6, 15.7, and 15.8.

An interesting difference emerges out of these three tables. Specifically, defense counsel and judges place greater emphasis on increasing explanation of terms used while probation officers feel that the most appropriate changes are translating everything into plain English and working with the judges so that they will speak plain English. The position taken by judges and defense counsel seems to reveal a satisfaction with the structure of the system and

Table 15.6 Changes to Simplify Legal Language Probation Officers

What changes would you propose to simplify legal language?

Proposed changes*	Frequency
Translate all terms into plain English	8
Work with judges	6
Convince legal actors of need for plain English	3
Place onus on court to explain	2
Send explanatory pamphlet with summons/notice	2
Increase probation involvement	1
Do away with Latin terms completely	1
Develop rules for vocabulary used in juvenile court	1

* Multiple responses permitted
Number of interviewees = 15

Table 15.7 Changes to Simplify Legal Language Defense Counsel

What changes would you propose to simplify legal language?

Proposed Change*	Frequency
Explain all legal words	5
Standardize explanation of terms	2
No response	1
Make it mandatory to use plain terms	1
Have one person to explain legal terms and legal procedures	1
Make key actors responsible for explanation	1

* Multiple responses permitted
Number of interviewees = 15

Table 15.8 Changes to Simplify Legal Language Judges

What changes would you propose to simplify legal language?

Proposed Change	Frequency
Explain in plain English	1
Make it incumbent on judge to explain	1

Number of interviewees = 6

the desire to work *within* the system to achieve any changes in the use of language in the court. Increased explanation of language used can be accommodated within the existing structure. Probation on the other hand advocate more sweeping changes at the structural level. The desire to translate all language used in the court into plain English suggests a general dissatisfaction with the current use of language. Likewise the desire to work with the judges of the juvenile court so that they will speak plain English indicates the desire for reform on a much broader scale. The apparent differences on this particular issue might be a reflection of probation's ambiguous role within the changed Winnipeg juvenile court. Likewise it might indicate an opposition to a more legalistically oriented court.

CONCLUSION

This paper has attempted to present the results obtained from focused interviews conducted with probation officers, defense counsel and judges of the Winnipeg juvenile court. The literature suggested that understanding legal language is problematic for *most*, particularly juveniles. The key actor findings corroborated this position.

Acknowledging the difficulty juveniles face in trying to understand legal language is a feasible proposition. Beyond key actors support for the use of a plain and simple English in legal proceedings, certain structural changes may be necessary for a more effective communication between the juvenile and the court. Specifically, if the probation officer's role is primarily explanatory then a more active role may increase juveniles' understanding of legal language. Small numbers of cases in each courtroom would technically allow the judge more time to explain the language, process and procedure of the court to the juvenile. Structural changes such as these two *may* promote juveniles' understanding of legal language to a greater extent than the simplification of legal language. As the governing legislation is about to be surpassed by the YOA, it is particularly important to explore such suggestions.

Notes

1. This paper is excerpted from T.F. Smith-Gadacz, *Legally Speaking: The Potential For A 'Plain English' Movement in the Winnipeg Juvenile Court.* Unpublished MA Thesis, University of Manitoba, 1982.

2. Fifteen probation officers, either senior probation officers or intake workers, were interviewed. These two groups were selected because of their extensive contact with apprehended juveniles as well as the explanatory role which they play in the court process.

3. Fifteen defense counsel — five duty counsel, five retained counsel, and five legal-aid-clinic representatives — were interviewed. Lawyers included in the sample all had sizeable caseloads within the juvenile court. The total sample size was fifteen in order to make it equivalent to the sample size of probation officers.

4. The bench of the Family Division of the Manitoba Provincial Judges Court

is composed of sixteen judges. Ten of these are full-time while the other six are part-time. Six of the ten full-time judges were interviewed in this study.

5. Earlier work (Smith-Gadacz 1982) demonstrated that there are many examples of legal language in the Winnipeg juvenile court.

6. "Probation docket" courts were like informal meetings of juvenile, judge and concerned others which operated as late as October 1981. They can best be likened to a discussion between concerned parties.

7. In October of 1981 a provincial prosecutor was placed in every juvenile court in the city of Winnipeg. Previously, probation officers had assumed a quasi-prosecutorial role. The presence of a prosecutor denoted the departure from a more social-welfare model and a move toward a more legalistic model of functioning in the juvenile court. Equally important to note is that the time period preceding this change in the structure evidenced an apparent increase in the number of defense counsel representing juveniles.

8. The Manitoba Youth Centre is a closed detention facility for juveniles which is located in the city of Winnipeg.

9. A duty probation system is a relatively new system in the Winnipeg juvenile court. On each day of the week at the Manitoba Youth Centre one of the probation districts in the city has the majority of their matters heard. This does not mean that matters from other districts are not dealt with. If for example, it was a day when the South-West district was bringing its cases to court then one member of that district would act as duty probation officer meaning that they would be inside the court at all times. Often times the duty probation officer will take care of matters for other probation officers from their district office as well as other districts. This contributes to the more efficient use of the probation officer's time. Less time is wasted waiting for cases to come up in court. Likewise the judge can give instructions to any number of probation officers through the duty probation officer.

10. From April 1981 to February 1982, I was employed by the Solicitor-General of Canada as a courtroom observer (Winnipeg site) for the "National Study On The Functioning Of the Juvenile Court".

11. The idea of preparing a compendium of legal terms and legal phrases came from a suggestion given to me during an interview in which I was pretesting one of the key actor instruments. The interviewee suggested that all key actors I would interview would be very familiar with the language of the court. The familiarity, s/he speculated, might make it difficult for the respondant to isolate terms and/or phrases into the category of most important. Defense counsel and probation officers commented that having this list to prompt them did aid them in answering the question.

12. To adjourn *sine die* is to adjourn a case without a date, without a time on which it will be brought up again.

13. Supra, n. 12.

References

Aiken, Ray J. 1960. Let's not oversimplify legal language. *Rocky Mountain Law Review.* 32, 358–364.

Atkinson, J. and Paul Drew. 1979. *Order in court.* London: The Macmillan Press Ltd.

Bala, Nicholas and Kenneth D. Clarke. 1981. *The child and the law.* Toronto: McGraw-Hill Ryerson Limited.

Bankowski, Z. and G. Mungham. 1976. A power elite: The legal profession in process. *Images of law.* London: Routledge and Kegan Paul.

Danet, Brenda. 1980. Language in the legal process. *Law and Society Review,* 14(3): 445–564.

Ericson, Richard V. and Pat Baranek. 1982. *The ordering of justice — A study of accused persons as dependants in the criminal process.* Toronto: The University of Toronto Press.

Hackler, James. 1978. *The prevention of youthful crime: The great stumble forward.* Toronto: Methuen.

Juvenile Delinquents Act. 1929. R.S.C., 1970, Chapter J-3.

Matza, David. 1964. *Delinquency and drift.* New York: John Wiley and Sons, Inc.

Mellinkoff, David. 1963. *The language of the law.* Boston: Little, Brown and Company.

Merton, Robert K., Marjorie Fiske and Patricia L. Kendall. 1956. *The focused interview — A manual of problems and procedures.* Glencoe, Ill.: The Free Press.

Probert, Walter, 1972. *Law, language and communication.* Springfield, Ill.: Charles C. Thomas.

Rubin, Ted H. 1976. The eye of the juvenile court judge: A one-step up view of the juvenile justice system. In Malcolm Klein, *The juvenile justice system.* Sage Criminal Justice Annuals, Volume 5, Sage Publications, Beverly Hills, Ca.

Smith-Gadacz. 1982. *Legally speaking: The potential for a "plain English" movement in the Winnipeg juvenile court.* Unpublished MA Thesis, University of Manitoba.

Chapter 16

Cops Don't Always See It That Way*

Clifford D. Shearing

INTRODUCTION

This paper examines the beliefs about the public within the police culture. It argues that the almost exclusive emphasis on the "public as enemy" view found within the sociological literature on the police arises from a failure to distinguish between the public that policemen do things for and the public that they do things to. When this distinction is made, other, more paternalistic beliefs about the public are revealed.

One of the most consistent findings in the literature of the police is that the police view the public as a threat and see themselves as existing in an adversarial relationship (Buckner 1972, 5) with the public. (For an excellent review of the literature related to the police culture see Wexter 1973).[1] Manning, for example, in summarizing aspects of the police occupational culture notes the following postulates with respect to the relationship between the police and the public.

(1) People cannot be trusted; they are dangerous . . .
(2) You must make people respect you.
(3) Everyone hates a cop. . . . (Manning 1971, 156).

The first two of these propositions define what sociologists have come to regard as the central features of the antagonistic

* Revised version of a paper presented at the Canadian Sociology and Anthropology Association Meetings, Fredericton, New Brunswick, June 1977. Substantially revised from *Canadian Review of Sociology and Anthropology* 18(3) 1981. Clifford Shearing, Centre of Criminology, University of Toronto.

relationship that police perceive exists between themselves and the public, namely, that the public are dangerous (Westley 1953; Skolnick 1966; Wolfgang 1968; Wilson 1968; Dougherty 1969), and they are disrespectful of police authority (Westley 1971; Pilivan and Briar 1965; Reiss and Bordua 1967; Sykes and Clark 1975).[2] These two elements combine to define the public as an assailant who can injure the police, both physically and morally. Westley, in one of the earliest sociological studies on the police, captured the quality of this relationship when he argued that the police see the public as an enemy (Westley 1971). This metaphor of the public as an enemy, either explicitly or implicitly, recurs throughout the police literature.

Kirkham (1974, 119), for example, an American criminologist who became a policeman implicitly employs the public-as-enemy metaphor when he writes:

> Whatever the risk to himself every police officer understands that his ability to back up the lawful authority which he represents is the only thing which stands between civilization and the jungle of lawlessness.

Harris (1973, 55–56), in writing about police training, is more explicit:

> . . . the officer learned through sad experience that out groups . . . were not to be trusted, he seemed to imagine that the criminal was always watching him, just waiting. . . . The invisible enemy was not just the criminal; it included the citizen.

This notion that the public is an enemy has had profound implications for our understanding of the police. It has been used by sociologists as the principal factor in accounting for the police response to the public and each other as they go about their work. For example, the police organization has been characterized as expressing considerable in-group solidarity coupled with a secretiveness that excludes outsiders (Westley 1971, 111–118; Bittner 1970, 64). This characteristic is typically explained as a defensive strategy that policemen establish to deal with a hostile public (Westley 1956; Banton 1964; Whitaker 1964; Clark 1965; Clark and Gibbs 1965; McNamara 1967; Manning 1971; Buckner 1972). This argument is well stated by Harris who writes:

> Finding themselves barraged by a steady onslaught of criticism from many segments of the community — all of whom the policeman is supposed to be serving — police officers try to protect themselves by curling up individually and organizationally like the vulnerable porcupine. (Harris 1973, 28).

Not only has the conception of the public as an often dangerous and disrespectful enemy been used to explain police solidarity,
but it has been used to explain the police response to citizens in
police-citizen encounters, for example, their use of force and their
decision to enforce the law as a means of dealing with problems
(Banton 1964; Piliavin and Briar 1965; Wilson 1968; Reiss and
Bordua 1967; Sykes and Clark 1975).

In this paper I will argue that the conception of the public as
enemy is only one aspect of the police view of the public, albeit an
essential one, and that to deal only with this aspect distorts the
police view of the world and limits our understanding of the
relationship between the police and the public. To do this, I will
first describe the view of the public expressed by policemen
working within the communications centre of a Canadian police
department as they responded to calls from citizens for police
assistance. In this situation, while the perception of the public as
enemy did arise, it was not the only or the dominant meaning that
other researchers have found it to be.

This description will be followed by a consideration of the
reason for this discrepancy. Finally, a conception of the police view
of the public that incorporates both sets of findings will be
suggested.

THE RESEARCH

The research on which this paper is based took place within
the communications centre of a large Canadian police department
in 1972. The communications centre was the division within the
police department which received calls from citizens requesting
police assistance. The work of responding to calls was divided into
two jobs. A complaint officer received calls from citizens requesting police assistance, and made a decision as to whether the police
would respond. These officers then passed the request on to the
dispatchers for their attention. There were normally four to six
dispatchers working at a time and up to eight complaint officers.

This study focussed on the work of the complaint officers. As
policemen working in the communications centre alternated
between the jobs of complaint officers and dispatchers, the views
expressed by the complaint officers represent the views of the
policemen working in the communications centre (both dispatchers and complaint officers).

The findings presented here are based on informal focused
interviews with the complaint officers, together with the remarks

complaint officers made with respect to the calls they were dealing with and conversations between themselves and with policemen from other parts of the police department.

VICTIMS, COMPLAINANTS, WITNESSES, AND TROUBLEMAKERS

The public called the police for assistance with respect to a wide variety of problems (see Shearing 1975 for a description of the range and types of problems). In responding to requests for police assistance, the complaint officers classified the people involved in the problem in terms of their relation to it: people in trouble (victims), people reporting trouble (complainants), people who observed the trouble (witnesses), and people causing trouble (troublemakers).[3]

Troublemakers were the people that the police, in responding to problems, would often be required to deal with by doing something *to* them. The complaint officers, however, seldom dealt directly with troublemakers. They dealt fundamentally with victims and complainants; the people whom the police, in responding to problems, would be doing something *for*.[4] The people they came into contact with were people who wanted help and who saw the police as a helper they could turn to for assistance.[5] In talking about "the public", complaint officers referred to the people requesting police help: the people the police do things for rather than to. This relationship of helper and helped provided the framework within which the complaint officers defined the public. They saw themselves as experts who understood trouble and knew when and how help should be provided; they saw the public as people in need of help. The specific characterizations complaint officers used to describe the public all acquired their meaning with reference to this overriding relationship.

THE PUBLIC ARE HELPLESS AND STUPID

Above all what the complaint officers commented on most about the public was their utter helplessness and stupidity.[6] As one of the complaint officers remarked, "some of them don't have enough brains to pound sand." The public's stupidity was, the complaint officers believed, expressed in almost all their activities associated with the problem they brought to the police. They believed, for instance, that many of the problems citizens called the police for were problems they had brought on themselves and that could have been avoided had the caller had "an ounce of brains."

Not only did the policemen in the communications centre believe that many of the problems the public faced were of their own making, but they also believed that many of the problems they sought police help for were trivial problems that any reasonably competent human being with a modicum of initiative should have been able to handle themselves. The complaint officers frequently used noise complaints as illustrations of this aspect of the public's helplessness.

> It makes you sick, all you get on weekends are noisy parties. Why don't they go and bang on doors themselves?

> Those barking dog and noisy party calls are a pain. Why can't they deal with them themselves?

> So why did he have to call us? The guy's a neighbour. Why doesn't he go and ask him to shut up his bloody dog himself?

Not only did the public report problems to the police that they should have been able to solve themselves, but complaint officers felt, they were often so helpless and incompetent that they were not even able to ask for police help without assistance.

> You have to be another Larry Solway sometimes. You have to put words in their mouths just to find out where they live or their phone numbers.

While the public's stupidity was defined in large measure in terms of their frequent inability to prevent and deal with minor problems on their own, it was also seen as arising from the public's naivity about the world of the police. The public, as a result of the dramatization of the police role in novels, films, and television dramas, complaint officers believed, had developed unreasonable expectations as to what the police could do in resolving problems.

> Some people think a policeman's uniform will make everything all right. But it only quietens things down for a little while. It really doesn't accomplish anything.

> It's futile sending an officer out anyway. There's nothing he can do even if he finds her.

> Another domestic; probably can't do much about it.

> We send out a car and they get the kids to disperse. But they probably come right back again as soon as the car's gone.

The public were, the complaint officers believed, not only naive about the police organization and resources, but also about the definition of problems. The area in which this was, the complaint officers felt, most obvious, was in the public's definition of emergencies: the public simply did not know what an emergency was and constantly exaggerated trivial incidents by calling them emergencies. Complaint officers, for example, frequently pointed out that what a citizen defined as an emergency often proved on closer examination, to be no more than a noisy party or a minor traffic accident.

THE PUBLIC ARE DEMANDING

While it was the public's helplessness and incompetence which impressed them most, it was the public's frequently demanding attitude that was the communications officers' most constant source of annoyance. People requiring police assistance, they believed, were frequently disrespectful because they demanded help rather than requested it. This demanding attitude annoyed the complaint officers because they felt it was an expression of the failure on the part of the public to accord them the respect they, as professionals and expert helpers, deserved. This demanding attitude suggested to them that the public regarded them as servants who could be ordered to do things rather than as professionals whose help could be requested, but should not be demanded.[7] The resentment that complaint officers felt towards a demanding public was expressed in the communications centre in remarks such as the following comment by one of these policemen to a colleague:

> Send out a car immediately. It really bugs me when they say that.

The complaint officers were particularly resentful of the demanding attitude callers sometimes took when the callers were defined as citizens of particularly low status, for example, non-English speaking immigrants.

> The thing that bugs me is getting a call from a person who can bearly speak English, but demands a car "right away". The two things that they know are "dollar" and "send police right away", and they don't even speak the language. The woman had only called ten minutes ago so I said, "There are two million people in the city and you are only one of them."

The complaint officers saw themselves as professionals and believed that the public too often, by being demanding, did not acknowledge this status. For the complaint officers, this meant that the public frequently did not know their place. Their attitude towards these people was much the same as that of whites in the southern United States and countries like Rhodesia and South Africa to blacks who "don't know their place"; they regarded them as "uppity" much as one regards precocious children.

THE PUBLIC ARE EXPLOITERS

While people who brought trivial problems to the police were often regarded as simply incredibly helpless and stupid, some callers were seen as not helpless but lazy and exploitative. These callers were regarded as "using" the police and as not really as helpless as they would have one believe. Often this was seen as laziness or perhaps a fear of doing things for oneself.

> Very often people call about barking dogs because they do not want to get involved themselves. They want to leave it to the police to do something. Complaints about barking dogs just misuse the police. In the vast majority of cases, it is probably quite unnecessary to involve the police, expect as a last resort. The thing to do would be to go directly to the dog's owner and ask him to take the dog inside or quiet it down some other way.

At other times, however, the complaint officers felt that the public was deliberately trying to "use" the police.

> We're not running a taxi service for them. That's not an emergency. They don't have money for the subway, but they have money for other things. As soon as you mention ambulance to them, they go off because they think they might have to pay for it.

Besides individuals who tried to exploit the police, the complaint officers felt that certain businesses used the police to make money for themselves. For example, insurance companies, they believed, used the police to do their investigating for them; investigating that the companies should, the complaint officers believed, have done themselves, as they were being paid to do so by their clients. The worst offenders in this regard, the complaint officers felt, were the alarm companies who "had the nerve" to get the police to respond to *their* alarms for them.

> Alarm companies, they use the police. They get us to do their work for them.

> God damn phony outfits. They call the owner and he says not to tell the police anything so our car sits there at the scene waiting and waiting for someone to show.

If the image that came to mind in describing the police response to the public's demanding attitude was that of a precocious child, the metaphor that comes to mind in describing the complaint officers' views of the public's exploitative tendencies is that the public are like "spoilt children".

THE COMPLAINT OFFICERS WERE PATERNALISTIC

What unifies the meanings that the complaint officers ascribed to the public is a pervasive paternalism that arises out of their definition of their relationship with the public as between helpers and people requesting help. The complaint officers above all saw the public (victims, and complainants) as helpless incompetents. While they derided and ridiculed the public for this helplessness and incompetence, they also expected it and criticized them for being too "uppity" when they were not appropriately helpless and submissive and for exploiting the police if they felt they were presenting themselves as more helpless than they really were. Underlying each of these meanings lies a paternalism that colours each meaning which must be taken into account if the complaint officers' definition of the public is to be appreciated. Thus the disrespect for their status of experts that the demanding attitude the public sometimes took, as well as the disrespect implied in the public's tendency to exploit the police was not the disrespect of an enemy, but rather the disrespect of occasionally recalcitrant children. Such recalcitrance is part of the lot of most parents but it seldom is seen as a threat to the parent-child relationship. Similarly, the lot of the complaint officer was to deal with a public who were fundamentally helpless and stupid and occasionally demanding and exploitative. Throughout, however, the police remained the helper and the public, the helped.

THIRD AND FOURTH CLASS CITIZENS

In contrast to "the public" who called for help and who were seen as sharing, to a greater or lesser degree, the meanings we have identified, the complaint officers distinguished "third and fourth class citizens", or as they sometimes called them, "the people from the slum areas", or simply the "scum".

That is a pretty run down area, as you could hear from old gravel voice. They're at the very bottom of the ladder — third and fourth class citizens.

When you've worked in the area, you learn that they haven't seen soap for weeks. They and their houses are filthy, dirty. In _____, if you get involved in something, you never know whether you'll get out O.K.

Pick up one garbage can at X. Imagine getting a station detail to X — you'd be surprised to get out alive.

Complaint Officer: There was a murder at X yesterday, you know.
Fellow Officer: That's not a murder, that's a "local improvement", but if you called it that you'd have to pay taxes on it.

That's the first clown of the night. I'd like to go down and arrest the bum myself. I can't stand those pigs.

The complaint officers did not view "the scum" as part of the public. "The scum" deserved no *help* from the police, and they should, in their view, get none. "The scum", they felt, should not be included as part of the public they were to "serve and protect".

First Complaint Officer: They should close down the division and put a fence around it. Everyone there deserves each other.
Second Complaint Officer: Yeah, you better believe it.
Third Complaint Officer: You could say the same for division X. They're the same sort.

"Third- and fourth-class citizens" were troublemakers that the police did things *to* rather than *for*. "The sum" was not, they believed, in a helper/helped relationship with the police and they tended to reject any attempts to so define their relationship with them. The "third and fourth class citizens" in the complaint officers' opinions, contributed nothing to society but took everything they could from it. They not only exploited the police whenever they could, but they "ripped off" everyone with whom they came in contact. The "third class citizens" lived off the public. They were troublemakers. They were the enemies of the public. As such they were also the enemies of the police. "The scum" were undeserving and as troublemakers they were dangerous.

The "third and fourth class citizens" stood in sharp contrast to the public. They were the enemy both of the public and the police and as the enemy they were both feared and despised. They not only deliberately and systematically exploited the police, but they threatened the police as individuals, and as an institution, in the same way that they threatened society, and the values the police symbolized and stood for. "The scum" gave no quarter and deserved none.

The meanings the complaint officers ascribed to "the scum"

coloured and defined their disrespect for the police in the same way as the meanings they ascribed to the public coloured the complaint officers' interpretation of their disrespect. The disrespect the "scum" showed the police was the disrespect of an enemy, while that shown by the public was that of a simpleton.

THE PUBLIC AS ENEMY VERSUS THE PUBLIC AS SIMPLETON

These findings indicate that policemen in the communications centre studied distinguish between two "publics"; the public they did things for, and with whom they interacted within a helper/helped relationship and the "public" they did things to and whom they control. This distinction corresponds to the two aspects of the police role noted by Cummings et al (1964): a manifest control and a latent supportive aspect. The supportive aspect of the police role has been frequently noted by sociologists who have argued that policemen frequently spend a considerable proportion of their time providing support as opposed to exercising control (Banton 1964; Wilson 1968; Black 1968; Reiss 1971).[8] However, in studying police decision making, sociologists have tended to view the police primarily in terms of the consequences of their actions for the definition of people and events as criminal. This emphasis has focused sociological attention on the control aspect of the police role, that is, the things that the police do *to* others. Sociological research has focused on those members of the police organization most directly involved in dealing with troublemakers — patrolmen and detectives — and within this context the control aspect of these activities has been examined. Thus, for example, where the relationship between the complainant has been studied it has been examined primarily from the point of view of the complainant's influence on the actions the police take to control the situation; that is, what they do to troublemakers (see Reiss 1971). This focus has resulted in a systematic bias in our understanding of police work and our conception of the relationship between "the public" and the police. Only "the public as enemy" aspect of the police perception of the people they deal with has been emphasized.

In studying police work within a communications centre, we have focussed on a situation in which the supportive, as opposed to the control aspect of the police role is most apparent. This has enabled us to observe and describe an aspect of the police view of "the public" that has been neglected in the literature on the police. This aspect of the police definition of "the public", while readily visible within a communications centre is, however, we would suggest, not restricted to this situation. The paternalistic view of the public we have described is the view corresponding to the supportive aspect of the police role; it is the view the police hold of those people that they do things for as opposed to the people that they do things to. As such, it will, we suggest, be found in all situations of people work, just as the view of "the public" as enemy was found within the communications centre. What will vary, however, from situation to situation, is the extent to which policemen will highlight one or other view of "the public". In situations in which the police concentration is on doing things to troublemakers, the "public as enemy" view will be more frequently expressed (for example, in detective work). In contrast, in situations where the police focus is on providing help for people (for example, a communications centre), the emphasis will be on the paternalistic view. In both sets of situations, both images of "the public" will apply, because both "publics" and both types of relationships will always be relevant. What will differ is the focus of attention on one "public" or the other, and this will be reflected in the views about "the public" that are expressed in the situation.

The definition of two "publics" by the police and the shifting relevance of one public versus the other perhaps accounts for the discrepancy between the findings of field studies and surveys with respect to the police view of the public. Koenig (1975) has noted that survey research findings tend to depict a much more amiable relationship between the police and the public than the public as enemy image suggests. He reports, in presenting his own findings, that:

> . . . the R.C.M.P. do not appear to be overwhelmingly cynical. While it is true that there frequently are substantial minorities holding cynical views about the public, a majority believes that most people are basically honest, keep out of trouble with the law, and that their local area is comparatively safe (Koenig 1975, 38–39).

In discussing the variation in attitudes of Royal Canadian Mounted Policemen to the public, Koenig presents data that provides some support for our argument that the view which public policemen *express* depends on which "public" is most immediately relevant to them. For example, Koenig found that as a policeman's rank increases he becomes less cynical. The same, he found, holds for length of service. He also found that policemen in isolated detachments tended to be more cynical than those working in urban areas (see Koenig 1975: Chapter Three). For each category of policemen that Koenig found to be relatively more cynical it appears likely that the policemen concerned are more directly involved with troublemakers than the policemen in contrasting categories. Policemen on patrol tend to have to deal with troublemakers more frequently and more directly than policemen in administrative positions and in jobs like those in a communications centre. Indeed, a number of detectives have suggested to the author that, despite the popular crime-fighting image of detective work, patrolmen in fact have more contact with troublemakers than detectives, who in investigating a case tend to have more frequent contact with witnesses and prosecutors than they do with troublemakers.

Consequently, it is not surprising to find that uniformed patrolmen are more cynical about the public than other policemen or that new policemen and those of low rank tend to be cynical as these policemen tend to work as patrolmen. Similarly the greater cynicism among traffic enforcement officers is not surprising as for the traffic policemen every motorist is a potential trouble-maker. Finally, policemen in isolated areas, one would suspect, are likely to find themselves less involved in the number and range of helper services that urban policemen become involved in (see Pepinsky 1976, 94–95 for discussion of urban policemen's work). In smaller communities people are likely to rely on community resources to deal with troubles that are not seen as demanding state intervention. Policemen in isolated communities could thus find themselves involved with proportionally more "real" trouble-makers than their city counterparts.

Notes

1. This review has been published in an abbreviated form in Boydell et al. 1974.

2. For a useful summary statement of the police response to perceived public disrespect, see Rock 1973, 1982; and Pepinsky 1976, 63–65.

3. See Emerson and Messinger (1972) for an excellent discussion of the social organization of trouble and the roles that are associated with it.

4. This distinction between people one does things for and those one does things to is a distinction that extends beyond the police to other service occupa-tions. Hughes notes the general applicability of this distinction to service occupa-tions when he writes:

> To understand them (service occupations) one must understand the system, including the clients and their wants. People and organizations have problems: they want things done for them — for their bodies and souls, for their social and financial relations, for their cars, houses, bridges, sewage systems; and they want things done to the people they consider their competitors or their enemies (Hughes, 1971, 422).

5. For a discussion of the notion of "someone to turn to", see Sacks 1967.

6. It must be noted that in making these and similar comments, complaint officers did not present them as essentially descriptive comments, but as operational strategies indicating the working assumptions that they used in responding to the public.

7. In this regard, see Zakuta's (1970) discussion of the status implications of requests and orders. He argues that one requests help from people of higher status but one orders people of lower status.

8. The tendency to categorize police activity as controlling or supportive — for example, as order maintenance or law enforcement (Wilson 1969, 13) — or policemen in terms of the activities they undertake — for example, law officer or peace officer (Banton 1964) — does not follow from Cumming's distinction between two aspects of the police role. Indeed we would argue, it misrepresents police work. Police activity can be, and indeed usually is, both controlling and supportive. How it is defined will depend on the point of view from which it is viewed. From the complainant's point of view, if the police decide to do something *for* him, the action taken is supportive. In offering this support, however, the policeman may well be controlling another by doing something to him. For a criticism of attempts to categorize police action in terms of the support/control dichotomy, see Shearing and Leon 1977.

References

Banton, M. 1964. *The policeman in the community*. London: Tavistock.

Becker, Howard S. 1973. *Outsiders: Studies in the sociology of deviance*. New York: Free Press.

Bittner, Egon. 1970. *The functions of the police in modern society*. National Institute of Mental Health, Chevy Chase, Md.

Buckner, H. Taylor. 1972. Police culture. Paper represented at the Canadian Sociology and Anthropology Association meetings in Toronto, June.

Clark, A.L. and J.P. Gibbs. 1965. Social control: A reformulation. *Social Problems* 12:398–415.

Clark, J.P. 1965. Isolation of the police. *Journal of Criminal Law, Criminology and Police Science* 56:307–319.

Cumming, Elaine, Ian Cumming and Laura Edell. 1964. Policeman as philosopher, guide and friend. *Social Problems* 12:276–286.

Dougherty, R.C. 1969. Requiem for the Centre Street mafia. *Atlantic Monthly* 223:109–114.

Emerson, R.M. and Sheldon L. Messinger. 1972. A sociology of trouble. Paper presented at the Annual Meetings of the Society for the Study of Social Problems. New Orleans, Louisiana, August.

Harris, R. 1973. *Police academy: An inside view*. New York: Wiley.

Hughes, Everett C. 1971. *The sociological eye: Selected papers on work, self and the study of society*. Chicago and New York: Aldine and Ather.

Kirkham, George L. 1974. A professor's street lessons. *F.B.I. Law Enforcement Bulletin* 35:14–22, March.

Koening, Daniel J. 1975. R.C.M.P. views of themselves, their jobs, and the public. Report submitted to the Justice Development Commission Office of the Attorney General, Province of British Columbia.

Manning, Peter K. 1971. The police: Mandate, strategies and appearances. In Jack D. Douglas (Ed.), *Crime and justice in American society.* New York: The Bobbs-Merrill Company.

McNamara, N. 1967. Uncertainties in police work: The relevance of police recruits, background and training. In D.J. Bordua (Ed.), *The police: Six sociological essays.* New York: John Wiley.

Pepinsky, Harold E. 1976. *Crime and conflict: A study of law and society.* New York: Academic Press.

Piliavin, I. and S. Briar. 1964. Police encounters with juveniles. *American Journal of Sociology* 70:206–214.

Reiss, Albert J. and David J. Bordua. 1967. Environment and organization: A perspective on the police. In David J. Bordua (Ed.), *The police: Six sociological essays.* New York: John Wiley.

Rock, Paul. 1973. *Deviant behaviour.* London: Hutchinson University Library.

Sacks, Harvey. 1967. *The search for help: No one to turn to.* Ann Arbor, Mich.: University Microfilms.

Shearing, Clifford D. 1974. Dial-A-Cop: A study of police mobilization. In Ronald L. Akers and Edward Sagarin, *Crime prevention and social control.* New York: Praeger Publishers.

Shearing, Clifford D. and Jeffrey Leon. 1977. Reconsidering the police role: A challenge to a challenge of a popular conception. *Canadian Journal of Criminology and Corrections* October, 331–345.

Sykes, Richard E. and John P. Clark. 1975. A theory of deference exchange in police-civilian encounters. *The American Journal of Sociology* 81:584–600.

Westley, William A. 1953. Violence and the police. *American Journal of Sociology* 59 (July):34–41.

———. 1956. Secrecy and the Police. *Social Forces* 34:254–257.

———. 1971. *Violence and the police: A sociological study of law, custom and morality.* Cambridge, Massachusetts: M.I.T. Press.

Wexler, Mark N. 1973. *Police culture: A response to ambiguous employment.* Master's Dissertation, Department of Sociology, University of Western Ontario.

———. 1974. Police culture: A response to ambiguous employment. In C.L. Boydell, C.F. Grindstaff and P.C. Whitehead (Eds.), *The administration of criminal justice in Canada.* Toronto: Holt, Rinehart and Winston.

Whitaker, B.C.G. 1964. *The police.* London Eyre and Spotteswood.

Wilson, J.Q. 1968. *Varieties of police behaviour: The management of law and order in eight communities.* Cambridge: Harvard University Press.

Wolfgang, M. 1968. The police and their problems. In A.F. Brandstatter and L.A. Radelet (Eds.), *Police and community relations: A source book.* Beverly Hills: Glencoe.

Zakuta, Leo. 1970. On "Filthy Lucre". In T. Shibutani (Ed.), *Human nature and collective behaviour.* Englewood Cliffs: Prentice-Hall.

Chapter 17

Contradictions in Canadian Prisons: Some Aspects of Social Control Mechanisms

Brian D. Maclean

The late sixties and early seventies witnessed an unusual frequency of hostage takings and other violent disturbances within Canadian prisons. In 1976, a Parliamentary Subcommittee was assigned the task of investigating the Canadian Penal System in an attempt to understand the causes and conditions which fostered these occurrences. In its *Report to Parliament*, this Subcommittee stated:

> Society has spent millions of dollars over the years to create and maintain the proven failure of prisons. Incarceration has failed in its two essential purposes — correcting the offender and providing permanent protection to society . . . (Supply and Services Canada 1977).

Clearly, a contradiction exists between the purposes of the prison system and the consequences of its operation and maintenance. To be specific, official rhetoric regarding the purpose of the penal system changes from election to election and official to official. As the philosophy of legislators changes over time, so too do official goals of incarceration. Nevertheless, despite ongoing changes in rhetoric two things remain constant. These are (1) an increasing allocation of resources unaccounted for by inflation and/or growth of prison populations; (2) the continual failure to achieve the various officially stated goals of the penal system (MacLean, no date). One major reason or this continual failure despite increased resource allocations is, perhaps, presented by the

---

* Ph.D. candidate, Department of Sociology, University of Saskatchewan.

Canadian Committee on Corrections (Ouimet 1968) who identify two contradictory purposes of the Canadian Penal System:

1. to contain the offender in custody for the duration of his sentence (modified somewhat by remission and parole), and
2. to assist the offender in preparation for his permanent return to the community as a lawful, productive citizen.

The contradiction between these functions can be simply stated: control over offenders cannot be achieved simultaneously with treatment that ensures successful reintegration into the community (Griffiths and Verdun-Jones 1980). As a result of this contradiction between objectives, many researchers have concluded that the fate of the penal system is failure.[2] While there is little doubt that prisons make the attempt to resolve this contradiction, informed researchers generally agree that control of the inmate population emerges as the primary goal of the prison. In order to determine if, in fact, this goal is being achieved, we must look at the available data for disturbances, riots, escapes etc., in Canadian Prisons to see if they are decreasing.[4]

Statistics regarding hostage-taking incidents, acts of violence, prison riots, etc., have only been published since 1970. The Solicitor General's *Annual Report* (1974/1975, p.55) states: ". . . incidents from 1970 are tabulated because of their significance as a societal problem." This can be read as an alarming increase in these types of incidents. Table 17.1 gives a report of hostage-taking incidents for the six-year period 1970–75, while Table 17.2 provides hostage-taking incidents as well as other types of disturbances for the period 1975-1978.

As can be seen from Table 17.1 and 17.2, there has been a rash of hostage-taking incidents during the decade 1970–1980. (Of interest is that for the year 1975, one table reports eleven while

Table 17.1   Hostage-Taking Incidents, 1970–75

Year	No. of Hostage Incidents	No. of Inmates Involved	No. of Hostages Taken	No. of Hostages - injured (1) - killed (2)
1970	5	19	5	(1) - 1
1971	4	many	10	nil
1972	3	10	4	(1) - 1
1973	5	16	9	nil
1974	nil	—	—	—
1975	11	13	39	(1) - 3 (2) - 1

SOURCE: Solicitor General Canada. *Annual Report* 1974/75. p. 55.

Table 17.2 Hostage-Taking Incidents and Other Disturbances, 1975–78

Type of Incident	1975	1976	1977	1978
Inmate Deaths				
Murder	4	7	8	5
Suicide	8	5	11	6
Natural Causes	15	15	9	15
Hostage Taking	10	28	6	5
Major Disturbances	4	8	5	2
Assaults on Staff	n/a	n/a	25	33
Assaults on Inmates	n/a	n/a	n/a	53
Escapes				
Number of Incidents	48	61	54	71
Inmates Involved	62	71	78	88

SOURCE: Solicitor General Canada. *Annual Report* 1978/79. p. 126.

n/a = not available

the other reports ten, indicating the difficulty one encounters in obtaining accurate and precise data.) Given the primary goal of prisons has been to obtain a greater degree of control,[5] one can readily see that less and less control is actually the case. Escapes show a steady increase which is not particularly surprising considering that most of these would be taking place in the lesser security institutions.

Clearly, authorities are losing rather than gaining social control in Canadian prisons. This development may be acceptable to some, despite the costs involved, if at least prisons were serving to rehabilitate prisoners or at least to reduce the crime rate. Neither of these goals are being met, however, as pointed out by the Parliamentary Subcommittee (MacLean, no date). How is it that the increased professionalism in prisons is actually losing rather than gaining ground? At the turn of the century, there were on the average 300 inmates in each of ten prisons supervised by one-sixth their number in staff. Today we have on the average less than 200 inmates in each of approximately sixty prisons supervised by more staff than prisoners. Nevertheless, there are more violent disturbances or less social control today with an excess of resources compared to sixty years ago with a minimum of resources. (MacLean, no date). The obvious question is: why?

In an attempt to answer this question, the discussion will focus firstly, on some of the major social control mechanisms employed in Canadian prisons and attempt to explain why they have proven to be inadequate. Secondly, I will examine the contradiction which exists between formal and informal social control mechanaisms. (It must be pointed out here that the contradictory nature of the inmate versus penal authority value systems tends to make these two groups view formal social control mechanisms differently. While this point will be developed at a later point, it should be kept in mind during this portion of the discussion.)

FORMAL SOCIAL CONTROL

Parole

One method by which the institutional authorities maintain social control is through the possibility of early release. The parole system was inaugurated in 1959 to facilitate this process. While the authority to grant parole rests with the National Parole Board and not with the prison personnel, the institutional authorities do make reports which recommend either favourably or unfavourably any individual for a parole. Parole is not automatic contrary to publicly held myths concerning its universal application. Rather, when an individual becomes eligible for parole, the Parole Board gathers information from various agencies in the community as well as the institution and then determines whether parole will be granted.

Basically, there are two types of parole for which the inmate may apply, and one form of parole, mandatory supervision, which is automatically granted to the inmate normally after the completion of two-thirds of his original sentence. (Mandatory supervision will be discussed later in the section regarding Good Conduct Remission.) The two forms of parole for which the inmate must apply are: (a) full parole, and (b) day parole.

Full Parole and Day Parole

In the normal course of events, an inmate becomes eligible for full parole after one-third of his sentence has been served. For offences such as murder, and other crimes for which a life sentence has been imposed, the eligibility is stated in the sentence. For example, a twenty-five year minimum sentence carries a parole eligibility date of twenty-five years after the day sentence was passed. Life sentences other than murder carry an eligibility for parole of ten years after sentencing. Full parole means that the individual is released into the community under the supervision of a parole officer, and certain restrictions are placed upon him. He must remain in the community under these conditions until the sentence he is serving expires.

Eligibility for day parole is determined as being one year prior to the individual's full parole eligibility date. Day parole is similar to full parole; however, the restrictions are much greater and the individual generally resides in a halfway house or community correctional centre where he must abide by the house rules which include curfew, signing in and out, etc.

To the casual observer, this system may appear as one which provides the inmate with an opportunity to be released into the community earlier in his sentence. However, certain contradictions become apparent when one views this system from the perspective of the inmate. Firstly, of the factor from which the Parole Board actually determines whether or not to grant parole, institutional conduct seems to be of minor significance. According to one senior member of the Parole Board, more crucial to the decision are factors such as the individual's prior record, and his propensity toward criminal behaviour, or, more importantly, violent criminal behaviour. In considering these variables and their importance, one can readily see that the parole system is more likely to be favourable to first offenders. Considering that the *Solicitor General's Statistical Handbook* (1975) indicates that approximately 73 percent of all federal inmates have been incarcerated before, one sees that the remaining 27 percent who are first offenders are more likely to receive parole. This figure roughly coincides with the number of actual paroles granted. In 1972, the Parole Board published a five-year study of recidivism in parolees. During the period of investigation about 25 percent of the inmates in prison, were actually released on parole (Solicitor General, Statistics Division 1972) and this figure appears quite stable over time.

Clearly, the parole system can only serve a social control function, then, to 25 percent of the inmates population in Canada. Inmates spending several years in federal institutions come to realize this fact and as such recognize the parole system as being a sham. This idea is further reinforced when individuals actually see those released on parole being returned shortly after having failed to abide by the parole regulations. It is precisely this form of selective perception, viz. contact with the parole failures rather than the parole successes, which further helps to weaken the effects of this social control mechanism. As a result, for the majority of those individuals housed in federal correctional facilities, the promise of parole is considered to be a broken one.

Good Conduct Remission

Perhaps the social control mechanism about which the public is most grossly misinformed is that of good conduct remission or "time off for good behaviour". There seems to be a popularly held myth that if an inmate is of satisfactory conduct throughout his period of incarceration, he will be rewarded by having a portion of his sentence cancelled. In fact, time off for good behaviour is an illusion.

Prior to 1978, inmates were granted one-quarter of their sentence as statutory remission automatically, and an additional three days per month earned remission could be credited to the individual providing he was of good conduct and industry. This was not always the case. At one time, inmates could earn one day for every week of the sentence they served. The present system allows a maximum of fifteen days per month to accrue to the credit of the individual. The remission is earned and statutory remission has been abolished since 1978. Included in the fifteen days are five days for industry, five days for institutional conduct and five days for participation in institutional programs. Essentially, this means that if an inmate works and conforms in his behaviour, regardless of his participation in programs, he will earn the maximum allowable remission which totals exactly one-third of his original sentence. This does not mean, however, that after completing two-thirds of his sentence an inmate is free.

Crucial to the concept of good conduct remission is mandatory supervision, first initiated in August 1970 (Solicitor General, *Annual Report* 1977/78). Essentially, once an inmate is at the point in his sentence where the only portion remaining unserved is that represented by good conduct remission, he is released into the community under mandatory supervision if he so desires. Mandatory supervision is no different than full parole in that the individual has the same restrictions placed upon him. While this appears to be beneficial to the inmate on the surface, in reality he has gained very little. Of the types of parole classifications, mandatory supervision has the worst success rate. The official reason for this situation is that those inmates under mandatory supervision are those who were never granted another form of parole because they are the higher risks. Thus, it is little surprise that the rate of forteiture is higher in this group (Solicitor General, *Statistics Handbook* 1975). Whatever the reason, it can be seen that despite the fact an individual has been of satisfactory conduct and earned his remission, the probability that he will be forced to return to prison to serve the balance of his sentence is quite high. For example, in 1979/1980, 1,093 persons had their mandatory supervision revoked while 1,843 persons were under mandatory supervision during the same period — a failure rate of approximately 60 percent (Solicitor General, *Annual Report*).

The idea of mandatory supervision is thus questionable and continues to be a thorn in the side of the National Parole Board. Inmates have come to equate mandatory supervision with being put out in the backyard on a leash. They fully recognize that good conduct remission is a political instrument utilized to:

    (a) maintain behaviour control; and
    (b) satisfy the public that the corrections system is
        humanitarian.

Given these attitudes, it is little wonder that good conduct remission does not serve to control behaviour to a large extent with most inmates.

Transfers

The correctional system has witnessed an amazing growth of correctional facilities in recent history. Specifically, the construction of lesser-security institutions represents the adoption of policy designed to control the behaviour of inmates. Firstly, they provide hope of transfer to prisons in which conditions and environment are much more relaxed as a reward for conforming behaviour on the part of inmates who are incarcerated in maximum-security institutions. Secondly, the threat of being transferred to maximum security acts as a deterrent for nonconforming behaviour on the part of those inmates incarcerated in minimum- and medium-security institutions. Finally, the construction of two super-maximum special handling units in the later 1970s represents a threat for the control of behaviour for inmates in maximum security institutions. (Coupled with this threat is the idea of dissociation or segregation which will be discussed in detail later.)

In practice, the idea of transfer as a control mechanism is not as meritous as it appears in policy. One must recognize that inmates classified as maximum-security usually spend a great deal of their sentences in that environment before being considered for transfer. Several consequences result. Firstly, these inmates have formed strong bonds with others in the same situation, and being transferred means to leave one's friends behind as well as starting all over again in a new environment. A good number of inmates seem quite content to forget the idea of transfer altogether and complete their sentences in maximum security where they are socially more comfortable. Secondly, those inmates who, "play the game" and obtain transfers, as well as those initially classified as lesser-security are generally looked upon with contempt by those maximum-security types who maintain a more rebellious self-image. As a result, the threat of transfer to maximum security has a much more controlling effect on the behaviour of medium-security inmates. This is perhaps the major reason why maximum-security institutions have been the most difficult to control. In any event, the limitations upon the efficacy of this method of controlling behaviour are readily obvious.

Temporary Absences

Similar to the parole system is the system of temporary absence. Temporary absence may be granted to individuals serving an aggregate sentence of less than five years at the discretion of the institutional director. An escorted temporary absence may also be granted by the director of the institution. For all sentences exceeding five years or sentences for which the crime involved was violent in nature, unescorted temporary absence may be granted only at the discretion of the Parole Board.

Temporary absences may be granted for a variety of reasons, from the death of a relative to humanitarian reasons. Any inmate has the option to apply for temporary absence at any time; however, the granting of these is far from being automatic. As with parole, many factors are considered. Chiefly, support of relatives, other community support, past record, institutional behaviour, etc., are factors which influence the decision. When one considers that most inmates have serious prior records in federal institutions, and that many have no family and certainly no community support, the idea of temporary absence becomes an illusion for them. These inmates fully recognize they have no hope of ever being granted a temporary absence. This is especially true in the maximum- and supermaximum-security institutions. Most inmates have come to recognize the temporary absence as a carrot-on-a-stick approach to behaviour control and as such this mechanism is of little value in maintaining what the administration would consider to be conforming behaviour.

Inmate Pay System

Except for the bare necessities of meals, clothing, etc. inmates are required to purchase articles necessary for daily living.

Examples would be: cigarettes, writing paper, and postage stamps. Inmates are not allowed to purchase these articles with their personal funds. The method by which inmates accumulate funds for purchasing canteen articles is by payment for their labour. Inmates are assigned work while incarcerated and are paid a mere pittance for their efforts. For example, prior to May 1981, inmates earned from a low of $9.00 to a high of $14.00 every two weeks depending upon the grade level they had attained. Furthermore, a total of $2.50 every two weeks was placed in a savings account to be accumulated for postrelease spending. The official logic behind this program is to give the inmate training in budgeting, etc. Furthermore, as with other amenities, the fact that the inmates have it means that the threat of its forfeiture can be used to control behaviour. It does not require a chartered accountant to recognize that this form of budgeting deviates to a high degree from a normal environment. The fact that the allowance is so small has been the major reason for a complete and illicit economic system to evolve in order to make up the financial deficit inherent in this system. Thus, contraband money, articles, and drugs have replaced the gold standard in prison populations. Inmates, therefore, have come to realize that this system is an attempt to control their behaviour. The emergence of this illegal economic system has further reduced any controlling effects of the pay system on inmate behaviour.

The fact that a new inmate pay scale, initiated in May 1981, was the cause of three prison riots in British Columbia as well as several other disturbances across the country best illustrates the futility of the kind of logic employed in the development of programs of this nature. When one considers that the new pay scale is designed to control behaviour but in fact sparks widespread violent behaviour within the prison populations, one can come to no other conclusion than the inmate pay system is ineffective in terms of behavioural control.

Penitentiary Services Regulations

The Commissioner of Penitentiaries is given authority under the Penitentiary Act to administer the daily operations of the correctional system. The principle vehicle by which the Commissioner facilitates this is the Penitentiary Service Regulations. Included in this set of procedures is the provision for disciplinary measures to be taken against inmates who have been found guilty in disciplinary court of breaking one of the prison rules. The implementation of the 1976 Parlimentary Subcommittee's recom-

mendation to have disciplinary court presided over by an independent chairperson has resulted in little effect upon inmate
attitudes toward the court. Essentially, upon the finding of guilty,
the chairperson has the following options available to him in the
imposition of a sentence. (Penitentiary Service Regulation, 2.29):

a) dissociation;
b) forfeiture of good conduct remission;
c) loss of privileges;
d) downgrading;
e) fines;
f) admonishment.

The reason why the independent chairperson has had little effect
is because inmates are seldom acquitted when brought before the
court. As a result, no inmates have any respect for this instrument
of authority. Rather they view it as a "Kangaroo Court" which
serves to facilitate the harassment of inmates by prison staff.
Furthermore, the types of sentencing which are carried out have a
negligible effect on the inmates behaviour since, as has already
been discussed, that which is being forfeited has little value to the
inmate in the first place. With the exception of dissociation, which
only physically controls the inmate, the other forms of punishment are purely figurative and the inmates recognize disciplinary
court as being a sham.

Dissociation

The increase of the use of social control mechanisms is
perhaps best illustrated by the phenomenon known as dissociation
(solitary confinement). Although statistics showing the use of
dissociation are not available, some trends can be identified from
various reports. The only statistics indicating the number of
persons being held in dissociation are for 15 November 1974. On
that day, 139 inmates were under that classification. Of those, 56
had been dissociated for a period exceeding twelve months, and
one had been dissociated for a period exceeding three and one-half
years. (Vantour 1975, 20). The fact that Commissioner's directives state that people can only be dissociated for thirty days as a
result of being found guilty of a disciplinary offence is, perhaps,
one reason why statistics are not available.

The correctional investigator's reports have consistently
made recommendations regarding the abusive use of this social
control mechanism. The first reprot of the correctional investigator since the office was inaugurated in 1973 recommends:

that a special study of the use of dissociation in Canadian penitentiaries be
made to determine:
a) whether it is useful as a punishment
b) whether it is the most efficient way of providing protection to certain
   inmates
c) whether some or all dissociated inmates could be detained in other small
   structures which provide adequate security; but outside the main
   institution (Hansen 1973/74, 45).

The recommendations were successful in that they prompted
a study, the *Vantour Commission* in 1975. The *Vantour Report* devotes a
whole chapter to apologizing for the lack of statistics (pp. 13–16),
not unlike those given by the authors of the *Statistical Handbook*
previously cited. Of the fifty-seven recommendations made by the
Vantour Commission, they recommend that administrative
segregation be maintained, that institutions should maintain
accurate statistics, and that further scientific research should be
focused on the effects of sensory deprivation (pp. 90–91). Of these
recommendations, only those designed to ensure security have
been implemented.

The correctional investigator report of 1977 (two years after
the *Vantour Report*) states:

> The conditions in dissociation have not improved during the last four years.
> If anything, they are worse. Amenities are fewer and contact between one
> human being and another has been reduced to a minimum in some insti-
> tutions . . . (Hansen 1977, 13).

Clearly, dissociation is a brutal and severe form of punishment designed to control inmates' behaviour. In another form, viz.
segregation, the physical surroundings are a little better but the
isolative factor remains constant. Dissociation and segregation
can be utilized at the discretion of the director for the "maintenance of good order and discipline in the institution" (Penitentiary Service Regulation, 2.30(1)(a)). In this case, inmates may be
held indefinitely. Also, inmates may be segregated into protective
custody. Protective custody offers refuge to those inmates whose
lives are endangered by a falling out with other inmates. Typically
this is due to either sexually related offences or to providing
information to the administration for certain favours. The rapid
growth of protective custody in the past ten years indicates
another control mechanism. That is, inmates will be provided
refuge in exchange for information which allows the administration the opportunity to gain more control over the general
population. Contrary to official reasons for this growth, such as
gambling debts, etc., this mechanism is clearly one designed for
control.

The number of inmates, however, who are dissociated against their will for purposes of administration is also quite high, although lack of available data prevents any evaluation of the effectiveness of this form of control policy. While one may argue that prolonged dissociation may contribute to the number and severity of hostage-taking incidents, for example, this assumption cannot be supported empirically because accurate records are not kept by the correction service. It is my own knowledge, however, that the major hostage-taking incident in 1975 which resulted in the death of a prison employee in British Columbia was executed in part by the one individual, cited in the 15 November 1974 statistics on dissociation, who had been dissociated for three and one-half years. By June 1975 this period would have increased to four years. Were better record-keeping practices employed by the penal system as a whole, and were those records made available, then perhaps, scientific research would be able to determine correlations of this nature, adding to a more general theory. Until these statistics are available, however, research of this nature becomes futile.

Any analysis of dissociation must show that far from controlling violent behaviour it fosters more of the same, thus losing all credibility as an effective control device. To the extent that it is effective, i.e., keeping violent individuals away from other prisoners, that merit is lost when one realizes the individual must be released some day into society at large which must then deal with the problem created by this beastial form of punishment. However, in the case of long-term offenders and lifers, more violent behaviour such as hostage takings are sure to take place in an attempt to escape this miserable form of existance.

Behaviour Modification Techniques

During the 1950s behaviour modification began gaining credibility as a discipline. The primary reason for this development is that in response to a challenge, behaviour modification experts began to show success with some populations such as behaviourally handicapped or "retarded" populations with whom more traditional forms of psychotherapy had miserably failed.[6] As a result of these early successes, prison authorities became interested in the idea that behaviour-modification programs may, in fact, serve to control prison populations. Since that time behaviour-modification programs have been implemented in prisons throughout the continent.

Central to the effectiveness of any behaviour-modification

program are the principles of positive reinforcement and immediacy (Martin Pear 1978, 17–32). Positive reinforcement can be defined as any stimulus which maintains a behaviour (Ibid. 18–19). In order for maintenance to be strengthened reinforcement should be delivered immediately following the behaviour. Punishment and negative reinforcement are not effective for changing behaviour. Unfortunately, it appears that punishment and negative reinforcement are exactly the mechanisms employed in prisons. The idea of punishment is fairly straightforward. For example, if an inmate does something incorrect, he is forced to forfeit some or all of his "privileges". Negative reinforcement can be defined as the withdrawal of an aversive stimulus following the emission of a desirable behaviour (Ibid. 201).

Prison administrators tend to use what they consider to be positive reinforcers. These include many of the mechanisms discussed to this point e.g. parole, transfers, inmate pay, etc., as rewards contingent upon desirable behaviours. As has been illustrated, however, these rewards are clearly not reinforcers to the perspective of the inmates, since they do not maintain any form of desirable behaviours. If anything, the inmates view themselves as being in an aversive situation. That is to say loss of freedom and a prison environment are not desirable to most people. By reinstating step by step what the inmates feel is theirs to begin with, viz. more freedom, increased amenities, etc., the prison authorities are only lessening the degree of averseness which the inmate feels. This is precisely negative reinforcement, and according to the principles of behaviour modifiers is not an effective means of changing behaviours.

"Frequently, the goal of effective behaviour modification in prisons, is the preservation of the institutions' authoritian control" (Stolz et al. 1978, 710). This is not to say that behaviour modification when designed and applied properly is not effective — quite the contrary. The sad fact, however, remains that institution personnel are not sufficiently trained in this field and that the premise upon which the programs are designed by the Department of Corrections contradicts the actual perspective of the inmates. In the United States,

> the Law Enforcement Assistant Administration (LEAA) withdrew its support from these programs. An LEAA spokesman claimed . . . "staff did not have the technical and professional skills to screen, evaluate or monitor such programs" (Ibid. 710).

Furthermore, one can safely assume that the administrators lack the same skills when developing these programs. This fact becomes clear when one recognizes that, in actuality, they are based

on negative reinforcement and punishment. Given this information, one can readily see the fallacy in this approach toward
behavioural control. Nevertheless, in Canada this approach can
still be identified in many inmate programs even though in the
United States LEAA has discontinued any support in this area.

Token Economies

One clear example of the way in which behaviour-modification programs are misapplied is the use of token economies.[7]
Those institutions which utilize token economies, pay the inmates
with little chips of plastic which they can then cash in at the
canteen in exchange for desired articles. This approach is quite
effective when dealing with "retarded" populations who have
been conditioned to the tokens as reinforcement immediately
after the emission of a simple desirable behaviour such as tying
shoelaces. In the prisons, however, desired behaviours are much
more complex and reinforcement does not take place for as long as
two weeks. Given this approach, the tokens are more likely to be
reinforcing a more immediate and simple behaviour such as going
to the Dome at the proper time to collect them. Once again the
theoretical advantages of this program are lost in the practical
application within a prison environment.

Racial Segregation

Those Canadian prisons which house large proportions of
native offenders tend to segregate them from the white population. This is accomplished generally by assigning them to specific
ranges and workshops. As a result, some cell blocks house native
offenders only and some cell blocks house white offenders only.
Furthermore, some work gangs are entirely composed of one
group or the other. Officially, the reason given is to prevent racial
conflict from developing. In actuality, however, these arrangements serve to foster and maintain racist attitudes in both groups.
As a result, they differentiate themselves in many other ways.
Thus, if the white population wants to riot over a specific issue,
the native population may not see this as crucial to them or vice
versa. Therefore, the institutional authorities have effectively
split the population, preventing full-scale disturbances from
taking place to some degree. This strategy loses its effectiveness, however, because racial segregation is not universal and

interaction of a friendly nature certainly occurs between both groups. Nevertheless, in some respects, this strategy is probably the most effective of all the social control mechanisms.

Amenities

To the lay person, life in prison seems pretty soft. Prisoners watch T.V., play at sports, go to movies, attend socials, etc. What more could a prisoner want?

Essentially, the increase of amenities such as these serve two purposes: (a) they give the impression that prison life is humanitarian; and (b) they are used as social control mechanisms.

Two factors are important in terms of the control function. The first is that by making these amenities communal, inmates must be in certain places at certain times to enjoy them. This lessens the need for supervison and ensures less potential trouble, especially if the inmates must be in the range or in their cell to watch television, for example. The second factor is that by increasing the number of amenities available to inmates contingent upon specified behaviours, the lack of those behaviours can be dealt with by removing the amenity. This idea is effective in most cases of daily living, but the fact that inmates have much to lose in the form of amenities such as cold soft drinks does not seem to deter riotous behaviour to any great extent.

INFORMAL SOCIAL CONTROL

The foregoing discussion analyzes some of the major mechanisms employed in Canadian prisons in order to maintain social control. While the list discussed is not exhaustive, it does cover some major strategies. A number of reasons why these mechanisms are not very effective in maintaining control have also been discussed. Perhaps, the major reason that Canadian prisons do not achieve the desirable level of social control rests in the contradiction between formal and informal social control. Formal social control mechanisms can be defined as those measures taken by the administration to control behaviour, while informal social control can be defined as those processes by which the inmates control the behaviour of other inmates. The contradiction stems from the fact that these two forms of control are diametrically opposed to one another. That is to say that the behaviours which the institutional authorities view as conforming, the inmates view as deviant, and the behaviours the inmates view as conforming the institutional authorities view as nonconforming. Thus a new arrival in the penitentiary is faced with a real dilemma of how to behave. An example may serve to illustrate. The institutional authorities would reward an individual for coming forward to provide information about illicit drug use in the prison. The reward may consist of favourable recommendation for parole, transfer, etc. The inmates, on the other hand, would punish the individual. In a volatile and violent environment such as a prison setting, inmate punishment could very easily be murder or, at minimum, violent assault. Unlike outside society where informal control is attained via mechanisms of shunning, ostracism, etc., inmate justice is swift and violent.

In other words, the emergence of an inmate subculture within prisons serves to undermine the efficacy of administrative social control policies. The only valuable research regarding the inmate subculture in a Canadian context is found in the work of W.E. Mann (1967, 1). Mann notes:

> The success of . . . policies has also been drastically circumscribed by the development of a normative system and separate sub-culture largely hostile to administrative personnel and their objectives. Numerous [Researchers] have noted that the most serious block to the . . . efforts of correctional personnel in penal institutions is the development of this sub-culture with its own distinctive folkways, mores, rituals and value system. Thus, the Warden of a British Columbia institution stated: "The bane of every correctional institution is the sometimes subtle but always strong opposition of the inmate sub-cultures to staff philosophy and goals" (Braithwaite 1966, 98).

Clearly a contradiction not only exists between the value systems of the subculture and penal authorities, but the social structure of the prison setting contributes to this contradiction. Therefore, new prisoners soon discover that within the walls of the prison exists a small but total society to which they must socialize themselves. During the course of this resocialization they will learn and internalize new attitudes and values as well externalize behaviours stemming from these. However, since there pre-exists a certain social structure, the new inmates must discover a position and feel comfortable somewhere within that structure. Contrary to literature regarding an inmate code and the coercive way in which inmates must adopt it, inmates internalize a value system from which certain behaviours are a consequence. For the most part, inmates do not behave in the manner expected of them as a result of their fear of punishment from other inmates. Rather, they adopt and support a new set of values particular to the primary group to which they are resocialized. While certain values are constant throughout the superstructure of the various inmate primary groups, other values are variable and can be actually contradictory between these groups. This small group structure, therefore, is crucial to the adoption of a value system by the newcomer. Ironically, most academic literature on the subject contradicts this viewpoint.[8] Irwin (1977, 257–67) is one researcher whose work in this area has led him to accurately conceptualize the inmate social structure in his analysis; however, this point has not been accepted by other researchers in the field (Griffiths et al. 1980, 220). At any rate, the inmate social structure consists of many small primary groups, while the overall prison social structure is comprised of basically two groups — guards or prison staff and inmates. Each of these two groups are visibly and physically separate — visibly because they both wear identifiable uniforms, and physically because they associate only with those persons wearing the same uniforms. A newcomer to prison quickly recognizes the social distance between the two groups and tends to identify with those wearing the same uniform viz. other inmates. Furthermore, personal histories, language, culture or subcultural characteristics, social similarity, etc., all serve to facilitate this identification process with smaller primary groups. Essentially, these two groups are in a permanent state of conflict. For example, the prison staff wish to keep the inmate in prison, while the inmates wish to leave, etc.

This contradiction between the two groups in most cases speeds up the process by which newcomers internalize inmate values, attitudes and behaviours while fostering increasing levels of animosity between the individual and prison staff. Those newcomers who do not internalize the cognitions of other inmates are soon weeded out (by them) and end up either in protective custody or the prison hospital.

There are, of course, a number of violent offenders in prisons. This fact can lead to high levels of paranoia in the prison population. This is witnessed by the fact that almost every inmate has access to a homemade weapon of some sort at any given moment. Weapons may be fashioned from almost anything. Iron bars, homemade knives, and bars of institutional soap in heavy woolen socks have all be utilized. Although these weapons are crude, they are also very effective in the amount of physical damage they are capable of inflicting. All of this can lead to some inmates conforming purely out of fear of reprisal rather than just simple peer pressure. When in prison, an inmate soon learns who his friends are. Leaving prison alive at the end of one's sentence begins to take on much more importance than committing a deviant act by inmate standards just to obtain a favourable mention from prison staff.

Clearly, these coercive elements, perceived or real, have a much more powerful influence over inmate behaviour than anything the authorities could dream up, although, generally speaking, most inmates conform to the expected behaviour of their peers because they come to believe in them.

Many inmates in Canadian prisons are there as a result of drug-related offences. This means that many are not only amenable to but crave for illicit use of drugs as a way of temporarily escaping this hostile environment. Illicit drug use is quite common in prison. Inmates soon learn the ways and means of obtaining or arranging to receive illicit drugs. Due to the fact that, if detected, drug use commands heavy punishment from the authorities, newcomers will have difficulty obtaining drugs (unless they are well known) until others become confident that they can be trusted. This trust can only be established through the internalization of inmate values and attitudes and by conforming to acceptable inmate behavioural patterns. Since the inmates themselves control the flow of drugs, and since drugs represent a powerful reinforcer for inmate behaviour, the inmates themselves have much greater control over their peers' behaviour than the prison authorities do with their selection of reinforcers.

It can be seen from this discussion that social acceptance among the inmate population and the reinforcers at their disposal become strong motivations for conforming behaviour. It is precisely because this conforming behaviour violates institutional rules in the more extreme cases that the authorities must attempt to develop strategies which overcome or decrease these motivations. To this date they have been unsuccessful and in all probability the degree of control they desire will never be met due to the influence and effectiveness of informal social control mechanisms employed by the inmate subculture.

Since the informal social control mechanisms are more effective than the formal policies, how is it that except for those which are isolated (although frequently), disturbances do not develop daily? Why are our prisons not in a constant state of chaos? One answer to this question is that sometimes the inmates and staff have similar goals. The smooth-running daily operation of the prison is one example. Drug traffic serves as an illustration. If there existed continuous repercussions of riotious behaviour, then drug traffic would be severely impeded. While authorities are aware of drug traffic, some inmates feel they fail to restrict it purposefully because it helps to maintain a quieter atmosphere.

Essentially, then, sometimes both groups compromise their positions in order to maintain a more peaceful environment in which both groups can achieve some of their goals. The effectiveness of this strategy depends somewhat upon the degree of power the inmate subculture possesses over the individual inmates. Mann (1967, 139) notes that:

> an authoritarian regimented and custodial emphasis on the part of guards and administration leads to the development of a hostile inmate subculture with all its attendant pressures to buck the system and support delinquent codes and attitudes.

In fact, much research has indicated that the formal organizational structure of the prison is related to the subsequent organizational structure and strength of the inmate subculture.[9] The emergence of the "Living Unit concept" is an attempt to both reorganize the formal structure as well as weaken the inmate subculture. It has been Canada's response to these findings, and is regarded by some as the panacea for the problems of inmate social control.

Living units are smaller formally organized sections of the inmate population. Each unit has an independent group of officers who attempt to present themselves as friends of the inmates rather than their keepers. In keeping with this image, they do not wear uniforms but, rather, regular civilian clothing. Any administrative decisions regarding the inmate are funnelled through the living-unit officers who are supposed to know the inmates on a more personal level as a result of interaction with them as well as their observations of the inmate's interaction patterns with other inmates in the unit. The fact that the units are smaller and observed more closely allows the living-unit officer the opportunity to counsel inmates individually when it appears they may be moving toward greater levels of committment to inmate values.

The living-unit system has met with varying degrees of success. To the extent that it has been effective, this is true for the lesser-security institutions. In fact, maximum-security institutions do not utilize living units. The recent construction of two maximum-security institutions in Alberta and British Columbia with an architectural design suitable for the living-unit system, resulted in flat failure to implement that system when the prisons were filled. Because the inmates were maximum-security, they strongly opposed the living-unit system to the extent that it was abolished, despite the special architectural design. As with the other formal measures examined in this discussion, the living-unit system can be validly questioned as an effective behavioural control device.

SUMMARY AND CONCLUSIONS

From the above discussion, it can be concluded that our prison system operates under a host of contradictions. Some of these have been analyzed in an attempt to understand why social control in Canadian prisons proves to be a failure mainfesting itself as hostage takings, violent disturbances, escapes, etc.

As Clair Culhane notes in *Barred From Prison:*

> No objective examination of the best prison system can avoid the conclusion that it is primitive, coercive and dehumanizing. No rational, let alone scientific appraisal of treatment or rehabilitative programs within the prison setting, can assess them as anything but a total sham. The best efforts of correctional personnel are doomed to frustration and failure, whether measured by the recidivism rates or any other reasonable standards of "progress" (See Margous in Culhane).

Prison administrators must recognize this propensity toward failure, and it becomes fairly evident that their main concern is getting through each day with as little difficulty as possible. Attempts at social control range from the physically coercive to the psychological brutal, and these methods must be legitimated somehow to the public at large. The way in which this is generally accomplished is by presenting them as humanitarian. This discussion has demonstrated that far from being humanitarian, the control strategies employed in Canadian prisons are based on coercion and deception — a deception through which most inmates are able to see. If the penal system must fail in its rehabilitative function because it is contradictory to the control function, then the converse also follows. That is, the penal system must also fail in the control function because it contradicts the rehabilitative function despite the emphasis placed on control. The contradiction between formal and informal control has been discussed as another major factor related to this inevitable failure.

Yet, prisons still operate despite their proven failure in the past and prospect of failure in the future. This observation may lead one to conclude that there exist other objectives of the penal system that are as yet latent and undetected. It would, therefore, seem from the above discussion that research in this area would be warranted. Perhaps, this line of inquiry may prove fruitful in explaining the continued maintenance of Canada's penal system when so much evidence indicates that it is failing.

Notes

1. Data for this discussion was secured by a combination of methods which includes:
(1) secondary data,

(2) observations of inmate interactions and behaviours within the institutional setting, and

(3) informal and unstructured interviews with inmates within the institutional setting.

For the most part, this discussion deals with male offenders. Lack of secondary data regarding female offenders is due to their underrepresentation in correctional facilities. When included, data on the female offender is generally not distinguished. All other forms of data collection were also employed on male offenders only. While some of the major issues discussed in this paper can also apply to the female offender, the generalization of male attitudes and experiences to their female counterparts is not warranted.

2. See for example, Tittle, C. "Prisons and Rehabilitation: The Inevitability of Failure" in *Social Problems* vol. 21, 1977 pp. 388–394. Duffee, D. and Fitch, F. *An Introduction to Corrections: Policy and Systems Approach*, Goodyear, publ. Pacific Palisades Calif.: 1976.

3. See for example MacLean, B. "The Canadian Prison System: An Industry," unpublished paper. Also see Thomas, C. and Petersen D. *Prison Organization and Inmate Subcultures* Bobbs Merrill Publ.; Indianapolis: 1977.

4. On the issue of Available Data, *The Statistical Handbook of the Canadian Criminal Justice* states: "As with all statistical system which are primarily administrative in nature, problems arise when one wishes to use that data base for nonadministrative purposes. Statistical reports not essential to the day to day operations have a tendency to come in late or be less than ideally accurate." From: *Statistics Handbook — Canadian Criminal Justice,* Information Systems and Statistics Division, Solicitor General Canada: 1975, p. 52.

5. I have argued elsewhere that an increasing allocation of federal resources to the Canadian Penal System has been utilized primarily to obtain greater levels of control. See MacLean, B. "The Canadian Prison System: An Industry." Unpublished paper.

6. For a discussion of the history of behaviour-modification program see Martin and Pear, 1978.

7. For a discussion of token economies and the way in which they should be implemented for the most effective results see Martin, G., and Pear, J. *Behaviour Modification: What It Is and How To Do It,* Prentice Hall, Publ., New Jersey: 1978, pp. 336–364.

8. See for example Sykes, G. and Messinger, S. "The Inmate Social Code", Johnston et al., Eds. *The Sociology of Punishment and Correction,* John Wiley and Sons, Pubs., New York: pp. 401–408.

9. For example see Grosky, "Organizational Goals and the Behaviour of Informed Leaders" in *American Journal of Sociology,* Vol. LXV, No. 1. July, 1949, pp. 59–67. Also see Street, D., Vinter, C. and Perrow, C. *Organization For Treatment.* Free Press, Publ., New York: 1966.

References

Braithwaite, J. 1966. Treadmill or treatment. *The Canadian Journal of Correction.* January.

Griffiths, C., J. Klein and S. Verdun-Jones. 1980. *Criminal justice in Canada: An introductory text.* Vancouver: Butterworths.

Hansen, I. *The annual report of the correctional investigator 1973/74.*

———— . *The annual report of the correctional investigator 1976/77.*

Irwin, J. 1976. The changing social structure of the men's prison. In Greenberg (Ed.), *Corrections and administration: Selected readings.* St. Paul West Pubs.

MacLean, B. *The Canadian penal system: An industry.* Unpublished paper.

Mann, W.E. 1967. *Society behind bars: A sociological scrutiny of Guelph reformatory.* Toronto: Copp Clark.

Margous, E. Conneticut bar journals. 1972, 46(3). In C. Culhane, *Barred from prison.* Vancouver: Pulp Press, 1979.

Martin, G. and J. Pear. 1978. *Behaviour Modification: What it is and how to do it.* New Jersey: Prentice-Hall.

Ouimet, R. (Chairman). 1969. *Report of the Canadian Committee on Corrections — toward unity: Criminal justice and corrections.* Ottawa: Information Canada.

Solicitor General Canada. *Annual report 1974/75.* Ottawa: Supply and Services Canada.

———— . *Annual report 1977/78.* Ottawa: Supply and Services Canada.

———— . *Annual report 1978/79.* Ottawa: Supply and Services Canada.

———— . *Annual report 1979/80.* Ottawa: Supply and Services Canada.

———— . 1972. *Parole recidivism study.* Statistics Division. Ottawa: Supply and Services Canada.

———— . 1975. *Statistics handbook — Canadian criminal justice.* Information Systems and Statistics Division. Ottawa: Supply and Services Canada.

Stolz, S., L. Wienckowski and B. Brown. 1978. Behaviour Modification. In N. Johnston and L. Savitz (Eds.), *Justice and correction.* New York: John Wiley and Sons.

Supply and Services Canada. 1977. *Subcommittee on the penitentiary system in Canada, report to Parliament.* M. MacGuigan (Chairman), Ottawa: Supply and Services Canada.

Vantour, J.A. *Report of the study group on dissociation.* Solicitor General Canada. Ottawa: Supply and Services Canada.

Chapter 18

The Growth of Punishment: Imprisonment and Community Corrections in Canada*

John Hylton

For most of the past century in the United States and other Western countries, it has been common practice to incarcerate virtually all offenders committed to the state for supervision. Today this is no longer true. A radical shift in correctional programming has occurred over the last thirty years. The modern corrections system is characterized by the widespread use of community programs. This use is based on a clearly articulated philosophy, and the state is extensively involved in creating and sustaining these "alternative programs". These facts constitute clear evidence of a major departure from traditional penal practices. In many jurisdictions, offenders in community programs now outnumber offenders in institutional programs by two, three, or even four to one.

The emergence of noninstitutional programs on a large scale has meant that, more than any other time, it is appropriate to speak of "systems" of correctional programs. Yet, most correctional research has been concerned with whether community or institutional programs graduate more offenders who subsequently recidivate and not with questions of a systemic nature. Unfortunately, little effort has been directed at assessing how community programs affect other correctional programs or how policies and practices in the larger criminal justice system respond to development in the corrections field. As a result, many questions about community corrections remain unanswered and much

* Saskatchewan Social Services, Revised version of a paper originally presented in *Crime and Social Justice*, No. 15, 1981.

of the conventional wisdom, particularly as it relates to the nature and extent of state involvement in social control, has not been critically analyzed.

In this paper, two questions about community corrections are singled out for discussion: Are institutional programs being replaced by community programs? What effect do community programs have on the size of the correctional system? Much of the data for the analysis of these questions is drawn from a case study of the Canadian province of Saskatchewan.[1] The limited size of its correctional system (the provincial population is less than one million), the development over the past twenty years of community programs for a substantial proportion of offenders under supervision, and the availability of data respecting program utilization, make the Saskatchewan corrections system ideal for the type of analysis undertaken here. In addition, reference will be made to a small but growing literature about the impact of community correctional programs in a number of other Western countries.

ARE INSTITUTIONAL PROGRAMS BEING REPLACED BY COMMUNITY PROGRAMS?

In recent years, the role of "alternative" programs in reducing reliance on institutional care for offenders has received much attention. The President's Commission (1967), for example, argued that community programs were "an important means for coping with the mounting volume of offenders" (38) and, because of their effectiveness, they could be expected to "reduce court dockets and correctional case-loads" (205). In a similar vein, the National Advisory Commission on Criminal Justice Standards and Goals (1973), noting the "urgent need for reducing the population of jails and juvenile detention facilities", argued that community programs could be used as "a substitute for the institution" (12). Moreover, we are told that the use of community programs in some jurisdictions has permitted both reductions in imprisoned populations and the closing of correctional institutions altogether (Scull 1977; National Advisory Commission on Criminal Justice Standards and Goals 1973). These popular beliefs about the impact of community programs are also evident in the frequent calls for the abandonment of existing institutions and for moratoria on the construction of new ones.

Concerns have also been expressed about an overreliance on prisons in Saskatchewan. A Corrections Proposals for Saskatchewan (Department of Social Services 1975), the provincial government's official position respecting the future of corrections in the province, advocates major efforts to "arrest and reserve the emphasis on incarceration and custodial care" (9). Beliefs in the ability of community programs to replace institutional programs are clearly evident. Current plans call for the number of institutional beds to be reduced by some 100. This is over 10 percent of the total institutional capacity in the provincial correctional system. Instead, community programs are to be employed.

From the foregoing comments, one might expect the expansion of community programs to be associated with a decreased reliance on correctional institutions. However, an analysis of the Saskatchewan case, which is reported in detail elsewhere (Hylton 1981; forthcoming a), suggests this may not always be the case. Table 18.1 sets out figures respecting the utilization of correctional institutions in Saskatchewan from 1962 to 1979. The average daily counts in the correctional institutions and the admissions to the correctional institutions have been controlled for changes in the Saskatchewan population, and the resulting rates are also shown in Table 18.1.

A linear trend analysis of the Saskatchewan case confirms that institutions are not being abandoned. The average daily count per 100,000 population in Saskatchewan institutions increased from 55.23 in 1962 to 84.87 in 1979 — an increase of some 53% in 18 years. This linear trend is statistically significant (R squared = .41, p. .01). On average, the predicted rate of increase in the average daily count each year was 1.06 per 100,000 population.

Analyses which rely on utilization figures for correctional programs are very sensitive to "operational definitions" (Waller and Chan 1976). By employing average daily counts, the actual number of persons incarcerated each year may be obscured. For this reason, admission data for Saskatchewan were also examined. The results (see Table 18.1) indicate that a steady increase in admissions to correctional institutions occurred in Saskatachewan between 1962 and 1979. The number of admissions per 100,000 population increased from 434.85 in 1962 to 688.72 in 1979 — an increase of some 58%. This linear trend was statistically significant (R squared = .58, p. .01). On the average, the predicted rate of increase each year was 9.09 admissions per 100,000 population.

There is no evidence that institutions are being abandoned in Saskatchewan. The provincial prisons process more offenders now than at any other time in their history and they process a larger proportion of the total provincial population. The analysis also suggests that further increases can be expected in the future. Importantly, this expansion of institution-based strategies of

Table 18.1 Utilization of Saskatchewan Provincial Correctional Institutions, 1962–1979

Year	Total Saskatchewan Population	Average Daily Count[a]	Average Daily Count (Rate per 100,000)	Sentence Admissions[b]	Average Admissions (Rate per 100,000)
1962	916,176	506	55.23	3,984	434.85
1963	939,466	487	51.84	4,013	427.16
1964	935,005	571	61.07	4,563	488.02
1965	943,799	633	67.07	4,743	502.54
1966	951,434	550	57.81	4,436	466.24
1967	959,310	528	55.04	4,659	485.66
1968	962,376	565	58.71	5,136	533.68
1969	963,878	643	66.71	5,186	538.03
1970	948,370	542	57.15	4,339	457.52
1971	938,527	527	56.15	4,893	521.35
1972	934,607	572	62.20	5,528	591.48
1973	923,181	540	58.49	5,056	547.67
1974	922,487	534	57.89	4,623	501.15
1975	931,921	527	56.66	4,791	514.10
1976	949,463	609	64.14	4,810	506.60
1977	961,526	743	77.27	5,516	573.67
1978	970,510	733	75.53	5,738	593.30
1979	976,734	829	84.87	6,727	688.72

SOURCE: Adapted from Annual Reports of Saskatchewan Social Services, 1962–1979.

a The average daily count is calculated by averaging the daily count in each correctional institution for the year and then summing the average daily count of the four correctional institutions in Saskatchewan.
b Includes those admitted to the four provincial correctional institutions for the purpose of serving a sentence.

social control occurred concomitantly with the expanded use of "alternative" programs. While some might argue that community programs reduced the numbers which would have been institutionalized had no alternatives been available, it is clear that, in Saskatchewan, they have not replaced the institutions.

Analyses of other correctional systems in Canada and elsewhere suggest that the Saskatchewan case is not unique. In Ontario, Canada's most populous province, for example, one research report has concluded that the introduction of community programs has not been accompanied by a reduced reliance on correctional institutions (Davis 1980). Moreover, in the federal penitentiary system, which is responsible for offenders sentenced to a period of incarceration in excess of two years, a steady increase in the number of prisoners has occurred since 1960 (Ministry of the Solicitor General 1976.)

In the United States, some declines in imprisonment rates at the state and federal levels were evident during the 1960s when community programs were rapidly expanded (Scull 1977). However, it is by no means clear that the counts in state and federal prisons actually reflect the number of offenders incarcerated in the United States. Locally administered jails, detention centres and reform schools, or other institutions (e.g., for the mentally ill) may have compensated for some or all of the apparent decreases. Lerman (1975) has shown, for example, that during this period, local administrators were enticed by state and federal governments to retain offenders in local jurisdictions. Thus, decreases in one part of the system may have been compensated for by increases in other parts. In any case, if decreases did occur during the 1960s, they were short lived. By the early 1970s, prison utilization figures had reached their former levels, and recently the American Correctional Association (1980) reported that numbers in state and federal insitutions had reached an all-time high for the fifth consecutive year. This increase in rates of imprisonment is now being widely recognized (Lerman 1975, 1980; Rutherford and Bengur 1976; Pabon 1978; Messinger 1976). Moreover, the U.S. and Canadian experience parallels that in a number of other Western countries where there have been attempts to substitute community-based programs for prisons (Smith 1980; United Kingdom Prison Services 1979; Snare 1979).

IS THE SYSTEM GETTING LARGER?

In the past, proponents have argued that the effectiveness of community programs relative to institutional programs would be evidenced in the constriction of the correctional system. Offenders treated in community programs, it was believed, would recidivate less often than offenders who were institutionalezed. The total number of offenders under the supervision of the correctional system could thus be reduced, it was argued, if community strategies were adopted. These beliefs are especially evident in the reports of major task forces and commissions advocating the expanded use of community programs in the U.S. and Canada. Many have interpreted the widespread use of community programs as an indication that the correctional system is somehow getting smaller or, at the very least, that it is not getting any larger.

In recent years, a number of authors have been concerned that the end result of community correctional programming may not be to reduce the size of the correctional system, as suggested by popular thinking. Vinter et al. (1976), for example, have argued that community programs may not be substitutes for traditional programming, but rather, they may serve to expand the state's control over individual behaviour and freedom. Rutherford and McDermott (1976), in a similar vein, have cautioned that diverson programs may expand the state's "net of control". And Messinger (1973) has warned that the system may be expanding, not only in terms of absolute numbers, but also in terms of the proportion of the total population under supervision. That community programs may expand the social control apparatus of the state has been the subject of much recent discussion (Cohen 1977, 1979; Pabo 1978; Greenberg 1975; Morris 1974).

Unfortunately, the "expansion hypothesis" has not often been subjected to empirical test. Vinter, Downs and Hall (1976) point out that an adequate analysis requires longitudinal data on the number of offenders handled outside the correctional system. This type of data has not generally been available. Data on the number of offenders being processed in other systems are particularly difficult to obtain. Any analysis based solely on statistics for the criminal justice system is bound to result in a conservative estimate of the total number of offenders being processed. To this writer's knowledge, no study has overcome all of these methodological problems; however, the work of Vinter, Downs and Hall and that of Blomberg (1978, 1977) warrant mention here.

Vinter, Downs and Hall did not come at the expansion question in a straightforward way. They examined the relationship between the use of community programs and the use of correctional institutions in the United States. They reasoned that if community programs were replacing correctional institutions, then those states high in community programs would have a less than average use of correctional institutions. If, on the other hand, community programs were being used to supplement institutional programs, then states high in community programs might also have above average use of institutional programs. The study concludes that the total number and the proportion of the population under supervision of the juvenile correctional system has increased and that community programs are the means by which this increase has occurred.

Blomberg (1978) has suggested that diversion practices in the juvenile justice system are being applied to a large number of offenders who previously might have been released outright and without supervision. The end result, he believes, is an increase in the number of juveniles and their families under supervision. In his own case study of a juvenile diversion program in California, Blomberg observed a 32 percent increase in the number of persons "in the system" after the first year of operation (Blomberg, 1977). Blomberg's findings have been replicated in a number of other studies (Bohnstedt 1978; Klein et al. 1976; Dunford 1977; Gibbons and Blake 1976; Kutchins and Kutchins 1975; Seitz et al 1978).

These studies suggest that the system may be expanding and the community programs may play an integral role in this expansion. Unfortunately, the empirical evidence is scant. The extent of system expansion is not yet clear, nor are the factors that affect the size of the correctional system well understood. Moreover, the available evidence bears on the juvenile justice system, but the adult correctional system may well be different.

Any attempt to estimate the total number of offenders under supervision of a correctional system will inevitably be complicated. In Saskatchewan, however, because of its limited size and the limited number of correctional programs, accurate estimates of correctional program utilization could be computed. Virtually all offenders under supervision of the Saskatchewan correctional system are included in the statistical compilations of four major programs: the correctional institutions, probation, the program of community training residences (CTR's) and the community service program for defaulters (the Fine Option Program). By adding the daily counts in these programs, an estimate of the total number of offenders under supervision could be obtained. Since only data respecting admissions and discharges were available for the Fine Option Program, this program was not included in this part of the analysis.

As Table 18.2 indicates, the rate per 100,000 population under supervision of the Saskatchewan correctional system increased from 85.46 in 1962 to 321.99 in 1979 — an increase of 277% in 18 years. A linear trend characterizes the actual observations exceptionally well, since the R squared value is .95 — a value which is significant at greater than the .01 level. On the average, the predicted yearly increase in the population under supervision at any one time was 15.26 per 100,000.

Table 18.2   Persons Under Supervision of the Saskatchewan Correctional System 1962-1979 (estimated)

Year	Average Daily Count In Institutions	Year end Probation Caseload	Year end CTR Count	Total	Total (Rate per 100,000)
1962	506	277	—	783	85.46
1963	487	356	—	848	89.73
1964	571	432	—	1,003	107.27
1965	633	586	—	1,219	129.16
1966	550	519	—	1,169	122.87
1967	528	651	—	1,179	122.90
1968	565	697	—	1,262	131.13
1969	643	732	—	1,375	142.65
1970	542	859	—	1,401	147.73
1971	527	1,097	—	1,624	173.04
1972	572	1,430	—	2,002	214.21
1973	540	1,606	38	2,184	236.57
1974	534	1,784	50	2,368	256.70
1975	527	2,007	58	2,592	279.14
1976	609	2,033	63	2,705	284.90
1977	743	2,283	43	3,069	319.18
1978	733	2,162	43	2,938	302.73
1979	829	2,268	48	3,145	321.99

SOURCE: Adapted from Annual Reports of Saskatchewan Social Services, 1962-1979.

An analysis of admission figures was also undertaken. For all practical purposes, admission to the correctional system in the province of Saskatchewan between 1962 and 1979 occurred via the institutions, probation or the Fine Option Program. Simply counting the admissions to each program, however, would result in some double counting. Probationers, for example, are breached, and if incarcerated, they would show up as both a probation intake and an institutional admission. Similarly, not all offenders in the Fine Option Program complete their work assignment, and some are subsequently placed on probation or incarcerated.

Fortunately, statistics on the number of offenders not completing the Fine Option Program were available. The failures could be subtracted from the total number of admissions to avoid double counting. As for offenders who had their probation revoked, their numbers turned out to be so small that they could safely be ignored. In 1974-75, for example, there were only nineteen offenders who had their probation revoked. Unfortunately, reliable data on the number of revocations could not be obtained for each year. Therefore, the revocation problem was ignored in the calculation of the estimates.

Estimates of the total admissions to the correctional system were derived by adding the sentence admissions to the correctional institutions, the probation intake, and the number of Fine Option admissions for each year from 1962 to 1979. The number of Fine Option failures was then subtracted from this total. These figures, as well as the corresponding rates per 100,000 population, are set out in Table 18.3.

Table 18.3 Admissions to the Saskatchewan Correctional System, 1963–1979 (estimated)

Year	Sentence Admissions to Institutions	Probation Intakes	Fine Option Completions	Total Admissions	Total (Rate per 100,000)
1962	3,984	412	—	4,396	479.82
1963	4,013	536	—	4,549	484.21
1964	4,563	627	—	5,190	555.08
1965	4,743	845	—	5,588	592.08
1966	4,436	998	—	5,434	571.14
1967	4,659	971	—	5,630	586.88
1968	5,136	1,027	—	6,163	640.39
1969	5,186	1,686	—	6,872	712.95
1970	4,339	1,955	—	6,294	663.67
1971	4,893	1,577	—	6,470	689.38
1972	5,528	1,797	—	7,325	783.75
1973	5,056	2,253	—	7,309	791.72
1974	4,623	2,383	—	7,006	759.47
1975	4,791	2,370	655	7,826	839.77
1976	4,810	2,561	1,624	8,995	947.38
1977	5,516	2,796	2,920	11,232	1,168.14
1978	5,758	2,626	3,789	12,173	1,254.29
1979	6,727	2,720	3,614	13,061	1,337.21

SOURCE: Adapted from Annual Reports of Saskatchewan Social Services, 1962–1979.

As can be seen from Table 18.3, the number of admissions per 100,000 population increased from 479.82 in 1962 to 1337.21 in 1979 — an increase of 179%. The linear trend analysis indicates there was a steady increase in the number of admissions throughout the period from 1962 to 1979. On average, the rate of increase each year was 43.99 admissions per 100,000 population. This linear trend characterizes the actual observations very well, since the R squared is .84 — a value which is significant at greater than the .01 level.

Convincing evidence of a steady increase in the size of the

Saskatchewan correctional system has been presented. This finding obtained whether admission or daily average figures were employed and whether "raw" data or rates per 100,000 population were used. The "expansion hypothesis" has thus received strong support. Throughout the period under study, both the number of persons under supervision of the correctional system and the proportion of the total provincial population under supervision increased dramatically.

There can be little question that the expanded use of community programs in Saskatchewan provided the means by which the correctional system expanded. Although the utilization of correctional institutions did increase in the period from 1962 to 1979, the expanded use of community programs was far more significant. Whereas 65% of those under supervision of the correctional system were incarcerated in 1962, by 1979 only 26% of those under supervision were incarcerated. Similarly, admissions to correctional institutions in 1962 accounted for 91% of all admissions to the provincial correctional system; however, by 1979, admissions to correctional institutions accounted for only 52% of the total.

TOWARDS AN UNDERSTANDING OF SYSTEM EXPANSION

In this paper, I have argued that community correctional programs in Saskatchewan do not have some of the impacts that popular beliefs suggest they ought to have. At the same time, however, they have other dramatic impacts that have not received much attention. When the use of community programs was expanded in Saskatchewan, no corresponding decrease in the use of correctional institutions could be observed. Rather, the utilization of correctional facilities, whether measured in terms of daily counts or admissions, increased steadily. Community programs, it appeared, permitted the correctional system to expand at a tremendous rate, with the result that an ever larger proportion of the population was under some form of supervision by the state. During the eighteen years examined in the study, the rate of persons under supervision of the correctional authority on a given day nearly tripled. Moreover, research examining other correctional systems in the Western world, while not as definitive as the analysis of the Saskatchewan case, suggests that the observed patterns in the expansion of social control are not unique to a small Canadian province.

Many observers of correctional practices, when asked to account for the recent popularity of community correctional programs, would point to the inhumanity and ineffectiveness of correctional institutions and the exorbitant costs associated with this method of social control. These observers would have us believe that the deficiencies of institutional care and the merits of community programs have only recently come to light. In fact, however, it has been shown that criticisms leveled at correctional institutions today are no different from those clearly articulated more than 150 years ago (Rothman 1971, 1980; Scull 1977; Powers 1959; Foucault 1977; Rusche and Kurchheimer 1939). Moreover, alternatives to incarceration are not a recent phenomenon, but date back over a century (Dressler 1959; Newman 1968). These ideas are hardly new. In addition, serious questions can be raised about the extent to which the community alternatives are as cost efficient, effective and humane as the rhetoric would have us believe (Hylton forthcoming b). If we are to understand the factors that have contributed to a rather sudden departure from traditional penal practices, we must go beyond these popular beliefs.

Fiscal restraint has been a pervasive constraint on all public-sector human-service programming in recent years. The effects of fiscal restraint can be seen everywhere — discontinued programs, programs modified so as to restrict the scope of services, the introduction of eligibility criteria or the tightening up of existing criteria, etc. Fiscal restraint poses special problems for the correctional system. Correctional administrators, unlike administrators in many other human-service programs, cannot usually control the rate of intake into their system. This intake function is more directly related to the decisions of the police and the courts. Thus, even in a time of fiscal restraint, methods for dealing with offenders coming into the correctional system must be developed.

In one of the few attempts to systematically assess the evolution and subsequent impact of the community corrections movement, Scull (1977) has argued that the radical changes in correctional practices are intimately bound up with what O'Connor (1973) has termed "the fiscal crisis of the state". Building on O'Connor's analysis, Scull has argued that advanced capitalist countries, such as the U.S., Britain and Canada, have been required to socialize more and more of the costs of production. This is most clearly evident in the development of the welfare state. According to Scull, welfare capitalism creates structural pressures to curtail spending, including spending on costly systems of segregative control such as mental hospitals and correctional institutions. At the same time, the development of the welfare state makes available a system for managing elements of the "surplus population" in the community. These constraints and pressures, it is argued, lead the state to divest itself of expensive institutions and to develop an alternative system of "care" in the community. The arguments about the ineffectiveness and inhumanity of correctional institutions that, in the popular view, account for the rise of community corrections are, according to Scull, an ideological camouflage that allows economy to masquerade as benevolence.

There is little doubt that cutbacks in spending have dramatically affected human-service and social-control programs in Canada. Bergeron (1979) examined spending on such programs in Canada between 1962 and 1976. He found that, beginning in the early 1970s, "spending for social programs in relation to both total government spending and GNP decreased" (17). In Saskatchewan, Riches (1979) examined provincial government expenditures common in the late 1960s and early 1970s were replaced by a climate of restraint characterized chiefly by a tighter rationing of resources.

The climate of restraint influenced planning for corrections programming in Saskatchewan. During the period of restraint, existing community programs (e.g., probation) underwent a tremendous expansion and new community programs (e.g., CTR's and Fine Option) were developed. The cost considerations were explicit. In the provincial government's Corrections Proposal for Saskatchewan (Department of Social Services 1975), which was the culmination of a community corrections movement that had begun in the province some years earlier, the provision of corrections programs at a reasonable cost is identified as a primary interest of the state in considering alternative policies. By demonstrating a "reasonable cost-benefit ratio" (3), it is argued, the government could assure the general public that its interests were being safeguarded.

The role of community programs in reducing the costs of correctional supervision is clearly evident in Saskatchewan. With the development of community programs, expenditures on correctional services (and on correctional institutions in particular) declined as a proportion of total expenditures on human-service and social-control programs administered by the Department of Social Services. As can be seen from Table 18.4, both the corrections budget and the budget for correctional institutions consumed a smaller percentage of the total department budget following 1968. While increased expenditures did occur, the budget for corrections was less than half what would have been expected for 1977, had corrections received a level of support comparable to that in 1968.

Table 18.4 Total Corrections Expenditures and Expenditures for Correctional Institutions as a Percentage of Total Departmental Expenditures 1966–1977 (thousands of dollars)

Year	Total Departmental Budget	Corrections Expenditures	Corrections as % of Total	Expenditures for Institutions[a]	Institutions as % of Total
1966	20,030.1	1,552.9	7.8%	1,502.1	7.5%
1967	19,931.6	1,680.5	9.4%	1,632.0	8.2%
1968	18,500.0	1,860.6	10.1%	1,794.0	9.7%
1969	20,952.1	2,071.1	9.9%	1,979.6	9.4%
1970	22,552.7	2,191.4	9.7%	2,191.2	9.7%
1971	28,907.6	2,453.5	8.5%	2,453.5	8.5%
1972	33,239.9	2,775.9	8.4%	2,775.9	8.4%
1973	44,822.2	3,144.8	7.0%	2,118.2	7.0%
1974	85,179.8	3,847.3	4.5%	3,609.0	4.2%
1975	108,104.9	4,717.9	4.4%	4,318.6	4.0%
1976	138,486.7	5,684.2	4.1%	5,223.3	3.8%
1977	155,188.3	7,512.4	4.8%	6,106.7	3.9%

SOURCE: Adapted from Department of Social Services (1966–1977).

a These are gross expenditures

Smaller increases in corrections funding were made possible by the development of corrections programs outside the walls of traditional institutions. This is clear when the direct costs to the correctional system of community and institutional programs are examined. In 1978, for example, the cost of probation supervision was approximately $400 per man-year in Saskatchewan, whereas the cost of institutional care was approximately $9,100 per man-year, or nearly twenty-three times as much. From these figures it can be estimated that the costs of providing institutional services to the 2,300 probationers under supervision at any one time in 1977 would have been over $20 million. Since this amount is nearly three times the total corrections budget for 1977, it is clear that vast increases in expenditures would have been required had probation services not been available. In all probability, demands to reduce excessive expenditures would have resulted in some offenders being released outright and without supervision. From this perspective, community programs may be seen not as an alternative to incarceration but as an alternative to outright release.

Scull's analysis suggests that the state, in order to minimize costs, divests itself of expensive programs and even neglects elements of the population that formerly were the subject of obtrusive social-control strategies. The most straightforward way of accomplishing such savings in the corrections field would be to release some offenders outright from institutions while channeling other offenders into inexpensive modes of supervision in the community. Yet, the findings reported in this paper indicate that community programs have not reduced reliance on correctional institutions but, instead, have served to greatly expand the proportion of the population under state supervision. While many clients are channeled into modes of service that are inexpensive, the social-control apparatus as a whole has expanded and the costs associated with the maintenance of the corrections system have continued to increase. Thus, it is clear that savings have not accrued to the state as a result of the creation and use of community programs. Scull's analysis must be taken further in order to account for the expansion which has been occurring.

O'Connor's analysis of the fiscal crisis makes comprehensible the cutbacks in social services and the desire to reduce expenditures on "deviant" populations that have come to characterize many Western societies in recent years. Yet, the fiscal crisis has an impact on much more than social-service and social-control programs. In North America, other symptoms of the fiscal crisis include high and growing rates of unemployment, levels of inflation that are unprecedented in recent decades, soaring interest rates, and economic instability in both the domestic and international spheres. These conditions have led to a swelling in the ranks of the "industrial reserve army". A larger and larger proportion of the population is either unemployed or unemployable. In Canada, the unemployment rate increased by 58 percent between 1974 and 1978 alone, while in Saskatchewan the corresponding increase in the unemployment rate was 75 percent (Saskatchewan Bureau of Statistics 1979). Yet, government programs to maintain even subsistence levels among those who are marginal to the market economy are eliminated or cut back. These conditions in the labour market markedly influence the nature and extent of the state involvement in domestic pacification and control.

Rusche (1978) has pointed out that criminal law and criminal courts are almost exclusively directed against persons whose class backgrounds include poverty, neglected education, and unemployment. These individuals, he argues, commit crimes of desperation often because of hunger, deprivation or frustration. Increased law violation can thus be expected to occur, he predicts, when larger proportions of the population are forced to cope with deteriorating social and economic conditions. Overwhelming evidence collected since the initial formulation of this theory, much of which has been summarized by Kornhauser (1978) and Taylor, Walton and Young (1973) has shown the importance of these factors in explaining the distribution of crime.

Increased pressure on the state to intervene in the process of socialization and social control is brought about by the advancement of capitalism. The crime rates discussed by Rusche are but one symptom of a larger crisis. In capitalist societies, as Spitzer (1975) has pointed out, the growth of constant capital (machines and raw material) in the production process is accompanied by an expansion in the overall size of the relative surplus population, because the increasingly technological character of production removes ever larger numbers from productive activity. These individuals become marginal to the market economy. In order to ensure the orderly accumulation of capital, this increasingly widespread marginality requires intervention in the processes of socialization and social control. But, since capitalism brings about a dissolution of traditional institutions responsible for integration and social regulation — such as the family, the church, and the community — bureaucratic institutions become more and more important means for differentiating and controlling both those caught up in and those marginal to the market economy. As Braverman (1974) has pointed out, it is not only that whole new strata of the helpless as dependent are created, but that the family and community cannot bear such encumbrances if they are to survive in the market economy. Therefore, the care of the increasingly deviant and dependent population becomes institutionalized, often in inhumane and oppressive ways.

The foregoing analysis emphasizes the ever-increasing need for state involvement in domestic pacification and control that is brought about by advanced capitalism. Yet, it is important to point out that the nature of the state's intervention is not fixed over time. Rather, it is influenced by social and economic conditions. Every system of production, according to Rusche and Kurchheimer (1939), tends to discover punishments which correspond to prevailing productive relationships. In a period of fiscal crisis, when there is pressure on the state to expand its activities in domestic pacification and control, inexpensive methods of supervision are required for larger and larger proportions of the total population. The state, in such circumstances, appears to reserve expensive segregative controls for the increasing numbers who are believed to seriously threaten existing productive relationships. At the same time, the state develops inexpensive community-based strategies of supervision to cope with the increasing proportion of the population that is marginal to the market economy.

There is a danger that the needs in advanced capitalism for both costs efficiency and the expansion of social-control activities may produce an array of punitive sanctions for offenders. Many of the most punitive sanctions (e.g., capital and corporal punishment) are very "cost-effective". In addition, Rusche (1978, 4) contends:

> . . . all efforts to reform the punishment of criminals are inevitably limited by the situation of the lowest socially significant proletarian class which society wants to deter from criminal acts.

For Rusche, penal sanctions, in order to act as a deterrent in the face of deteriorating social and economic conditions, will need to become more punitive. While this labour-market theory has justifiably been criticized as too simple and mechanistic (Jankovic 1977; Melossi 1978), the relationship between the nature of social-control processes and the labour market cannot be disputed. We should expect the crisis of advanced capitalism to be accompanied by greater emphasis on the control of crime and the punishment of offenders.

The restoration of capital punishment in many states, the legislating of mandatory sentences, and the lengthening of prison terms in recent years, all indicate that criminal justice policy is becoming more punitive in the United States. The treatment of offenders has also been changing in Canada. Theories of innate criminality, such as "the criminal personality", are increasingly being used to justify punitive policies and practices even though such theories have no empirical support (Keller 1980; Hylton forthcoming c). Juveniles are being "scared straight" by those who believe terrorizing the young will "cure" them of their criminal dispositions. "Opportunity models" and "responsibility models" that blame offenders for the circumstances in which they find themselves are increasingly popular among corrections workers. Moreover, expenditures on policing in Canada have continued to rise at an unprecedented rate, even while social services are being cut back. Expenditures on policing now make up two-thirds of all expenditures on the criminal justice system in Canada (National Task Force 1979). There is an increasing willingness to trade off individuals rights and freedoms for a measure of state supervision.

There is evidence that a right-wing ideology has emerged to justify more punishment. Platt and Takagi (1977) for example, have shown that a brand of intellectuals they call the "new realists" have provided the justification for punitive policies and practices by arguing that only tougher state repression will preserve law and order. This ideology has obviously found favour with those who run the criminal justice system and with some segments of the public in both the U.S. (Stinchcombe et al. 1980) and Canada (Fattah 1978; Hylton and Matonovich 1979, 1980).

Community correctional programs make an expansion of state involvement in social-control activities economically viable. The development of inexpensive social-control programs that catch up an increasing proportion of the total population and the emergence of a right-wing ideology that justifies the use of such programs must be viewed within the context of the crisis of capitalism and the changing requirements for domestic pacification and control that this crisis brings about. So long as correctional research is preoccupied with how programs differentially affect offenders there will continue to be widespread ignorance about the way larger structural exigencies influence modern correctional practices.

Notes

1. Saskatchewan is located on the Canadian prairies and it lies north of Montana and North Dakota. The provincial population of less than one million is spread over a land mass of some 220,000 square miles. Saskatchewan is still primarily a rural province, although a pattern of increasing migration from rural to urban areas has been evident in recent years. Until recently, the economy has been almost totally dependent on agriculture. In the last decade, however, there

has been some diversification. Development of the resource industries (oil, natural gas, uranium, potash, coal and forest products) has been the key to diversification; however, some expansion has also been evident in the manufacturing and service sectors. In Saskatchewan, the only socialist party in North American ever to govern a political unit larger than a municipality has dominated provincial politics for over twenty years. The party, originally known as the CCF or Cooperative Commonwealth Federation, was elected in 1944 and, but for two elections in the 1960s, it has remained in power ever since. The party is now known as the NDP or New Democratic Party.

References

American Correctional Association. 1980. Record high for number of inmates. *On the Line* 3, 5 (July).

Bergeron, Michel. 1979. *Social spending in Canada: Trends and options.* Ottawa, Canada: Canadian Council on Social Development.

Blomberg, Thomas. 1978. Diversion from juvenile court: A review of the evidence. In F. Faust and P. Brantingham (Eds.), *Juvenile justice philosophy,* 2d ed. Minneapolis: West Publishing Company.

_____. 1977. Diversion and accelerated social control. *Journal of Criminal Law and Criminology* 68, 2 (June).

Bohnstedt, M. 1978. Answers to three questions about juvenile diversion. *Journal of Research in Crime and Delinquency* 15, 1 (January).

Braverman, Harry. 1974. *Labor and monopoly capital: The degradation of work in the twentieth century.* New York: Monthly Review.

Cohen, Stan. 1979. The punitive city: Notes on the dispersal of social control. *Contemporary Crises* 3.

_____. Prisons and the future of control systems: From concentration to dispersal. In M. Fitzgerald et al. (Eds.), *Welfare in action.* London: Routledge and Kegan Paul.

Davis, S.L. 1980. *The seduction of the private sector: Privatization in Ontario corrections.* Ottawa, Canada: School of Social Work, Carleton University.

Department of Social Services. 1975. *A corrections proposal for Saskatchewan.* Regina, Canada: Department of Social Services.

Dressler, D. 1969. *Practice and theory of probation and parole,* 2d ed. New York: Columbia University Press.

Dunford, F. 1977. Police diversion, an ilusion. *Criminology* 15, 3 (November).

Fattah, Ezzat, 1978. Moving to the right: A return to punishment. *Crime and Justice* 6, 2.

Foucault, M. 1977. *Discipline and punish.* New York: Pantheon.

Gibbons, D. and G. Blake. 1976. Evaluating the impact of juvenile diversion programs. *Crime and Delinquency* 22, 4 (December).

Greenberg, D. 1975. Problems in community corrections. *Issues in Criminology* 10, 1 (Spring).

Hylton, John. Forthcoming a. Community corrections and social control: The case of a Saskatchewan, Canada. *Contemporary crises.*

_____. Forthcoming b. Rhetoric and reality: A critical appraisal of community correctional programming. In Shedon Messinger and Egon Bittner (Eds.), *Criminology review*, Yearbook 3. Beverly Hills, Ca.: Sage.

_____. Forthcoming c. Innate criminality revisited. *Canada's mental health.*

_____. 1981. *Reintegrating the offender: Assessing the impact of community corrections.* Washington, D.C.: University Press of America.

Hylton, John and Rae Matonovich. 1980. *Public attitudes towards crime and the police in Moose Jaw.* Regina, Canada: Prairie Justice Research Consortium, University of Regina.

_____. 1979. *Public attitudes towards crime and the police in Regina.* Regina, Canada: Regina Police Department.

Jankovic, I. 1977. Labor Market and Imprisonment. *Crime and Social Justice* 8 (Fall-Winter).

Keller, Oliver. 1980. The criminal personality of Lombroso revisited. *Federal Probation* 44, 1 (March).

Klein, M. et. al. 1976. The explosion in police diversion programs: Evaluating the structural dimensions of a social fad. In M. Klein (Ed.), *The Juvenile Justice System.* Beverly Hills, Ca.: Sage.

Kornhauaser, Ruth. 1978. *Social sources of delinquency.* Chicago: University of Chicago Press.

Kutchins, H. and S. Kutchins. 1975. *Pretrial diversionary programs: New expansion of law enforcement activity camouflaged as rehabilitation.* Presented at Pacific Sociological Association Meetings, Hawaii.

Lerman, Paul. 1980. Trends and issues in the deinstitutionalization of youths in trouble. *Crime and Delinquency* 26, 3 (July).

_____. 1975. *Community treatment and social control.* Chicago: University of Chicago Press.

Melossi, Dario. 1978. Book review: George Rusche and Otto Kirchheimer, punishment and social structure. *Crime and Social Justice* 9 (Spring-Summer).

Messinger, Sheldon L. 1976. Confinement in the community: A selective assessment of Paul Lerman's treatment and social control. *Journal of Research in Crime and Delinquency* 13, 1 (January).

_____. 1973. The year 2000 and the problem of criminal justice. Presented at the Conference on Criminal Justice Meetings, Chicago.

Ministry of the Solicitor General. 1976. *Statistical handbook: Selected aspects of criminal justice.* Ottawa, Canada: Ministry of the Solicitor General.

Morris, Norval. 1975. *The future of imprisonment.* Chicago: University of Chicago Press.

National Advisory Commission on Criminal Justice Standards and Goals. 1973. *Task force report: Corrections.* Washington, D.C.: U.S. Government Printing Office.

National Task Force on the Administration of Justice. 1979. *Report.* Ottawa, Canada: National Task Force on the Administration of Justice.

Newman, Charles. 1968. *Sourcebook on probation, parole, and pardons.* 3d ed. Springfield, Ill.: Charles C. Thomas.

O'Connor, J. 1973. *The fiscal crisis of the state.* New York: St. Martin's Press.

Pabon, E. 1978. Changes in juvenile justice: Evolution of reform. *Social Work* 26, 6 (November).

Platt, Tony and Paul Takagi. 1977. Intellectuals for law and order: A critique of the new realists. *Crime and Social Justice* 8 (Fall-Winter).

Powers, Edwin. 1959. Halfway houses: An historical perspective. *American Journal of Corrections* 21, 4 (July).

The President's Commission on Law Enforcement and Administration of Justice. 1967. *Task force report: Corrections.* Washington, D.C.: U.S. Government Printing Office.

Riches, Graham. 1979. *Spending is choosing: Restraint and growth in Saskatchewan's personal social services 1966–1977.* Regina, Canada: Social Administration Research Unit, University of Regina.

Rothman, David J. 1980. *Conscience and convenience: The asylum and its alternatives in progressive America.* Boston: Little, Brown and Company.

————. 1971. *The discovery of asylum: Social order and disorder in the new republic.* Boston: Little, Brown and Company.

Rusche, Georg. 1978. Labor market and penal sanction: Thoughts on the sociology of criminal justice. *Crime and Social Justice* 10 (Fall-Winter).

Rusche Georg and Otto Kirchheimer. 1939. *Punishment and social structure.* New York: Russell and Russell.

Rutherford, A. and O. Bengur. 1976. *Juvenile diversion.* Washington, D.C.: U.S. Government Printing Office.

Rutherford, Andrew and Robert McDermott. 1976. *Juvenile diversion.* Washington, D.C.: National Institute of Law Enforcement and Criminal Justice.

Saskatchewan Bureau of Statistics. 1979. *Saskatchewan economic review.* Regina: Saskatchewan Bureau of Statistics.

Scull. Andrew T. 1977. *Decarceration: Community treatment of the deviant — A radical view.* Englewood Cliffs, New Jersey: Prentice-Hall.

Seitz, S. et al. 1978. *The Des Moines exemplary project: Final report.* Washington: CEAA.

Smith, D. 1980. Reducng the custodial population. *Home office research bulletin* 5.

Snare, A. 1979. *Crime and criminal justice in Norway during the last twenty years.* Oslo: University of Oslo.

Spitzer, S. 1975. Toward a Marxian theory of deviance. *Social Problems* 22, 5.

Stinchcombe, Arthur L. et al. 1980. *Crime and punishment: Changing attitudes in America.* San Francisco: Jossey-Bass.

Taylor, Ian, Paul Walton and Jock Young. 1973. *The new criminology.* New York: Harper and Row.

United Kingdom Prison Services. 1979. Report of the Committee of Inquiry Into the United Kingdom Prison Services. London: HMSO.

Vinter, Robert, et al. 1976. *Time out: A national study of juvenile court programs.* Ann Arbor: University of Michigan Press.

Vinter, Robert, George Downs and John Hall. 1976. *Juvenile corrections in the States: Residential programs and deinstitutionalization.* Ann Arbor, Michigan: University of Michigan Press.

Waller, Irvin and Janet Chan. 1976. Prison use: A Canadian and international comparison. In Ministry of the Solicitor General, *Statistical handbook: selected aspects of criminal justice.* Ottawa, Canada: Ministry of the Solicitor General.

Part IV

Theoretical Issues and Criminological Concerns

Introduction

In this final section of the book we present four articles which deal with current theoretical issues in the field of criminology. These offerings challenge you the reader to apply some of the knowledge of basic processes in the creation of deviance and criminality and the operation of law which have been explored in the previous sections of the book. Undergraduates should not be dismayed if the articles require much of them in terms of understanding, they are meant to provide starting points for more in-depth contemplation of processes, responses, and concepts in the three areas which this book addresses. Further illumination of some of the issues raised in this section, and indeed in the reader as a whole may be found in Robert Silverman and James Teevan's excellent book, *Crime in Canadian Society*.

Two articles by criminologist Robert Menzies highlight this section. The first examines the controversy surrounding Black's theory of law. Black is one of the most oft-quoted scholars of law in this decade; his theory of law is the subject of close scrutiny in this finely crafted article. Menzies' second contribution is an attempt to return realism to the consideration of class, calculus, and crime in criminological research. Stephen Webb, another West coast academic provides us with a valuable analysis of deterrence theory. The question of whether deterrents are effective has been with us since the beginning of the criminological enterprise and is likely to remain the subject of much debate, both public and private. Webb's article does much to fuel that debate, but also to reorientate our ideas concerning deterrence.

Our closing article is by three criminologists from the University of Ottawa. Juliani, Jayewardene and Talbot offer the reader an examination of the teaching of the applied criminology. This is the field which prepares young people to utilize their knowledge of criminology in whatever field of endeavour they should come to enter. It is an important article in the Canadian context, as more universities begin to offer undergraduate programs in criminology which are geared to the fostering of practical skills in undergraduates and graduates to fill the needs of the corrections, research, policy, academic, business and other fields. Criminology and criminology-related programs at the universities of Alberta, Simon Fraser, Ottawa, Toronto, Regina, and perhaps soon at Newfoundland are vital and growing not only in student numbers but in their influence on the shape of all the criminological enterprise which must be carried out in Canada.

Chapter 19

A Farewell to Norms: Black's Theory of Law Revisited

*Robert J. Menzies**

INTRODUCTION

The history of the sociology of law has hardly been replete with radical challenges to the reigning paradigms. From the time of Aristotle and Plato, the dominant themes have surrounded the role of value and norm in law. Consensus theorists have supported the ideology of universal normative entrenchment in law, wherein legal form provides a mirror image for valued standards which prevail within and across social systems. Conflict theorists, as well, argue for the notion of value-laden law; conversely, however, the conflict paradigm views law as systematically reflective of the moves of dominant groups — groups who utilize the resource of power to crystallize their interests within the legal apparatus. Both theoretical paradigms, nevertheless, are unified in the axiom that normative and legal systems interpenetrate. According to traditional jurisprudence of both the left and right, neither the creation, the mobilization, nor the analysis of law can be detached from the ideological and prescriptive systems in which the legal machinery is embedded.

Donald Black's *The Behaviour of Law* (1976) represents a staggering challenge to this conventional wisdom. By divesting the study of law of its normative content, Black has fomented a potential revolution in the field of sociological jurisprudence. For Black, law, like any social fact, is an accumulation of behaviours — in this case, the behaviours of individuals and groups who exert governmental social control. In the Durkeimian tradition, law behaves according to laws and properties which are discoverable, like any social facts, through methods similar to those in the physical sciences. Most dramatically, the study of law — the field of sociological jurisprudence — is radically altered within Black's paradigm. Evaluative and prescriptive methods do not belong to the analysis of legal systems. Like the proverbial doomsday

* Department of Criminology, Simon Frazer University.

weapon, law is neither good nor evil. Moreover, it is the mandate of the social scientist not to utilize law as a vehicle for social engineering, nor to assess its applicability as a method of dispute settlement or social ordering, but rather to measure and predict its quantity. For Black, then, the jurisprudent is transformed into a jurometrician.

This conception has stimulated considerable debate among legal sociologists, particularly among members of the Berkeley School. For example, Nonet (1976) has termed Black's theory of law "prescribed ignorance". Eder (1977) has suggested that the book is "nothing more and nothing less than systematized commonsense". Stinchcombe is more eloquent in his critique:

> Black has a "classic" esthetic. He voluntarily cripples his intellect by giving up certain intellectual advantages, much as a string quartet gives of the blare of brasses, and tries to see how much social theory he can write without the blare of the intentions of people, and without recourse to distinctions among types of law and legal action. (1977, 129).

On the other hand, Nader (1976) has hailed *The Behaviour of Law* as a "crashing classic". Koch terms the book "a long-awaited synthesis of sociolegal scholarship, presenting a general model of the behaviour of law in social life and laying a conceptual foundation for future comparative research on law in history, sociology, and ethnography" (Koch 1977, 149). Sherman, quite simply, describes Black's monograph as "the most important contribution ever made to the sociology of law — that and more" (1978, 11). In accounting for Black's uneven impact upon the sociolegal field, it is important to consider the framework within which the theory has been constructed, as well as the structure and dynamics of the theory itself. In the following sections, this review will attempt to place *The Behavior of Law* within theoretical/historical context, before proceeding to examine the book in more detail, and critically analyze its more controversial postulates.

THE BACKGROUND

Black's book represents a return to Durkheimian notions of the study of law and social control. It is the delineation and pre-diction of social facts, rather than the examination of motivation, value, and nuances of commitment by social actors, which to Black constitutes the stuff of which the sociology of crime and control is made. What Turk (1979, 17) characterizes as a "positivistic perspective" informs Black's conception of law as a contingent social phenomenon, a reified and tangible essence which varies quantitatively across time and space according to other vagaries of a number of macrolevel social features. When the tools of social science are sufficiently refined to gauge the degree of stratification, differentiation, organization, culture and social control in a given society, the amount of law inherent in social life should be wholly predictable, when derived from an equation which includes these variables.

For Black, the conduct of social inquiry must be disengaged from the normative considerations which have dominated the discipline of sociological jurisprudence. In an early article, Black's theoretical commitment to a "de-ideologized" study of law and deviance was made clear (1972). According to Black, in order to construct a general theory of social control, it would be necessary to excoriate both programmatic concerns of social policy, and the idea that sociology could boast the mandate of lobbying legal activism through the vehicle of law reform (compare Feeley 1976). Law is, in fact, neither more nor less than governmental social control (1972, 104). To argue, with Selznick (1968) and the Berkeley School (Nonet 1976) that the goal of legal sociology is to assess the "effectiveness" of a corpus of legal rules, is to confuse "factual and normative discourse" (Black 1972, 1096). Law is knowable, but only as a system of behaviour. With Marx (see Balbus 1977; Quinney 1972) Black views written law, and prescriptive codification of normative life, as an ideological smokescreen, which mystifies the empirical playing out of law and deviance in the real world. In fact, it is the phenomenon of governmental social control itself which is most open to legal insight and measurement.

> Law can be seen as a thing like any other in the empirical world. It is crucial to be clear that from a sociological standpoint, law consists in observable acts, not in rules as the concept of rule or norm is employed in both the literature of jurisprudence and in every-day legal language. From a socio-logical point of view, law is not what lawyers regard as binding or obliga-tory precepts, but rather, for example, the observable dispositions of judges, policemen, prosecutors, or administrative officials. Law is like any other thing in the sense that it is as amenable to the scientific method as any other aspect of reality. No intellectual apparatus peculiar to the study of law is required. (Black 1972, 101).

While the delineation of an ideal role for law may have a place in philosophy and the "technocratic sciences" (1972, 100), the legal sociologist's mandate is to trace the function of the *mobilization* of law on the front lines of human discourse. This entails an enforced *limitation* of the scope of legal sociology. First, since only the phenomenon, as a second-order construct (Schutz 1967) can be known and measured, any attempt to uncover a Kantian essence underlying this behaviour is misplaced effort. Second, it is the empirical referent — the behavioural residue to any sociological construct — which is the cutting ground of legal research. Ideological artifact is turned into social fact only when normative discourse is sifted out of the realm of scientific inquiry. Third, following Weber (1966), Black insists that a social problem, "once selected . . . should be pursued non-electically" (1972, 102). That is, value judgments, the election of preferred lines of research and policy, have no purchase in sociology.

The roots of Black's general theory of law lie in a wedding of two apparently discordant traditions: first, the rational/positive school of grand social theory, and second, the American legal realism of Holmes and Llewellyn. The rational/positive approach seeks to take ideographic vagary — the error term of human choice — out of the construction of pure theory. In abstracting one's postulates to the highest possible level of generalizability, the theorist seeks to divorce, in Parsons' words, social structure from social action. In order to contruct a theory of deviance and control which applies to the entire range of social and historical conditions, motivation and intent are treated as constants, while choice and discretion and unexplained variances external to the equation.

> A pure sociology of law does not study humans in the usual sense. It studies law as a system of behavior. Taken in this sense, law feels nothing. It has no joy or sorrow or wonderment. Scientifically conceived as a social reality in its own right, law is no more human than a molecular structure. It has no nationality, no mind, and no ends proper to its nature. (Black 1972, 105).

Black's theory rests on the assumption that general, discernible *laws* exist, which enable the prediction of the quantity of law. The sociology of law and deviance is a scientific enterprise, from which quantity rather than quality is the end product. There is no fundamental distinction between the conduct of physical sciences, and the kind of sociology that Black proposes. Social institutions are external to individuals, whether deviants or law enforcers. Since sociological knowledge cannot penetrate to the inner workings or purposes of law generation and deviance production, it must be restricted to the mapping of the general patterns of objective social control.

This is a rationalist approach to the study of law, which, according to Unger:

> . . . starts with the selection of a few general premises about human nature, chosen for the explanatory power of the conclusions they make possible

rather than for their descriptive accuracy. From these postulates it draws a growing string of consequences by a continual process of logical deduction and conceptual refinement, as well as by the introduction at many points along the way of certain empirical assumptions about nature and society. Rationalist social science aspires to become a system of propositions whose interdependencies are governed by precise logical notions of entailment, consistency, and contradiction. (Unger 1976, 11).

Like the positivist tradition in criminology (see Taylor et al. 1973, 10–30), a rational legal theory seeks to denormatize, to eclipse ideology from the study of jurisprudence. Only analysis freed from values could reveal social causes and legal effects. This position is supremely naturalistic and claims mastery over the laws which dictate social order. This is a modern perspective seeking to transcend the moral mess in which mundane human values and commitments are played out; "modernity appears not only as the birth place of but also the graveyard of ideologies; while ushering in a multitude of ideological blueprints, the modern age also made the "end of ideology" a permanent item on its agenda" (Dallmayr 1977, 5). Positive human science provides the conceptual framework for a value-free sociology of law:

> Implicit in positivist science is a critique of ideology as a source of rational knowledge. Ideology, but its attachment to value and programmatic action, is necessarily less rational than science. Detached from value and action, science can more rationally master the laws of human nature. Thus ideology is destroyed or at least severely limited by its own commitment to rationality (Pfohl 1980, 22).

Like Popper (1957), Black adopts a universal paradigm for social science, which attacks the assumptions of historicism, i.e., that the social fact is historically produced and contingent. The theorists can construct an objectivist language which breaks roots with the peculiaristic social and normative systems in which theory is born. "[T]he rationalist strategy is not only antihistoricist, it is also antinormative. This methodological program starts with the assumption that social phenomena can be explained without reference to the understanding social actors have of these social facts" (Eder 1977, 134).

At the same time, the tenets of legal realism form a second theme imported into Black's theory of law. Legal realism advances the notion that legal scripture and normative statements are meaningless to an understanding of the "living law". As Holmes wrote:

> The life of the law has not been logic; it has been experience. The felt necessities of the time, the prevalent moral and political theories, institu-

tions of public policy, avowed or unconscious, even the prejudices which judges share with their fellow men have had a good deal more to do than the syllogism in determining the rules by which men should be governed. (1881, 1)

Legal realism demands a stripping away of jurisprudential speculation, and an acute awareness by the theorist that law exists in behaviour rather than in prescription. "Before rules, were facts; in the beginning was not a Word, but a Doing" (Llewellyn 1931, 1222). This paradigm provides a target for Black's theory of law. Law exists not in the rulings of appeals court justices or the pages of governmental legislation or the policies of police, courts, penitentiaries and other judicial agencies, but rather in the application of and subjection to governmental social control in real life contexts. Coupled with the tradition of rationalist/positivist social science, legal realism constituted the conceptual framework within which Black's theory was spawned. It is to the structure of the theory itself that the discussion now turns.

THE THEORY

In *The Behaviour of Law*, Black's central proposition is that law must quantitatively be treated as a dependent variable, which recedes and expands in lockstep with the stratification, morphology, organization, culture, and social control of a given societal context. Law has a life, literally, as it traverses social time and space. Every governmental sanctioning activity is an instance of more law; every retraction of governmental control entails less law.

> Law is a quantitative variable. It increases and decreases, and one setting has more than another. It is possible to measure the quantity of law in many ways. A complaint to a legal official, for example, is more law than no complaint ... A trial or other hearing is itself an increase of law, and some outcomes are more law than others: a decision on behalf of the plaintiff is more law than a decision on behalf of the defendent, and conviction is more law than acquittal ... More generally, the quantity of law is known by the number and scope of prohibitions, obligations and other standards to which people are subject and by the rate of legislation, litigation, and adjudication (1976, 3).

Stratification predicts the quantity of law. Hierarchically arranged societies experience more law than egalitarian groups. For Black's purpose, stratification is "the vertical aspect of social life ... It is any uneven distribution of the material conditions of existence . . . and the means by which these are produced (Ibid, 11). Law varies directly with (1) the mean vertical distance between socioeconomic groups, (2) the degree of vertical segmentation, (3) asymmetry in the distribution of resources, and (4) social forces which militate against mobility. Moreover, law varies across vertical space. Economically high-ranking groups experience more law than the dispossessed. Finally, law has vectorlike qualities; every incidence of law embodies an origin, a direction, and a point of application. In relation to stratification, downward law is greater than upward law; in an encounter between two differentially ranking individuals or groups, the lower-ranking party is more likely to be the target of legal forces. The greater the vertical distance between two parties, the more downward law will be applied.

Law also varies in relation to morphology, "the horizontal aspect of social life, the distribution of people in relation to one another, including their division of labor, networks of interaction, intimacy, and integration" (Ibid, 37). The degree of functional specialization — or differentiation — explains law. The relationship between law and differentiation is curvilinear; both undifferentiated and symbiotic societies experience less law than intermediate groups. In addition, law is distributed according to radial location; highly integrated individuals and groups have more law than those on the periphery. Law can be centrifugal (radiating from the centre to the periphery) or centripetal (from the periphery to the centre); there is more centrifugal than centripetal law.

Law can be predicted by culture, which Black defines as "the symbolic aspect of social life, including expressions of what is true, good, and beautiful . . . It . . . includes ideas about the nature of reality . . . conceptions of what ought to be, what is right and wrong, proper and improper . . . (and) finally . . . culture includes aesthetic life of all sorts" (Ibid, 16). Like law, culture has an objective and quantitative existence independent of human value, experience and motivation. The amount of culture in a society, or a group within a society, predicts the amount of law. Culturally rich groups mobilize more law; law moves more from positions of dense culture to positions of low culture, than the reverse. The cultural distance between two parties predicts the amount of law which flows between them. Furthermore, culture can be defined in terms of conventionality; conventionals experience more law than unconventionals. More law flows proportionately from conventionality to unconventionality; the imbalance of the flow increases with the radial distance between the applier and the target of governmental social control. Finally, social settings differ in the content of their culture; law varies in a curvilinear fashion with cultural distance, "law is less likely at the extremes, where there is little or no cultural diversity, and also where it is great" (Ibid, 74). Law, therefore, can be predicted by observing the amount, the frequency (conventionality), and the diversity in culture.

The quantity of law varies directly with the quantity of organization in a society, defined as "the corporate aspect of social life, the capacity for collective action" (Ibid, 85). More law flows from high to low organization, than in the opposite direction. All other things equal, the likelihood of being subject to governmental social control varies inversely with the centralization, or bureaucratization, or incorporation of one's group.

An inverse relation obtains between law and other forms of social control. Nongovernmental social control measures the respectability of the members of social groupings, and includes "etiquette, custom, ethics, bureaucracy, and the treatment of mental illness" (Ibid, 105). Settings with less informal regulation require the superimposition of law to govern human interaction. Individuals and groups possess more or less respectability ("the more social control, the less respectability" (Ibid, 111); predictably, law varies directly, and other social control inversely, with respectability. Law is greater in a direction toward *less* respectability, and as the normative distance increases between law-mobilizing respectables and law-receiving nonrespectables, the quantity of law is augmented.

Black defines anarchy as "social life without law, that is, without governmental social control. It is a quantitative variable, the inverse of law" (Ibid, 123). Being the absence of law, anarchy is predicted by those variables which predict law. Anarchy exists in two forms: first, communal anarchy ("where people are equal, symbiotic, intimate, homogeneous, and unorganized" (Ibid, 125)), and second, situation anarchy ("where people are again equal and unorganized, but where they are independent of one another instead of symbiotic, complete strangers instead of intimates, and heterogeneous instead of homogeneous" (Ibid, 125)). Black predicts that the historical increase in law will reverse, that anarchy will return, as social life "evolve(s) into something new, neither communal nor situational as before, but a synthesis of the two" (Ibid, 132). The evolution of societal structures will engineer the "demise of law" (Turk 1979).

> To some degree, anarchy will return. But it will be a new anarchy, neither communal nor situational, and yet both at once. If these trends continue, then, law will decrease. It might even disappear (Black 1976, 137).

A CRITIQUE

The validity of sociolegal theory must rest ultimately *not* on its eloquence, but on its utility, its explanatory value, and its goodness-of-fit with conditions in the empirical universe. Black's *Behavior of Law* erects a propositional structure on a number of theoretical and epistemological underpinnings which may be unable to survive rigorous critique.

Consider the relationship between quantity and quality of law. In a purely Durkheimian formulation, Black views law as social fact, as matter, which expands and contracts, accumulates and disperses, according to its placement within a matrix of social conditions. Yet, at the same time, he suggests that governmental social control can vary qualitatively, aggregating into discrete legal forms. Depending on structural conditions, law may be conciliatory, therapeutic, compensatory, or penal. While Black suggests that macrosociological conditions which foster *more* law also generate law more likely to be *penal*, nowhere is this relationship adequately exploited. Nor is it clear that Black's allowance for "styles of law" (1976, 4) does not defeat his efforts at maintaining a coherent and consistant system of operational postulates. "While it is true in principle that differences normally thought of as qualitative can be turned, at the discretion of the analyst, into quantitative ones and vice versa, there are problems in such transformation which must be solved if one wants to avoid severe loss of information, gross conceptual simplification, and distortion of the original questions (Rueschemeyer 1978, 1041). Black, by failing to elaborate on his notion of "legal style", leaves the reader without a model for converting style into quantity. How much corporate law is equal to how many debtor-creditor cases? Is one therapeutic civil commitment comparable to one sentence of imprisonment in a criminal court? In the tradition of grand theory, Black, by attempting to extrapolate beyond the perimeters of any one form of law — civil or criminal, public or private, substantive or procedural — has usurped the comparative power of his postulates.

All sociological theory — even macrolevel, positive theory — must retain some conception of human nature. By abstracting to a level of generalization beyond human value or intent, Black introduces predictability and refinement, while sacrificing what could be gained by microanalysis. As Stinchcombe writes, "Once in a while something that is all muddy with people's intentions in it becomes remarkably clear and orderly when they are taken out. Usually, though, productive social theories simplify and aggregate intentions, rather than eliminate them from the theory altogether" (1977, 130). There is, in Black's theory, an inconsistency in insisting that all institutional life is behaviour, while denying the theoretical relevance of the behaviour of individual human agents who make that institutional existence possible.

At the level of theoretical structure, several problems can be raised. For example, many of Black's propositions might be dismissed as tautological (Eder 1977, 137). Consider, for example, the proposition "law varies directly with organization." Law is defined as governmental social control; government is a form of organization; under Black's definitions, there is no conveivable logical instance in which a governed society could produce less law than an acephalous society; the proposition, for all intents, is untestable. As Michaels writes: "In stating that law is governmental social control and no law is anarchy, Black has invented a simple tautology, a dichotomous system of classification, but not a theory. Everything becomes true by definition" (1978, 11).

This problem can be expanded to the issue of operationalizing the quantity of law itself, particularly in its relation to other forms of social control. Recall that Black writes "law varies inversely with other forms of social control" (1976, 107). One might conceive how this could be measured cross-sectionally, or on a cross-jurisdictional basis. However, when expressed in longitudinal or historical terms, the relationship becomes obscured. It is logically impossible, in Black's theoretical structure, for *both* law *and* other forms of control to expand in lockstep. Yet it is clear that the posited inverse relationship does not always hold (see Cohen 1979; Donzelot 1979; Foucault 1977); Black is simply in error here. Moreover, it is not clear what is meant operationally by "quantity of law". "In claiming an evolutionary increase in law . . . does he mean an absolute increase in law, a per capita increase in law, or an increase in the proportion of types of behaviour that is subject to law?" (Sherman 1978, 14).

Like many theories (see Black, 1969), the theory of law is subject to the fallacy of *ceteris paribus*. To each proposition concerning a relationship between structure and law, is addended an implicit "all other thing being equal". Of course, in the world of "living law", all other things are very *un*equal. Black has constructed a bivariate theory in a multivariate causal universe. The dynamic interactions among independent macrolevel variables are left unexplored. Black is like a student exposed to an introductory statistics course who ecstatically runs dozens of one-way cross-tabulations to the chagrin of his instructor who is more learned in the ways of partial correlation and statistical control. There are undoubtedly a few higher-order propositions which would subsume most of the individual relationships suggested by Black.

In examining the relative weight of different independent variables under different conditions, some would increase in explanatory power, some would be attenuated, some would disappear altogether when controls were introduced. For example, one might hypothesize that both integration and conventionality would recede significantly as legal indicators, when stratification was controlled for. While at an abstract level the variables may appear discrete, there is surely an "empirical overlapping of some of the concepts" (Sherman 1978, 14).

Equally problematic is the contingent nature of law avowed by Black. The "black box" approach in explaining law, as argued by the jurisprudential sociologists, ignores the role of law in social engineering, as an independent variable, or at least the feedback mechanisms which characterize a *reflexive* rather than unilaterally causal relationship between social structure and law. To limit one's theory to a statement such as "X causes law to increase at time A" ignores the possible effect of that same law on X at time A–1. If we are to follow Black (1969) the establishment of causality is an empirical impossibility, and must be restricted to armchair theoreticians. Moreover, not only the causal contingencies of an increase in law, but also the increase itself, becomes problematic when empirically operationalized. As Sherman (1978) suggests, complex, and sometimes inverse relations may prevail between prescription, mobilization, and disposition of law. Any theory purporting to account for increases and declines in the quantity of law, must allow for the fact that law is internally partitioned, and that certain variables may predict only certain levels of legal construction and enactment.

Possibly most crucial is the lack of a systematic account of the relationship between social control and deviance. Implicitly, if not at a manifest level, Black's book is as much a theory of deviance as a theory of law. Black argues that his positive conception of law is a more scientific substitute for deviance theories which rely on the motivation, values, cognition, and conduct of "the deprived, the marginal, the subcultural, and the "labeled" (Sherman 1978, 14). Black's theory of deviance is strongly phrased. If law is contingent on stratification, morphology, and other structural variables, then deviance is contingent upon law; in fact, deviant behaviour is defined simply as that conduct to which law is applied. "The quantity of social control also defines the rate of deviant behaviour" (Black 1976, 9). Once again, Black's emphatic unicausality becomes troublesome. The quantity of law may also be contingent upon the amount of deviance; one need not renounce one's critical perspective to make this assertion. Moreover, the hypothesis that law and deviance flow in opposite directions may have exceptions.

What Quinney (1979) terms "crimes of domination" describe instances where the application of law is in itself deviant, where criminality and social control are monodirectional.

The credibility and impact of the theory of law rest directly on derivative empirical research. Black's postulates were fashioned in a format which would supposedly facilitate operationalization. To date, research based upon the theory has been equivocal in its support for Black. Chan (1980), in a study of 325 juveniles in a suburban Canadian setting, conducted a loglinear analysis to predict whether contacts with police would result in caution or charge. Vertical location was operationalized by socio-economic status, respectability by prior police record, conventionality by demeanour, and organization by victim type. In support of Black, Chan found that the actual conduct of the juvenile (i.e., seriousness of offence) was not an important predictor of outcome. On the other hand, socio-economic status, prior record and demeanour were all included in the model which provided the best hierarchical fit to police reaction (defining the quantity of law applied to the offender).

Gottfredson and Hindelang (1979a) were less supportive of Black. Utilizing National Crime Survey victim data in the United States, the study's criterion for the quantity of law was whether the victim reported an offence. The Gottfredson and Hindelang findings are summarized below.

1. Stratification (victim's rank) was not correlated with reporting.
2. Morphology, measured by place size (city/town/rural) failed to support Black; integration, measured by marriage, was related to reporting; measured by employment, it failed to correlate.
3. Culture (educational level) has a weak positive correlation with reporting.
4. Black is supported regarding organization; organizations report more victimizations proportionately than individuals.
5. Other social control (measured by urban/suburban/rural setting): reporting behaviour is homogeneous across all levels of urbanization refuting Black.

Gottfredson and Hindelang found that the seriousness of the offence, as gauged by the Sellin-Wolfgang scale (1964) was a more consistent predictor of the "quantity of law" than the postulates of Black's theory. In response, Black (1979) writes that the victimization survey employed by Gottfredson and Hindelang embodied an inadequate formulation of the dependent variable; in asking respondents to enumerate "crimes" to which they have been subjected, the survey builds an evaluative (read: "normative") component into the research. The victimization survey neglects the original conceptualization of an incident as crime; this is one element in the processual quantification of law in any given case.

> (Gottfredson and Hindelang's) study . . . shows only what the labels predict, not what predicts the labels. It shows only whether people called the police when they considered an incident worthy of police attention, not whether some incidents were more or less likely to be considered worthy of this attention in the first place. (Black 1979, 21).

Black's response to Gottfredson and Hindelang raises a dilemma central to the operationalization of the theory's propositions. The mobilization of law is a sequential, longitudinal process, comprising a series of discretionary decisions rendered by official actors at various levels in the legal process (see Chambliss and Seidman 1971). In gauging the quantity of law applied to an individual or group in any legal context, there are two options: (1) the "proximally conditional" model (Gottfredson and Hindelang 1979b, 28), i.e., how much additional law is experienced at STAGE X, given a measurable amount of law at STAGE X–1?, and (2) the "only initially conditional" model (1979b, 29), i.e., how much law has been applied *altogether*, up to and including STAGE X? It is clear that a general theory of law would employ the second model; the dependent variables in a macrosociological equation must represent the *totality* of law encountered by an individual or group in an identifiable context. But at present, Black's theory can only be applied as "proximally contingent"; the relative increase in law can be compared only for individuals and groups at the same stage in the process. Only by introducing *evaluations* of legal impact can different kinds of law be compared. How much civil litigation is equal to how much probation? Is denial of bail more law than revocation of parole? Because of their more wide-ranging ramifications, are decisions made early in the process more productive of law than those made once the individual's legal fate has, to a degree, been determined? The theory of law, at its present point of development, cannot resolve these issues. The ephemeral nature of the dependent variable — at the same time that a claim to radical objectivity is maintained — ultimately defeats the theoretical purity of Black's propositions.

Braithwaite and Biles (1980) support these contentions through the use of Australian victimized data. Proportion of reported victimizations was established as the criterion variable in this study. A range of independent variables — including city size, victim income, education, mobility, victim-offender relationship, etc. — were disaggregated across the criterion, with similarly equivocal results. Braithwaite and Biles regard such research as, as best, a limited and cross-sectional approach to longitudinal theory. "These are only very partial tests of a theory meant to apply to many other domains. The theory is relevant to the social construction of the event as crime which occurs prior to a decision about reporting to the police, to a number of stages of processing through the criminal justice system which are subsequent to reporting to the police, and to an infinitely wider range of justifiable types of conduct than the eight which are the subject of this paper and the four which are the subjects of Gottfredson and Hindelang's paper (Ibid, 337). Myers' work in Indiana (1980) has supplied further empirical disconfirmation of Black's general postulates. Myers incorporates a multiple regression analysis to determine the relative weight of Black's indicators, on a composite index for quantity of criminal law visited upon accused felons in the criminal courts. As with Gottfredson and Hindelang (1979), Chan (1980), and Braithwaite and Biles (1980), the theory of law achieves only circumscribed verification. On three barometers — validity, predictive power, and generality — Myers disputes the applicability of Black's theory for sociolegal inquiry. The dilemma resides most particularly in the antireductionistic nature of the theory. By positing a theory which envelops *all* variants of social control, and *all* contingencies for state and customary response to deviance, Black has inadvertently forestalled the potential for researching concrete instances of that control. More critically, he has rendered such work irrelevant, by abstracting and elongating the notion of law, to a strataspheric position unmuddied by the error terms of discretion, human agency and judicious, idiosyncratic choice.

CONCLUSION: SOCIAL AND THEORETICAL STRUCTURALISM

Black's theory of law is an impressive attempt at a synthesis of legal scholarship. In the grandest tradition of grand theory, Black has erected an imposing monument to structural jurisprudence. The monolithic flavour of the theory of law touches on one of the most powerful controversies in sociological thought. Theorists have a long history of ambivalence toward the structural paradigm. From Parsons on the right to Althusser on the left, structural theorists have exercised a tendency to train a wide-angle lens on social institutions such as law. In their wake, human actors become interchangeable, intentions dissipate, consciousness is somehow rendered epiphenomenal, materialist explanations wither away. Consciousness itself is structuralized, becoming in the process "epistemologically inert" (Thompson 1978, 18).

Needless to say, this formulation has much appeal to rationalist studies in the sociology of law. If legal and social forms can be neatly crystallized into rarified conceptual units, one might successfully circumnavigate the irritating unpredictability of human agents on the front lines of legal mechanisms. In turn, the problem of values in legal analysis conveniently disappears, since "ideological state apparatuses" (Althusser 1971) are treated as constants and, therefore, have no role to play in accounting for variance in either legal systems or their modes of arbitration. Moreover, law can be pencilled in at the extreme right end of the path diagram. That is, in a structuralist model, law is a contingent, acted upon, but maintaining no independent energy of its own creation. There is no warrant here for any variety of dialectical analysis. Nor can structuralists entertain the notion that law may be mobilized to affect social structure, that law may both reform and in turn be subject to reform.

What remains from Black's theory is an arid, immutable portrayal of legal structure, sociological methodology, and the study of jurisprudence. In a very real sense, *The Behavior of Law* and its sequels (Black 1983a, 1983b) if valid, would function to foreclose the most fruitful line of investigation available to students of law. Legal sociologists are primarily in the business of tracking the relationship among three phenomena: (1) social forces and institutions, (2) the legal and judicial apparatus, (3) concrete decision making and problem solving behaviour of agents, officials, deviants, and disputants. A structural legal theory, such as Black's, erases perforce a third of this theoretical model. Most ironically, a sociology of law founded on Black's work would, to a large extent, define sociologists out of the judicial terrain. It is the legal task of the sociologist to identify the location at which constraint meets license (Giddens 1976, 161), to interrogate the interaction between rule of law and rulings of officials. When the latter are rendered theoretically superfluous, sociolegal investigation can be left to lawyers, demographers and statisticians. Black's is a sociology of law which has abdicated its sociology. To quote E.P. Thompson paraphrasing Dickens:

> As if an astronomical observatory should be made without any windows, and the astronomer within should arrange the starry universe solely by pen, ink and paper, so [Professor Black], in his observatory . . . had no need to cast an eye upon the teeming myriads of human beings around him, but could settle all their destinies on a slate . . . (Thompson 1978, 192).

References

Althusser, L. 1971. *Lenin and philosophy.* London: New Left Books.

Balbus, I.D. 1977. Commodity form and legal form: an essay on the "relative autonomy" of the law. *Law and Society Review* 11: 571–588.

Black, D.J. 1972. The boundaries of legal sociology. *Yale Law Journal* 1: 1086–1100.

———. 1976. *The behavior of law.* New York: Academic.

———. 1979. Common sense in the sociology of law. *American Sociological Review* 44: 18–27.

———. 1983a. Crime as social control. *American Sociological Review* 48, 1 (February): 34–45.

———. 1983b. *Toward a general theory of social control.* New York: Academic.

Blalock, H.M. 1969. *Theory construction: From verbal to mathematical formulations.* Englewood Cliffs, N.J.: Prentice-Hall.

Braithwaite, J. and D. Biles. 1970. Empirical verification and Black's *The Behavior of Law. American Sociological Review* 45, 2 (April): 334–337.

Chambliss, W. and R. Seidman. 1971. *Law, order and power.* London: Addison-Wesley.

Chan, J. 1970. A multivariate analysis of the behavior of law. Presented at the Annual Meeting of the American Sociological Association. New York.

Cohen, S. 1979. The punitive city: notes on the dispersal of social control. *Contemporary Crises* 3: 339–363.

Dallmayr, F. 1977. Ideology, marxism and phenomenology. Presented at Symposium on Sociology and Ideology. Purdue University.

Donzelot, J. 1979. *The policing of families.* New York: Random House.

Eder, K. 1977. Rationalist and normative approaches to the sociological study of law. *Law and Society Review* 12: 133–144.

Feeey, M.M. 1976. The concept of laws in social science: a critique and notes on an expanded view. *Law and Society Review* 10: 497–523.

Foucault, M. 1977. *Discipline and punish: The birth of the prison.* New York: Pantheon.

Giddens, A. 1976. *New rules of sociological method: A Positive critique of interpretrative sociology.* London: Hutchinson.

Gottfredson, M.R. and M.J. Hindelang. 1979a. A study of The Behavior of Law. *American Sociological Review* 44: 3–18.

———. 1979b. Theory and research in the sociology of law. *American Sociological Review* 44: 27–37.

Holmes, O.W. 1881. *The common law.* Boston: Little, Brown and Company.

Koch, K.E. 1977. A general theory of law. Review of D.J. Black, *The behavior of law. Science* 197: 149–150.

Llewellyn, K. 1931. Some realism about realism — responding to Dean Pound. *Harvard Law Review* 1222.

Michaels, P. 1978. Review. Donald Black, *The behavior of law. Contemporary Sociology* 7: 10–11.

Myers, M.A. 1980. Predicting the behavior of law: a test of two models. *Law and Society Review* 14, 4 (Summer): 835–858.

Nader, L. 1976. Introduction, to D.J. Black *The behavior of law.* New York: Academic.

Nonet, P. 1976. For jurisprudential sociology. *Law and Society Review* 10: 525–545.

Pfohl, S. 1980. Ideology and criminological theory: criminalizing the body, mind, society and state. Presented at Meetings of the North Central Sociological Association. Dayton, Ohio.

Popper, K. 1957. *The poverty of historicism.* Boston: Beacon Press.

Quinney, R. 1972. The ideology of law: notes for a radical alternative to legal oppression. *Issues in Criminology* 7: 1–35.

_____. 1979. *Class, state and crime.* New York: McKay, 2d edition.

Rrueschemeyer, d. 1978. Review. Donald Black, *The behavior of law. American Journal of Sociology* 83: 1040–1042.

Schutz, A. 1967. *The phenomenology of the social world.* Chicago: Northwestern University Press.

Sellin, T. and M. Wolfgang. 1964. *The measurement of delinquency.* New York: Wiley.

Selznick, P. 1968. The sociology of law. *International Encyclopedia of the Social Sciences* 9:50.

Sherman, L.W. 1978. Review. Donald Black, *The behavior of law. Contemporary Sociology* 7: 11–15.

Stinchcombe, A.L. 1977. Review. Lawrence M. Friedman, *The legal system.* Donald Black, *The behavior of law. Law and Society Review* 12: 129–131.

Taylor, I., P. Walton and J. Young. 1973. *The new criminology.* London: Routledge and Kegan Paul.

Thompson, E.P. 1978. *The poverty of theory and other essays.* London: Monthly Review Press.

Turk, A.T. 1979. Conceptions of the demise of law. In P.J. Brantingham and J.M. Kress (Eds.), *Structure, law and power: Essays in the sociology of law.* Beverly Hills: Sage.

Unger, R.M. 1976. *Law in modern society.* New York: Free Press.

Weber, M. 1966. *The theory of social economic organization.* New York: Free Press.

Chapter 20

Deterrence Theory: A Reconceptualization

*Stephen D. Webb**

The Deterrence model is drawn from the so-called "classical school" of criminology in which man was seen as fundamentally hedonistic and therefore deterrable from crime only by swift, sure, and severe punishment. Recent investigations have focused on these factors and endeavoured to determine if in fact deviance is inversely related to the celerity, certainty, or severity of punishment.

While the model is exceptionally simple, the evidence to date is ambiguous and inconsistent. It is proposed that the fault lies, in part, with both the simplicity of the model and the methods used to test it. First, virtually all recent research has focused on general rather than specific deterrence, and second, the deterrence doctrine has been examined largely from a social rather than a psychological perspective. Yet as Erickson, Gibbs and Jensen have recently pointed out, the deterrence doctrine is in fact a psychological theory. Thus, tests of the theory using social variables, such as arrest or incarceration rates, are most likely inappropriate. Rather, attention should focus on perceptual variables such as perceived risk.

Similarly, recent examinations of the deterrence model have been concerned largely with the pressure to stop or deter offending through various sanctions. There has been a general assumption that the pressure to commit an offense is fairly constant. Clearly it is necessary to be more sensitive to the fact that different offenders experience vastly differential pressures to offend

* Department of Sociology, University of Victoria. Revised version of a paper in *The Canadian Journal of Criminology*, 22 January 1980.

and *ipso facto* are differentially deterrable. Finally the model assumes a "rational man", and the fact that many offenses are the result of irrational and unintentional acts is largely ignored.

Rational choice processes, based on a calculation of relative pleasure or pain, are far too simple to provide an adequate explanation of behaviour. Criminal behaviour, like noncriminal behaviour, is more realistically viewed as a result of an individual's desires and needs relative to the groups to which he belongs or aspires, as well as his definition of the situation relative to a multitude of factors including opportunity, formal and informal sanctions and hedonistic considerations. As Schur has stated, "Concentration on hedonistic calculation does justice to neither the unconscious nor the situational and subcultural learning processes that may be involved in crime." Thus, with the usual conditions of certainty, severity and celerity of punishment, a number of additional factors specific both to the individual and the situational context must be considered before even a rudimentary prediction can be made regarding the differential deterrability of offenders.

MARGINAL GROUPS

A fundamental assumption implicit throughout the arguments presented here is that considerations of punishment or threat of punishment are generally inconsequential in preventing most of the population from engaging in serious criminal activites. What keeps most people law abiding are the prescriptions and proscriptions for conduct that are internalized in the socialization process — not the written law and its sanctions. Thus only the "inadequately" or "abnormally" socialized "individual fits the model of classical criminology and is deterred from expressing deviant impulses by a nice calculation of pleasures and punishments." This, of course, is impossible to document but it does point to the likelihood that most persons need not be deterred from serious criminal activities. In this regard, Zimring and Hawkins have developed the concept of marginal groups, i.e., the "would be" criminals, "a body of persons objectively on the margin of a particular form of criminal behaviour".[1] Deterrent threats and punishments are seen as relevant only to the criminal groups and those persons in the marginal category, whereas the remainder of the population will be relatively unaffected by legal deterrents and in this regard it is quite unrealistic to expect a holistic response by the general population to various deterrent measures.

> Clearly, the effectiveness of alternative sanction policies is likely to be determined by the response they evoke from the particular criminal and marginal groups concerned.

Unfortunately, this fact has been lost sight of in most recent research.

While it should be clear that a distinction can be made between the general law-abiding populace, on the one hand, and the marginal and criminal groups on the other, a further distinction should be made between the last two groups. To speak of deterrence seems to assume a specific level of commitment to legal or criminal norms which in turn is a function of the degree and kind of socialization experienced, coupled with "pressures" within the system. The individual's commitment, therefore, can vary widely depending upon the influence of these and other factors. Whether an individual violates a law usually will depend, then, upon whether he has internalized that law as a norm, whether he merely pays it deference or whether he is complying with different criminal standards. Of course, compliance may result from a conscious desire to comply because of some sort of moral influence, or it may result from a rational calculation of the hazards involved in noncompliance.

Thus, it seems useful to distinguish between the three groups: the law-abiding segment of the population to whom legal deterrents are largely inconsequential; the marginal group who are likely to be most sensitive to legal threats and punishments; and the criminal group who would likely fall somewhere between the other two groups in terms of their responsiveness to legal sanctions.[2]

OFFENDER MOTIVATION

The concepts of deterrence and punishment cannot exist in a vacuum; they are related to specific kinds of acts and the meaning these acts have for the individual. The motivation of the offender is crucial to understanding the deviant act, for s/he either complies with or violates the law depending, largely, upon his/her personal and situational motivations. It is likely, then, that a direct relationship exists between an offender's motivation to deviate and the differential influence of certain sanctions in deterring him, or his differential resistance to the deterrent threat of punishment.

Perhaps the most important distinction to be made in this regard is that between "expressive" and "instrumental" motivations to act and by extension, expressive and instrumental acts.

Instrumental motivation is a disposition to engage in behaviour in order to attain some specific goal, whereas expressive motivation is a disposition to engage in behaviour for the pleasure or gratification it provides, rather than as a means to an end. Furthermore, it has been argued that since instrumental acts are rationally motivated they may be responsive to certain deterrent measures. Expressive acts, on the other hand, being impulsive and less rational in nature, are unlikely to be responsive to legal sanctions.

This characterization of acts as either expressive or instrumental is somewhat oversimplified for it ignores certain acts which may be planned but are nevertheless nondeterrable. We believe a more useful distinction could be made between impulsive or spontaneous acts and compulsive acts in which the individual is irresistibly driven toward some irrational behaviour. In terms of the dichotomization of expressive and instrumental behaviour, compulsive acts do not fit neatly into either category for they may be both irrational and goal directed. For example, kleptomania or drug addiction are both conditions leading in many cases to compulsive criminal acts which are, at the time of the offense, virtually nondeterrable. On the other hand, compulsive and impulsive acts differ in that, over time, compulsive acts would tend to be more predictable and to some extent more amenable to prevention through intensive treatment of the offender. But if we retain our original emphasis on the calculative, rational type of behaviour which should be responsive to legal sanctions then behaviour which is either compulsive or impulsive in its motivation can be eliminated from consideration since by definition it is largely nondeterrable.

To summarize, deterrence through legal sanctions is relevant to only a limited segment of the population. Changes in the severity, certainty or celerity of punishments is largely inconsequential to both the law-abiding population and those offenders who may be characterized as impulsive or compulsive in their motivation to deviate. Only the instrumental offenders and that marginal group of potential offenders can be characterized as theoretically responsive to legal sanctions (see Table 20.1).

Table 20.1 Applicability of the Deterrence Model

Population Subgroup	Type of Act		
	Instrumental	Compulsive	Impulsive
Law-Abiding	No	No	No
Marginal	Yes	No	No
Criminal	Yes	No	No

The implications for deterrence research should be obvious. The effect of sanctions in achieving general deterrence cannot be measured using the general population. The effectiveness of deterrence policies can only be measured among instrumental and potential offenders. Yet, it should go without saying that these groups, even when contemplating or engaging in similar types of acts, will be differentially deterrable, depending upon a complex variety of personal, situational and perceptual factors.

DETERRENCE IN THEORY BUT NOT PRACTICE

Given the above problems, the inconsistencies of reported research seem quite understandable. What is required at this time is the development of a less simplistic model to deal with the deterrence question. If it can be accepted that only a limited segment of the population is affected by deterrence measures then our next task is to determine why those offenders who ar deterrable in theory are not deterred in practice. To achieve this goal, attention focuses first on the traditional factors of severity and certainty of punishment and second on selected extralegal factors which appear to have considerable salience for the deterrence issue. Finally a typology is constructed to examine types of offenses and their differential deterrability depending upon both legal and extralegal or behavioural dimensions.

TOWARD A TYPOLOGY OF DETERRENCE

In regard to the deterrability of any type of offense the first question which must be asked is whether the offense was impulsive or compulsive in nature. If the answer is affirmative to either then the act is essentially nondeterrable. These two criteria, then, constitute the first two categories of the vertical axis in Table 20.2. Murder, the first offense category on the horizontal axis, has been classified as impulsive but not compulsive. This, of course, is an oversimplification for some murders may be either compulsive or instrumental in motivation. Yet for the vast majority of cases, murder remains a largely spontaneous and impulsive act and it is the general rule rather than the exception that the technology is meant to highlight. Thus, in this case murder is classified as nondeterrable and characterizing the offense in terms of the other legal and extralegal factors becomes superfluous insofar as a deterrence theory is concerned.

Table 20.2 Types of Offenses and Legal and Extralegal Dimensions Influencing the Differential Deterrability of Offenders[1]

Legal & Extralegal Factors	Type of Criminal Act					
	Murder	Chronic Drunkeness	Prostitution	White Collar	Amateur Shoplifting	Organized Crime
Offender Motivation[2]						
Impulsive	Yes	No	No	No	No	No
Compulsive	No	Yes	No	No	No	No
Legal Sanctions						
Severity	High	Moderate	Low	Low	Low	Moderate
Certainty	High	High	Moderate	Low	Low	Low
Celerity	High	High	Low	Low	Low	Low
Other Extralegal conditions						
Criminal Self-image	Low	Low	Moderate	Low	Low	High
Criminal-life Organization	Low	High	High	Low	Low	High
Group Support	Low	High	High	Low/Moderate	Low	High
Differential Association	Low	High	High	Low	Low	High
Moral Commitment to the Law	Moderate/High	Moderate	Low	Moderate/High	Moderate	Low

[1] The table should be read as follows: In regard to murder, most offenders are impulsive but not compulsive; the legal sanctions are severe, and the risk and swiftness of punishment are high; the offender will not likely have a criminal self-image nor will his life be organized around his criminal offending; he will be unlikely to receive group support nor will he associate with other murders; and finally his moral committment to the law will be moderate to high.

[2] Where offender's motivation is either impulsive or compulsive the offense is nondeterrable. The legal sanctions can act to deter only those offenses where the extralegal conditions have low salience.

The second offense on the horizontal axis is chronic drunkenness and in this case is classified as largely compulsive. Thus this
type of deviant behaviour is unlikely to be significantly influenced
by legal sanctions and again the extralegal factors are inconsequential. But to the extent chronic drunkenness is not compulsive then the extralegal factors significantly complicate the
picture. The effect of these additional factors is perhaps better
viewed in regard to the third offense category, prostitution.

Prostitution and the remaining offense categories discussed
here are classified as neither impulsive or compulsive in motivation. Thus, theoretically at least, they should be responsive to legal
sanctions if the sanctions are certain and severe enough. But a
brief scan of the various offense categories suggests they differ
considerably in their responsiveness to deterrence measures. This
would appear to be the case even if each offense had identical
sanctions attached to it and if the risk for apprehension or conviction were also identical. If this is in fact the case then the deterrability of different types of acts must be determined by the
extralegal as well as the legal factors. An examination of these
factors would allow us to determine why many offenses which are
deterrable in theory are not deterred in practice.

Severity: Writing in the late eighteenth century, Bentham
argued that for an individual any act (when considered by itself)
had four determinants. These were the intensity, duration,
certainty or uncertainty, and propinquity of the pleasure or pain
associated with the act. The first two of the determinants are
what we now refer to as severity while propinquity is synonymous
with the celerity of punishment.

Often it has been argued that the best way to keep people law
abiding is through increasing the severity of penalties to the point
where no one would dare risk violation of the law. Such proposals,
of course, rest on the false assumption that it is possible to increase
punishment *ad infinitum*. Not only is this impossible, but extremely
severe penalties become a matter of moral justification. Traditional sentiments of justice, decency and compassion impose limits
on the punishments that will be tolerated by the populace. Thus,
while extremely severe punishments may theoretically provide
maximum deterrence they are not a feasible alternative, for
neither court nor jury would be likely to impose such sanctions.
Excessively severe penalties may also engender a general hostility
toward the legal institutions and as Andenaes points out,

> with general enmity toward the penal code, it will lose its force, and
> impunity will be the real consequence of the law's always threatening the
> most severe punishment.

These considerations aside, however, what is known about the effect of varying degrees of severity in deterring offenders or potential offenders? Because the model is inherently untestable, i.e., measuring suppressed and therefore unobservable acts, attention has focused on the differential incidence of offending or recidivism under differing standards of punishment. In regard to "specific" deterrence, the evidence is relatively consistent in showing that severity of punishment, whether measured through intensity or duration, has little or no effect in deterring criminals from further offenses. Indeed, incarceration may engender further and more serious offending through both labelling processes and the criminal skills and norms which may be learned in prison.

Studies of the relationships between severity and crime rates are inconsistent in their findings although most report little or no effect. At the individual level the evidence suggests that severity has an effect only when certainty of punishment is high. Overall, certainty of detection and punishment are generally accepted as having a greater deterrent impact than the relative severity of the punishment.

Certainty: Criminal behaviour is usually assumed to be rational and calculative and therefore prevented or acted out depending upon the perceived risk of apprehension and punishment on the part of the offender or potential offender. That is, the greater the risk of being caught and punished the lower the probability of law violation. The objective risks of detection, however, are immaterial for it is the risk as subjectively calculated by the offender that will most influence his subsequent behaviour.

Earlier research focused on objective risks and generally found a moderate relationship between it and various crime rates. More recent studies, however, have concentrated on subjectively perceived risks and the weight of opinion suggests it may have a deterrent effect, although a number of studies conclude its direct effects may be nil or specific to certain types of offenses.

It can hardly be accepted that there are standardized risks, objectively or subjectively, in law violation. Rather, the relative risk of being detected, apprehended and convicted, operates as a deterrent (if at all) depending upon the types of offense and the specific offender. Attempts to determine the effectiveness of certain sanctions are fruitless without reference to other variables. Deterrence is a highly relative concept and can be examined and interpreted only within a matrix of dependency upon other factors. This can be demonstrated most easily by examining the specific types of offenses in regard to the severity and certainty of their sanctions.

Looking at Table 20.2 we see that for murder, both the severity of legal penalties and the likelihood of their being applied are relatively high. Yet, as argued previously, for most murders this has little relevance since the acts are largely impulsive and the offender does not rationally consider the consequences of his actions. While the penalties are significantly lower for chronic drunkenness, because of the compulsive nature of the offense it is similarly nondeterrable by legal sanctions. Prostitution, however, presents a much different picture for it is theoretically deterrable. One reason it is not deterred to a great extent may be due to the fact that sentences are light and there is only moderate risk associated with the offense. Yet even when governments have attempted to increase both the severity and certainty of punishments for prostitution they have not been especially successful in eliminating the offense. Some might argue, however, that the penalties were simply not severe enough to attain a critical level for deterrence. This may be true enough but there is always the question of what the community will tolerate in regard to severe punishments. In the final analysis, we must assume that prostitution, like many other instrumentally motivated offenses, is not particularly responsive to legal sanctions at least at a level acceptable to the community.

What other dimensions, then, are important for deterrence and how might we distinguish different types of offenses in regard to them? The prospects for deterrence will vary with both the individual and situational context in which the offense is contemplated and a number of factors reflecting these dimensions have been postulated. These factors, arranged along the vertical axis of Table 20.2, provide a scheme for understanding why certain crimes differentially deterrable in theory are not deterred in practice. Following Gibbs we term these factors "extralegal conditions," in this case meaning conditions that may engender or foster crime in a manner independent of criminal sanctions. The remainder of the extralegal conditions to be dealt with here are drawn from a variety of sources although primary reliance has been on the criminal behaviour systems developed by Clinard and Quinney.

1. **Criminal self-image:** Indicates the degree to which the offender or potential offender conceives of himself as a criminal. To the extent the criminal self-concept exists it will be difficult to prevent that person from engaging in criminal acts.

2. **Criminal life organization:** Indicates the degree to which the person's life is organized around his offending behaviour. If this is high then, again, there are unlikely to be feasible alternatives for the person and it is likely he will remain as a career

offender regardless of the legal sanctions. "Habituation" is a closely related concept and is used by Gibbs to indicate a situation whereby law-abiding behaviour may become habitual (e.g., observing speed limits) and thereby act to prevent law violation. We would argue that the same concept can be used to explain some law violation, that is, habitual offending behaviour may be viewed as a condition generating further offending.

3. **Group support:** Refers to the degree to which the offender has the support of his reference group. Again, if the offender receives support and/or encouragement from significant others then his behaviour will be reinforced.

4. **Differential association:** If a person associates with others engaged in criminal behaviour, not only will his own offending be condoned but within that group he will likely learn the skills and rationalizations to support further criminal activities.

5. **Moral commitment:** The findings of recent research indicate that moral commitment to the law is an important variable which acts as a good predictor of offending behaviour as well as specifying the relationship between other extralegal factors and crime. To the extent a person has a high moral commitment to the law he will be less likely to engage in criminal behaviour regardless of the legal sanctions involved.

There are at least three other factors which do not fit neatly into the above scheme but which nevertheless might help explain why a person refrains from or engages in criminal actions independent of legal considerations. The first and most obvious of these is the **individual's knowledge of the law.** It is widely supposed that before there can be a legal deterrent a person must be aware that a threat exists. While there can be no deterrent effect if an individual has absolutely no knowledge of a law this is seldom the case, at least insofar as serious offenses are concerned. Further confounding the picture is the fact that those persons with the greatest knowledge of the law are often those already in conflict with it. For this group at least, it might be hypothesized that knowledge of the law varies directly with criminal behaviour.

The second condition refers to the **opportunity for crime commission and the ease with which it might be carried out.** Other things being equal, we might expect that persons confronted with an easy opportunity to engage in some criminal activity might do so whereas the person confronted with many obstacles would be more likely to refrain from the behaviour, or even never consider it in the first place. In this sense, ease and opportunity can actually engender the criminal response. This, of course, is the reasoning behind crime prevention programs such as environmental design or the "lock your car" type of messages.

The third factor is **social stigma and the labelling process.** Many persons may refrain from criminal activites, again independent of legal sanctions, because of the stigma attached to being identified as a criminal. In fact the anticipation of the stigma and social condemnation may act as the greatest deterrent for the so-called potential offenders. On the other hand, however, while many persons may "refrain from crime to avoid stigmatization, those who are punished may commit even more crimes because of stigmatization." This involves the labelling process and secondary deviation whereby persons labelled as criminal are forced to associate with others carrying the same stigma and over time come to identify themselves as criminal. Thus stigmatization must be viewed as an extralegal factor that may either prevent or generate crime independent of legal sanctions.

Categories of crime: At this point it seems useful to return to Table 20.2 and examine the types of crime in regard to the dimensions we have delineated above. Many different types of either crimes or criminals could be utilized in this typology. Clinard and Quinney used social rather than legal types of criminal behaviour and while many of other types are too broad for our purposes, we have retained their emphasis on criminal behaviour systems. The categories used here are not meant to be exhaustive of all types of criminal behaviour. Rather only a few types are presented for illustrative purposes.

In order to demonstrate how the typology is composed it might be helpful to examine a single crime type in regard to the legal and extralegal dimensions. Earlier we noted that prostitution was neither compulsive nor impulsive in its characteristic motivation, and therefore was theoretically deterrable. The severity and certainty of sanctions attached to the offense were then examined and it was argued that penalties are low and risk only moderate with harassment considered part of the job. It might be supposed that greater risk and stiffer penalties could deter some prostitution but the most important question focuses on why the behaviour is not more responsive to legal sanctions than it is. In other words, why is it that prostitution, like many other instrumental offenses cannot be greatly influenced by the law? The answer must reside in those extralegal factors of self image, group support, etc., suggested above.

The criminal self-image of the female prostitute is probably moderate for most but would certainly be strengthened by contact with law enforcement agencies. The prostitute's life is usually organized around her profession and she would receive significant support from other prostitutes, pimps and the members of other deviant subgroups, with whom she would associate. Thus in Table

20.2 prostitution would be classified as high on criminal-life organization, group support and differential organization while being classified as low on moral commitment. These factors, then, help us understand why even certain instrumental offenses are unlikely to be deterred by the criminal law. When illegal behaviour constitutes a way of life for a person or if there is strong group support for his activity and his moral commitment is low it is unlikely that the law will have a great impact on him. Thus if one wishes to deter or prevent a specific offense, attention must focus on these extralegal factors rather than the simple imposition of criminal sanctions. This, of course, is not an easy task for it is virtually impossible to alter such things as group support, self-image, commitment, etc., in order to achieve compliance. Indeed, it appears little can be done in these areas to alter offense patterns. Yet if we look across Table 20.2 to the category "amateur shop-lifting" we see that the salience of our extralegal factors is "low". In this case deterrence could probably be achieved by increasing the risks and penalties as well as decreasing the opportunities for the offense. But, again, such a legal response could be expected to have little impact on the category of "organized crime".

SUMMARY

In the final analysis, any consideration of differential deterrence must be based on the conclusion that it is the person's perception of the deviant act (or offending behaviour) as well as the situation in which it occurs and as it relates to him as an individual and as a member of certain groups, that will determine his attitudes and, therefore, his adherence to the legal proscriptive and prescriptive expectations of society. Those acts classified as impulsive or compulsive in motivation are simply not responsive to legal sanctions. And even for many instrumental offenses, deterrence or compliance is not determined by laws and sanctions; rather, it is the individual's perception of the act or behaviour and the situation in which it occurs which are the crucial variables in determining or understanding human action, whether criminal or noncriminal. Thus the legal system can have little effect in reducing many types of crimes unless it considers the situational motivation of the offender. And as Chambliss has pointed out, "Ironically, most of the criminal-legal effort is devoted to processing and sanctioning those persons least likely to be deterred by legal sanctions."

The typological scheme presented here provides a relatively simple theoretical model for understanding the differential deterrability of offenders and offenses. It is not meant to be exhaustive but rather is offered as an exploratory tool within which modifications and additions can easily be made. For the short run it may provide a scheme within which findings may also be classified and from which hypotheses may be generated. It may also provide a blueprint for policy although it more likely points to the essential normalcy of certain types of offending and their fundamental nondeterrability without extremely authoritarian legal and economic measures.

Notes

1. Not the least of these is the existence of alternatives. As Zimring has suggested, "When other means exist to satisfy the drives that lead to crime, the prospect for deterrence is brighter than when acceptable substitutes do not exist: the man who can either steal or work to eat is surely more responsive to legal threats than the man for whom stealing is the only way to eat" (Reference #27).
2. The possible utility of using the Clinard and Quinney typology as a framework for the examination of deterrence was originally suggested to the author by J. Kitay.

References

Andenaes, Johanes, 1952. General prevention — Illusion or reality. *Journal of Criminal Law, Criminology and Police Science* 43 (July):176–198.

Antunes, G. and L. Hunt. 1973. The impact of certainty and severity of punishment on levels of crime in American States. *Journal of Criminal Law and Criminology* 64(4):486–493.

Bentham, Jeremy. 1948. *A fragment on government and an introduction to the principles of morals and legislation.* Oxford: Basil Blackwell.

Chambliss, William J. 1967. Types of deviance and the effectiveness of legal sanctions. *Winsconsin Law Review* 67 (Summer):703–719.

Clinard, Marshall B. and Richard Quinney. 1967. *Criminal behaviour systems: A typology.* New York: Holt, Rinehart and Winston.

Erickson, Maynard L., Jack P. Gibbs and Gary F. Jensen. 1977. The deterrence doctrine and the perceived certainty of legal punishments. *American Sociological Review* 42 (April):305–317.

Geerkin, Michael and Walter R. Gove. 1977. Deterrence, overload and incapacitation: An empirical evaluation. *Social Forces* 56 (December):424–447.

Gibbons, Don C. 1975. Offender typologies — Two decades later. *British Journal of Criminology* 15 (April):140–156.

Gibbs, Jack P. 1975. *Crime, punishment and deterrence.* New York: Elsevier.

Grasmich, Harold G. and Steven D. McLaughlin. 1978. Deterrence and social control. *American Sociological Review* 43 (April):272–278.

Longshore, Douglas. 1977. Deterrence: The effects of moral commitment and anticipated punishment on criminal activity. Unpublished manuscript, 1977.

Morris, Norval. 1951. *The habitual offender*. Cambridge, Mass.: Harvard University Press.

Parsons, Talcott and Edward A. Shils. 1951. *Toward a general theory of action*. New York: Harper and Row.

Ross, H. 1976. The neutralization of severe penalties. *Law and Society Review* 10:340–410.

Schur, Edwin M. 1968. *Law and society*. New York: Random House.

Silberman, Matthew. 1976. Toward a theory of criminal deterrence. *American Sociological Review* 41 (June):442–461.

Steffensmeir, Darrell J. and Robert M. Terry (Eds.), 1975. *Examining deviance experimentally*. Port Washington: N.Y.: Alfred Pub. Co.

Teevan, James J., Jr. 1972. Deterrent effects of punishment: The Canadian case. In C.L. Boydell et al. (Eds.), *Deviant behaviour and societal reaction*. Toronto: Holt, Rinehart and Winston, 153–165.

———. 1976. Deterrent effects of punishment: Subjective measures continued. *Canadian Journal of Criminology and Correction* 18 (April):152–160.

Tittle, Charles R. and Charles H. Logan. 1973. Sanctions and deviance: Evidence and remaining questions. *Law and Society Review* 7 (Spring):371–392.

Toby, Jackson. 1964. Is punishment necessary? *Journal of Criminology, Criminal Law and Police Science* 55 (September):332–337.

Wilkens, Leslie T. 1966. Persistent offenders and preventive detention. *Journal of Criminology, Criminal Law and Police Science* 57 (September):312–317.

Zimring, Frank and Gordon Hawkins. 1968. Deterrence and marginal groups. *Journal of Research in Crime and Delinquency* 5 (2):100–114.

Zimring, Frank. 1971. *Perspectives on deterrence*. Rockville, Md.: National Institute of Mental Health.

Chapter 21

Class, Calculus and Crime: Some Realism About Rank and Order in Criminological Research

Robert J. Menzies*

Our primary aim is to discover how some social structures exert a definite pressure upon certain persons in the society to engage in non-conforming rather than conforming conduct. If we can locate groups particularly subject to such pressures, we would expect to find fairly high rates of deviant behavior in those groups, not because the human beings comprising them are compounded of distinctive biological tendencies but because they are responding normally to the social situation in which they find themselves. Our perspective is sociological (Robert K. Merton 1957, 147).

Today the onslaught continues — with five offences being recorded every minute. There is a vicious crime of violence — a murder, forcible rape, or assault to kill — every two and a half minutes; a robbery every five minutes; a burglary every twenty-eight seconds; and fifty-two automobiles are stolen every hour (J. Edgar Hoover 1969).

INTRODUCTION: WHY STATISTICIANS SHOULD NEVER TALK ABOUT CLASS

Sociologists of deviance and delinquency have long been enamoured with the study of the relationship between class and crime. The publication of Bonger's *Criminality and Economic Conditions* (1916) was

* Department of Criminology, Simon Fraser University.

the first in an extended corpus of works equating (and equivocating) the social economy with criminality. Of particular interest is the penchant among criminologists to generate quantitative formulae, yielding rigorous equations which purportedly delineate the proportion of criminal variance explained by social class (Akers 1964; Hirschi 1969; McDonald 1968; Short and Nye 1957), the intersection between cultures of poverty and areas of crime (Morris 1957; Shaw and McKay 1969; Wolfgang et al. 1972), and the criminogenic features of absolute and relative inequality (Clinard and Abbott 1973; Lewis 1976; Smith 1965). As McDonald (1976) has pointed out, class is a sociological indicator which is serviceable to both conflict and consensus theorists. The former incorporate the theme of class structure into accounts of the politicization of proletarian deviance (e.g., Gordon 1971; Inciardi 1980; Reasons 1974; Taylor et al. 1973, 1975), crimes of accommodation (Quinney 1977), and the inarticulate brutalization of lumpenproletarian surplus labour (Bonger 1916; Marx and Engels 1968). Consensus theorists integrate social class into systems which highlight conflict between normative and cultural structures (Cloward and Ohlin 1960; Cohen 1965; Merton 1957), social coincidence of defect and disenfranchisement (Banfield 1968; Ferri 1917; Lombroso 1871), and the salience of discernible crime-generative cultural/moral practices within lower-class culture (e.g., Eysenck 1970; Miller 1958; Trasler 1962).

Theoretical investment in the grounding of crime in the political economy is, therefore, well understood. What is less comforting is the discovery that the notion of social class is more a construct than an index. It is socially, culturally and morally mediated, it embodies both subjective and objective properties, and it is highly resistant to sophisticated operationalization. Importing conceptions from the classical theorists (e.g., Dahrendorf 1959; Gramsci 1970; Marx and Engels 1968; Schumpeter 1942; Weber 1966) is of questionable value, given the macroscale of thought and the historically specific character of class; even among more contemporary writers (Kolko 1962; Miliband 1969; Ollman 1971; Wright 1973), indicators of political and economic stratum tend to dissolve at the point of quantification. For criminologists, this rather bleak characterization of the area has been something less than paralyzing. Braithwaite (1981), for example, was able to locate 216 studies which included treatments of the relationship between "class" and crime.

It would be illusory — and adulatory to the extreme — to suggest that sociologists of crime have resolved the methodological problematics of class where their colleagues have failed. In fact, through an implicit definitional sleight of hand, researchers have been able to have their class and eat it too. According to Tittle et al. (1978), the emphasis, following the work of mainstream theorists (e.g., Laumann 1966; Nisbet 1959; Ossowski 1963; Rose 1958), has subtly shifted from class to stratum. While manifestly retaining a stated fidelity to the predictive power of social class, criminologists' cooptation of the more flexible economic registers of stratification has generated a spate of literature in the field over the past two decades. Class has been operationalized using such indices as "the percentage of the adult male population of the area who are in lower class occupations, the percentage unemployed, the percentage of welfare, the percentage below some poverty line, or some combination of these" (Braithwaite 1981, 36).

GETTING PAST THE REPORTS: AN INTRODUCTION TO THE DELINQUENCY NUMBER RACKET

Beyond the conceptual encumbrances referred to above, the social topography of class and crime is fraught with a litany of methodological and empirical concerns. Traditional reliance upon the proliferation of institutionally generated numbers has been accompanied by an aficionado's urge to reify the rates, to place self-evidentiary closure on what are in fact the products of social transaction of "praxiology" (Cicourel 1968, 27). In his consideration of the significance of crime rates, Sellin wrote three decades ago: "[t]he value of criminal statistics as a basis for measurement of criminality in geographic areas decreases as the procedures take us farther away from the offense itself" (1951–489). As is well documented, both the absolute quantity and the relative composition of deviance are rendered less meaningful as persons and information are circulated through the "deviance corridor" (Rubington and Weinberg 1973). The "social transformation of deviance" (Buckner 1970), or the "certification process" (Tepperman 1977) engineers a carnival mirror image of the phenomenon for criminality consumers.

As a technical implement of detection, patented by the academic community, the official statistic has seen better days. The assemblage and tabulation of "crimes known to the police" is akin to driving a thin straw into the vast reservoir of deviance which abounds somewhere beyond the constable's less-than-vigilant gaze. Crime rates are "produced" through the convergence of criminal event and official response (Black, 1970). "Official statistics have been shown to be unreliable indicators of crime in the population (e.g., Box 1971) and can best serve as measures of the behaviour of the organization which produces them (Kituse and Cicourel 1963), or as clues for further investigation" (West, W.G. 1979, 248–249). Literature on police discretion (e.g., Black and Reiss 1967; Goldman 1963; Hohenstein 1969; McEachern and Bauzer 1967; Piliavin and Briar 1964) have underscored the selective and telescopic reality of institutional control. Studies of reporting procedures have unearthed tales of thirteen-fold increases in reporting crime subsequent to administrative change (Reid 1976, 73). Organizational investment in predetermined numeric products (Zeisel 1963), political resolve for the manufacture of crime waves (Bell 1960), dark figures which are asymetrically open in the upper strata (Pearce 1976, 90–97), the obscurity of interaction among criminal, victim, and agent (Wheeler 1967), vagaries of definition (Hagan 1977, 34), and the technical ambiguities of base rates, demographic nuances, and jurisdiction-specific counting formulae (Hagan 1976, 69–70; Nettler 1978, 57–68) are all cited as corruptors of the reliability and validity of official crime rates. Morris and Hawkins suggest that "our present criminal statistics are an undefined sample of an artificial universe of heterogeneous elements" (1970, 34). The enormity of the error term has motivated researchers such as Beattie (1960) to renounce the use of crime statistics altogether.

As a corrective to the cavernous gap between the essence and appearance of official numerology, criminologists have succeeded in assembling an array of devices for shining light on the dark figure. Ethnographers (Becker 1963; Humphries 1970; McCord and McCord 1959; Miller 1967; Polsky 1967; West, W.G. 1979) have gained proximity to the phenomenon, sacrificing quantitative rigour for descriptive detail, and seeking to construct an appreciative (Matza 1964) account of the deviant enterprise. The use of "unofficial" sources of statistics has occasionally surfaced in the literature, for example in Cameron's (1964) study of boosters, snitches and five-fingered discounts.

Victimization studies, while circumscribed by expense and competence, have been efficacious in highlighting the ineluctable gap between the criminal event and its announcement. While the rank-ordering of incidence and prevalence, from victims' presentations, tends to parallel that of official registration, the absolute rates range wildly, and the disparities vary with the type of crime (Biderman et al. 1967; Ennis 1967). Explanation for the non-reporting of crime differs across studies, from failure by the public to mobilize official agents (Ennis 1967; Schneider 1975), to selective response by the police (Biderman et al. 1967). Small-scale studies in the Canadian context (Curtis 1970; Koenig 1976) report similar discrepancies and accounts.

468 DEVIANT DESIGNATIONS: CRIME, LAW AND DEVIANCE IN CANADA

The most animated excursion into the realm of the dark figure has been generated by the discovery of the self-report study. In the 1940s findings by Wallerstein and Lyle (1947) and Porterfield (1943) of the ability of delinquents to tell us what they do, ushered in a transformation in delinquency research that was almost Copernican in its dimensions. An avalanche of studies ensued, which comprised a number of variants on the main theme of scale construction and pencil sharpening. Debate raged over the methods appropriate for maximal memory eliciting, lie detection, neutralization of researcher bias and threat, relative efficacy of interview versus questionnaire, and perfection of robust reliability and validity checks. Summarized by Nettler (1978, 97), there have evolved six general methods of delivering self-reports to adolescents:

1. Asking people to complete anonymous questionnaires (Akers 1964; Christie et al. 1965; Dentler and Monroe 1961; Elmhorn 1965; McDonald 1968; Nye and Short 1957);
2. Asking people to complete anonymous questionnaires identified in a circuitous fashion and validated against later interviews or police records (Voss 1963);
3. Asking people to confess to criminal acts on signed questionnaires validated against police records (Hirschi 1969; McCandless et al. 1972);
4. Asking people to complete anonymous questionnaires validated against follow-up interviews and the threat of polygraph tests (Clark and Tifft 1966);
5. Interviewing respondents (Belson et al. 1970; Gold 1966; Reiss and Rhodes 1961; Waldo and Chiricos 1972); and
6. Interviewing respondents and validating their responses against official records (Erikson, 1971; Erickson and Empey 1963).

The attraction of the self-report resided in the ready availability of respondents, whether institutionalized or culled from the population-at-large. In addition, the comparability with official statistics reinforced the disreputable status of the latter among researchers. For example, Murphy et al. (1946) reported that less than 1.5 percent of law violations were reported to the police. The distinction between achieved status (measured by self-reports) and ascribed status (measured by official statistics) became a dominant theme, which was to have impact upon the development of early social reactions accounts of deviance-production (Becker 1963; Erikson 1966; Kitsuse 1962; Lemert 1951). As indicated by Reiss and Rhodes, "it is clear that there is no simple relation between ascribed social status and delinquency" (1961, 737).

At the same time, the promissory mission of victimization and self-report studies was scarcely impervious to methodological critique. Surveys of victims were beset by insoluble sampling difficulties, nonparticipation, selective participation, unbalanced interpretation, and memory lapse (Hagan 1977, 37–38; Skogan 1974). Self-report studies have been the object of critique directed at the same sources of internal invalidity, in addition to the questionability of external reliability, validity, generalizability, and inference. For example, Farrington (1973) discovered that one-fourth of admitters, upon further interrogation, later denied their delinquency. Gold concluded that 17 percent of his sample were "outright liars" (1966). In an attempt to evaluate the predictive power of his test, Farrington wrote "to correctly identify 24 future delinquents, it would be necessary to misidentify 53 future nondelinquents" (1973, 110). The generalizability of findings is often constrained by the unique properties of the sample (see Dentler and Monroe 1961; Voss 1966). Crucially, the distinction between "delinquent" and "nondelinquent" subsamples is generally an artifact of arbitrary cutting-points devised by the researcher (e.g., Chambliss and Nagasawa 1969). In fairness, nonetheless, Elliott and Ageton (1980, 96) suggest that "available research seems to support both the validity and reliability of the method" (see Clark and Tifft 1966; Dentler and Monroe 1961; Elliot and Voss 1974; Erickson and Empey 1963; Hirschi 1969; Nye and Short 1956).

In the following discussion of the relation between class and crime, we are inheriting, then, a compendium of inconsistency and complexity which at the least taxes credulity. As Quetelet asserted (1842), "the social mapping of delinquency is inseparable from the tools of the cartographer." Under conditions of doubt, the most productive methodological route entails harnessing the full range of available implements, delivering at least an approximation of a Popperian unity of methods to the social problem. As well — and this is critical — the assumptions and tools of the researcher should be collapsed back into the range of investigation: alternative methods and resources should be rendered problematic dependent variables (Cicourel 1968; Douglas 1967). Discrepancies in the demarcation of a social condition or relation which are elicited by variable methods, should be reintroduced not only to the methods themselves, but to the domain assumptions, theoretical formulations, and rules-in-use exploited by the investigator. With this in mind, we turn to the literature on class, crime and delinquency.

SOCIAL CLASS AND CRIMINALITY: FACT AND FIAT

Conventional wisdoms abound in the empirical world of delinquency research. Frequently, competing conventions may exist in parallel, each trying for territorial rights in the pursuit of some uniform truth. The role of social class of explaining delinquency embodies this competitive property, and for good reason. As noted above, the claims of most theories of crime are in some measure contingent upon establishing some manner of relationship, negative or positive, among class, criminal behaviour, and social control. In (admittedly crude) summary, the consensus theorist maintains a stake in the discovery of an inverse relation between criminality and class, and a null relation between social reaction and class. The "pure" labelling theorist (Becker 1963; Erikson 1966; Kitsuse 1962; Scheff 1966; but see Downes 1978; Ericson 1975; Lemert 1973) anticipates a null relation between class and "rulebreaking" (Becker 1963), and an inverse relation between class and official intervention. The critical criminologists (Doleschal and Klapmuts 1973; Quinney 1977; Taylor et al. 1973, 1975; but see Quinney 1970; Turk 1969) forecasts a negative correlation between class and *both* delinquent behaviour and institutional intervention. These hypotheses are summarized in Table. 21.1:

Table 21.1

	Class by Behaviour	Class by Reaction
Consensus	-	0
Labelling	0	-
Conflict	-	-

The official statistics on delinquency and criminality are, on the whole, unequivocal in establishing an inverse relationship between index crimes and social class. Exceptions are infrequent (Erickson 1973; Williams and Gold 1972). At both a composite and individual level, the "predatory" crimes, as institutionally detected, are concentrated in the lower class. As summarized comprehensively by Braithwaite (1981), the research findings are nearly unanimous among studies of the relationship between social class and officially recorded *adult* crime (e.g., Bannister 1976; Cameron 1964; Chimbos 1973; Glueck and Glueck 1934; Green 1970; Willett 1971; Wolfgang 1967), the relationship between social class of *area* and officially recorded *juvenile* crime (e.g., Bordua, 1958; Burt 1944; Glueck and Glueck 1966; Gold 1963;

Lander 1954; Reiss and Rhodes 1961; Shaw and McKay 1969; Wolfgang et al. 1972), and the relation between social class of *area* and officially recorded *adult* crime (Clinard and Abbott 1973; Porterfield 1952; Shaw and McKay 1969). Corroboration is to some extent available in victimization surveys (Hindelang 1978), and ethnographic observational data (Miller 1967; Short and Strodtbeck 1965). Miller's research, in particular, attempts a definitive articulation of the class/crime relation: "[i]ts patterning was so decisively related to social status that status differences as small as those between lower class 2 and 3 had marked influence on the frequency" (Miller 1967, 37).

The official indices have been criticized fundamentally vis à vis the "ecological fallacy" (Robinson 1950) inherent in much of the research (Tittle et al. 1978, 644). A number of the above studies examined relationships between class and crime for geographic area, rather than individuals (e.g., Lander 1954; Shawa and McKay 1969). The self-fulfilling prophecy of deployment intensity by police (Chambliss 1975) may function to elevate lower-class official rates in a spurious fashion. Indices of class and crime rates were desperately unsophisticated in several of these studies (see Tittle et al. 1978, 645). In addition, research such as that by Wolfgang et al. (1972) employed broadly-based census tract data, which could be at best marginally specifiable to individual class or delinquency.

The bulk of the controversy, however, resides in the findings of self-report studies; while it is generally conceded that lower-class persons are comparatively more likely to be arrested for criminal offences (but see Tittle et al. 1978, 650), it is the convergence of this "processing" measure and the "real" patterning of behaviour which is of theoretical significance. Whether lower-class juveniles and adults report more crime than other strata is, apparently, contingent upon who does the reporting. Elliott and Ageton, for example, assert that ". . . self-report studies generally find no differences in delinquent behaviour by class or race" (1980, 95). This perspective was adopted particularly by the earlier researchers in self-report studies (e.g., Nye et al. 1958; Murphy et al. 1946; Wallerstein and Lyle 1947) who were impressed by the considerable middle-class constituency within the "dark figure". A number of more recent studies have indicated similar nonsignificant differences between middle- and lower-class confessors (Bachman et al. 1970, 1978; Elliott and Voss 1974; Empey and Erickson 1966; Gold 1974; Gold and Reimer 1974; Williams and Gold 1974). Empey and Erickson (1966) suggested that it was the character, rather than the volume of crime which varied across status frontiers, with lower-class stealing, driving without licenses, and consuming drugs; middle-class youths destroying property; and upper-class delinquents "defying parents".

In his recently published article, Braithwaite (1981) constructs a rather convincing demolition of the "no-difference" finding among self-report studies. First, he refers to the disparate means by which the variable "class" has been operationalized — for example, "status of parent" as opposed to "status of child". Second, several of the findings of nonrelation (eg. Box and Ford 1971; Cohen and Short 1971; Erickson 1974; Polk et al. 1974) have been conducted in rural settings, where the subjective conditions of class may have an experientially different connotation. Third, methodological deficiencies prevail in several studies (see Hirschi and Selvin 1967, 108–109). Fourth, as Hirschi (1969) indicates, research which focusses on the distinction between working- and middle-class (counterposed to lower- and middle-class) delinquency is less likely to uncover class differences. Fifth, the inclusion of numerous trivial items on questionnaires, such as "theft of less than two dollars" (Hirschi 1969) functions to exaggerate officially nondetectable (as opposed to undetected) bad manners and norm violation (as opposed to rule breaking) by middle-class youth (Box 1971; Gold 1963). Sixth, as revealed by Elliott and Ageton (1980), the truncation of item frequencies to "three or more incidents" obscures the relatively higher prevalence of lower-class delinquents in the upper frequency ranges, as well as the general correlation found throughout the literature among class, frequency and seriousness of intransigence. Braithwaite concludes that "the failure to find significance in a large number of studies is a result of the contamination of measures with items measuring behaviour not normally punishable by law, the setting of lower class cutting points too high, or the choice of a small sample which is disproportionately middle-class to the exclusion of the very lowest social class groups" (1981, 46).

The self-report studies which generate confirmatory findings for an inverse relation involve both juvenile (Belson 1969, 1978; Cernkovich 1978; Elmhorn 1965; Johnstone 1978; McDonald 1968; Phillips 1974) and adult respondents (Reiss and Rhodes 1961; Walberg et al. 1974; West, D.J. 1973). Following her British study of 1,000 London schoolboys, McDonald was led to conclude "from the American studies . . . evidence . . . both supports and denigrates the theory that the working class is more delinquent than the middle class . . . (whereas) almost all of the literature on delinquency in Britain is in favour of the view that the working class is more delinquent (1968, 19). Reiss and Rhodes offered similar qualifications in reporting their investigations of 9,238 white boys in Tennessee, suggesting cultural homogeneity as an intervening variable: ". . . more homogeneous status groups (produce) the largest proportion of delinquents for any status group" (1961, 720). Parenthetically, the two most-cited Canadian self-report studies arrive at diametrically opposed conclusions; whereas Tribble (1972) found higher reporting among lower socio-economic groups, LeBlanc (1975) revealed no significant difference.

A recent article by Tittle et al. (1978), using associational and multivariate analysis, attempted to identify variables contributing to the relationship between class and crime among studies in the literature. The authors reported only a slight inverse overall relationship between class and crime (gamma=.09). Most dramatically, in a time-series analysis, while only minor fluctuations in the relationship prevailed among *self-report* studies over the forty-year period, for *official data* the *direction* of relation had shifted to a slight *positive* association between class and apprehended crime for studies conducted in the 1970s. Tribble et al. conclude that "over the past three decades social class differences . . . have become less important as predictors of criminality" and further (citing Giddens 1973, among others), they suggest the influence of a "putative reduction in class differentation" (1978, 652). Braithwaite (1981, 47–48) looks askance regarding the obvious methodological flaws in this study, but he neglects the fundamental issue involved here. To conclude that alterations in the hierarchical distribution of official statistics denotes a generalized "societal massification" is first a disastrous misinterpretation of class, and second, a myopic equation of differential institutional treatment with a structurally biased sociolegal system. In fact, equal processing of unequal persons may be a requisite for the legitimation of a hegemonic legal structure (Balbus 1973; Habermas 1973; Turk 1976). The equilibration of officially counted crime across social classes in the 1970s — if this can be established by more rigorous research — is more likely an accommodative kneejerk on the part of criminal juridical forces, who can rely on alternative class control embodying nonofficial norm enforcers, mental health and welfare institutions, and exhaustive community absorption of lower-class deviancy (see Scull 1977; Matthews 1979).

This argument entails a wholesale refocussing of the class/crime relationship, and may indicate that the notion of class — beyond the stated "technical" and definitional misinterpretations — may in its present form be conceptually useless as an epidemiological indicator of rates of crime. This observation spills over, for example, into studies of class bias in police work (eg. Black 1970; Black and Reiss 1970; Piliavin and Briar 1964; Weiner and

Willie 1971), and sentencing behaviour among judges (eg. Bernstein et al., 1977; Hagan 1974; Terry 1967) which indicate an absence not only of differential perception, but also of any systematic differential processing of lower-classs offenders. "Once the seriousness of the instant offense and prior record of the offender are taken into account, apparent class bias plays only a minor role in the generation of official data" (Hindelang et al. 1979). Similarly, Williams (1980) in an extensive review of the literature, indicates that differential class processing is apparent only in capital cases, in rural areas, in Southern states, and prior to 1950. What he fails to observe is that the areas of nondifferential processing (ie. northern cities, in the 1960s and 1970s) coincide with the social conditions under which class conflict has been most apparent (see Balbus 1973).

This conception, moreover, obliges us to return to the contingencies sketched in Table 21.1, to add a final cell which completes the set of interactions to the favour of the critical theorist. The fourth possibility, of course, is absence of relation *either* between class and criminal behaviour, *or* between class and differential processing. Within the framework of an symmetrically imposed sociolegal framework, neither behaviour nor process is a necessary (as opposed to sufficient) condition for class bias. The very existence of a system built around the predominance of downward law renders the two "independent" variables (and for that matter, the entire table) of secondary or epiphenomenal impact.

In addition, the obsession in the literature with legal mobilization — to the exclusion of law generation — obscures the class bias inherent in the *non*processing of white collar and corporate rule violators. Confined within the framework of a methodological reliance on police-generated statistics, households reporting victimizations by vandals, and questionnaires furnished to school children, research on the distribution of criminality is, by fiat, excluded from penetration into upper-world malfeasance. Distinctions unearthed between suburban and slum children are intrinsically meaningful and scientifically valuable, but such work fails to grasp the inextricable reflexivity between the microlevel selective enforcement of legal standards, and the macrolevel establishment (or inhibition) of legal-normative standards to be enforced. Gordon, for example, notes that "[t]he economic loss attributable to Index Crimes against property — robbery, burglary, and so on — are one-fifth the losses attributable to embezzlement, fraud, and unreported commercial theft" (1973, 166). To date, criminal statistics are unavailable on the Schwendingers' lexicon of crimes against humanity (1973, 113–146). And not surprisingly, few self-report questionnaires have been distributed to oil executives, in order to gauge the correlation between net annual profits and likelihood of falsely advertising, damaging the environment, or providing unsafe working conditions for employees.

THE ALTERNATIVE FORMULATION OF OFFICIAL STATISTICS: BACK TO KITSUSE AND CICOUREL

Eighteen years ago, Kitsuse and Cicourel (1963) suggested a wholesale re-think of the role of criminal statistics in the sociological enterprise. In essence, they insisted that the "rate-producing processes" (1963, 132) themselves become an object of investigation. The authors were building on a formulation offered earlier by Merton:

> There is little in the history of how statistical studies nor the incidence of juvenile delinquence [six] come to be collected that shows them to be the result of efforts to identify either the sources or the contexts of juvenile delinquency. These are social bookkeeping data. And it would be a happy coincidence if some of them turned out to be in a form relevant for research (Merton 1956, 32).

In the seminal article by Kitsuse and Cicourel was the implanation of a novel perspective on criminal materials, which elevated the level of inquiry to encompass the process of data compilation, assimilation and announcement as the *primary* sociological subject matter. "Validity" and "reliability" were rendered meaningless as barometers of crime and its correlates. "To reject . . . statistics as 'unreliable' because they fail to record the 'actual' rate of deviant behavior assumes that certain behavior is always deviant independent of social actions which define it as deviant" (Kitsuse and Cicourel 1963, 137). This premise led to the natural corollary that crime recording was an integral feature of the certification paradigm, that registrars of deviance were close cousins to official agents of social control, and that — relevant to the present subject matter — a search for official deviance along any social contour (including class/stratum) would by definition be successful, independent of that behaviour's "actual" incidence. Cicourel, in a later study based upon this theme, wrote "[t]he meaning of official statistics . . . must be couched in the context of how men, resources, policies, and strategies of the police, for example, interpret incoming calls, assign men, screen complaints, and routinize reports (1968, 28). This notion by no means invalidates the search for alternative realities embodied in self-report and victimization studies. The result is rather, to redirect and thrust, from the "mutual convergence of methods for best approximate reality", to the apprehension that all methods are equally valid, but measuring different features of the deviant world. The division of strategies allows the researcher — for example, the student of social class and crime — to penetrate the accounts, definitions, constructs, and rules-in-use of either the deviant or the deviance reactor. Subjectivity is reintroduced to the notion of acquiring knowledge about crime, class, race, or any other element in the criminal enterprise; ". . . official statistics . . . are sociologically relevant data" (Ibid., 139).

This recasting of criminological conceptions of the datum has encountered three divergent reactions among the research community. First, among mainstream criminologists, it has been ignored. Statistics are regarded as indices, not as variables which might have causal or correlative properties of their own. Second, ethnomethodologists (Cicourel 1968; Douglas 1967, 1970; Garfinkel 1968; Pfohl 1978; Sacks 1963; Scott and Douglas 1972) have engaged with the problem-solving practices of control agents in rendering statistics intelligible; the statistic itself, outside of its social construction, is of little interest. Third, some critical criminologists have urged a return to the statistic itself as an absolute indicator of manifest, functional social control. Turk writes ". . . a criminality rate is . . . not synonymous with such counts as 'persons arrested by the police' and 'arrests by the police', but is that proportion of a social category which has been defined as 'criminal' by the actions of legal norm enforcers" (1969, 105). Similarly, Taylor, Walton and Young insist that radical criminology entails:

> . . . a return to the empirical examination of official statistics and other recorded material, with the aim in view of unpacking the inequitable and class-based nature of crime, imposition of law and police activity (Taylor et al. 1975, 33).

CONCLUSION

A tracing of one substantive issue in delinquency research — the relationship between crime and social class — requires an understanding of the theoretical, ideological, and even epistemological underpinnings of the conceptions employed, as well as a comprehension of the production and distribution of technologies and methods available to the criminologist. This paper began with a treatment of the traditional research on the class/crime correlate, attempted to expose some of the conceptual investments and theoretical limitations impeding such inquiry, and proceeded to suggest a resensitization to the criminal statistic as a flexible social phenomenon with properties capable of amending some of the more critical flaws in empirical research.

References

Akers, R. 1964. Socio-economic status and delinquent behavior: a retest. *Journal of Research on Crime and Delinquency* 1:38-46.

Bachman, J., S. Green and I. Wirtanen. 1970. *Youth in transition: Vol. II.* Ann Arbor: Institute for Social Research, University of Michigan.

Balbus, I. 1973. *The dialectics of legal repression.* New York: Russell Sage.

Banfield, E. 1968. *The unheavenly city.* Boston: Little, Brown and Company.

Bannister, S. 1976. Education and employment histories in a group of young offenders. In United Nations Social Defense Research Institute, *Economic crises and crime.* Rome: U.N. Publication No. 15.

Becker, H. 1963. *Outsiders.* Glencoe: Free Press.

Bell, D. 1960. *The end of ideology.* New York: Collier.

Belsen, W. 1969. The extent of stealing by London boys and some of its origins. Survey Research Centre, London School of Economics.

_____. 1978. *Television violence and the adolescent boy.* Westmead, Eng.: Saxon House.

Belson, W. et al. 1970. *The development of a procedure for eliciting information from boys about the nature and extent of their stealing.* London: London School of Economics and Political Science, Survey Research Centre.

Bernstein, I., W. Kelley and P. Doyle. 1977. Societal reaction to deviants: the case of criminal defendants. *American Sociological Review* 42:743-755.

Biderman, A. et al. 1967. Report on a pilot study in the district of Columbia on victimization and attitudes toward law enforcement. Field Survey I. President's Commission on Law Enforcement and the Administration of Justice. Washington: G.P.O.

Black, D. 1970. Production of crime rates. *American Sociological Review* 35:733-748.

Black, D. and A. Reiss. 1967. Patterns of behavior in police and citizen transactions. Section I of *Studies of crime and law enforcement in major metropolitan areas* (Vol. III). Washington: G.P.O.

_____. 1970. Police control of juveniles. *American Sociological Review* 25:63-77.

Bonger, W. 1916. *Criminality and economic conditions.* Boston: Little, Brown and Company.

Bordua, D. 1958. Juvenile delinquency and "anomie": an attempt at replication. *Social Problems* 6:230-238.

Box, S. 1971. *Deviance, reality and society.* London: Holt, Rinehart and Winston.

Box, S. and J. Ford. 1971. The facts don't fit: on the relationship between social class and criminal behavior. *The Sociological Review* 19:31-52.

Braithwaite, J. 1981. The myth of social class and criminality reconsidered. *American Sociological Review* 46:36-57.

Buckner, H. 1970. Transformations of reality in the legal process. *Social Research* 37:88-101.

Burt, C. 1944. *The young Delinquent*. New York: D. Appleton.

Cameron, M. 1963. *The booster and the snitch: Department store shoplifting*. Glencoe: Free Press.

Cernkovich, S. 1978. Value orientations and delinquency involvement. *Criminology* 15:443–457.

Chambliss, W. 1978. *Criminal law in action*. Santa Barbara: Hamilton.

Chambliss, W. and R. Nagasawa. 1969. On the validity of official statistics: a comparative study of white, black and Japanese high-school boys. *Journal of Research in Crime and Delinquency* 6:71–77.

Chimbos, P. 1978. A study of breaking and entering offences in "Northern City" Ontario. *Canadian Journal of Criminology and Corrections* 15:316–325.

Christie, N. et al. 1865. A study of self-reported crime. In K. Christiansen (Ed.), *Scandinavian studies in criminology I*. London: Tavistock.

Circourel, A. 1968. *The social organization of juvenile justice*. Heinemann: London.

Clark, J. and L. Tifft. 1966. Polygraph and interview validation of self reported deviant behavior. *American Sociological Review* 31:516–523.

Clinard, M. and D. Abbott. 1973. *Crime in developing countries*. New York: Wiley.

Cloward, R. and L. Ohlin. 1960. *Delinquency and opportunity: A theory of delinquent gangs*. Chicago: Free Press.

Cohen, A. 1955. *Delinquent boys: The culture of the gang*. Chicago: Free Press.

Cohen, A. and J. Short. 1971. Crime and juvenile delinquency. In R. Merton and R. Nisbet (Eds.), *Contemporary social problems*. New York: Harcourt, Brace, Jovanovitch.

Courtis, M. 1970. *Attitudes to crime and the police in Toronto: A report on some survey findings*. Toronto: Centre of Criminology, University of Toronto.

Dahrendorf R. 1959. *Class and class conflict in industrial society*. London: Routledge and Kegan Paul.

Dentler, R. and L. Monroe. 1961. Social correlates of early adolescent theft. *American Sociological Review* 26:733–743.

Doleschal, E. and N. Klapmuts. 1973. Toward a new criminology. *Crime and delinquency literature* 607–626.

Douglas, J. 1967. *The social meanings of suicide*. Princeton University Press.

Douglas, J. (Ed.), 1970. *Deviance and respectability: The social construction of moral meanings*. New York: Basic.

Downes, D. 1979. Praxis makes perfect: a critique of critical criminology. In D. Downes and P. Rock (Eds.), *Deviant interpretations*. London: Martin Robertson.

Elliott, D. and S. Ageton. 1980. Reconciling race and class differences in self-reported and official estimates of delinquency. *American Sociological Review* 45:95–110.

Elliott, D. and H. Voss. 1974. *Delinquency and dropout*. Lexington, Mass.: D.C. Heath.

Elmhorn, K. 1965. Study in self-reported delinquency among school-children in Stockholm. In K. Christiansen (Ed.), *Scandinavian studies in criminology I*. London: Tavistock.

Empey, L. and M. Erikson. 1966. Hidden delinquency and social status. *Social Forces* 44:546–554.

Ennis, B. 1967. *Criminal Victimization in the United States: A Report of a National Survey*.

President's Commission on Law Enforcement and the Administration of Justice. Washington: G.P.O.

Erickson, M. 1971. The group context of delinquent behavior. *Social Problems* 19:114–129.

_____. 1973. Group violations, socio-economic status and official delinquency. *Social Forces* 52:41–52.

Erickson, M. and L. Empey. 1963. Court records, undetected delinquency and decision-making. *Journal of Criminal Law, Criminology and Police Science* 54: 456–469.

Ericson, R. 1975. *Criminal reactions. The labelling perspective.* Lexington: Saxon.

Erikson, K. 1966. *Wayward puritans.* New York: Wiley.

Eysenck, H. 1970. *Crime and personality.* London: Paladin.

Farrington, D. 1973. Self-reports of deviant behaviour: deviant or stable? *Journal of Criminal Law and Criminology* 64:99–110.

Ferri, E. 1917. *Criminal sociology.* Boston: Little, Brown and Company.

Garfinkel, H. 1968. *Studies in ethnomethodology.* New York: Prentice-Hall.

Giddens, A. 1973. *The class structure of the advanced societies.* New York: Harper and Row.

Glueck, S. and E. Glueck. 1934. *Five hundred delinquent women.* New York: Kraus Reprint.

_____. 1966. *Juvenile delinquents grown up.* New York: Kraus Reprint.

Gold, M. 1963. *Status forces in delinquent boys.* Ann Arbor: Institute for Social Research, University of Michigan.

_____. 1966. Undetected delinquent behavior. *Journal of Research in Crime and Delinquency* 13:27–46.

Gold, M. and D. Reimer. 1974. *Changing patterns of delinquent behavior among Americans 13 to 16 years old – 1972.* Report #1 of the American Survey of Youth, 1972. Ann Arbor: Institute for Social Research, University of Michigan.

Goldmana, N. 1963. *The differential selection of juvenile offenders for court appearance.* New York: National Council on Crime and Delinquency.

Gordon, D. 1971. Class and the economics of crime. *Review of Radical Political Economics* 3:51–75.

_____. 1973. Capitalism, class and crime in America. *Crime and Delinquency* 19:163–185.

Gramsci, A. 1970. *Prison notebooks.* London: Lawrences and Wishart.

Green, E. 1970. Race, social status and criminal arrest. *American Sociological Review* 35:476–490.

Habermas, J. 1973. *Legitimation crisis.* Boston: Beacon.

Hagan, J. 1974. Extra-legal attributes and criminal sentencing: an assessment of a sociological viewpoint. *Law and Society Review* 8:357–383.

_____. 1977. *The disreputable pleasures.* Toronto: McGraw-Hill Ryerson.

Hindelang, M. 1978. Race and involvement in common law personal crimes. *American Sociological Review* 43:93–109.

Hindelang, M., T. Hirschi and J. Weis. 1979. Correlates of delinquency: the illusion of discrepancy between self-respect and official measures. *American Sociological Review* 44:995–1014.

Hirschi, T. 1969. *Causes of delinquency.* Berkeley: University of California Press.

Hirschi, T. and H. Selvin. 1967. *Delinquency research: An Appraisal of analytic methods.* New York: Free Press.

Hubenstein, W. 1969. Factors influencing the police disposition of juvenile offenders. In T. Sellin and M. Wolfgang (Eds.), *Delinquency: Selected studies.* Toronto: Wiley.

Hoover, J. 1969. The faith of free men. In R. Knudten (Ed.), *Criminological controversies.* New York: Appleton-Century Crofts.

Humphries, L. 1970. *Tearoom trade.* Chicago: Aldine.

Inciardi, J. (Ed.), 1980. *Radical criminology: The coming crises.* Beverly Hills: Sage.

Johnstone, J. 1978. Social class, social status and delinquency. *Sociology and Social Research* 63:49–72.

Kitsuse, J. 1962. Societal reaction to deviant behavior: problems of theory and method. *Social Problems* 9:247–256.

Kitsuse, J. and A. Cicourel. 1963. A note on the uses of official statistics. *Social Problems* 11:131–139.

Koenig, D. 1976. Correlates of self-reported victimization and perceptions of neighbourhood safety. In D. Brusegard and L. Hewitt (Eds.), *Social indicators in Canada.* Edmonton: Government of Alberta.

Kolko, G. 1962. *Wealth and power in America.* New York: Praeger.

Lander, B. 1954. *Towards an understanding of juvenile delinquency.* New York: Columbia University Press.

Laumann, E. 1966. *Prestige and association in an urban community.* Indianapolis: Bobbs-Merrill.

LeBlanc, M. 1975. Middle class delinquency. In R. Silverman and J. Teevan (Eds.), *Crime in Canadian society.* Toronto: Butterworths.

Lemert, E. 1951. *Social pathology: A systematic approach to the theory of sociopathic behavior.* New York: McGraw-Hill.

———. 1978. *Human deviance, social problems and social control.* Englewood Cliffs: Prentice-Hall.

Lewis, O. 1966. *La Vida: A Puerto Rican family in the culture of poverty.* New York: Random House.

Lombroso, C. 1971. *L'homme criminal.* Paris: Felix Alcan.

Marx, K. and F. Engels. 1968. *Selected works.* London: Lawrence and Wishart.

Matthews, R. 1979. Decarceration and the fiscal crisis. In R. fine et al. (Eds.), *Capitalism and the rule of law.* London: Hutchinson.

Matza, D. 1964. *Delinquency and drift.* New York: Wiley.

McCandless, B. et al. 1972. Perceived opportunity, delinquency, race, and body build among delinquent youth. *Journal of Consulting and Clinical Psychology* 38:281–287.

McCord, W. and J. McCord. 1959. *Origins of crime: A new evaluation of the Cambridge-Somerville youth study.* New York: Columbia University Press.

McDonald, L. 1968. *Social class and delinquency.* London: Faber and Faber.

———. 1976. *The sociology of law and order.* London: Faber and Faber.

McEachern, A. and R. Bauzer. 1967. Factors related to disposition in juvenile police contacts. In M. Klein (Ed.), *Juvenile gangs in context: Theory, research, and action.* Englewood Cliffs: Prentice-Hall.

Merton, R. 1956. In H. Witner and R. Kotinsky (Eds.), *New perspectives for research on juvenile delinquency.* Washington: G.P.O.

———. 1957. *Social theory and social structure.* Glencoe: Free Press.

Miliband, R. 1969. *The state in capitalist society.* London: Weidenfeld and Nicholson.

Miller, W. 1958. Lower class culture as a generating milieu of gang delinquency. *Journal of Social Issues* 14:5–19.

_____. 1967. Theft behavior in city gangs. In M. Klein (Ed.), *Juvenile gangs in context: Theory, research, and action.* Englewood Cliffs: Prentice-Hall.

Morris, N. and G. Hawkins. 1970. *The honest politician's guide to crime control.* Chicago: University of Chicago Press.

Morris, T. 1957. *The criminal area: A study in social ecology.* London: Routledge and Kegan Paul.

Murphy, F. et al. 1946. The incidence of hidden delinquency. *American Journal of Orthopsychiatry* 16:686–695.

Nettler, G. 1978. *Explaining crime.* Toronto: McGraw Hill.

Nisbet, R. 1959. The decline and fall of social class. *Pacific Sociological Review* 2:11–17.

Nye, I. and F. Short. 1957. Scaling delinquent behavior. *American Sociological Review* 22:326–331.

Nye, I., F. Short and v. Olsen. 1958. Socioeconomic status and delinquent behavior. *American Journal of Sociology* 63:381–89.

Ollman, B. 1971. *Alienation: Marx's conception of man in capitalist society.* New York: Cambridge University Press.

Ossowski, S. 1963. *Class structure in the social consciousness.* New York: Free Press.

Pearce, F. 1976. *Crimes of the powerful.* London: Pluto Press.

Pfohl, S. 1978. *Predicting dangerousness: The social construction of psychiatric reality.* Lexington, Mass.: Heath.

Phillips, J. 1974. The creation of deviant behavior in high schools: an examination of Cohen's general theory of subcultures. Ph.D. dissertation, University of Oregon.

Piliavin, I. and S. Briar. 1964. Police encounters with juveniles. *American Journal of Sociology* 70:206–214.

Polk, K., D. Frease and F. Richmond. 1974. Social class, school experience and delinquency. *Criminology* 12:84–96.

Polsky, N. 1967. *Hustlers, beats and others.* Chicago: Aldine.

Porterfield, A. 1943. Delinquency and its outcome in court and college. *American Journal of Sociology* 49:199–208.

_____. 1952. Suicide and crime in the social structure of an urban setting. *American Sociological Review* 17:341–349.

Quetelet, A. 1842. *Treatise on man.* Paris: Bachelier.

Quinney, R. 1970. *The social reality of crime.* Boston: Little, Brown and Company.

_____. 1977. *Class, state and crime.* New York: McKay.

Reasons, C. 1974. *The criminologist: Crime and the criminal.* Pacific Pallisades: Goodyear.

Reid, S. 1976. *Crime and criminology.* Hinsdale, Ill.: Dryden.

Reiss, A. and A. Rhodes. 1961. The distribution of juvenile delinquency in the social class structure. *American Sociological Review* 26:720–732.

Robinson, W. 1950. Ecological correlation and behavior of individuals. *American Sociological Review* 15:351–357.

Rose, A. 1958. The concept of class and American Sociology. *Social Research* 25:53–69.

Rubington, E. and M. Weinberg. 1973. *Deviance: The interactionist perspective.* New York: Macmillan.

Sacks, H. 1963. Sociological description. *Berkeley Journal of Sociology* 8.

Scheff, T. 1966. *Being mentally ill: A sociological theory.* Chicago: Aldine.

———. 1972. *Labeling madness.* Englewood Cliffs: Prentice-Hall.

Schneider, A. 1975. *Crime and victimization in Portland: Analysis of trends 1971–1974.* Eugene, Oregon: Oregon Research Institute.

Schumpeter, J. 1942. *Capitalism, socialism and democracy.* New York: Harper.

Schwendinger, H. and J. Schwendinger. 1975. Defenders of order or guardians of human rights? In I. Taylor, P. Walton and J. Young (Eds.), *Critical criminology.* London: Routledge and Kegan Paul.

Scott, R. and J. Douglas (Eds.). 1972. *Theoretical perspectives on deviance.* New York: Basic.

Scull, A. 1977. *Decarceration. Community treatment and the deviant — A radical view.* Englewood Cliffs: Prentice-Hall.

Sellin, T. 1951. The significance of records of crime. *Law Quarterly Review* 67: 489–504.

Shaw, C. and H. McKay. 1969. *Juvenile delinquency and urban areas.* Chicago: Univeristy of Chicago Press.

Short, J. and I. Nye. 1957. Reported behavior as a criterion of deviant behavior. *Social Problems* 5:207–213.

Short, J. and F. Strodbeck. 1965. *Group and process and gang delinquency.* Chicago: University of Chicago Press.

Skogan, W. 1974. The validity of official crime statistics: an empirical investigations. *Social Science Quarterly* 55:25–38.

Taylor, I., P. Walton and J. Young. 1973. *The new criminology: For a social theory of deviance.* London: Routledge and Kegan Paul.

———. 1975. *Critical criminology.* London: Routledge and Kegan Paul.

Tepperman, L. 1977. *Crime control: The urge toward authority.* Toronto: McGraw-Hill Ryerson.

Terry, R. 1967. The screening of juvenile offenders. *Journal of Criminal Law, Criminology and Police Science* 68:173–181.

Tittle, C., W. Villemez and D. Smith. 1978. The myth of social class and criminality: an empirical assessment of the empirical evidence. *American Sociological Review* 43:643–656.

Trasler, G. 1962. *The explanation of criminality.* London: Routledge and Kegan Paul.

Tribble, S. 1972. Socio-economic status and self-reported juvenile delinquency. *Canadian Journal of Criminology and Corrections* 14:409–415.

Turk, A. 1969. *Criminality and legal order.* Chicago: Rand McNally.

———. 1976. Law, conflict, and order: from theorizing toward theories. *Canadian Review of Sociology and Anthropology* 13:282–293.

Voss, H. 1963. Ethnic differences in delinquency in Honolulu. *Journal of Criminal Law, Criminology and Police Science* 54:322–327.

———. 1966. Socioeconomic status and reported delinquent behavior. *Social Problems* 13:314–327.

Walberg, H., E. Yeh and S. Paton. 1974. Family background, ethnicity and urban delinquency. *Journal of Research in Crime and Delinquency* 11:80–87.

Waldo, G. and T. Chiricos. 1972. Perceived penal sanction and self-reported criminality: a neglected approach to deterrence research. *Social Problems* 19:522–540.

Wallerstein, J. and C. Wyle. 1947. Our law-abiding law-breakers. *Federation Probation* 25:107–112.

Weber, M. 1966. *The theory of social and economic organization.* New York: Free Press.

Weiner, N. and C. Willie. 1971. Decisions by juvenile officers. *American Journal of Sociology* 77:199–210.

West, D.J. 1973. *Who becomes delinquent?* London: Heinemann.

West, W.G. 1979. Serious thieves: lower-class adolescent males in short-term occupation. In E. Vaz and A. Lodhi (Eds.), *Crime and delinquency in Canada.* Toronto: Prentice-Hall.

Wheeler, S. 1967. Criminal statistics: a reformulation of the problem. *Journal of Criminal Law, Criminology and Police Science* 58:317–324.

Willett, T. 1971. *Criminal on the road.* London: Tavistock.

Williams, F. 1980. Conflict theory and differential processing: an analysis of the research literature. In J. Inciardi (Ed.), *Radical criminology: The coming crises.* Beverly Hills: Sage.

Williams, J. and M. Gold. 1972. From delinquent behavior to official delinquency. *Social Problems* 20:209–229.

Wolfgang, M. 1967. Criminal homicide and the subculture of violence. In M. Wolfgang (Ed.), *Studies in homicide.* New York: Harper and Row.

Wolfgang, M., R. Figlio and T. Sellin. 1972. *Delinquency in a birth cohort.* Chicago: University of Chicago Press.

Wright, E. 1973. *The politics of punishment.* New York: Harper and Row.

Chapter 22

Teaching Applied Criminology in Canada

T.J. Juliani, C.H.S. Jayewardene and C.K. Talbot*

In 1938 Thorsten Sellin contended "the term Criminology should be used to designate only the body of scientific knowledge and the deliberate pursuit of that knowledge. What the technical use of knowledge in the treatment and prevention of crime might be called, I leave to the imagination of the reader. The term 'crimino-technology' is not likely to suite him" (Sellin 1938). This notwith-standing, there has been a move to make criminology an applied rather than a pure discipline. Even before the term Criminology was coined, when the study of crime and criminals fell almost exclusively within the purview of law, the suggestion was made by Gabriel Tarde, supported by Enrico Ferri, at the first Inter-national Congress of Criminal Anthropology in Rome in 1885, "that students should be admitted to criminal law courses only provided they first became members of a prisoners' welfare society and made weekly visits, either individually or as a group, to prisons" (I.S.C. 1959).

When criminology began to be taught at universities, it was taught as a subdiscipline in Sociology, Psychology and Social Work, mainly with a theoretical and research orientation. The courses were organized so as to provide knowledge regarding crime and criminality in such a manner as to promote a scientific understanding of the phenomenon (Jayewardene and Durie 1975). Following general beliefs extant at that time and extant even today, it was believed that the criminology graduate was capable, because of his possession of a broad and liberal education, of

---

* Department of Criminology, University of Ottawa. Revised version of a paper published in *The International Journal of Comparative and Applied Criminal Justice*, Vol. 5, 6, Sept. 1982.

performing effectively in any and every position of responsibility related to his discipline. However, when he was taken out of the ivory tower where he was engrossed in the pursuit of an elusive truth and thrust rudely into an arena where he must engage in the pursuit of equally elusive criminals, he and his colleagues were found only capable of engaging in a "collective fraud" convincing governments, penal institutions, police and the like of an ability to control a phenomenon which they were really unable to control (Grabbiner 1973).

Dissatisfaction with the content and direction of traditional criminology, we are told, led to a reassessment of goals, a reevaluation of methods, and a redefinition of concepts, if not in an obvious and revolutionary fashion, in an unobtrusive and evolutionary manner (Taylor et al. 1973). The evolution has shown two distinct tendencies. One has been the adoption of a normative orientation focusing not on why people called criminals did certain things, as the traditional criminologists were wont to, but on why certain members of society insisted on criminalizing others. The other has been the adoption of an applied orientation focusing on the treatment of offenders and the many problems associated with it. Condemned as correctionalism in the United States (Taylor et al. 1973) applied criminology was left to become the Canadian contribution to the discipline (Jayewardene 1973). In the United States, attempts had been made since almost a half century ago to introduce educational programs with what Glaser calls a professional perspective, concerned with the preparation of students for practice in the field rather than a disciplinary perspective, emphasizing learning and research for the advance of theory and understanding independently for their usefulness for practice (Glaser 1978). Most of these programs, however, were either not implemented or lasted only a few years (Swank 1972). The few of the later ones that did survive attempted to bridge the gap between the academic pursuite of criminology and the professional dimensions of the field mainly by encouraging research on actual problems in criminal justice while developing a curriculum based on the premise of a solid base of academic excellence (Lejins 1965). Even in Canada this idea prevailed. Though it was generally accepted that a university program in criminology should be geared to supplying potential candidates for recruitment into the different segments of the criminal justice system through a practice-oriented education (Grygier 1962), the possibility of linking theory to practice through the provision of research and consultative services to agencies dealing with offenders was not overlooked (Szabo 1963).

The concept of applied criminology demands that the

knowledge that is imparted to the student should serve a specific purpose with the specificity defined in terms of the tasks the individual educated is claimed to be proficient to perform. This definition involving specificity calls for the limitation of the traditional claim of competence for graduates from an undefined anything and everything to a well-defined something. The transformation from a nebulous general competence to a more or less tangible specific competence carries the implication that education comprises two basic forms. First, there is education for job performance or education that would enable an individual to perform better at the level at which he is. Then, there is education for career development, or education that will enable the individual to perform well at the level into which he hopes to move so that promotion would entail a movement not from a level of competence to a level of incompetence but between two levels of competence (Jayewardene and Jayasuriya 1981). As the process of education cannot be separated from its contents, what is and can be taught in a classroom must unavoidably be that which is amenable to description and analysis and presentation by the human voice, supplemented by visual aids. The practical application of education demands the use of "talents that we gain by experience, intuitions that come by practice, the confidence developed by success, the humility that failures press on us and the wisdom that tempers logic" (Parr 1978), all of which are not classroom items.

In delivering the keynote speech for the 1981 Education Week, the Ministry of Colleges and Universities for Ontario noted that "recent research indicates that most Ontario residents view career preparation as the top priority of secondary schools. About one third of Ontario residents are dissatisfied, in some way, with the educational system. Our hypothesis is that some people are dissatisfied because they feel secondary schools are not helping young people make the transition from school to career, whatever that career might be" (Ministry of Colleges and Universities 1981). The Ontario Ministry of Colleges and Universities is promoting the concept of "Cooperative Education" in which the community's workplace becomes the students' classroom. This program is operating at a secondary school level and credited toward secondary school education. It has also been introduced at the college and university level in some disciplines to enable the student to learn through working and at the same time to earn enough to support himself during his learning period. It is hoped that the combination of the work experience and the instruction received in the class would result in an education program that meets the needs of both the student and the workplace. The concept of applied criminology also calls for this work experience. It calls for this work experience, but only as an adjunct to a solid core of theory and a basic training in research. In consequence, the field situation should not be isolated from the classroom but should be under academic control. This control is necessary to provide students with real opportunities for learning rather than the agencies with additional manpower for their routine tasks, to fully coordinate the classroom learning and the field experience, and to maintain the student posture, the fact that he is a student learning, not a general citizen evaluating, nor another employee working (Hyenes 1968). What must constitute an integral part of the practical training is "to indicate to students how the concepts learned in the classroom could be utilized in a real life setting, how skills and techniques are developed to achieve the overall objectives of the system, how the operation of one individual or groups of individuals influence and are influenced by the operations of others" (Talbot 1978).

Traditionally, a university provides education at three levels — the Bachelor's, the Master's and the Doctor's — which are supposed to indicate not only the acquisition of an increasing quantum of knowledge but also possession of an increasing competence. This is in terms of the competency involved in the concept of a broad and liberal education. When a slightly more specific competency is considered necessary, diploma or certificate courses are provided. When education is geared to the provision of a specified knowledge as in the disciplines of medicine, engineering, law and the like, imparting a professional education as opposed to an academic one, knowledge for job performance as opposed to knowledge for the sake of knowledge, the levels signify basic knowledge required and varying degrees of specialization. In applied criminology too, programs at the undergraduate level, the graduate level, and at the postgraduate level, could be developed but these must be developed not only to reflect the implied hierarchical differentiation of knowledge but also to satisfy the needs of the field to reflect, perhaps, the hierarchical differentiation of personnel. Thus, a Certificate program in Criminology could be designed to provide a level of academic background in criminology for persons actively engaged in the field of criminal justice desiring to improve their professional effectiveness. Candidates in the certificate program would follow a specific course of study designed to improve job performance, to supply an academic background to augment a practical experience. Although the program would be geared to job performance, its successful completion should be considered as an initial diploma designed to stimulate graduates toward further development. Then, there could be a Bachelor's program to ensure continuity. The format should be that of a general arts degree. This format appears to be necessary in view of the fact that criminology is still essentially a multidisciplinary discipline, drawing on a multitude of disciplines, each injecting into the discipline its peculiar viewpoint, and not as yet an interdisciplinary one where all these viewpoints have been well integrated. Any stress of one approach at the expense of another, while being academically satisfactory and even desirable, might be disastrous from the point of view of a practical program. Such a situation would promote conflicts and debates about the parameters and paradigms of the subject and detract from the eclectism that appears necessary for applied criminoiogy at the present. The Bachelor's degree could have an Honours component where an emphasis on both research and practice would introduce the student to the way in which academic knowledge could be utilized to handle practical problems. The full thrust of the applied criminology program could commence at the fourth, or Honours year, of study at the undergraduate level and continue extensively at the graduate level. Restriction of its thrust at the under-graduate level is suggested because it is possible for an individual to integrate theory and practice only once he has acquired a sufficiently sound basic framework.

In the planning of a curriculum for applied criminology one should perhaps proceed with the realization that the education offered is designed to direct the professional behaviour of the student in a particular direction and that the success of the educational process is dependent on the proper management of learning. In consequence, the first step in the development of an applied program is the definition of the job that the student would be called upon to perform so that the educational goals and objectives of the program could be derived. To be educationally useful the definition of the jobs must involve an identification of their functional components. If one is to draw from the educational experience of medicine, one finds that there are three methods available for the formulation of this definition. First is the approach advanced by the Institute of Medicine which comprises description of the essential attributes of the services to be provided (Institute of Medicine 1978). The second approach, adopted by Hansen and Reeb (1970) in their development of a curriculum outline for the primary care of children, is to outline the educational content of the tasks as deduced from a systems model of the service system. The third approach is one that could be derived from time motion studies to obtain a composite picture of what the job entails (Berman et al. 1966). Whatever method may be adopted the basic idea is to determine first what it is that the trained individual has to do and second, what knowledge, skills and attitudes are needed for the individual to perform competently. The identification of the education objectives would indicate the learning experiences required and the teaching methods desired. The curriculum could, consequently, be planned so that the opportunities for the requisite learning experiences are maximized. Thus, if report writing is a desired experience, it should be made a component of as many courses as possible. Similarly, if interaction with people or working in stressful situations are demanded, as many opportunities as possible for the student to acquire such an experience should be provided. Once implemented, the learning experiences and teaching methods must be evaluated with the results of the evaluation not only fed to the students but also used to review and revise the program.

Pertinent to the development of a curriculum are two other considerations. The first refers to the teaching style adopted by the instructor. As far as criminology is concerned these have been identified as (1) didactic, where the teacher tells the learner, usually asserting his authority; (2) socratic, where the teaching is through a question-answer process with each answer of the learner triggering the next question of the teacher; and (3) the case conference method, where the learning is promoted by discussion of actual problems encountered using stimulated models of trial and error (Jayewardene 1976). Each method has its own peculiar advantage and disadvantage, and instructors differ in their preference of teaching style. The second consideration refers to the stance of the student, his psychological rather than his educational needs. Here it is claimed that students in applied criminology programs, especially if they happen to be adults, "(1) . . . respond best to a non-threatening learning environment where there is a good teacher-learner relationships; (2) . . . want to assess themselves against a relevant standard to determine their educational needs; (3) . . . want to select their own learning experience — to be self directing; (4) . . . prefer a problem oriented, . . . approach to learning; (5) . . . want to apply their knowledge and skills immediately; (6) . . . want to know how they are progressing; and (7) . . . want to contribute from their reservoir of knowledge and skills to help others to learn" (Fabb et al. 1976). The courses of instruction, thus, would have to be geared to meet (1) the educational demands of the profession; (2) the teaching styles of the instructors; and (3) the psychological needs of the students; if an applied program is to be successful. The calibre of the program would perhaps be improved if a counselling component was introduced to the work experience to help the student to understand his own behaviour (Royal College of Practitioners 1972).

The viability of an applied program depends largely upon the ability of the training students to secure employment in the system, and the level of the program must necessarily be that which ensures maximum employability. The first task in the organization of a program of applied criminology, consequently, must comprise an assessment of its input and output needs. The relevant questions here become: who enters the program? when? what? for? why? and with that expectation? The answers define the input needs of the program. Before these questions can be answered there is another set of questions to which answers must be provided. These questions are: who exits from the program? why? to what? with what capacity? and with what expectations? The answers to these questions define the output needs (Mueller 1972). For the assessment of the output needs the personnel structure of the métier has to be first analyzed. As far as the criminal justice system is concerned, there are essentially three segments: the police, the courts, and corrections. The courts involving the judges, the prosecutors and the defenders, have most of their personnel training needs met by schools of law. Applied criminology consequently has to cater to the ends of either the police or corrections. In corrections it was found that the personnel employed at the field level were structured to comprise a bottom, or line-staff rank with a supervisor, both of whom were responsible for the performance of custodial duties. At the top was the management rank, drawn partly from the middle-management rank and partly from a fourth, or counselling, rank.

The crucial element in an applied program of criminology is the field work component, not as a separate part isolated from the theory the student is taught in the classroom but as an integral part of the program complementing the theoretical expositions in practical demonstration. The organization of field work, consequently, plays a very important role. Here, there are a number of problems but the main one relates to the conception that both the field and the student has of the relationship between fieldwork and employment. To the field, the field work offers an agency "a unique method of staff recruiting which allows them to evaluate a potential employee in a manner which is precluded by the usual personnel procedures". To the student it offers an opportunity "to learn the etiquette and methods of navigation" that would permit him to sail safely in what may be otherwise dangerous and troubled waters. In both cases the prime objective of training and learning, "of testing the metal of theory against the heat of practice" gets forgotten (Talbot 1975). In this connection, it is perhaps important to remember that any applied program of studies seeks to reconcile two contrasting views of a university. On the one hand there is the view that it is basically "a haven of cognitive rationality", a place for the preservation of cultural heritage and civilization and the advancement of knowledge. On the other hand there is the view that it is a "supermarket of services and occupational training", a vehicle for general education and the preparation of students for professions. Both these views promote the university as an institution for the perpetuation of the existing system. Proponents of an applied program of studies in a university seek to convert it into a place where the experience of the past would indicate the direction of the future, not in terms of what should but in terms of what could be done. In the training of the youth of today for the world of tomorrow with the knowledge of yesterday, it is easy to follow the well-trodden path and seek to perpetuate the existing system. It is also easy to stray into the woods and discover a new path which is no more than a track to the old.

The failure of universities to prepare students to design and implement the social change that is necessary is an accusation that is justly laid against them. Programs of applied studies must do more than prepare students to get into occupational slots. They must, while providing students with the basic skills for job performance, endow them with a sensitivity for detecting the need for change and equip them with the ability to effect that change. "Programs, no matter how well designed or sound in theory, are only as good as that which is put into practice. It is the highest of self deception to inaugurate a program of high-sounding phrases while actually continuing to do business at the same old stand, in the same old way, with the same old procedures". Pearl made this reference to correctional programs (1962). It is equally applicable to training or educational ventures especially in corrections where the conservative nature of the activity of bringing them back into the fold tends to make a program of applied criminology a procedure for the production of "specialized correctional plumbers keeping the criminal justice sewers operational" (Talbot 1975).

References

Bergman, A.B., S.W. Dassel and R.G. Wedgewood. 1966. Time motion study of practicing paediatricians. *Paediatrics* 38:254.
Fabb, W.E., M.W. Heffernan and W.A. Phillips. 1976. *Focus on learning in family practice.* Melbourne: Royal Australian College of General Practitioners.
Glaser, N. 1978. Graduate training needs: Professional perspective. *ASA Footnotes* 6:1.

Grabbiner, B.E. 1973. Dialogue with Marie-Andree Bertrand. *Issues in Criminology* 8:31.

Grygier, T. 1962. Education of correctional workers: A survey of needs and resources. *Canadian Journal of Corrections* 4:137.

Hansen, M.F. and K.G. Reeb. 1970. An education program for primary care. *Journal of Medical Education* 45:1007.

Heynes, R. 1968. The university as an instrument of social action. In Mittner and Johnson: *Colleges and Universities as Agents of Social Change*. WICHE.

International Society of Criminology. 1959. *The university teachng of social sciences: Criminology*. Paris: UNESCO.

Institute of Medicine. 1978. *Report of a study: A manpower policy for primary health care*. Washington: National Academy of Science.

Jayewardene, C.H.S. 1973. *The integration of theory and practice in the training of criminologists*. Canadian Congress of Criminology, Regina, June.

_____. *A clinical case conference model for staff training*. Ottawa: Criminology Ottawa.

Jayewardene, C.H.S. and H. Durie. 1975. The teaching of criminology in Canada. *Criminology Made in Canada* 3:181.

Jayewardene, C.H.S. and D.J.N. Jayasuriya. 1981. *The management of a correctional institution*. Toronto: Butterworths.

Lejins, P.P. 1965. The criminology program at the University of Maryland. *Criminologica* 3:25.

Mueller, G.O.W. 1972. *Differential distribution of pedagogic responsibilities in the training of human resources for criminology*. American Society of Criminology, Caracas, November.

Parr, J.G. 1978. About the boundaries of instruction. *OUPID Newsletter* 21:2.

Pearl, A. 1962. *Quality control in evaluative research of correctional programs*. National Institute on Crime and Delinquency, Seattle.

Royal College of General Practitioners. 1972. *The future general practitioner: Learning and teaching*. Suffolk: Laverham Press.

Sellin, T. 1938. *Culture conflict and crime*. New York: Social Research Council.

Swank, C. 1972. *A descriptive analysis of criminal justice doctoral programs in the United States*. Ph.D. Dissertation, Michigan State University.

Szabo, D. 1963. Criminology and criminologist: A new discipline and a new profession. *Canadian Journal of Corrections* 5:28.

Talbot, C.K. 1975. Theory and practice in applied criminology. *Acta Criminologica Japonica et Medicinae Legale* 41:153.

Talbot, C.K. 1978. *Field practice manual*. Ottawa: Department of Criminology, University of Ottawa.

Taylor, I., P. Walton and J. Young. 1973. *The new criminology*. London: Routledge and Kegan Paul.

Topping, C.W. 1929. *Canadian penal institutions*. Toronto: The Ryerson Press.

_____. 1981. *Skills 2/2*. Published by the Ministry of Colleges and Universities, Ontario.

About the Authors

THOMAS FLEMING holds a B.A. (Soc.) and an M.A. (Crim.) from The University of Toronto. He was Canada Council Fellow. He received his doctorate from The Department of Sociology of The

London School of Economics. He has taught at The London School of Economics, and the University of Toronto. Currently, he is Assistant Professor in The Department of Sociology, University of Alberta. His research interests include crime, deviance, social control, the sociology of law, mental disorder, the media, contemporary culture, and social institutions.

L.A. VISANO holds a B.A. (Soc.) and an M.A. (Crim.) from The University of Toronto. He has held numerous fellowships and scholarships during his academic career. He is currently Ph.D. candidate in The Department of Sociology, University of Toronto, where his work concerns the network and careers of male street prostitutes. He has taught at Ryerson Polytechnical Institute, and the University of Toronto, and is involved in a number of community committees in the Toronto area. His research interests include crime, deviance, law and social control, ethnic relations, and urban sociology.